THE 20TH CENTURY LEGAL PHILOSOPHY SERIES

IV

THE LEGAL PHILOSOPHIES OF LASK, RADBRUCH, AND DABIN

LONDON : GEOFFREY CUMBERLEGE
OXFORD UNIVERSITY PRESS

20TH CENTURY LEGAL PHILOSOPHY SERIES: VOL. IV

THE LEGAL PHILOSOPHIES OF LASK, RADBRUCH, AND DABIN

TRANSLATED BY
KURT WILK
Associate Professor of Government
Wells College

INTRODUCTION BY
EDWIN W. PATTERSON
Cardozo Professor of Jurisprudence
Columbia University

CAMBRIDGE · MASSACHUSETTS
HARVARD UNIVERSITY PRESS
1950

PRINTED IN THE UNITED STATES OF AMERICA

GENERAL INTRODUCTION TO THE SERIES

By the Editorial Committee

This book is one of the 20th Century Legal Philosophy Series, published under the auspices of the Association of American Law Schools. At its annual meeting in December, 1939, the Association authorized the creation of a special committee "for the purpose of preparing and securing the publication of translations on the same general lines as the Modern Legal Philosophy Series, sponsored by this association at the annual meeting thirty years ago . . . the materials to represent as nearly as possible the progress of Continental Legal thought in all aspects of Philosophy and Jurisprudence in the last fifty years."

Whereas the earlier Series was a very daring venture, coming, as it did, at the beginning of the century when only a few legal scholars were much interested in legal philosophy, the present Series could be undertaken with considerable assurance. In 1909 only a few of the leading law schools in this country included Jurisprudence in their curricula, and it was usually restricted to the Analytical School. By 1939 Jurisprudence was being taught in many law schools, and the courses had been broadened to include not only Analytical Jurisprudence, but also the Philosophy and the Sociology of Law. The progress in logical theory, in ethics, and in social science between 1909 and 1939 was without doubt an important factor in the expansion of Jurisprudence. In 1939 there was not only the successful precedent of the earlier Series, now completely out of print, but also the known rise of a very substantial body of interested readers, including students and practicing lawyers as well as professional scholars. This thoroughly admirable change, especially in the English-speaking countries, has been widely recognized as productive of a great enrichment of Anglo-American law. The Modern Legal Philosophy Series has been justly credited with a major part of that influence by making readily available the Continental jurisprudence of the last century.

The primary task of the legal philosopher is to reveal and to maintain the dominant long-run influence of ideas over events, of the general over the particular. In discharging this task he may help his generation to understand the basic trends of the law from one generation to the next, and the common cultural ties of seemingly disparate national legal systems. He may, again, create from these common ideal goods of the world's culture general theories, beliefs, and insights that will be accepted and used as guides by coming generations. The works of great legal philosophers serve not only the needs of the practitioner and other utilitarian ends; they also contribute abundantly to our theoretical knowledge. Indeed, in a deeper sense, we have come to understand the superficiality of setting utility against theory. The day is past when jurisprudence can defensibly be regarded as a curious hobby or as "merely cultural" in the sense that the fine arts contribute to the rounded education of a gentleman at the Bar. The issues are now correctly formulated in terms of whether one wishes to be a highly competent lawyer or a technician. Since the question, thus put, is obviously rhetorical, it is but another mode of asserting the considered judgment of those best qualified to pass on such matters, that the science and philosophy of law deal with the chief ideas that are common to the rules and methods of all positive law, and that a full understanding of any legal order therefore eludes those whose confining specialties keep them from these important disciplines.

The recent revival of interest in American history also reminds us emphatically that the great Fathers of the Republic, many of them lawyers, were men of universal intellectual outlook. They were as thoroughly grounded in French thought as in English. Grotius and Pufendorf were almost as widely read as the treatises on common law. Indeed, Jefferson and Wilson, to select two of the many great lawyers who come to mind, were able philosophers and social scientists. They apparently regarded it as essential to the best conduct of their professional careers to study philosophy and, especially, jurisprudence, Jefferson remarking that they are "as necessary as law to form an accomplished lawyer." The current movements in politics and economics have raised innumerable problems which, just as in the formative era of the Republic, require for their solution the sort of knowledge and skills that transcend specialization and technical proficiency. They call for a competence that is grounded in a wide perspective, one that represents an integration of the practitioner's technical skills with a knowledge of the various disciplines that bear directly on the wise solution of the present-day problems; and these are by no means confined to public affairs — they equally concern the daily practice of the private practitioner. With many such legal problems, with methods relevant to sound solutions, with the basic ideas and values involved, the eminent legal philosophers whose principal works appear in this Series have been particularly concerned. If it seems to some that the literature of jurisprudence is rather remote from the immediate practical problems that occupy the attention of most lawyers, it is necessary to reassert our primary dependence for the solution of all such problems upon theory — a truth that has been demonstrated many times in the physical sciences but which holds, also, in the realm of social problems. The publication of such a Series as this rests on the premise that it is possible to discover better answers than are now given many problems, that a closer approximation to truth and a greater measure of justice are attainable by lawyers, and that in part, at least, this can be brought about through their greater sensitivity to the relevant ideals of justice and through a broader vision of the jurisprudential fundamentals.

In the General Introduction to the first Series, it was noted that "The value of the study of comparative law has only in recent years come to be recognized by us. Our juristic methods are still primitive, in that we seek to know only by our own experience, and pay no heed to the experience of others." As the nations are drawn closer together by forces not wholly in human control, it is inevitable that they should come to understand each other more fully. The legal institutions of any country are no less significant than its language, political ideals, and social organization. The two great legal systems of the world, the civilian and the common law, have for some years been moving toward what may become, in various fields of law, a common ground. The civilian system has come more and more to recognize actually, if not avowedly, the importance of case-law, whereas the common law system has been exhibiting an increasing reliance on legislation and even on codes. In a number of fields, e.g., commercial law, wills, and criminal law, there is such an agreement of substantive principles as to make uniformity a very practical objective. While economic interests will undoubtedly provide the chief stimulus to that end, in the long-range view the possibility of focusing the energies of leading scholars and lawyers, the whole world over, on the same problems is the most inviting ideal of all. The problems of terminology, legal methods, the role of precedent, statutory interpretation, underlying rationale, the use of different types of authority, the efficacy of various controls and their operation in diverse factual conditions, the basic issues concerning the values that are implemented — these and innumerable other fundamental problems of legal science and philosophy may and should receive collaboration on a scale never before attainable. The road to the attainment of these objectives is not an easy one, but if any such avenue exists it is surely that indicated by the best literature in jurisprudence.

These fundamentals are also invaluable aids to better understanding of one's own law. On the side of insight into legal methods and substantive doctrines alone, the gain is immeasurably great. The common lawyer, at least until very recent times, was wont to accept a rigorous adherence to the rule of precedent as axiomatic in any modern system. He was apt to regard the common law through Blackstonian eyes; and he can hardly be said to have been even initiated into the criticism of statutes from other perspectives than those required by an unquestioning acceptance of the primacy of case-law. The gains should be no less great as regards organization of the substantive law. A century and a quarter ago John Austin remarked that the common law was a "mess." Although much progress in systematization has been made since that time, we still have a great deal to learn from our civilian friends — particularly from those who have attained wide recognition for their jurisprudential analyses of the common problems of modern legal systems. In addition, there is that vast illumination to be had from the discovery that other advanced legal systems, representing cultures of high achievement, sometimes apply to the solution of many problems different rules of law and even different basic doctrines than does our own. What better avenue to sound criticism of our legal system, what easier road to its early enrichment than by way of intimate knowledge of the innumerable ideas, some identical with our own but otherwise enunciated, some slightly divergent, others directly opposite, that are supplied so generously in the works of legal philosophers!

With the above objectives in view, the Editorial Committee, appointed early in 1940, immediately took up its task. For almost an entire year it engaged in active correspondence with practically all the legal philosophers in the United States, with many European, including English, legal philosophers; and, later on, when the Committee decided to include in the Series a volume devoted to Latin-American jurisprudence, there was much correspondence with legal philosophers of the various countries of Latin America. In addition, like activities centered on the engagement of translators qualified to translate correctly great works of jurisprudence into readable English. Anyone who has undertaken such translation will realize the difficulties involved, and the very high competence that is required. The Committee was able to set very rigorous standards in this regard because of the presence in the United States of an exceptionally able group of European legal scholars, some of whom had for many years been well versed in the English language.

In making its selection of works for inclusion in this Series, the Editorial Committee has been guided in part by the originality and intrinsic merit of the works chosen and in part by their being representative of leading schools of thought. The first Series, the Modern Legal Philosophy Series, had made available some of the work of nineteenth-century European legal philosophers — including Jhering, Stammler, del Vecchio, Korkunov, Kohler, and Gény. That Series and other publications had brought Duguit to the English-reading public. In 1936 the Harvard University Press published a translation of Ehrlich's *Fundamental Principles of the Sociology of Law*. The present century has also seen the rise of a number of brilliant legal philosophers who have attained very wide recognition. Among those whose inclusion in this Series was clearly called for were Max Weber, Kelsen, Petrazycki, Radbruch, the French Institutionalists, chiefly Hauriou and Renard, the Interests-Jurisprudence School centering around Heck, and some others. The opinion of the Committee as to these men was abundantly confirmed by the numerous communications received from legal philosophers of many countries, and the chief problem was to decide which of their works should be translated. But distinction in jurisprudence is not confined to a few writers, and any choice solely on the basis of scholarly merit would be enormously difficult, if not impossible. The Committee, like its predecessors, sought "to present to Anglo-American readers, the views of the best modern representative writers in jurisprudence . . . but the selection has not centered on the notion of giving equal recognition to all countries. Primarily, the design has been to represent the various schools of thought." (General Introduction to the Modern Legal Philosophy Series.) Some schools of thought have been much more productive than others; especially has this been true of those of Legal Positivism and Sociology of Law, which number many very able representatives. Without further presentation of the numerous phases of this problem, it may be stated that the Committee, whose members represent various legal philosophies, has endeavored to make the best selection possible under the conditions of its appointment, the objectives set before it, and the rigorous restriction resulting from the size of the Series.

The success of such a project as this required considerable assistance of many kinds, and the Committee is pleased to acknowledge the abundant aid extended to it. Our greatest debt is to the late John H. Wigmore, whose broad experience as Chairman of the Editorial Committee of the Modern Legal Philosophy Series was placed at our disposal, and who advised us frequently on many problems that arose in the initial stages of the work. As Honorary Chairman of this Committee until his death on April 20, 1943, he participated in many of its conferences and took an active and highly important part in launching the project and assuring its success. It was Mr. Wigmore who, in the early uncertain days of the enterprise, interested his former student, a Trustee of Northwestern University, Mr. Bertram J. Cahn, and Mrs. Cahn to contribute a substantial sum to defray the expenses of translation. The publication of the Series involved the expenditure of a considerable sum of money, and would have been impossible had not the Committee received a very substantial subsidy from Harvard Law School. No less a debt does the Committee acknowledge to the authors who contributed their work and, in some instances, their close personal collaboration. The translators have earned the Committee's admiration for their splendid achievements in the face of serious obstacles and with very little financial assistance to ease their task. We of the Committee wish, also, to give our very hearty thanks to the many legal philosophers, American, Continental, English, and Latin-American, who made many valuable suggestions and encouraged us greatly by their interest in the project. They are far too numerous to be named, as are those many persons in various positions, some of them rather humble ones, who lightened our tasks by their kindly aid. Finally the Committee acknowledges the special help given by Harvard Law School, the University of San Francisco Law School, Columbia University Law School, and Indiana University Law School. Each of the first two schools provided at its own cost a member of its faculty to serve as a translator, as well as stenographic assistance, and the other schools provided considerable stenographic, clerical, and other help. To each of the above persons and institutions the Committee gives its grateful thanks for assistance, without which the publication of this Series would not have been possible.

CONTENTS

II. GUSTAV RADBRUCH: LEGAL PHILOSOPHY

III. JEAN DABIN: GENERAL THEORY OF LAW

PART ONE. THE CONCEPT OF LAW

INTRODUCTION

By Edwin W. Patterson *

The significant contributions to the general theory of law which are translated in this volume have, along with their many differences and conflicts, a common theme and a common level of discussion. The common theme may be stated as the relation of values to positive law. The common level is the plane on which the jurist's judgments of value eventuate in law-making, in the implementation of values by legislation or case law. Each of these three writers tries to place law in the context of some more general and abstract philosophy. Here they part company. For Emil Lask and Gustav Radbruch the starting point of legal philosophy is to be found in the work of Immanuel Kant. For Jean Dabin the basic context is the philosophy of St. Thomas Aquinas. All three of them seek to relate the values of positive law to a world outlook.

The common theme above stated signifies another point on which they generally agree, the maintenance of the distinction between the "Is" and the "Ought." This distinction is here twofold. The "Is" of postive law, the law of the state, is distinguished from the values (justice, the common good, expediency, certainty, etc.) which that law ought to embody and implement, but which it may, on the other hand, limit or partly reject. This distinction is well brought out in Dabin's treatment of what he calls "legal method." On the other hand, the "Is" of societal facts, of sociology, economics, psychology, and even prevailing social morality, presents the materials, raw or partly prefabricated, of evaluations, judgments of Oughtness, which in turn may or may not be given effect through positive law. In Lask and Radbruch this distinction appears in the opposition between "reality" and "value" and in the concept of "transempirical value." In Dabin it appears in the opposition between the "given" and the "construed," which is, roughly, that between the materials of law-making and the law-maker's technique. All three emphasize the difference between the role of the ethical philosopher and that of the practical law-maker. None is prepared to justify a law on merely traditional or historical grounds.

Yet the "Is" and the "Ought" are not divorced in these philosophies of law. No claim is made, as in Kelsen's pure theory of law,[1] that a

* Cardozo Professor of Jurisprudence, Columbia University.

[1] See Kelsen, General Theory of Law and State (1945), in this Series.

general theory of law can or should be developed by excluding values and societal facts as extraneous elements. Lask tries to place legal science among the cultural sciences, and in so doing to determine the meaning of cultural science. Radbruch and Dabin discuss the purpose and justification of such legal conceptions and rules as those relating to property, contract, and penalty. Aided by the excellent supplemental notes provided by the translator, Professor Kurt Wilk, the reader who is familiar with Anglo-American law will, I believe, find these discussions the most interesting parts of the book.

The common level of discussion in Radbruch and Dabin is that of law-making and systematic interpretation rather than that of the judicial process, the application of law to individual cases. Lask, a philosopher who abandoned the study of law, is frequently on a higher level of abstraction. Perhaps all three were somewhat influenced by the Free Law movement [2] or by the Jurisprudence of Interests [3] of the early twentieth century; if so, none of them touches upon those movements. In another view, the level of discussion is more abstract and remote from law at the beginning and at the end. Lask is the most abstract and difficult to grasp. Radbruch begins with the more abstract part of his discussion, and ends his volume with delightful comments on particular topics. Dabin begins with the more concrete parts of this theme — the concept of law, legal method — and ends with natural law and justice. Between the poles of neo-Kantianism and neo-scholasticism they meet on a common ground, the meanings and evaluations of legal doctrines and institutions. No one of these men has, I think, founded a new and original philosophy of law; yet each has added something to the philosophical system from which he started by adapting it to twentieth-century culture. Each in his own way illustrates the familiar dictum that the most enduring aspect of philosophy is not its solutions but its problems.

Lask

Emil Lask's *Habilitationsschrift*,[4] submitted to the faculty of philosophy of the University of Heidelberg in 1905, was his only published work in the field of legal philosophy. He had previously given up the study of law for the study of philosophy, in which he was deeply influenced by the German philosopher, Rickert. Yet Lask's single work

[2] See essays in Science of Legal Method (Modern Legal Philosophy Series, vol. IX; Boston, 1917).

[3] The Jurisprudence of Interests (trans. Schoch), vol. II in the present Series.

[4] That is, his thesis submitted for admission to the academic profession.

on legal philosophy, here translated, had a considerable influence upon German jurists, among them Gustav Radbruch, who became an instructor (*Privatdozent*) at Heidelberg shortly before Lask did. Lask's essay thus provides the general philosophical background for Radbruch's treatise.

Lask's general objective, as he tells us at the close of his essay, is to explore the "methodology" of legal philosophy and legal science. By this he means not the methods of the legislative process or the judicial process — subjects which he scarcely touches upon — but rather the place of legal philosophy and legal science in the general scheme of cultural sciences. The latter are sciences of value; they deal with culture in its relation to values. What is a value? Lask nowhere defines the term. He uses it as elemental, basic and therefore undefinable, just as Bentham used the term "interest." Lask does, however, give a contextual meaning to "value" by the way in which he uses the term. The "critical theory of values" regards empirical reality as the only kind of reality. Values are "trans-empirical," that is, they are not inherent in or logically deducible from empirical reality, but are derived by a mental operation upon reality. Since the mind can operate only by the use of categories or types, "typical values," that is, types of value, are the subject matter of legal philosophy. Yet Lask assigns a somewhat equivocal status to "individual values." At one point he says that individual value is an inexplicable idea, since value implies a standard of appraisal. Yet a little further on he defends the conception on the ground that there is no reason why the "universality" of a value "should be bound to the logical structure of a general concept and why it is not as compatible with the logical structure of incomparable singleness and individuality."[5] This passage seems difficult to reconcile with the Kantian theory of cognition by means of universals. Kant did, indeed, hold that the ultimate test of morality was to be found in the individual conscience; but he placed the individual under a duty to make an evaluation of his proposed act by constructing a general principle in accordance with the categorical imperative: "Act according to a maxim which can be adopted at the same time as a universal law."[6] Lask's "individual value" is the value of a concrete, individual case rather than of an individual person.

Lask, like Radbruch, introduces a theory of meaning which is not explicitly formulated but which seems to have been derived from the German philosopher, Heinrich Rickert. Lask brings in the conception of levels of meaning, a common device in twentieth-century philosophy,

[5] *Infra*, p. 5.

[6] KANT, THE PHILOSOPHY OF LAW (trans. Hastie, 1887) 34.

when he says that reality is a "substratum" of typical values. The "social value," which is one kind of typical value, is intermediate between the empirical substratum and the individual value. The individual evaluation is to be made by applying social standards to the empirical facts.

Lask's essay shows the struggle of Kant's followers, who were (and probably are) numerous in Germany, to convert Kant's eighteenth-century rational individualism into a twentieth-century social philosophy of law. Rudolf Stammler, at the beginning of the present century,[7] tried to do this by making the end of the legal order a social ideal which was ultimately dependent on individual ethics: A community of men willing freely. In such an ideal community life, says Lask, the ultimate ends of the community would have to be recognized intuitively by each individual and fulfilled spontaneously. But this is merely an ideal. Order in the community requires formal prescriptions which, Lask says, take no account of the moral complications of individual cases. The new world outlook proclaims "transpersonal values," objective typical values. Lask does not quite decide whether law is merely a means to the attainment of individual values or, as an embodiment of social values, has a separate purpose. He does not say, as Jhering did, that the social values of community life are essential to the realization of individual values, that man lives alone and also in society.[8]

At all events, legal philosophy, as a theory of typical values, permits two types of operations on the "formal" value: (1) Absolute meanings may be systematized, remaining within the realm of value. (2) Particular realizations of a value may be considered, as in politics. Radbruch's book partly fulfills the former task, by developing a classification of values into individual, transindividual, and transpersonal, and it brilliantly fulfills the latter by showing the realizations of value in significant concepts and doctrines of modern law. Besides legal philosophy, says Lask, there is legal science, a subordinate discipline, which is a cultural science because (following Rickert) it is a product of the theoretical relation of immediate reality to cultural meanings. This does not mean that law is a "social science" as that term is used by American sociologists. The German "cultural science"[9] is a broader term than social science.

[7] STAMMLER, THE THEORY OF JUSTICE (trans. Husik, 1925), Modern Legal Philosophy Series, vol. VIII.

[8] See JHERING, THE LAW AS A MEANS TO AN END (trans. Husik, 1924), especially pp. 344–345.

[9] See Translator's note (a) to Lask's Introduction.

Legal science, in the broad sense, may look at law in two distinct ways: One, as a "vital social process," a cultural factor; the other, as a complex of normative meanings, of dogmatical contents. The former leads to a social theory of law; the latter to jurisprudence, of the analytical type but still pursuing its task of relating the contents of legal norms to cultural meanings. Lask's twofold division may be compared with that between the sociology of law and sociological jurisprudence, which it substantially though superficially resembles. Lask's social theory of law is basically different from the sociology of law, which is regarded by most of its adherents as an empirical or natural science. For Lask the difference between natural science and cultural science is as profound as that between reality and value.

On one point Lask differs with Kant, namely, on the "externality" of law. Kant distinguished morals from law in that the latter deals only with external conduct. Lask points out that Kant did not adhere consistently to this distinction since, in his philosophy of law, he tried to reduce all legal relations to relations of the human will. Thus a contract is a union of the wills of the parties and the law gives effect to their individual wills. Lask remarks that Kant overshot his mark in this respect but he does not indicate how much of the Kantian will theory he would retain. Legal science, as a study of normative meanings, includes not only the systematic connections between the contents of legal norms (as in a standard legal treatise, for instance) but also the ideal (theoretical) comparison of juridical meanings with the prejuridical substratum of the law, that is, the concrete and abstract realities of culture and of ordinary life. Law should be given a social interpretation. The individual will is no longer the key to unlock all doors.

Lask seems to see around a good many corners which he does not purport to explore. His sense of wholeness, his endeavor to relate law to a world outlook, and his failure to use illustrations drawn from legal doctrines, together with the lack of a clear structural organization in the presentation of his ideas, will doubtless make his essay difficult for some readers to understand. The foregoing commentary is intended for such readers. If it does not suffice, they may do well to pass over Lask until after they have read Radbruch.

Radbruch

Gustav Radbruch is distinguished as lawyer, political leader, jurist, and legal philosopher. He takes from German idealism, especially from Lask, as much as he needs of general philosophy in order to develop a critique of the values involved in the important legal doctrines, institutions, and problems of his time. His service as Reich Minister of Justice of the German republic under the ill-starred Weimar Constitution gave him experience with the practical workings of politics, law, and government. Because of his political views he was removed during the Hitler regime from his academic post as professor of law at Heidelberg; he was restored to it after the cessation of World War II.

Radbruch's book, like the German Civil Code, is divided into a general part and a special part. The general part (Sections 1–15) presents the foundations of his legal philosophy and some of the broadest value-relating aspects of law. The special part (Sections 16–29) discusses such familiar subjects as legal personality, ownership, contract, marriage, penal law, and international law. His concluding topic, prophetically, is war.

Radbruch's first assumption is that legal philosophy is a part of general philosophy, hence the legal philosopher must begin by demonstrating the assumptions of general philosophy. The first of these is the distinction between reality and value. In our immediate experience this distinction is blurred. The primitive man sees in the thunderstorm a warning from the gods; the modern man sees in it an interference with his plans for golf or a picnic. Events come to us colored with our personal evaluations. Only by an effort of the mind can we separate reality from value. The meteorologist does this when he considers the thunderstorm as a consequence of the meeting of air currents under certain conditions of temperature, barometric pressure, and vapor density. Such is the "value-blind" attitude of the scientist toward reality. The scientist, however, does not discover reality; he creates it. Here Radbruch follows the Kantian theory of cognition in its reformulation by post-Kantian German philosophers. The mind in separating reality from value creates both. While I may remark in passing that this seems to push a good idea too far, it is a basic epistemological assumption which affects Radbruch's analysis and terminology throughout most of his book.

In contrast with the value-blind attitude of science is the deliberately evaluating attitude which characterizes logic, ethics, and aesthetics. That ethics and aesthetics are evaluating disciplines one would have no doubt; it may seem somewhat unusual to classify logic as an evaluating science. Symbolic logicians would be rather surprised, though John Dewey's instrumental logic is avowedly normative, that is, it purports to tell men how they *ought* to think in order to get the best results. At any rate, Radbruch's inclusion of logic among the evaluating disciplines gives us a clue to his conception of value.

In addition to these two attitudes toward value, Radbruch finds two others: The value-relating attitude and the value-conquering attitude. The former is the methodical attitude of the "cultural" sciences, which include the humanities, history, and the social sciences. The value-conquering attitude belongs to religion, which calls for love or mercy regardless of the worth or worthlessness of the individual. To these four attitudes toward value correspond four realms of what is given: Existence (value-blind), value (evaluating), meaning (value-relating), and essence (value-conquering). The philosophy of law is chiefly concerned with value and the science of law with meaning.

The relation between these last two is expressed in another way. Law is a cultural phenomenon, a fact related to value. The "concept" of law (which is distinguished from its validity) can be determined only as something which "means" to be just, however short of that end it may fall. Legal science deals with law as a cultural fact; legal philosophy, as a cultural value.

Radbruch's philosophy of law is "relativist." Two main assumptions underlie his relativism: That value judgments, conclusions of value, cannot be logically derived from facts; and that legal philosophy can clarify the end by considering the means. It may arrive at a single world 'look of the ultimate end of law, or it may try to develop all possible outlooks as starting points of legal evaluation. It may thus present the antinomies of conflicting values implicit in a legal situation, and leave it to the individual to draw his decision from the depths of his own personality, his conscience. Here Radbruch, like a good German, falls back upon a passage from Goethe. This attitude of "antinomism," of the presentation of antinomies to be resolved by the individual conscience, exemplified throughout the book, is characteristic of Radbruch's critical discernment and his tolerance.

While Radbruch regards all law as oriented toward justice, he recognizes that justice alone does not explain the content of all legal norms. A second element of the idea of law is expediency, suitability to a purpose. Questions of expediency cannot be answered absolutely but only relativistically, in relation to one's views of the law and the state. A third element of the idea of law is legal certainty. The law, as an ordering of society, must be one order over all members of society; it must prevail over their various disagreements. To do this it must be laid down by an agency able to carry through what it pronounces; it must be positive. Thus legal certainty requires positive law. At this point one may wonder why certainty was not included under expediency; legal certainty is expedient for many branches of the law, such as property, contracts, and criminal law. The reason, I think, is that Radbruch conceives of legal certainty primarily as peace and order, as putting an end to the babble of conflicting views or the war of all against all. Thus he says that the existence of a legal order is more important than its expediency or even its justice. Yet the conflicts between them do not end with the establishment of law. His discussion of the "tensions" between these three elements of the idea of law is the core of his antinomic philosophy of law.

When he comes to discuss the "validity" of law (Section 10), Radbruch seems to blur the distinction between reality and value which he took to be fundamental. He outlines three doctrines of the validity of law: The juridical, the sociological, and the philosophical. The first is that of the judge and the lawyer who trace the validity of all legal norms to the constitution; but they have no way of testing the validity of the constitution unless they resort to an extra-juridical (or, to use Kelsen's term, a meta-juridical) test. Here the sociological doctrine purports to provide an answer, but Radbruch rejects it as merely descriptive and not a justification of the legal order. It is hard to see why he feels it necessary to reject the juridical-sociological explanation of the validity of law. His conclusion is that law is valid *if* it can be carried through effectively *because* that is the only way to provide legal certainty, peace and order.

Radbruch leaves no doubt of his rejection of Kant's attempt to state all legal relations in terms of the individual will. For instance, in his discussion of contracts (Section 19) Radbruch rejects the idea that the courts, in enforcing a contract, merely give effect to the will of the obligor. Agreeing with Jhering, he says that the "obliging" will is the will of yesterday, while the "obliged" will is the will of today and tomorrow. How far ought the law to prescribe that the obligation of a contract be governed by the will of the obligor, and how far by his declaration? Here the interests of private autonomy are opposed by those of the security of trade and commerce, the individualistic by the social view of law. This is substantially the opposition between the subjective and objective theories of contract in Anglo-American law.

Radbruch's book is written in an urbane and gracious style, rich in classical and historical allusions. Its fundamental starting points are those of nineteenth-century German idealism, which it tries to adapt to the movement for the socialization of law of the early twentieth century. There is evidence that, in its three editions, it won a high prestige among the German intellectuals of the 1920's and 1930's. Ironically enough, the third edition appeared in 1932, shortly before the accession to power of Adolf Hitler. The Nazi regime engulfed its tolerant rationalism and led the German people down the path of war, which to Radbruch is the negation of law and reason. The reader may ponder for himself why this happened.

DABIN

Jean Dabin has devoted his career to law teaching and productive legal scholarship. Since 1922 he has been a member of the faculty of law at Louvain in Belgium. His works cover a wide range of law and legal philosophy, and have been honored both in his own country and abroad.

Dabin's work is of interest to American readers for several reasons. First, he builds his General Theory of Law (the work here translated) upon one of the major philosophies of western civilization, the scholasticism of St. Thomas Aquinas (1225–1274). Secondly, he adapts the principles of Thomism to modern social conditions and modern systems of thought, even departing in detail from some of the pronouncements of the Doctor Angelicus. Thirdly, he displays the same tactful tolerance that the Doctor did toward rival systems of thought, not denouncing or berating them as heresies but trying to persuade the reader by reason to take a different view. In this respect he differs from some American scholastic writers. Fourthly, and not least important, Dabin is chiefly interested in the philosophy of positive law, the reasons of policy and expediency which serve to explain the systems of legal norms of modern states. His level of discussion, as was said above, is that of law-making and interpretation; he does not view the arena of litigation, where the law is confronted with a complex situation of fact. Hence some of his "solutions" will seem to the American case lawyer a bit oversimplified. Dabin stops short of what, since Cardozo's memorable work,[10] has been known in this country as "the judicial process."

As some readers may be unfamiliar with scholasticism, it seems well to give a brief though inadequate outline of the legal philosophy of St. Thomas Aquinas. The three main topics, which the reader will encounter throughout Dabin's book, are natural law, justice, and the common good. Governing the universe, both animate and inanimate, is God's Eternal Law. Natural law as a principle or principles of human conduct is so much of the Eternal law as man can perceive by the use of his reason. Natural law, when rightly discovered by reason, is universal, absolute, eternal, immutable. Justice has to do with man's duties toward others. Here St. Thomas followed Aristotle in distinguishing between commutative justice, the "man-to-man" justice of civil litigation, and distributive justice, the distribution of the good of the community among its members according to their personal merit. "Legal

[10] CARDOZO, THE NATURE OF THE JUDICIAL PROCESS (1921).

justice," a third kind discussed by Dabin, has to do with the duties of the subject to the political community. The "common good" takes its meaning from Aquinas' definition of human law as "an ordinance of reason for the common good, made by him who has care of the community and promulgated."[11] The common good of the community is the end or purpose of human enactments. Dabin takes the common good to include the fitness or expediency of law for a particular community and for the limitations and needs of the legal order which is to fulfill it. Since he is concerned chiefly with the jurist's art or technique of making and interpreting law in a modern state, he gives the common good greater prominence in his discussion (though not greater significance in his theory) than the other two concepts.

This emphasis appears in the basic organization of Dabin's book into three parts: The "concept" of law, legal method, and a third part on natural law and justice. Instead of beginning with an exposition of natural law and justice as the logical fundamentals of positive law, he begins with the conception of law as he finds it in modern states. At many points throughout the first two parts he speaks of natural law and justice in relation to the jurist's work but refers the reader to his later discussion of those topics. Even one who does not follow his views of natural law and justice will be enlightened by his scholarly, prudent, and illuminating interpretation of the values implicit in modern law.

At the outset Dabin envisages the law of a state, as expressed in its statutes, juridical customs, and the precedents of its tribunals (case law), as the "realities" on which his conception of law is based. Other realities, the state, the conduct of officials, the societal facts of a given community, are related to law. He finds the expression, "positive law," unsatisfactory to express the "concept" of law, because the adjective "positive" traditionally means something that is accidental, arbitrary, or capricious. These are qualities which Dabin is unwilling to include in his concept of law. At this point one may compare Dabin's conception of law with Holland's definition (derived from Austin) of a law as "a general rule of external human action enforced by a sovereign political authority." One can find in Dabin all of the characteristics that Holland ascribes to a law. A law is a general rule. Its subject matter is external human conduct rather than conscience or belief. It has the authority and sanction of the state. Dabin substitutes for "enforced" the lesser requirement that there be obedience to the law of a state in general, in the great majority of instances to which it might

[11] 8 St. Thomas Aquinas, The Summa Theologica (Dominican Friars trans., London, 1927), 8 (*Ia IIae*, qu. 90, art. 4).

be applied. He has some difficulty with the Continental doctrine that a law can be abrogated by desuetude, especially because Aquinas in one passage intimated that a law can be set aside by a conflicting usage; yet Dabin eventually rejects this doctrine. Likewise, a law does not cease to be a law even though public officials in the exercise of their discretion choose not to enforce it. Thus Dabin's conception of the validity of law resembles that of the English analytical jurists, from Austin to Holland.

Dabin even finds the same trouble spots in the imperative (positive) conception of law that other writers have found. Do the parties to a contract create individual legal norms for themselves? Disagreeing with Kelsen, Dabin says not, because law must have the character of generality (No. 57). Are constitutional provisions which grant certain powers to and impose certain duties upon the three major branches of the government, but which cannot be enforced by any recognized kind of legal sanction, really laws? The highest court under the guise of interpretation may negate a provision of the constitution. Or the highest legislative body may neglect to do something (e.g., reapportion legislative representatives to districts on the basis of population as determined by the latest census) in direct contravention of a constitutional requirement. Dabin, refusing to regard such constitutional clauses as merely hortatory political principles, calls them "imperfect laws" (*leges imperfectae*). International law, for the same reason, is imperfect law.

But Dabin's "concept of law" includes more than Holland's definition of law because Dabin is not satisfied to determine the validity of law; he seeks to determine also its end or objective. This he finds in the common good. The primary end of the state is to provide order in society; the law is a necessary means to that end. *Ubi societas, ibi jus.* This relation gives the state its rightful claim to sovereignty over all other social groups and the law of the state, inasmuch as it is supreme, is the only true law (No. 12). Here Radbruch and Dabin are moving on nearly parallel tracks.

Dabin means by "legal method" something a good deal different from the method of the Jurisprudence of Interests [12] and from the methods represented by books on that title published in the United States.[13] The latter are concerned with the judicial process, the interpretation of statutes, the application of the formal sources of the law. Dabin discusses the questions, how and from what materials is law constructed? The end of the law is to promote the temporal common good; the means

[12] *Supra*, note 3.

[13] For example, *supra*, note 2.

to this end is legal technique. Because law is "instrumental" in character it differs fundamentally from morals (No. 132); morality is an end in itself, not a means even to beatitude. Dabin's definition of the temporal public good (No. 136) resembles the interpretation which two American pragmatists, Professors John Dewey and James H. Tufts, have given to Jeremy Bentham's utilitarian end of law, "the greatest happiness of the greatest number." They defined it: "Social conditions should be such that all individuals can exercise their initiative in a social medium which will develop their personal capacities and reward their efforts."[14] Although there are differences, in each case the end is that of a social philosophy of law.

Dabin devotes a good deal of space — too much, for American readers — to refuting the positions taken by two distinguished French legal philosophers of the early part of this century. François Gény's thesis was that the law is partly "given" and partly "construed"; partly "science" and partly "technique." Dabin tries to show that the law is wholly "construed," that it is a creation of jurists guided by prudence toward a temporal end, the common good. He likewise rejects the social-psychological conception of Léon Duguit, another French legal philosopher. The jurist (by which Dabin means the prudent law-constructor) does indeed obtain the raw materials of his art from morals, from customs, and other conditions in society; but he transforms them into something new, to his own end and with his own technique. For example, the jurist has to draw firm lines where life knows only gradual shadings; he must consider the requirement of proof, since it is futile to enact a law in such terms that no one can produce proof of the facts necessary to invoke its application. The jurist has to consider the practical convenience and enforceability of his law. Dabin's illustrations of "technique" seem a good deal like Radbruch's examples of the work of "legal science." However, the difference in terminology signifies a difference in fundamentals and some differences in treatment.

Dabin's exposition of natural law follows, as far as I can tell, the orthodox scholastic tradition. Natural law is a rule of human conduct deduced from the nature of man as revealed in the basic inclinations of that nature under the control of reason. Since human nature is identical in all men and invariant in all times and places, the precepts of natural law are universal, immutable, certain, admit of no doubt or discussion (No. 203). He recognizes, however, a difference of opinion as to whether the secondary principles of natural law have these qualities; the present trend is to recognize that only the "primary principles" are so endowed. The primary principle of natural law is: Seek the good

[14] DEWEY AND TUFTS, ETHICS (1932) 276.

and avoid evil. He recognizes a familial natural law and a political natural law, having for their subject matter, respectively, duties of members of the family toward each other and duties of subjects and officials to each other. He denies, consistently with his conception of (positive) law, that there is a "juridical natural law"; juridical law must always be conditioned by the circumstances in which it is to operate. Yet civil laws that are contrary to natural law are bad laws, and "do not answer to the concept of law" (No. 210). God and the Church lay down positive moral rules which complete and render more precise the "given" of the moral natural law. A legal rule positively contrary to morals must be condemned as contrary to the public good. As examples, "historic or imaginable," he mentions laws ordering apostasy, dueling, abortion, euthanasia, and laws prohibiting gifts, testamentary or *inter vivos*. Moreover, a legal rule which tends to discourage virtuous acts or to encourage vicious ones is contrary to morals (No. 246). Still, the civil law need not sanction every command or prohibition of morals, for morality imposed under the threat of coercion ceases to be morality (No. 248). On the whole, Dabin's treatment of "natural law" characterizes it as ethics rather than law.

Professor Kurt Wilk's knowledge and understanding of European legal systems, philosophies, and literatures has greatly enriched this translation. Wherever an author's allusion would be unfamiliar to most American readers, he has inserted a translator's footnote (lettered and indicated as such) to explain it. On the assumption that most American readers will not readily understand Latin expressions, these have been translated except where they have become common terms of American law. Professor Wilk's training in American law (as well as in German law) has enabled him to use the closest American analogue to some of the legal concepts and doctrines discussed by Radbruch and Dabin. To him is due the credit for a clear and accurate translation. Yet it is only fair to say that the present writer has suggested some idiomatic and stylistic changes which were designed to make the translation smoother reading. The final product is, in minor part, a result of collaboration. Our purpose has been to make the volume as easy to read as would be compatible with the nature of the subject matter and fidelity to the author's ideas.

COLUMBIA UNIVERSITY,
NEW YORK
December, 1949.

TRANSLATOR'S NOTE

By Kurt Wilk *

In presenting to American readers contributions to general legal philosophy by scholars of other countries, the translator's task must be to make each author's thought as fully accessible as possible without violating or altering it.

In the following translations of works by Emil Lask, Gustav Radbruch, and Jean Dabin, an effort has therefore been made to present the three writers in readable English and in terms familiar to an American lawyer, yet to preserve, as much as rendition in another language will permit, the cast of each writer's reasoning, the significance and uniformity of his terminology, the shadings of meanings in his arguments, and something at least of the flavor of his personal style.

Different problems have been presented by the style and terminology of each of the three authors, differing as they do in their national and personal backgrounds in law, philosophy, and civilization. Each one draws his material and illustrations of course largely from the institutions of his part of the world and from conceptions developed in the juristic and philosophic literature in his own language. Wherever possible, equivalent English terms have been chosen for such materials or concepts. In the choice of equivalent English terms, Anglo-American legal, political, and social institutions and ideas have been freely resorted to where their general significance and their meaning in the context sufficiently resemble those of their Continental counterparts. Only where the distinctive meaning of the Continental term is involved has it been retained, if necessary with an appropriate brief explanation. Only in such passages, to give one example, has the term "causa" been used rather than "consideration." The translator has preferred to reproduce the author's thoughts, and the terms his language offered him or imposed upon him, in equivalent and readily understandable English rather than simply transcribing and then explaining them. Where insertion of explanatory matter in text passages or footnotes could not be avoided, all additions made by the translator have been enclosed in brackets or otherwise indicated.

Apart from the material which each author has drawn from the law and life familiar to him, the style of each reflects his grounding in a distinctive philosophical tradition — that of Kant and Hegel in the Germans, and that of St. Thomas in the Belgian — and the individual

* Associate Professor of Government, Wells College.

way in which he has projected and developed it for the problems of his time and environment. Lask's highly abstract, conceptually and terminologically precise yet complex and original reasoning proceeds in the self-assured, severe and pregnant sentences of technical philosophical German of the turn of the century. While built on these foundations, Radbruch's thoughts reflect the broad understanding humanism and the practical concerns of the legal scholar and statesman of the Weimar Republic, which are expressed in the mellower phrases of his polished German with its wealth of literary and cultural connotations. The fixed scholastic categories and rubrics of Dabin's exposition are set forth in careful didactic French with occasional academic rhetoric that shows but rarely the stress of contemporary Nazi-Fascist pressure on the landmarks of established and reinterpreted Thomistic doctrine. Each of these styles of writing offers a different kind of challenge to reproduction in English that the American student may find clear and readable.

The texts of the three works included in this volume, Lask's *Rechtsphilosophie*, Radbruch's *Rechtsphilosophie* (third edition), and Dabin's *Théorie générale du droit*, have been translated in full. The authors' annotations have also been translated in full except for certain omissions in the voluminous footnotes to Professor Dabin's work. These omissions include many of the sometimes lengthy Latin passages quoted and some of the detailed polemics, quotations from and modifications in the thoughts of other writers not familiar to American readers. In all cases, the complete references have been preserved in the footnotes in order that the interested reader may pursue them if he wishes to. All omissions are indicated by three periods.

In all three works, the original divisions and their headings have been preserved. Subheads have been added by the translator in the essay by Lask and have been taken from the table of contents and from page headings in the book by Radbruch and, with some abridgements, from the analytical table of contents of the book by Dabin. The authors' footnotes have been numbered consecutively for each chapter or section; footnotes added by the translator have been indicated by similarly consecutive letters and enclosed in brackets. Where the author uses terms or passages in a language foreign to him, or words in his own tongue for purposes of etymological discussion, these have been retained in their original language, with translations added where necessary. Citations have been preserved as given by the authors though adapted in form to American legal usage as far as practicable; in a few cases, references to editions in English of works cited have been added, such as to volumes published in this Series and in the first Modern Legal Philosophy Series.

The translator has been fortunate in the close contact he had throughout his work with Professor Edwin W. Patterson, of the School of Law of Columbia University. Professor Patterson read the entire manuscripts of the three translations and contributed numerous valuable comments and detailed recommendations for improvements, without ever fettering the translator's freedom of judgment. His suggestions have resulted in a clearer and smoother text in too many places to indicate them in detail; and the exchange of views with him has guided and aided the translator in his endeavor to produce English editions that would be both accurate and readable presentations of the ideas of the three writers.

Wells College K. W.
Aurora-on-Cayuga, New York

I

LEGAL PHILOSOPHY

By EMIL LASK

1905

Emil Lask was born on September 25, 1875. He passed his youth in Falkenberg in the province of Brandenburg, Germany, and he began the study of law at the University of Freiburg (in Baden) but soon changed to philosophy under the influence of Professor Heinrich Rickert. He continued his studies at the University of Strassburg, where Wilhelm Windelband and Paul Hensel were then professors of philosophy. His dissertation for the degree of Doctor of Philosophy, which he received from Strassburg, was "Fichte's Idealismus und die Geschichte" (1902). His second work, the one here translated, entitled RECHTSPHILOSOPHIE, was a contribution to the ***Festschrift*** for Kuno Fischer, a collection of essays by various authors published under the title, DIE PHILOSOPHIE IM BEGINN DES 20. JAHRHUNDERTS (1st ed. 1905; 2d ed. 1907). It was also published separately in pamphlet form (Heidelberg, 1905). He became Privatdozent at Heidelberg University in January 1905, and later Professor Extraordinarius at the same university. He never returned to legal philosophy. His later works were in general philosophy; among them were DIE LOGIK DER PHILOSOPHIE UND DIE KATEGORIENLEHRE (1911), and DIE LEHRE VOM URTEIL (1912). He died on May 26, 1915, as a sergeant in the German army in World War I. His collected works were published in three volumes, 1923–24, under the editorship of his pupil, Eugen Herrigel.

LEGAL PHILOSOPHY[a]

INTRODUCTION

OURS IS A TIME engrossed with the problems of social life. Yet true speculation in the field of legal and social philosophy at present shows but little independence; it still leans heavily upon the great systems created by German idealistic philosophy. This may justify our frequent references to Kant and Hegel in presenting those modern theories of legal philosophy which have retained some contact with the ultimate questions of world outlook (Chapter I). However, the position of legal philosophy at the beginning of the twentieth century is not hopeless, despite its lack of originality as to the fundamental problems. For the methodological trend, most promising after its lively beginnings in very recent times (Chapter II), will force legal philosophy to recognize anew that any controversy about the method of empirical cultural sciences[b] leads beyond mere methodology and finds its definitive solution only in a system of transempirical values.

CHAPTER I

THE PHILOSOPHY OF THE LAW

A. The Method

Only in the nineteenth century has legal science achieved its full independence and apparently final deliverance from metaphysical speculation. Between the "philosophical" and "historical" schools there has

[a] The following is a translation of RECHTSPHILOSOPHIE by Dr. Emil Lask (HABILITATIONSSCHRIFT DER HOHEN PHILOSOPHISCHEN FAKULTÄT DER RUPRECHT-KARLS-UNIVERSITÄT ZU HEIDELBERG ZUR ERLANGUNG DER VENIA LEGENDI VORGELEGT Heidelberg, 1905. Carl Winter's Universitätsbuchhandlung). The footnotes, the subheadings and textual matter enclosed in brackets [ ] are by the Translator. The original — except for the list of "References" at the end — has no footnotes.

[b] This is a literal translation of the German term. Sciences (*Wissenschaften*) in German terminology include not only the natural sciences but also what some German philosophers call spiritual sciences (*Geisteswissenschaften*) and Lask and other German philosophers call cultural sciences (*Kulturwissenschaften*), namely, the humanities, history, and social sciences. The German term for culture (*Kultur*) embraces all creations of the human mind as distinct from purely natural phenomena; it thus includes all aspects of civilization as well as of culture in the narrowest sense of the word, often with emphasis on the spiritual rather than on the technological aspects.

since existed a clear distinction, but also a mutual distrust that is still strong. Those who are not content with a "general theory of law" or other generalizing sublimations of the results of empirical science but dare, even today, to challenge legal philosophy to fathom the law's absolute significance and its relation to other absolute values, from the outset incur the grave suspicion of the "heresy of natural law." Indeed, the vital question of modern legal philosophy has always been this, must any nonempiristic philosophy of the law coincide with the old metaphysics of the law which has been discredited by the splendid development of positive science?

Natural law inquired into the absolute meaning of law and justice. Thereby it established a principle in the world history of ideas which cannot be substantially dimmed in its imperishable significance by any corrections, indispensable as these may be from the methodical point of view. Its absolute, transcendental philosophical tendency is shared by any conceivable speculation on values, no matter how "critical."

Reality and Value. But the metaphysics of natural law and the critical philosophy of law differ fundamentally in determining the relationship between value and reality. This difference bears directly upon life; yet it is grounded in deep contradistinctions of theoretical philosophy. It opens the way to a clear demarcation between natural law and a legal philosophy free of metaphysics. The critical theory of values differs from any Platonistic two-worlds theory in that it regards empirical reality as the only kind of reality, but at the same time as the scene or the substratum of transempirical values or meanings of general validity. It therefore admits only a one-world theory of law, recognizing but a single kind of law: empirical legal reality. But the necessary distinction between value and its empirical substratum entails a basically two-dimensional approach; this is the dualism of philosophical and empirical methods. Philosophy regards reality from the viewpoint of its content of absolute values, while empirics regards it from the viewpoint of its factual contents. In this view, the philosophy of the law must be concerned with legal values while empirical legal science must be concerned with legal reality.

Legal Philosophy as Theory of Typical Values. However, the fundamental character of the philosophy of the law needs to be clarified further by some general remarks on the modes or forms in which values appear to us. From the standpoint of a critical dualism of value and reality, a formal logical distinction may easily be made between what may be called two coinages of value, or two states of value. A value may either be *individual,* that is, as unique as the infinitely manifold empirical substratum of reality to which it is attached; or else it may be *common,* that is, belonging to a plurality of distinct contents of reality. Almost all philosophy is concerned with the latter kind of values, that is, common or typical values. Its task is quite properly to reveal the systematic articulation of the ideal universe, the realm of super- and subordinated formal meanings of this kind, such as theoretical, ethical, aesthetical ones. But that typical values should be the only logical form of values is a mere prejudice, though one dignified by its age. There is absolutely no reason, and no one has ever attempted to show, why the absolute validity, the universality of a value, should be bound to the logical structure of a general concept and why it is not as compatible with the logical structure of incomparable singleness and individuality. The sublimity of a value is in no way affected by this second possibility. The individual value may have meaning in a sphere as high above all empirical reality, and hovering over it at the same altitude, as the typical value. The individual value shares, as a formal logical attribute, the singleness but not the infinite variety of empirical reality. Only a most imperfect analogy, at best a sort of parallel structure, would in this case exist between value and reality. Even the individual value, say, an individual value chain composed of individual value links, must, no matter how it may rank teleologically in its relation to the formal values, leave behind any specific definiteness of the several typical meanings of values (theoretical, ethical, etc.). Any isolation, particularity, and, as it were, indigence of contents must be transformed into concrete wholeness, complete penetration and homogeneity.

This is sufficient to show that legal philosophy, as the theory of the specific value of the law, can, like logic, aesthetics, philosophy of religion, and the other branches of philosophy, be only a theory of typical values. We do not at this point ask whether there is a peculiar value of the law, susceptible of coördination with other values, or what else may be the relationship of the value of law to other values. For the time being, we merely stress the methodical relation of the typical value to empirics. As indicated above, even the individual value falls short of the infinite variety of the fullness of empirical content. The typical value is still further removed from that which is concretely given, since it embodies the absolute standard of an unlimited number of instances of its realization. Thus it acquires the character of a value formula, in contradistinction to the single value, which is not repeatable. Just as the theory of logical judgments fathoms the universal formula of meaning which any judgment must contain in conformity with its absolute purpose of attaining truth, so the philosophy of law searches for the universal formula of legal value. It searches for the formal absolute objective of any historically given law, the systematically articulated complex of postulates applicable to any empirical legal reality, or in Stammler's words, the law of the law, the right law. The philosophy of law looks for the transcendental locus or typical value-relation of the law; it inquires into the law's position in the context of a world outlook.[a]

It is therefore too broad and ambiguous to define the philosophy of law as the theory of the "concept of law." The formation of concepts is always the product of a certain method. Thus, a "concept" of law is formed not only in philosophy but also in the various distinct sciences dealing with laws. There are a philosophical, a juridical, and a social concept of law.

Formal Natural Law. So far, the most general criteria of speculation about values have been elaborated only to the extent indispensable for a clear contrast with the metaphysical trend of natural law. Rational metaphysics is opposed to the critical distinction between value and reality, and to the doctrine that historical facts are not to be derived from any abstract value formula. For it is directed at a hypostasis of transempirical values as real independent vital forces, thus combining and confounding value and reality.

In this sense, any natural law is metaphysical rationalism; it hypostatizes legal values as legal realities. Yet for a firm grasp of that core of all natural law, agreement must first be reached as to what "empirical reality" as contrasted with mere value may mean in the field of law. To answer this question, we need not enter into an investigation of the concept of reality in the cultural sciences. We may provisionally confine ourselves to dividing the complex concept of legal reality into *formal* positiveness and *material* positiveness — following the discussions of Bergbohm and his predecessors such as Hegel, Stahl, and Bruns. Corresponding to that division, natural law may in turn be divided into a formal and a material confusion of value and reality.

The formal positiveness of the law is nothing but a kind of validity. In this case, then, a kind of validity appears as "empirical reality" and, consequently, as a product of the reification common in natural law. The hypostasis in this case transfers one kind of validity into another, absolute normativeness into empirical normativeness; in short, it transforms the reasonableness of the law into the external obligation of the law. For its external absolute obligation upon the organs and the mem-

[a] This is the literal translation of the German term *Weltanschauung*, which Lask uses to denote the basic theory of the world as a whole that underlies a particular philosophy.

bers of the community is essential to the positive legal norm. Hence the thesis of formal legal positivism that the only reason why that positive normativeness is binding is the authority of a human community. This connection between community authority and obligation represents the formal criterion of the law which is broken down by natural law. For natural law assumes that the external obligation upon the members of the community issues directly from the *absolute* significance of a legal postulate, that is, from its purely ideal dignity. Natural law thus is emanatist.[b] It eliminates the criterion of the community authority and replaces it with reason as a higher formal source of law, from which "law" emanates without and against any human enactment, so that law conflicting with reason becomes formally void.

It is Bergbohm's merit to have traced this formal natural law, and to point out even suspicious tendencies toward a belief in natural law in modern jurisprudence. However, an explicit profession of natural law is confined today almost entirely to Catholic legal philosophy, represented by von Cathrein, von Hertling, Gutberlet, and others.

Material Natural Law. But there have also been theories of past and present legal philosophy which may be properly characterized as natural law, although they expressly deny the metaphysical doctrine of the sources of law. Unless any belief in absolute standards of law, any kind of speculation about values, is to be confounded with natural law, natural law must be understood as material as well as formal, as opposed in both respects to critical speculation about values. Just as formal natural law beclouds the form of legal reality, namely, the specific normative character of law, so natural law in a material sense must be fatal to the material element of the positive in law, or to the empirical content of the law. In this case, the reality that is subjected to a metaphysical hypostasis can consist only in the fullness of individual content and the concrete historical conditions of the positive legal rules, in the very element that in the critical view constitutes the transcendental prerogative of empirical reality. The exponent of natural law believes that out of a system of abstract values he can deduce a stock of legal norms, the contents of which need not be individualized any further and are suitable for introduction as law anywhere, regardless of concrete historical connections. He may quite possibly regard such a complex of proposed rules as complete and exhaustive only as to its contents, at the same time believing that it acquires the formal quality of law only through its enactment by positive legislation. This would amount to an exclusively material natural law, whereas natural law in

[b] That is, it assumes that law flows from a higher essence.

a formal sense is likely always to involve the material element too. This material element is usually in the minds of those who blame natural law for proposing an ideal code valid for all times and peoples.

Natural law is unhistorical rationalism and metaphysics; yet it need by no means coincide with naturalistic metaphysics. The naturalistic undercurrent which so often appears in the history of natural law theories must rather be understood as a mere variety of the material doctrine of natural law. Indeed, the immutable value of reason may serve as the speculative principle to get and isolate abstract partial contents out of the concrete fullness of what is given; but so may unchanging "nature." Abstract formulae of natural law, and not value formulae, are thus precipitated as independent realities. Indeed, the term "natural law" contains several meanings of "nature," which are rarely distinguished sufficiently. First — and especially in the formal version of natural law — "nature" implies universal validity or the absolute, as contrasted with the mere relative validity of human enactment. Secondly, it implies the generality of contents, either of reason or of nature, as contrasted with individual particularity.

It is necessary to narrow the meaning of natural law down to a hypostatizing metaphysics as distinct from a theory of absolute values in general. Only from this point of view may the unanimous opposition of positive science to natural law be justified on the most general epistemological grounds. To be sure, all polemics against the unhistorical character of natural law suffer from an insufficient distinction between the formal and material aspects, as Bergbohm, again, has recently shown. Bergbohm himself wants to test the historical method exclusively by the criterion of a formal-positivistic theory of the sources of the law. But this theory is at best connected with the historical principle loosely, namely, to the extent that the concept of the positive source of law involves the assumption of a law-forming process that is "perceptible externally" and "demonstrable historically." Otherwise, the predominant interest of the entire opposition to natural law is formalistic and is directed toward purifying the concept of law, however empiristic that concept may be. On the whole, therefore, this interest may be termed empiristic or positivistic rather than historical.

Critical Legal Philosophy as a Philosophy of Positive Law. Nearly all adherents of absolute value principles in the legal philosophy of the nineteenth century — such as Stahl, Trendelenburg, and Lasson — were affected by empiricism, the empirical approach. At least they have tried to reconcile speculation with positive legal science. Most recently, Stammler both put law into the context of absolute purposes and took "formal regularity" or "objective rightness" for a mere standard or absolute postulate of law, an aim for the legislator and not a norm externally obligatory upon the social life of men. Critical speculation about values which thus complies with Bergbohm's requirement is a philosophy of positive law.

At present, the distinction between concern with value and with reality, emphasized especially by Windelband as the fundamental principle of all philosophical reflection, gains increasing recognition among legal and social philosophers. This above all is bringing about a firmer grasp of the aims of legal philosophical research. Almost the entire pre-Kantian natural law, unable to get away from typically naturalistic vagueness, stealthily substituted a value significance for the general laws of nature. The necessarily resulting lack of orientation and the arbitrariness of the naturalistic principles of selection were castigated by Hegel and many after him, like Stahl and Lasson. Most recently, Marxist naturalism provoked a methodical "return to Kant" in the field of social philosophy. This "neo-Kantian movement," to use Vorländer's term, is led by Cohen, Natorp, Stammler, and Staudinger. It now begins to spread also within socialism, including among its adherents Marxists such as Struve and Woltmann. It fights against the absolute rule of a "genetic" explanation, which it wants to supplement rather than supplant with a systematic consideration of how absolutely to justify causal events. In the group of neo-Kantians, there appears a strong intellectualism in posing philosophical questions. It tends toward taking all problems of value for purely epistemocritical or methodological ones. In the discussion regarding the "regularity" and supreme "unity" of the social, frequently the meanings of social philosophical method, of the absolute significance of the social itself, and of the methodical form of empirical social science shade imperceptibly into one another. But the borderline between philosophy and empirics is always strictly observed.

Closely connected methodically with the conception of critical legal philosophy is another problem, which has also been suggested anew by Stammler. This is how to justify a theory of politics governed by absolute standards, as distinct from the empiristic discipline carrying the same name [i.e., politics]. Legal philosophy, as a theory of typical values, belongs to the systematic sciences of values. Therefore, the context of meanings into which it inquires is disparate from any context of reality quite apart from the general disparity between value and reality. It also lacks that partial parallelism of structure which exists between individual values and empirical reality. Nevertheless, even the typical value is in one way, as it were, turned toward reality; for reality may be considered as at least the substratum of the typical value. Consequently, any theory of typical values permits two possible operations upon the formal value. On the one hand, the absolute meanings may be systematized among one another, thus remaining within the realm of the values themselves. On the other hand, the particular realizations of a value may be considered. This explains the relation of legal politics, which alone in the last analysis interests Stammler, to purely systematical legal philosophy. In politics, the value is considered from the viewpoint of its particular realization; the value turns into a norm or postulate. The value-concept actually precedes the norm-concept. However, in any legal philosophical thought there is immanent the idea of introducing values into life as something to be realized through the human will. It is therefore not surprising that in this field the normative background of the value concept is immediately at home. Politics, then, differs from pure systematization in that it confronts the individual case with the formal value and examines whether what is individually given conforms with the formal ultimate purpose.

Historism. By comparing legal philosophy and legal metaphysics we have seen that empiricism is by no means rejected but rather confirmed and established by critical speculation about values. But we must as strongly emphasize the reverse: speculation must at once turn against the same empiricism, and especially historical empiricism, when the latter presumes to pose as philosophy. Indeed, there is at present a widespread delusion that out of the basic ideas of the "historical school" a world outlook may be gained, especially in the field of social and legal philosophy.

At first sight, the separation between the evaluating and the non-evaluating approach seems in fact to be obliterated by the existence of the historical cultural sciences, if one reflects that these disciplines operate upon reality with regard to objective cultural meanings. Yet, as Rickert has pointed out, their complex empiristic character must be most strongly emphasized. For their regard to cultural meanings must be taken not in the sense of a direct value judgment, but rather in that of a purely theoretical value relation, serving as a means of mere transformation of reality. The task of the cultural sciences does not consist in establishing the absolute validity of cultural meanings. Rather does it consist in working out the mere empirical and temporal factuality of the appearance of cultural meanings. This, to be sure, is already a product of methodological selection, compared with the original materials of reality. He who would draw standards of value from history would, to be consistent, have to take everything as valuable that the historian as a scholar deems significant for the presentation of historical connections. In more methodological terms, he would simply have to take for absolute the product of an empiristic trend. As a matter of fact, historism is nothing but an empirical scientific method posing as a world outlook; it is an inconsistent, uncontrolled, dogmatic way of evaluation. In this it exactly resembles naturalism.[c]

However, it may seem that historism is wronged by such a characterization. Does not the concept of *individual* values mean that historically concrete individuality has invaded the very realm of values, thus establishing historical evaluation? This assumption, however, would rest on a gross delusion. To be sure, a parallelism of structure, a certain formal logical analogy, which exists between individual values and empirical reality, also exists between individual values and historical factuality. In both, what is individual appears to be isolated and elevated because of its significance. But such similarity is by no means identity. If one were to call individual values historical, he should as well take the entire systematic philosophy, logic, ethics, aesthetics, philosophy of religion, for a part of the natural sciences; for undoubtedly a certain formal logical analogy also exists between the typical value and the generality of the laws of nature. He who confounds individuality of values and historical factuality overlooks the immense gap which separates meaning and being. The unique development of culture, as a mere product of historical conception-building, is interconnected temporally, causally, factually. Consequently, it does not suppress the element of temporality and the brutal fortuity of empirical events. In the region of value connections, on the contrary, there can be no question of time relations. In this respect, individuality of values does not differ from the system of typical values. Indeed, all attacks by evaluative Platonism against the possibility of individual values originate in the belief that individuality of value could not but result in taking for absolute what is merely given in time.

Historical factuality, then, remains the same everywhere in its merely temporal structure. So it does not afford a criterion to isolate the absolute value, but merely offers the value a scene of action. It need not be denied that historical factuality may well serve as a means of orientation in the search for the absolute value. But this is acceptable only in the sense in which empirical reality generally serves as the substratum of all contemplation of values, including systematic contemplation. Even the individual value is produced, and the unique chain of such values is construed, by a creative process, by viewing the value apart from

[c] That is, it resembles a variety of what Lask calls the material doctrine of natural law, in which the value character of law is reduced to terms of natural phenomena by "materialistic metaphysics"; cf. *supra* p. 8.

temporality. It follows that even the concrete or individual value cannot be simply taken from historical reality as such. Only this basic and formal methodical relation matters here. In a popular and inexact way, one may speak of absolute historical values. But it is the philosopher's duty to look through the *quaternio terminorum* [d] contained in such expressions. By these formal distinctions, the substantial significance of historical scholarship is not depreciated by a hair's breadth. Indeed, in denying historism it may be conceded that even empirical history-writing is ultimately regulated by the belief in absolute individual values. But this would only confirm, not that a world outlook may be gathered from history, but rather that history may be gathered from a world outlook.

Historism is the exact counterpart of natural law, and this constitutes its significance in principle. Natural law wants to conjure the empirical substratum out of the absoluteness of value; historism wants to conjure the absoluteness of value out of the empirical substratum. It is true that natural law by its hypostatization of values destroys the independence of the empirical. But its basic belief in transhistorical, timeless values has not been an error, refutable by the historical enlightenment of the present, as many think; rather has it been its immortal merit. Historism, on the other hand — not by any means history itself nor the historical view of the law — destroys any philosophy, any world outlook. It is the most modern, most widespread and most dangerous form of relativism, the levelling of all values. Natural law and historism are the two rocks of which legal philosophy has to steer clear.

B. The Various Trends

The starting point of all recent legal philosophical speculation is a definition which has been adhered to by Kant. According to it, law is the external regulation of human conduct for the attainment of conditions that are inherently valuable. On this common ground, two possibilities of fitting law into contexts of values have emerged. Either the ultimate purpose of law was traced exclusively to the perfection of the individual ethical personality, and the meaning of the life of the community was measured solely by the fulfillment of this ideal; or else the view prevailed that the order and institutions of the common existence of humanity contained their own inherent values which need not in any way be derived from individual ethics. The importance for legal philosophy of this contrast in world outlook is manifest. Law, in its empirical position, doubtless belongs in the realm of the "social" institutions. This

[d] Literally: Quaternion of terms; i.e., a fourfold or multiple ambiguity of terms.

unquestioned empirical-social significance of law may be correlated to an absolute value only if there is a typical value peculiarly "social" along with the typical value of individual ethics. Otherwise, law is just mechanically related to a typical value of individual ethics that is foreign to the law's own social structure. But in so far as a peculiar value corresponds to the sphere of social ends of the law, the law itself may finally be taken for more than a means, namely, as an element in the articulated structure of the "objective spirit." [e] Even in this view, however, the law need not at all be taken for an absolute ultimate end.

The Problem of the Value of the Social: Kant v. Hegel. Those who have speculated from and beyond the individualism of Kant and the eighteenth century may be called legal-philosophical Hegelians. They have proposed to characterize ethical individualism as *social* philosophical atomism. For according to Kant, value, notwithstanding its trans-individual validity, is exclusively attached to the individual personality. This being so, all superstructures which may possibly be built upon and connect the isolated value centers are excluded from the region of absolute value. In contrast with such a purely personalistic system of values, the new world outlook first of all proclaimed transpersonal values. It confronts the personal typical value with what may be called an objective typical value. Going back to Plato, the absolute ethical demand is directed not toward the will and deed of the person, but toward the objective order of the "moral world" itself. The perfection of this order, and not that of the individual human being, is the ultimate end of social existence. Hegel has attempted to combine this "substantial morality" idea of antiquity with the individualism of Christianity and of modern times in a supreme synthesis. He recognizes the right of individual freedom but only as one of the fused "elements," a link necessarily joined in the structure of the whole. The entire legal philosophy of the nineteenth century has exerted itself to maintain a distinct absolute meaning of social relations without having to give up the recognition of the individual as an absolute end in himself, which had been fought for and won by the eighteenth century. At present, this philosophical struggle has not been brought one step nearer to its conclusion. In particular, there remain unsolved all questions as to whether the transpersonal value of social life is to be treated as a subspecies of ethical value, or to be coördinated with other values, or to be classified as a distinct group of "cultural values." All discussions of individual and social ethics, of social questions, of the state and the law, of nationalism and cosmo-

[e] A Hegelian term meaning the realm of the spirit as objectified, collective and developing.

politanism, and all beginnings of cultural philosophy, have fundamentally turned on whether the typical value of the social is to be assigned an independent position in a comprehensive system of values.

Stammler as a Kantian. At present, Stammler may be regarded as representative of legal philosophical Kantianism. To be sure, he emphasizes that the social coexistence of men must be viewed as the peculiar subject matter of specifically social scientific knowledge, constituted by special methodological categories. Nevertheless, in Stammler's view, the social ideal and the absolute task of the legal order are to be exclusively subservient to the norm of individual ethics. In his writings we meet the decisive argument of Kantianism: man's absolute law being his free will, motivated solely by the sense of duty, the ultimate end of social life can only consist in uniting the duty-bound wills of all in the "community of men of free will." The absolute in all social institutions thus is found in the "community" in the sense of a mere coexistence of individual morality, a fusion of what may be deemed universally valid in the endeavors of the members of the community. This is precisely the view which has led individualistic legal philosophy at all times to elevate the contract, as an agreement between the wills of ethically autonomous beings, to the single principle justifying social institutions. Although in the interest of methodology Stammler has emphasized the peculiar empirical structure of the social, to it there corresponds no peculiar value structure.

Socialism and Kant. This distinction between the empirical structure of society and the value-structure of the social sheds light on the recent attempts to connect socialism with the "community idea" of Kantian ethics. They could succeed only because what was presented as socialistic world outlook in no way transcends the scope of individualistic ideas. "Humanity" in Kant's view does not mean the concrete community of men but the abstract value of man. Kantian ethics requires that we esteem all fellow-men not as members but rather as representatives of humanity. It involves no other "idea of community" than that of Stammler. By the same token, the whole controversy about individualistic, as opposed to socialistic, economic organization may be carried on as an internal affair within a purely individualistic world outlook. To be sure, there are socialist systems in which a centralized economic organization is demanded as the necessary consequence of a world outlook which is "social" in the sense of value. Lassalle and Rodbertus, as followers of Fichte and Hegel, argue for the intervention of the state in business on the ground that humankind as a whole is to fulfill its tasks, which can be realized only by the race and not by the individual. Here there is a belief in an independent basic type of community life, a longing for a peculiar glory and perfection of human collective existence.

The Social as a Specific Value: Hegelianism. Hegelianism, by rendering the system of ultimate social ends far more concrete, has become especially significant for a renovation of legal philosophy. As Schelling, Hegel, Schleiermacher, Stahl, Trendelenburg, and the school of Krause have constantly emphasized, there have now been discovered an abundance of specific ends and models, a new world of life purposes and destinations, which do not belong to the isolated individual but are peculiar to the living conditions of the human community as such. The legal order is to be closely adapted to the rich articulation of these ends and "goods" and to the "world economic ideas" expressed therein. In itself, accordingly, it is to be integrated into an "organic whole" or an "organism." The destination (τέλος) immanent in particular relationships of life, such as property, family, rank, class, or state, is to provide the "objective and real principle of legal philosophy."

This view has been combined with arguments against deriving the social universe exclusively from the concept of will and personality, yet these arguments are by no means directed against Kantian ethics itself. Not only are the Kantian and Hegelian ways of evaluation co-predicable, and in need of complementing each other, but also, in the view of Hegelian legal philosophy, the idea of the personality as the supreme purpose (τέλος) of the legal order must be included in the stock of common ethical ideas.

Ramifications of Hegelianism: Jhering, Gierke. It is interesting to note a parallel to the reaction against the philosophical reduction of all legal institutions to collective communities based on the will and on freedom. This parallel is the attack of positive [legal] science, led especially by Jhering in the middle of the nineteenth century, upon the formalistic legal concept of the will. Jhering himself mentioned Krause's philosophical school as a predecessor, though one without much influence, in the struggle against the so-called will theory. Of greater influence on positive science, however, were the speculations of Schelling, Hegel, and also, according to Ahrens, of Stahl. They, together with the predominant influence of the historical school, contributed to a more vital conception and a more concrete treatment of the law. On the other hand, the profound effect of the abstract view of Rousseau, Kant, and Hegel on positive legal science is also universally recognized.

The ramifications of speculations concerning the structure of the social world, extending from the pure theory of values to the methodological problems of the formation of concepts, may also be shown in the development of the idea of the corporation. Gierke well demonstrated that the atomizing individualistic spirit of the Enlightenment [f] has proved its worth in the field of jurisprudence by smashing the concepts of all associative legal institutions. Conversely, legal science, and especially public law doctrine, has often resorted to the world outlook of Hegelianism to establish its opposition to the exclusive rule of individualistic legal principles. As far as the methodological problems can be traced at all to the ultimate issues of world outlook, the legal concept of the association, as represented by Gierke, may indeed find its only speculative foundation in the idea of a specifically social typical value and not in individualistic ethics. For only on the assumption of a specifically social system of ends is it ultimately possible to construe independent totalities of values that differ from the sum of individual value structures.

However, the deep-rooted connection between methodological and pure problems of values must not lead us to overlook the formal discrepancy which always exists between empirical and philosophical formations of concepts, by virtue of their basically different objectives. Consequently, a clear-cut distinction must be made between the more concrete theory of ends, which was initiated by Stahl and others, and the empirical-teleological doctrine, now generally accepted, of the social function of the law and its dependence on the interests of society. Indeed, these empirical relations are not denied even by the ethical individualist. He only denies that any absolute relations of value correspond to them. He will either insist that no such relations could extend into the region of values; or he will admit such a relation only between law and the value of the individual personality. In either case, he will reject the opposite view as taking for absolute mere empirical phenomena having only relative validity. Yet this objection need not deter legal philosophical Hegelianism as such. As a matter of formal method, the objection affects one sphere of values no less than the other. For fundamentally, the dualism of philosophic and empirical approaches applies to the totality of possible subjects of experience; even the processes of the will which are the material of individualistic ethics present an empirical aspect. Now a line must be drawn unequivocally between those elements of empirical reality which are solely empirical and those in which some value element may be found. But where to draw that line

[f] *Aufklärung*, the Age of Reason, the eighteenth century.

is among the axiomatic and incontrovertible choices of any consistent world outlook.

Hegelianism eliminates, along with the philosophical dogma of the will, another consequence of Kantian legal philosophy. In the individualistic view, the law, as to its social structure, must be entirely outside the sphere of values. Strictly speaking, it can then be understood only as a mechanism which, while empirical in itself, serves to maintain transempirical ends of [individual] freedom. If it is to be characterized in transcendental terms at all, it can be expressed only by negative predicates, all of which are derived merely from its contrast with morals. To be sure, the Kantian school has never been content in strict consistency to define the substantial essence of the law as merely contrary to ethical inwardness, as mere outwardness and enforceability. It has always been governed also by the conviction that the law itself partakes of the sanctity of the ends it serves. This may quite distinctly be traced in Kant himself. His analysis of all empirical legal relations and institutions into so many plainly intelligible relations of freedom can hardly be harmonized with his insistence on the outwardness of the law. As against Kant's vacillation, Fichte's much stricter deduction of the concept of law from a logical analysis of the "material rational being," the "definite material ego," doubtless has the advantage of consistency. The empirical coloring of some legal concepts, which Fichte was the first to deduce transcendentally, especially of the concept of personality, may be found also in Hegel and Stahl. At the present time, a metajuridical *a priori* basis of the law, consonant with Fichte's immanent idealism, has especially been sought by Schuppe. In his view, the legal approach stops at affirming the individual "concretion of consciousness in space and time," without proceeding to the ethical evaluation of what is good in itself, or of consciousness as such. In his fundamental legal-philosophical constructions, Schuppe never departs from the characteristic scheme of Kantianism, namely, the opposition between abstract value-generalizations and individual empirical-concrete instances, and the exclusive explanation of law by a comparison with ethics.

The Specific Social Value of the Law. Only with the introduction of a typical value that is specifically social is the law itself as a social phenomenon established in the sphere of values. Therewith it may aquire some, if possibly small, positive significance even in transcendental terms; there may be found in it valuable articulations of common human life albeit in primitive and externalized form. In this sense — though in a more empirical-sociological context — Jellinek characterized the law as the "ethical minimum." He expressly noted that such an evaluation of law is necessarily outside the scheme of individual ethics. Similarly, Hegelians such as Lasson depicted law as the human spirit still submerged in naturalness, as the first stage of reason and morality. This view was represented splendidly by Stahl, who is still influential.

In order to show the necessity of a legal regulation of the life of the community, one may resort in the first place to the fiction of the complete interpenetration of individual moral action and the objective system of ethical ideas. In the ideal state of a perfect equilibrium of human community life, the ultimate ends of the community would at any moment have to be recognized intuitively by the individuals and fulfilled by them in dutiful spontaneity. A corresponding fiction has been set forth by intuitive reason in the critical thought of theoretical philosophy. This fiction serves to put into especially clear relief the only way in which we may attain the theoretical aim, that is, by splitting cognition into general conceptions and concrete perceptions. Analogously, the practical ideal may remind us that any order of the community that we may experience can be maintained only by establishing formal prescriptions that take no account of the moral complications of the individual case. In addition, the maintenance of the moral world requires the enforceability and external prevalence of legal imperatives. These features, together with the abstract nature of the law, establish its rigid traditional character, as an organization of life outlasting the successive generations and the historical changes of a people. It also follows from its abstract nature that the legal order is able to express the ideas contained in the common ethos not in full concrete substance but only in the barest of outlines.

Once we assume the law to represent at least a minimum of the common ethical ideas, even if it be the most abstract and formal structure within the social typical value, the decisive step is taken beyond its merely negative characterization in Kantian legal philosophy.

Hegel. Determination of the transcendental place of the law in a system of social typical values was first attempted in the philosophy of Hegel. That attempt dominated nineteenth-century thought in so far as it was susceptible to influence by such speculations. In Hegel's view, the legal order appears as a well-defined link in the chain of progressively concrete objective cultural purposes and represents a peculiar stage of the development of the "spirit." In this view, the most concrete "law," the law of the universal spirit, prevails as absolutely sovereign over all more abstract rules and rights. Yet Hegel, idolizing as he did objective transpersonal institutions, was far from taking for absolute those forms of cultural life which are merely legal. Rather he might be charged with an unjustified aversion to all abstract and "formal" legislation, which led him to regard what is systematic and typical in values as a mere first step, imperfect and in need of supplementation to attain the absolutely saturated totality and homogeneity of value. This is shown by his view that the "person" in the legal sense was the abstract personality or legal capacity, absolutely identical in all men, as distinguished from living human individualities. He always characterized the person as an atom torn out of the substance of its spiritual contexts. For he was unable ever to regard the abstract otherwise than as something alienated from true concrete endlessness — as something empty, and thus somehow negative. He compared the viewpoint of the law with the world outlook of late Hellenism, when the vain and rigid self, the self-satisfied individuality, proudly defiant, stepped out of the life of substantial morality. What in Stoicism was the "in itself" of mere reflection has become reality in the law. The mission of Romanism in world history was to bend the concrete individuality under the power of abstract freedom and the abstract state, and at the same time to incorporate the concrete images of the individual peoples in the abstract concept of the state and to "crush" them under this universality, thus gathering all gods and all spirits into the pantheon of world dominion.

At this point it may be anticipated that Hegel's theory is also the root of the methodological version of legal formalism which is found frequently in nineteenth-century jurisprudence. This, however, will be discussed in the following chapter.

Those thinkers, then, who postulate a concrete prototype of social life, have always tended to believe that the legal order, being merely regulatory and organizing, is but a surrogate for the social ideal. How often has been cited Plato's statement that the abstract law, which is the same throughout, is inadequate to govern justly the inequality and unending restlessness of human affairs. A defense of all revolutions and *coups d'état* has been attempted with Fichte's argument that the forms of social order which admit of rational systematization, the goods in the possession of which the ages "faithfully continue on the road on which they have set out," are only means, conditions, and scaffolding of "what patriotism really desires, the flowering of the eternal and divine in the world." Lagarde, often agreeing with Fichte, saw the doom of the present era in the impersonal constraint of laws which paralyze the creative energy of men and of nations, in the rule of the state's institutions and constitutions, in the "*caput mortuum* [g] of mankind."

[g] Dead head, i.e., the head that rules us from the grave.

Tönnies, Simmel. In our time, Tönnies has discussed the abstract character of law as no mere methodological problem and has tried to fit the law into a total picture of the social universe. His picture of the late Rome resembles Hegel's: Rule over the world assimilates all cities to the one city, polishes off all jarring differences and inequalities against one another, gives everybody the same attitudes, the same money, education, and avarice. The law creates the concept of the legal "personality," a fiction and construction of scholarly thought; this "mechanical unity" does not underlie concrete multiplicity, as the unity of organic essence; it rather stays above it, as a conceptual generic unity, a *universitas post rem* and *extra res.*[h] More and more in the last few centuries the law has been stripped of its organic character; more and more it has been serving the principle of "society," that is, a condition in which the individuals are removed from all primitive and natural combinations and enter into mutual relations only through abstract rational considerations of profit and reward. By this construction of social rationalism, the idea of society, as conceived by classical economic theory and as given philosophical influence by Hegel's speculative appraisal, is carried to its most extreme philosophical formulation. The system of social abstractions is contrasted by Tönnies with the "community" as the organic type of the social. The latter is structurally analogous to Hegel's conceptions of the substantial spirit and the moral totality. But it differs from Hegel's purely cultural philosophical tendency by its much more naturalistic color, its emphasis on the natural and original. While all community life rests upon the universality and unbroken unity of vital interests, the law creates the technical forms for isolating and separately pursuing specialized purposes. It is only for such purposes, as for instance the purely economic ones, that capricious individual wills, with their essentially separate spheres having only that single point in common, may coöperate. Within Christian civilization, too, according to Tönnies, the law, and especially Roman law, has been the ready instrument for the emancipation of individuals from all original community ties; and this universal disintegrating and leveling process has culminated in the modern state, which has turned from a true community of living into a societal-capitalistic union.

Simmel's view of the law, though expressed only occasionally, resembles that of Tönnies. The law is considered to be a symptom of the growing rationalization of life which is especially marked in the present age. It is deemed comparable to intellectualism, on the one hand, and to money, on the other, in that it is indifferent toward individual

[h] Universality after the thing and outside of things.

peculiarities and draws an abstract, general factor out of the concrete totality of experiences. However, Simmel believes that the modern process of depersonalization affects only the external aspects of life. He believes that the personality, while permitting certain particles of its being to be more and more subordinated to impersonal organizations, retains an unassailable nucleus, and that nucleus is sharply distinct from any fractions that may be splintered off from it and is not to be reduced to a mere object.

The Idea of Justice. Along with such tendencies to view the law as embodying a formalism hostile to any originality of individuals and of civilization, there has always survived the speculative recognition of a specific positive value-significance of the law. This has at all times found its most universal expression in the idea of justice. But it would be futile to attempt a uniform definition of justice. For that term simply is intended to state what is absolute and *a priori* in the law, and so it covers whatever any world outlook may require of the law.

In a narrower sense, the concept of justice has come to be used in theories of the criminal law. The idea, once influential, that the punishment of the offender restores the majesty of the law, goes back to Kant and Hegel. For such "absolute theories of criminal law" can never be substituted the "relative" ones. In criminal law, too, the questions of the ultimate meaning and of the empirical "purpose" of an institution may well be kept apart.

If justice is really to express a specific and intrinsically valuable idea, any resort to it as a concept implies a fundamental departure from ascribing value exclusively to the individual personality, a departure toward an idealizing view of community life. Even a legal philosophy of Kantianism — indeed, that of Kant himself — thus contains the starting point of a trend beyond social-philosophical individualism.

Hermann Cohen. This becomes apparent in the philosophy of the Kantian Cohen. In his view, law is to provide the methodical orientation for ethics, whereas ethics provides the substantive foundation of law. Legal science and political science furnish the "methodical model" for the ethical concepts of the unity of pure values, the unity of action and personality, the "true unity of the will." For, compared with the individual person, the "legal person" is less liable to be confused with its material substratum, which in this case consists of a plurality of individuals. Therefore, the "legal person" may serve as a model of purely ideal "universality," which as a distinct unit stands out from the material details of its underlying discrete and divisible reality. Quite in accord with Hegel, the particularities of races and classes are deemed to represent only societal "plurality" or collectivity and ultimately to constitute elements of mere nature, which are to be subjected to the "compelling unity of the state." Indeed, Cohen goes so far as to construe the fundamental concepts of ethics "with exclusive regard to the law and the state." The ethical acts of the state itself are the laws, which in their sanctity and their unqualified universality must be taken to be the indispensable guides for the self-reflection of the pure will. In Cohen's view, the formalism of the law becomes a symptom of its absoluteness as value, its purity, and its *a priori* character. Law and justice are the true realm of transempirical purposes. They deliver the will from its discordance and incalculability, from the limits of caprice and selfishness. The law and the state are creations of the mind, they are ethical cultural concepts. The people, on the other hand, is a product of nature; thus, even patriotism retains the naturalistic flavor of a "widening the circle of one's affections," despite the sublimity of the cultural concept of the fatherland. The purely cultural Hegelian concept of the people is rejected by Cohen. In his view, the formal idea of justice triumphs over any more concrete evaluation.

The Position of the Social in the System of Typical Values. So at present the views as to the absolute significance of the law are still far apart; and the fitting of law into a system of cultural values remains a task for the philosophy of the future. Only the definition of legal philosophy as a theory of *typical* values has proved true in the various trends of this discipline. However, it is necessary to point out that the Hegelian concept of the social world, no matter how "concrete" are its terms, is in two respects purely formal. First, the value connotation of the "objective spirit" must be kept apart from the empirically concrete. The term "concrete," when applied to a value, is but a symbol to indicate a certain coloration of the value. Consequently, even the concrete value cannot be construed rationalistically as an empirical particularity. Secondly, the social is distinct from any individual values. Its character is that of a typical value, since it comprises ideal postulates for which validity is claimed in any conceivable community life, in any social reality whatever.

Thus, the social is formal as against the empirical substratum of values and formal also as against the individual value. It occupies a peculiar intermediary position in the realm of values. It seems a concrete world of new transpersonal values when it is compared with the exclusive uniformity of the individual personality type; and it appears abstract or formal as a generality of values that admits of repetition when it is compared with the totality of a unique value. A conclusion from this intermediary position has been drawn by Windelband. As he has pointed out, the social values seem substantive from the viewpoint of the duty of the individual; but they seem formal as against any individual total definition of society itself. The outstanding historical example of the same relationship is offered by the social ethics of Plato. It is a model of the concrete view of the state. Yet it remains within the limitations of Grecianism, without advancing to the principle of the unique chain of values, which Schelling has been first to call specific to Christian speculation.

The "concrete" character of the social typical value again raises the same complication as the confusion of the unique character of values with historism. It is now understandable why historism, which lives on confounding the empirically concrete with the concrete value, has become so seductive especially in the field of legal and social philosophy. What historism implies in an unreflecting way of evaluation was made explicit and dogmatized in the philosophy of the restoration.[1] In that philosophy, the forms of state organization which have empirically grown and become legitimate provide the unchangeable bars at which any criticism that measures by standards of absolute value must stand silent. The sharpest contrast with any such acceptance of given political facts as absolute may be found in the theory of Hegel, with its inexorable attack upon the vacuity of mere finiteness, upon the unreason of the single empirical "this." Never, therefore, should we forget Kuno Fisher's words at the end of his work on Hegel, where he shows that throughout the nineteenth century nothing has been more profoundly opposed to the political tendencies of the restoration than the philosophy of Hegel, the evolution of the universal spirit in its conscious, logically developed form.

CHAPTER II

THE METHODOLOGY OF LEGAL SCIENCE

In the first chapter we have dealt with the formation of legal philosophical concepts and with the concept of law itself as value. In order to throw light on the philosophical "method" by contrasting it with the empirical method, we had to compare philosophy and empirics. To this end, we had to establish their common denominator, approaching both from the viewpoint of contemplation, theory, knowledge, or science. The methodology of philosophy deals with the question of the value of philos-

[1] *Restauration*, i.e., the restoration of the Bourbons and other royal families after the fall of Napoleon I.

ophy as a *science*. Thus, the theory of the form of philosophical science may be compared to the theory of the special forms of empirical science, that is, to methodology in its narrower sense.

From a strictly methodical point of view, the methodology of empirical legal science belongs not to the philosophy of law but to the philosophy of science. For the type of value with which it is directly concerned is not that of the law but that of science. It need not be pointed out how well nevertheless this section of the special theory of science in substance fits into the frame of "legal philosophy." Indeed, the logic of science is at present the most cultivated field of legal philosophy; and positive legal science has rendered important contributions to it.

Thus the entire subject-matter of legal philosophy may be subordinated to the uniform concept of philosophy as the critical theory of values. It may be divided into the theory of the value of legal philosophy as science (Chapter I, a), the theory of the value of law itself (Chapter I, b), and finally the theory of the value of legal empirics as science (Chapter II).

Cultural Sciences: Historical and Systematic. Legal science is a branch of the empirical "cultural sciences." Therefore, recent inquiries in this group of sciences may serve as the most general foundation for a methodological critique of legal science. In the first chapter, we have touched upon the view of Rickert that the world contemplated in the cultural sciences is the product of a purely theoretical relation of immediate reality to cultural meanings. In order to clarify for our orientation the communicating lines between the logic of legal science and the basic concepts of the cultural sciences, we have first of all to distinguish between a historical and a systematical tendency within the cultural sciences. From the complexity of given facts, typical cultural elements are selected by the systematic disciplines. In history, those typical cultural elements are submerged in individual events of unique and indivisible significance. In the systematic disciplines, on the contrary, they remain explicitly isolated in their formal structure and are elevated to become guiding concepts of the several disciplines. To avoid misunderstanding, it may be added that these sciences of general concepts are sufficiently distinguished from the natural sciences by the complete disregard of cultural meanings in the abstractive and systematizing principle of the natural sciences.

We have repeatedly mentioned the parallelism of methodological and pure value-problems; it may be found between the unique character of value and the historical method, and it may also be found, analogously, between the systematic theories of philosophy and of the empirical-cultural sciences. Insight into this parallelism may again save us from confounding the empirical cultural concept, which serves as the selective principle of a particular science, with that concept of culture which represents absolute value and world outlook. We have found the affirmation of a peculiar structure of the social sciences compatible with the denial of an independent structure of social values, as for instance in Stammler's view. Generally speaking, it is at least conceivable thus to segregate the group of cultural sciences for purely methodological purposes without at the same time admitting absolute cultural values. Therefore, we must distinguish between the methodological-empiristic "cultural meaning" and the absolute "cultural value," at least as a matter of formal method. This is necessary even though the cultural value may serve as a regulative principle of all empirical cultural sciences in the same sense as we admitted the unique character of value as a regulative principle of empirical historiography.

Scientific and Prescientific Thought. From the epistemological point of view, reality appears as a product of syntheses of categories. Methodology transfers that Copernican standpoint to the selective creations of the several sciences. For instance, it regards the atoms and laws of nature as products of conceptions formed by the natural sciences; and it regards the events of world history or phenomena of law, politics, and economics as products of conceptions formed by the cultural sciences. It is not easy for the untrained eye always to adhere strictly to the basic Copernican idea. The objection seems so easy that after all the great historical events are not allotted their world historical role merely by the historian, and the several types of cultural significance, such as economics, law, language, etc., are not set off, one from the other, merely by the scholar. Indeed, even the methodologist cannot but acknowledge that the primitive disciplining of the materials which he encounters at the start represents, so to speak, work preparatory to the activity of the scholar. But no matter how far in a particular case such "prescientific conceptions," to use Rickert's term, may be advanced, they must always lack the truly conceptual exactitude and scientific strictness. In any case, therefore, there will always remain the task for the scholar to develop indefinite beginnings into precise, conceptually fixed results, for instance, to separate exactly the different cultural types and to evolve their refined systematic ramifications in the several disciplines. Granted, then, that the elaboration of a specifically cultural scientific world in part goes back to prescientific thinking, this can but limit and disguise the Copernican mission of science without ever really calling it in question.

The fact of prescientific elaboration prevents our directly taking, as the material of the cultural sciences, the immediately given reality. Between it and the ultimate aim of a science there enters a world already related to cultural meanings, comparable to a half-product; and this complex cultural reality, and not the original reality which is free of any kind of value relation, becomes the material of the cultural sciences proper. However, the boundary lines between prescientific and scientific elaboration are blurred. Also, very often the work broken off by the prescientific mind is resumed in the same direction, albeit rectified and perfected, by science. For this reason, the viewpoints of methodological critique may be transferred from the scientific to the prescientific function. Thus, from a one-sided methodological standpoint not only the cultural sciences but also the several cultural fields themselves may be regarded as coagulations of theoretical reason, which embody "conceptions," though prescientific ones. As a result, methodology may possibly take for the subject of its investigation something other than forms of *science*. It may be directed not only at the cultural sciences but, at times, straight at "cultural reality"; not only at the social sciences but at the social itself and, accordingly, at the law, etc. This result is odd and may seem contradictory. Nevertheless, even such methodological investigation as is directed at the cultural forces themselves must of course not be confused with the several sciences dealing with the same subject. For methodology is distinguished by its peculiar intention, with all the questions it raises being turned into problems of the formation of concepts. It will later be shown that the methodology of prescientific and that of scientific concepts of law in particular must not be basically separated.

Legal Science as a Systematic Cultural Science. As regards the classification of the systematic cultural sciences, we confine ourselves here to a general suggestion that the various cultural types which constitute the guiding concepts of the several disciplines may be not merely coördinate but possibly also super- and subordinate. Thus, for instance, all cultural types may well involve the element of the social, which in its complete isolation and unadulterated purity could be grasped only by an ultimate, most abstract analysis. That analysis would then be the "sociology" postulated by Simmel, which would start from the final results of the other disciplines and constitute their "general part." [a]

The idea of the formalistic cultural discipline discloses in dim outline

[a] That is, it would contain the general concepts common to all of them. A "general part" often precedes the part or parts dealing with special topics in German legal codes and treatises.

the methodological structure of any kind of legal science. Cutting homogeneous sections out of the complex cultural material in which they are embedded in concrete connections constitutes the most general scheme of the kind of science to which legal science, among others, belongs. The isolation of the field of law and its hypostasis as a vital force of separate reality is a product of the prescientific mind. Here again, it is the task of science to give conceptual sharpness to the prescientific process of selection. It is the task of methodology to meet the hypostasis with the Copernican point of view, to realize that the demarcation of a specific field of law is a transformation — partly prescientific and partly scientific — of epistemological "reality" into an abstract world related to particular cultural meanings.

The Dualism in Legal Science: Law as Cultural Meaning and as Cultural Reality. Now we cannot advance a step in the methodology of legal science without first noting the methodical dualism which pervades all inquiry into law and which may justly be called the ABC of juridical methodology. At the present time, a distinction between jurisprudence and social theory of law has been urged especially by Jellinek. He has been followed by Kistiakowski, Hold von Ferneck, and others. In preceding authors, e.g., Knapp, Jhering, and the Russian jurist Pachman, we find but few suggestions of this fruitful contradistinction. Kistiakowski aided the fight against methodological syncretism by logical theories of the concept of judgment and viewed the social scientific concepts as precipitates of different purposes of knowledge.

The basis of the methodical dualism of legal science is this, that the law may be either regarded as a real cultural factor, a vital social process, or examined as a complex of meanings, more exactly of normative meanings, with regard to its "dogmatical contents." To be sure, even the social theory of the law, like all formalistic cultural sciences, isolated something abstract out of the concrete social totality, though that abstraction does not in reality exist in any way separate from the extralegal environment. Yet despite that clear recognition of its abstract character, we project the law as conceived by the social sciences on the screen of reality, as it were, just as we project on it all "real" cultural phenomena. We argue that the law need only be combined with certain other partial realities in order to appear at once as the full living reality. In the same way, as soon as we start thinking about it methodologically, we see across the distance that separates even the complex and allegedly concrete cultural reality from the *concretissimum* of epistemological reality. Nevertheless we do not cease to regard this methodically prepared cultural world as reality, although it is diminished in substantiality and disfigured, as it were, by its relation to cultural meanings. Probably everybody will admit this without hesitation as regards the concrete historical realities.

But we do not hesitate to call "realities" even the subject matters of the several formalistic cultural disciplines, which are infinitely farther and more artificially removed from what, in the epistemological sense, is the original substratum of reality. We form the peculiar concept of a cultural reality, in this case abstract partial reality, which we contrast with the concrete cultural realities of history. At this point, the logic of the formalistic cultural disciplines is confronted with one of its most difficult tasks. For it must throughout face the question how far the work of the cultural sciences penetrates only to the "realities" which are related to cultural meanings, and how far it aims ultimately at the realm of pure isolated meanings themselves. The contrast of reality and meaning, which Lotze believes may be traced as far back as Plato, must here be made fruitful for methodology in a quite limited empiristic sense.

Jurisprudence and Social Theory of Law. In one field, this has already been accomplished with the greatest success, namely, for legal science, by the separation of social theory and jurisprudence. The law in the social sense is deemed a "real" cultural factor; the law in the juridical sense is deemed a complex of mere meanings of thought. Consequently, the abstract character of the juridical world must be assumed in a more complicated sense than that of the subjects of social theory. The social theorist or the legal historian draws a "real" borderline between the law and the customs, habits, and other expressions of the life of a people. But there is absolutely no sense in thinking that a norm — which possesses mere validity — could complement other aspects of cultural life so as to form an independent reality. To the lawyer, therefore, the drawing of the borderlines in sociology and legal history is, as a matter of concepts, a mere presupposition and preparatory work — even though, as a matter of scientific technique, he may collaborate in it himself. For his only concern is to connect systematically the conceptual *contents* of those norms which have been, by a process of social theory, recognized as "law." The thesis of *juridical* "legal formalism," therefore, can refer only to an ideal comparison of juridical *meanings* with the prejuridical "substratum" of the law, which must always consist in the concrete and abstract *realities* of culture and of ordinary "life." So the isolating and systematizing tendency of jurisprudence is different from the typological method of most other social sciences. It will be more fully characterized hereafter.

Among the best known theories of law in terms of social science is the doctrine of Marxism. Recently, the Marxist Karner has stated that the only worth-while undertaking of legal science is to fit the law into the causal connection of all non-legal phenomena, to examine its "social efficacy," as against any mere dogmatic-technical treatment of juridical materials. In the second half of the nineteenth century, a universal revolt, supported by economists, arose against the absolute rule of what was thought to be a "dogmatism" that disregarded the real vital relationships. This lively movement in legal science is clearly reflected in the gradual development of Jhering's writings. However, the methodology of the sociological legal theories is part of the general logic of the cultural disciplines of the social sciences, so it cannot be further considered in this essay which is confined to the methodology of jurisprudence.

Relation Between the Ought and the Is. In contrasting inquiries into reality with those into meanings, we face the most confusing aspect of the parallelism of philosophical and empiristic scientific tendencies. The idea seems only too obvious that there is an ultimate speculative opposition between the Ought and the Is, between norms and laws of nature, between normative and genetic viewpoints. Indeed, this universal methodical dualism has frequently been used to characterize jurisprudence — e.g., by Jellinek, Kistiakowski, Kohlrausch, and Eltzbacher. Yet methodological boundary lines could not be blurred more fatally than by opposing jurisprudence as a "normative science" to the purely empirical disciplines. To such an opposition we would be imperceptibly led if the indubitable analogies and parallels caused us to overlook the ambiguity of the concept of the norm, the cleavage between its philosophical and its empirical significance. To be sure, the subject matter of jurisprudence, as of philosophy, is not what exists but what signifies, not what is but what ought to be, what commands obeisance. But in philosophy the character of the Ought is grounded in absolute values for which there is no empirical authority. In jurisprudence, on the contrary, its formal ground is its positive establishment by the will of the community. In this connection, Stammler and Eltzbacher have justly emphasized the element of factual existence, of what is empirically given. This element is relevant not only in the theory of the social Is of the law — as it occasionally appears in Jellinek and Kistiakowski — but also and especially in the theory of the juridical Ought of the law. Only the formal theory of natural law, which derives the juridical Ought directly from the absolute value, could have cause to align jurisprudence with the "normative sciences" of logic and ethics. In our view, however, jurisprudence can only present the unique method of purely empiristic operation upon an imagined world of meanings.

Legal Science and Prescientific Thought. Turning to a closer view of the juridical method, we must first observe that nowhere does the prescientific formation of concepts play so great a part as in the legal field. Apart from science itself, there is no cultural phenomenon which could be remotely compared to the law as a formative factor of concepts. The law itself establishes far-reaching distinctions between itself and extralegal reality. It forms concepts of so high a technical perfection that they can often be distinguished only by degrees from scientific concepts. As a result, nothing more is left to scientific elaboration, in some instances, than the mere continuation of the formative process begun by the statute. Conversely, scientific conclusions have in all epochs been embodied in legal codifications. All attempts at a theory of juridical method so far, from Jhering to the present, have recognized this concept-forming spirit inherent in the law. So they have frequently made no distinction, not even in terminology, between a logic of law and a logic of legal science.

Legal Science as a Teleological Science. Juridical methodology in the broader sense, as a critique of the formation of concepts by both law and legal science, has two principal subjects. In the first place, it examines the peculiar and uniform attitude of law and jurisprudence to the prelegal substratum of life and culture, and the transformation of the prelegal material into legal concepts. In the second place, it examines the systematic connection of the juridical concepts themselves, or the form of the system of jurisprudence.

The principal success of the modern beginnings of a logic of legal science has been to render conscious and explicit, in methodological thought, the teleological principle which jurisprudence has always applied. Jellinek, in particular, has tried to utilize Sigwart's discussion of teleological unifying principles for a "critique of juristic judgment." Indeed, even the substratum of the law hardly ever coincides with what is originally given psychophysically. Since it belongs in the field of practical life, of the social and economic and higher coöperative formations, it is interspersed throughout with teleological elements. Rickert, applying Jhering's ideas, has characterized the purpose of law as the principle determining the legally "relevant" conceptual elements. G. Rümelin and Zitelmann have pointed out that here as always it is the task of science to overcome the indefinite generality of prescientific thought. Methodology is still to fathom how jurisprudence, praised for its conceptual exactness, arrives at such precision within the value-bound limits of its teleological method. This much, however, has been recognized by most lawyers and legal philosophers since Savigny,

Puchta, and Stahl: that a distinction must be made between the concepts taken over unchanged by the law, those modified by the law, and those newly created by the law, and that everything embraced by the law loses its naturalistic freedom from value relationships. Even physical objects are embraced by the law not in their total qualities, but only by the sum total of those aspects of theirs which are subject to the dominion of the will. This was most strongly emphasized by Gierke when he compared Roman and Germanic legal concepts. "Property" no more coincides with the physical thing than the "person" does with the human being. In the same way, all the subjects accessible to the law are covered, as it were, with a teleological web, which cannot be more fully discussed here. Its methodological significance is this: the juridical pattern of the world makes possible wholly different articulations, which are unheard of in the epistemological and naturalistic views and often even in the common-sense view of life; it offers new syntheses, new principles of unification and individualization. What is continuous in the naturalistic view may be discrete in the juridicial view; what is but a collective plurality, naturalistically speaking, may legally be a unit distinct from any mere sum. The indispensable prerequisite for an understanding of the legal principles of unification is an inquiry into the conceptions of things and collectivities in the social sciences. This has been quite neglected until not long ago and a new stage has been reached only with recent enlightening investigations by Kistiakowski.

The specifically juridical attitude toward reality is made up of two mutually pervading elements. The real substratum is transformed into a spiritual world of pure meanings, under the guidance of teleological relationships; at the same time, the totality of what may be experienced is unraveled into mere partial contents. This decomposing function of law and legal science has been brilliantly described by Jhering. His *Spirit of the Roman Law*, a work justly renowned as the first comprehensive investigation of legal formalism, may be regarded as mediating between some elements of the legal philosophical speculation of Hegel and the positive science of the nineteenth century. A first attempt — though one overreaching its aim — to determine the peculiar character of juridical abstraction and isolation may be found in Kant's and Hegel's reduction of all legal relations to relations of the human will. The generally accepted dogma of the discovery of the abstract personality by the Romans, which Lassalle elaborated, has been mentioned in the first chapter. But in other connections, too, Hegel throughout recognized the formalism and "practicability" (Jhering) of the law and its technical fitness to be realized easily and uniformly. Like Hegel, Jhering depicted the position of Rome in world history, the conflict between the principle of nationality and the principle of the abstract state and law, through which the peoples of that period were "crushed and pulverized." Jhering supplemented the excellent concise statements of Puchta by a minute description of the generalizing and equalizing tendency of the law, and of its splitting up of the immediately given total sensations, with which the law's certainty, its uniformity, and its elevation above the mere emotional standpoint, are closely connected.

Objective Law and Subjective Rights in Legal Science. Our discussion so far might perhaps create the impression that methodology is concerned with the law only in its complete, concise, codifiable form, as a complex of norms or as what is "law" in an objective sense. It might seem as if law and prelegal reality confronted each other as spheres that are nowhere contiguous and only comparable in the abstract by the logical relations of their contents. For we have not yet pointed out that the variety and individuality of real life also comprehend the legal "right" in the subjective sense,[b] namely, the law in the form of "individual, concrete" legal relations and other subjective legal situations. This aspect of the relationship between law and reality, too, must be illuminated by methodological critique. Thus there arises the new problem of the entanglement of legal significance and real substratum in the *individual* case. The law in this individualized and concretized, temporary state, too, must be conceived of as a realm of pure meanings and must be separated from the concrete bearers of these meanings, to whom it usually adheres. This endeavor is faced with a general phenomenon the exact structure of which is still little investigated and is accessible only to the decomposing approach of the methodologist: abstract contents are entwined with their concrete bearers, which creates the deceptive appearance of a real existence of the former by themselves and thus always causes their hypostasis in the naive mind. Such a deceptive appearance of independent existence recurs in all spheres of knowledge: in the "concrete" cultural reality as against reality in the epistemological sense; in the abstract partial realities as against the complex cultural realities; and again in meanings — e.g., legal meanings — as against the psychophysical realities of culture and life which serve as their substratum. In this connection, Marx discussed the shibbolethic character of the commodity; and Simmel has dealt in detail with the "real abstrac-

[b] The distinction referred to in this passage is that between "law" and "legal right" or "legal relation." German legal terminology distinguishes law as "objective" from legal rights as "subjective," since both "law" and "right" are expressed by the same German term ***Recht.***

tions," the symbolizing, as it were, of abstract social functions in objective institutions. In the field of the natural sciences, analogous crystallizations of mere quantitative relationships into concrete structures may be found, for instance, in astronomical objects, and similar relations exist between pictures of geometrical figures and the purely mathematical relationships which they express. The latter example may serve especially well to illustrate our juridical problem. In the real material individuality of, say, a circle we must first disregard the empirical instrumentalities of the picture, such as paper and ink, blackboard and chalk, etc., in order to arrive at the mathematical individuality of this figure. In the same way, we must first deduct from the real complex of, say, an individual sale the physical events, the accompanying mental occurrences, the particularities, of the historical situation, etc., in order to penetrate to the juridical individuality of this contract. Brodmann has well stated the complex character of the juridical facts of the case, the constant interplay of living reality and legal meaning that always occurs in legal transactions and their legal consequences, exercises of rights or violations of rights, etc. — all of which are but seemingly concrete. Schlossmann, Thon, Zitelmann, and others also have noticed this peculiar commingling of the worlds of the Is and the Ought and their interplay, which very nearly recalls the metaphysics of occasionalism; and they have endeavored to grasp the conceptual forms of origination, disappearance, involution, in short, of connection in the "legal world." Zitelmann maintains that there is a causal connection of legal phenomena, but, as he himself adds, it is a "peculiar juridical" causality which is merely analogous to "natural" causality and coincides with "no other formation of the causal theorem." Schuppe, on the contrary, wants to apply the categories of thing and causality to the psychophysical and legal worlds without any distinction; for in his logic all that matters is the possibility of connecting mental contents uniformly, in whatever manner it may be. So, too, in the field of criminal law, a methodological revision has now begun of what constitutes the facts of the case. Kohlrausch and Hold von Ferneck argue against confusing the factual occurrence as the "real substratum" with its "juridical aspect," which, as Hold von Ferneck well puts it, never loses its abstract character "despite its concretion."

The entanglement of the concretized world of the law with living reality is of concern directly to juridical decisions and indirectly to legal science. Emphasis on this entanglement should above all prevent one from misunderstanding that the sharp contrast between the worlds of existence and validity may be confined one-sidedly to law in the objective sense, law identical with the meanings of norms, or that, on the other hand, it may be based on a "general theory of law" concerning the relation between law and legal rights.

Legal Science and Psychology. The teleological tinge of all legal concepts may best be studied in the alterations and introjections, unjustified from a mere naturalistic and psychological standpoint, to which mental realities are necessarily subject in the legal order. In the juridical view, mental existence, just like the corporeal world, serves as mere material to be worked upon for projection into the practical world of action. Jurisprudence thus serves especially well to prove that the disciplines which are misleadingly called "spiritual sciences" [c] by no means consist of an analysis of mental phenomena. Jellinek has pointed out that to determine the basic juridical concepts it is indispensable to examine the use which the legal order may make of the volitional acts of individuals. Indeed, there is hardly a single juridical problem where the methodological approach has not labored under an insufficient distinction between the purely psychological concept and the very variable juridical concept of the will.

Here, a wide field is open to the methodology of the future. There has been as yet no attempt at separating the truly psychological-naturalistic and the teleological elements in the juridical elaboration of psychological concepts. To be sure, such an undertaking could hardly be expected of jurisprudence since neither the logic of psychology nor psychology itself has as yet arrived at generally recognized conclusions. Perhaps such a distinction between psychological and teleological elements may aid both sciences to gain a fuller methodological knowledge of themselves. For the practical element which is fused with the psychical concepts and which naturalistic psychology has to disregard, attains its highest possible degree of precision in jurisprudence.

It may be suggested in passing that the controversy between the doctrines of will and of purpose can be settled only by close attention to the teleological formation of concepts, which is equally relevant here. This controversy, made famous by Jhering, has become immeasurably worse confounded because a clear answer has never yet been given, despite all attempts, to this question: whether purpose lies "beyond" the dogmatic legal concepts and therefore belongs only in the field of social theory, as Laband insists, or whether it involves metajuridical social factors overlapping into the juridical formation of concepts.

Recently, fortunate indications of the beginnings of a gradually pervading insight into the inadequacy of methodological psychologism have appeared in the field of criminal law. Liepmann has expressed the

[c] See Translator's note b, Introduction.

view that the solution of the problem of causation in criminal law depends on the recognition of specifically juridical selective principles. Kohlrausch has sought to utilize the principle of teleological formation of concepts, which Jellinek postulated, especially as applied to the concept of the consequences of a criminal act, as a "segment of the series of empirical consequences under a juridically relevant viewpoint." All this inaugurates the correct view that the legally relevant "adequacy" of causation can be determined only by practical criteria which rest on considerations of expediency and justice; for instance, by the "foreseeability" or "calculability" of a result which must be ascertained by "objective prognosis after the event," as pointed out frequently in the literature of civil and criminal law. The much disputed question whether the "philosophical" concept of causation is applicable to jurisprudence may perhaps be solved by recognizing that a precise epistemological concept of causation may serve as the point of departure but not as the goal of inquiries in criminal law. Most vigorously M. E. Mayer has turned against the absolute rule of naturalism in criminal law. Adopting Windelband's and Rickert's classifications of sciences, he regards jurisprudence as a kind of cultural science of value relations, though he seeks to approximate some elements of systematic criminal jurisprudence to the "ideographical" method.

Legal Science and Ethics. Finally, the relation between ethics and jurisprudence also is subject to a methodological critique. We need only recall concepts like willful violation of duty, intent, responsibility, or freedom of the will. In this case, the "prejuridical" would belong in the realm of values. The methodological delimitation here would turn on comparing philosophical and empiristic concepts.

The Problem of Legal Personality. Connected with the problems of teleological psychology is the old problem of the legal person and of the relation between individual and collective personalities. Here, Jellinek's solution may well promise to clarify the issue. According to him, the substratum of both the individual and the collective personalities appears in the naturalistic view as an aggregate or swarm of unconnected realities, while in the prejuridical-teleological view each appears as an independent unit, coherent in our thought because of its purpose relationships, namely, a unified individual and a unified association. These teleological formations of prelegal realities are properly adopted by the law, which in the same sense, in the realm of legal meanings, coins the concepts of individual and of collective personality. "Person" in neither case is a fiction, but in either case is a scientific abstraction. In law, there are only "legal" persons. Instead of contrasting "physical" with "legal persons," which involves a μετάβασις εἰς ἄλλο γένος,[d] we must contrast the legal individual personality with the legal collective personality. If, at the same time, the concept of teleological unity of the will is utilized for the personality problem, the teleologically unified will of a collective person, distinct from the sum of its members, will no longer seem to be a mythological personification.

Gierke and Laband. In our context, the controversies of positive science serve only as illustrations of very general methodological views. Therefore, on the subject of the legal person, we may also refer to the controversy between Gierke and Laband. From a purely methodological point of view, the investigations of Gierke are especially significant because they expressly recognize the abstract character of the legal world and yet deliberately pose the problem of the *degree* of legal formalism, that is to say, the difficult question of the adhesion of legal concepts to the prelegal substratum. The legal order, while modifying and leveling the articulation of the prelegal world, is able to transfer the latter's particularities and distinctions to a certain degree into the sphere of juridical meaning. Such an adhesion of the law to its substratum may be traced in two directions. First, the law may retain a certain nucleus of what is psychophysically given; for instance, natural distinctions between things or between mental phenomena may somehow effectively reach into the world of legal thought. Or, secondly, the law may adapt itself to the teleologically shaped realities of life and culture. Here it is important that the relationships of life present material which has already been formed typically and thus prepared for legal regulation, as has been noted by Jhering, Jellinek, and Lasson. As examples of the different degrees of intensity in the adaptation of the law to the variety of the forms of life, we may mention the contrasts between principles of generalization in Romanistic and Germanistic, or in civil and public, law. Rosin and Stoerk measure the degree of formalism by the greater or lesser homogeneity and uniformity of purposes.

Likewise the controversy between Laband and Gierke is marked by the contrast of Romanistic and Germanistic tendencies. Gierke objects — sometimes, indeed, in metaphysical terms — to Romanistic jurisprudence on the ground that it proceeds as if there were no other substratum of the concept of personality than the unconnected and merely coördinated individuals, and that it entirely neglects in any way to indicate in the legal sphere the prelegal social interdependence of individuals in associations. Laband has replied that the peculiar relationship be-

[d] Transition into another kind.

tween individuals as members of associations is one of the very elements which belong to life exclusively and can have no corresponding expression in the juridical concept of personality. However, one cannot understand why the structures of social substratum and legal personality should be wholly disparate just in the matter of interdependent membership, why there should be no legal doctrine of those personal relations between the collective person and the individual persons which differ from the legal relations possible between unassociated individuals. Gierke demands a finer adaptability of juridical doctrine and thus keeps an opening for the influx of new ideas into the formation of law. Yet he does not thereby seek to bridge the gap between law and reality. Indeed, he expressly distinguished the social centers of life which form "the factual basis of legal personality" from their appearance as "association-persons" in "the field of law."

Again, a more uniform approach to the question how far juridical formalism is to be extended without harm may result only from constant close contact of methodology with epistemology. Such contact may fix an epistemological concept of reality as the point from which to ascertain clearly the different distances between the several layers of the formation of concepts and their common foundation of reality, on which they are, as it were, superimposed. Only then may the structure of the dovetailing scientific syntheses, and especially their "objectivity" and "subjectivity," be clarified.

The Independence of Jurisprudence as a Science. While a certain agreement exists on the relation of the world of legal concepts to the prelegal substratum, views about the formal character of jurisprudence as a science and a system still differ widely. This cannot be regarded as exclusively peculiar to legal science, since the "technique" of the law itself elaborates the juridical material in highly systematic perfection. So it is not surprising that doubts have long been raised as to the character of jurisprudence as a science.

No matter how this question may be answered by a uniformly fixed concept of cognition in the cultural sciences, this much may be taken for granted, that jurisprudence in one essential respect at any rate is more independent than any other technology. In every other technology, the purely theoretical knowledge that is utilized for its practical purposes is derived elsewhere, to wit, from the natural sciences. Jurisprudence, on the contrary, creates everything necessary to fulfill its practical task in a peculiar world of concepts all its own, which it is well worth while to illumine methodologically. To be sure, methodology will always be forced to recognize the practical mission of law in life as a system-forming factor. It must never go so far as to view the logical in the law otherwise than as interwoven with the practical. The demand for an exact investigation of the logical structure of legal science is by no means a plea for a "jurisprudence of concepts," which is justly derided.

Jurisprudence and Statutes. An independent significance may first be ascribed to jurisprudence in a formal sense, that is, independence from the law, and more especially from statute law. The statute points the direction which legal science is to follow; but in a way it merely claims the position of material that is subject to interpretation and to an examination of its reliability. Law [as the body of legal norms] and statute are disparate. Not the statute but the law is the subject matter of legal science. The statute, like the customary law, the judicial application of the statute, and other clues, is only one of the indicia from which jurisprudence must ascertain the underlying system of legal norms truly "valid" at a certain time and in a certain community, "intended by the legislature" and so indeed "positive." This work of jurisprudence is in part creative. To give even an approximate picture of all present discussions of statutory interpretation, use of analogies, lacunae in the law, statute and customary law, statute and the judiciary, etc., would go beyond the scope of this sketch.

Jurisprudence and the Non-juridical Scientific Systems. The material independence of jurisprudence consists in the peculiarity of the contents of specifically juridical forms of systematization, as distinct from the systematic forms of other sciences. The methodology of the present proves least fruitful when it is expected to explain this material independence of jurisprudence. Jhering's discussion of the "precipitation of legal rules into legal concepts" may still be counted among the most successful characterizations of the juridical way of thought, despite all the justified objections that have been raised against its flowery natural-science terminology. There are a number of thoughtful investigations of the transformation of the original imperative form into the form of the scientific judgment and conception, the dissection of the composite into its simplest elements, the juridical "construction," etc. Nevertheless, it seems as if the real secret of the form of the juridical system has not yet been objectivated in a logical expression, though it has been felt immediately by the specialist to whom it has become familiar by professional scholarly practice. Again, there have been discussions of the very general logical schemes common to all sciences, such as deduction, reduction, induction, classification, as applied to jurisprudence, e.g., by

G. Rümelin, Wundt, and especially recently Radbruch. Such attempts at a first logical mastery of the legal material are doubtless instructive. However, they have not always sufficiently clearly characterized the individual juridical shadings of those formal logical principles. Here, too, the one-sided orientation so far of logic toward the natural sciences has been very harmful to methodology. Frequently, it is overlooked that the basic teleological character of the law, which governs the function of juridical elaboration applied to the prelegal substratum, similarly, if in a more complex way, also governs the operations that develop the juridically fashioned material into higher systematic formations.

Legal History. A complex methodological position is occupied by legal history. To determine it exactly we must construct the concept of the historical cultural discipline with relatively systematical elements. This would be analogous to the concept of a historical science with relatively natural-science elements, which has been examined by Rickert. Special additional difficulties arise from the fact that legal history as a discipline may be regarded as the history either of social legal reality or of juridical legal reality, and then again as a history of doctrines, which would constitute a branch of the history of sciences. It has been frequently noted, e.g., by Jhering and Arnold, that legal history, unless exclusively concerned with doctrine, must tend to take juridical abstractions in connection with the totality of life.

Comparative Law; "General Theory of Law." Finally, the logic of jurisprudence has also methodologically to analyze the present demand for a "general theory of law," that is, for a "general doctrine" applicable to legal science in its entirety. In this connection, it is erroneous to assume that empirical research may be suddenly transformed into "philosophy" by merely increasing and generalizing the process of systematization. This frequent error has already been attacked by Stammler and must be opposed.

The dualism of the social science approach and the juridical approach also prevails in the highest concepts of the theory of legal scientific principles. It creates a split between a general social theory of the law and a general jurisprudence, both of which are now still undivided and confounded with a lot of other fragments of sciences in the "general theory of law." General jurisprudence may command two complementary instruments: the comparative treatment of doctrines, which covers all historical legal systems, and the elaboration of the fundamental juridical concepts out of the analysis of the more special concepts. However, comparative law may be treated from the viewpoint not only of juridical doctrine but also of ethnology and sociology; and these contrasts cut across the distinctions between systematic and historical methods. Furthermore, comparative legal science may connect the "rationally cognate," which is quite different from research directed toward actual connections at a definite time between different legal systems, that is, toward the exclusively historically cognate, e.g., the "history of Aryan tribal laws," as has been well stated by Leist.

The general theory of law is dealt with here as a mere subject of methodological examination. It follows that not only the approach of social science and cultural history to the living connections of the law with other vital forces is put outside of philosophy, but also the most general juridical problems concerning the relation of law and the state, law and compulsion, objective law and subjective right, etc., are left to empirical science.

Not those problems but only the purely methodological attempts of jurisprudence at understanding its own essence were to be dealt with in the preceding pages. So far, the methodology of legal science consists only in a number of scattered remarks. But the expectation that they will in future be joined in a coherent whole is justified by the trend toward logical self-reflection which just at present is becoming strongly apparent in jurisprudence.

REFERENCES

Chapter I: The Philosophy of the Law

AHRENS, H., NATURRECHT ODER PHILOSOPHIE DES RECHTS UND DES STAATES. 6. Aufl. 2 Bde. (1870.)

BERGBOHM, C., JURISPRUDENZ UND RECHTSPHILOSOPHIE. (1892.)

CATHREIN, V., MORALPHILOSOPHIE. 4. Aufl. 2 Bde. (1904.)

COHEN, H., ETHIK DES REINEN WILLENS. (1904.)

GIERKE, O., JOHANNES ALTHUSIUS. 2. Ausg. 1902.

JELLINEK, G., DIE SOZIALETHISCHE BEDEUTUNG VON RECHT, UNRECHT UND STRAFE. (1878.)

LASSON, A., SYSTEM DER RECHTSPHILOSOPHIE. (1882.)

SCHUPPE, W., GRUNDZÜGE DER ETHIK UND RECHTSPHILOSOPHIE. (1882.)

SIMMEL, G., PHILOSOPHIE DES GELDES. (1900.)

STAHL, FR. J., PHILOSOPHIE DES RECHTS. 4. Aufl. 3 Bde. (1870.)

STAMMLER, R., WIRTSCHAFT UND RECHT NACH DER MATERIALISTISCHEN GESCHICHTSAUFFASSUNG. (1896.)

——— DIE LEHRE VON DEM RICHTIGEN RECHTE. (1902.)

TÖNNIES, F., GEMEINSCHAFT UND GESELLSCHAFT. (1887.)

TRENDELENBURG, A., NATURRECHT AUF DEM GRUNDE DER ETHIK. 2. Aufl. (1868.)

CHAPTER II: ON THE GENERAL METHODOLOGY OF THE CULTURAL SCIENCES

DILTHEY, W., EINLEITUNG IN DIE GEISTESWISSENSCHAFTEN. 1. Bd. (1883.)

MÜNSTERBERG, H., GRUNDZÜGE DER PHILOSOPHIE. 1. Bd. (1900.)

RICKERT, H., DER GEGENSTAND DER ERKENNTNIS. 2. Aufl. (1904.)

——— DIE GRENZEN DER NATURWISSENSCHAFTLICHEN BEGRIFFSBILDUNG. (1896/1902.)

——— KULTURWISSENSCHAFT UND NATURWISSENSCHAFT. (1899.)

SIMMEL, G., DAS PROBLEM DER SOZIOLOGIE. SCHMOLLERS JAHRBUCH FÜR GESETZG. VERW. UND VOLKSW. Bd. 18. (1894.)

——— DIE PROBLEME DER GESCHICHTSPHILOSOPHIE. (1892.)

WEBER, M., DIE "OBJEKTIVITÄT" SOZIALWISSENSCHAFTLICHER UND SOZIALPOLITISCHER ERKENNTNIS. ARCH. F. SOZIALW. U. SOZIALPOL. Bd. 1. (1904.)

WINDELBAND, W., GESCHICHTE UND NATURWISSENSCHAFT. 3. Aufl. (1904.)

On the Methodology of Jurisprudence[1]

ARNOLD, W., KULTUR UND RECHTSLEBEN. (1865.)

BIERLING, E. R., JURISTISCHE PRINZIPIENLEHRE. 2 Bde. (1894. 1898.)

BRODMANN, E., VOM STOFFE DES RECHTS UND SEINER STRUKTUR. (1897.)

ELTZBACHER, P., ÜBER RECHTSBEGRIFFE. (1900.)

——— DIE HANDLUNGSFÄHIGKEIT. 1. Bd. (1903.)

GIERKE, O., DAS DEUTSCHE GENOSSENSCHAFTSRECHT. 3 Bde. (1868–1881.)

——— DIE GENOSSENSCHAFTSTHEORIE UND DIE DEUTSCHE RECHTSPRECHUNG. (1887.)

——— DEUTSCHES PRIVATRECHT. 1. Bd. (1895.)

——— LABANDS STAATSRECHT UND DIE DEUTSCHE RECHTSWISSENSCHAFT. SCHMOLLERS JAHRB. FÜR GESETZG., VERW. U. VOLKSW. Bd. 7. (1883.)

HOLD VON FERNECK, A., DIE RECHTSWIDRIGKEIT. (1903.)

JELLINEK, G., DIE RECHTLICHE NATUR DER STAATENVERTRÄGE. (1880.)

——— GESETZ UND VERORDNUNG. 1887.

——— SYSTEM DER SUBJEKTIVEN ÖFFENTLICHEN RECHTE. (1892.)

——— ALLGEMEINE STAATSLEHRE. 1900.

JHERING, R., GEIST DES RÖMISCHEN RECHTS. 4. u. 5. Aufl. 3 Tle. (1881–1891.)

[1] The following writings have been selected solely because of their methodological elements. [Author's footnote.]

——— Der Zweck im Recht. 2. Aufl. 2 Bde. (1884/1886.)

——— Unsere Aufgabe. Jahrbücher für Dogmatik des heutigen römischen und deutschen Privatrechts. 1. Bd.

Karner, J., Die soziale Funktion der Rechtsinstitute. (1904.) (Marx-Studien hrsg. v. Adler und Hilferding.)

Kistiakowski, Th., Gesellschaft und Einzelwesen. (1899.)

Knapp, L., System der Rechtsphilosophie. (1857.)

Kohlrausch, E., Irrtum und Schuldbegriff im Strafrecht. 1. Tl. (1903.)

Laband, P., Beiträge zur Dogmatik der Handelsgesellschaften. Zeitschr. f. d. ges. Handelsrecht. Bd. 30. (1885.)

Leist, B. W., Altarisches jus gentium. (1889.)

Liepmann, M., Einleitung in das Strafrecht. (1900.)

Mayer, M. E., Die schuldhafte Handlung. (1901.)

——— Rechtsnormen und Kulturnormen. (1903.)

Meumann, G. A., Prolegomena zu einem System des Vermögensrechts. (1903.)

Pachmann, S., Über die gegenwärtige Bewegung in der Rechtswissenschaft. (Aus dem Russischen übersetzt.) (1882.)

Puchta, G. F., Cursus der Institutionen. 1. Bd. 10. Aufl. (1893.)

Radbruch, G., Der Handlungsbegriff in seiner Bedeutung für das Strafrechtssystem. (1904.)

Rickert, H., Zur Lehre von der Definition. (1888.)

Rosin, H., Souveränetät, Staat, Gemeinde, Selbstverwaltung. Annalen des Deutschen Reiches. (1883.)

Rümelin, G., Juristische Begriffsbildung. (1878.)

Schuppe, W., Der Begriff des Rechts. Grünhuts Zeitschr. f. d. Privat- u. öffentl. Recht d. Gegenw. Bd. 10. (1883.)

Stoerk, F., Zur Methodik des öffentlichen Rechts. (1885.)

Thon, A., Rechtsnorm und subjektives Recht. (1878.)

Wundt, W., Logik. 2. Bd. 2. Abt. 2 Aufl. (1895.)

Zitelmann, E., Irrtum und Rechtsgeschäft. (1879.)

II

LEGAL PHILOSOPHY

By GUSTAV RADBRUCH

1932

Gustav Radbruch was born in 1878 at Lübeck, Germany. In 1904 he became a Privatdozent at the University of Heidelberg; in 1914 he transferred to the University of Königsberg in Prussia (where Immanuel Kant had lived and taught more than a century before), as Professor. In 1919 he transferred to the University of Kiel, and in 1926 to Heidelberg. He was a member of the Reichstag under the Weimar Constitution from 1920 to 1924, and during this period was Minister of Justice of the German Reich in the cabinets of Chancellors Wirth and Stresemann, as a Social Democrat. On political grounds he was dismissed from his academic post at Heidelberg in 1933. In 1945 he again became Professor of Criminal Law and Legal Philosophy at Heidelberg. He is the author of the following works: EINFÜHRUNG IN DIE RECHTSWISSENSCHAFT (7th and 8th ed. 1928); RECHTSPHILOSOPHIE (3d ed. 1932), the work here translated in full; KULTURLEHRE DES SOZIALISMUS (2d ed. 1927); PAUL JOHANN ANSELM FEURBACH, EIN JURISTENLEBEN (1934); GESTALTEN UND GEDANKEN, eight essays (1945); DER GEIST DES ENGLISCHEN RECHTS (2d ed. 1947). A valuable commentary on English jurisprudence — Bentham, Austin, and Maine — is found in Radbruch, *Anglo-American Jurisprudence through Continental Eyes* (1936) 52 L. Q. REV. 530. He is now (August 1949) living at Heidelberg.

To

HERMANN KANTOROWICZ

Veterrima quaeque, ut ea vina, quae vetustatem ferunt, esse debent suavissima verumque illud est, quod dicitur, multos modios salis simul edendos esse, ut amicitiae munus expletum sit. — CICERO, *De Amicitia*

[What is oldest, as with those wines which show their age, must be sweetest; and it is true what people say, that many measures of salt must be eaten together to make good the gift of friendship.]

AUTHOR'S PREFACE [a]

Every writer at some time reaches the point when he feels he ought to clean up and close up and make the remaining time of his life available for other tasks. This book is to bring to a close this author's legal philosophical works.

It is called a third edition of the OUTLINES OF LEGAL PHILOSOPHY.[b] The second edition was published in 1922 as a mere reprint of the first edition; it was dated back to the year of the first edition, 1914. A new edition was necessary and a revision impossible at that time, when the need for a thorough transformation after the upheavals of war and revolution was already recognized. Dating the reprint back was to express that the book in that form did not pretend to set forth the state of the author's thought at the time of its publication.

The revision now submitted is based on a rewriting of the entire book. It is a new book rather than a new edition. Some sections of the General Part (§§ 11–14) and the entire Special Part (§§ 16–20)[c] have been added. In this Special Part the author proposes not to exhaust the topics in all their aspects but only to approach them from the viewpoints set forth in the General Part and thus to test the General Part. However, political philosophy, to the extent that it can be separated from legal philosophy, has been eliminated. The portions dealt with in the old book also have undergone manifold changes. Many corrections have been made; for example, justice has been conceded a greater significance, as opposed to the expediency of the law. Elsewhere there have been omissions, such as the discussion of the problem of freedom of the will, not because they appeared incorrect, but because they seemed to the author dispensable in this context. Much that once needed detailed discussion could be cut down. Many a passage, possibly the whole accent of the book, has changed, because after nearly twenty years what sounded natural from the young man's lips would have sounded false to him from his lips after growing older. Maybe some will like the old book better

[a] The numbered footnotes are those of the author; the lettered footnotes have been added by the translator, who has also in some instances added to the author's text or footnotes explanatory matter enclosed in brackets [ ]. In the original work (RECHTSPHILOSOPHIE. DRITTE, GANZ NEU BEARBEITETE UND STARK VERMEHRTE AUFLAGE, 1932) the author's footnotes began with number 1 on each page. It was impractical to preserve this numbering, hence in this translation the footnotes are numbered or lettered consecutively within each section.

[b] [GRUNDZÜGE DER RECHTSPHILOSOPHIE.]

[c] [*Sic* in the German text. Actually, the Special Part embraces secs. 16–29.]

than the new one. But the old book is not out of the world either, and it is to be supplemented and not supplanted by the new book.

Now as before, however, the author professes the same way of thought: that rationalism which "intends to remain in the night that people call enlightenment" (Larenz), and that relativism which "can be disposed of as plainly unscientific" (Sauer). He does not follow the irrationalist fashion of the times. By rationalism as represented in this book he does not mean, to be sure, that the world divided by reason leaves no remainder. But he sees his task in rationally revealing ultimate conflicts and not in irrationally befogging them. To relativism the author attributes even greater significance at present than at the time this book was first published. For relativism is the conceptual presuppositon of democracy. Democracy refuses to identify itself with a definite political view; rather it is ready to leave leadership in the state to any political view that was able to obtain a majority, because it does not know of any unequivocal criterion for the correctness of political views nor does it acknowledge the possibility of a standpoint above the parties. Relativism, which teaches that no political view is demonstrable — and none refutable — is apt to counteract that self-righteousness which is usual in our political controversies: if no partisan view is demonstrable, each view is to be fought from the standpoint of an opposite view; yet if none is refutable either, each is to be respected even from the standpoint of the adverse view. Thus relativism teaches both determination in one's own attitude and justice toward that of another.

This legal philosophy as a modest contribution in 1914 belonged to those works which set legal philosophical efforts going again after decades of standstill, during which Rudolf Stammler alone held the banner of legal philosophy aloft. Since then an immense literature has sprung up. The author declares himself unable to discuss that literature in this book. He also deems it superfluous to quote it exhaustively, in view of the wealth of bibliographical references in other treatises (Stammler, Sauer).

He wants to suggest to students the How rather than the What of legal philosophy, less to tie them down to conclusions than to guide them to legal philosophical thinking. But to those who strive with him, and especially to the friend whom he best liked to think of as his reader, he addresses that verse of Horace:

Vive, vale. Si quid novisti rectius istis,
Candidus imperti; si non, his utere mecum.[d]

RADBRUCH

[d] [Live and be strong! If you know what is more correct than these presents, candidly then impart it; if not, make use of this with me.]

LEGAL PHILOSOPHY

Section I

Reality and Value

When we think about the world, it tumbles,
Breaking into wild and rugged parts.
But we join them to a bridge of beauty
Quietly again within our hearts. — *Richard Dehmel*

Legal philosophy is a part of philosophy. Therefore it is indispensable first to demonstrate the general philosophical assumptions of legal philosophy.[1]

In what is given, the unformed raw material of our experience, reality and value are drastically commingled. We experience men and things affected with value, that is, with worth and worthlessness, without reflecting that such worth and worthlessness originate from ourselves, the spectators, and not from those very men and things. The nobility of a man lights his face up like a halo. The rustling boughs of old oaks give us a thrill of the sacred. We think we observe the poison in the poisonous plant and scorn it as a moral malignancy.[2]

Value-Blind, Evaluating, Value-Relating, Value-Conquering. The first achievement of the mind consists in the ego withdrawing from and confronting what is given, and thus distinguishing reality from value. The mind learns how its evaluating consciousness may be sometimes screened off and sometimes deliberately put in. Thus, on the one hand, by a value-blind attitude of ours, the realm of nature is created out of the chaos of what is given; for nature is nothing but that which is given, as it presents itself when cleared of falsifying evaluations. Contrariwise, in a deliberately evaluating attitude, the mind becomes conscious of the standards of such evaluation, viz., the norms, and of their interconnection, which makes up the realm of values that confront nature. The value-blind attitude, applied methodically, is the essence of natural

[1] The background of the following discussion is formed by the philosophical doctrines of Windelband, Rickert, and Lask. In particular, Lask's Rechtsphilosophie (reprinted in his 1 Gesammelte Schriften (1923) 275 *et seq.*) [translated in the present volume] has guided this discussion and the present book.

[2] Cf. Eduard Spranger, Lebensformen (5th ed. 1925) 37.

scientific thought; the evaluating attitude, carried through systematically, characterizes the philosophy of values and its three branches: logic, ethics, and aesthetics.

There are, however, two more attitudes, which are complementary to and in different ways intermediary between the value-blind and the evaluating attitude. These are the attitude that relates values and the attitude that conquers values. First, the value-relating attitude may be illustrated by some concepts resulting from it.

The concept of science[a] is not identical with the concept of truth; the science of an age embraces not only its scientific achievements, but also its scientific errors. But the reason why we use the concept of science to include its labors regardless of their failure or success is that they all at least aimed and claimed to be truth: science is anything given that, whether attaining or missing the truth, still has the significance, the meaning, to serve the truth. In the same way art, in the sense in which it is the subject-matter of the history of arts, is not sheer beauty, but a mixture of style and tastelessness, joined in a unified concept only by the quest for beauty that is common to all its creations. Morals, in the sense in which it is dealt with, say, in anthropology, includes also the errors of conscience, but only because these, too, meant to strive for the good which they actually missed. All those and many other concepts are included in the concept of culture. This concept therefore has the same structure as those component concepts. As described by the historian, culture is by no means pure value, but rather a mixture of humanity and barbarism, taste and tastelessness, truth and error; but in all its phenomena, whether hampering or promoting values, whether missing or realizing values, it is never thought of without relation to value. Culture is not realization of value, yet it is whatever has significance or meaning for the realization of values; or, in Stammler's words, it is "striving for the right."[3] Thus it appears that the value-relating attitude is the methodical attitude of the cultural sciences.

Lastly, the value-blind, evaluating, and value-relating attitudes are complemented by the religious attitude which conquers values. Religion is ultimate affirmation of whatever exists, smiling positivism that pronounces its "Yea" and "Amen" over all things, love without regard to the worth or worthlessness of what is loved, beatitude beyond happiness or unhappiness, mercy beyond guilt and innocence, peace higher than reason and its problems, the "gay metaphysical light-mindedness"

[a] [On the meaning of science (*Wissenschaft*) and culture (*Kultur*) in German terminology, see translator's note to LASK, LEGAL PHILOSOPHY, *supra*, *Introd.*, n. (6), p. 3.]

[3] LEHRBUCH DER RECHTSPHILOSOPHIE (2d ed. 1923) sec. 29, n. 1.

(Scheler) of the children of God whom "everything must serve to the good." This passage from the New Testament is in harmony with the conclusion of the story of creation: "And God saw everything He had made, and lo, it was very good." [4]

Religion means conquest of worthlessness, and therewith necessarily also conquest of the value, which is conceivable only as worth opposed to worthlessness: worth and worthlessness become no longer of *different* validity and are, therefore, *in*different. "He who would treasure everything alike, in this his life attains the state of everlasting bliss" (Angelus Silesius). But with the contrast between value and worthlessness cancelled, there is also cancelled the contrast between value and reality. What is adverse to value is either still valuable in some ultimate sense or else altogether unessential. For we speak of the essence of a thing [5] when we think of value as the principle of its being.

In conquering the contrast between value and worthlessness, however, religion presupposes that very contrast. Otherwise its lovely indulgence would in no way differ from the dull indifference of the attitude that is blind to values. A subject of religious affirmation is only what first, as worth or worthlessness, has passed through the realm of values: nature lies on this side, religion lies on the other side of the realm of values. Religion springs from the unbearableness of the contrast between value and reality — and it must spring from that unbearable contrast anew at any instant and never become a permanent state lest its conquest of values sink down to blindness toward values. It is not like a monastery which one enters never to emerge from again, but rather like a wayside chapel where one leans the wandering stick against the wall for brief meditation and prayer.

Thus, to these four attitudes there corresponds a fourfold formulation of what is given: existence, value, meaning, and essence. The relation of these four realms may also be expressed in these terms: Nature and ideal, and two connections across the gap between them, the never-to-be-completed bridge of culture and the ever instantaneously accomplished flight of religion: Work and faith.

We now have to fit the law to these four viewpoints.

Legal Science, Legal Philosophy, Religious Philosophy of the Law. Law is a creation of man, and like any human creation it can be understood only by its idea. Just try to define a human creation as simple as, say, a table, otherwise than by reference to its purpose! For instance:

[4] On this passage, cf. MAX BROD, 1 HEIDENTUM, CHRISTENTUM, JUDENTUM 64 *et seq.*

[5] LASK, LOGIK DER PHILOSOPHIE (1911) 7: "Superexistence."

a table is a top plate with four legs. Against such a definition, it would at once be objected that there are tables with three legs or with one leg and even folding tables without legs so that only the top is essential to a table. But the top of the table is nothing but boards joined together, differing from other such boards by absolutely nothing else than their purpose; which results in a definition of a table as, say, a contrivance on which to put something for those sitting at it. Thus a view of human creations that is blind to purposes, that is, to values, is impossible; so, then, is a value-blind view of the law or of any single legal phenomenon. A natural science of crime, as striven for by criminal anthropology, would be possible only if first a natural concept of crime could be substituted for the concept of crime that is related to a legal value. It would be a miracle beyond all miracles if a concept formed by relation to values, such as that of law or that of crime, could be made to coincide with a natural concept arrived at by a value-blind approach.

Law can be understood only within the framework of the value-relating attitude. Law is a cultural phenomenon, that is, a fact related to value. The concept of law can be determined only as something given, the meaning of which is to realize the idea of law. Law may be unjust (*summum jus — summa injuria* [b]); but it is law only because its meaning is to be just.

The very idea of law, however, which is the constituent principle of, and also the standard of evaluation for, legal reality, belongs to the evaluating attitude.

But even this evaluating attitude does not have the last word that may be spoken about law. There remains the possibility of declaring the law valuable and yet ultimately, "before God," utterly unessential, as in the Sermon on the Mount; and, conversely, there remains the possibility of anchoring the law not only in the realm of values but in the most absolute essence of things, as in classical antiquity. These attitudes, however, belong to the value-conquering view.

There emerge, then, three possible views of the law: the value-relating view, the view of law as a cultural fact, which marks the essence of legal science; the evaluating view, the view of law as a cultural value, which characterizes legal philosophy; and the value-conquering view of the law, the view of its essence or its nonessentiality, which is the task of a religious philosophy of law.

[b] [The utmost law is the utmost wrong.]

Section 2

Legal Philosophy as the Evaluating View of Law

Man is not born to solve the problems of the world, but rather to search where the problem begins and then to keep within the limit of what can be understood.
— Goethe to Eckermann

Legal philosophy, then, is the evaluating view of the law, the "theory of the right law" (Stammler). The method of this, our evaluating view of law, is characterized by two features: methodical dualism and relativism.

Methodical Dualism. 1. Kantian philosophy has taught us that it is impossible from what is to derive what is valuable, what is right, what ought to be. Never is anything right merely because it is or because it was — or even because it will be. This disposes of positivism, which derives what ought to be from what is; of historism, which derives it from what was; and even of evolutionism, which derives it from what is about to be.[1] Even if we recognize a certain trend of development we do not thereby demonstrate that its goal is right and that "swimming against the current" is wrong; Don Quixote was a fool, but a noble fool. "I love men wanting the impossible!" Statements concerning the Ought, evaluations, judgments, may not be based inductively on statements concerning existence, but may only be based deductively on statements of the same kind. The view of values and the view of existence lie side by side, like distinct closed circles. This is the essence of methodical dualism.[2]

To be sure, it is just in the field of legal science that the claim is being made, the right rule should be derived from the "nature of things." This claim may indeed be supported on certain grounds. The legal ideal is an ideal for the law and, more especially, for the law of a certain time, a certain people, and certain sociological and historical conditions. The idea applies to a certain material, is oriented toward that material, and

[1] This evolutionary point of view was advocated for purposes of legal policy by Franz von Liszt in an article in (1906) 26 ZEITSCHRIFT FÜR DIE GESAMTE STRAFRECHTSWISSENSCHAFT 553 *et seq.*, which was much discussed at the time; for a summary of discussions thereof, see Radbruch in 27 ZEITSCHRIFT FÜR DIE GESAMTE STRAFRECHTSWISSENSCHAFT 246, 742, and Kantorowicz in 4 ASCHAFFENBURGS MONATSSCHRIFT FÜR KRIMINAL-PSYCHOLOGIE 78 *et seq.*

[2] The term "methodical dualism" as here used is opposed only to methodical monism; it includes methodical triadism, which will be discussed below, sec. 3 subdiv. 9.

thus it is in turn partly determined by the material which it is to govern. Just as the artistic idea accommodates itself to the material, differing according to whether it is to be embodied in bronze or in marble, so adjustment to the material is innate in any idea. We call this relation the "material qualification of the idea," deliberately adopting the double meaning of the term: qualified *by* the matter because qualifying *for* the matter.[3] The material qualification of the idea has been illustrated with regard to the legal idea by Eugen Huber in his theory of the "realities of legislation" and also by François Gény in his theory of the given factors (*donnés*).[4] Now one is tempted to identify this material qualification of the idea with a preformation of the idea in the material. Indeed, it is psychologically possible to visualize the idea both in and out of the material. Thus, Michelangelo may have seen, vision-like, the figure of David in that rough-hewn marble block out of which he delivered it. The same applies where the jurist decides according to the "nature of the thing."[5] But thus to visualize the idea in the material which it is intended to form is a lucky case of intuition and not a method of cognition. For methodical knowledge it remains true that statements concerning the Ought can only be derived deductively from other statements concerning the Ought and cannot be based inductively on facts of existence.

However, this nonderivability of the value from reality indicates only a logical, and by no means a causal, relationship. (So, incidentally, does the material qualification of the idea.) Methodical dualism is not intended to imply that evaluations or judgments are not influenced by existing facts. Doubtless acts of evaluation are the causal result, the ideological superstructure, of existing facts, for instance, of the social environment of those who do the evaluating. The sociology of knowledge has taught us how ideologies are determined by their social settings.[6] We are here concerned not with the *causal* relation between existing facts and value judgments, but rather with the *logical* relation of existence and value. We state, not that evaluations may not be caused by existing

[3] Cf. Lask's theory of the differentiation of meanings, LOGIK DER PHILOSOPHIE (1911) 57 *et seq.*, 169 *et seq.*, and also Radbruch, *Rechtsidee und Rechtsstoff* (1923–24) 17 ARCHIV FÜR RECHTS-UND WIRTSCHAFTSPHILOSOPHIE 343 *et seq.*

[4] Eugen Huber in (1914) 1 ZEITSCHRIFT FÜR RECHTSPHILOSOPHIE 39 *et seq.*, and RECHT UND RECHTSVERWIRKLICHUNG (1921) 281 *et seq.*; François Gény, 1 SCIENCE ET TECHNIQUE EN DROIT PRIVÉ POSITIF (1922) 96 *et seq.*, 2 *id.* (1915) 370 *et seq.*

[5] On the history of the concept of "nature of the thing," see ISAY, RECHTSNORM UND ENTSCHEIDUNG (1929) 78 *et seq.*

[6] Cf. MANNHEIM, IDEOLOGIE UND UTOPIE (1929); and *Wissenssoziologie*, in HANDWÖRTERBUCH DER SOZIOLOGIE (1931).

facts, but rather that they may not be logically grounded upon them. An entire structure of ethical ideas may have originated from the class resentment of its founder; yet within the system of his ethics that resentment has no place, and the systematic reasoning of that ethics is not refuted merely by unmasking its origin in causes not consistent with its reasoning. In discussing a theory, the psychological causes of its origin must not be introduced unless the purpose be to terminate the discussion, to demonstrate that further discussion is futile because thoughts are shown to be so tenaciously tied to existence as to preclude any understanding.

It may be objected that such a view, confined to the ideal content of evaluations and disregarding their existential basis, is concerned with the unessential, with "mere ideologies" and not with real and effective forces; that legal philosophy is but the struggle of political parties, which is ultimately the struggle of economic interests raised to the level of the spirit; and that it is therefore a mirage, without essence of reality. But — as will be shown later in analyzing the Marxian view of history — if legal philosophy is spiritualized politics, and politics is a spiritualized class struggle, such spiritualization unchains an autonomy of the spirit and thus enables the spirit to react upon the forces that are spiritualized. The ideas do not fight the struggle of the interests all over again in the clouds like the Valkyries above the battlefield; rather, like the Homeric gods, they descend to the battlefield and fight, powerful forces themselves, side by side with the other forces. Granted that, on the one hand, legal philosophy is the struggle of political parties transferred into the realm of the spirit; on the other hand, the struggle of political parties in turn represents a grandiose legal philosophical discussion. All great political changes were prepared or accompanied by legal philosophy. In the beginning there was legal philosophy; at the end, there was revolution.

Relativism. 2. Statements concerning the Ought may be established or proved only by other statements concerning the Ought. For this very reason, the ultimate statements concerning the Ought are incapable of proof, axiomatic. They may not be discerned but only professed. So in an argument between opposite affirmations of ultimate statements concerning the Ought, between opposite views of values and the world, there can be no decision of scientific unequivocality. It has been said that the scientific view of values may indeed teach what one is able to do and willing to do, but not what one ought to do. More precisely, science in the field of the Ought can achieve three things:

First, it may establish the means necessary to realize the end that ought to be attained. To be sure, we call guidance in the choice of the right means for a legal end not legal philosophy but legal policy. But consideration of means as conditioned by a legal end may involve a view not only from the end toward the means, as in legal policy, but also conversely from the means back toward the end. That is to say, the import of the end may be fully clarified only by showing the means indispensable for its attainment and the incidental effects which they inevitably entail. Such consideration of the means with a view to clarifying the legal end they are to realize is legal philosophy.

Secondly, it is the task of legal philosophy not only to think a legal value judgment through down to the remotest means for its realization, but also to clarify it up to its ultimate presuppositions of world outlook. Legal philosophy raises the Kantian question: how is this particular value judgment possible, that is to say, what presuppositions must be recognized in order consistently to permit this value judgment? Just as the paleontologist aims to reconstruct the entire skeleton of an ancient animal out of some bone remains, so the legal philosopher is to develop, out of a single legal evaluation, the entire system of values implied therein. However, as the first-mentioned consideration is not one for the sake of the means, so the present consideration is not one for the sake of the presuppositions, but rather for the sake of the legal evaluation which they involve. He who evaluates is to be made conscious that in approving a particular end of the legal Ought he must accept not only the means connected therewith by causal necessity but also the more general evaluations involved therein by logical necessity. In both directions, he is to be given full insight into the bearing of that end.

Thereby, thirdly, it becomes possible systematically to develop the conceivable ultimate presuppositions and, consequently, all starting points of legal evaluation. This permits an exhaustive presentation of the systems of legal evaluation as contrasted and related with one another, and a topical arrangement of the possible legal views within the framework of a topical arrangement of conceivably possible ways of world outlook. Thus we may establish, not indeed *the* system of legal philosophy, but the complete systematization of its possible systems.

It does not avail to call this method a purely empirical and therefore not a philosophical procedure. Our method does not stop at the mere happening of factual legal philosophical evaluations. Rather it examines their meaning, and not only their subjective, actually intended meaning, but their objective, signifying meaning. What the evaluating individual intended by his evaluation is but the starting point of this method. The aim of its thought is what according to that starting point he should have intended in causal and logical consistency. Its task is not to register thoughts about legal ends, but to clarify and possibly thereby to correct them. By making the individual conscious of the objective meaning of what he desires, it will either confirm him in his value judgment by more profound supporting argument or else conversely shake him by insight into the distance between the intended and the true meaning. In either case, it will serve life by knowledge.

To be sure, relativistic legal philosophy cannot relieve the individual of choosing between the legal views developed systematically out of the opposing ultimate presuppositions. It is limited to presenting to him exhaustively the possibilities of decision, but it leaves his decision itself to the resoluton he draws from the depth of his personality — by no means, then, to his pleasure, but rather to his conscience. It limits itself in this way because in its view the response to the ultimate value judgments must be *ignorabimus*.[a] Even if the response were to be a mere *ignoramus*,[b] it would persist in its method, trusting to have done at least useful spade work, by its systematic development of the possibilities of world outlook, preparing the way for the genius who one day might be able to decide between them with scientific exactitude.

The method which is here presented is called relativism,[7] because its task is to determine only whether any value judgment is right in relation to a particular supreme value judgment, within the framework of a particular outlook on values and the world, but not whether that value judgment and that outlook on values and the world are right in and of themselves.[8] Relativism, however, belongs to theoretical and not to

[a] ["We shall not know."]

[b] ["We do not know."]

[7] Or "problematicism," as in WINDELBAND, EINLEITUNG IN DIE PHILOSOPHIE (1914) 219.

[8] The outstanding representatives of relativism are GEORG JELLINEK, ALLGEMEINE STAATSLEHRE (3d ed., 5th printing, 1929); MAX WEBER, GESAMMELTE AUFSÄTZE ZUR WISSENSCHAFTSLEHRE (1922; cf. MARIANNE WEBER, MAX WEBER (1926) 328 *et seq.*); and HANS KELSEN, ALLGEMEINE STAATSLEHRE (1925), 38 *et seq.*, 369 *et seq.* The present author has evolved this fundamental view of his in exchanging views with the man to whom this book is dedicated [Hermann Kantorowicz]; besides many other of his utterances, see KANTOROWICZ, ZUR LEHRE VOM RICHTIGEN RECHT (1909). About, and mostly against, the ideas advocated here, cf. EMGE, ÜBER DIE GRUNDLAGEN DES RECHTSPHILOSOPHISCHEN RELATIVISMUS (1916); LEONARD NELSON, DIE RECHTSWISSENSCHAFT OHNE RECHT (1917) 123 *et seq.*; MAX SALOMON, GRUNDLEGUNG DER RECHTSPHILOSOPHIE (2d ed. 1925) 53; LEONH. COHN, DAS OBJEKTIV RICHTIGE (1919) 96 *et seq.*; Münch in 1 BEITRÄGE ZUR PHILOSOPHIE DES DEUTSCHEN IDEALISMUS (ed. by Hoffmann and Engert, 1919) 135 *et seq.*; M. E. MAYER, RECHTSPHILOSOPHIE (1922) 21 *et seq.*, 67 *et seq.*; BINDER, PHILOSOPHIE DES RECHTS (1925) 112 *et seq.*; LARENZ, RECHTS- UND STAATSPHILOSOPHIE DER GEGENWART (1931) 66 *et seq.*; Ernst von Hippel in 12 ARCHIV DES ÖFFENTLICHEN RECHTS (NEUE FOLGE) 408 *et seq.*; HERRFAHRDT, REVO-

practical reason. It implies a renunciation of the scientific establishment of ultimate decisions and not a renunciation of the decision itself.[9] Our relativism is not cognate to Pilate of the Gospel, in whom practical as well as theoretical reason becomes mute: "What is truth?" It is cognate rather to Lessing's Nathan, to whom the silence of theoretical reason is the strongest appeal to practical reason: "May each of you vie with the other then in bringing out the power of the gem in his own ring." For relativism may be based on different foundations of world outlook. The relativist may forego a decision of his own in presenting ultimate evaluative decisions because he doubts the rightness of all of them alike — that is the skepticism of Pilate. Or he may do so because he firmly believes in the rightness of one of them but is unable to demonstrate it — that is the agnosticism of Nathan.[10] Still a third view is possible, which resembles the agnosticism of Nathan in combining relativism with activism. The relativist may also forego his own decision between conflicting evaluations because he accords equal right to all of them; that is, to each of them in its exclusive character as a duty of its representative; because he believes that what is mutually exclusive to our minds is compatible, indeed requisite, to a higher mind. This is antinomism, which has once been illustrated in a beautiful statement by Walter Rathenau: "We are not composers but musicians. So everyone may play

---

LUTION UND RECHTSWISSENSCHAFT (1930) 24 *et seq.*; MEZGER, SEIN UND SOLLEN IM RECHT (1920) 4 *et seq.*; SILBERSCHMIDT in (1930–31) INTERNATIONALE ZEITSCHRIFT FÜR THEORIE DES RECHTS 142 *et seq.*; MANIGK in (1930) JURISTISCHE WOCHENSCHRIFT 236 *et seq.* ("tolerable only as something provisional"); Graf Dohna in 31 KANTSTUDIEN 8 *et seq.* ("that the paths of this relativism . . . never cross those of the critical theory of law, so that they may well run side by side, as two entirely different views"); RIEZLER, DAS RECHTSGEFÜHL (1921) 79 ("In my opinion, the view of the relativity of value judgments . . . can be effectively fought only by demonstrating the validity of an absolute standard of value and thus raising an absolute legal ideal. Indeed, such attempts have been frequently made, though they have not succeeded"); RÜMELIN, DIE GERECHTIGKEIT (1920) 56, n. 2 ("This starting point of relativism may be hardly refutable"); Stammler, *Rechtsphilosophie*, in DAS GESAMTE DEUTSCHE RECHT 19 *et seq.* ("This is basically a feeble and miserable philosophy"). — The most illuminating discussion of the problem is to be found in EDUARD SPRANGER, DER SINN DER VORAUSSETZUNGSLOSIGKEIT IN DEN GEISTESWISSENSCHAFTEN (1929).

[9] The best proof is the great ethical personality of Max Weber. When Max Weber rejects, as a gross misunderstanding, the interpretation of his standpoint as relativism (MARIANNE WEBER, [MAX WEBER] 339), he thinks of that relativism which denies not only the possibility of a cognition of values but also the belief in values.

[10] Such a "moderate" relativism is advocated by ANRATHS, DAS WESEN DER SOG. FREIEN WISSENSCHAFTLICHEN BERUFE (1930) 200 *et seq.*, with valuable conclusions on the professional work of the lawyer; cf. Radbruch in 7 JUSTIZ 52 *et seq.*

his instrument as beautifully as he is able to; he is even permitted variations, if only all chords sound. All instruments are equally necessary. None need worry about harmony: that is created by another one." But relativism may also invoke the great name of Goethe. On January 22, 1811, he wrote to Reinhard, after having read a "comparative history of the philosophical systems": "In reading this work, I understood again what is also very explicitly stated by the author: that the different ways of thought are founded upon the difference of men, and that for this very reason a general uniform conviction is impossible. Now if one knows on what side he stands, he has done enough; he then is calm toward himself and fair toward others." That Goethe's relativism resembles not the skepticism of Pilate but the agnosticism of Nathan is testified by his beautiful "Gentle Xenion":

> If only I could know it, forsooth!
> I'd gladly walk the way of the Lord.
> If I were led to the house of truth,
> I'd stay there of my own accord.

Section 3

The Trends of Legal Philosophy

> *Where many contradictions whir,*
> *There I should like it best.*
> *How funny! Each one will contest*
> *The other's right to err. — Goethe*

The legal philosophy which rests on methodical dualism and relativism will now be shown to result from the legal philosophical development of the past century. The legal philosophical trends will accordingly be characterized not by their objective positions but only by their methodological peculiarities.

Natural Law Doctrine. 1. All legal philosophy from its inception to the beginning of the nineteenth century was a doctrine of natural law. To be sure, the term "natural law" embraces fundamentally different phenomena. The natural law of classical antiquity hinged upon the opposition of nature and enactment, that of the Middle Ages upon the opposition of divine and human law, and that of modern times upon the opposition of legal compulsion and individual reason. Sometimes natural law serves more profoundly to confirm enacted law; sometimes, conversely, it aids the fight against enacted law. But in all its forms it is marked by four essential characteristics, though these are differently emphasized at different times: It provides legal value judgments that are definite in content. These value judgments, according to their source — nature, revelation, or reason — are of universal validity and unchangeable. They are susceptible of cognition. Once known, they prevail over conflicting enacted law: natural law is superior to positive law.

The claim of natural law to deduce legal rules of universal validity, unchangeable and definite in content, cannot be deemed refuted purely empirically, by the usual reference to the colorful variety of the legal views of different ages and nations. The theorist of natural law would justly reject any conclusion as to what ought to be that is drawn from what is, that "vulgar appeal to ostensibly conflicting experience" (Kant). In the variety of legal views he would find only the variety of error as against the single truth of natural law: *error multiplex, veritas una.*[a] The decisive blow against natural law has been struck not by legal history and comparative law but by epistemology; not by the historical school, but by critical philosophy; not by Savigny but by Kant. Kant's critique of reason has shown that reason is not an arsenal of finished theoretical cognitions, of ethical and aesthetical norms ready to be applied, but rather the mere power to arrive at such cognitions and norms; that it is not a complex of answers, but rather one of questions, of points of view from which what is given is to be approached; of forms which need to be filled with a given substance, of categories which need to be applied to a given material, in order to yield statements or judgments of definite content. Those cognitions or evaluations which are definite in content are never produced by "pure" reason, but always only by its application to something definitely given. Therefore, they are never universally valid but always are valid only for these given data. Consequently, we may indeed grant that there is universal validity in the *question* concerning the "natural," that is, the right law; but to any of the answers to it we may concede validity only for a given state of society, for a definite time and a definite people. Only the category of right, just law, but none of its applications, is universally valid. If it is desired to retain the name, "natural law," for the "right law" that is characterized only by the unity of the categorial form, it must be contrasted with the old-style unchangeable natural law as a "natural law with changing content" (following Stammler) or, as it has been called, a "cultural law."

Now if, contrary to the relativistic view, right law were unequivocally cognizable, whether it be old-style natural law or natural law with

[a] ["Error is manifold, truth is one."]

changing content, the conclusion would be inevitable that where it confronts conflicting enactments these must fade away like the exposed error that is confronted with revealed truth. However much it has been attempted, no sound reason can be conceived why an enacted law should retain its validity after being found indubitably unjust. It will be shown below that the validity of enacted law can be founded only upon the indiscernibility of the right law. Contrariwise, a representative of the view that there is an unequivocally cognizable natural law must, to be consistent, deny the two-dimensionality of the legal world; he must identify "material" and "formal natural law" (to use Lask's terms), or the rightness and the validity of law. He is unable to concede to enacted law any independent reason for existence besides natural law; he arrives at a complete absorption of enacted law by the right law, of legal reality by legal value, of legal science by legal philosophy.

Historical School. 2. The historical school proposes the extreme opposite to the natural law doctrine: the absorption of the right law by enacted law, of the legal value by legal reality, of legal philosophy by legal science. This at least is the first impression of the program of the historical school; it seems as if it rejected all legal evaluation, all legal philosophy, along with that of natural law, as if it wanted science to confine itself positivistically to purely empirical examination of historical legal reality. In fact, it later worked out in this sense. Yet always, driven by an ineradicable philosophical need, it stealthily readmitted the evaluating view even where it ostensibly banished it. A more attentive second glance shows that even the historical school denies, not all evaluation of the law, but only the *differentiating* evaluation of the several historical legal phenomena; that it values them all equally highly because in its view the necessary product of history and of the spirit of the people appears upon that very ground to be right. Its basic feature is reverence for all that is and has grown, but also for all that is growing, piety in respect of all reality. Not unjustly has it been characterized, not only as quietism, but also as pietism, as a "pietistic trend" (Thibaut). This would show that the background of the historical school is a religious philosophy of the law, rather than a value philosophy of the law. But even the differentiating evaluation of the several legal phenomena could not be avoided permanently by the historical school. Consistently, it should pronounce all positive law equally right, since none can be conceived that is not the necessary product of its historical and national environment — including even the legislative products of the natural law period. Yet the historical school is led by its struggle against natural law to pass very definite judgments of worthlessness on natural law, enlightenment, revolution, and the "arbitrariness of the legislator," and equally definite judgments of positive value on an organic formation of law by the "internal, quietly working forces," the "national spirit." "He who is thoroughly convinced of the organic view of the law and the state will only too easily and gladly forget that hurricanes and earthquakes are no less part of the regular course of nature than is the quiet growth of animals or plants." [1] The legal positivism which is blind to values, and the value-conquering religious philosophy of the law, thus turn imperceptibly into a legal philosophy of romantic color and even a legal policy of conservative direction.[2] Indeed, Friedrich Julius Stahl, the theorist of conservatism, found the nucleus of historism not in its "view of the factual, how law originates, but in its view of the ethical, how it ought to originate and what its contents ought to be"; accordingly, he called his own doctrine a "philosophy of the law from the historic point of view." [3]

As a matter of fact, the gradualness of historical development without any leaps or bounds is a need *a priori* of historical cognition. A historical event is historically perceived only if it has been demonstrated as a continuation and not as an interruption of the historical process. No matter how defiantly a historical deed may break away from all tradition in the minds of the doers, as a deed that is done it becomes irrevocably subject to that necessary form of historical scientific thought, that category of gradualness without breaks. In the subsequent historical view, even the most arbitrary Will is inevitably revealed as a Must, that necessarily originated in long ripened conditions, just as the boldest conquest of gravity, the proudest triumph of the pilot, still remains inescapably enclosed in this world with its gravity. Yet the historical view may claim to be applied only to the subsequent consideration of the deed that is done; applied as a norm to an active human being, the demand that one regard oneself in creative politics as being bound by history brings history itself to a standstill. The error of all historism, then, rests on elevating a category of historical cognition to a norm of political action.

Hegel. 3. At first glance, a close relation seems to exist between the methodical monism of the historical school, which claims to know reality

[1] Anton Menger, Das bürgerliche Recht und die besitzlosen Volksklassen (4th ed. 1903) 13.

[2] Cf. Rothacker, Einleitung in die Geisteswissenschaften (2d ed. 1930) 60 *et seq.*; Zwilgmeyer, Die Rechtslehre Savignys (1929) 32 *et seq.*

[3] Late writings most characteristic of the program of the historical school are J. J. Bachofen, Selbstbiographie and Antrittsrede (reprint, 1927).

alone, and the Hegelian philosophy of law with its famous motto of all philosophy of identity: "All that is rational is real; and all that is real is rational." In fact, Hegel shares the historical school's antagonism to natural law. Unlike the doctrine of natural law, his philosophy does not oppose individual legal reason to legal reality, but rather finds rational law in historical legal reality.[4] "All that is rational is real." Despite this common antagonism, however, his profound opposition to the historical school is unmistakable. Whereas the historical school bases the identification of reality and value on the belief in God's inscrutable counsels which pervade history, Hegel rests it on the dialectical construction that traces reason unfolding itself in the historical process: "All that is real is rational." Reason stands against the national spirit, rationalism against irrational romanticism. This objective opposition was reflected in sharp personal arguments between the Hegelians and the historical school. Hegel called Savigny's hostility to codification "one of the greatest insults that could be offered to a nation or to that profession" (viz., the legal profession). From the opposite side, Hegel's theory was called the "hostile power" (Stahl), nay, a "frivolous philosophy" (Puchta). There, the potentialities of radical developments inherent in Hegelianism were clearly felt.[5]

Marx-Engels: Materialistic View of History. 4. Those developments were of greatest consequence in the "materialistic view of history," which was established by Karl Marx and Friedrich Engels.[6] Hegel identified Is and Ought, but in regarding reality as reason unfolding itself he regarded the Ought as the determining and the Is as the determined aspects of that unity. Historical materialism, on the other hand, retained the identification of Ought and Is but regarded the Ought, or what Karl Marx calls consciousness, as determined by existence. "Thereby, Hegelian dialectic was turned upside down or rather, since it stood on its head, downside down, and on its feet" (Friedrich Engels).

[4] In this sense, LASSALLE, 1 SYSTEM DER ERWORBENEN RECHTE (1861) 70, says: "Natural law itself is historical law."

[5] The last system of legal philosophy in the spirit of Hegel was published by Adolf Lasson in 1882. The so-called Neo-Hegelianism of KOHLER, LEHRBUCH DER RECHTSPHILOSOPHIE (3d ed. 1923) and BEROLZHEIMER, SYSTEM DER RECHTS- UND WIRTSCHAFTSPHILOSOPHIE (5 vols., 1904 *et seq.*), on the contrary, has little to do with Hegel. Hegelianism without dialectics is no Hegelianism.

[6] Writings in which historical materialism is applied to and tested by historical experience are more important than the immense literature *about* historical materialism. As to the law, cf. KARL RENNER, DIE RECHTSINSTITUTE DES PRIVATRECHTS UND IHRE SOZIALE FUNKTION (1929) and E. PASCHUKANIS, ALLGEMEINE RECHTSLEHRE UND MARXISMUS (1927).

The economic view of history involves a twofold doctrine: on the one hand, a doctrine of ideology, and on the other hand, a doctrine of necessity. On the one hand, it submits a historical hypothesis: "that the economic structure of society in each case forms the real foundation upon which the entire superstructure of legal and political institutions and of religious, philosophical and other views of any historical period is to be ultimately explained." On the other hand, it contains a political prognosis: that the economic development of natural necessity will lead to a socialist economic and, consequently, legal order. In this historical-causal and not merely teleological foundation of socialism, its foundation not upon its desirability but upon its future necessity, historical materialism finds the transformation of socialism "from Utopia to science." It seems as if the first of these two propositions turns legal philosophy into a dependent part of social philosophy and the second turns social philosophy itself into an empirical social science.

But both propositions need to be limited. On the one hand, in the course of later elaboration or clarification of historical materialism, the autonomy of ideology, including the sphere of law, has been restored. Karl Marx himself calls the ideal "the material as transformed and translated in human brains," without however specifying the form which the material assumes in human brains. And Friedrich Engels later says both of them had "neglected the formal while considering the substantive aspect." [7]

An example may serve to illustrate the conversion of the material when "transformed and translated" into the ideal. The demand for civil liberty and its fulfillment originated in the interest and the power of the ascendant bourgeoisie. But the liberty which it intended was not only liberty for itself but liberty for all — for the very reason that it demanded that liberty as its right. Legal right essentially involves the claim of justice; justice, again, demands generality of the law and equality before the law. To claim something as of right thus implies that one concede to the other what one claims for himself. Because the bourgeoisie claimed liberty as of right, that liberty became liberty for all and could result also in freedom of organization for the struggling proletariat and thus could turn into an instrument of combat against the very bourgeoisie in the interest of which it had had its origin.

This example shows two things. First, the "transformation and translation" of economic interests and powers into the cultural form of the law unchains an autonomy of the law which cuts loose more and more from the dominion of economic interest. Second, this autonomously un-

[7] Letter to Mehring of July 14, 1893.

folding law is able in turn to react on the very relationship of economic power from which it originated, so that economic basis and legal ideological superstructure affect each other mutually.[8]

On the other hand, with the independence of legal philosophy within the social sciences thus restored, criticism has also been directed against the identification of social philosophy and social science, of Is and Ought, of an inescapable trend and a desirable goal of development. No doubt the overwhelming propagandist weight of the Communist Manifesto rests precisely on this, that its authors, unlike their utopian predecessors, based socialism not on well intended but impotent humanitarian grounds, but on the firm foundation of a probable and irrefutable calculation, proposed with conquering intellectual self-confidence, and depicted as an irresistible fate which discourages any resistance and lends wings to every hope. Yet there is no doubt either that the doctrine of the future necessity of socialism is able to confirm socialist convictions but unable to establish them in the first place. In truth, the socialist advocates socialism not because he knows its coming is inevitable but because he feels the present state of society is wrong, an "exploitation" or "oppression," while the socialist state of society is demanded by justice. In truth, socialism is not only a prognosis but also a battle-cry, not only a prophecy but also a program, not fatalism but policy. Since socialism is no longer condemned to wait but is called upon to act, this activistic insight more and more enters into its theory. Consciously or unconsciously, the empirical-causal view of historical materialism strives for its complement in a teleological social and legal philosophy of socialism.[9]

General Theory of Law. 5. Thus, in historism, in Hegelianism, and in materialism, the flame of philosophy burst through the positivism which threatened to quench it; the evaluating view burst through the view of existence. Then the flame was really extinguished: we enter the decades of legal positivism. No longer do people search for the legal value in legal reality; they rather pronounce any evaluating view of the law unscientific and deliberately confine themselves to the empirical investigation of the law. Legal philosophy is replaced by the general theory of law, the top story, only now completed, of positive legal

[8] Cf. Friedrich Engels' letter to Conrad Schmidt of October 27, 1890, which happens to refer to the law for exemplification; also Radbruch, *Klassenrecht und Rechtsidee* (1929) 1 ZEITSCHRIFT FÜR SOZIALES RECHT 75 *et seq.*

[9] The outstanding example of this trend of thought is HENDRIK DE MAN, PSYCHOLOGIE DES SOZIALISMUS (1926); cf. Radbruch, *Überwindung des Marxismus?* (1926) GESELLSCHAFT II 368 *et seq.*

science. Its task is to examine the most general legal concepts common to several legal disciplines, possibly also to rise above the national legal order and compare cognate legal concepts of diverse legal orders, and even to go beyond the field of law and to investigate its relations to other cultural fields.[10]

This purely empiristic general theory of law would deserve mention here only as the euthanasia of legal philosophy were it not for the ineradicable philosophical impulse that does penetrate it almost against its will.

To a large extent, the legal concepts developed by that theory are not merely shown inductively to be common to all given legal orders; they are concepts that may be discerned *a priori* to be valid for any conceivable legal order. It will be brought out later that concepts such as legal subject and legal object, legal relation and legal wrong, and indeed the very concept of the law itself, are not accidental possessions of several or all legal orders but are necessary prerequisites if any legal order is to be understood at all as legal. Such concepts are no longer parts of an empirical general theory of law but rather belong to a philosophy of positive law — though, to be sure, of *positive* law only. Once gathered from a critical analysis of positive law, they can never escape the magic circle of positive law nor lead to an evaluation of positive law. To be sure, they too belong to an evaluating view, the subject of which, however, is not the law but rather the cognition of the law. The question which they answer is not, when is a law right, but rather, how may a law be correctly discerned. They belong to juridical epistemology, to theoretical philosophy, and not to legal philosophy as a branch of practical philosophy.

Jhering. 6. The general theory of law would be inconceivable without Rudolf von Jhering. He, however, transcends positivism too definitely to be appraised within its framework. In his mind, all motifs of thought so far discussed were gathered and joined in that argumentation out of which arose the renascence of legal philosophy and the revision of juridical method which we have experienced.

Jhering completed and conquered the program of the historical school. His genius completed it by showing, in the "Spirit of the Roman Law,"[b] the connection of the law with the national spirit, which the historical school laid down as a program but never undertook to demon-

[10] The program of the general theory of law was devised by KARL BERGBOHM, JURISPRUDENZ UND RECHTSPHILOSOPHIE (1892). Its principal representatives were Ernst Rudolf Bierling, Adolf Merkl, and Karl Binding.

[b] [The reference here is to Jhering's book, DER GEIST DES RÖMISCHEN RECHTS.]

strate specifically. But he also conquered it, by finding that the purposeful will rather than the dim urge is the force that carries on the development of the law. "Purpose is the creator of the entire law," and "Fighting thou shalt find thy right" — those are the leitmotifs of his works, "Purpose in the Law" and "The Fight for the Right." [c] To the irrationalism of the historical school he again opposes rationalism. But unlike Hegel he establishes rationalism in the very field of the historical school: not as "a logical dialectics of conception" but rather as "the practically compelling dialectics of purpose"; not as a philosophical but rather as a historical-sociological doctrine. For, at least in his way of presentation, Jhering did not yet conquer empirism. Quite characteristically, he called purpose the "creator" of law. What he referred to is not the transempirical idea of purpose, which possibly may be quite ineffective in the factual development of the law yet is to provide the standard for appraising it. Rather it is the empirical event of the statement of a purpose by men. Purpose in this sense is not the opposite, but a subdivision, of cause: the purposive cause, *causa finalis*. He, too, resting upon the foundation of methodical monism, knows but one scientific approach: the causal one. The teleological approach as he understands it is nothing but the causal view applied especially to the causation of human action. Sometimes, though, it would seem as if Jhering semi-consciously used that fictional approach, made familiar to legal philosophy by the theory of the social contract, in which the ground of justification is spoken of figuratively as a cause of origin. Thus, where he talks of the causal relation of a legal institution to the empirical act of stating a purpose, he would seem to have meant its teleological relation to the trans-empirical idea of that purpose. Under the guise of the sociologist, he would seem to be in truth a legal philosopher. Be that as it may, Jhering needed to take but one step to progress from sociology to legal philosophy. Once he viewed himself not only as the contemplative spectator of strangers stating purposes but as an actor in the development of the law who himself states purposes, he would have had to face not the factual statement of the purpose but the demanding purpose itself and to see empirical legal reality confronted with a normative legal standard. He would then have had to perceive the dualism of the views of legal reality and legal value, and finally to conquer the utilitarianism of partial purpose statements in an ultimate absolute idea of purpose. He took this step when, in "Fun and Ear-

[c] [The reference here is to Jhering's works, DER ZWECK IM RECHT (1877–1883), partly translated as THE LAW AS A MEANS TO AN END (Modern Legal Philosophy Series, 1913), and DER KAMPF UMS RECHT (1872), translated as THE STRUGGLE FOR LAW (1879; 2d ed. 1915).]

nest," [d] he confronted the constructions of "conceptual jurisprudence" with the teleological formation of concepts, thus recognizing the lawyer as a creative collaborator in the development of the law; and the continuation of the work on "Purpose in the Law" would surely have arrived at the necessary conclusion of methodical dualism if death had not taken the pen from the author's hand.

Thus, Jhering leads from the irrationalism of Savigny through the rationalism of Hegel close to the conquest of that methodical monism which those two have in common.

Stammler. 7. The reëstablishment of legal philosophy, the restoration of an independent view of legal value beside the investigation of legal reality, based on the methodical dualism of Kantian philosophy, was the great work of Rudolf Stammler.[11] To be sure, Stammler posed rather than solved the problem of legal philosophy. With tenacious perseverance and unafraid to repeat the same discussions over and over again, he well-nigh hammered two ideas into the legal philosophical consciousness of his time: that beside the investigation of positive law there must be developed, in full independence, the "theory of the right law," but also that this theory of the right law represents only a method and not a system of legal philosophy. The theory of the right law will not and cannot develop a single legal rule that could be proved right as of universal validity. It buys the universal validity of its concepts at the price of their purely formal character. Thus, it is less a legal philosophy than a logic of legal philosophy, and epistemology of the view of legal values, a critique of legal reason. It is an extremely valuable entrance wing to any legal philosophy but not the main structure itself.[12]

[d] [The book here referred to is his SCHERZ UND ERNST IN DER JURISPRUDENZ (1884).]

[11] WIRTSCHAFT UND RECHT (5th ed. 1924); LEHRE VOM RICHTIGEN RECHT (2d ed. 1926); THEORIE DER RECHTSWISSENSCHAFT (2d ed. 1923); LEHRBUCH DER RECHTSPHILOSOPHIE (3d ed. 1928); *Rechtsphilosophie*, in DAS GESAMTE DEUTSCHE RECHT (ed. by Stammler, 1931); RECHTSPHILOSOPHISCHE ABHANDLUNGEN UND VORTRÄGE (1925). The following may be selected from the comprehensive critical literature about Stammler: MAX WEBER, GESAMMELTE AUFSÄTZE ZUR WISSENSCHAFTSLEHRE (1922) 291 *et seq.*, 556 *et seq.*; M. E. Mayer in (1905) KRITISCHE VIERTELJAHRSSCHRIFT FÜR GESETZGEBUNG UND RECHTSWISSENSCHAFT 178 *et seq.*; BINDER, RECHTSBEGRIFF UND RECHTSIDEE (1915); ERICH KAUFMANN, KRITIK DER NEUKANTISCHEN RECHTSPHILOSOPHIE (1921) 11 *et seq.* In accord with Stammler: in particular, Graf Dohna in 31 KANTSTUDIEN 1 *et seq.* I adhere to every word of recognition and reservation in the fine appraisal of Stammler by SOMLÓ, JURISTISCHE GRUNDLEHRE (1917) 45, n. 2.

[12] MAX SALOMON, GRUNDLEGUNG DER RECHTSPHILOSOPHIE (2d ed. 1925) and C. A. EMGE, VORSCHULE DER RECHTSPHILOSOPHIE (1925), GESCHICHTE DER RECHTSPHILOSOPHIE (1931) may be mentioned here as having started, like

Relativism. 8. Here begin the endeavors of those who cannot forget that legal philosophy in its great ages always had the task of serving life by setting up or clearing the goal of great political movements, and who therefore want to lead legal philosophy out of the charmed circle of incessant inquiry into its own method, to a system replete with definite value judgments. To be sure, no legal philosophy can steal away from the insight, established by Kant and reaffirmed by Stammler, that only what is of formal character is subject to universally valid cognition. If legal philosophy is to be directed toward a system and not merely a method, it cannot but renounce the universal validity of the system. On the other hand, if it is not to stop with the arbitrariness of a particular system, it is left with no choice but to develop a system of systems without deciding between them. This, then, is the task of legal philosophical relativism. Man's urge toward knowledge will attempt again and again to break through this relativistic self-limitation; the most recent past, too, has produced quite a number of such attempts. Relativism welcomes every such attempt as a clarification of a particular legal philosophical decision, as the deeply personal illustration of one among the systematic possibilities, without which indeed a relativistic legal philosophy would have to remain a realm of shadows, colorless and shapeless. But relativism cannot help rejecting the pretended universal validity of any such attempt and demonstrating its ties to very definite basic assumptions of world outlook.

Cultural Philosophy. 9. But there is still another direction in which legal philosophical development has pressed on beyond the narrow framework of Stammler's legal philosophy. Stammler thinks that the law and the idea of law must be strictly distinguished and the concept of law may be derived without any reference to the idea of law. As we have seen above (§ 1), no work of man can be understood without reference to an idea, not even a table, far less the law. The concept of law can be defined only as the reality tending toward the idea of law. But back of this view of the concept of law, there is the basic assumption that, contrary to Stammler's doctrine, the mere antithesis of Is and

---

Stammler, from the Marburg Neo-Kantian school of Cohen and Natorp. According to Salomon, legal science is "legal problematics," a demonstration of legal problems, with positive law constituting but a complex of definite possibilities of solutions. These problems are the subject of mere legal technology, while legal philosophy is the theory of the idea of law as the preliminary question of legal problematics. Emge sees the subject of legal philosophy in the logical premises to which legal science owes its peculiar character.

Ought, of reality and value, is not enough; that between the statement of reality and the appraisal of values a place must be saved for the relation to values, that is, between nature and ideal, a place for culture. The idea of law is value, but the law is a reality related to value, a cultural phenomenon. This marks the transition from a dualism to a triadism [e] of approaches (disregarding here the fourth, that is, the religious approach). That triadism turns legal philosophy into a cultural philosophy of the law.[13]

Other Trends in the Legal Philosophy of the Present. 10. A legal philosophy, based on methodical triadism and relativism, we regard as the result of the course of development of legal philosophy as heretofore described. Beside it, however, the previous stages of that development are at present also holding their ground.[14] The theory of natural law has survived, and indeed acquired new vigor.[15] Imposing in its consistency and imperturbability, the natural law of the Middle Ages, in the form of Catholic legal philosophy, still towers over the present age.[16] And the rational law of enlightenment has been resurrected in a system, based on Kant and Fries, which impresses by its unshaken belief in reason.[17] Another courageously unseasonable follower of the tradition

[e] [The author's term is *Trialismus*, corresponding to *Dualismus*.]

[13] This trend of legal philosophy was established by Emil Lask (*supra*, sec. 1 n. 1) and is represented by Max Ernst Mayer, Rechtsphilosophie (1922); Wilhelm Sauer, Lehrbuch der Rechts- und Sozialphilosophie (1929), Grundlagen der Gesellschaft (1924); Tsatsos, Der Begriff des positiven Rechts (1928); Ravà, Compiti della filosofia di fronte al diritto (1907), Introduzione alla filosofia del diritto (1919). Cf. Angerthal, Untersuchungen zur Kulturidee in der neueren Rechtsphilosophie (Thesis, Königsberg, 1929), but also the sharp criticism by Kelsen in (1916) 40 Schmollers Jahrbuch 1180 *et seq.* Triadism and relativism are combined, as in this book, by Kantorowicz; cf. his Rechtswissenschaft und Soziologie (1911) 21 *et seq.*, and his *Staatsauffassungen* (1925) 1 Jahrbuch für Soziologie 101 *et seq.*

[14] Cf. Larenz, Rechts- und Staatsphilosophie der Gegenwart (1931); Recaséns Siches, Direcciones contemporáneas del pensamiento jurídico (Barcelona-Buenos Aires, 1929).

[15] Griess, Naturrechtliche Strömungen der Gegenwart (Thesis, Freiburg, 1926); *Jus naturae et gentium, eine Umfrage* (1925) 34 Zeitschrift für Internationales Recht 113 *et seq.*

[16] For example, cf. Cathrein, Recht, Naturrecht und positives Recht (2d ed. 1909); von Hertling, Recht, Staat und Gesellschaft (4th ed. 1917); Mausbach, Naturrecht und Völkerrecht (1918); Hölscher, Sittliche Rechtslehre (2 vols. 1928).

[17] Leonard Nelson, System der philosophischen Rechtslehre und Politik (1929) 85 ("Justice is law"). Cf. my review in (1925) Juristische Wochenschrift I, 1252–1253.

of enlightenment founds the "eudemonistic principle" he advocates upon an "intuition resting on the broadest possible empirics," upon a metaphysics on an empirical basis.[18] Again, the much discussed Hegelian renaissance has spread its powerful influence, with one Hegelian even turning away from the point of Kantian criticism which he had previously accepted.[19] However, Hegel's philosophical adversary, Schopenhauer, has also been rediscovered recently for legal philosophy.[20] On the other hand, the general theory of law has found a remarkable presentation, in the changed form of a "juridical basic theory." [21] This theory makes a distinction between the merely general juridical concepts, which are of universal empirical validity, and those basic juridical concepts which are presuppositions of any conceivable legal science. Another legal philosophy of positive law, if legal philosophy at all, is to be found in the so-called pure theory of law,[22] a peculiar combination of positivism with its seeming opposite, the "normlogical" theory of the Ought. In its inexorable unmasking of all hypostases and fictions, it seems to take up the challenge of an original philosopher of the school of Ludwig Feuerbach: [23] that as the "high police of knowledge" it should "destroy" all "legal phantasms," and finally "annihilate itself." From the pure theory of law, connections are more and more frequently established with the phenomenological investigation of the law.[24] Phenomenological "observation of the essential," directed toward the "nature of the thing," need not involve a value judgment: The determinations of the Ought which are made by positive law may with good reason deviate from the laws of existence ascertained by phenomenology.[25] So the problem of a phenomenology of the law would appear to be one different from that of value philosophy of the

[18] ARTHUR BAUMGARTEN, RECHTSPHILOSOPHIE (1929), DIE WISSENSCHAFT VOM RECHTE UND IHRE METHODE (2 vols. 1920, 1922).

[19] JULIUS BINDER, PHILOSOPHIE DES RECHTS (1925) 67: In Hegel "we find what we have looked for in vain in Kant: the reality of ideas in the empirical world, and history as the process of the appearance of the idea in reality." His previous book, RECHTSBEGRIFF UND RECHTSIDEE (1915), however, had aligned Binder with the trend characterized *supra*, n. 8.

[20] GEORG STOCK, RECHTSPHILOSOPHIE (1931).

[21] SOMLÓ, JURISTISCHE GRUNDLEHRE (1917, 2d ed. 1927).

[22] Introduced by Hans Kelsen in his book HAUPTPROBLEME DER STAATSRECHTSLEHRE (1911, 2d ed. 1923), and since represented in numerous writings by Kelsen and his disciples.

[23] LUDWIG KNAPP, SYSTEM DER RECHTSPHILOSOPHIE (1857).

[24] First represented by ADOLF REINACH, DIE APRIORISCHEN GRUNDLAGEN DES BÜRGERLICHEN RECHTES (1913), who was followed by Felix Kaufmann, Fritz Schreier, Gerhart Husserl, and Wilhelm Schapp.

[25] Thus at least REINACH, *op. cit.* 133.

law.[26] Finally, too, the cry for the Leader [*Führer*] has found its echo in legal philosophy: a "pragmatic legal theory" is founded on the "basic conception of leadership"; it is concerned less with the idea than with the person who will creatively produce the idea out of "the inner experience of necessity." [27] No mention in detail can here be made of foreign legal philosophy, especially the highly developed Italian and French legal philosophy.[28]

There are as many languages as there are voices, hardly understandable to one another any more; there is much keen shrewdness; but rare are the playful side lights of refined wit or the terrifying and blessing flashes of melancholy wisdom, and rarest is the seal of classical simplicity which plainly proves itself.

Section 4

The Concept of Law

He who shies away from the idea finally does not even have the concept.—Goethe

The question of the concept of law seems at first glance to belong to legal science and not to legal philosophy. Indeed, legal science has again and again attempted to get the concept of law inductively out of the various legal phenomena; and there can be no doubt as a matter of principle that it is possible by comparing the various legal phenomena to get the general concept underlying all of them. However, in such a manner we may only get the concept of law, but we cannot reason it out. General concepts, as many as one pleases, may be derived from experience, such as, all men with a certain initial or with a certain date of birth. But the generality of such concepts, in relation to a larger or smaller circle of individual facts, does not guarantee their value. That they are not accidental but necessary general concepts, that is, efficient and fruitful ones, can never be shown by way of generalizing induction.

[26] Other questions than those of legal philosophy are also answered by Ernst Weigelin in his investigations of the "ethics of reality," Einführung in die Moral- und Rechtsphilosophie (1927).

[27] Wilhelm Glungler, Prolegomena zur Rechtspolitik (2 vols. 1931), and others.

[28] E.g., cf. Giorgio Del Vecchio, Lezioni di filosofia del diritto (1930), and in France the recently established Archives de Philosophie du Droit et de Sociologie juridique.

That the concept of law is such a *necessary* general concept is to be demonstrated now, by the manner in which it is derived.

Law: The Reality Directed Toward the Idea of Law. The concept of law is a cultural concept, that is, a concept of a reality related to values, a reality the meaning of which is to serve a value. Law is the reality the meaning of which is to serve the legal value, the idea of law. The concept of law thus is oriented toward the idea of law.[1]

Now the idea of law can be none other than justice. *Est autem jus a justitia, sicut a matre sua, ergo prius fuit justitia quam jus,*[a] reads the gloss on 1.1 *pr. Dig.* 1, 1. But we are also justified in stopping at justice as an ultimate point of departure, for the just, like the good, the true, or the beautiful, is an absolute value, that is, a value that cannot be derived from any other value.[2]

Justice As the Idea of Law. One might be tempted to regard justice merely as a form in which the moral good appears. Indeed, this is correct if justice is regarded as a quality of man, a virtue, as in Ulpian's words: *constans ac perpetua voluntas jus suum cuique tribuendi.*"[b] Yet such justice in a subjective sense cannot be defined but as the sentiment directed toward objective justice, in the way in which veracity, for instance, is directed toward truth. Objective justice alone is in question here. But the object evaluated by objective justice is quite different from the object toward which the moral value judgment is directed. Always, what is morally good is but a human being: a human will, a human sentiment, a human character. Even social ethics evaluates man, in his relations with other men to be sure, yet it does not evaluate those relations themselves. But just, in the sense of objective justice, can be only a relation between human beings. The ideal of the moral good is represented by an ideal human being; the ideal of justice is represented by an ideal social order.

[1] *Accord:* BINDER, RECHTSBEGRIFF UND RECHTSIDEE (1915) 60 ("Everything wherein the *a priori* norm of law, or the idea of law, functions is law"); GURVITCH, L'IDÉE DU DROIT SOCIAL (1931) 96: "The notion of law is . . . essentially linked to the idea of justice. The law is always an attempt with a view to realizing justice"; also DEL VECCHIO, FILOSOFIA DEL DIRITTO (1930) 158: "The logical form (of the law) does not at all tell us what is the sense of an affirmation of the just or unjust; it is, in short, the token of juridicality." Against the view presented here: SOMLÓ, JURISTISCHE GRUNDLEHRE (1917) 131 *et seq.*

[a] [But law issues from justice as from its mother, as it were, so there has been justice prior to law.]

[2] On the concept of justice, see MAX RÜMELIN, DIE GERECHTIGKEIT (1920); DEL VECCHIO, LA GIUSTIZIA (2d ed. 1924).

[b] [The constant and perpetual will to allot to everyone his right.]

From another point of view, too, justice is of two kinds. We may call "just" either the application or observance of a law, or that law itself. The former kind of justice, especially the justice of the judge true to the law, might better be called righteousness. Here, at any rate, we are concerned not with that justice which is measured by positive law, but rather with that by which positive law is measured.

Justice in this sense means equality. But equality itself admits of different significations. On the one hand, as regards its object, it may be related to goods or to men: the wage that corresponds to the value of the work is just, but so, too, is the punishment that is meted out to one man and the other alike. On the other hand, as regards its standard, equality may be absolute or relative: the wage equal to the work, as against the punishment of several men proportionate to their guilt.

Both distinctions are combined in Aristotle's famous doctrine of justice. Absolute equality between goods, e.g., between work and wage, or between damage and compensation, is called by him "commutative" justice. Relative equality in treating different persons, e.g., taxation according to ability to bear the tax, or relief according to need, or reward and punishment according to merit and guilt, is the essence of "distributive" justice. Commutative justice requires at least two persons, while distributive justice requires at least three. The two persons in the former case confront each other as co-equals; but of the three or more persons in the latter case one, who imposes burdens upon or grants advantages to the others, is superior to them. Commutative justice is justice in the relation of coördination; distributive justice is to prevail in the relation of super- and subordination. Commutative justice is the justice of private law; distributive justice is the justice of public law.

This is sufficient to clarify the mutual relation between the two kinds of justice. Commutative justice is justice between persons co-equal as to their rights. Therefore, it presupposes an act of distributive justice which has granted to those concerned equality of rights, equal capacity to act, equal status.[3] Distributive justice, then, is the prototype of justice.[4] In it we have found the idea of justice, toward which the concept of law must be oriented. This is not to say that law could be explained exhaustively

[3] So, too, EMGE, GESCHICHTE DER RECHTSPHILOSOPHIE (1931) 34 *et seq.*

[4] Moreover, unlike distributive justice, commutative justice is meant to represent not an absolute value at all but only a process of expediency which serves the highest possible simultaneous fulfillment of two egoisms. Cf. PASCHUKANIS, ALLGEMEINE RECHTSLEHRE UND MARXISMUS 143–144, but on the other hand also the fine paper by Ernst Marcus in (1925) 2 MOSLEMISCHE REVUE 13 *et seq.*, describing equivalence as the common root of the laws of nature, juridical laws, and moral laws.

by founding it upon justice. On the one hand, the principle of distributive justice does not say who is to be treated as equal and who as unequal; rather it presupposes that, from a viewpoint which it does not of itself provide, equality or inequality has already been established. Equality, indeed, is not something that is given; things and men are as unequal "as one egg is to another." Always equality is but an abstraction, from a certain point of view, of a given inequality. On the other hand, from the idea of distributive justice we may gather only the relation and not the kind of the treatment of different persons: we may gather whether theft in relation to murder is less severely punishable, but not whether the thief is to be hanged and the murderer to be broken upon the wheel or whether the thief is to be fined and the murderer to be committed to the penitentiary. In either direction, justice needs to be complemented by other principles if rules of right law are to be derived from it.[5] Justice is not the exhaustive principle of law. It is rather the specific principle of law, that which governs the determination of the concept of law: law is the reality the meaning of which is to serve justice.

Equity. In the struggle to govern law, however, justice is rivaled by equity.[6] The dilemma that equity is to be better than justice and yet not quite opposed to justice, but rather a kind of justice, has troubled men as early as Aristotle's famous chapter V 14[c] of the Nicomachean Ethics. But again Aristotle already indicated the solution that justice and equity are not different values but different ways to arrive at the unitary value of law. Justice regards the individual case from the viewpoint of the general norm; equity in any individual case looks for the proper law of that case, which, however, must also be susceptible of being elevated finally to a general law; for equity as well as justice is ultimately generalizing. Thus, in the distinction between justice and equity, we again confront the previously suggested methodical distinction between a deductive derivation of the right law from general principles and an intuitive grasp of the right law out of "the nature of the thing." Equity is the justice of the individual case. So regard to equity does not compel us to vary our formula: that law is the reality the meaning of which is to serve justice.

[5] The merely formal character of justice is illustrated by the example of justice of taxation by F. K. Mann in FESTGABE FÜR SCHANZ (1928) 112 *et seq.*

[6] Cf. MAX RÜMELIN, DIE BILLIGKEIT IM RECHT (1921); BINDER, PHILOSOPHIE DES RECHTS 396 *et seq.*

[c] [In the Oxford translation of the NICOMACHEAN ETHICS (W. D. Ross, 1942), the passage on "equity" is in Book V, sec. 10.]

Derivation of the Concept of Law. The foregoing would indicate what approach to take in determining the concept of law, but it would not yet give us the determination of the concept itself. We want to know of what kind that reality is that is intended to serve justice; and we are indeed able to draw conclusions from that meaning of legal reality back to the essence of legal reality. Justice means rightness as related especially to the law. By virtue of this material qualification of the idea, we are able to draw from the idea conclusions as to the matter for which it is valid.

The realities the meaning of which is to serve ideas are of the psychological nature of evaluations and demands. Thus, they represent a peculiar kind of reality, intermediate between the idea and the other realities. As psychological facts, they belong to reality themselves; but at the same time they rise above the other realities by applying standards and raising demands. Of this kind are conscience, the cultural phenomenon related to the moral idea; taste, that related to the aesthetic idea; and reason, that related to the logical idea. The factual phenomenon which in the same way corresponds to the legal idea is the precept. It, too, may be said to have the same peculiar character of reality, that is, both positivity and normativity. Furthermore, the precept as a reality related especially to the idea of law (i.e., justice) shares with justice its subject of reference: the mutual relations between men. It is social in character. As it is the essence of justice ultimately to shape those relations in the sense of equality, so it is essential to the legal precept in its meaning to be directed toward equality, to claim to be susceptible of generalization or to be general in character. A precept addressed to an individual human being or an individual relationship, say, a "measure" according to Article 48 of the Reich Constitution [of 1919],[d] is nevertheless a legal rule if its individual character is due merely to the fact that its legal terms apply only to that individual person or relationship; that is, if only the substratum of the precept is individual in character, but not, if the precept itself is individual in character. We summarize the essence of the legal precept as both positive and normative, both social and general. In this sense we define law as *the complex of general precepts for the living-together of human beings.*

[d] [Art. 48, the "dictatorship article" of the Constitution of Weimar, provided in part as follows: "If in the German Reich public safety and order are to a considerable extent disturbed or endangered, the Reich President may take the measures requisite for the restoration of public safety and order; if necessary, he may intervene with the aid of the armed forces." "Of all measures taken according to . . . this article the Reich President shall immediately advise the Reichstag. Upon the demand of the Reichstag the measures shall be repealed."]

This determination of the concept of law has not been obtained inductively from the various legal phenomena but has been derived deductively from the idea of law. It is thus not juridical but prejuridical; that is, in relation to legal science, it is *a priori* in nature.[7] The concept of law is not an ordinary and accidental concept, but is a necessary general concept. The law is law not because the various legal phenomena may be classified under it; rather, contrariwise, legal phenomena are "legal" only because they are embraced by the concept of law. The concept of law has not been set up above the legal phenomena by themselves, democratically as it were, but it has assumed its rule over them "by the grace of God," that is, by the grace of the idea. Only when the chaos of what is given is considered from the viewpoint of the concept of law is the juridically essential separated from the juridically unessential, as water and land were separated by the creative word. If, in the words of Savigny, law is taken for "the very life of men, viewed from a particular aspect," or considered from a particular point of view, this point of view constitutive of the legal universe is the *a priori* concept of law.

A Priori Legal Concepts. However, the concept of law comprises a number of particular legal concepts which share its *a priori* nature, that is, the quality of being not products but instruments of legal science, not accidental generalizations of empirical legal phenomena but indispensable categories of juridical thought. Thus, from the nature of law as both positive and normative there results the concept of the legal rule, and with the legal rule result the concepts of its elements. It may be said *a priori* (that is, in advance) that there can be no legal rule that does not rule something, thus involving both the something and the ruling: the state of facts and the legal consequence. Inseparably bound up with the qualities of positivity and normativity, too, is the question of where law is created, the question of the source of law. There is no law that does not owe an answer, and is not able to give an answer, to the question of the origin of its normative character. From the normative character there results the twofold possibility of acting in accordance with it or against it, and therewith result the concepts of legality and illegality, before which again each legal fact has the *a priori* duty to identify itself. From the validity of the law for the living together of men, their mutual relations, there follows that its contents must be to establish legal relations, and as their elements, legal duties and legal rights, subjective rights.[e] No legal order is conceivable that may not be resolved into legal

[7] "A relative *a priori* of legal science," Somló, Juristische Grundlehre 127.

[e] [On "subjective legal rights" as distinguished from "objective law," see translator's note 16, Lask, Legal Philosophy, chap. II, *supra*, p. 32.]

relations, rights and duties. Again, rights and duties are not conceivable without subjects to whom they belong, nor without objects to which they relate. Legal subject and legal object are again concepts which cannot be dispensed with by one legal order while being used by another but which are necessary to any conceivable law.

Later on in our discussions we shall meet still further legal concepts *a priori*. For the *a priori* is a relational concept, characterizing a relation of certain concepts to certain factual materials. Thus, the legal concept as an *a priori* concept fully unfolds only against the fullness of legal facts; and these unfoldings can no more be exhaustively enumerated in advance than can the facts with which the legal concept will be confronted. So the idea of a "table of categories," that is, a symmetrical schedule of innumerable *a priori* legal concepts,[8] cannot be realized.

Section 5

Law and Morals

Incidentally, people have always tried to keep the moral laws as vague as possible. Why are they not fixed in writing or print, like the divine and the civil laws? Perhaps because an honestly written moral law would have to include also the rights of men. — *Strindberg*

From the concept of the law as determined by us, it must be possible exhaustively to derive the distinction between law and other kinds of norms. That distinction will be worked out here for the most closely related kinds of norms, viz., morals and custom.

To confront law with morality, as is most often done, is to compare incommensurable quantities. Law is a cultural concept; morality is a value concept. As the idea of justice becomes a cultural reality in the law, so the idea of morality becomes a cultural reality in morals, that is, in the psychological factuality of the conscience. What is comparable is either two value concepts, viz., justice and morality, or two cultural concepts, viz., law and morals.

Usually the distinction between law and morals is couched in the slogan: "Law is outward, morals are inward." Concealed in that formula, however, are four different meanings.

Outwardness and Inwardness of the Directions of Interest. 1. The contrast of "outwardness v. inwardness" has been referred to the *sub-*

[8] Stammler, Theorie der Rechtswissenschaft (1911) 222–223.

stratum of law and morals, in the belief that external conduct is subject to legal, while internal conduct is subject to moral, regulation: *cogitationis poenam nemo patitur.*[a] Indeed, this statement seems at first to follow necessarily from the view of law as a complex of rules for the living together of men, since there is no living together except where the individual actively enters into relations with other individuals.

However, legally relevant internal conduct is often known to legal experience. Either internal conduct may govern the legal treatment of a particular corresponding external conduct, e.g., forms of culpability, good faith; or occasionally internal conduct by itself alone may produce legal results, e.g., tutelary education may be decreed when the "mental welfare" of a child is endangered.[b] On the other hand, moral evaluation is as little confined to internal conduct as legal evaluation is to external acts; indeed, merely internal conduct is outside of moral evaluation. Just as the "pious wishes" which are never followed by deeds, or the "good resolutions" with which the path to hell is paved, are not accounted as meritorious, so consistently no guilt must be found in the "evil desire," the troubling "temptation." [1] The passive life of impulses itself is morally irrelevant; what is morally relevant is only the active will wrestling with it. But the will is distinguished from impulses precisely by its activity. Action alone attests its existence. So the field where morals apply may rightly be sought in the very actions of men.

So moral judgments may apply to external conduct and legal ones to internal conduct. There is no field of internal or external conduct that

[a] [Nobody suffers punishment for his thoughts.]

[b] [The German Civil Code, sec. 1666, provides in part: "If the mental or bodily welfare of the child is endangered by the father abusing his right to care for the person of the child or neglecting the child, or becoming guilty of dishonorable or immoral conduct, the court of guardianship shall take the measures necessary to avert the danger."

Subsequently, the Reich Youth Welfare Act of 1922, sec. 63, provided for tutelary education if, among other cases, "the preconditions according to sec. 1666 . . . of the Civil Code exist and removal of the minor from his previous environment is necessary to prevent his corruption while he cannot, in the discretion of the court of guardianship, be suitably placed elsewhere."

Tutelary education was defined in sec. 62 of this Act as follows: "Tutelary education shall serve to prevent or counteract corruption and shall be administered in a suitable family or educational institution under public supervision and at public expense."]

[1] "Bad thoughts, indeed! We cannot prevent the birds from flying over us. But we can prevent them from building nests on our heads!" — Luther (quoted in a letter by Th. Fontane). "Thoughts have come, that is not my fault and I did not bid them come. I did not know they were evil. Then I have struggled with the thought, and I shall not weary as long as I live." — Otto Ludwig (quoted by WEIGELIN, MORAL UND RECHTSPHILOSOPHIE 60 n. 1).

could not be subjected to both moral and legal evaluation. But what appeared at first as a distinction of the subject matter of morals and law may be maintained as a distinction of their respective *directions of interest*: external conduct is of interest to morals only inasmuch as it attests internal conduct; internal conduct enters the scope of law only if it suggests external conduct that is to be expected. For instance, in the doctrine of the criminal law reform movement which regards the criminal act essentially as a mere symptom of the criminal sentiment of its perpetrator and deems that sentiment the true ground of punishment, the criminal sentiment in turn is legally relevant only as the possible source of further criminal acts.

Again, as the sentiment is legally relevant only as a symptom of future acts, even acts are inaccessible to legal regulation if they come into question solely as symptoms of sentiments. Relations which find expression in acts but in which the acts are relevant not as what they are but according to what they mean, what they reveal of the actor's soul, must be left exclusively to moral evaluation. Thus, for instance, law has withdrawn from friendship, since among friends external conduct is a secondary matter without significance of its own, and of significance only if and insofar as it discloses a sentiment, as a "token of friendship." Leo Tolstoy, considering all conduct between one man and another significant only as the expression of a community of love among men, consistently refused to justify any intervention of the law and the state. This noblest form of anarchism is rooted in the aversion to conceding to soulless externals even the most limited value of their own; in the superbly one-sided thought that anything external is worth only as much as it contains of the soul; and in the deep feeling that the lawyer may lose his own soul by his professional habit of casting only side-glances, as it were, at living human souls as the incidental sources of their deeds, which alone are legally essential. "The external, hustling, useless activity which consists in fixing and applying the external forms of life hides from people the truly essential inner activity, the change of the mind, which alone is able to improve life." It is the essence and the mortal sin of the law and of its representatives "to believe that there are relations in which men may be dealt with without love; but there are no such relations." [2]

Outwardness and Inwardness as to the Subjects of Purposes. 2. The antithesis "outwardness v. inwardness" may also aim at the subjects of

[2] TOLSTOY, DAS GESETZ DER GEWALT UND DAS GESETZ DER LIEBE (1909) 102; AUFERSTEHUNG Pt. II, chap. 40. Cf. the fine book by BORIS SAPIR, DOSTOJEWSKY UND TOLSTOI ÜBER PROBLEME DES RECHTS (1932).

the purposes of law and morals. The legal value characterizes an act as good for living together, the moral value as simply good. Legal value is the value of an act for others or for all others; moral value is the value of an act pure and simple. The scholastics used to say that morals is *ab agenti* [c] while law is *ad alterum*.[d] Consequently, the legal obligor is always confronted with an obligee, an interested claimant, whereas to the moral duty such an obligee is attached only as a symbol when it is called a duty toward the God in one's own breast, toward one's own conscience, toward humanity in one's own person, toward one's better self. In the field of law one may talk of duty as an obligation that is owed; but the moral duty is not thus owed to a creditor, but is duty pure and simple. Even the so-called duties toward others are not to be understood in the sense that their fulfillment could be claimed by those others. "Whosoever smite thee on thy right cheek turn to him the other also; and if any man will sue thee at the law and take away thy coat, let him have thy cloak also": these commandments are not intended to grant a right to the smiting and the cloak but illustrate the very nothingness of any right on either side. Petrazycki has deemed the "imperative-attributive" nature of the law and the purely imperative nature of morals the basis of their distinction; and it is no accident that the juridical approach is attacked in the very person of Petrazycki by Tolstoy in the last of his writings, when Tolstoy wants in a purely ethical way to found all human relations upon the spontaneous overflowing fullness of love and not the compelling pressure of a claim.[3]

Outwardness and Inwardness of the Modes of Obligation. 3. Again, the opposition of outwardness and inwardness seems to signify a difference in their modes of obligation. Morals require one to do his duty out of a sense of duty; the law permits other motives as well. Morals are satisfied only by a sentiment that is in accordance with the norm, law by mere conduct according to regulations; or in the words of Kant: morals require "morality," law requires only "legality."

This distinction is correct, but it is incorrect to regard it as a distinction between modes of obligation. A duty of mere legality is a con-

[c] [From the actor.]

[d] [Toward another.]

[3] L. V. PETRAZYCKI, ÜBER DIE MOTIVE DES HANDELNS UND ÜBER DAS WESEN DER MORAL UND DES RECHTS (1907); TOLSTOY, ÜBER DAS RECHT, BRIEFWECHSEL MIT EINEM JURISTEN (1910). On Petrazycki, cf. Gurvitch in (1931) ARCHIVES DE PHILOSOPHIE DU DROIT 403 *et seq.* DEL VECCHIO, FILOSOFIA DEL DIRITTO 171 *et seq.*, also bases the distinction between law and morals essentially on this characteristic: "that that concept of bilaterality is the key to the vault of the juridical structure."

tradiction in itself if by duty one understands the relation of a will subordinate to a norm — and any other definition appears hardly possible.[4] If one is to recognize "duties" of legality one must concede that the body may be obliged without simultaneous obligation of the mind; one must agree to call duty the relation of the substratum of a norm to the norm, no matter of what kind that substratum may be, and thus to talk of the obligation of the thought by the logical norm and of the aesthetic duty of the marble toward the chisel.

Morality and legality, accordingly, do not involve a distinction of the modes of obligation, but mean precisely this, that the moral norm alone has a substratum that may be obliged, namely, the will, while the substratum of the law, namely, conduct, is of necessity insusceptible of obligation. The distinction, then, is merely one between the substrata, the fact that morals alone regard the individual and his motives while the law regards living together, which covers only the external (and but indirectly also the internal) conduct of the individual and not his motives as such. But if legality is thus understood it is not peculiar to law, but is common to all values that do not regard the individual and his motives, including the logical and aesthetical values. Consistently the viewpoint of legality must then be brought to bear on judging the aesthetic value of a work of art or the logical value of a scientific work like the value of a legal act, regardless of the motives of its creator. From this viewpoint, the cultural achievement of mankind loses nothing in value because it is largely the product of human ambition, and contrariwise the "bad musician" does not improve because he is such a "good man."[5]

Norm and Imperative. It follows from this consideration that the original nature of legal norms is that of standards measuring the living together of individuals and not of commands directed to the individuals, that it is primarily composed of "evaluative norms" and not of "determinative norms."[6] Still the law intends not only to judge human conduct, but also to bring about human conduct conforming to law and to prevent human conduct conflicting with law. The legal standards are, therefore, transformed into "imperatives," i.e., prohibitions and commands determining the human will — not by any means "determinative

[4] As a matter of fact, BINDER, RECHTSNORM UND RECHTSPFLICHT (1912) and LÖWENSTEIN, DER RECHTSBEGRIFF ALS RELATIONSBEGRIFF (1915) 57 *et seq.*, banish the concept of duty from the field of law.

[5] How far this interpretation of legality is in accord with Kant himself has been examined by HAENSEL, KANTS LEHRE VOM WIDERSTANDSRECHT (1926) 32 *et seq.*

[6] The very great significance of this view for the criminal law doctrines concerning wrong and culpability is familiar.

norms" evaluating the human will. But the distinction between norm and imperative needs fuller elaboration.[7]

It may best be illustrated by any sentence combining a norm with an imperative, when normative contents appear in imperative form.[8] "Do your duty!" Let us separate the meaning of that sentence from what carries it, the declared from the declaration. We then get, on the one hand, an existential structure, definite in time and space, brought about and effective by way of causation, a sequence of tones which sounds here and now, originating in a certain psychological process in the speaker and producing another such process in the listener. On the other hand, we get a nontemporal, nonspatial, noncausal content of significance, a moral necessity which is valid independently of the place, the time, and the effectiveness of that declaration. That sentence, then, is an imperative inasmuch as it exists and is effective, and a norm inasmuch as it signifies and is valid; it is an imperative inasmuch as a Will is asserted thereby, and a norm inasmuch as an Ought is stated therein. Both are combined in the instant sentence though by no means in every other case. The norm is nonreality intending to be realized; the imperative is reality intending to be effective. The norm intends to be an end, the imperative only a means to an end. The norm as an end has not been fulfilled before compliance with the norm itself; the imperative, as a mere means to an end, is executed upon compliance with its purpose, whether by its own motivating force or without its intervention by a previously existing motivation in the same direction. The norm requires a conduct complying with the norm from a motive complying with the norm; the imperative is satisfied by a conduct complying with the imperative no matter how motivated. In other words: the norm requires morality, the imperative legality — but again, even as regards that secondary imperative form of the law, legality is by no means a mode of obligation, since the very essence of the imperative is not to oblige but to determine, not to be valid but to be effective.[9]

Outwardness and Inwardness of the Sources of Validity. 4. Finally, the outwardness of law and the inwardness of morals have been looked

[7] According to the following elaboration of the concepts, Kant's "categorical imperative" is in truth a norm.

[8] The imperative form as here understood includes any form in which motivation is aimed at by the spoken or written word, that is, the intended imperative and not only the grammatical imperative. The following scale illustrates the growing imperative vigor of the command forms of the language: Come! — You shall come! — You will come! — You come! French legislative language prefers the imperative future (*sera puni*); German, the imperative present (*wird bestraft*).

[9] *Contra*: BRODMANN, RECHT UND GEWALT (1921) 13–14; KELSEN in (1916) 40 SCHMOLLERS JAHRBUCH 1234 *et seq.*

for in the difference of their sources of validity. "Heteronomy" has been ascribed to law because it approaches its subjects as a foreign will, obliging from the outside; "autonomy" has been ascribed to morals because moral rules are imposed on anyone only by his own moral personality.[10] Yet a heteronomous obligation, an obligation by a foreign will, is a contradiction in itself. A Will may produce a Must if it is accompanied by the power to enforce; but neither a foreign Will nor even one's own Will may ever produce an Ought. We can understand the term "autonomy" only if by the obliging self of the self-obligation we understand not any Will, not even the desire of conscience, indeed, no empirical psychological reality whatever, but the moral personality, a purely normative, ideal, and unreal structure, in other words, the obligatory norm itself; what obliges us is not our conscience but the norm that speaks through it. So one arrives at the dilemma: either to regard the law as Will — which means to do without establishing its Ought, its obligatory force, its validity; or else to consider the law as an obligatory and valid Ought — which means to establish its validity as autonomous, as demanded by its subject's own moral personality.[11]

The foregoing is sufficient to suggest that along with all distinctions between law and morals there must also be relations between them. This is not to say, however, that law is the "ethical minimum" (Georg Jellinek) or the "ethical maximum" (Gustav Schmoller): an ethical minimum extensively, on the ground that it raises only some moral duties to a legal duty, and intensively, on the ground that it is content with outward compliance without requiring inner sentiment; or an ethical maximum because of the law's compulsive force to carry it through as contrasted with the physical powerlessness of morals. Both views ignore the possibility of tragic conflicts between law and morals, which may result from the character of the law as enactment and of morals as inner conviction, in the case of the criminal who acts upon his convictions. Rather, law and morals coincide but partially and accidentally in the contents of their demands. The relation between the two spheres of norms consists rather in this, that morals, on the one hand, constitute the end of the law and, on the other hand, for that very reason are the ground of its obligatory validity.

Morals as the Ground of the Validity of Law. 1. In morals alone may the obligatory force of the law be grounded. It has been shown that

[10] On the question of heteronomy or autonomy of the law, see Darmstaedter, Recht und Rechtsordnung (1925).

[11] *Accord*: Rudolf Laun, Recht und Sittlichkeit (Hamburg University Rector's Address, 1925).

from legal rules as imperatives, expressions of a will, we may possibly derive a Must but never an Ought. Of legal norms, legal Ought, legal validity, legal duties, we may speak only when the legal imperative is endowed by the individual conscience with moral obligatory force. The false notion that the founding of legal validity on morals renders that validity dependent on the rightness of the law, in the sense of natural law, or on the assent of the individual conscience, in the sense of anarchism, remains to be dispelled later, when the problem of validity is discussed. What must be shown here is that our view does not by any means obliterate the distinction established between the respective contents of law and morals, or incorporate law as a mere province in morals, or turn the legal norm into a moral norm of some particular content. The naturalization of the legal duty in the realm of morals represents an instance of a more general phenomenon, which has as yet been too little examined: the investment of the same material with a twofold value character. Thus, the logical value of truth becomes the object of another evaluation, viz., the ethical one, it turns into a moral good, when it is set up as the subject of the virtue and duty of veracity. Of this kind are all "cultural duties," by which working values, such as truth in the form of science, or beauty in the form of art, are turned into tasks of moral action; of this kind are also certain duties of "social ethics," including especially justice in which right law, or righteousness in which positive law, is conceived as a moral good. Just as the independence of the logical laws concerning the value of truth, or of the aesthetical laws concerning the value of beauty, is not impaired but truly recognized by setting them up as moral goods, so the laws peculiar to the legal sphere are fully preserved when this sphere is annexed by morals. Kant is right in saying: "that all duties, simply because they are duties, belong to ethics; yet legislation concerning them is not for that reason always contained in ethics, but as to many of them it falls outside of ethics." [12] Here morals submit to a foreign legislation, give way to the specific dialectics of another province of reason, subscribe, by acceptance in blank, as it were, to a content of duties still to be established in another sphere of norms. Morals stamp law and justice as moral tasks, but leave the determination of their contents to an extramoral legislation.

Morals as the Goal of Law. 2. But this moral sanction of law is possible only because the law, notwithstanding any possible variance of its contents from morals, still tends toward morals as its end. To be sure,

[12] METAPHYSIK DER SITTEN (ed. by Vorländer, 1907) 22–23.

it cannot intend to serve the realization of moral duties by providing them with the sanction of legal duties; for it is precisely because the moral norm is to be complied with for its own sake that it cannot gain anything by being accompanied by imperatives of another kind that have the same contents. The law serves morals not by the legal duties it imposes but by the rights it grants. The face which law turns toward morals is that of its rights rather than that of its duties.[13] It grants rights to individuals so that they are the better able to comply with their moral duties. We may recall, for instance, the similar justification of ownership which is sought in Article 153 of the Reich Constitution [of 1919]: "Ownership obliges. The use of property shall at the same time serve the common good." Thus only may we explain the passionate ethical stress upon the subjective right, the fact that the thought of "My right!" just like the thought of "My duty!" inspires that sense of sublimity which the individual soul experiences whenever it becomes humbly aware of being pervaded by a transcendent consciousness, of humanity in man. While elsewhere moral pride is always combined only with what one wrests from himself, in the subjective right it is combined with what one wrests from others; urge and interest, fettered everywhere else by the norm, here are, contrariwise, released by the norm. My right is basically the right to do my moral duty — and therefore, conversely, it is my duty to defend my right. In his right, one fights for his duty, his moral personality. Thus, Jhering could preach the "fight for the right" as a straight duty of "moral self-preservation." To be sure, the ideal type of the fight for the right, the fight in which one defends his moral personality in the form of his interest, admits a development toward two opposite extremes. One the one hand, it may rise to a pure fight for one's moral personality, regardless of one's own interest, involving even one's self-destruction (Michael Kohlhaas).[e] On the other hand, it may sink to the level of a naked struggle of interests without any moral background, nay, to the mere struggle for power of an empty self-righteousness, bare of the substance even of an interest (Shylock). Indeed, the law is but the possibility of morals, and for that very reason it is also the possibility of the immoral. Morals can only be rendered possible, and cannot be enforced, by the law, because of necessity the

[13] The question whether the right or the legal duty represents the primary form of the law is, therefore, to be answered differently in legal philosophy and in jurisprudence. In jurisprudence the logical sequence runs thus: from the objective law, the legal duty; from the legal duty (possibly) a (subjective) legal right; but in legal philosophy, it runs as follows: for the sake of the moral duty, the subjective right; for the sake of the subjective right, the objective law and the legal duty.

[e] [The hero of a novel by Heinrich von Kleist.]

moral act can only be an act of freedom; but since law can render morals only possible, it inevitably must also render possible the immoral.[14]

Thus, the relation of morals and law represents a relation rich in tension. At first, law is just as foreign, just as differentiated from and possibly opposed to morals as the means always is in relation to the end; it is only subsequently that, as the very means for the realization of moral values, the law partakes of the worthiness of its end and is thus incorporated in morals with the reservation that it operates according to its own rules.

Section 6

Law and Custom

A mighty antipode of sincerity among men is urbane courtesy. The greatest misery of the wise and the greatest happiness of fools rests on conventions. — Franz Schubert

The attempts to distinguish law and custom as concepts have always failed. It has been said that law is made while custom grows. That view could be refuted simply by pointing to customary law. Again, law has been regarded as enforceable and custom as susceptible of only voluntary compliance. Against this view it could be pointed out, on the one hand, that there are numerous unenforceable legal duties. Among them are not only the duties, in international law and in constitutional law, of the highest organs of the state (*quis custodiet custodes*?),[a] but also many a duty of individual members of the legal community (Reich Code of Civil Procedure, sec. 888 para. 2.[b]) On the other hand, it could be pointed out that the psychological compulsion, which is indeed indispensable to the validity of law, is no less an attribute of custom than of law, as is shown, for instance, by a restaurant in which the drinking of

[14] Similarily: Max Ascoli, Intorno alla concezione del diritto nel sistema di Benedetto Croce (1925) 35: the purpose of the law: to preserve in man the possibility of becoming good; 41 *et seq.*, nevertheless, amorality of the law.

[a] [Who is to watch the watchers?]

[b] [This section is among the provisions of the Code for the execution of judgments for specific performance of acts or omissions. Sec. 888 para. 1 provides in part: "By order on motion, the trial court may by fines or imprisonment compel the judgment debtor to perform an act which cannot be performed by a third party, where the act depends exclusively upon the will of the debtor." Sec. 888 para. 2 provides: "This provision is inapplicable to judgments to contract a marriage, to resume matrimonial life, and to render services under a contract of service."]

wine is "required" or by a poster to the effect that "the public is invited to inspect our goods with no requirement to make purchases." [1]

The futility of all attempts so far to draw a line between law and custom suggests that it is impossible to do so. That impossibility may in fact be proved. Cultural concepts, being concepts related to values, can be defined only with the aid of the idea of the value toward which they are oriented. Thus, we have defined morals as the reality the meaning of which is to represent the idea of the good, and law as the reality the meaning of which is to serve justice. But the idea of a value toward which custom might be oriented cannot be found, which excludes any commensurability between law and morals on the one hand and custom on the other. Custom cannot be coördinated with the other cultural concepts; it has no place in the system of cultural concepts.[2]

Antinomic Character of Custom. Custom, then, is not related to law and to morals systematically; but it is related to them historically. It is the common anterior form in which law and morals are contained, still undeveloped and indistinct, the "state of indifference from which the forms of law and of morality issue in different directions" (Georg Simmel). Thus, the custom of giving alms develops into the moral duty of charity, on the one hand, and into the institution of the poor law, on the other. It is the destination of custom to be absorbed by law and by morals after having prepared and rendered possible both law and morals.

This character of custom as a preparatory school of law and morals explains the degeneration of custom which occurs as soon as law and morals have evolved as independent cultural forms and separated from each other. Then custom becomes a mixed product, intrinsically absurd, of legal and moral evaluations. The outwardness of law may be attributed to it as correctly as the inwardness of morals, in all their respective meanings. On the one hand, custom shares the outwardness of law: it is concerned only with external conduct; it obliges only in the interest of an outside obligee; its commands approach their addressee from the outside; and it is satisfied if he obeys them outwardly no matter what his motive. On the other hand, it also claims the inwardness of morals: it sets store not by the handshake but by the sympathy attested thereby; one owes it not to others but to oneself to observe the decencies; our

[1] Neither has the problem been brought any nearer to a solution by Stammler's concept of the "conventional rule." The claim of custom to be valid is rather more "autocratic" than that of the law.

[2] *Contra:* Weigelin, Sitte, Recht und Moral (1919) 91 *et seq.*; Baumgarten, 1 Wissenschaft vom Recht (1920) 190.

social conscience and not a book of etiquette imposes our "social obligations" upon us; only he who respects custom is a gentleman, while he who just "follows" it externally is an upstart. Yet these mutually exclusive views are inseparably combined in custom, namely, by means of a fiction, by the "conventional lie." People have tacitly agreed to behave as if back of the outwardness of custom there were a corresponding inwardness; back of appearance, a reality; back of the greeting, devotion; back of the contribution expressed in four figures, the "generosity" which has become a hackneyed form. People have agreed with the sophisticated grin of augurs to take paper for gold without raising the painful question of its backing. But just because custom combines the twofold force of outer and inner mode of obligation, even if only by fiction, it is much more powerful than are morals and law. "Not morality rules the world, but a hardened form thereof, custom. The world as it has come to be forgives a violation of morality more readily than one of custom. Happy the times and the peoples where custom and morality still are one! All the struggles occurring in large and in small affairs, in general and in particular, turn on cancelling the contradiction between these two and rendering the rigid form of custom fluid for inner morality, on redetermining the coin according to the inner value it contains," as Berthold Auerbach says. But the most impressive criticism of custom — as well as of law — has been made by Leo Tolstoy. Again and again we meet in his novels the contrast between the goodness without form of the lower classes of the people and the forms without goodness of "society."

Social Function of Custom. Along with its moral genuineness, however, custom loses also its social function. Unlike "good old custom," "refined manners" are no longer popular custom but the custom of a class; custom was "rural-moral," decorum is "urbane"; custom was rustic, courtesy is courtly; custom was a matter of the "community," convention is a matter of "society" [3] — or rather of the society page. Custom worked to unite the people, convention works to split the people. Convention expresses the will and the ability to be counted as belonging to a certain upper stratum of society, the masonic greeting of the initiated which is changed as soon as once the uninitiated learn it and make use of it. So, whereas custom was enduring as a bond between changing generations, convention is subject to fashion. For we call fashion the endeavor of the "upper" class to distinguish itself by external marks from the "lower" class, the more and more accelerated race of the lower

[3] Cf. Tönnies, Die Sitte (1908).

in competing with the upper class, which finds itself forced again and again to change those tokens of its higher dignity as soon as the lower class, too, has appropriated them. This class character of convention is shown, more clearly than by anything else, by the fact that convention is required to be known and mastered rather than complied with. For convention is quite unlike moral rules, which cannot be violated at all except consciously, and unlike legal prescriptions, where culpability is, if anything, aggravated by consciousness of wrongdoing. Convention, contrariwise, least forgives the booby who "doesn't know what is proper," but in everything smilingly indulges the playboy who knows how gracefully to disregard a conventional form.

Yet it would be a mistake even after the separation of law and morals to deny any social function to custom. Even in "society" there still survive numerous fragments of "community," social classes and primitive peoples where custom preserves its unbroken unity and where it still has to fulfill its educational work. Again, just as in the life of the group the rule of custom prepares its transformation into morals (and into law), so morals are brought home to the individual in his education first in the form of custom. No education in its beginnings can do without the categorical norm: "That is not done" — which after all is a reference to custom. But this function which custom still discharges at present does not detract from our previous statement that it is not systematically coördinate with law and morals but is historically antecedent to them — just as battle-ax and javelin are still in use today, yet should not appear in a systematic science of arms, except in the historical introduction.

Section 7

The Purpose of Law

Falk: "Do you think that men are created for states? Or that states exist for men?" Ernst: "Some seem willing to affirm the former. But the latter may well be more true." — Lessing

Our discussions have shown that justice is the specific idea of law, sufficient to unfold the concept of law, but that it does not exhaust the idea of the law. For two reasons, justice alone has been found to be insufficient for legal rules of definite contents to be derived from it. Justice demands that equals be treated equally, different ones differently according to their differences; but it leaves open the two questions, whom to consider equal or different, and how to treat them. Justice determines only the form of law. In order to get the content of the law, a second idea must be added, viz., expediency. The question of justice has been raised and answered independently of questions of expediency or suitability for any purpose, including the purpose of the state. But within the framework of the question of the purpose of law, the state for the first time enters the scope of our investigation. Since law, or an essential part of it, is the will of the state, and the state, or an essential part of it, is an institution of law, the questions of the purpose of law and the purpose of the state are inseparable.

In raising the question of the purpose of law, we do not indeed seek empirical statements of the purposes which may have produced the law, but rather seek the transempirical idea of purpose by which law is to be measured. The answer to this question we may obtain only by considering what values may be said to be absolutely valid in the same way as the absolute value of the just, and which of these, beside the value of the just, law is intended and is suitable to serve. We may, however, be content to point to the traditional triad of ultimate values, the ethical, logical, and aesthetical ones, the ideals of the good, the true, and the beautiful, because it is evident that law may intend to serve only one of them directly, namely, the ethical value of the good.

To be sure, the ethical value of the good takes in the other absolute values in the way described above (sec. 5, *supra*); the logical value of the true and the aesthetical value of the beautiful, by entering the theory of ethical goods as ends of ethical action, are invested again with an — ethical — value character. The theory of ethical goods and the theory of ethical duties are mutually dependent in that, on the one hand, the fulfilling of moral duties finds its reflection in a moral good, viz., the moral personality, and, on the other hand, the moral goods, such as truth, in turn call forth requirements of moral duties such as veracity.[1]

Individual Values, Collective Values, Work Values. Now the ethical goods which result in this way are not all attainable simultaneously. Rather, we can serve one only at the price of neglecting or even violating the others. This becomes apparent at once when we realize the substrata of the different ethical goods.

In the whole sphere of the world of experience, there are only three

[1] "The moral may be perceived as the form of the Ought attached to the value contents of life. In substance, however, it is the personal direction toward the supreme objective value of our own inner essence." SPRANGER, LEBENSFORMEN (3d. ed. 1922) 257–258.

kinds of subjects susceptible of absolute worth: individual human personalities, human collective personalities, and human works. According to these substrata we may distinguish three kinds of values: individual values, collective values, and work values. Individual value is the personality. Ethical, too, is the value of which collective personalities, if they are recognized, are susceptible. The aesthetic and logical values reveal themselves in the works of the arts and sciences as work values.

It may now be easily shown that one is unable to serve all these values equally. "Only he who purely serves the cause has personality in the field of science. And this is so not only in the field of science. We know of no great artist who ever did anything else but serve his cause, and it alone." [2] Thus the work values demand the opposite of what the individual values require: not personality but objectivity. In the field of the individual value of the moral personality, there prevails an "ethic of sentiment," e.g., truth at any price; in the field of collective values, there prevails an "ethic of responsibility," e.g., diplomatic lies for the sake of the common weal.[3] Thus the collective values demand the opposite of what the individual values require. "One asks: What happens afterwards? The other asks but: Is it right?" as Theodor Storm says, if in another sense. Finally, hardly soluble tensions exist between the purpose of the power of collective personalities and the purpose of culture. "Now power is in itself evil no matter who wields it. Inevitably one gets into the hands of those forces which are least concerned just with the continued flowering of culture." [4] Thus the collective values demand the opposite of what the work values require.

Three Alternatives of World Outlook. So one has to reach a decision whether to allot first place in the hierarchy of values to the individual, the collective, or the work values. According to the decision, as to whether the way of life, and in particular of the law and the state, is to aim at one or the other of those groups of values, we distinguish indi-

[2] MAX WEBER, WISSENSCHAFT ALS BERUF (1919) 13.

[3] MAX WEBER, POLITIK ALS BERUF (1919) 56–57. An example of sacrificing the ethic of sentiment for the sake of the ethic of responsibility may be found in WERA FIGNERS ERINNERUNGEN: "Reason advised to join the comrades who took the path of political terror. Feeling drew us back into the world of the wretched and disinherited. It was only later that we recognized that that mood was the urge toward a morally pure life, toward higher personal values. After an inner struggle we mastered our feeling, our mood; we renounced the moral satisfaction that life and work in the country would have given us, and stepped into the rank and file of the comrades who were our superiors by political instinct."

[4] JAKOB BURCKHARDT, WELTGESCHICHTLICHE BETRACHTUNGEN (3d ed. 1918) 96.

vidualistic, transindividualistic, and wholly transpersonal views.[5] Let us illustrate the opposition of these views in a series of pithy sentences, each of which has been pronounced categorically in the author's belief of its incontrovertibility.

Popper-Lynkeus: "The disappearance from the world, without or indeed against his will, of any individual, no matter how insignificant, who did not intentionally endanger the life of anyone else, is incomparably more important than all political, religious or national events and the entire scientific, artistic and technical progress of all centuries and all peoples taken together." Schiller: "Everything may be sacrificed to the state except that to which the state itself is but a subservient means. The state itself is never an end, it is important only as a condition under which the end of mankind may be attained, and this end of mankind is nothing but the full development of all the faculties of man." These individualistic attitudes are confronted by equally brusque transindividualistic ones: that absolute morality is nothing else "than the absolute life in the fatherland and for the people"; "the absolute moral totality, nothing else than the people itself"; the state, "the basis and the center of the other concrete aspects of national life, the arts, customs, religion, and sciences; all spiritual activity has but the purpose to become conscious of that consolidation" (Hegel). "The (Italian) nation is an organism with purposes, life, means of action, which in force and duration surpass those of its separate or grouped individual members; it is a moral, political, and economic unit which is integrally realized in the (Fascist) state" (Mussolini, *Carta del Lavoro*). The transpersonal view is expressed in the statement by Kurt Eisner: "I for one value my life not so highly as a creation of eternal art and do not estimate art so low as to be worth less than living beings," and also in the other, indescribably harsh sentence: "A statue by Phidias counterbalances all the misery of the millions of slaves of antiquity" (Treitschke), and in the early words of Plutarch: "We cherish a work and despise its maker." When the temple on the Nile island of Philae was sacrificed to irrigation works, Sir George Birdwood publicly complained about it. Thereupon he was asked by Sir George Knollys: "What would Sir George Birdwood do if he were alone in a burning house with a living child and Raphael's Dresden Madonna?" Sir George Birdwood replied he would prefer the Dresden Madonna.[6] On the other hand, it has been

[5] In another, more widespread terminology, individualism is contrasted with universalism; cf. e.g., G. JELLINEK, ALLGEMEINE STAATSLEHRE (3d ed.) 174; WINDELBAND, EINLEITUNG IN DIE PHILOSOPHIE (1914) 64; SPANN, HAUPTTHEORIEN DER VOLKSWIRTSCHAFTSLEHRE (20th ed. 1930) 26 *et seq.*

[6] Analysis of this example in SPRANGER, LEBENSFORMEN (3d ed. 1922) 285.

said by Friedrich Nietzsche: "Great men without works are perhaps more badly needed than great works for which such a price of human lives must be paid." And Gerhart Hauptmann during the War [of 1914–1918] said in answer to an attack by Romain Rolland concerning the destruction of works of art by acts of war: "All honor to Rubens, but I am among those who are pained far more deeply by the shot-through breast of a human brother."

Let us now cast in conceptual forms the oppositions we have illustrated.

In the individualistic view, work values and collective values are subservient to personality values. Culture is but a means to cultivate the person; the state and the law are but institutions to secure and promote individuals.

In the transindividualistic view, personality values and work values are subservient to collective values, morality and culture to the state and the law.

In the transpersonal view, personality values and collective values are subservient to work values, morality as well as law and the state to culture.

The ultimate ends may be summarized by the slogans of freedom, for the individualistic view; nation, for the transindividualistic view; and culture, for the transpersonal view.

Three Views of the Law. Law and the state, in the individualistic view, are relations between the individuals; in the transindividualistic view, they are a totality above the individuals; in the transpersonal view, they are relations of the individuals to something outside their selves, to their common labor, their common work.

The transindividualistic doctrine illustrates its view of the state and the legal community by the analogy of the organism: as in the human body, so in a good state the whole does not exist for the members but the members exist for the whole.

The individualistic view uses as illustration the analogy of the contract.[7] Like the organism doctrine, the contract doctrine does not apply to the actual state. It means, not that real states have been created deliberately by way of contract, but only that a right state must be able to be conceived as originating in a contract between its members. The contract "is by no means necessarily to be presumed as a fact"; "rather is it

[7] That the contract theory is to be exclusively attached to the individualistic view is denied by Guterman in his review of this book in 41 ARCHIV FÜR SOZIALWISSENSCHAFT UND SOZIALPOLITIK 507.

a mere idea of reason, which, however, has its undoubted practical reality, viz., to bind every legislator so to make his laws that they *could* have originated in the united will of a whole people, and to regard each subject who is desirous of being a citizen, *as if* he had agreed to join in such a will. For this is the touchstone of the legality of any public statute" (Kant). So the contract theory declares the state justified not because, but rather if, it may be conceived as originating in a contract, because only then, indeed, it may be regarded as in the interest of every one of its members. Therefore, wherever the contract theory uses the term "will," one must insert the term "interest" for which the former figuratively stands, if one is to understand the contract theory correctly.[8]

Again, the transpersonal view not infrequently uses the analogy of a building being erected by workers who are joined together neither by a whole including them nor by direct relations connecting them, but by the common labor they perform and by the common work that is to be produced thereby.

As technical terms, finally, following in part Ferdinand Tönnies, we propose the word "society" for living together as constructed on the basis of individualism, "collectivity" for the collective structure viewed transindividualistically, and "community" for the transpersonal form of human relations. Whereas society and collectivity are direct social relations and structures, the community is a structure the social coherence of which is brought about indirectly by a common cause.

Dialectic Relation of the Three Views of the Law. Society, collectivity, and community are related to one another dialectically. Each of them turns into the other. Each can be attained only by striving for another.

The ultimate end of society is the personality, but personality is among those values which can be attained only if they are not striven for. Personality is but the unexpected reward of selfless devotion to the cause; it is a matter of gift and grace alone. "Whosoever will save his life shall lose it, and whosoever will lose his life shall find it." Personality is acquired only by self-forgetting objectivity. The boy who ardently endeavors to practice a character handwriting certainly gets an ugly handwriting, but never a characteristic one. So he who strives directly

[8] Therefore, it is no improvement upon but only another expression of the basic idea of the contract theory to base the state on *negotiorum gestio* [a quasi contract in civil law, arising from a transaction in behalf of another without his request] rather than on contract, as proposed by THEODOR HERZL, JUDENSTAAT (6th ed.) 72 *et seq.*

to become a personality may well become a dandy with a mirror in his hand, but never a personality.

But what applies to the personality also applies to the collectivity, the nation. National character likewise cannot be attained by ever so ardent direct efforts, it is but a matter of gift and grace. A people becomes a nation not by striving after a peculiar national character but by self-forgetful devotion to universally valid tasks. Deliberate "regional art" and "patriotic poetry" will always remain second-rate artistically. But art occupied with the great subjects of mankind is also inescapably national. A German truth, a German God, do not exist as ends of German endeavors, but what a German does for the sake of a cause becomes inescapably German. Nation as well as personality are categories subsequently applied by history; they are not ideals for cultural action.

So both society and collectivity refer to work and community. But work and community in turn refer back to society and collectivity, in an interdependency the ring of which cannot be broken. Just as a personality can be developed only by objective devotion to work, so the truly great work in turn is but the overflow of a rich personality: "His work is greatest who can do no other." And just as the personality, so the nation is the precondition of any true community of work. Indeed, the end of community labors is not the isolated work, not the book that gathers dust in the library or the statue that lies buried in the earth, but rather culture, i.e., the articulated whole, the living unity in which all cultural ends are joined. But that unity rests not in the works themselves but in the consciousness uniting them, and not in an individual consciousness which would be altogether unable to grasp its fullness but in the collective consciousness of the nation which embraces the individuals and joins the generations.

So it is but emphasis on one link in a closed ring, and not a break in the ring, to point sometimes to the individual personality, sometimes to the collective personality, and sometimes to the culture of work as the ultimate end of individual and collective life. These three possible views of the law and the state result from emphasizing different elements of an indivisible whole.[9]

The Transpersonal View in Particular. But empirically they are embodied in the political parties. Only the idea of the culture of work is not expressed in the policies of any particular party. It is not a program

[9] These explanations show that I by no means "hypostatize a relative contrast into an absolute one," as I am reproached with doing by Erich Kaufmann, Kritik der neukantischen Rechtsphilosophie (1921) 71 note.

but a feeling for a way of life — such as the way of life of the [German] Youth Movement, which is expressed in the word "community." Since transpersonalism in a peculiar way combines individualistic and trans-individualistic elements, it may provide the background of personal conviction for all party attitudes. But no state as yet has formed itself in accordance with transpersonalism, which for empirical reasons seems to be adequate to partial legal communities only, such as universities, religious orders, or the Catholic Church, and not to the total legal community of the state. To be sure, transpersonalism, too, has the idea of a form of government attached to it, viz., the state organized by occupational Estates. But where that idea of the state of transpersonal work, the *stato corporativo*, has been realized, it has become the mere façade of a state of transindividualistic power. And yet it is with the transpersonal standard that nations are subsequently measured by history. The urge to self-preservation of living peoples wants the state to serve them, as individuals or as collectivities. But history on the contrary appraises states according to what remains when men and peoples have passed: according to their works.

In the following pages, however, no attempt will be made to construe in a vacuum the ideal image of a state oriented toward the transpersonal culture of work.[10] Rather, the individualistic and transindividualistic views of the state and the law will be demonstrated in the ideologies of parties in which they have become embodied historically.

Section 8

Legal Philosophical Theory of Parties

Nobody stands in the air above the parties. You fools are
Roaming between the foes, sure to be hit in the clash. — Adolf Glasbrenner

In the following pages, we shall deal with partisan views, that is, with the ideologies of parties. It may be objected that in regarding the ideology of a party we do not regard the party from its most essential aspect; that the interest of the party alone is real, and the ideology of the party is a mere pretext, merely the fine façade of that interest.

[10] Suggestions in that direction in Radbruch, Kulturlehre des Sozialismus (2d ed. 1927) and Radbruch, *Wilhelm Meisters sozialpolitische Sendung* (1919) 8 Logos 152 *et seq.*

Significance of the Party Ideologies. Let us assume for the moment that a party has really been founded upon mere political interests without any coöperation of political ideas. Even such a party is of sociological necessity forced to provide itself with an ideology, i.e., at least to pretend that its special interest coincides with the general interest. To be sure, such a party ideology at first is nothing but the enchanting dress that covers the bareness of the interest, but it is sociologically bound soon to become more than that. For the ideology of a party is directed not only toward fighting the adversary but also toward enlisting new adherents. Around the nucleus group which is bound to this party by an interest there gathers an ever-expanding circle of party members whose adherence depends not on the interest but on the idea of the party and who therefore insist on the consistent and complete carrying out of the idea even at the expense of the interest, thus binding the party to the idea which in turn bound them to the party.

There is still another way in which the idea of a party grows beyond its interest. The armies in the struggle of parties must extend their ideal fronts farther and farther lest they be outflanked. The competition between the parties forces each of them to have planks concerning *all* the questions of public life, even those which are connected with its original interest only loosely or not at all. Thus a party platform comes to include more and more demands that are called forth only by ideological motives and not by sociological conditions.

At the moment the interest appeals to the idea it in turn delivers itself up to the logic of that idea, which now goes on to unfold according to its own law, possibly even against the interest that called it into service. Like a ghost, the spirit may perhaps be called at will but may not be sent back home at will. The interest cannot use the service of the idea without in turn becoming subservient to the idea. Of sociological necessity, the interest unwillingly becomes the vehicle of the idea. Hegel sees the "trick of reason" in its making the unwilling interests work for it.

So, in turning now to the ideologies of parties, we are concerned not with a mere phantom but with a really effective sociological force.[1]

Individualism. The individualistic view of the law and the state has been the first to have its precipitation in a party ideology, indeed, in a

[1] On the following, cf. BINDER, PHILOSOPHIE DES RECHTS 288 *et seq.*; also M. E. MAYER, RECHTSPHILOSOPHIE 71 *et seq.*, and, concerning his views, M. Salomon in (1924–25) 18 ARCHIV FÜR RECHTS- UND WIRTSCHAFTSPHILOSOPHIE 431 *et seq.*

series of different ideologies. The point from which those ideologies radiate in different directions is the concept of the individual.[2]

One may at first be inclined to locate the individual, as the starting point of individualism, in the empirical particular human being. But from the concrete individual with all his fancies, whims, and spleen, there is no way at all that would lead to a legal and political order serving all equally ("To please everyone is impossible"), but only one to the denial of any law and any state. Max Stirner, who started with the "single one," i.e., the concrete ego, consistently had to end in anarchism. Anarchism is that form of individualism which assumes to be able to start from the empirical, concrete individuality.

So the law and the state cannot aim at serving the real particular human being with all his inclinations, no matter how unreasonable and immoral. But no more can they be oriented toward the ideal image of the perfectly moral and reasonable man. It is of the essence of reason and morality that they cannot result from legal compulsion but can only be achieved in freedom. This wrecked enlightened despotism, which constituted another form of individualism,[3] for it wanted to serve the individuals — serve them even against their wills — and to enforce the unenforceable: reason and morality. Enlightened despotism is that form of individualism which makes the morality and reason of individuals the objects of direct compulsion.

The Concept of the Individual. The concept of the individual, then, at which liberalism as well as democracy aims, must be the mean between the empirical individuality and the moral personality. This is the natural individual inasmuch as he may become a moral personality, the personified idea of the capacity for morality: personified freedom. Hence there result the progressively more precise statements: that the law ought to serve the individual — the law ought to render possible individual morality — the law ought to effect individual freedom — as far as it can

[2] The individual as the subject of the purpose of the legal norm and the individual as the point of attack for the motivating force of the legal norm are different problems. The former is dealt with here, while the latter is discussed in my lecture DER MENSCH IM RECHT (1927). How the Romans thought of man in the law in the latter sense has on one occasion been stated by Goethe: "They were really interested in man only inasmuch as something can be gained from him by force or by persuasion" — the very clever and very selfish man, *homo oeconomicus*, who until today has also remained *homo juridicus*. How the Romans, on the other hand, regarded the individual as the subject of the purpose of the legal norm has been shown by Hegel in the statement quoted below, n. 5.

[3] *Contra:* Guterman in 41 ARCHIV FÜR SOZIALWISSENSCHAFT UND SOZIALPOLITIK 506.

effect it, that is, not inner freedom but the outward liberty which inner freedom presupposes, the deliverance from the motivating force of societal surroundings, whether it consist in the terrorism of the fight of all against all or in the suggestions of the social environment.

In one sense, therefore, the individual of the individualistic view of the state is the isolated individual, who is connected with other individuals by no bond but the bonds tied by the law itself. Thus in the individualistic view the social phenomenon of law purports, speaking paradoxically, to destroy the social, i.e., the fact that every one is determined by all or by some others, and to replace it with a side by side grouping of free individuals without contacts. Expressing it less paradoxically, it purports to replace the wild-grown irrationalism of manifold tangled social ties with a rational minimum system of legal relations. The legal maxim runs: "Law separates but does not make friends." We sense that delivering effect or, if a hyperbole is permitted, that antisocial function of the law whenever in personal relationships that are hard to disentangle we regard it as the last way out to look at the matter in a "purely business," i.e., a purely legal, way.[4]

However, the individual of legal philosophical individualism, being but personified liberty, at the same time implies the equality of all individuals. Whereas difference, peculiarity, "individuality" mark the empirical individual and the moral personality ("Each owns an image of what *he* ought to become" [a]), the legal philosophical individual, conceived as the mere capacity of empirical individualities for individualized morality, is as such incapable of any individualizing characteristic. He is an individual without individuality, comparable and frequently compared to the atom of the natural sciences, forever equal in a thousandfold multiplications and infinite reflections. "Man in the abstract, the most artificial, most regular, most refined of all machines, is construed and invented, and he looks like a ghost in true and sober bright daylight" (Tönnies).[5]

[4] Schopenhauer compares human society to a society of porcupines which crowd together in order to warm one another but must keep apart lest they be hurt by one another's quills. The middle distance which they finally discover Schopenhauer calls human courtesy. He might also have said: the law, conceived individualistically.

[a] [Quotation from a poem by Angelus Silesius.]

[5] Hegel, PHILOSOPHIE DER GESCHICHTE (Reclam ed.) 361, shows how the Romans created this concept of the individuality: "The abstract general personality did not yet exist (among the Greeks), for the mind had first to develop to that form of abstract universality, which harshly disciplined mankind. Here in Rome we now find that free universality, that abstract liberty, which on the one hand sets the abstract state, politics, and power above the concrete individuality and fully subordinates the latter, and on the other hand creates the personality confronting that

The abstract nature of the legal philosophical individual may be most aptly illuminated by the picture of the social contract. That contract does not indeed mean the real agreement of real wills of real men, but fictitiously takes for intended what anyone *reasonably* cannot be unwilling to intend, since it is in his *true* interest. The contracting party of the social contract thus is fictitiously taken for a purely rational being who knows, and is solely determined by, his true interest. The social contract is entered into not by real men, but by unending repetitions of one abstract rational scheme.

As a result, the individualistic view of the state appears to some so very unindividualistic — that is to say, if the term is related not to the individual but to individuality. In the individualist view, moral individuality, just because it is a value of the highest order, and law and the state are mere means subservient to it, may realize itself only beyond the juridical sphere; while empirical individuality may occur in the legal order only in the general form of a personified capacity for the moral, or of personified freedom, which is the form of the individual without individuality. So it is precisely in individualism that individuality falls outside, both hither and yon, of the idea of law.

Liberalism and Democracy. Liberalism and democracy, differing from anarchism and enlightened despotism because of their different concept of the individual, are distinguished one from the other by a different evaluation of the individual.[b] The earlier characterization of democracy as "left liberalism," that is to say, a more intense kind of liberalism, was misleading. That liberalism and democracy differ not merely in degree but in kind is indicated by the opposition of their most extreme forms: anarchism as utterly intensified liberalism, and socialism as democracy thought through to a conclusion, namely, continued beyond politics into economics. This opposition in world outlook between liberalism and democracy is now to be worked out step by step from its political repercussions.

Democracy requires the unconditional rule of the will of the majority; liberalism demands the possibility of the individual will maintaining itself under certain circumstances even against the will of the majority. To liberalism, the starting points of political philosophical thought are

---

universality — the freedom of the ego in itself, which must be well distinguished from the individuality. For personality is the basic determinant of the law, it comes into existence mainly in property, but is indifferent to the concrete determinations of the living spirit, with which individuality is concerned."

[b] [The term "liberalism" is used throughout this work in the specific sense of the nineteenth-century *laissez-faire* conception of the state.]

the rights of man, the fundamental rights, the rights of liberty of the individual, those portions of his natural freedom antecedent to the state which are brought into the state with the unconditional claim for respect because the state's task and its justification consist exclusively in their protection: "The ultimate end of any political society is the preservation of the natural and imprescriptible rights of man" (Declaration of 1789). In the democratic view, on the contrary, the individual's freedom that is antecedent to the state is put by him completely at the disposal of the will of the state, the will of the majority, in consideration of and in exchange for merely the opportunity to take part in forming that will of the majority. From that difference of fundamental views there follow quite different principles of political organization of liberalism and of democracy, involving the long misunderstood antagonism between Montesquieu and Rousseau. Liberalism pays homage to Montesquieu's doctrine of the separation of powers, which intends to play the two pretenders for absolutism, monarch and majority, against each other in favor of the unimpaired rights of individual liberty; democracy with Rousseau rejects the separation of powers because it combats that absolutism of the majority which is the very goal of democracy.

Here majority, there liberty; here participation in the state and hence possibly in the majority, there freedom from the state; here "free citizenship," there "civil liberty"; here rights of political liberty granted by the state, there natural liberties left at rest by the state; here equality of the rights of liberty granted, there a liberty, equally left to all, to use very different natural abilities, an equal start in the race which soon changes into inequality; here the thought of equality outweighs that of liberty, there contrariwise the thought of liberty outweighs that of equality. For it is to be understood, after all that has been said, that this distinction involves not the elimination of the liberal by the democratic element or vice versa, but the predominance of one or the other in what fascist terminology calls the "demo-liberal" mixture.

And so we are able to penetrate to the opposition in world outlook from which the aforementioned particular oppositions result. In algebraic terms: democracy attributes to the individual but a finite value, liberalism an infinite one. Consequently in democracy the value of the individual may be multiplied, the value of the majority of individuals exceeding that of their minority; on the contrary, the infinite individual value of liberalism, of conceptual necessity, cannot be surpassed even by the value substance of no matter how large a majority. That different evaluation of the individual seems to be founded on the different structure of the ethical concept of value on either side. To the liberal, it appears that in principle the moral value may be completely fulfilled in a single individual. Every individual is called upon to realize the moral value that is for all equal and complete, hence unsurpassable and therefore infinite. To the democrat, on the contrary, the moral value acquires its content only by its application to the many different individuals, and a different content for each individual. Only in an infinite number of individuals may the entire wealth of the moral world be displayed.

Social View of the Law, and Socialism. To liberal and democratic individualism, however, there must be added social individualism. It originated in the criticism of political and civic equality contrasting with social and economic inequality, which is the essence of "demo-liberal" individualism. In social reality, the liberty of property, equal for all, turns for the owner of means of production from a mere dominion over goods into a dominion over men, and for the propertyless classes into serfdom to property. The liberty to contract, equal for all, turns for the property-owner into liberty to dictate, and for the man without property into defenseless subjection to dictation. Political rights, equal for all, mean a power many times increased in the hands of the propertied groups that are able to fill the coffers of parties and finance the press, as compared with the propertyless. But this criticism against merely legal formal equality is in the last resort directed against the isolated individual without individuality, from which the demo-liberal view starts. It implies the postulate that law and the state be oriented toward the concrete individual in society [6] — not, indeed, toward the individuality of every single being, from which, as has been shown, no way at all leads to any conceivable view of law and the state, yet neither toward the abstract generic concept of man thought of as personified liberty; but rather toward a plural number of social types, such as the employer and the employee, the laborer and the office worker.[7] Thus only the social view of law and the state renders the differences of social power, the individual's position of power or powerlessness, visible to the juridical eye. Thereby it creates the possibility of taking them into account legally, of differentiating in the treatment of the socially powerful and

[6] KARL MARX, ZUR JUDENFRAGE: "The emancipation of man is accomplished only when the real individual human being takes the abstract citizen back unto himself and, as an individual human being in his empirical life, in his individual work, in his individual relationships, has become a generic being; only when man has recognized and organized his *forces propres* as social forces and therefore no longer separates social force in the form of political force from himself."

[7] Cf. Radbruch, *Von der individualistischen zur sozialen Rechtsauffassung* (1930) 13 HANSEATISCHE RECHTS- UND GERICHTSZEITSCHRIFT 457 *et seq.* (also: (1931) ARCHIVES DE PHILOSOPHIE DU DROIT 387 *et seq.*).

the powerless, of supporting the weak and curbing the strong; it replaces the demo-liberal idea of equality with the social idea of equalization. So the social law in this characterization represents the victory of equity over strict justice.

While the social idea aims at the equalization of social inequality, socialism demands its removal by removing its cause: private ownership of the means of production. Yet socialism, like the social idea, is a form of legal philosophical individualism. In the economic view, socialism may be opposed to individualism because the former does not regard economic life as consisting of free individuals working with and against one another, but wants to subject it to transindividual regulation. But in the legal philosophical view, all that matters is that that transindividual regulation, too, is intended in the last resort to serve the individuals. Thus, even the Communist Manifesto culminates in the ultimate goal of an "association in which the free development of everyone is the condition of the free development of all." The paradox, that that goal of liberty for all is to be reached by means of limiting the liberty of all, the socialist view shares with all other individualist views. It is the basic problem of legal philosophical individualism, with which even the doctrine of the social contract had to wrestle. Again, from the relation of socialism to "bourgeois" individualism there follows the duality of its tactical trends: the form of transition to the socialist commonwealth, the dictatorship of the proletariat, is understood, on the one hand, as democratic majority rule, and on the other, as minority rule of a proletarian *élite*. In the one form, then, the socialist idea is entwined with the demo-liberal idea; in the other, it involves the belief in the necessity for a separation, at least a transitional one, from the form of popular government under the law.

Conservatism. It was only much later that the individualistic party ideologies were opposed by a transindividualistic conservative party ideology.[8] The former are aggressive, the latter defensive ideologies. The individualistic parties wanted to reform the political facts in accordance with their ideology; the conservative parties support the existing political facts by a subsequent ideological construction. Consequently, the individualistic ideologies are rational, the conservative ones irrational: historical or religious. To the former, the state is composed of its parts like a machine; to the latter, it is shaped by a mysterious vital force like an organism. The picture of the organism, the rule of the head over the limbs, serves conservatism to illustrate its doctrine: that, just as the

[8] Cf. Mannheim, *Das konservative Denken*, 57 ARCHIV FÜR SOZIALWISSENSCHAFT UND SOZIALPOLITIK 68 *et seq.*, 470 *et seq.*

organism maintains its identity in changing its cells, so the people unites not only its present but also all its past and future members as "a holy bond between the generations" (Treitschke); that for this reason alone not the people sets up its ruler but the ruler is set up over the people; that he rules in the name of the whole and not at the mandate of the individuals, receiving his sanction not from below, by the will of the people, but from above, by history and religion, by legitimacy and the grace of God, by the charisma of the leader.[9] "Authority, not majority," says Stahl; and Mussolini replaces the triad of 1789 with the new one of "Authority, Order, Justice" — with justice understood in the Platonic sense of the order of estates.

Almost more important even than the conclusions from the organic theory of the state as to the position of the ruler are its implications for the position of the individual. Individualistic legal philosophy starts from individuals and sums of individuals; transindividualistic legal philosophy starts from individualities and collective wholes of individualities. In the image of the organism there is proposed a richly articulated state with manifold intermediate formations between the whole and the individuals, multiformity and inequality of functions, differentiation in kind and rank between the regions and localities, racial groups, classes and individuals. Thus, in the conservative ideology, unlike the individualistic one, individuality has its place. The individual of the individualistic view of the state was abstract, isolated, and without individuality. Conservatism, since it thinks of the individual not as isolated but as member of an organism, is able to understand him as individuality. His freedom is not the liberty equal for all, the abstract opportunity for each and every thing, but the freedom fully to work within his limited peculiar character for the collective best; not freedom from everything, but freedom for something, hence freedom without equality. Whereas individuality had no place in individualistic ideology precisely because it was the ultimate end thereof, it has its place in conservative ideology

[9] The same political function that was fulfilled hitherto by the organic theory of the state is now being assumed by the doctrine of integration (SMEND, VERFASSUNG UND VERFASSUNGSRECHT, 1928). As against the organism doctrine, it emphasizes the thought that "the individual, to be sure, lives in the whole, but the whole no less lives in the individual" (LITT, INDIVIDUUM UND GEMEINSCHAFT, 3d ed. 1926, 284). The whole lives only by being experienced ever again by the individuals. In the doctrine of integration, then, the organic view of the state is actualized, turned from the static into the dynamic, from the substantial into the functional. But the political function of the doctrine of integration, like that of the organic theory, consists in its suitability for founding even non-democratic constitutional forms upon the will of the people, not indeed the will of the popular majority, but the integrating will of the folk, a popular community which cannot be determined and controlled by numbers and hence can largely be construed at will.

precisely because it constitutes but a means at the service of the collectivity. But the collective whole itself, like the individual, is an individuality. The individualistic idea, starting as it does with the individual without individuality, cannot consistently come to a final stop before reaching its ultimate end in mankind without nationality. In the transindividualistic view, an ultimate end is reached in the individuality of the national whole. So conservative thought leads to the twofold articulation of the world in nations and of the state in occupational estates.

At present, however, the conservative idea of the state and the law is expressed but with refractions in the parties that are closest to it. Peculiarly essential to conservatism is that historical or religious monism which finds value in reality. Parties which confront reality with an ideal, if only the ideal of a past, necessarily lack that structure of conservative thought. But their divergence from the conservative way of thought is aggravated still further when they are not even able to demand the complete restoration of the past but confront the present with a new ideal of the future enlaced with elements of the past. This divergence becomes very profound indeed if they pursue their aim not with constitutional but with revolutionary, nay, counterrevolutionary means. Even in the political picture of the future drawn by these parties, we can as yet trace only the general conservative-organic-transindividualistic features. Fundamentally, we may reduce it to the readily available but ambiguous catchword: "The common weal before selfish interest." [c] All specific demands are in the nature of agitation rather than a program. In accordance with their irrational way of thought, these parties do not demand political power to realize a preëstablished program but say conversely: first power, then the program! So the program of Fascism prior to its seizure of power is completely included in the slogan: *Italia a noi!* [d] And even the constitutional scheme of occupational estates which it adopted after its seizure of power has justly been described as "not a coherent system of state but merely an adroitly devised instrument of simple dictatorship." [10]

Political Catholicism. Finally, an intermediate position between the transindividualistic and the individualistic parties is occupied by political Catholicism. The Evangelical [Protestant] and Catholic views of the church are related to each other exactly like the individualistic and transindividualistic ideas of the state. In the Evangelical view, the

[c] [A slogan contained in the Twenty-five Points which were the program of the Nazi party.]

[d] [Italy shall be ours!]

[10] Cf. Ludwig Bernhard, Der Staatsgedanke des Faschismus (1931) 42.

church is a human institution for the service of the individual souls, who alone are religiously valuable. In the Catholic view, on the contrary, the church, quite apart from any value it may have for the sanctification of the individual souls, is an institution established by God Himself, with a transindividualistic religious value of its own. The state in the Catholic view is imbedded in, or at any rate attached to, the church as thus understood. So it may be regarded as "authority by God" and hence touched by a reflected glow of that transindividualistic value of the church; but it may also be regarded as a secular state and a mere instrumentality of individualistic purposes of security and welfare. Therefore, it is possible for Catholicism to join the right as well as the left, the transindividualistic as well as the individualistic parties.

To this extent our party setup may be illuminated by legal philosophy. To this extent, then, it has objective foundations. Through the thicket of further splits between parties, through the coppice of the minor parties, no light can show a way.

Section 9

Antinomies of the Idea of Law

Did you ever think a thought through to its conclusion without hitting upon a contradiction? —Ibsen

We now look back at the road we have traveled thus far.

Justice, Expediency, Legal Certainty. From the concept of the law, a cultural concept, that is, a concept related to value, we were pressed on to the value of the law, the idea of the law: Law is what, according to its meaning, is intended to serve the idea of the law. The idea of the law we found in justice; and we determined the essence of justice, of distributive justice, as equality: equal treatment of equal, and correspondingly unequal treatment of different, men and relationships. We were able, indeed, to orient the concept of the law toward justice; yet we were unable thereby to obtain the guiding thought from which exhaustively to derive the content of law. For while justice directs us to treat equals equally, unequals unequally, it does not tell us anything about the viewpoint from which they are to be deemed equals or unequals in the first place; moreover, it determines solely the relation, and not the kind, of the treatment. Both questions may be answered only by referring to the purpose of the law. Thus to justice there was added, as a second element of the idea of the law, expediency or suitability for a purpose. However, the question of purpose and expediency could not be answered unequivocally but only relativistically, by the systematic development of the different views of law and the state, the views of the different parties. Yet that relativism cannot remain the last word of legal philosophy. The law as the order of living together cannot be handed over to disagreements between the views of individuals; it must be one order over all of them.

So we are confronted with a third postulate concerning law, ranking with the other two, a third element of the idea of the law: legal certainty. The certainty of the law requires law to be positive: if what is just cannot be settled, then what ought to be right must be laid down; and this must be done by an agency able to carry through what it lays down.[1] So, most oddly, the positivity of the law itself becomes a prerequisite of its rightness: to be positive is implicit in the concept of right law just as much as rightness of content is a task of positive law.

Of the three elements of the idea of law, it is the second, expediency, to which relativistic resignation applies. But the other two, justice and legal certainty, are above the conflicts between views of law and the state, above the struggle of the parties. It is more important *that* the strife of legal views be ended than that it be determined *justly* and *expediently*. The existence of a legal order is more important than its justice and expediency, which constitute the second great task of the law, while the first, equally approved by all, is legal certainty, that is, order, or peace.[2] So, too, all equally submit to the postulate of justice. The entire political struggle of the day represents an endless discussion about justice. That he withholds from others what he claims for himself; that he has to grant others what he takes for himself; that he is not entitled to demand for himself what otherwise could be demanded by others as well: that is the kind of objections, demands, and refutations that fly like shuttlecocks incessantly back and forth between the politician and his political antagonist. But they rest on the tacit assumption on the part of all disputants that what is right for one is fair for another — which is the idea of justice. The idea of justice is absolute; it is

[1] This line of reasoning is concurred in by MAX RÜMELIN, DIE RECHTSSICHERHEIT (1924) 3.

[2] "Peace, security — these are the first benefits the law is to afford us. Even if we should be in profound, irreducible disagreement on the higher ends of the law, we could nevertheless arrive at an understanding so as to make it achieve these intermediate ends in which we are all interested." CUCHE, CONFÉRENCES DE PHILOSOPHIE DU DROIT (1928) 19.

formal, indeed, but universally valid withal. Like legal certainty, it is a nonpartisan postulate; but upon the view of the state and the law, the party attitude, it depends how far these postulates are to precede or rank below other postulates concerning the law, to what extent expediency or justice of the law is to be sacrificed to legal certainty or conversely legal certainty is to be sacrificed to them. Universally valid elements of the idea of the law are justice and legal certainty; a relativistic element, however, is not only expediency itself but also the rank of the three elements relative to each other.

Our investigation has been pressed irresistibly from one element of the idea of the law to another: the three elements of the idea of law require one another — yet at the same time they contradict one another.[3]

Tensions Between the Three Ideas of Legal Value. Justice and expediency raise opposite demands. Justice is equality; equality of the law demands generality of the legal rule. Justice generalizes to some degree. But equality is not given in reality; always, equality is but an abstraction from actual inequality, taken from a certain point of view. Still, from the point of view of expediency, every inequality remains essential; expediency is bound to individualize as far as possible. So justice and expediency become contradictory. The contradiction is illustrated, for instance, by the conflict between administration and administrative courts, the struggle between the tendencies of justice and expediency in criminal law, and, in another field, the contradiction between pedagogic and disciplinary requirements in all mass education. This relation of tension, however, is irremovable.[4]

But a contradiction arises also between justice and expediency, on the one hand, and legal certainty, on the other. Legal certainty demands positivity, yet positive law claims to be valid without regard to its justice or expediency. Positivity is a fact, positive law presupposes a power that lays it down. So law and fact, law and power, while opposites, enter into a close relation all the same. But legal certainty not only requires the validity of legal rules laid down by power and factually carried through; it also makes demands on their contents: it demands that the law be capable of being administered with certainty, that it be practicable. It frequently impresses the law with features that conflict with individualizing expediency. For instance, it draws sharp lines where

[3] Cf. Radbruch, *Die Problematik der Rechtsidee*, in the yearbook (1924) Die Dioskuren 43 *et seq.* Concerning the "relation of tension" between justice and legal certainty, see also Petraschek, Rechtsphilosophie des Pessimismus (1929) 181 *et seq.*, 408–409.

[4] Cf. Isay, Rechtsnorm und Entscheidung (1929) 135 *et seq.*

life knows only flowing transitions, or it defines a state of facts by external symptoms instead of the really intended inner facts.

Indeed, the demands of legal certainty may ultimately conflict with the conclusions from that very positivity which is required by legal certainty. Thus, in the interest of legal certainty, customary law or revolutionary law, in derogation of previous positive law, may be considered valid once it has succeeded at the expense of such previous law. This phenomenon in the field of legal validity is paralleled also by phenomena in the contents of the valid law itself. Just as, in the interest of legal certainty, illegal facts may destroy and create (objective) law, so for the sake of legal certainty legal (subjective) rights may arise from, and be terminated by, illegal facts.[a] In the interest of legal certainty, *res judicata* renders even the substantially wrong decision valid for that particular case — and renders the wrong precedent valid possibly even beyond the particular case.[5] In the statute of limitations, title by adverse possession,[b] the protection of possessory estates in private law, and the *status quo* in international law, even the illegal situation is given the effect of destroying or creating rights in the interest of constancy, that is, of certainty in legal life.[6]

One might be tempted to settle the conflict between justice, expediency, and legal certainty by proposing a straightforward division of labor between the three principles according to their fields of operation. By justice we would test whether a precept is cast in the form of law at all, whether it may at all be brought within the concept of law; by expediency we would determine whether its contents are right; finally, by the degree of legal certainty it affords we would judge whether to ascribe to it validity. As a matter of fact, we determine by the standard of purported justice alone whether a precept is at all legal in nature, whether it accords with the concept of law.[7] But the contents of the law are governed by all three principles. To be sure, the bulk of legal contents is governed by the principle of expediency; but even these legal

[a] [On "objective law" and "subjective legal right" see translator's note b, LASK, LEGAL PHILOSOPHY, chap. II, *supra*, p. 32.]

[5] The "ideal of universal agreement," which W. JELLINEK, SCHÖPFERISCHE RECHTSWISSENSCHAFT (1928) has proposed for judicial decisions, also belongs in this connection.

[b] [The term used in the German text is *Ersitzung*, the Roman *usucapio*, which was adverse possession begun in the good faith belief in one's ownership at the time of acquisition.]

[6] *Contra:* M. RÜMELIN, DIE RECHTSSICHERHEIT (1924) 24, n. 4.

[7] This, of course, does not prejudge their admissibility [legality]: thus, Art. 48 of the Reich Constitution [of Weimar, 1919] authorizes [dictatorial] "measures," which because of their individual nature do not bear the character of law.

contents are modified by justice, as, for instance, when a doctrine derived from expediency demands application even beyond the range of its expediency on grounds of legal equality. Moreover, there are a number of legal provisions which are dictated by no expediency at all but solely by justice or legal certainty. Equal protection of the laws or the prohibition of *ad hoc* tribunals, for instance, rests on requirements not of expediency but solely of justice. And required solely by the demand for legal certainty are the so-called "directing norms," [8] which completely fulfill their purpose by just being there without any purpose governing their specific contents. They are legal rules the opposite of which would be just as right and which only purport to provide a uniform regulation, no matter which; e.g., the traffic rule "Keep right!" which fulfills its purpose of preventing collisions no better than would the opposite rule, "Keep left!" [9] Finally, too, it will appear that even the validity of positive law that is unjust and wrong cannot be maintained unqualifiedly; hence the question of validity may be considered not only from the standpoint of legal certainty but also that of justice and expediency.

Antinomic Character of Legal Philosophy. So our result is this, that the three aspects of the idea of law, justice, expediency, and certainty of the law, jointly govern law in all its aspects, although they may sharply contradict one another. To be sure, different ages will be inclined to lay decisive stress upon one or the other of those principles. So the government by prerogative [c] [of enlightened despotism] sought to raise the principle of expediency to sole dominion, unhesitatingly pushing aside justice and legal certainty in its administration of law by cabinet fiats. So the age of natural law tried to conjure the entire contents of the law out of the formal principle of justice and at the same time therefrom to derive the validity of law. So, with fatal one-sidedness, the past age of legal positivism saw only the positivity and certainty of the law and caused a long standstill in the systematic examination of the expediency, not to mention the justice, of enacted law, for decades nearly silencing legal philosophy and legal policy. But the very one-sidedness

[8] Cf. MARSCHALL VON BIEBERSTEIN, VOM KAMPF DES RECHTES GEGEN DIE GESETZE (1927) 116, 123.

[9] Such directing norms would be needed even in a community of perfect beings who would fully know and fulfill the duties of justice. It is therefore incorrect to explain the law merely as a makeshift remedy for human sinfulness, destined to disappear whenever the human race should arrive at the summit of sinless morality. Even the "heavenly hosts" cannot do without parade regulations.

[c] [See *infra*, sec. 26, note a.]

of each of the successive legal ages serves to illustrate the contradictory many-sidedness of the idea of law.

We have shown contradictions without being able to resolve them. We consider this no defect of a system. Philosophy is not to relieve one of decisions, but to confront him with decisions. It is to make life not easy but, on the contrary, problematical. A philosophical system is to resemble a Gothic cathedral in which the masses support each other by pressing against each other. How suspect would be a philosophy that did not consider the world a purposeful creation of reason and yet resolved it into a rational system with no contradiction! And how superfluous any existence if ultimately the world involved no contradiction and life involved no decision! [10]

Section 10

The Validity of Law

"Thou shalt because I will" is nonsense; but "Thou shalt because I shall" is a correct syllogism and the basis of all law.—Seume

In the conception of legal certainty, the problem of the idea of law touches the problem of the validity of law, which we now explicitly present for discussion.[1] The question of the validity of law is the question of the "normativity of the factual" (Georg Jellinek): How can a norm issue from a fact, a legal Ought issue from the legal will of the state or society, since it seems that a Will, if accompanied by power, can produce a Must but can never produce an Ought?

Juridical Doctrine of Validity. 1. To be sure, in legal science that Will is questioned, not as to its mental factuality but solely as to the significance of its contents. Yet the only possible way to express the contents of a command without referring back to the fact of commanding, is by the words: "This ought to be!" The meaning of a Will separated from its psychological foundation is an Ought, that is, the content of an imperative, a norm that is neatly cut out of the factuality of the giving

[10] So, too, A. Baumgarten refers to the "antinomic structure of the universe," RECHTSPHILOSOPHIE 34, and professes a "philosophy of contradictions," 1 DIE WISSENSCHAFT VOM RECHT (1920).

[1] On the problem of the validity of law, cf. EMGE, VORSCHULE DER RECHTSPHILOSOPHIE 81 *et seq.*, and BURCKHARDT ORGANISATION DER RECHTSGEMEINSCHAFT (1927) 163 *et seq.*

of the command. So legal science, of methodological necessity, conceives the contents of the law as something valid, an Ought, something obligatory.[2]

But in searching for the ground of that validity, the juridical doctrine of validity at some point necessarily encounters the factuality of an authoritative Will that cannot be further derived anywhere. It will derive the validity of a legal rule from other legal rules, that of an ordinance from a statute, that of a statute from the constitution. But the constitution itself can and must be taken by such a purely juridical doctrine of validity for a *causa sui*.[a] It may well explain the validity of a legal rule in relation to other legal rules, but never the validity of the highest legal rules, the fundamental laws, and hence never the validity of the legal order as a whole. Legal science is purely immanent; it is caught and confined within a particular legal order, the meaning of which alone it is called upon to understand. Accordingly, it may forever measure the validity of a legal order by that very order's claim to validity only, but can never decide impartially about the claim to validity of one of these legal orders in relation to other orders.

Thus it is helpless when faced with "collisions of norms" in all their numerous forms. In the conflict between custom, morals, and law, it can forever side only with the law, which is its given subject-matter, and can never serve as an impartial judge above the disputing parties. The conflict between domestic and foreign laws it cannot decide impartially but only in accordance with the claim of validity of the domestic law, the so-called "international private law" or "international criminal law,"[b] which is of course part of the national law. In the controversies between statute law and customary law, between the law of nations and municipal law, between the state and the church, between legitimity and revolution, in the "struggle of the old with the new law" (G. Jellinek), it can forever plead only the one-sided claim of the part it serves, like an

[2] At this point, the very involved line of reasoning concerning the problem of the legal duty may be summarized once again. *Legal philosophy* cannot on its own strength establish the idea of legal duty. It knows the law in its normative form as a standard only and as an imperative in a purely factual cast alone (*supra*, sec. 5, pp. 81–83). What is legally prescribed turns into a duty only by being elevated to a moral duty, that is, within the field of ethics. The legal duty is thus established as a moral duty, and not a true legal duty (*supra*, sec. 5, pp. 84–85). True legal duties exist only in *jurisprudence*, which is concerned with the content of meaning of the legal imperatives. That content of meaning, separated from the fact of the Will that carries it, can be understood only as an Ought that establishes duties — and only in the limited sense which will presently be described in the text above.

[a] [Cause of itself.]

[b] [These Continental terms are equivalent to "conflict of laws," denoting the legal rules governing the choice of law.]

attorney, but can never pass objective judgment. Indeed, it would be unable on cogent grounds to deny the validity even of the imperatives of a paranoiac who believes himself to be king. Only from the standpoint of *one* legal order can it ever criticize the claim of validity of another one — *tamquam e vinculis sermocinari* [c] (Bacon) — but it can never on its own strength establish why it takes the standpoint of just that legal order. So it is unable on its own strength even to justify the choice of its field of work. The subject-matter of its work must be assigned to legal science by an extra-juridical approach.

Sociological Doctrine of Validity. 2. For an impartial choice between all those colliding norms, then, a jump from the world of meaning into the world of existence seems inevitable. Valid is that legal order which succeeds in rendering itself factually effective, whether it has won for itself the minds of those subject to it by long, convincing, and habituating influence or has been forced upon them by compulsion and punishment. What is required for the validity of a legal order, however, is not its efficacy in every particular case; it is sufficient that it is carried through in the average of cases.

This emphasis on the typical suffices to indicate that such a doctrine of validity is sociological-historical, or descriptive, and not juridical-philosophical, or normative. Normative doctrines of validity aim at establishing the validity of the law in all particular cases. But the validity of the law as against a particular individual cannot very well be based on its being effective usually, that is, against others. Still another feature shows the descriptive nature of this doctrine of validity. It is compelled, corresponding to the degrees of efficacy, to assume degrees of validity, and hence to assume the validity, differing by degrees, of two simultaneous legal orders in conflict with each other. But a normative doctrine of validity aims precisely to decide between such conflicting legal orders with respect to their validity.

The Power Theory. The historical-sociological doctrine of validity [3] appears in two versions: the power theory and the recognition theory. According to the power theory, the law is valid because it is the command of a power which is able to carry it through. But command and power imply only a Will and a Can, so they may call forth at most a Must but not an Ought on the part of the addressee, possibly obedience but never a duty to obey. Just as a worthless paper (according to

[c] [Discoursing in jail, as it were.]

[3] On the distinction between juridical and sociological doctrines of validity, cf. MAX WEBER, WIRTSCHAFT UND GESELLSCHAFT (2d ed. 1926) 368 *et seq.*

Merkl's apt comparison) acquires no validity by one with a pistol in his hand forcing it upon someone else for payment, so an imperative does not become valid against him who, gnashing his teeth, is forced to submit to it, and still less against him who sneers at it, knowing how to evade it. For if the law is valid only because it is backed by power, it cannot be valid where that power fails. Accordingly, not to be caught would mean not to have offended, as in Spartan morals; and with the statute of limitations run, at the latest, the deed would not only cease to be punishable but cease to be wrong.

However, an analysis of the concept of power is enough to lead one beyond the power theory. Power is not bounded by force. Power is spiritual: [4] in the last analysis, all power is power over souls. "The ruler is raised but by the obedient" (Schiller).[5] Yet the greatest power is the law: "Even the strongest one is not strong enough unless he transforms his power into law, and obedience into duty" (Rousseau); and therefore law is the best "policy of force" (Jhering). Nay, your very force is nothing but my fear: *Qui potest mori non potest cogi* [d] (Seneca). All power rests on the recognition, willing or unwilling, of those subject to it.

The Recognition Theory. So under our hands the power theory has changed into the recognition theory. To refute this theory, which bases the validity of law on the consent of those subject to the law, the objection has been raised that it destroys the legal bond by making it dependent upon the pleasure of those who are to be bound: *sub hac conditione "si volam" nulla fit obligatio* [e] (*Dig.* 44, 7, 1, 8). Thus, it is said, it causes the law to fail precisely where it should stand the test: against the criminal, who by transgressing the law withdraws his consent to it in what seems the most unequivocal manner. But that objection overlooks the fact that recognition is a function not of the will but of feeling, belonging in the field not of mental spontaneity but of mental passivity; that it no more rests with us to find something right or wrong than to find something beautiful or ugly, good or evil, true or false; that just as we cannot at will switch off our taste, conscience, or reason, so even the

[4] "Do you know what surprises me most in this world? The impotence of material force. There are only two things in the world, the sword and the spirit. In the long run, it is always the spirit that will conquer the sword." Napoleon I after the Russian campaign.

[5] *Oboedientia facit imperantem* [Obedience makes the ruler]. On these alleged words of Spinoza, see W. Jellinek, Grenzen der Verfassungsgesetzgebung (1931) 16, n. 29.

[d] [He who knows how to die knows how not to be forced.]

[e] [Subject to this condition: "If I should wish to," no obligation is created.]

criminal cannot shake off his sense of law, which binds him to a norm, simply by transgressing it. Often, indeed, the criminal by his very crime expresses his recognition of the law he violates. The thief injures the property of another in order to get property of his own, thus in principle recognizing the legal institution of property and, consistently, all that is necessary to protect that property — hence recognizing his own culpability. For the forged document, the forger claims the very public faith that he shakes by his forgery, thus recognizing the legal good he violates and, consistently, the protection of the law which turns against himself.

Yet these examples also suffice to indicate that the recognition theory does not stop with the psychological factuality of recognition but rather imputes as indirectly recognized what one cannot consistently fail to recognize. As in the doctrine of the social contract, so in the recognition theory, what is in the "true interest" of the individual is fictitiously taken to be willed by him. If we discard that fiction, if we base the validity of the law not on the fictitious recognition of its validity by those subject to it but on their true interest in its validity, we complete the transition from the historical-sociological to the philosophical doctrine of validity.

Philosophical Doctrine of Validity. 3. But does not such a philosophical doctrine of validity necessarily identify the valid with the right law, the right with the valid law, positive validity with absolute validity? Does it not relapse into the errors of natural law, which denied the validity of wrong law just because it is wrong and ascribed validity to right law just because it is right?

No doubt, if the purpose of the law and the means necessary to attain it could be known with scientific clarity, the conclusion would be inescapable that that natural law, once it was scientifically recognized, must extinguish the validity of positive law deviating therefrom, just as the disclosure of truth must extinguish the exposed error. The validity of demonstrably wrong law cannot conceivably be justified. However, any answer to the question of the purpose of law other than by enumerating the manifold partisan views about it has proved impossible — and it is precisely on that impossibility of any natural law, and on that alone, that the validity of positive law may be founded. At this point relativism, so far only the method of our approach, enters our system as a structural element.

Ordering their living together cannot be left to the legal notions of the individuals who live together, since these different human beings will possibly issue contradictory directions. Rather, it must be uniformly governed by a transindividual authority. Since, however, in the relativistic view reason and science are unable to fulfill that task, will and power must undertake it. If no one is able to determine what is just, somebody must lay down what is to be legal; [6] and if the enacted law is to fulfill the task of terminating the conflict of opposing legal views by authoritative fiat, law must be enacted by a will which is able also to carry it through against any contrary legal view. He who is able to carry law through thereby proves that he is competent to enact law. Conversely, he who does not have enough power to protect every one of the people against anybody else has no right to command him either (Kant). The first promise of a revolutionary government is to reëstablish and maintain the "safety and order" which the revolution has just disturbed — this is the first of its promises because only by maintaining safety and order may a revolutionary government legitimitize itself. Charles Martel asked Pope Zachary: "Should he who has the power also be king?" The Pope answered in the affirmative,[7] upon the ground: *ne conturbaretur ordo.*[f] "He is lord who keeps us quiet" (Goethe, *Faust*, Part II, Act IV) — that is the "fundamental norm" upon which the validity of all positive law is based. It has been expressed in these words: "If in a community there is one who has supreme power, his commands shall be obeyed," or, more briefly, as in Rom. 13:1: "Let every soul be subject unto the higher powers." [8]

[6] That is, lay down what ought to be legal, and not what is right, which would be contradictory in itself. The competency of the holder of power to enact law may indeed make a certain legal veiw the basis of the legal order but cannot pronounce it a universally valid legal truth; it may terminate the struggle of the legal views for power but not the controversy between them as opinions. On the contrary, the very relativism which calls upon power to choose between the validity of legal views demands that that power leave the field open for controversy between legal views as opinions. It requires legality of behavior but also freedom of criticism and of propaganda. This has very properly been said, in complementing the statements in this book, by Guterman in 41 ARCHIV FÜR SOZIALWISSENSCHAFT UND SOZIALPOLITIK 508.

[7] RANKE, ÜBER DIE EPOCHEN DER NEUEREN GESCHICHTE, Lecture 8, sec. 3.

[f] [Lest order be disturbed.]

[8] Cf. WALTER JELLINEK, GESETZ, GESETZESANWENDUNG UND ZWECKMÄSSIGKEITSERWÄGUNG (1913) 27 *et seq.*, and GRENZEN DER VERFASSUNGSGESETZGEBUNG (1931) 16; also his note 1 in GEORG JELLINEK, ALLGEMEINE STAATSLEHRE (3d ed.) 264. Kelsen, too, says "that by the basic norm only an authority whose norms are obeyed by and large may be set up as an authority creating law," and he finds in the basic norm "the transformation of power into law," NATURRECHTSLEHRE UND RECHTSPOSITIVISMUS (1928) 65. [Translated in KELSEN, GENERAL THEORY OF LAW AND STATE (1945) 437.] Rom. 13:1 was in fact referred to, after the Revolution [of 1918], by the [German Catholic] Center Party, through Deputy Groeber in the National Assembly [of Weimar], Feb. 13, 1919: "In our opinion, any authority is by the grace of God, no matter whether it is monarchical or republican."

So the connection between power and law, the origin of law in a breach of law, the theory of the accomplished fact in international law, the normativity of the factual, are now established philosophically. Yet this is by no means a relapse into the sociological doctrine of validity. The law is valid not *because* it can be carried through effectively; rather, it is valid *if* it can be carried through effectively, *because* it is only then that it can afford legal certainty. The validity of positive law, then, is based upon the certainty which it alone possesses; or, circumscribing the sober term "legal certainty" by weightier verbal formulae, upon the peace it creates between conflicting legal views, upon the order that terminates the struggle of all against all. Positive law is to "establish peace in action during the war of opinions, during the struggle of philosophers" (Anselm Feuerbach). Justice is the second great task of the law, while the most immediate one is legal certainty, peace, and order. "I'd rather commit an injustice than tolerate disorder," said Goethe and also: "It is better that you suffer wrong than that the world be without law." [9]

Antinomies of the Doctrine of Validity. But such cannot remain the last word of legal philosophy on the question of validity. Only this has been established, that legal certainty too is a value and that the legal certainty which positive law affords may justify even the validity of unjust and inexpedient law. Not established, though, has been any absolute precedence of the demand of legal certainty, which is fulfilled by any positive law, over the demands of justice and expediency, which it may possibly have left unfulfilled. The three aspects of the idea of law are of equal value, and in case of conflict there is no decision between them but by the individual conscience. So the absolute validity of all positive law as against every individual cannot be demonstrated. It would indeed be miraculous if something real should have value and validity throughout. The individual conscience usually will, and properly may, deem an offense against positive law more objectionable than the sacrifice of the individual's own legal conviction,[10] but there may be "shameful laws" which conscience refuses to obey. At the time of the

[9] The same kind of legal sense is aptly described by THEODOR FONTANE, MEINE KINDERJAHRE: "As long as revolutionary struggles fall short of certain victory, I follow all these insurgencies with greater or less disapproval, founded, I would say, not on my legal sense but on my sense of order." Fontane sees its basis "in a certain sense of order, a natural claim to be made in view of superiority of numbers or power."

[10] The value of legal certainty is put too low as against legal conviction by MARSHALL VON BIEBERSTEIN, VOM KAMPF DES RECHTES GEGEN DIE GESETZE (1927).

Socialists Act[g] the [German Social Democratic] Convention of Wyden resolved to amend the Platform of Gotha to read that the party strives for its aims by *all* means, and no longer merely by all *legal* means.

To be sure, "every lawyer always ought to deem best any existing legal constitution and, if it is amended by superior authority, then the one succeeding it" (Kant). The judge, charged with interpreting and serving the positive legal order, ought not to know any but the juridical doctrine of validity, which deems the law's meaning of validity, its claim to validity, equal to real validity. It is the professional duty of the judge to validate the law's claim to validity, to sacrifice his own sense of the right to the authoritative command of the law, to ask only what is legal and not if it is also just. To be sure, the question may be raised whether this very duty of the judge, this *sacrificium intellectus*,[h] this devotion in blank of one's own personality to a legal order the future changes of which one cannot even anticipate, is morally possible. But however unjust the law in its content may be, by its very existence, it has been seen, it fulfills one purpose, viz., that of legal certainty. Hence the judge, while subservient to the law without regard to its justice, nevertheless does not subserve mere accidental purposes of arbitrariness. Even when he ceases to be the servant of justice because that is the will of the law, he still remains the servant of legal certainty. We despise the parson who preaches in a sense contrary to his conviction, but we respect the judge who does not permit himself to be diverted from his loyalty to the law by his conflicting sense of the right. For the dogma is of value only as an expression of faith, while the law is of value not only as a precipitation of justice but also as a guarantee of legal certainty, and it is preeminently as the latter that it is entrusted to the judge. A just man is worth more than a merely righteous, merely law-abiding man; but we do not usually call judges "righteous" but only "just," since a righteous judge by that very token, and by that alone, is also a just judge.

Yet the judge, who is in conscience bound to consider all enacted law valid, may be faced by a defendant who is bound by his conscience to regard unjust or inexpedient law as invalid although it is enacted.[11] Against the latter, the law may prove its power but can never demonstrate its validity. That case of the "criminal from conviction" proves a truly tragic case precisely because there is no solution for it. Duty de-

[g] [German statute, 1878–1890, containing sweeping repressive measures against socialists.]

[h] [Sacrifice of the intellect.]

[11] "I swore to observe the constitution *conscientiously*; but what if my conscience demands of me *not* to observe it?"—Bismarck to Crown Prince Friedrich Wilhelm. Cf. ZECHLIN, BISMARCKS STAATSSTREICHPLÄNE 60 *et seq.*

manded the crime of the perpetrator, duty demands the sentence of the judge, and duty may possibly demand that one submit to the penalty incurred for the crime committed out of duty — for the sake of the law's inviolability, of legal certainty. Socrates thought and acted thus when he scorned escape from the execution of the miscarriage of justice: "Do you think that a state can survive, and is not indeed destroyed, where sentences that are pronounced are without force and are invalidated and frustrated by individuals?" [12]

Section 11

Philosophy of History and the Law

The stone patiently suffers the forming chisel, and to the musician who touches them the chords respond without resisting his fingers. The lawmaker alone works at a self-acting, resisting material — human freedom. — Schiller

The theme of the philosophy of history is history from the viewpoint of the realization of values, history as the road toward, or again the wrong road away from, value. So the problem of the philosophy of history in relation to the law (or the philosophy of legal history) is to contemplate, in the reality of historical events, the realization of the concept, the idea, and the validity of law (which in three spheres of problems have formed the theme of our discussions so far).

The Law as a Form of Culture. 1. "Law" is not only the category antecedent and basic to any legal contemplation, not only the form of thought outside of which nothing legal can be conceived, but also the real form of culture which comprehends and molds every fact in the legal universe. For a new legal trend is realized not in a legal vacuum but either by reinterpretation of existing legal institutions or by insertion of new legal institutions into a given legal system. In either case, it is built into the architecture of a tremendous legal structure, altering it in details only, and is inescapably qualified by its style. Law as a conceptual category is expressed in reality by the law as a real form of culture.

Form and Material of the Law. The question thus raised in the philosophy of history concerns the relation between the matter and the

[12] Cf. Alsberg, Der Prozess des Sokrates (1926) 27–28.

form of the law, between the *donnés* and the *construit* [a] (Gény), between the *realia* of legislation and their legislative formation (E. Huber). It has been answered by manifold different estimates of the formative power of the legal form and the resisting power of the legal matter.[1]

The theory of natural law assumes that the resisting power of the matter against the idea may be put at zero. It completely volatilizes the matter of the law. In its view, the material of the legal idea is not a definite historical situation but the state of nature; and that state of nature is depicted not as a sociological relationship, but rather as an unsociable side-by-sideness of individuals; the first creation of social relations between them being reserved to the legal idea, unhampered by any preëxisting sociological ties. And since the theory of natural law knows no resistance of historical or sociological matter, it denies the changeability of the legal idea, which indeed could spring only from its material concrete element and not from the quite empty and hence quite universal pure form. So natural law affirms a legal ideal that is everywhere everlastingly the same.

It is the merit of the historical school to have overthrown that doctrine of the omnipotence of the legal form. What is given by the "national spirit" is stressed at the expense of the formative forces of reason. That the resistance of matter may indeed not be put at zero is shown by the simple reflection that the decisive movements in the social world are outside of the influence of the law. The legal order can command the individual only; it can gain influence on social processes but indirectly, by way of the individual, and hence to a very limited extent; processes of mass psychology, for instance, it cannot dominate. And it cannot at all effect natural events. Thus economic life being both a natural and a social process, both technical and economical, moves essentially uninfluenced by law and is in turn apt to react upon the law.[2]

As a result of such considerations, the doctrine of omnipotence has been opposed by the doctrine of powerlessness of the law. In the materialistic view of history, law is a mere mode of appearance of the economic life, hence the legal form is a mere mode of appearance of legal matter. In calling law the form of the economy, this view refers not to the formative but to the formed form, not to a form into which the matter is pressed, but to one which it assumes, not to innermost essence but to outward appearance. It regards law as historically and

[a] [That which is given and that which is construed.]

[1] Cf. Radbruch, *Rechtsidee und Rechtsstoff* (1923) 17 ARCHIV FÜR RECHTS- UND WIRTSCHAFTSPHILOSOPHIE 343 *et seq.*

[2] Cf. RENNER, DIE RECHTSINSTITUTE DES PRIVATRECHTS UND IHRE SOZIALE FUNKTION (1929) 145 *et seq.*

sociologically conditioned throughout, without any formal element of universal validity. In this sense, Marx-Engels note, in their *Draft of a German Ideology*: [b] "Never forget that law has no more a history of its own than has religion."

As has been shown previously (sec. 3, pp. 63–65, even historical materialism has been compelled to recognize that the forms of culture, and in particular the legal form, follow laws of their own. It does not simply identify the ideal with the material but regards the ideal as a transformation and translation of the material into a new form, without, however, giving sufficient attention to the formal aspect of this process. For our part, we have established that the legal form is the form of justice, that is, of equality and generality, and that by this form any purposeful endeavor that wants to utilize the law is inescapably seized and is deprived of the sole dominion of its set purpose. The question of the philosophy of history concerning the relation between the form and matter of the law thus is to be answered by saying that each law is a product of legal matter and legal form, with now the formal, now the material, element prevailing. Typical are Roman law on the one hand and Germanic law on the other.

Closely connected with the doctrine of the exclusively material determination of the legal form is another doctrine in the philosophy of history, the doctrine that not only every legal content but the legal form itself is transitory, the Marxist doctrine of the "withering away of the law." According to it, the juridical world outlook is the "classical world outlook of the bourgeoisie" (Engels), which superseded the theological world outlook of feudalism; in the proletarian transitional state, this civil law with its affectation of justice is to be replaced with a class "law," "without any make-up," i.e., with the legal form deliberately discarded, which would then in the classless society be completely submerged and make room for a mere "administration of goods." Justice is only the ideological reflection of the market with its *do ut des*,[c] destined to disappear with the individualist market economy. To be sure, the justice which is referred to there is but the justice of private law, commutative justice. By stepping beyond the "narrow horizon of civil law" (Marx) and of commutative justice, there would then be established but the exclusive dominion of another justice, the distributive justice of public law; or, in other words, the entire law would be rendered public and the individualistic would be merged in the social law. So even the socialist commonwealth will be a government of laws,[d] though one gov-

[b] [ENTWURF EINER DEUTSCHEN IDEOLOGIE.]

[c] [I give that you give.]

[d] [Cf. *infra*, sec. 26, n. a.]

erned by distributive instead of commutative justice. The living together of human beings without any legal form at all is inconceivable.[3]

The Realization of the Idea of Law. 2. The question of the realization of the idea of law in history may be raised in two ways. It is possible to start from the legal ideas of the several parties and trends of world outlook and to examine how far history serves to realize each of them. To each view of the law and the state there would then correspond a particular philosophical construction of history. One may cite as examples, of a liberal philosophy of history, Kant's *Idea of a Universal History with Cosmopolitan Intent*; [e] of a socialist philosophy of history, the Communist Manifesto; of a transindividualistic philosophy of history, L. von Ranke's lectures before King Max of Bavaria and his *Political Conversation*; [f] and of a transpersonal philosophy of history, Jakob Burckhardt's *Observations on World History*.[g] But, on the other hand, it is also possible to discuss the question in what way ideas, and in particular legal ideas, influence history at all, whether in the form of deliberate statements of purposes by individuals or in the form of unconscious social processes.

Deliberate and Unconscious Development of the Law. The answer to this question, which goes back to the opposition between Hegel and Savigny,[4] can only be this, that the idea of law has become a progressively more deliberate and more purposeful motive power of history. This development may be characterized by different slogans: as the development from the national spirit to the will of the state, from the "organic" growth of law to "purpose in the law" and to the "fight for the right" (Jhering); [h] or, considering the social institution by which norms are laid down, as the development from community to society (Tönnies); or, again, considering the form taken by the legal position of the individual, as the development from status, the state in which one

[3] Cf. PASCHUKANIS, ALLGEMEINE RECHTSLEHRE UND MARXISMUS; also Radbruch, *Klassenrecht und Rechtsidee* (1929) 1 ZEITSCHRIFT FÜR SOZIALES RECHT 75 *et seq.*, and Kelsen in (1931) 66 ARCHIV FÜR SOZIALWISSENSCHAFT UND SOZIALPOLITIK 449 *et seq.*

[e] [IDEE EINER ALLGEMEINEN GESCHICHTE IN WELTBÜRGERLICHER ABSICHT.]

[f] [POLITISCHES GESPRÄCH.]

[g] [WELTGESCHICHTLICHE BETRACHTUNGEN.]

[4] Hegel against Savigny: "Barbarians are governed by urges, customs, emotions, but are not conscious of it. By the law being enacted and known, everything accidental of emotion or belief, the form of revenge, pity, selfishness, is cancelled, and thus only does the law attain its true destination and acquire its honor." Cf. ROTHACKER, EINLEITUNG IN DIE GEISTESWISSENSCHAFTEN (2d ed. 1930) 62–63.

[h] [*Supra*, sec. 3, n. c.]

is born, to contract, the social situation created by one's own will (Henry Sumner Maine).

To be sure, the statements of purposes which progressively replace instinctive acts do not necessarily correspond to absolute ideas of such purposes; they may be purely egoistic and arbitrary statements. Yet frequently the deliberately egoistic statements of purposes, like the instinctive acts, unconsciously become the instruments of universally valid ideas of purposes. The fact has been described by Wundt, who called it the "heterogony of purposes," and by Hegel, who spoke of the "trick of reason." Our description above (sec. 8, pp. 97–98) of the relation between ideology and interest in party activities presents an illustrative example. Based on that sociological fact of *sic vos non vobis*[i] is the theory of liberalism, the theory of the prestabilized harmony of universal self-interest and common weal, which has been "transformed and translated" into lyrics by Rückert: "When the rose adorns itself, it adorns the garden." Again, the Marxian theory of necessity, of the inevitable development toward socialism by social forces which by no means deliberately aim at a socialist order of society, rests on the same thought. The materialistic view of history represents, not indeed a subjective idealism of ideal motives, but an objective idealism of victorious ideas. In the words of Karl Marx: Thought may not press toward reality, yet reality contrariwise presses toward thought.

The inevitable development in the formation of law from the instinctive to the purposeful, from the irrational to the purposive rational, may be evaluated in different ways. The view that the rationality of things and of relations is superior to any individual reason cannot but respond to that naturally necessary development with an attitude of cultural pessimism. The other view that there is no rationality in things and relations other than that which rational individuals have imparted to them, cannot but hail that same development with cultural optimism as the victorious procession of reason through history, as progress without end.[5]

Theory of Legitimacy and Theory of Catastrophes. 3. Finally, too, the idea of legal validity is susceptible of consideration by the philosophy of history. From the viewpoint of the juridical doctrine of validity, one may examine not only the relation of one legal rule to another within a certain legal order, say, of a statute to a constitution, but also the relation of the historically succeeding legal orders to one another. Applied

[i] [Thus it is you (who act) though not for yourselves.]

[5] However, it must be stated here that the great theorist of the "community" does not by any means draw conclusions of cultural pessimism from the irresistible development from community to society; Tönnies in (1925) 49 SCHMOLLERS JAHRBUCH FÜR GESETZGEBUNG, VERWALTUNG UND VOLKSWIRTSCHAFT 188 *et seq.*

to history, the juridical doctrine of validity turns into the principle of legitimacy, the postulate that each new legal order must have evolved from its predecessor in a legal way, and the negation of any legal order that cannot be justified from the legal order preceding it. "Law must remain law."

Yet "any law there is in present mankind has come about against legal form" (Fichte). "How many existences in the political world of today are not rooted in revolutionary soil?" (Bismarck).[6] There is only one legitimate development uninterrupted through millennia: the chain of ordinations reaching from the apostles to every individual Catholic priest. So the theory of legitimacy is no more able to do justice to the problems of the philosophy of history than the juridical doctrine of validity is to those of legal philosophy. Law cannot originate in law alone; again and again law grows from wild roots. There is an original creation of law, a first generation of law out of factuality, lawmaking by law-breaking, new legal ground on congealed revolutionary lava.

The two opposite views might be called Neptunism and Vulcanism in the philosophy of history, the theory of continuity and the theory of catastrophes of legal history. They are forms in which the more comprehensive views of historism and rationalism appear. Legitimism corresponds to the view in which gradual progress without jumps, a category of historical thought, is turned into a norm of political action (sec. 3, p. 62, *supra*). Quite in accordance therewith, legitimism raises the juridical doctrine of validity, a form of legal scientific thought, to a political doctrine. Against this it may be said that even the historical catastrophe does not fall out of history, that it, too, becomes subject to the subsequent insight into its long prepared, historically necessary causation. To that historical continuity, however, there also corresponds a legal continuity. Unchanged above all catastrophes of the law stands the legal principle that at any time he is called upon to lay down law who is able to enforce the law (sec. 10, p. 117, *supra*). Revolution results in this, that other social forces succeed to the supreme authority of power provided by that "fundamental norm." But the fundamental norm itself reigns unchanged above any change of forces. Its effect is that the new revolutionary government represents the legal successor of the former legitimate government. Only thus can it be understoood that a revolutionary change in the form of government does not affect the identity of the state itself, e.g., that imperial Germany and republican Germany represent the same German Reich.[7]

[6] 1 GEDANKEN UND ERINNERUNGEN (1898) 176 — in that detailed correspondence with Gerlach concerning the principle of legitimacy.

[7] Cf. ANSCHÜTZ, REICHSVERFASSUNG (3d revision, 10th ed., 1929) 8 *et seq.*

Section 12

Religious Philosophy of the Law

Nec ulla nobis magis res aliena quam publica.[a] — *Tertullian*

Religion is the behavior which conquers values; by conquering worthlessness it conquers the opposition of value and reality, identifies value and reality, justifies all existence; it is the emotional theodicy (sec. 1, pp. 50–51, *supra*). The theodicy expressed in concepts we call religious philosophy, as contrasted with the philosophy of values. Both the approach of the philosophy of values and that of religious philosophy may be applied to every subject matter — including the law.[1]

Yet the complete identification of value and reality which is proposed cannot be achieved by a human mind. An expedient of religious philosophy with regard to facts which can be understood neither as valuable nor as nonexistent is the concept of the unessential: the worthlessness which defies any attempt at conquering it is regarded as nonexistent in a deeper sense, as without essence. But it is not worthlessness alone that may appear unessential in the view of religious philosophy. Even what has been established as valuable by the philosophy of values may be unessential from the most absolute point of view of religious philosophy: "before God." So the question of the religious philosophy of the law is whether law is not only valuable but also essential.

Early Christianity. A mythology of the law in pre-Christian antiquity would show us religious, definitive, essential significance closely spun all around the law and the state. To Christianity in its original form, on the contrary, law and the state appeared quite remote from God, quite unessential, quite nugatory. Says Jesus: "Who hath set me above you to settle your inheritances?" The story of the penny of tribute must not by any means be read as expressing anything but the profound indifference of Jesus toward political and legal matters: As far as I am concerned, do render unto Caesar the things which are Caesar's, if only you render unto God the things that are God's — the emphasis is solely upon the second half of the sentence. In the parable of the laborers in the vineyard, a great gesture puts the question of law and justice far aside in favor of goodness and mercy. And when the fraudulent behavior of the

[a] [And no affairs are more foreign to us than affairs of state.]

[1] Cf. Radbruch, *Über Religionsphilosophie des Rechts*, in Radbruch and Tillich, Religionsphilosophie der Kultur (2d ed. 1921).

unjust householder is chosen, with superb sarcasm, as a parable for the preparation for rendering account to God, Jesus' view of the unessential character of legal evaluation is expressed with a sharpness which is only made more cutting, almost terrifying, precisely because this is not the theme of the parable. Is the difference between right and wrong, between ownership and theft, really so very great? Mammon in any form is "unjust mammon" — this is the intended view which is the unexpressed basis of the parable, nay, almost its expressed basis: for the Lord praised the unjust householder for having acted cleverly. The just and the unjust understand each other perfectly, Jesus feels; they are related by a secret underground family resemblance and sympathy, like forester and poacher, inquisitor and delinquent. Coming to close quarters with another, one cannot help having something in common with him; the method of defense is prescribed by the method of attack: so the way of law is necessarily governed by wrong; law, at best a relative good, is inextricably bound up with wrong in a sphere of common sinfulness. Only against this background can we fully understand those deeply moving words, the most radical revaluation of all values for all times: "Do not resist evil!" Do not quarrel about the coat, give up the cloak also! Yourselves turn your cheeks to the blow! To be proved right or to suffer wrong — both are equally unessential. Essential in the mutual relations between men is only love. The life of the community enters the scope of religion not as the result of a legal order above the individuals but only as the radiation of Christian charity of the individuals. The community of men in its essence is no legal community but a pure, anarchic community of love: "Ye know that they which are accounted to rule over the gentiles exercise lordship over them; and their great ones exercise authority upon them. But so shall it not be among you: but whosoever will be great among you, shall be your minister: and whosoever of you will be the chiefest shall be the servant of all." [2]

In the later developments three different attitudes have been taken toward this purely negative religious philosophy of the law.

Tolstoy. 1. Leo Tolstoy has taught us to regard the law not only as unessential but even as anti-Christian. Any outward thing is significant only as a radiation of inwardness; but the law, valuing outwardness for its own sake and touching inwardness with a mere side glance, diverts

[2] The question of the relation between law and religion reappears as an intra-theological problem in the form of the question of the relation between God's justness and goodness. Cf. ESPOSITO, LINEAMENTI DI UNA DOTTRINA DEL DIRITTO (1930) 145 *et seq.*

one from what alone is needed.[3] Yet radical as may seem Tolstoy's complete negation of the law, his Christian anarchism, the Sermon on the Mount itself is much more radical still. For more radical indeed than the passion which undertakes to fight against the compulsion of law is the superior contempt which refuses to engage in a fight and rather extends the commandment against resisting evil, not only to wrong but also to the compulsion of law, and not only (as in Tolstoy) to active but also to passive resistance. Obedience to authority because resistance to it would attribute an undue significance to that whole question, which is religiously indifferent — that is the standpoint of the Sermon on the Mount.

Catholicism. 2. Catholicism, on the contrary, concedes a relative religious significance to law and the state. The thought of natural law is renewed and given religious color, and natural law is related, at least as a preliminary step, to the ethics of love of the Sermon on the Mount. Comparable to the state of Estates, there is established a gradation of spiritual estates, of which each has its own ethics and the highest only has the full duties of the ethics of Christian love. At one of the lower steps of this structure, the state and the law also find their place, hence they glow in a reflection of religious significance. Law and the state are not anti-Christian, as in Tolstoy; they just are not yet fully Christian. The law is valued even more highly: for the church in the Catholic view possesses a legal order not arbitrarily made by man but established by God Himself. There is a *jus divinum*[b] which is not only of secular and provisional but also of transcendental and absolute validity. As long as people were content to see in religion not so much a direct inner relation of the individual as a relation of the united collective body of Christendom to God, the contradiction between the evaluation of law by the philosophy of values and by religious philosophy could be considered fully resolved.

Reformation: Luther. 3. But the Reformation wanted again to relate each individual directly to God. Each individual is faced eye to eye with the ultimate demands of the Christian ethics of love. So the possibility of regarding law on the one hand and the full ethics of love on the other as spheres of duties of different estates is broken asunder; the conflict between the standpoint of law and the Sermon on the Mount is again put into each individual human breast. Legal philosophy and religious phi-

[3] Cf. Boris Sapir, Dostojewsky und Tolstoi über Probleme des Rechts (1932) 65 *et seq.*

[b] [Divine Law.]

losophy stand again independently side by side and in a contradiction to each other that cannot and must not be veiled: on the one hand, the ethic of the sanctity of law, of legal self-preservation, of the fight for the right; on the other, the doctrine of the unessential character of law, of nonresistance, of the reprobation of legal controversies. Yonder the sword, wrath, and sternness, sheer punishing, prohibiting, judging, and sentencing, to force down the bad and protect the pious; here mercy and charity and sheer forgiving, sparing, loving, serving, doing good, peace and joy — Luther's strong soul obviously delights in the tension between these opposites. He has expressed them by the opposition between the morals of office and personal morals, without, however, assigning to the morals of office a fixed field not to be entered by personal morals. It has always been the way of religious renewal and religious heroism to sweep like storm and fire through the area in which worldly life expected to be able to unfold under its own law undisturbed by religion — from Jesus to Tolstoy. Religion, being revolutionary and respecting no human enactment, does not permit its jurisdiction to be limited by the fences of civil morals; nor did Luther intend it to do so. Luther's formula means not the conquest, but the very sharpest demonstration of an unconquerable contradiction. We are challenged to live in the world of the law and the state fully conscious of its being conditioned and threatened by the absolute religious postulate, to live in it as in a foreign country, as if we did not live in it. Law and the state possess but a provisional significance; in the last resort they are unessential.[4]

The unessential in the law, proclaimed by the Sermon on the Mount, has been deepened by Tolstoy to the anti-essential, limited by Catholicism in the sense of the relatively essential, and restored by Luther in the sense of the but provisionally essential and ultimately unessential.

However, Christian religious philosophy with its doctrine of the unessential character of the law and the state is by no means able to unhinge the doctrines of the philosophy of values concerning the positive value of the law and the state. Law and the state are unessential only inasmuch as all worldly life is unessential, from an other-worldly standpoint, "before God." But the philosophy of values, including legal philosophy, assumes a standpoint within this world and passes value judgments within this world, conscious of being enclosed in the conditions of worldly life. Either standpoint has its natural foundation: the entanglements of worldly man in society contrasts with the ultimate terrible

[4] The profession of nothing more than this Lutheran view of the relation between Christianity on the one hand and the state, law, and war on the other caused the "Dehn case" [involving the alleged pacifism of a Protestant minister in the German republic]. Cf. GÜNTER DEHN, KIRCHE UND VÖLKERVERSÖHNUNG (1932) 84–85.

loneliness of the woman who gives birth and of the human being who dies. "We work together by hundreds, we love by twos, we die alone" (Iwan Goll).

Section 13

The Psychology of the Man of the Law

Jurisprudence, dressed in the traditional [German] color of the faculty of law, speaks:
"Red is the law so that its rules
May live in my disciples' veins.
If logic gives them all their tools,
The righteous cause will end in chains!" — Karl Heinsheimer, Festspiel.

Eduard Spranger has coined the concept of psychology as a spiritual science.[a] [1] Contrary to the efforts of psychology as a value-blind natural science, this psychology relates mental processes to values. It investigates mental processes as directed toward cultural values, as forming or understanding structures of meaning, in short, as spiritual achievements. It examines what structures of the mind, or "forms of life," are requisite for a spiritual achievement of a certain kind. Forms of life which Spranger describes as ideal types are theoretical man, economic man, aesthetic man, social man, political man, and religious man.

Objective Law as a Form of Life.[b] These types do not include juridical man or "the man of the law." According to Spranger, his is not a simple structure but a complex formation, a mixture of the social and theoretical structures.[2] We too regard the form of life of the man of the law as a complex formation, since the very idea of law, to which it is related, represents a complex formation, the trinity of justice, expediency, and legal certainty. Now Spranger correctly says that "what has been called purpose in the law is not itself legal in nature," but rather social, political, cultural; to that extent, then, the law has no peculiar corresponding form of life besides the social, political, theoretical, and aesthetic ones. But the remaining two elements are specific legal values, which cannot be reduced to other values. Inasmuch as the form of life specific to the

[a] [On the term "spiritual science," cf. translator's note b, Lask, Legal Philosophy, *Introduction*, in this volume, *supra*, p. 3.]

[1] Cf. Eduard Spranger, Lebensformen (3d ed. 1922) 3 *et seq*.

[b] [On "objective law" and "subjective legal right" see translator's note b, Lask, Legal Philosophy, chap. II, *supra*, p. 32.]

[2] Cf. Spranger, *op. cit.* 326 *et seq*. On the psychology of the man of the law, cf. also Riezler, Das Rechtsgefühl (1921).

man of the law is determined in its structure by justice, this form may be ranked with the forms of life elaborated by Spranger. Again — using Spranger's terms — justice determines the structure of the man of the law in a twofold sense: as ideal justice and as positive justice, i.e., as legal certainty.

Justice and legal certainty impress different, indeed, contradictory, stamps upon the man of the law. Justice is apt to establish a transpositive and progressive, while legal certainty is apt to establish a positivistic and conservative, attitude toward the law. With the sense of justice, there contrasts the "sense of law" as a sense of order. As a layman, the man of the law is oriented rather toward justice; as a lawyer, he is oriented rather toward legal certainty. The former — again using Spranger's terms — is rather a "legal idealist," the latter rather a "legal formalist" or, speaking without a value judgment, a "legal realist." For this very reason, it may be said that the sense of law of laymen and lawyers must be measured by opposite criteria: the sense of law of the lawyer, by how hard he finds it to put up with an injustice of enacted law; the sense of law of the layman, by whether he is able at all to put up with an injustice of enacted law in the interest of legal certainty.

If we want to illustrate the two forms of life of the man of the law by personalities, we may think, on the one hand, of Schiller, who challenges us to reach toward heaven and bring down its inalienable and inviolable lofty rights [3] (and yet who also praises holy, blessed order); and, on the other hand, of Goethe, who would rather commit an injustice than tolerate disorder (and yet who deplores that the law that was born with ourselves, alas! is never talked about).

Both mental structures of the law degenerate unless they penetrate each other. On the one hand, there is the Philistine of order, whose embodiment in office is the bureaucrat and whose civic image Goethe himself has presented in the Easter Promenade in *Faust*; on the other hand, there is the unchained fanatic of justice. Justice, as we have seen, is an empty category that may be filled with the most varied contents. So the madness of justice without purpose may dress the utmost monstrosity up as an ideal (Robespierre). Justice is a polar value, which needs resistance if its essence is to prevail. Justice that is not again and again wrested from love becomes injustice, just as mercy would become unsteady weakness were it not in turn to be wrested again and again from justice. Justice without love hardens into self-righteousness, upon which the suppressed vital forces sooner or later terribly revenge themselves. In the figure of Angelo in *Measure for Measure*, Shakespeare has

[3] Locke's "appeal to Heaven"; cf. DEL VECCHIO, GIUSTIZIA (2d ed. 1924) 73 n. 1.

presented to us the image of the zealot of the law who slips into self-righteousness and injustice, the rebellion of suppressed desires running wild against the self-righteous norm.

Yet both legal certainty and justice involve still further common dangers because they equally require human lives to be measured by concepts. As against the steady flow of the stream of life, the concept stands out as discontinuous; and as against the concrete nature of the phenomena of life, it stands out as general. It is possible to say, without becoming paradoxical, that there is no such discontinuity in the stream of life, no particularity of separate actions at all, that there is only the constant totality of a human being or rather the flowing totality of his life. Life and man are no more composed of particular acts than the sea consists of particular waves. They are totalities; the individual acts are movements, flowing into one another, of one indivisible whole. Perhaps those men who are seized by the machinery of the law are most profoundly tormented by their impotent experience of having the picture of an act, and the total picture of a life out of which that act is forcibly torn, distorted precisely because that act is viewed in isolation and the life originating it is viewed from the aspect of that accidental detail. Yet it is of the inalienable essence of legal science to intend to see but the particular trees and not the wood.

Moreover, the lawyer always looks at the individual human being and the individual case through the glasses of the general legal concept, through a close veil, as it were, which permits him to see but the roughest outlines — just like blindfolded Themis.[4] To illustrate how poorly the law grasps the reality of a life, it is sufficient to compare the biography of a great human life with its juridical condensation. To the man of the law, what is left of Goethe consists of his birth and death certificates, the document of his admission to the bar, his marriage license and the birth certificate of his son, the recordings of his house on Frauenplan and of his cottage on the Stern, the contracts concerning the publication of his works, and his appointment as a privy councilor! So what is juridically essential in a concrete individuality is but its most abstract quality — its very quality of being one concrete individual. Legal thought requires attention to be given to the most concrete life and yet only to its most abstract outlines. Roman law excels Germanic law essentially because of its superior power of abstraction, which thus cruelly simplifies the fullness of life. The lawyer must be able to see only a juridical scheme in a living human being. It was this that caused Tolstoy to pronounce his judgment of damnation over the lawyers: "that

[4] On this symbol, see E. von Moeller in (1905) Zeitschrift für christliche Kunst 107 *et seq.*, 142 *et seq.*

all these people think there are circumstances in life where a direct relation of man to his fellow-man is not needed." [5] This attitude of the man of the law is also referred to by Spranger, who ascribes to him "the closest relation to the scholar" and to the scholar's striving for theoretical universality of rules. Indeed one is tempted to call him most closely related of all to the mathematician. Just as the mathematician may see only the spatial and numerical relationships in all colorful reality, so the lawyer too may give attention only to very definite rough outlines in the picture of life that is so rich in colors and forms. As a matter of fact, Savigny has characterized legal science as an "arithmetic of concepts"; and, in a more recent book on the question of aptitude for the legal profession, it is maintained that a poor mathematician is a poor lawyer.[6]

This is far from implying that a good mathematician is a good lawyer. The degenerate form of the "ivory tower" jurist suggests precisely the professional habits of one who has so long been used to having to disregard the full flow of life that he has altogether forgotten to regard it. This degenerate form comes into existence when the man of the law in his concern with justice and legal certainty forgets the third aspect of the idea of law, viz., expediency. In thinking of justice and legal certainty, the man of the law comes close to theoretical man; in thinking of expediency, he becomes related to social man and even to political man.

Subjective Right as a Form of Life.[c] So far we have oriented the figure of the man of the law toward objective law. But he may also be viewed with reference to subjective right. In the former relationship, his outstanding personification is the judge; in the latter, he becomes personified in the fighter for a right, whose characteristic sense of law is the sense of his own right. That sense is most clearly understood when it is compared with its opposite: conscience.[7]

One must first become fully aware of the problematic character of that duality of ethical voices in every human breast: one ethical legislation forever imposing duties alone, and another authorizing claims; one binding the will, and the other contrariwise unchaining it; the former abhorring interest and fettering selfishness, and the latter justifying in-

[5] Cf. SAPIR, DOSTOJEWSKY UND TOLSTOY (1932) 78 *et seq.*

[6] HOLLENBERG, JURIST OHNE EIGNUNG (1931).

[c] [See translator's note b, *supra*, this section, p. 130.]

[7] Contrariwise, ISAY, RECHTSNORM UND ENTSCHEIDUNG (1929) 90, declares the sense of law and the moral sense to be "essentially one," and RÜMELIN, RECHTSGEFÜHL UND RECHTSBEWUSSTSEIN (1915) 30, says the sense of law "shares one source with conscience." Neither, however, refers to the feeling of one's *own* right.

terest and allying itself with selfishness. Let us for a moment hark to their dialogue:

Says conscience: "Whosoever smite thee on thy right cheek, turn to him the other also; and if one man will sue thee at the law and take away thy coat, let him have thy cloak also." But the sense of law replies: "Do not let your right be trampled underfoot by others. He who makes himself a worm cannot afterwards complain of being trodden upon" (Kant). Resumes conscience: "But I say unto you that ye resist not evil!" But the sense of law insists: "I'd rather be a dog than a man if I am to be trodden upon!" (Kleist). And again conscience: "Love your enemies, bless them that curse you." And against this the sense of law: "The fight for one's right is a command of moral self-preservation" (Jhering). "Blessed are the peacemakers," says conscience, but the sense of law rejoins: "He who feels the law on his side must act roughly; a polite law won't mean anything" (Goethe). This does not silence conscience; only we cannot continue to listen to their unending dialogue, loath as we are to leave the last word with one or the other party.

Sense of Law and Conscience. Every one of us is the scene of the seemingly irreconcilable conflict of two ethical systems: a system of duty and love, peace and humility, and a system of right and honor, fight and pride. Since the acceptance of Christianity, the moral world and the moral life of each individual are rent in two: beside our Christian conscience, there abruptly stands our pre-Christian sense of law. We are, say, pious Christians and at the same time convinced adherents of dueling; or we believe equally in the God of love and the right to war. Down to its last depths, this contradiction has been traced by Ibsen's dramatized ethical casuistry. Again and again — in Mrs. Alving, in Rosmer, in the master-builder Solness — the suppressed rights of life maintain their ethical claims against the antivital tyranny of duties; again and again the "trolls," the ancient gods whom Christianity has degraded to monsters, rebel against the despotism of Christian conscience.

Not until Kant has it been possible systematically to reconcile the two hostile ethical worlds. He did so by the same line of reasoning to which Jhering later lent his fiery eloquence: by characterizing the fight for the right as the fight for the possibility of fulfilling moral duties, as moral self-preservation, and thus attributing a content of moral duties to the law. Yet the equilibrium between conscience and sense of law, as described by Kant or Jhering, between the "modest firmness" which always remains conscious of the subservience of right to duty and the "robust conscience" which is not so burdened by duties as to forget to claim its right, is an ethical ideal, to be sure, but not a psychical reality. Sense of law and conscience are tied to characterological conditions which are as different and incompatible as their respective pathological cultures, the delusion of right of the querulous and the delusion of sin of the melancholic; so different indeed that they will hardly ever be found in equal strength in the same man. Actually, sense of law and conscience have been characterized as the centers of two fundamentally different human types, the anger type and the anguish type.[8] The reader need only examine those who surround him — at the first glance, those predominantly gifted with conscience will set themselves clearly apart from those prevailingly gifted with a sense of law, the gentle from the wrathful, the kind from the strong, the saints from the heroes, the sneaks from the brawlers, the sheep from the goats. Therefore, even after Kant, philosophers who regard themselves less as creators of universal systems than as moral teachers with a mission to remedy one-sidedness by opposite one-sidedness, will again and again build ethics exclusively upon the sense of law or, conversely, exclusively upon conscience. The former will praise rights as the noblest of duties, the other will deny any right to rights. In our days, the first has been done by Nietzsche, the second by Tolstoy. The noble man, says Nietzsche, "must count his privileges and their exercise among his duties." Not to resist evil, defenselessly to suffer wrong, is our part, according to Tolstoy.

But the rarity of a well-developed sense of law is to be explained not only by the fact that it demands an equally well developed conscience at its side; in addition, the sense of law, quite different from conscience, presupposes an active intellect. We are told of our duty in a particular case by our conscience without having first had to become conscious of the general maxim on which it is based. Of our right, on the contrary, we become conscious only by recalling the general norm from which it flows. For the moral norm applies to men in isolation, the legal precept to men in relation to one another; and whereas the moral duty demands of me recognition regardless of whether it claims validity for others in the same situation, a right, by its very concept, I may attribute to myself only if I am ready to concede it to others in the same situation. Without such generalization, claims can be raised only through a feeling of arbitrariness and not through a feeling of right. So the sense of law requires a nimble mind that is able to shift from the specific to the general and back from the general to the specific. The fighter for rights is characterized by a peculiar mixture of intellectualism, which alone is able to raise the particular to generality and thus to judge it according to

[8] Cf. Kornfeld, *Das Rechtsgefühl* (1914) 1 ZEITSCHRIFT FÜR RECHTSPHILOSOPHIE 135 *et seq.*

justice, and of passion, which alone is able to fill the abstract thought of justice with the effective fire of individual life.

Spranger has proposed to describe the fighter for his right, in contrast with the man of the law, as a power type. In this sense, even the impotent type of man who struggles in vain, say, against the force of *res judicata*, appears as a frustrated power type, a passive form of the power type. Yet this does not adequately characterize the fighter for his right. The peculiarity of this power type consists precisely in combining power in the service of an interest with the consecration of ethical value, merging within a single form interest and value, which elsewhere are always opposites. The tremendous explosive effect of the sense of law rests precisely on its combining into a single force the two opposite forces of man, value-consciousness and desire. This explains also why the sense of law, more than other senses, is liable to be overemphasized and so to become diseased. Thus, it has been shown that the manifold "relief neuroses" of our time are really "law neuroses," diseases of the sense of law.[9] But the sense of law is only too apt to deteriorate not only in the direction of exaggerated intensity but also in that of pollution. Envy, desirous of having what another has; jealousy, unwilling to let another have what one does not have oneself; and vindictiveness, anxious to make another suffer what one has suffered oneself, dress up in the demands of equality and justice, whether from hypocrisy or from self-deception; and the legal power contained in the right degenerates into a lust for power which is anxious to affect the adversary, detached from any interest. We speak of chicane when a right is thus to be realized for its own sake alone, with no regard to its moral or even utilitarian purposes; and *The Merchant of Venice*, if indeed it is to be mounted upon a legal philosophical formula after famous models, resembles many another story of the wise judge in showing how the law, contradicting itself in a chicane, restores itself as it were by a counter-chicane — so strong is its inherent moral purposiveness.

So the description of the man of the law has recalled to us again what we have previously faced in various ways: that the law is in labile balance, ever threatened and forever to be restored anew, in the midst of polar tensions.

[9] Cf. von Weizsäcker in (1929) 2 DER NERVENARZT 569 *et seq.*

SECTION 14

AESTHETICS OF THE LAW

To you, the Muses willingly
Hand roses down from every bill and deed,
And yet you serve two lords more bitterly
Opposed than love of Christ and Mammon's greed. — *Goethe to H. P. Schlosser*, 1774

Law may make use of art, and art of law. Like every cultural phenomenon, the law needs bodily means of expression: language, gesture, dress, symbol, building. Like any bodily means of expression, the bodily expression of the law is subject to aesthetic evaluation. And, like any phenomenon, the law as subject-matter may enter the arts, the specific field of aesthetic evaluation. So an aesthetics of the law is required.[1] So far, however, it has been formulated only in beginnings and fragments.

In the early epochs of peoples, when separation and autonomy of the cultural fields were unknown, not only law, custom, and morals, or law and religion, but also law and art were closely connected, nay, contained in one another. As to those periods, we may pursue "poetry in the law" with Jakob Grimm, "humor in the law" with Otto Gierke, or the mythological forms of the idea of law, Themis and Dike, with Hirzel. With the separation of the cultural fields, however, law and art too have more and more fallen apart and even into hostile opposition. Poetry is not exactly on good terms with the law. Law, the most rigid of the cultural structures, and art, the most changeable form of expression of the changeable spirit of the times, live in natural hostility, as witnessed by numerous utterances of poets about the law and by the frequency of young poets giving up the legal profession.[2]

Art of the Law: Aesthetics of Forms of Legal Expression. But that very separation of law from art has perhaps served to clarify the specific aesthetic value of the law which it does not owe merely to an admixture from the foreign sphere of art. This could be demonstrated clearly in the language of the law, which was able to develop only when the law

[1] Cf., above all, THEODOR STERNBERG, 1 EINFÜHRUNG IN DIE RECHTSWISSENSCHAFT (2d ed. 1912) 178 *et seq.*; also GEORG MÜLLER, RECHT UND STAAT IN UNSERER DICHTUNG (1924); HANS FEHR, DAS RECHT IM BILDE (1923); DAS RECHT IN DER DICHTUNG (1931).

[2] Cf. RADBRUCH, EINFÜHRUNG IN DIE RECHTSWISSENSCHAFT (7th and 8th ed. 1929) 207–208.

was segregated strictly from other cultural fields and which by that very development gained its aesthetic peculiarity, due, to be sure, to its manifold renunciations.

The language of the law is frigid, renouncing any emotional tone; it is blunt, renouncing any argumentation; it is concise, renouncing any intention to teach. Thus there comes into existence a lapidary style of self-imposed poverty, a style which cannot be surpassed as an expression of the self-assured consciousness of power of the commanding state and which in its utterly sharp precision could serve as a style model to an author of the rank of Stendhal.[3]

Whereas the language of the law is the cold lapidary style, by odd contrast, glowing rhetoric is the language of the fight for rights, of the fighting sense of law. The sense of law combines in itself two seemingly contradictory elements: feeling, which elsewhere is usually attached to the concrete and obvious only, and the abstract generality of the legal rule. For the fighter for a right is characterized by that peculiar mixture of coldness and ardor, of generalizing intellectualism which reduces the particular case to its principle and individualizing passion which burns through the wrong it opposes as something singularly monstrous. So the adequate form of expression of legal controversy is rhetoric, the essence of which is to endow the general with the obviousness and effectiveness of the particular, whereas poetry contrariwise bestows upon the particular the symbolic significance of universality.

Still other aesthetical values are to be found in the judicial opinion and in legal science. We are satisfied with a correct solution of a legal question, but we enjoy only an "elegant" solution. Rudolf Sohm extols the faculty of Celsus "in the particular legal case to develop the general rule which, cast in the most concise form of language, soaring with the force of winged words, like a flash of lightning illumines the landscape far and wide." Sohm thus manifests his aesthetic pleasure in a scholarly quality which preëminently characterized that incomparable teacher himself. This elegance of judicial solutions may be expressed by the formula: *Simplex sigillum veri,*[a] which suggests that beauty is regarded as the indicia of truth, an aesthetical value as the criterion of a logical one.

On that pleasure in the elegant solution of what seem hopelessly knotty judicial tangles there feed the numerous stories of "wise judges" which may be found in the literature of all peoples. Their effect is due to the surprise which is caused by seeing the evidently appropriate decision conjured up from seemingly insignificant words or facts.

[3] Cf. RADBRUCH, *op cit.* 35 *et seq.*

[a] [Simplicity is the seal of truth.]

The Law in the Arts: Law as an Artistic Subject. Therewith we have already turned from the artistic expression of law to law as a subject-matter of the arts. The quality which cannot but render law an alluring artistic subject is the variety of its inherent antitheses, the opposition of Is and Ought, of positive and natural law, legitimate and revolutionary law, freedom and order, justice and equity, law and mercy, etc. So those artistic forms which essentially express antitheses will be especially attracted to the law; in particular, the drama, from Sophocles' *Antigone* to Shakespeare's *Merchant of Venice* and *Measure for Measure.* Georg Jellinek [4] has shown how the drama of antiquity glorifies the sanctity and inviolability of objective law, while the modern drama sympathizes with the rebellion of the subjective sense of law against the legal order. To the art of today, positive law is either the hard fate which shatters the individual, or the oppressive force against which a higher justice raises the banner of revolt, or perhaps simply the stupidity of bureaucracy at which the wit snaps his fingers with pleasure.

This also suggests the other form besides the drama that is especially suited to express the antitheses of the law: in literature, the satire, and in the plastic arts, the caricature. A good lawyer would cease to be a good lawyer were he not fully conscious, at any moment of his professional life, of both the necessity and the profound questionability of his profession. So the serious lawyer sees without displeasure those mockers who fill the margins of his statute books with all sorts of ironical question and exclamation marks, such as Anatole France; he likes even more to see those ponderers among the poets whose doubting humanism touches the fundamentals of justice, such as Tolstoy or Dostoevsky or the great caricaturist of justice who is both a mocker and a ponderer, Daumier. Only the Philistine feels at every moment unquestionably useful as a member of human society. The shoemaker of Socrates knew what he was in this world for: to make shoes for Socrates and others; Socrates only knew that he did not know it. But our burden as lawyers is heaviest: we are to believe in the profession of our life and yet at the same time, in some deepest layer of our being, again and again to doubt it.

[4] 1 AUSGEWÄHLTE SCHRIFTEN UND REDEN (1911) 208 *et seq.* Cf. also Radbruch, *Mass für Mass,* in LÜBECKISCHE BLÄTTER, Sept. 6, 1931 (FESTSCHRIFT FÜR DEN LÜBECKER JURISTENTAG).

SECTION 15

THE LOGIC OF LEGAL SCIENCE

What is the truth that those mountains bear — is it a lie to the world at their feet? — Montaigne.

Having completed our considerations of legal philosophy in a strict sense, we focused the law upon the contexts of the philosophy of history, of religious philosophy, of psychology as a spiritual science, and of aesthetics. Into ethics we had fitted the law previously when we considered the purpose of law. It remains to speak of the law as a subject of logic, of the methodology of legal science.

Legal Science and Sciences Concerned with Law. The sciences the subject-matter of which is the law we shall call sciences concerned with law. Of these, we shall call legal science in a strict sense that science concerned with law which works at the law by means of the specifically juridical method. This legal science proper, viz., systematic, dogmatic legal science, may be defined as the science concerned with the objective meaning of positive legal orders. This characterizes its special position among the other sciences concerned with law.

1. Its subject is made up of positive legal orders. It is a science concerned with valid and not with right law, with the law that is and not the law that ought to be. It is thereby distinguished from those sciences concerned with law the subject matter of which is the law that ought to be, viz., from legal philosophy as the science concerned with the purpose of law, and from legal politics as the science concerned with the means to attain that purpose.

2. Legal science in the strict sense deals with legal orders and not with life under law, with legal norms and not with legal facts. Therewith it is so delimited as to exclude research into legal facts — from papyrology to criminology. The legal order, the legal norms, are concepts directly related to values; as given, their meaning is to serve justice. Life under law, the legal facts, are concepts indirectly related to values; as given, their meaning is to correspond to that legal order, to those legal norms, which in turn are oriented toward the idea of justice.

3. Legal science is a science concerned with the objective meaning and not the subjective meaning of law. It determines how the law is to be understood and not necessarily how it was intended. The existence of law, the thoughts which its authors intended to put into it and the thoughts which its expounders actually gathered from it, the law as a

caused and causative fact, is dealt with not by legal science in the strict sense but by the "social theory of law" (Georg Jellinek) [1]: legal history,[2] comparative law, sociology of law.

The work of legal science proper, of dogmatic, systematic legal science, is done at three stages: interpretation, construction, and system.

Interpretation. The essence of juridical interpretation is best clarified by comparing it with philological interpretation. August Boeckh has characterized philosophical interpretation as "knowing the known"— thinking again what has been thought before. Philological interpretation is directed toward determining a fact, the subjectively intended meaning, the thoughts actually thought by actual men which are basic to the spiritual work that is the subject of the interpretation — a purely empirical method. But juridical interpretation is directed toward the objectively valid meaning of the legal rule.[3] It does not and cannot stop at determining the meaning intended by the author of the law, for the simple reason that each enactment is participated in by many authors, resulting in a possible multiplicity of views of participants on the meaning of the law; whereas juridical interpretation, serving the administration of justice, must of necessity work out a single signification of the law. But even if all participants were of one mind, this would not necessarily determine the authoritative meaning of the law. Legislators are not the authors of the law; the legislative will is not the collective will of those participating in the making of the law; it is, rather, the will of the state.

Now the state speaks not in the personal utterances of those who participate in lawmaking but solely in the law itself. The legislative will coincides with the will of the law. It signifies but the personified total content of legislation, the content of the law reflected in a fictitious single consciousness. So the legislative will is not a means of interpreting but the goal and the result of interpretation; it is an expression for the *a priori* necessity of a systematic interpretation, free of contradictions, of the entire legal order. It is therefore possible to determine as the legislative will what never existed in the conscious wills of the authors of the law. The interpreter may understand the law better than its creators understood it; the law may be wiser than its authors — indeed, it *must*

[1] Cf. KANTOROWICZ in 1 ERINNERUNGSGABE FÜR MAX WEBER (1925) 93 *et seq.*

[2] On the relation between legal history and dogmatic legal science, see FRANZ SOMMER, 1 KRITISCHER REALISMUS UND POSITIVE RECHTSWISSENSCHAFT (1929) 216 *et seq.*

[3] MARCK, SUBSTANZ- UND FUNKTIONSBEGRIFF IN DER RECHTSPHILOSOPHIE (1925) 77, regards the opposition of subjective and objective meaning as a mere "distinction of degrees."

be wiser than its authors. The thoughts of the authors of a law necessarily have gaps, cannot always avoid obscurities and contradictions; yet the interpreter must be able to derive a clear and uncontradicted decision from the law in any conceivable legal case. For, as stated in the [French] Civil Code and implied in any other code, "a judge who refuses to render a decision under the pretext that the law fails to cover the case or that it is obscure or inadequate may be prosecuted for denial of justice." So juridical interpretation does not think again what has been thought before, but thinks through what has been thought of. It starts with the philological interpretation of the law, only to go quickly beyond it — like a departing ship which is first piloted on her prescribed way through the waters of the port but then takes her own course under her captain's orders at the open sea. It passes by imperceptible steps from interpretation in the spirit of the legislator to rules which the interpreter himself "would lay down as a legislator," as provided in the famous introductory section of the Swiss Civil Code. It is an insoluble mixture of elements theoretical and practical, perceptive and creative, reproductive and productive, scientific and transscientific, objective and subjective. To the extent, however, that interpretation is practical, creative, productive, transscientific, it is determined in each case by the changing requirements of the law. Therefore, the legislative will, which it aims at and results in determining, is not fixed by interpretation as a definite content for all times but remains able to respond with new meaning to new legal requirements and questions under the conditions of changing times; it must be understood not as a single act of the will, which once called the law into being, but as the changeable permanent will which keeps the law in existence. Says Hobbes: "Not he by whose authority the law was first made but he by whose authority it continues to be law is the legislator." This view is symbolized by the legend of Solon voluntarily exiling himself after completing his codification: the empirical legislator leaves the field to the ideal legislator who lives only in the law itself.

To understand this peculiar character of juridical interpretation fully one must not judge it by the empirical model of philological interpretation. One must rather keep in mind that philological interpretation is a late product in the history of knowledge, juridical interpretation being less closely related to it than to incomparably older forms of interpretation. In primitive periods people attributed to the word a power independent of the speaker's thoughts and, as it were, magic.[4] To them the word of the oracle, for instance, was the receptacle of a hidden mean-

[4] ". . . where the word was so important, having been a spoken word" (GOETHE, DIVAN).

ing which, unrecognizable to the uninitiated, was illumined, lightning-like, only by its realization. How many fairy tales have been founded upon the ambiguity of words of which the speaker was unconscious! We speak of a freak of nature where a natural phenomenon has by accident been made to carry a meaning: a cave of stalactites representing a hall of columns, or two rocks representing monk and nun. So the word, too, was a freak of nature in primitive times, permeated by a significance unbeknown and unintended. So it is only consistent that in those times even nature, lacking knowledge and intention, was regarded as carrying significant meaning, and natural phenomena were taken for symbols, that not only the creations of the human mind but also the natural phenomena were subjected to anthropomorphous interpretation. Thus, St. Augustine said that "prophetic power is spread throughout the world," and even Goethe observes: "One is justly pleased when inanimate nature produces a symbol of what we love and venerate."

This way of interpretation, directed toward the meaning that transcends consciousness, was elevated to a scientific method by the scholastics. Well known is their doctrine of the fourfold meaning of the scriptures:

Littera gesta docet; quid credas, allegoria;
Moralis, quid agas; quo tendas, anagogia.[a]

To be sure, in getting at an allegorical, a moral, and an anagogical meaning back of the literal meaning, according to the doctrine of inspiration, they professed to disclose thoughts actually thought, not indeed by the human authors of the holy scriptures, but by God Himself.[5]

In a nonscientific manner, this way of interpretation has survived into our own days. In the clergyman's sermon the individual words of holy scriptures under the impression of the particular situation are made to gleam in ever new significations regardless of their original meaning. Indeed, the indelible vitality of the biblical word rests on its susceptibility to this wealth of interpretation. Even from profane words playful profundity likes to elicit a deeper meaning back of the intended one. Goethe in his *Divan* expresses multiple meaning in a gracious picture: "The word is a fan! Between its ribs a pair of beautiful eyes look out; the fan is a lovely gauze." And in the magazine *Die Jugend* (1899, No. 6), the following fine passage can be found:

It has always been one of my purest pleasures when from the superficiality of thoughtless words a plummet could be cast into the depths of things and

[a] [The letter tells you what happened; allegory, what to believe; the moral, how to behave; anagogy, whither to tend.]

[5] Cf. HANS VOLLMER, VOM LESEN UND DEUTEN HEILIGER SCHRIFTEN (1907).

the nonsensical provided the frame for an undreamt-of sense. This is not malicious arrogance but modesty, for it implies something like comfort and hope that even our wisdom, which we so often have to doubt, may leave room for a meaning, hidden from us, which higher spirits in friendly interpretation ascribe to it — since in case of doubt the better intention is always presumed in favor of the accused.

This passage was signed with the initials G. S.; it was written by Georg Simmel.[6]

However, juridical interpretation is distinguished from those intuitive forms of interpretation by its utterly rational nature. It is not a magical or a mystical interpretation, nor a play of profundity, but a logical interpretation. Assuming that logic originated in the sophists' instruction in rhetoric, scientific logic originally was the logic of advocates; for rhetoric is the act of proving and refuting in alternating orations, especially in forensic orations. Now in that logical art of deriving proof and refutation from the law, the question is not what the lawmaker has thought of but what may be made of the text of the law for this cause. The search is not for the meaning actually intended by the lawmaker but for what may be imputed to him, hence for a meaning that is gathered from the law although it was not put into it.[7]

Such rational, advocatory interpretation of the law solely out of the law itself is most closely related to that Biblicism of early Protestant theology which wanted to establish nothing without the Holy Scriptures and everything upon the Holy Scriptures.[8] Luther himself stressed that parallel: "A lawyer talking without his text is disgraceful, but much more disgraceful is a theologian talking without his text."[9] But jurisprudence need not rest the legitimacy of its method solely upon this after all rather questionable relation to an obsolete method of theology. It may also feel in the very good company of thoroughly modern branches of knowledge.

[6] Cf. SIMMEL, HAUPTPROBLEME DER PHILOSOPHIE (Göschen editions, 1910) 71–72.

[7] Cf. STROUX, SUMMUM JUS, SUMMA INJURIA. EIN KAPITEL AUS DER GESCHICHTE DER INTERPRETATIO JURIS (1926).

[8] Cf. RADBRUCH in 4 ARCHIV FÜR SOCIALWISSENSCHAFT UND SOZIALPOLITIK 355 *et seq.*

[9] Leibniz: *Merito partitionis nostrae exemplum a Theologia ad Jurisprudentiam transtulimus, quia mira est utriusque Facultatis similitudo* [We have justly transferred the example of our division from theology to jurisprudence, because of than was suggested by the above-mentioned scheme (*supra*, pp. 140–141). Cf. SCHÖNFELD, VOM PROBLEM DER RECHTSGESCHICHTE 4 SCHRIFTEN DER KÖNIGSBERGER GELEHRTENGESELLSCHAFT (1927) 351.

In the study of literature, there prevailed until recently philological interpretation, research into the author's actual thoughts on the basis of all his utterances about his work, his drafts, his diaries, his letters — say, "Goethe philology." But this investigation into the subjectively intended meaning is more and more relegated to the background as against an investigation into the objectively valid meaning of the poem. Authors themselves testify that the content of their works is not exhausted in that subjectively intended meaning, that to themselves upon later rereading their own works there often occur new and unexpected meanings. Such understanding of the work exclusively out of the work itself may apply not only to a particular poem but also to the total work of a writer, his *oeuvres*. This method then results in a new form of biography. Traditional biography passed from the personality to the work, understood the work as an emanation of the personality. This new biography derives the personality solely from the work. It is biography based on the work. Thus has Goethe been presented to us by Gundolf: "The artist exists only inasmuch as he expresses himself in the work of art." Thus, again, Kant has been presented by Georg Simmel, who concerns himself "not with the real historical man" Kant "but with an ideal phenomenon that lives only in the achievement itself as an expression or symbol of the objective, inner coherence of its parts." To such a biography, the creator of the work is not the dead human being who once created this work, but the eternal poet or thinker who lives in this work, changing as long as he lives and giving new answers to the new questions of new times — just as according to that Hobbes passage the lawmaker is not he by whose authority the law was first made but he by whose authority it continues to be law.

Not only the history of an individual mind but also that of a collective spirit may be and frequently is based on its work.[10] The history of philosophy, or the history of dogmas, once used to endeavor to determine psychologically the actual influence upon one thinker of other thinkers. Since Hegel, on the contrary, it sets itself the task, irrespective of biographical-psychological connections, of developing the objective relationships between systems of thought, of comprehending their historical succession as a logical process, of understanding the development from one system to another as if it had occurred in a single mind, of interpreting the movement of the objective spirit as if it were the work of one

[10] Legal history, too, may be worked out as history of the spirit, as investigation into the movements of objective meaning. It then is closer to dogmatic legal science than was suggested by the above-mentioned scheme (*supra*, pp. 140–141). Cf. SCHÖNFELD, VOM PROBLEM DER RECHTSGESCHICHTE 4 SCHRIFTEN DER KÖNIGSBERGER GELEHRTENGESELLSCHAFT (1927) 351.

mind — just as the same "spirit of the lawmaker" back of the change in laws changes and yet persists.[11]

However, the examples we have submitted to the reader may still be insufficient to dispel the impression that the suggested kind of transempirical interpretation may be a conjuring trick which gets more and different things out of a vessel than were put into it. Is it really possible and plausible that one can gather a meaning from a work of the mind which was not put into it by its author? Simple examples suffice to answer this question in the affirmative. A riddle, too, may have a second unintended solution besides the one envisaged by its author, the second being just as correct as the first one. Again, a move in a game of chess may possibly have a meaning in the context of the game that is quite different from the one attributed to it by the player. Now such a move in a game of chess, not dependent upon the player alone, is any sentence that we speak. "The language thinks and invents for us" — which means that by thinking and speaking I fit my thoughts into a world of thought governed by specific laws of its own. Just as truly as I am unable to create anew a language and a world of thought all by myself, I submit whatever I utter to the specific laws of the world of thought in which I have to move, and with every utterance I form conceptual connections which I cannot remotely anticipate. Says Goethe: "A word that is uttered enters the circle of the other forces of nature which work of necessity." In this, the spiritual does not differ from the physical world. In utilizing the laws of nature I at the same time surrender to them — so, too, the laws of logic become my masters as soon as I utilize them. Thus under certain conditions the meaning my utterance was to have is not at all the meaning it has — and not merely because I did not succeed in expressing the intended meaning but rather because any meaning is a mere partial meaning in an infinite context of meaning and calls forth immeasurable effects in this context of meaning: "What he weaves no weaver knows." One is moved to be modest and yet infinitely exalted by one's consciousness of each of his thoughts being fitted into an immeasurable context of meaning, into the world of the "objective spirit" of which any subjective mind is but part and parcel.

Construction and Systematization. But it still remains to be made clear what are the specific, "logical" laws which guide us in ascertaining objective meaning. To understand means to grasp a cultural phenomenon

[11] "The entire succession of men, during the course of so many centuries, is to be regarded as one man who always lives on and learns continually." — Pascal. "The history of knowledge is a great fugue in which the voices of the nations make their appearances one after the other." — Goethe.

precisely as a cultural one, viz., in its relation to the corresponding cultural value. Hence legal scientific understanding, in particular, means a grasp of the law as a realization of the concept of law, viz., as a given something the meaning of which is to realize the idea of law, viz., an attempt at the realization of the idea of law.

It follows that the task of legal science is to work out its material in two ways: categorially, to present the law as realization of the *concept* of law and of its component legal categories; and teleologically, to depict the law as attempted realization of the *idea* of law. This twofold work is called "construction" and, where it relates not only to a single legal institution but to the totality of the legal order, "system." So there are two kinds of construction and systematization: categorial as well as teleological.[12] Thus, adjective law is construed teleologically when procedural rules are reduced to definite principles, such as the maxims of cognizance within the pleadings[b] or cognizance by judicial inquisition;[c] on the other hand, it is construed categorially when procedure is conceived as a legal relationship, as under the doctrine of the right to legal protection.[d] Thus, again, in introducing us to criminal law, the doctrine of the purpose of punishment offers a teleological construction, while the theory of norms[e] offers a categorial construction. Still further, the treatment of administrative law once used to be purely teleological, following the method of political science as contrasted with the juridical method established by Otto Mayer. Moreover, in the structure of the legal system, categorial viewpoints alternate with teleological ones. For instance, the distinction between public and private law is categorial, while labor law and the law of business regulation are teleological conceptions. A purely categorial discipline is the general theory of law. And corresponding to the emphasis on the categorial or the teleological task

[12] Cf. Radbruch, *Zur Systematik der Verbrechenslehre*, 1 FESTGABE FÜR FRANK (1930) 158 *et seq.*, and also Hegler, *Zum Aufbau der Systematik des Zivilprosessrechts*, FESTGABE FÜR HECK, RÜMELIN, SCHMIDT (1913) 216 *et seq.*

[b] [*Verhandlungsmaxime*, the original civil law maxim that the scope of trial and decision is determined by the allegations and demands of the parties.]

[c] [*Offizialmaxime*, the statutory civil law maxim that the scope of trial and decision may be changed by judicial official initiative and inquisition.]

[d] [*Rechtsschutzanspruch*, the right to have claims existing under substantive law adjudicated and enforced by legal process, which is considered a basic procedural right by many German authorities on adjective law, following WACH, DER FESTSTELLUNGSANSPRUCH (1888).]

[e] [The theory that any prescription of a penalty implies or presupposes a normative legal rule forbidding an act to be committed or requiring an act not to be omitted; proposed by BINDING, DIE NORMEN UND IHRE ÜBERTRETUNG (2d ed. 1890–1920), and many other authorities on German criminal law.]

of legal science, formalistic and finalistic epochs have followed each other in constantly changing succession in the history of legal science.[13]

Legal Concepts. To the three, or rather two, steps of juridical work, ascertainment of meaning and categorial and teleological elaboration of meaning, or interpretation on the one hand and construction and systematization on the other, there correspond two kinds of legal concepts. On the one hand, there are the concepts of which the legal rules are composed, especially the concepts used in setting forth states of facts in the terms of statutes and which are clarified by interpretation, the "legally relevant concepts." On the other hand, there are the constructive and systematic concepts by means of which the normative content of a legal rule is grasped, the "genuine legal concepts." The former are predominantly concepts of facts, such as thing, taking away, intention; the latter are concepts of rights, legal relations, and legal institutions, such as the rights and duties of vendor and purchaser or the legal institution of the sale.[14]

As to the legally relevant concepts, the formation of legal concepts depends upon prescientific concepts. For the material of legal science is not the amorphous formlessness of raw data, but a reality preformed by means of prescientific, or at least extrajuridical, concepts. Legal science is largely conceptual work of the second degree, which owes its concepts to preparatory work done outside of legal science; for instance, it owes the concept of the fetus to biology, the concept of the vine louse to zoology. However, legal science adopts no extra-juridical concept without at the same time transforming it. The concept "fetus," while depending upon the biological concept known by that term, does not coincide with it. The law distinguishes it from the concept of man as a born human being, not according to strictly biological viewpoints, but in conformity with legal requirements; it regards the human being as fetus as long as the penalty against abortion suffices to protect it, as man when the stronger protection against killing becomes necessary. And the concept "vine louse," while it may be coextensive in zoology and legal

[13] Cf. Hermann Kantorowicz, *Die Epochen der Rechtswissenschaft*, in (1914–15) 6 DIE TAT 345 *et seq.*

[14] RADBRUCH, DER HANDLUNGSBEGRIFF IN DER BEDEUTUNG FÜR DAS STRAFRECHTSSYSTEM (1903) 29. This dualism of legal concepts seems to be identical with their "twofold relation to values" in ERIK WOLF, 1 STRAFRECHTLICHE SCHULDLEHRE (1928) 93–94: concepts related to the value of law, and concepts related to the value of legal science. The above distinction may also coincide with that between concepts of legal content and concepts of legal essence (Kelsen). *Contra:* SOMLÓ, JURISTISCHE GRUNDLEHRE 27 *et seq.*, contrasting the concepts of legal content with the juridical basic concepts, i.e., the legal concepts *a priori.*

science, is determined by different contents and characteristics in each: in legal science, the essential characteristic is the quality of the vine louse as a vineyard pest, which is quite unessential in zoology. So naturalistic concepts undergo a teleological transformation when taken over by legal science.[15] At the same time, this consideration shows that the three steps of juridical work overlap, that interpretation is not merely the prerequisite of construction and systematization but in turn often presupposes teleological construction and systematization.

Legal Science as an Understanding Cultural Science. The essence of legal scientific work has now been sufficiently clarified to enable us to fit legal science into the system of sciences as it appears from what has been said at the beginning of this book (sec. 1). Legal science is an understanding cultural science.[16] As such, it is characterized by three features: it is an understanding, individualizing, and value-relating science.

1. Legal science is an *understanding* science, directed not at the factuality of any particular intended meaning, but at the objectively valid meaningful significance of legal rules. Here we must recall conclusions developed before (*supra*, sec. 10, p. 112). Legal rules are imperatives. The imperative expresses a Will. But the objective meaning of a Will is an Ought. The content of meaning of an act of volition, disregarding the factuality of its having been willed, cannot be expressed in any other way but by an Ought. The subject-matter of legal science consists of facts, legal imperatives, rulings of the Will; but since legal science considers these facts not as such but according to their objective meaning, it treats them like rules of Ought, or norms. This may be expressed by saying that legal science has the subject-matter of an existential science and the method of a normative science,[17] provided one does not forget that in the last analysis it remains an existential, namely, a cultural science.

2. As a cultural science, furthermore, legal science is an *individualizing* science. It may appear strange that this very science, in which the concept of "the law" originated, is called an "individualizing" science and not a science of general laws, or "generalizing" science. To be sure, each particular legal rule is essentially general. Yet the subject-matter

[15] Cf. SCHWINGE, TELEOLOGISCHE BEGRIFFSBILDUNG IM STRAFRECHT (1930); also the numerous examples in the first edition of this book, 198 *et seq.*

[16] *Accord* (in addition to those cited *supra*, sec. 3, n. 13): ERIK WOLF, 1 STRAFRECHTLICHE SCHULDLEHRE 73 *et seq.*

[17] Opposing this characterization: KELSEN in (1916) 40 SCHMOLLERS JAHRBUCH 1225 *et seq.*

of legal science is not the particular laws but the legal order made up of those particular laws, the "historical and hence individual system" [18]; and the task of legal science is, not to advance beyond the peculiarity of the particular (say, German or French) legal system to rules common to all legal orders, but rather to understand these legal orders in their individuality.[19] Moreover, the particular legal case is not a mere example of a general law, as in the natural sciences, but contrariwise the law exists only for the sake of deciding the particular cases. In this teleological sense the law is, indeed, not the totality of norms but the totality of decisions.[20] From this there results the special interest of the lawyer in the precise scope, the limits and the borderline cases, of a law. It shows that his interest in a law, unlike that of the natural scientist, is not so much that in a general statement but rather that in a summarization of many individual statements by way of an economy of thought. Despite the laws that characterize the legal order, the character of legal science is idiographic.

3. Yet individualizing sciences would be drowned in the abundance of individual facts could they not resort to a criterion to distinguish the essential and unessential ones among those individual facts. This criterion is the relation to values. A cultural science embraces only those facts which bear a relation, friendly or hostile, to the cultural values toward which it is oriented, facts by which such values are promoted or hampered, by which they attain, or fail of, realization. However, this relation to values also involves the variability of the subject-matter of the cultural sciences. Every revaluation of the values to which that subject-matter is related involves a restratification of the respective subjects. Every new age withdraws the mark of essentiality from facts that theretofore were related to values, and contrariwise it causes facts theretofore indifferent to emerge into the value-relationship. In every age, for instance, the borderline shifts between facts truly historical and those merely antiquarian. Every age rewrites its history.

"With a Stroke of the Legislator's Pen . . ." So it is no wonder that every age must rewrite its legal science. Kirchmann in his celebrated lecture on *The Worthlessness of Jurisprudence as a Science* felt able to dispose of the scientific character of jurisprudence in the now famous

[18] Schönfeld, Vom Problem der Rechtsgeschichte 324.

[19] The unity of the *a priori* system of categories, by means of which the multitude of national legal orders is worked out, turns legal science into an invisible unit, notwithstanding its apparent division by nations. The unit in this sense may be characterized as "legal problematics," as in Max Salomon, Grundlegung der Rechtsphilosophie.

[20] Isay, Rechtsnorm und Entscheidung 29.

words: "With three amending words by the legislator, whole libraries are turned into waste paper." [21] Even earlier, Pascal said: "There is hardly anything just or unjust that does not change its quality with the change of climate. Three degrees of latitude farther removed from the pole, the whole jurisprudence is overthrown. A meridian determines truth, a few years determine property. The basic laws change: the law has its ages. Odd justice, limited by a river or a mountain! Truth on this side of the Pyrenees, error beyond!" Yet, according to what has been said above, the changeability of the subject-matter of legal science by time and place is no argument against its scientific character; otherwise, one would have to deny the scientific character of history by the same token. To be sure, it might be urged that the above argument against jurisprudence as science was intended to point out not simply that its subject is changeable but that it is changeable arbitrarily. Yet that stroke of the pen of the legislator which withdraws an old subject from and assigns a new subject to legal science is no more "arbitrary" than the stroke of the pen of the poet which changes the value judgments of aesthetics and thus compels a rewriting of the history of literature, or than the stroke of the sword of the general which changes the value judgments of politics and thus demands a rewriting of political history. That stroke of the pen is but a dictated stroke, dictated by history. The only difference between the changeability of the subject of legal science and the changeability of, say, that of historical science is this, that the change in the former case occurs suddenly by one historical act, and in the latter case mostly, if by no means always, by a lengthy historical development.

Turning to Special Problems. With these considerations, the general part of legal philosophy comes to an end. It remains to subject the key problems of the particular fields of law to legal philosophical study. Of necessity, the selection of the questions to be dealt with is to some extent arbitrary, since there is not a single subject that could not be dealt with both by the respective particular science and by philosophy. The selection has been made partly with a view to demonstrating, in problems especially suitable for this purpose, the fruitfulness of the concepts developed in the general part. Before attacking those chief problems of the various fields of law, however, legal philosophical clarity must be reached as to the basic divisions of all law.

[21] On Kirchmann, see, besides numerous apologists of legal science, especially STERNBERG, J. H. v. KIRCHMANN (1908).

SECTION 16

PRIVATE AND PUBLIC LAW

Jus privatum sub tutela juris publici latet.[a] — *Bacon*

The concepts "private law" and "public law" are not among the concepts of positive law which a particular legal order might just as well do without. Rather, they are logically precedent to any legal experience and demand validity at the outset of any legal experience. They are legal concepts *a priori.* Not in that sense that the distinction between private and public law was always recognized: Germanic law of old did not know it; it was adopted only with the reception of Roman Law. Again, not in the sense that every legal order must contain both fields of public and fields of private law: socialism would involve almost complete merging of private law in public law, while anarchism demands a legal order of pure private law. Still less in the sense that the boundary line between private and public law must be identical everywhere; the same phenomena (e.g., the employment relationship) belong now to private, now to public, law. Finally, not in the sense that each field of law must be susceptible of being classed unequivocally as private or as public law; in labor law, or in the law of business regulation, private and public law form an indissoluble mixture.[1] Rather, the concepts "private law" and "public law" are *a priori* only in the sense that with regard to any particular legal rule the question may be asked, and an answer demanded, whether it belongs to private or to public law.[2]

A Priori Character of these Concepts. Now legal concepts *a priori* must be derivable from the *a priori* concept of the law. In fact, the distinction between private and public law is anchored in the very concept of the law. The law as a complex of positive norms presupposes the existence of an authority laying down norms. But if the rules laid down for individuals living together, that is, rules of private law, are really to satisfy

[a] [Private law latently rests under the tutelage of public law.]

[1] Nor can the *a priori* character of these concepts be impaired by the fact, justly stressed by Kelsen in (1931) 66 ARCHIV FÜR SOZIALWISSENSCHAFT UND SOZIALPOLITIK 495, that the concept of private law must frequently serve as a screen to hide relations of dominion, such as that of the employer, which are in truth relations in the nature of public law.

[2] The same question is raised by BURCKHARDT, ORGANISATION DER RECHTSGEMEINSCHAFT (1927) 10 *et seq. Opposing* the *a priori* character, see also E. KAUFMANN, KRITIK DER NEUKANTISCHEN RECHTSPHILOSOPHIE (1921) 86–87.

the reason of existence of all positive law, viz., legal certainty, the authority laying down the norms must itself be bound by them. That obligation which binds the authority enacting norms in favor of the addressees of norms, an obligation in the relationship of super- and subordination, is necessarily of public law character.

But the distinction of private and public law is suggested not only in the concept of law, but even in the idea of law. Justice, being either commutative or distributive justice, i.e., either justice between coequals or justice in the relationship of super- and subordination, itself indicates its two substrata, private and public law.

So the concepts "private" and "public law" are *a priori.* But the relative value and rank of public and private law are subject to historical change, to evaluation according to a world outlook.

Liberal View. To liberalism, private law is the heart of all law, with public law as a narrow protective frame laid around private law and especially private property. The [French] Declaration of the Rights of Man and of the Citizen of 1789 regards the crown as an authority revocably granted by the nation for the benefit of all and not for the monarch's profit, but regards private property as a natural, imprescriptible, inviolable, sacred right: the absolute ruler was to leave his throne only to have absolute capital ascend it.

This relative rank, as between private and public law, which is assumed by liberalism is expressed in the ideas of the social contract doctrine. It involves "a compromise between private law and public law," [3] the attempt to trace super- and subordination in the state to an agreement between the originally coequal individuals, i.e., to dissolve public law fictitiously in private law. Liberalism carried to the extreme, namely, anarchism, seeks to dissolve public law in private law not only fictitiously but really. By refusing to recognize any obligation that is not self-obligation, it makes the social contract doctrine not only the political theory but also the principle of organization of social living together.

In positive law, the liberal view of the relative rank as between private and public law leads to that penetration of the coördinative ideas of private law into public law, which is of the essence of a government of laws. The state in its business relationships [*Fiscus*] is subjected to private law. It assumes the same position as the individual by becoming a party in criminal and administrative procedure. That controversial legal conception, the "public law contract," would involve the state placing itself on the same level as the individual.

[3] L. von Ranke, Politisches Gespräch (1924 ed.) 34.

Conservative and Social Views. Precisely contrary are the conclusions under the opposite view of the precedence of public over private law. From this standpoint, private law appears but as the scope left, provisionally and revocably within all-embracing public law, to private initiative, which is granted in the expectation that it will be used dutifully and may be withdrawn as soon as that expectation is not fulfilled. This is the transindividualistic-conservative standpoint; but on this question it is in fundamental agreement with the individualistic-social standpoint. They differ as to the reasons for the precedence of public law. The former maintains the definitive preëminence of the state over individuals, the latter the preëminence of the state as the protector of the economically weaker individuals. But out of these different reasons there follows the same relative rank as between private and public law.

Social Law. The social-legal view of that relation results from the essence of social law, its devotion to the individual as a social being.[4] Social law [5] renders visible the social differentiations of individuals, their social positions of power or powerlessness, and thereby enables the law to take them into account, to strengthen social impotence and curb social predominance. By so doing, it replaces the liberal idea of equality with the social idea of equalization; it brings to the fore distributive instead of commutative justice; and since equalization by distributive justice necessarily supposes a superior authority above the individuals, it supersedes self-help by the help of organized society, especially the help of the state. This, however, involves the emergence of that great figure of organized society, the state, behind even the most private individual legal relations and their private participants, as the third and chief participant, always observant, ready to intervene, and frequently intervening. It involves a conception of even the most private legal relation as more than merely a concern of the private persons participating therein, as a social-legal relation, which is a relation of public law.

In a social-legal order, therefore, private and public law are not juxtaposed with clear-cut boundary-lines but rather overlap. This admixture, this washing through of private with public law occurs above all in the fields of labor law and business regulation. If the former is to back up social impotence and the latter to put a curb on social predomi-

[4] Attention to this connection is drawn by KASPAR ANRATHS, DAS WESEN DER SOGENANNTEN FREIEN WISSENSCHAFTLICHEN BERUFE (1930) 8 *et seq.*

[5] On the manifold meanings of this word, see GURVITCH, L'IDÉE DU DROIT SOCIAL (1931) 154 *et seq.* The view of social law which is taken in the present book (see also *supra*, sec. 8, p. 103) comes closest to the view of DUGUIT, LES TRANSFORMATIONS DU DROIT PRIVÉ DEPUIS LE CODE NAPOLÉON (2d ed. 1920).

nance by means of social equalization through a power above the individuals, both must contain public and private law, distinguishable indeed but not separable.

What in objective law appears as the publicizing of private law, in subjective rights appears as the penetration of the private title by a content of social duties, such as was expressed as a program in the property clause of the Reich Constitution [of Weimar, 1919], Article 153: "Property obliges. Its use shall at the same time serve the common weal." So social law shows a structure similar to that of the feudal law of the Middle Ages. The latter, too, granted rights as the material basis of services, though the result was not that the right was granted for the sake of service but that the office was based on the right and in turn appeared as a privileged right. But the social law of the present is protected against a similar degeneration by the legal guarantees of the duty content of the right, if only by the guarantee of legislation standing ready to act, ever on the alert to limit or withdraw rights which are not exercised dutifully. Thus, above private property there is suspended the Damocles sword of expropriation, socialization, by the Weimar Constitution, Articles 153, 155, 156.[b]

Nothing expresses the character of a legal order as clearly as the relation in which it puts public and private law and the way in which it distributes the legal relationships between private and public law.[6] The overthrow of feudalism coincided with the growing consciousness of the distinction between private and public law. The development toward government by prerogative [c] was revealed in the freeing of public law from private law pollutions; the parallel though contrary development, the emergence of a government of laws, was revealed in the liberation of private law from public law ties. The no less epochal change we are now passing through, again in the opposite direction, from liberal to social law, is revealed in new public law restrictions being imposed upon private law, especially upon freedom of property and of contract.

[b] [Art. 153, sec. 2: "An expropriation may be resorted to only for the common good and on the basis of a law. It shall take place in exchange for due compensation unless a law of the Reich shall provide otherwise. . ." Art. 155, sec. 2: "Real estate, the acquisition of which is required to satisfy housing needs, to promote settlement and cultivation, or to advance agriculture, may be expropriated." . . . Art. 156, sec. 1: "The Reich may by law transfer to common ownership private economic enterprises suitable for socialization, without prejudice to compensation in analogous application of the provisions for expropriation. It may cause itself, the states or the municipalities to participate in administering economic enterprises and associations or otherwise secure a determining influence therein."]

[6] Cf. Martin Drath, *Das Gebiet des öffentlichen und des privaten Rechts* (1931) 3 ZEITSCHRIFT FÜR SOZIALES RECHT 229 *et seq.*

[c] [Cf. *infra*, § 26, n. a.]

Section 17

The Person

The emancipation of man is accomplished only when the real individual human being takes the abstract citizen back unto himself and, as an individual human being in his empirical life, in his individual work, in his individual relationship, has become a generic being . . . — Karl Marx

The thought of purpose, together with the thought of order, is inherent in the concept of law; hence not only the means-end relation, but also the thought of an end of ends, an ultimate and self-sufficient purpose, is involved in the very concept of law, as an indispensable form of legal thinking. If this is so, the concept of the person, the subject of the law,[a] must be deemed a category of legal thought which is not based upon nor confined to legal experience but is of conceptual necessity and universal validity. For "the subject of the law is a being that is considered by a certain historically given law in the sense of an end unto himself, while the object of the law is one that in the same situation is treated as a mere means to conditional ends." [1]

Person as a Concept of Equality. Ends unto themselves preclude any relation of rank among one another. Consequently, the concept of the person is a concept of equality. As has been shown above (sec. 8, pp. 98 *et seq.*), individualism, in regarding the individual human being as such an ultimate end of the legal order, does not see his concrete individuality; rather, the individual of individualism is an individual without individuality; he is nothing but individualized human freedom, and this concretion of freedom without individuality involves the equality of all individuals. As we have also seen, however (*supra*, sec. 8, p. 103), opposing this concept of an individual, divested of his peculiarity and hence relieved of his social context in the individualistic view of the law, there arose the social approach to the law, which replaces him with the concrete and social man, for instance, the employer and the employee, the laborer and the office worker, in their differentiations of social and economic power.

But the concept of the person, unaffected by this development, remains a concept of equality, whereby the powerful and the powerless,

[a] [In German legal terminology, "subject of the law" is synonymous with "legal person" and "object of the law" has the meaning of "property."]

[1] Stammler, Unbestimmtheit des Rechtsubjekts (1907) 28–29; Theorie der Rechtswissenschaft (1911) 194 *et seq.*

the haves and the havenots, the weak individual person and the mammoth corporate person, are deemed equal. Without that concept of equality, we could not conceive of private law; for, as we have seen, private law is the field of commutative justice, i.e., of the equal measure of exchanged performances, performances being commensurable only if the subjects who exchange them are deemed equal.[2] So both individualistic and social views of the law are bound to start with the concept of equality of the person. The social view by no means dissolves that concept of equality into the differentiated types of the employer, employee, laborer, office worker. Being an employer, employee, laborer, or office worker, in this view marks but different situations occupied by persons who are deemed equal. If back of those social types there did not stand the concept of equality of the person, we should lack the common denominator without which we could not conceive of any comparison and equalization, of any considerations of justice, indeed, of private law and, possibly, of law altogether.

These considerations sufficiently indicate the "artificiality of the subject of the law as against the real plenary subject." [3] Legal equality, equal legal capacity, which is of the essence of the person, does not inhere in human beings and human groups but is only attributed to them by the legal order. Nobody is a person by nature or by birth — as is shown by the legal institution of slavery. To be a person is the result of an act of personification by the legal order. All persons, natural as well as legal ones, are creatures of the law. Speaking quite strictly, the natural persons, too, are "legal persons." No controversy, then, is possible about the "fictitious," i.e., artificial nature of all persons, both natural and legal. The problem of the legal person — fictitious person or real group person? — is rather the problem of its metajuridical substratum. Is there a prejuridical being back of the legal person, like the human being back of the physical person, a being encountered by the law and simply endowed by it with legal personality? This is the problem on which the controversy about the nature of the legal person turns.

Teleological Interpretation of the Problem of the Legal Person. What alone that nature may be we are told by the legal philosophical concept of the person which precedes these considerations: to be a person means to be an end unto oneself. So a man is a person not because he is a

[2] Says Karl Marx: "In order to relate things to one another as commodities, the custodians of commodities must behave toward one another as persons." Cf. PASCHUKANIS, ALLGEMEINE RECHTSLEHRE UND MARXISMS (1929) 87 *et seq.*

[3] Cf. MARCK, SUBSTANZ- UND FUNKTIONSBEGRIFF IN DER RECHTSPHILOSOPHIE (1925) 117.

physical-mental living creature but because in the eyes of the law he represents an end unto himself. So, too, in order to show that groups of persons are entitled to legal personality, we need not show that like men they are biological beings, organisms, but need only show that like individual men they represent ends unto themselves. The "organic" theories of the legal person, on the contrary, search for a biological, instead of the teleological, substratum of the legal person. By way of hypostasis, they substitute naturalistic structures for units of purposes; or at best they hide teleological conclusions behind naturalistic language. It is true that even the legal philosophical definition of the subject of the law which is proposed above refers to a "being" that is deemed an end unto itself by the law. But the relation between being and end is the exact opposite to that assumed by the organic theories. The organic theories of the legal person try first to determine the being that is its substratum, in order then to hearken to its purpose. Contrariwise, the teleological doctrine derives the unity of the being from the independence of the purpose. However, in most cases nothing will at first be discovered back of the legal person but the plurality of the participating individuals, its members, its organs. To be sure, in a particular case there may be back of a legal person a sociological unit, a "community"; but that fact is irrelevant to the question concerning the "real" unit back of the legal person. For unity is never unity as such, it is but unity from a certain point of view. The unity of the substratum of the legal person must be unity from the point of view of its unified purpose. From the viewpoint of the unified transindividual purpose, the individual persons who gather together in order to realize it join in a unit with a common purpose. Accordingly, the real substratum of the legal person would be the individual persons joined in a "teleological unit" by a transindividual purpose that they serve.[4]

However, in our discussion so far, the preliminary question has not yet been answered whether individual human beings may have and pursue transindividual, superhuman, objective purposes, and whether, therefore, there may be specific purposes of legal persons that cannot be resolved into individual purposes of their participants. The answer depends on the fundamental legal philosophical attitude, on the decision between individualistic, transindividualistic, and transpersonal views of the law. The correlation between the three distinctive theories as well as the three different positive legal types of the person, and those three basic views of the law, is a splendid additional confirmation of that basic doctrine of ours.

[4] On teleological unity as the principle of the legal person, cf. GEORG JELLINEK, ALLGEMEINE STAATSLEHRE (3d ed., reprint of 1921) 171.

Savigny, Gierke, Brinz. The individualistic theory of the law is expressed in the fiction theory of the legal person. According to it, there are only individual purposes. "All law," says Savigny, oddly contradicting his basically romantic transindividualistic attitude, "all law exists for the sake of the moral freedom inherent in every single human being; therefore, the original concept of the person must coincide with the concept of the human being." Legal persons would then be persons without any specific substratum. The only subject of purposes is the individual human being. When human groups are endowed with legal personality, they are merely treated as if they were the subjects of purposes, are fictitiously taken for subjects of purposes, for men at large. Legal personality could then only mean separate legal bookkeeping as to certain particular individual purposes, a legislative technique to which no specific prejuridical substratum would correspond.

That individualistic theory of the legal person is opposed by the transindividualistic theory contained in Gierke's doctrine of the real-group person. If we divest it of its organic-naturalistic terms, we may reduce it to the affirmation of distinct transindividual group purposes which cannot be interpreted as merely adding up the individual purposes of the members of the group.

Finally, the theory of the legal person assumes transpersonal appearance in Brinz' theory of "property with a purpose." Here, too, specific purposes are ascribed to the legal person, yet they are not "personal" purposes, in the sense that they are not purposes either of individual persons or of group persons, but are transpersonal, purely objective purposes, say, cultural purposes. Person then means certain goods and men being bound to certain objective tasks, say cultural ones.[5]

Individualistic Fiction Theory, Transindividualistic Real Group Person, Transpersonal Property with a Purpose. Each of these three doctrines starts from a particular kind of legal person as its prototype, to which it tries conceptually to adapt the other types of the legal person. The fiction theory starts from the individual human being; the theory of the real group person, from the private and municipal corporation; the theory of the property with a purpose, from the charitable foundation[b] and the institution of public law. Whereas the fiction theory is compelled to construe the legal persons individualistically, the other two

[5] Hauriou's view of the *institution groupe* seems also to be of a transpersonal kind. Cf. Gurvitch in (1931) ARCHIVES DE PHILOSOPHIE DU DROIT 151 *et seq.*

[b] [Anglo-American law has no equivalent of this German type of legal person, the "foundation" (*Stiftung*) devoted to a cultural purpose. The closest analogy is the charitable trust.]

doctrines are compelled conversely to view even the natural person transindividualistically or transpersonally. In such a view, just as the subjective right turns into an office and a service, the individual's quality as a person means his quality as an organ, the individual being "a subject only inasmuch as he is considered an organ of the community." [6] In the operation of positive law, however, individual personalities, corporations, and institutions are without apology placed side by side as phenomena subject each to but one interpretation: individual personalities to an individualistic, private and municipal corporations to a transindividualistic, foundations and institutions to a transpersonal, interpretation.

Section 18

Ownership

That the man who possesses the Juno of Ludovisi should have the right to destroy her! — Friedrich Hebbel.

To regulate the relations between human beings in a world in which the supply of the goods of life is limited involves the regulation also of the relations of human beings to things, or of the distribution of things among human beings. Thus the law of property is established as a concept that no conceivable legal order can do without. Among the property rights, again, ownership represents such a category of legal thinking that is not based on but rather precedes any legal experience.[1]

A Priori Character of the Concept of Ownership. The multiplicity of possible ways of dealing with things cannot be fully divided up into a number of property rights of limited contents. There is needed a subjective right which places a thing at one's disposal without limiting him to definite ways of dealing with it — a right to the "last word" over the thing: ownership. Ownership contains the right of the owner to all particular ways of dealing. Compared with ownership, therefore, property rights of limited contents may be regarded as rights not in one's own things but only in those of another. Such rights are not conceptually necessary but are rather created by the particular legal order; ownership, on the contrary, is a form of thought indispensable to the

[6] Cf. Binder, Philosophie des Rechts (1925) 448.

[1] Cf. Stammler, Theorie der Rechtswissenschaft (1911) 253 *et seq.*

legal approach. It makes sense to confront any legal order with the question as to each thing: Who is its owner? The answer to that question, to be sure, is to be derived only from experience and is open to criticism. Ownership is an *a priori* legal category; not so, however, is private ownership or common ownership. Whether private or common ownership prevails we may learn from legal experience only; which of them ought to prevail, from legal philosophy only. The legal philosophy of private ownership, in particular, is expressed in the theories of ownership.[2]

Theories of Occupation and of Specification. The oldest and still most widespread philosophcial doctrines of ownership are, the theory of occupation and the theory of specification. Occupation, or the taking possession of ownerless things, expands the rule of man over nature. It turns a mere thing of nature into an economic and cultural good, thus creating a new piece of natural wealth. So occupation, without changing the thing that is taken over, also constitutes specification, for instance, in the case of "original production." However, according to what is called the theory of specification or theory of work in the stricter sense, a thing of nature is fully subjected to the rule of man not simply by taking but only by forming it, by working up the raw material. Accordingly, only work that produces goods creates the legal title of ownership.

But against the theory of work, of which the theory of taking possession has been shown to be a variety, two objections may be raised. In the first place, it may discharge its function to justify private ownership under very definite conditions only, namely, as long as the production of goods is still the work of the individual with his own means of labor: the artisan's work, the peasant's work, and especially mental work. But ever since production has been taking place in the factory or the large estate with another's means of labor, by dividing work and in that sense collectivistically, the same theory of work must inescapably lead to socialist conclusions, to the expropriation of him who owns the means of production and takes no part in the work, and to the common ownership of those who work. Thus, following the theory of work, sec. 950 of the [German] Civil Code provides that he who, by working up or transforming one or more materials, shall produce a new movable shall become the owner of the new thing. That provision, applied to the present state of economics, would mean socialism were it not for the interpretation that by him who works up or transforms the material is to be understood he in whose name, and not he by whose hands, the

[2] Cf. DIEHL AND MOMBERT, AUSGEWÄHLTE LESESTÜCKE ZUM STUDIUM DER POLITISCHEN ÖKONOMIE, vol. 14: DAS EIGENTUM (1924).

work is done. Thus, again, the 1931 encyclical of Pius XI on the social order, recognizing work as a title to possession, immediately adds the limitation that "naturally" only such work as a man does in his own name has the power to create ownership.

Besides this substantive objection concerning their double-edged character, a methodological objection must also be raised against both the theories of work and of occupation. Both justify the acquisition of property on the assumption of the existing institution of private ownership but do not justify that institution itself. They answer the question: Who ought to be private owner? but not the question: Ought there to be private ownership? The answer to the latter question can be obtained only from the fundamental view of the ultimate ends of the legal order. Ownership, like law itself, may be regarded as serving either the individuals, the owners themselves, or society; accordingly, the individualistic and social theories of ownership may be distinguished.[3] The individualistic theory of ownership corresponds to the view of liberalism and democracy. In the social theory of ownership conservatism and socialism meet, differing from each other in that social ownership in the socialist view again ultimately serves the individual or the "society" made up of the individuals, while in the conservative view its ultimate end is the social whole, the collectivity. The individualistic view corresponds to the Roman, while the conservative-social view corresponds to the Germanic, concept of ownership.

Individualistic Theory of Ownership: Goethe. The individualistic theory of ownership or, as we may also call it, the "personality theory" of ownership, has found its noblest expression in Goethe. He has lived it and he has deliberately molded and clearly expressed what he lived. Instead of many passages, two may be quoted:

> Epimetheus: "How much, indeed, is yours?"
> Prometheus: "The circle filled by my activity.
> Nothing above and nothing underneath."

And again:

> Faust: "If you inherit ancestors' estates,
> Earn what you would possess.
> What you use not, is burdening, valueless;
> The moment can use but what it creates."

Here, a dynamic view opposes the static view that private ownership, once acquired, is permanently established. Ownership needs continuous

[3] Thus JHERING, 1 DER ZWECK IM RECHT (4th ed. 1904) 404 *et seq.*

"integration," to use this fashionable term. It needs ever again to be made effective, utilized, and thus acquired and created anew; it is a work wrought continuously in ever renewed occupation and specification. Doubtless Goethe in this doctrine of ownership thought of what he loved most of his property, his collections. They represent one of his great works, and not the least among them: in them, too, he let his personality fully live, work, and express itself, in them he became aware of ownership as expansion and expression of the personality, as projection of the personality. Oriented toward and penetrated by the personality, such ownership becomes an organic whole in which each single piece of property gains in value, even in economic value, by its coördination in sets of related things. There emerges a new unit which is more valuable than the sum of its parts; by its very existence, ownership becomes productive. The collector's mentality often represents only one aspect of this "chemically pure" ownership: the "collector of rarities" enjoys not so much the thing itself as its sole possession, the exclusion of others. But in Goethe the joy of possession and the enjoyment of the thing are finely balanced. Says he to the Chancellor von Müller: "I need possession to get the true concept of the objects. Only possession permits me to judge calmly and impartially, free from the illusions which are fed by the desire for a thing. And so I love possession for the sake not of the thing possessed but of my education, and because it makes me calmer and thereby happier." Possession of things for the sake of full enjoyment of things! Yet his enjoyment of things attains its fullness only in communication with others. It is the collector Goethe who in his *Years of Wandering* [a] has coined the unsurpassed formula for his individualistic theory of ownership, and for its turn toward the social doctrine of ownership: "Possession and the common good"—which means: possession *as* a common good.

According to the personality theory, ownership is not the rule of man over things but a relation between man and things. Not only man has his dignity, the thing too has a dignity of its own. Not only does man utilize the thing, the thing in turn demands something of man; it demands to be taken care of and not to be wasted, to be utilized and enjoyed, all according to its value; in a word, it demands love. So the relation between man and property approximates that between man and man, not only where such property consists in domestic animals, which any non-lawyer is loath even to call chattels, but also where it is represented by lifeless objects. The religious person expresses this relation of mutual duties between man and thing, this claim of the thing to

[a] [His novel WILHELM MEISTER'S WANDERJAHRE.]

be not only possessed but dealt with according to its own law, when he speaks of a "gift from God." As a gift from God the "daily bread," in particular, partakes of the sanctity of the bread which in the eucharist is transformed into the body of the Lord.[4] So the mother prohibits her child from playing with bread, telling him the legend of the punishment meted out to those who violate this prohibition.[5] This veneration of the bread was relied upon cleverly by Mussolini for the promotion of domestic agriculture, by celebrating a festival in honor of the bread.

However, these points have been made precisely in order to show how narrow is the field of application of the personality theory. That mental attitude which the personality theory of ownership assumes is conceivable only with regard to a small circle of things, to clothing and dwelling, books and collections, tools and handiworks. That doctrine fits into an economic world of artisans and peasants, and not one of factories, banks, and large estates.[6] In this latter world, the things that are appreciated for their own sake have changed into values and commodities which are appreciated only according to their price, which one has, not in order to possess them permanently, but rather to get rid of them as quickly as possible — thus truly "realizing" them only by turning them into money. Whereas in "ownership" the emphasis is on what is one's "own," the qualitative correlation of the thing with its owner, now an aggregate of things is conceived of as a "fortune" according to its monetary value only, as a quantitative power in the market of commodities. In a fortune, ownership is denatured: a fortune includes all that is worth money, and preëminently money itself; yet money is not really a thing any more but a claim to things, not unlike a chose in action. Thus, under our present economic system, things, money, and choses in action merge in a new conceptual unit, which does not coincide with but overlaps the old conceptual unit of ownership. This inadequacy of the concepts of the legal order of ownership as contrasted with the conceptual developments of the economic order, and the changed function of the concept of ownership in this economic order, have recently been impressively set forth.[7] Here they are of interest only from one point of view, namely, that apart from a quite narrow circle of things, owner-

[4] The view of ownership as "objective service of values" has been set forth beautifully by Brunstäd, *Das Eigentum und seine Ordnung*, in FESTSCHRIFT FÜR BINDER (1930).

[5] Cf., e.g., DEECKE, LÜBISCHE GESCHICHTEN UND SAGEN (5th ed. 1911) no. 216.

[6] The relative correctness of the theories of ownership each for a limited circle of economic goods is pointed out by Tönnies, *Eigentum*, in HANDWÖRTERBUCH DER SOZIOLOGIE.

[7] Cf. KARL RENNER, DIE RECHTSINSTITUTE DES PRIVATRECHTS UND IHRE SOZIALE FUNKTION (1929).

ship has lost the character of a mental relation and has turned into a mere purpose relation.[8]

Individualistic Theory of Ownership: Fichte. Still a second objection may be raised against the "personality" theory [of ownership]. Beccaria once called ownership a "terrible right." Indeed, ownership shows not only the affirmative aspect of the enjoyment of the thing but also the negative one of the exclusion of others; and in its sociological form as capital, ownership excludes others not only from a particular piece of property but from property altogether. The correlative to capital is the proletariat, the correlative to ownership in this form is the propertyless human being. So the unfolding of the personality in a very few is bought at such a price that it becomes impossible in numberless others. Hence the personality theory must be transformed if it is to afford not only an opportunity for the strong, as in liberalism, but also an equal chance for all, as in democracy. It must add to the right *of* ownership the right *to* ownership, that is, the right to work. This is done by Fichte, who reasons not as a socialist denying private ownership but as a democrat affirming private ownership. Private ownership grants the enjoyment of a thing to one, and excludes therefrom another. From the standpoint of democratic equality it is justified only to the extent that that enjoyment is universal and this exclusion is mutual. This thought is expressed in the assumption of a fictitious mutual agreement of guaranty of the owners. Just as the individuals guarantee one another their freedom in the social contract, so they guarantee one another their ownership in this property contract. But this contract can be considered to be concluded and valid only as between owners. The propertyless person has no interest in adhering to a contract by which he would merely promise to respect the ownership of others without gaining a claim to the respect of any legal goods of his own, so he cannot be fictitiously deemed a party to this contract. Therefore that property contract does not bind the propertyless. Everyone possesses his property only upon the condition that each man can live from his own property. From the moment anyone suffers want, nobody owns that part of his property which is needed to free the indigent one from his want. If but a single individual is excluded from ownership, ownership ceases to exist in society.

The legal philosophical fiction of the contract of owners hides the sociological fact that the economic order founded upon private ownership was indeed designed, and functioned without complaints, only for

[8] Tönnies accordingly distinguishes between property as the object of the essential will and property as the object of the elective will; cf. his *Das Eigentum* (SCHRIFTEN DER SOZIOLOGISCHEN GESELLSCHAFT IN WIEN, 1926) 19 *et seq.*

a state of society in which none but small owners faced one another in approximate equality. All parties were equally interested in maintaining the state of society. Where everyone may say to another: *Do ut des*,[b] everyone may also tell the other: *Habeas quod habeo*.[c] The mutuality of the commodities market produced the mutual recognition of ownership. As long as each economic unit was self-sufficient in the closed economy of the house, ownership was a relation to a thing rather than a relation to other men. Only when the thing becomes a commodity do we become more distinctly aware of the relation of our own thing to others and of another's thing to ourselves, of the claim to mutual respect for ownership, of ownership as a right between men. Yet this "mutuality" justification of ownership is at once lost after the economy of the free market, developing according to its own laws, has separated the owners and the propertyless and produced a class which no longer has any interest in recognizing the right of ownership.[9]

Social Theory of Ownership: Encyclical Quadragesimo Anno; Constitution of Weimar. However, even the individualistic theories of ownership were never purely individualistic. They were based on the assumption of a prestabilized harmony between individualistic selfishness and the common weal. The social theories of ownership differ from them by the recognition that this prestabilized harmony is an illusion, that the social function of ownership is not inseparably bound up with its individualistic one but needs to be specially implemented and safeguarded.[10] Recently, the social theory of ownership has found an authoritative expression in the above mentioned encyclical *Quadragesimo anno*. It distinguishes between the right of ownership and the use of property. The right of ownership expresses only the individual aspect of ownership, looking toward private benefit; the use of property expresses the social aspect of ownership, looking toward the common weal. The individual function of the right of ownership belongs to natural law, while the social function governing the use of property belongs to ethics and hence cannot be enforced by litigation — unless the ethical social duty

[b] [I give that you give.]

[c] [You may have what I have.]

[9] Cf. Paschukanis, Allgemeine Rechtslehre und Marximus (1929) 102 *et seq.*

[10] It is formalistic and not illuminating to call the social theory of ownership the "legality" theory. That term is designed to bring out that the law is not bound by prelegal natural law to regulate the right of ownership in a definite sense, but that it autonomously decides upon this regulation. But since the natural law against which the legality theory is directed bears the stamp of individualism, the legality theory itself can be understood only in the sense of the social theory of ownership.

of the owner has become the subject of positive legislation. But the legislator may and ought to regulate the use of property more strictly with regard to the requirements of the common weal; indeed (though this is stated in a somewhat inconspicuous passage of the encyclical) he may "reserve certain kinds of goods for the public hand because the excessive power connected with them cannot be delivered into private hands without endangering the public good." So the individualistic natural right of ownership, the social ethics of the use of property, and the liability to positive legal regulation requiring its use for social purposes and even taking it for social reasons, these three overlap in a compromise. It is interesting that this corresponds precisely to the regulation of the property clauses of the [Reich] Constitution of Weimar [of 1919]. In article 153 of the Reich Constitution, too, individualistic ownership is first guaranteed, but this guarantee is bound to the moral duty of social use: "Property obliges. Its use shall at the same time serve the common good." [d] "This clause binds the citizen but as a moral rule; the judge, as a rule of construction; the legislator, as a directive legal rule" (Giese). Thus the law directed by social viewpoints appears as the third power legally governing ownership: "Its contents and its limits depend on the laws." [e] Legislation is thus placed in a position to raise the "social mortgage of property" from the sphere of merely moral to that of legal validity. Thus the social function of ownership, though still left in the realm of ethics, turns into a potential legal duty. The social duties of ownership are put, not indeed under the sanction of a law now in force, but under the sanction of a law possibly to be enacted. Thus, even in the legal view of today, private ownership appears as an area of activity for private initiative, entrusted to the individual by the community, entrusted in the expectation of its social use, always revocable if that expectation is not fulfilled; hence, as a right conditional and limited, and no longer one justified in itself, limitless, "sacred and inviolable."

How far the social function of private ownership may be reconciled with its individualistic function or how far ineradicable individualistic abuses will force us to make use of the sanction of the social function of private ownership and to transfer to the community the private ownership of certain objects, such as land and the means of production, are questions of economic factual science and not of a legal-philosophical science of values. They are questions concerning not the purpose but its attainability. For that very reason, they are questions susceptible of an unequivocal answer, with which, however, we are not concerned.

[d] [*Ibid.* sec. 3.]

[e] [*Ibid.* sec. 1.]

Section 19

Contracts

Isn't it enough that this my spoken word
Forever should be governing my days?
Does not the world rush on in all its currents,
And I'm to be one whom a promise stays? — [*Goethe*], *Faust*

In the world of the law, title to property and chose in action represent as it were matter and force: The title to property is the resting, while the chose in action is the moving, element of the world of the law. The chose in action carries with it the germ of its death. It perishes when it attains its end in being fulfilled. Title to property, especially ownership, is intended to be permanent. It continues in being fulfilled. Therefore, life under law is static in character as long as it is based predominantly on title to property, but dynamic in character when the chose in action becomes its principal foundation.

Statics and Dynamics of Life under the Law. Static was life under the law while the order of work was still based on ownership, while the worker was the owner of the means and the products of work, or the master of work was the owner of the workers as slaves. Dynamic is life under the law of the capitalistic present. Ownership no longer affords merely power over things; it affords power over human beings; it turns into capital. In the capitalistic economic order, freedom of property becomes effective especially as freedom of contract. Ownership becomes the economic center of contractual relationships which grant power; the contractual relationships become "institutions connected with ownership," [1] with ownership attracting work, as in the contract of employment, or work attracting ownership, as in the loan.[a] Economic values are in incessant movement from one chose in action to another; their state of rest, their repose in a title to property becomes more and more abbreviated. Even their final economic status, the investment, assumes the legal form of the chose in action or the obligation. The dynamic restlessness of life under such a law, in which the objects of rights are incessantly on the move, is in sharp contrast with the static immobility of life under a law in which the objects of rights are normally tied to a definite point of the legal world.

[1] Cf. Karl Renner, *op. cit.*, 43 *et seq.*
[a] [E.g., an artisan becomes an enterpriser by borrowing capital from a bank.]

Now the lever of this whole moving world is the free contract. In order really to grasp its essence one does well to recall the position conceded to it by the system of natural law.

The Social Contract and the Contracts of Private Law: Fictitious Elements of the Contract. In the doctrine of natural law,[b] the contract was the foundation of all law, the solution of the basic problem of individualistic legal philosophy: How the law may serve the individuals exclusively and yet at the same time bind the individuals. To base the state with its legal power of command upon a contract of its members seemed to demonstrate all obligation ultimately as self-imposed obligation. The social contract seemed to succeed in reducing all heteronomy to autonomy and therewith in dissolving all public into private law.

Yet in truth heteronomy was by no means conquered, autonomy by no means established, least of all an autonomy as here intended. For, whereas autonomy elsewhere means that one is obligated only by a duty that one recognizes by one's self, autonomy here is understood in the quite different sense of one's self-created obligation. Now the contractual will is, indeed, the will to oblige oneself but is not itself the obligation. The will alone can never impose an obligation, neither upon another nor upon one's self; it can at most intend to produce the state of facts with which a norm superior to the will connects the obligation.[2] It is not the contract, then, that binds; rather is it the law that binds one to the contract. Contractual obligation is not suitable to serve as the basis of the obligation of the law; quite on the contrary, it presupposes the obligation of the law.

But the social contract remains heteronomous also in a much cruder sense: The individual's will that creates the contractual obligation and his will that is bound by that obligation, are not identical. Governed by the social contract are the real individuals; yet as contracting parties they are fictitiously taken to be the supposedly rational individuals, those who supposedly follow solely their own true interest. The social contract is intended not as a fact but as a standard. It is to affirm, not that the state originated in real contracts of real men, but that its value is to be measured by the success or failure of the attempt to conceive of it as originating in a contract of men who supposedly were purely rational beings. Thus, the social contract represents a heteronomous

[b] ["Natural law" here refers especially to the "natural rights" theories of the seventeenth and eighteenth centuries.]

[2] Cf. REINACH, DIE APRIORISCHEN GRUNDLAGEN DES BÜRGERLICHEN RECHTES (1913) 42 *et seq.*; BASSENGE, DAS VERSPRECHEN (1930) 10 *et seq.* [The argument here is based on Kant's basic thesis that one's duties can arise only from one's inner conviction, applying a norm.]

obligation of empirical individuals by the fictitious will of fictitious rational beings.

It is illuminating to compare the ordinary contract of private law with the social contract as thus analyzed. The contractual will in private law is hardly less fictitious than the will of the contracting parties of the social contract; indeed, in one respect it is even more fictitious. For the state is liable to be measured at any moment of its life by the standard of the social contract; thus the social contract must be thought of, not as concluded at some definite moment, but as capable of being concluded anew at any moment. The contract of private law, on the other hand, belongs to a definite moment of time. Yet it is binding permanently beyond that moment of time, and this means that the obliging will and the obliged will diverge in it to an even higher degree than in the social contract: The obliging will is the will of yesterday, the obliged one, the will of today and tomorrow. The obliged will is the fickle, empirical one, the obliging will is the will thought of as consistent, willing today what it willed yesterday — hence a fictitious will. The will therefore does not bind itself; rather, the changeable empirical will is bound to the fictitious permanent will. Contractual obligation is not autonomy but heteronomy.

One might object that in the contract of private law a fact must have existed at least once, namely, the real expression of the will of real men, while in the social contract the contractual fiction needs no factual point of reference. But this difference must be grossly exaggerated if it is to explain the contractual will as less fictitious in the contract of private law than in the social contract. For, on the one hand, the fiction of the social contract also refers to a fact: Only he who belongs to the state may be fictitiously taken to be a contracting party of the social contract; only to him may all that is included in the fictitious social contract be imputed as willed. On the other hand, in construing the real expression of the wills of the parties to a contract of private law everything is deemed willed that would consistently have to have been willed by them. Thus, to the contracting party in private law we impute, on the one hand, his will once expressed as continuing and, on the other, the consistent consequences of his expressed will as implicitly willed. So a good deal of the will of the contracting party is the legislator's will imputed to the party. The latter's will does not bind itself, but the law binds him to his will.

Will Theory and Declaration Theory. These considerations open the way for the view that as a matter of legal logic, or, at any rate, of natural law, it is not conceptually necessary to think of the contract of private law in terms of the will theory, which limits the obligation of the contract to the scope of what was actually willed by the contracting parties. It is not the will that binds; rather, insofar as the obligation of the contract is bound to the will, it is bound to it by the law. The legality theory proves true with regard to contracts as well as to ownership. Yet on the basis of the legality theory, there arises anew the controversy between the "will" theory and the "declaration" theory, as a controversy, not over legal-logical concepts, but about legal philosophical principles: How far ought the law to prescribe the obligation of the contract to be governed by the will, and how far by its declaration? In this controversy, the interests of private autonomy are opposed by those of the security of trade and intercourse, those of individual freedom by those of social peace, in short, the individualistic by the social view of the law.[3] The individualistic view of the law demands that, on the one hand, contracts are binding only as far as the contractual will extends (will theory) but, on the other hand, they are *always* binding as far as the contractual will extends (freedom of contract). To this doctrine, the social view of the law opposes two other rules: That the contract may bind one not only as far as one's will extends but also as far as the reliance of the other party upon one's declaration extends (declaration theory); and that contracts are not necessarily binding as far as the will extends but may be without binding force for many reasons (limitations upon freedom of contract).

Legal limitations upon freedom of contract have proved necessary because by a kind of dialectical process [c] freedom of contract had limited itself and frequently destroyed itself. From the outset, limits were drawn for it by the social area within which it moved, by the *milieu contractuel*.[4] For instance, in a contract of sale the price is determined not by the two contracting parties but by all those who enter into contracts about objects of the same kind; by the market. Moreover, only in a society of men of equal social power, a society of none but small owners, could freedom of contract be freedom of contract for all. When the contracting parties face one another as haves and havenots, the freedom of contract turns into freedom to dictate on the part of the socially powerful and bondage to dictation on the part of the socially impotent. Finally, the more the free capitalistic economy turns into a controlled one, the more the freedom of individuals to contract is curbed by the

[3] Cf. Gysin, *Das Rechtsgeschäft in der modernen Privatrechtsjurisprudenz* (1929) ZEITSCHRIFT DES BERNISCHEN JURISTENVEREINS, reprint, 38.

[c] [The "dialectical process" of Hegel: the resolution of conflicts in the course of history.]

[4] Cf. EMMANUEL LÉVY, LA VISION SOCIALISTE DU DROIT (1926) 99.

rule of groups. Freedom of contract itself first rendered possible the formation of groups of all kinds; now these groups in turn draw more and more narrow limits around freedom of contract.[5]

With juridical freedom of contract thus turning into social servitude by contract, the law is challenged to restore social freedom of contract by limiting juridical freedom of contract. Such statutory limitations upon freedom of contract are possible, and are, indeed, already in force, in the most manifold forms: In the form of provisions declaring void certain types of agreements; in the form of a power of avoidance conferred on particular public authorities; in the form of mandatory statutory requirements; in the form of collective bargaining impervious to modification by individual agreements; and, finally, in the form of duties to contract and of compulsory contracts. Whole new fields of law, such as labor law and business regulation, in the last analysis represent such limitations upon previous freedom of contract. Like ownership, freedom of contract is confined within the limits of the law, and the individual interest is therewith confined within the limits of the social interest, by the provision of Article 152 of the Reich Constitution [of Weimar, 1919]: "In economic intercourse, freedom of contract shall prevail in accordance with the laws." [6]

SECTION 20

MARRIAGE

Here, again, is the tragic fundamental phenomenon of life creating a form for itself which it finds indispensable yet which by the very fact of being a form is hostile to the mobility and to the individuality of life. The old form has been outlived, no new form has been created yet, so people think formlessness adequately expresses the impetus of life. — *Georg Simmel*

Nowhere is the "material qualification of the idea" (sec. 2, pp. 53–54, *supra*), the dependency of the "ideas" upon the *realia* of the law,[1] shown more clearly than in the law of marriage. Marriage confronts the law as

[5] Cf. Pappenheim, *Die Vertragsfreiheit und die moderne Entwicklung des Verkehrsrecht*, in FESTSCHRIFT FÜR GEORG COHN (1915) 291 *et seq.*

[6] On the above, cf. Darmstaedter, *Sozialwirtschaftliche Theorie und sozialwirtschaftliche Praxis des kapitalistischen Zeitalters*, 25 ARCHIV FÜR RECHTS-UND WIRTSCHAFTSPHILOSOPHIE 180 *et seq.*

[1] Cf. Eugen Huber, *Über die Realien der Gesetzgebung* (1914) 1 ZEITSCHRIFT FÜR RECHTSPHILOSOPHIE 39 *et seq.*

a natural and social state of facts of strong naturalistic and sociological autonomy, which the law cannot form autocratically but to which rather it has to adjust itself. It is not accidental that the Roman jurist chooses for an example of natural law, of the "nature of the thing" which even the lawmaker cannot escape, precisely the sexual community and the procreation and upbringing of children: *Hinc descendit maris atque feminae coniunctio, quam nos matrimonium appellamus, hinc liberorum procreatio, hinc educatio.*[a] The task of legal philosophy can only consist in showing how the law may and ought to adjust itself to marriage as a natural and social state of facts which must be regarded as given; to subject this very state of facts to a critique would be the task of a social philosophy of marriage.

The Problem: The Social Substratum of the Law of Marriage. That legal philosophical task, however, is rendered especially difficult at present because changes have appeared in that natural and social state of affairs which the legal philosophy of marriage is to presuppose as given. The natural foundations of marriage and the family, the sexual relation and the relation of descent, had been overlaid by a sociological layer which became determinative of the juridical form of marriage. Hence the latter is not unequivocally determined by the natural foundations. For instance, the naturalistically uniform sexual relation may be evaluated as legally recognized marriage or as legally rejected concubinage, and the naturalistically uniform relation of descent may be evaluated as legitimacy or as illegitimacy. Now the development which we are witnessing is the breakdown of that sociological intermediate layer, with the law of marriage thus more and more immediately resting upon the natural foundation of the factual situation of marriage.

How has that breakdown come about? In the precapitalistic development, house and home were still known as economic units, as original cells of the economic body, in handicraft as well as in agriculture. Man and wife, parents and children divided and joined in common economic tasks. Capitalism has torn asunder the productive community of the house, the home, the family. Stronger sociological structures, new economic units and enterprises, drew the individual members out of the family and turned each of them into a member of another economic unit. The man went to the mill, the wife helped in another household, the daughter worked as a salesgirl in a department store, the son perhaps as a clerk in an office — the family ceased to be a sociological struc-

[a] [Hence arises the conjunction of man and woman which we call marriage, hence the procreation of children, hence education. — This passage from Ulpian is to be found in Justinian's Institutes, I, 2, pr.]

ture with productive tasks of its own. Less and less it survived even as a consuming community. It was relieved of increasingly more of the economic tasks of consumption; spinning, weaving, and candlestick-making, washing, baking, and canning, the poultry yard and the vegetable garden, were separated from the economy of the house and turned over to distinct industrial enterprises; even the former tasks of education in the family were diverted to nursery homes, kindergartens, and schools. Thus emptied, the family lost the character of an organism, an individuality. The same tenement housed numerous families and dissolved them all into an amorphous and therefore clashing community of corridors and staircases. The family has lost its structure and has become an empty relation between family members, while around it new communities are about to form, communities of enterprises, of crafts, of political convictions. The endeavor to draw the cultural and juridical conclusion from that basically economic development, toward an individualistic dissolution of the family into its elements, is expressed in the feminist movement and the youth movement. Our whole problem of marriage and education today is embraced in that development of marriage and the family from communities to relations, in which man and wife, parents and children now face one another, eye to eye, connected by no objective tasks but by exclusively personal, psychological, and physical contacts.[2]

The social and natural state of affairs of marriage is difficult for the law to grasp, not only because it has begun to shift but also because it is extremely complex anyhow, because it presents the most diverse aspects to the law and the law may regulate it from the most manifold points of view. The law may view marriage as a sexual, erotic, or ethical community of life, as parentage, as a place for education and as a means of carrying out population policies, as a secular institution of the state, or as a religious institution of the church; and from each of these points of view the law of marriage could not but develop quite differently.[3] But all these legal views of marriage and the family may be divided into the two great groups, individualistic and transindividualistic views. In the individualistic view marriage appears, metaphorically, as a contractual relation entered into by the spouses; in the transindividualistic view, it is conceived of as the matrimonial state entered by the spouses. The former view starts primarily from the relation of the spouses to each other, the latter from their relation to the children.

[2] Cf. the description of the dissolution of the home, RENNER, *op. cit.* 34–35, and especially the touching picture of the proletarian family, *op. cit.* 133–134.

[3] Excellent statements, in the same direction, in GUNDOLF, GOETHE (10th ed. 1922) 566.

The Transindividualistic View of Marriage: The Encyclical Casti Connubii. The transindividualistic view of marriage is presented in superbly concise form in the Catholic doctrine of marriage, which has found its last expression in the encyclical on marriage *Casti connubii* of 1930. Like the code of the Church (Codex Juris Canonici, Canon 1013, sec. 1), the papal circular letter declares: "The primary purpose of marriage is the procreation and education of the child"; "purposes of the second order are mutual aid, manifestation of conjugal love, and regulation of the natural desire, purposes which the spouses are by no means prohibited from seeking, provided that the nature of the act and hence its subordination to the primary purpose, is not affected." That statement of the purpose of marriage governs the parts played in marriage by the will of the spouses, on the one hand, and by the norm, on the other. The liberty of the spouses "is concerned with this alone, whether those entering into marriage really intend to enter a marriage and to enter it with this particular person. But the essence of marriage is completely beyond the reach of human liberty so that anyone, once he has entered into marriage, is governed by its laws and essential qualities which derive from God." From this view of marriage as a matrimonial state superior to the will of the spouses, there follows the rejection of the conclusions that would have to be drawn from the contractual character of marriage: the legal equality of the spouses and the dissolubility of the marriage for a breach of the contract or by a contrary contract. The Christian marriage is "a symbol of the perfect unity between Christ and the Church"; and as Christ is the head of the Church, so the husband is the head of the wife; as Christ may not be divorced from the Church, so the spouses may not be divorced from each other. Finally, marriage both in its origin and its destination belongs to religion and the church: its origin is in the sacrament and its destination is "to take care of the preservation and expansion of mankind on earth, to bring up worshippers of the true God, and to turn the offspring to the Church of Christ."

The Transindividualistic View of Marriage: The Constitution of Weimar. Whereas in the Catholic view "the family is superior to the state," in accordance with the religious and ecclesiastic destination of the family, the political-conservative view orients marriage entirely toward purposes of the state. The marriage clauses of the Reich Constitution [of Weimar, 1919] are still influenced by this conservative view of marriage.[4] According to the Reich Constitution, article 119, just as accord-

[4] On the following, see Wieruszowski in *Nipperdey*, 2 GRUNDRECHTE UND GRUNDPFLICHTEN DER REICHSVERFASSUNG (1930) 72 *et seq.*

ing to Codex Juris Canonici, Canon 1013, sec. 1, marriage serves the twofold purpose of procreation and education of the child, being characterized as "foundation of family life" and of "the preservation and increase of the nation," with the first characterization obviously referring to the educational tasks of the family which are regulated in article 120.[b] But whereas in the Codex Juris Canonici these two purposes are subordinated to ecclesiastical religious points of view, in the Reich Constitution they are placed in the context of the secular state. The task of the family in population policies is characterized in the words: "preservation and increase of the *nation*"; so, too, the educational task is conceived entirely in the secular sense of the state, both as to its ultimate end, "social fitness," and as to its organs, "watched over by the community of the state." In the view of marriage of the Constitution of Weimar, as in that of the papal encyclical, the transindividualistic character of marriage is expressed in its direction toward the child, more emphatically in the assumption that its goal is "plenty of children," the "preservation and increase of the nation," that is to say, if not the greatest possible increase, at any rate no decrease in the population figures. No room is given in the Reich Constitution to the thought that conditions, especially economic conditions, might demand a limitation of population figures, or to the thought that on eugenic grounds the quality of the offspring might be preferable to its quantity. But a purely quantitative population policy is compatible only with a transindividualistic view of the state, in which the goal of the life of the state is seen, not in the happiness and perfection of individuals, but in the military and economic strength of the nation, in that expansive pressure of population against the frontiers which prevents it from yielding to the population pressures of other nations. However, one concession to the individualistic view of marriage has been made by the Reich Constitution: in the transindividualistic view of marriage, the superiority of the matrimonial state over the interests of the spouses is usually expressed in the superiority of the husband over the wife; the Reich Constitution, on the contrary, demands "equal rights of both sexes" in accordance with the contractual view of marriage.

[b] [Art. 119, sec. 1: "The Constitution affords especial protection to marriage as the foundation of family life and of the preservation and increase of the nation. Marriage rests on equal rights of both sexes." Art. 119, sec. 2: ". . . Families with plenty of children are entitled to equalizing consideration." Art. 120: "Education of the offspring for bodily, mental, and social fitness is a supreme duty and natural right of parents, whose activities are watched over by the community of the state."]

The Individualistic View of Marriage. While in the transindividualistic view marriage is regarded essentially as a community for propagation, in the individualistic view it is characterized as a community of love. The ascendancy of liberalism inaugurates the ideal of the love match, seeking its legal form in the favorite natural law concept of the contract.[5] Yet there is a contradiction between the love match and the legal form that is hard to reconcile. Eroticism, that most capricious and willful phenomenon, and law, the most rational and consistent order of human life, do not let themselves be joined like substance and form. Eroticism may be ecstasy or passionless, deliberate pleasure, it may be mysticism or light-hearted play; one thing only its very essence resists: "matrimonial duty." So it seems that the erotic marriage must be a marriage outside the law, a marriage not of compulsion but of conscience, indeed, not a marriage of conscience but "free love." It seems to range with a series of other phenomena from which the law has more and more consistently withdrawn because their essence is of human inwardness, inaccessible to legal compulsion: friendship and sociability, art and science, morals and religion.

But the denial of the law of marriage, the demand for free love, is not the last word even of an individualistic view of marriage. Eroticism confronts the law with a dilemma: Eros, transitory and changeable as a fact of emotion, lays claim in its exaltation to the permanence, nay, eternity, of its emotion. Though one may know of the transitoriness of love, each new love believes itself to be eternal. This belief of love in its eternity is like the will's consciousness of its freedom.[6] Just as the will is again and again experienced as free, no matter how irrefutably it is recognized as unfree, so the transitory love experiences itself again and again as eternal. Love in its transitoriness rejects legal bonds, yet in its claim to eternity it wants to bind itself and be bound. Thus Eros stands in a peculiarly ambiguous relation to legal marriage, both resisting it and seeking ultimate fulfillment in it. The law of marriage with all its bonds is therefore supported by the basic erotic conviction and will. Its task then would be to support this erotic conviction of eternity and this erotic will to eternity — not unlike the ethos which by presupposing freedom really produces freedom, saying: Thou canst for thou shalt. This task of the law of marriage is not infinite; it can be accomplished because the erotic relation in marriage imperceptibly becomes associated with a wealth of practical relations, which as permanent contents bridge the

[5] Cf. Friedrich Engels, Der Ursprung der Familie (20th ed. 1921) 70 *et seq.*

[6] On the problem of freedom, cf. the discussion of freedom of the will in my Grundzüge der Rechtsphilosophie (1914) 64 *et seq.*, which is not repeated in this edition.

gaps and changes in the erotic relation and outlast its dying down. Common interests of the most varied kinds, above all the common parental interests, substitute a firm, durable, increasingly stronger foundation for the original subjective and fragile emotional basis of marriage.[7]

Yet such a view of legal marriage cannot surmount its problems. Legal forms are usually cut out for the average case of the social phenomena; but the legal form of marriage as here depicted is oriented toward an ideal case. The present crisis in the law of marriage is due to precisely this, that that form of legal marriage, cut out for the ideal case, must become disastrous for the spouses when the ideal is not fulfilled, that is, not only in exceptionally unhappy but even in average cases. As a matter of consistency, that ideal justification of marriage involves the demand for its indissolubility, which must turn marriage into a prison if the illusive claim to eternity of the erotic experience fails to be confirmed later in the reality of common parental and other interests. So representatives of this view of marriage have found themselves compelled in varying degrees to make concessions to the transitoriness of Eros, which is never excluded by the claim to eternity. Such concessions include the demand for a relaxation of the law of divorce, the adoption of the "break-up" test rather than the culpability test as the ground for divorce, and proposals to introduce a temporary marriage, trial marriage, or companionate marriage.

Soviet Russia; Law of Marriage and Socialism. The most radical development toward the contractual marriage with almost no legal forms has taken place in the law of marriage of Soviet Russia.[8] It involves the informal establishment and the unconditional and informal dissolubility, of the matrimonial relationship. Its establishment requires no coöperation by the state; registration of the marriage facilitates its proof but is not a prerequisite of its existence. Marriage becomes a purely factual state; it is no longer a legal relation but only a state of facts with legal effects. In the "factual marriage," the contrast between what used to be marriage and what used to be concubinage is done away with; thus, on the one hand, the legally binding force of what used to be marriage is diminished but, on the other, the outlawry of concubinage is supplanted by legal safeguards. In marriage, according to its contractual character, there prevails the most complete equality of the

[7] On the preceding, cf. MARRIANNE WEBER, DIE IDEE DER EHE UND DIE EHESCHEIDUNG (1929).

[8] Cf. Freund, *Zivilrecht der Sowjetunion* (in HEINSHEIMER, ZIVILGESETZE DER GEGENWART; 1927), and the understanding and unprejudiced appraisal by AGNES MARTENS-EDELMANN in (1931) ZEITSCHRIFT FÜR RELIGION UND SOZIALISMUS 38 *et seq.*

spouses with reciprocal obligations of alimony and mutual shares in property acquired during marriage. Finally, dissolution of the marriage is possible, without the requirement of definite prerequisites or definite forms, on the ground of mutual consent or at the choice of either spouse; here, too, registration is only declaratory and not constitutive. "People think formlessness adequately expresses the impetus of life" (Simmel).

The Soviet Russian law of marriage is in accordance with the demands put forward as early as August Bebel's famous book on woman and socialism, *Die Frau und der Sozialismus*. He had spoken of marriage as a "private contract without intervention of a functionary." It may seem odd that socialism, elsewhere emphasizing the social character of legal relationships and the implications of social purposes even in relations of private law, strives to give the law of marriage a purely individualistic, non-state and desocialized form. But the individualistic dissolution of marriage and the family is not a demand of socialism; rather, as had been shown at the beginning of this section, it is the result of the capitalistic development. In its demands concerning the law of marriage, socialism, according to its tendency to adapt the legal form to social reality, simply draws the conclusions from a given social situation. However, it views the development of the law of domestic relations not simply as desocializing formerly social relations, but at the same time as substituting certain social structures for others. This true meaning of the socialist view of the law of domestic relations becomes clear to us if we cast a glance at the law of education. Under the [German] Civil Code, the right to educate is based on parental power, on an inherent right of the parents. The Reich Constitution [of 1919], article 120, also declares it "a supreme duty and natural right of the parents, whose activities are watched over by the community of the state." But the [German] Youth Welfare Act [of 1922] and Juvenile Courts Act [of 1923], in the purport of their regulations if not in their express terms, show a shift of the right to educate, from the parental power to the community, the state. According to their provisions, family education in the last analysis is education in trust for the community, entrusted on the assumption that it will be carried on in accordance with the interest of the community, and revocable if this trust is betrayed. So the new law of education limits the rights of the narrower social structure in order to expand those of the more comprehensive social structure. Thus it fits perfectly into the development of social law.

Coöperation or conflict of individual function and social function, which we have observed in the law of contracts, of ownership, and of marriage, are the leitmotifs also of the law of inheritance, with which the following section is concerned.

Section 21

The Law of Inheritance

One ought to be ashamed to die a millionaire. — *Carnegie*

An economic unit, such as an agricultural, industrial, or commercial enterprise, exists not only for the sake of the acquisitive interest of its owner but also in the "service of the common good." In view of this social function of the economic unit, its continuation after the owner's death appears desirable. A considerable unproductive expenditure of energy would result if the economic units, in which society organizes itself, should perish with the men who maintain them and should always have to be created anew by new men. In any society, therefore, the appointment of a new owner in the place of a deceased owner of an economic unit must be regulated by law. Any society needs an "order of succession."[1]

Freedom of Testation, Intestacy, Compulsory Distribution and Consolidation of Estates. The individualistic form of this order of succession is the law of inheritance. Like the law of ownership, the law of inheritance is built upon the conception of a prestabilized harmony of individual and social interests. According to this view, the interest of the decedent as expressed in his will and the interest of the family as basic to intestacy move together in the direction of the social interest. Howover, the insight into the illusory character of this assumption and the striving for a more reliable safeguard of the social function have so far prevailed much less in the law of inheritance than in the law of ownership. This may be due to the fact that the law of inheritance of today is an opaque compromise between opposite systems and principles. It combines the inheritance forms of free testation, of intestacy, and again of compulsory distribution and compulsory consolidation of estates.[2] Moreover, it is a tangle, almost impossible to unravel, of individualistic, social, and family purposes, the latter in turn being based either on

[1] On this and the following, see Karl Renner, Die Rechtsinstitute des Privatrechts und ihre soziale Funktion (1929) 134 *et seq.*

[2] These three forms of inheritance are distinguished according to Anton Menger, Das bürgerliche Recht und die besitzlosen Volksklassen (4th ed. 1908) 214 *et seq.*

a rather individualistic or on a rather transindividualistic view of the family.[3]

Individualistic View. The individualistic principle of the law of inheritance is freedom of testation. It represents freedom of ownership prolonged beyond death. Whereas discretionary succession thus appears as the primary form of the law of inheritance, legal succession in the absence of a will must be based on the presumption that the succession of the next of kin to the rights of the deceased corresponds to his unexpressed will.

But the law of intestacy as well as the law of the legitimate share[a] may be justified also on more immediate individualistic grounds, not indeed from the standpoint of the deceased but from that of the heir. At a time when sudden compulsion to make economic readjustments in life was still unknown, it used to be pointed out that the needs, the style of living, the personalities of those who shared the decedent's life had been formed on the basis of his property relations, that for this reason one was entitled to call his property a kind of family property and hence the members of the family, "trained for their pretensions," had a sociologically well-founded right to continue to enjoy the property of the head of the family even after his death.[4] But if this argument, which is focused all too much on the attainment of a "life without risk," could be approved at all, it would certainly apply only to the closest circle of relatives, those sharing the household of the deceased or supported by him. It would be insufficient to justify the present law of intestacy which does not limit inheritance to any degree of kinship, or the right of "laughing heirs" to inherit from a deceased with whom they were quite unconnected. The "large family" of all those related by the same blood and the same name has ceased to be a sociological reality, apart from family conventions which are rare in the nobility and rarer among commoners; thus unlimited intestacy has lost the ground on which it used to rest.[5]

[3] On the principles of the law of inheritance, cf. the summary by Böhmer in NIPPERDEY, 3 DIE GRUNDRECHTE UND GRUNDPFLICHTEN DER REICHSVERFASSUNG (1930) 262 *et seq.*

[a] [The "legitimate share" is the portion of a decedent's estate to which certain of his near relatives are entitled despite contrary provisions in his will. Laws of this type are frequently found in nations whose legal systems were founded on the Roman law. They are rare in common-law countries.]

[4] Cf. SCHÄFFLE, KAPITALISMUS UND SOZIALISMUS (1870), Lecture 4.

[5] Cf. the writings of the law reformer Georg Bamberger (King's Counsel at Aschersleben [Germany]), who was meritorious also in other fields: FÜR DAS ERBRECHT DES REICHES (1912); ERBRECHT DES REICHES UND ERBSCHAFTSTEUER (1917).

Transindividualistic and Transpersonal View. To be sure, the family functions of the law of inheritance may be understood not only individualistically but also transindividualistically. The family, then, is not merely the sum total of personal relations between relatives; it is a whole, superior to those human beings and beyond their personalities, which is not confined to the circle of those present personal relations, but in one unit gathers present and past generations across the distance of time, close and remote relatives across the distance of degrees. Symbols of a family as thus understood transindividualistically are the "clean escutcheon" and the "honest name" of the family to which the individual owes respect and sacrifice. But if the law of inheritance is to secure the material foundation for the sociological continuance of a family group as thus understood, the *splendor familiae*, the estate, must be preserved and not be split. Whereas the individualistic version of the family function of the law of inheritance requires the compulsory distribution of the estate, the transindividualistic version of that family function implies the compulsory consolidation of the estate, the entail, and the compulsory single heir.

At this point, however, opposition arises from the standpoint of the democratic view of equality, as successfully expressed in the Reich Constitution [of 1919], article 155, which requires the dissolution of entails. It is not only in the form of entail that the inheritance rights of a few create an immense number of "the disinherited" on the other side, that hereditary wealth means hereditary poverty at the other end of the social order. Upon the law of inheritance there depends, as Walter Rathenau says, "the very essence of our social stratification, the whole unchangeable, lifeless constancy of the distribution of national forces. The vital up and down of life which governs nature, the organic alternation of subservient and dominant members, the beneficent interchange of the golden vessels, are benumbed by this fatal power of the generations, which is the work of man. It condemns the proletarian to eternal service, the rich man to eternal pleasure." [6] Such considerations have again and again led to the demand that, even though private ownership be maintained, the right of private inheritance should be limited or abolished. If the evasion of laws to that effect, by such means as gifts *inter vivos*, can be prevented, such an abolition of the right of private inheritance would within a foreseeable time unite the entire national wealth in the hands of the state and establish socialism.

However, besides the motives of "family socialism" [above referred to], social justifications have been adduced to support the right of

[6] VON KOMMENDEN DINGEN (1917) 129.

private inheritance, and especially the compulsory consolidation of estates. We have seen that the meaning of the order of succession is to preserve, beyond the death of their founder, economic units that have once been built up. Consciousness of surviving in one's works is a strong incentive to economic and cultural creation. The principle of an order of succession as thus understood reads: "Only he who is called upon to continue the true purpose of the property may be an heir." [7] Yet in whom, it is asked, could the work of the deceased live on better than in those who have grown up in and with the sphere of action of the deceased or those whom he himself has trained to be his successors — his legal heirs or chosen devisees? [8]

No elaboration is needed to show that this social justification of the law of inheritance is incompatible with the existing law of inheritance, with the split-up of estates by compulsory distribution and the accident of unlimited intestate succession. But the law of inheritance has lost that social function not only from the viewpoint of the heir but also from that of the estate. In the prevailing mass of cases the estate represents no longer an entirety of goods devoted to a definite economic purpose, which could not be dissolved without loss, but rather a conglomeration, a sum, a formless mass of values. In the section on ownership, we have referred to the development from ownership to fortune, from quality to quantity. Now an accidental pile of values, a safe full of the most varied stocks, private and governmental bonds, and mortgage certificates is no economic unit that needs preservation. Only because the estate in most cases assumed that merely quantitative character could the compulsory distribution of estates be carried out at all. On the contrary, the economic units which need to be preserved throughout the changes of human beings have more and more passed from the hands of mortal physical persons to those of immortal legal persons, in the course of the widely heralded depersonalization of economics and objectivation of enterprises; they have thereby passed out of the sphere of the law of inheritance.

Thus the problems which have been brought out in the fields of the law of ownership and of domestic relations merge in the field of the law of inheritance, where they come to a head. All the present problems of the law of inheritance find expression in the Reich Constitution [of 1919], article 154: [b] The individualistic right of inheritance is confronted with the state's share in the estate, the individual function of

[7] Cf. Buschauer, DAS ERBUNRECHT (1918) 53.

[8] Cf. SCHÄFFLE, *op. cit.*

[b] ["The right of inheritance is safeguarded in accordance with civil law. The share of the state in the estate shall be determined by the laws."]

the law of inheritance is confronted with its social function, and the right of inheritance is placed under the axe of the law.

Section 22

The Penal Law

Whether he's to spare or punish,
He must see men humanly. — *Goethe*

In the theory of penal law it is traditional to distinguish doctrines concerning the justification and doctrines concerning the end, of punishment.

The Justification of Punishment. The quest for the justification of punishment sprang from the very particular historical situation of a time when the individual was faced by the state as something foreign, a state, not yet based on the popular will, in which he had no active part. In that situation, the punishment required by the purpose of the state was still in need of special justification in the eyes of the individual. For, as Kant says, "man may never be treated as a mere means to the designs of another and mingled with the objects of the law of property, being protected therefrom by his innate personality" — the state is simply "another" as against the individual! In such a view of the state, punishment by the state is justifiable in two ways only: by showing either that it is willed by the criminal himself or that it is deserved by him.

Theories of Consent and of Retaliation. The first theory, that of consent, was advocated by Feuerbach in his early days, in the sense of assuming an actual consent of the real criminal to his punishment. He who commits the crime, knowing the penal law — which Feuerbach requires as the presupposition of punishment — consents to the condition by engaging in the conditional act. On him, punishment may be imposed with the same right as entitles one to claim fulfillment of a contract once it is made. This empiristic doctrine is cast in a more spiritual form by assuming a contract which either is similar to the social contract or is possibly inserted therein as a clause. By such a contract, the individual, in the event he should commit a crime, has submitted in advance to punishment — not indeed the real individual, but the individual thought of as a rational being, to whom is imputed the consistent will to suffer the consequences of his actions. (We repeat what has been said before:) The thief, by violating another's ownership, wants to establish ownership of his own; thus he in principle affirms that the legal interest he violates is worthy of protection; consistently, he must approve the punishment of the disturber which is indispensable to protect that legal interest, hence his own punishment. The forger of a document claims for the forged document the very faith of the public which he himself violates by his forgery — thus, he again affirms what is implicit in the legal interest worthy of protection and in the legal provisions necessary for its protection, namely, the penal law under which he falls. By thus regarding as willed by the perpetrator through his deed what he consistently would have to will, the criminal, in Hegel's words, is honored as a rational being and the punishment is deemed his own right which his action involves.

While the theory of consent represents the individualistic justification of punishment, the theory of retaliation, the justification of punishment on the ground that it is deserved, is based on authoritarian lines of thought [1] — even though its principal representative is the great founder of autonomy: Kant. The justification of punishment by the theory of retaliation, independent of individual consent and individual interest, has been expressed in that famous parable of Kant's: "Even if a civil society dissolved itself upon the agreement of all its members (for instance, the people inhabiting an island resolved to break up and disperse throughout the world), the last murderer in jail would first have to be executed in order that everyone may suffer what his acts deserve and that blood-guilt shall not rest upon the people." Quite unexpectedly, "the people" appears here not as a sum of individuals but as carrying a transindividualistic value of its own, which outlasts the individual interests.

The End of Punishment. In both its forms, the justification of punishment without regard to the state belongs to the past. The state which is based on the popular will, whether on an arithmetical majority or on some other kind of "integration," faces the individual no longer as "another" but rather as "we all." The justification of the people's state as thus understood includes the justification of the punishment necessary for its preservation. So the doctrine of the justification of punishment is

[1] Cf. RICHARD SCHMIDT, DIE STRAFRECHTSREFORM IN IHRER STAATSRECHTLICHEN UND POLITISCHEN BEDEUTUNG (1912) 10. R. Schmidt finds a transindividualistic view in retaliation only in so far as it is a justification of punishment; he sees a liberal government-of-laws view in retaliation in so far as it is an end of punishment; cf. *infra*, n. 2

merged in the doctrine of the justification of the state. What remains is only the doctrine of the end of punishment, that is, of the necessity of punishment for the state or, speaking more precisely, for the state, society, or the legal order. These different possibilities of determining the end of punishment will unfold themselves as we proceed now to develop the idea of punishment from the idea of law and its threefold ramification in justice, expediency, and legal certainty.

Penal Law and Justice: Commutative and Distributive. 1. Justice offers first the form of commutative justice as a possible basis of punishment. Just as the price corresponds to the goods, the wage to work, compensation to damage, so punishment would then correspond to the crime — as retaliation. To be sure, in preceding discussions we have recognized commutative justice, justice between co-equals, as the justice of private law. In fact, subjecting punishment to the standard of commutative justice takes us back to a time when penal law was still private law, when the state inflicted punishment in lieu of the vengeance withheld from the injured, chiefly in order to give satisfaction to the injured. But even after penal law is reorganized as public law administered by the state in its own interest, it has not become nonsensical to measure punishment by commutative justice. For it is of the essence of a government of laws that the superior state in many relations shall betake itself to the level of co-equality with its citizens: in civil suits to which the treasury is a party, in criminal procedure, or before an administrative tribunal. So the doctrine of retaliation could be interpreted as a liberal, a government-of-laws view [a] of the penal law.[2] However, inseparably mixed with this view was an authoritarian-transindividualistic view — quite in accordance with the "national liberal" conception of the Bismarck Empire; witness Binding's theory of penal law, which is oriented entirely toward the conception of authority.

The theory of justice of the penal law contrasts with the theories of its ends. But they too lay claim to justice — though to distributive rather than to commutative justice. According to them, just punishment is not the punishment corresponding to the crime, but one criminal's punishment proportioned to another's in the proportion of their respec-

[a] [I.e., "liberal" in the sense of the nineteenth-century *laissez-faire* conception of the state. See infra, §26, and n. a.]

[2] I am abandoning my former one-sided transindividualistic interpretation of the retaliatory end of punishment, presented in my article in (1908–09) 5 ASCHAFFENBURGS MONATSSCHRIFT 1 *et seq.*, due to the convincing arguments of RICHARD SCHMIDT, DIE STRAFRECHTSREFORM IN IHRER STAATSRECHTLICHEN UND POLITISCHEN BEDEUTUNG (1912) 189 *et seq.* Cf. also DANNENBERG, LIBERALISMUS UND STRAFRECHT IM 19. JAHRHUNDERT (1925).

tive degrees of culpability. However, while the doctrine of retaliation may be fully developed out of the conception of commutative justice, the conception of distributive justice is not sufficient to derive therefrom the theories of the end of punishment. To be sure, distributive justice of punishment means that the equally incriminated ought to be punished equally, and the unequally incriminated in proportion to their incrimination. But it leaves us in doubt, on the one hand, by what standard we are to measure equality or difference of incrimination, whether by culpability, dangerousness, or what else. On the other hand, it tells us only the relation of penalties to one another but not their absolute severity and kind, only the place of any penalty within a given system of penalties but not that system of penalties itself; not whether that system should at the bottom start with jail and flogging and at the top end with cruelly aggravated death penalties or whether it should start at the bottom with fines and end at the top with life imprisonment. The answer to these questions, which the theory of justice leaves unanswered, can be derived only from the second element of the idea of law, that is, expediency. In thus reaching back to purpose and expediency, however, punishment at the same time steps out of the framework of the specific idea of law, justice, in order to become subservient to the purposes of the state and society.

Penal Law and Expediency: Theory of General Prevention. 2. Once again, in this connection, we meet a liberal, government-of-laws view of punishment, which, however, is related this time to the idea of expediency and the state, unlike the theory of retaliation which is related to the idea of justice and the law. This is the deterrent theory, in the form cast by Feuerbach. Indeed, in Feuerbach's thought on penal law, as in that of the period of Enlightenment, the deterrent theory paradoxically serves to bind penal law to the terms of the statute and its state of facts, and to safeguard the proportionality between crime and punishment. In this respect it is close to the theories of retaliation.[3] By the same token, both the deterrent and the retaliatory theories separate the deed from its perpetrator and the perpetrator from the human being. The concept of the perpetrator, on which penal law is thus based, corresponds to the concept of the person in private law. Just as in traditional private law, say, the laborer is the possessor of his ability to work, is the seller of the "commodity of labor," without any individuality of his own, so in a deterrent and retaliatory penal law the lawbreaker is the perpetrator of his deed, with no individuality of his own. The rela-

[3] The deterrent and retaliatory theories are closely related also in that both may be given a transindividualistic turn. Cf. *infra*, p. 188.

tionship created by penal law is thus turned into a partial relationship, entered into not by the whole human being but only by the perpetrator of this deed. Just as in the individualistic view of the employment relationship one sells as a commodity his ability to work, so in the corresponding view of penal law one expiates his crime.[4] In the merely partial nature of the relationship of penal law the liberal character of the retaliatory and deterrent theories is especially clearly expressed. For liberalism everywhere loosened the personal legal ties of man to his fellow men in their totality and replaced them with clear-cut partial relationships — in the relationship of penal law no less than in that of employment.

Expediency: Theory of Special Prevention. The liberal, government-of-laws theories of retaliation and deterrence contrast with the doctrine of custody and correction, which is the theory of social penal law. For, as shown above, it is peculiar to social as opposed to individualistic law that it is cut out not for the abstract and isolated individual, the person, the perpetrator, but for the concrete individual within society. Just as in labor law it has been recognized that the ability to work is not something separable from the human being but is the whole human being as seen from a particular point of view, so it is recognized in a social penal law that the crime is not separable from the human being but is again the whole human being from a particular viewpoint. The new penal law has been summed up in the slogan: "Not the deed, but the perpetrator"; one should rather say: not the perpetrator, but the man. It is the concrete human being with his psychological and sociological peculiarities that enters the ken of the law. From the viewpoint of the custodial and corrective theory, the concept of the perpetrator resolves itself into manifold characterological and sociological types: the habitual and the occasional, the corrigible and incorrigible, the adult and the juvenile, the fully and partly responsible criminals. So the new school of penal law may rightly call itself the "sociological school"; for it has put within the judicial ken facts that hitherto belonged only to sociology.

Expediency: Fascist Penal Law. However, the deterrent theory has experienced a rebirth, not indeed in its liberal, government-of-laws form which has just been described, but in a transindividualistic transformation: in the terroristic penal law of Fascism. The memorial attached to

[4] E. Paschukanis, Allgemeine Rechtslehre und Marxismus (1929) 149 *et seq.*, interprets the parallel relation as a sheer causal relation: The thought of retaliation is determined by the "basic form to which modern society is subject, namely, the form of equivalent exchange." *Contra:* Kelsen in (1931) 66 Archiv für Sozialwissenschaft und Sozialpolitik 483 *et seq.*

the new Italian Penal Code of 1930 quite explicitly starts from the Fascist view of the state as an organism. "The state represents no longer the arithmetic sum of its component individuals but the product, synthesis, and concentration of its constituent individuals, groups, and classes, with its own life, its own purposes, its own needs and interests, which reach and last beyond the lives of the individuals, groups, and classes and extend over all past, present, and future generations." The penal law of that state is characterized not as the defense of society (*difesa sociale*, in the sense of Ferri) but as the defense of the state itself (*difesa propria dello Stato*); it finds the means of such defense in the deterrence and incapacitation of criminals, which results from extremely numerous threats of capital punishment. "This state, which presupposes the superman as leader, assumes that men are not weak, helpless, needful of support, but that they are strong. The criminal is therefore basically dealt with as the rebellious enemy of the régime of the state, against whom the most important function of the penal power of the state is to deter him and render him harmless." [5]

Expediency: Soviet Penal Law. Another regeneration of terroristic penal law is to be found in Soviet penal law. The Soviet Penal Code of 1926 is the penal law of a state in transition, an odd mixture of authoritarian penal law, which corresponds to the dictatorship of the proletariat, and of social penal law which foreshadows and anticipates the classless society of the future. Corresponding to the social view of penal law, the Soviet law expressly declares that its "task is not to retaliate and to punish." But corresponding to the authoritarian view, it maintains that to deter, especially from political crimes, is no less an end of punishment than to keep in custody and to correct; and this end is embodied especially in the "supreme measure of social protection," the death penalty, which is copiously employed.

Even more characteristic than the admixture of authoritarian elements of penal law is the complete renunciation of government-of-laws guarantees in the Soviet Penal Code. Acts for which the statute threatens punishment are not crimes if in the individual case they lack the character of a danger to the common good; acts for which no punishment is threatened are crimes if they turn out to be dangerous to the common good: the clause *Nullum Crimen sine lege* [b] does not apply in Soviet Russia. Even the principle *Cogitationis poenam nemo patitur* [c] is im-

[5] Eberhard Schmidt, Strafrechtsreform und Kulturkrise (Staat und Recht, no. 79, 1931) 18.

[b] [No crime without a (previously enacted) law.]

[c] [Nobody suffers punishment for his thoughts.]

paired not only by penalizing preparatory acts generally but by even subjecting to the measures of social protection persons who "represent a danger by their connection with the environment of criminals or by their previous activities."

Penal Law and Legal Certainty. 3. If consistently carried through, the custodial and corrective theory would, indeed, lead to those conclusions, were they not precluded by the thought that forms the third part of the idea of law, namely, the conception of legal certainty. Undeniably, the theory of special prevention is complicated by the fact that it cannot by itself determine the shape of penal law, which is derived rather from the interplay of the special preventive purpose with the ideas of justice and legal certainty. That interplay, moreover, is largely counteraction. The tension within the idea of law is represented quite clearly within the particular problem of penal law. The idea of legal certainty saves the doctrine of special prevention from its extreme conclusion, from extending punishment even to preparatory acts, attitudes, and thoughts. Again, the conception of justice, which requires even unequal persons and circumstances to be treated to some extent equally, opposes the carrying of individualization to that ultimate extreme which would result from the conception of special preventive purpose. As against this antinomic formation of a penal law founded upon corrective and custodial punishment, the doctrine of retaliation discloses greater methodical efficacy: it serves both to justify punishment and to determine its purpose, it fulfills within itself both the conception of justice and that of legal certainty.

Finally, the legal institution molded upon the idea of retaliation doubtless represents "punishment," whereas a penal law consistently molded according to the theory of correction and custody ultimately ceases to be "penal." Indeed, Ferri's draft of a code, and again the Penal Code of the Soviet Union, consistently with the doctrine of special prevention, have replaced the name of "punishment" with other terms: "sanction," "measure of social protection." However, it need hardly be stressed that the concept of punishment is not a norm and limit determinative of the future shape of what used to be called "penal" law, any more than the methodical convenience of the doctrine of retaliation, which renders possible a single solution of all problems of penal law theory, is a criterion of truth. Indeed, on the contrary, the development of penal law may well turn out one day to step beyond penal law, with the reform of penal law opening not into an improved penal law, but into a corrective and custodial law that would be better than penal law, both more intelligent and more humane than penal law.

Section 23

The Death Penalty

Who gave you this power over me, hangman? — [Goethe, Faust:] Gretchen in jail

Only a transindividualistic view of the law is able to justify the death penalty; it alone can attribute to the state any right at all over life and death.

Transindividualistic Justification. Says Bismarck, in his speech of March 1, 1870: "A human force which feels within itself no justification from above is not strong enough to wield the executioner's sword." That the turn away from an individualistic view of the state provides the background for the re-introduction of the death penalty was expressed especially in the memorial on the new, Fascist, Italian Penal Code, in terms which celebrate the renewed death penalty as an outright triumph of this view of the state: "Such a reform represents another happy sign of the changed spirit of the Italian nation, of the regained virility and energy of our people, of the total liberation of our juridical and political culture from the influence of foreign ideologies directly involving the abolition of the death penalty." Those ideologies are expressly stated to be "the individualistic ideas which triumphed beyond the Alps," "the error of Kant's affirmation that the individual, as an end unto himself, may not be abased to the level of a means." "It is, on the contrary, true that society, regarded as an organism comprehending innumerable chains of generations, and the state which is its juristic organization, have ends of their own and live for their sake, while the individual is nothing but an infinitely small and transitory element of the social organism to the ends of which he must subordinate his acts and his very existence."

Death Penalty and Contract Theory: Beccaria, Rousseau, Kant. On the basis of the individualistic ideas condemned by Fascist Italy, the death penalty was opposed for the first time by an Italian, hitherto considered a glory of Italy: Cesare Beccaria (*On Crimes and Punishments*,[a] sec. 16). He proved the incompatibility of the death penalty with an individualistic view of the state, as embodied in the doctrine of the social contract. He argued that the death penalty contradicted the social

[a] [Dei delitti e delle pene.]

contract because life is an inalienable legal good, and suicide is reprehensible, hence any suicidal consent to the death penalty in the social contract is immoral and consequently void. To be sure, this argument would be conclusive only if in the [social] contract theory the justification of the death penalty were to depend upon its being actually willed by the culprit. It would not be conclusive if, as in the correct rational version of the contract theory, the death penalty is deemed justified provided it can be thought of as willed by the culprit, that is, provided he cannot rationally fail to will it because it is required by his own true interest. Once the disposal of one's own life is recognized as a mere symbolization of one's interest in his own death, no argument may be based on the inadmissibility of such disposal. The question of the justification of the death penalty may then no longer be whether the culprit is to be allowed to consent to the death penalty, but only whether he is able to consent thereto.

But Beccaria's opponent, Rousseau, makes the same mistake in his reasoning. Rousseau regards the consent to the death penalty in the social contract as legally valid because it is but a conditional consent, given only for the event, not at all to be expected, that one should commit a murder; that is to say, because one consents not to his death but to the quite remote danger of his death and because it is not immoral to submit to the danger of death in order to preserve one's life. "In order not to fall victim to a murderer, one consents to die if he himself should become a murderer. In this contract, far from disposing of his own life, one is only concerned with protecting it; and it is not to be presumed that any one of the contracting parties from the outset contemplates his being hanged" (*Social Contract*,[b] II, 5). So Rousseau arrives at the possibility of constructing an unobjectionable consent of the murderer to his own death by transferring that eventual consent back to a moment at which he did not yet consider becoming a murderer. Who would fail to see that, by this "having once consented," Rousseau turns the social contract into an act fixed in time, a historical fact, and thus unexpectedly slides back into the historical version of the contract theory which he so decisively rejects in the introductory words of the *Contrat Social?* If one sees in the social contract a mere fictitious picture, one must think of it as timeless, not as concluded once but as renewable at any moment. A just state must at any moment, with regard to any of its proceedings, permit an affirmative answer to the question whether it may be thought of as originating in the contract of all its members; hence even at the moment when the murderer puts his head upon the block. Therefore, under the contract theory the death penalty could be justified only if it

[b] [LE CONTRAT SOCIAL.]

could be proven that even at this moment the consent of the culprit to his death may be fictitiously assumed.

That desperate proof is indeed offered by Kant against Beccaria's "sophistry and pettifogging." [1] By an artifice characteristic of Kant's way of reasoning, he takes for a transcendental relation what in Rousseau appears as a relation in time. The consent alleged to have once been given by the culprit to the death penalty is replaced with the timeless judgment of his reason as to that penalty's necessity. For the contracting party to the social contract is to be found not in the empirical individual with his real will but in the very reason imputable to the empirical individual — it having been stressed again and again that the contract theory fictitiously takes for willed only what one cannot reasonably fail to will. "Therefore, when I draw up a penal law against myself as a criminal, it is the pure legal-legislative reason within myself (*homo noumenon*) that subjects me to the penal law as one capable of the crime, hence as another person (*homo phaenomenon*), along with all others in a civil society." Not indeed the criminal's empirical will, but his "own judgment with which one must of necessity credit his reason," necessarily consents to the death penalty even at the moment of its execution, according to Kant.

Yet even if the individual is viewed not in his empirical factuality but as concreted reason, he cannot be thought of as consenting to the death penalty.[2] As to any punishment that leaves the convict his mere life, in no matter how miserable a shape, the consent of his own reason, the interest of the culprit himself in his punishment, may in principle be proved: even life imprisonment leaves the convict still with a number of legal goods, protected by his own punishment which results in deterring others. But the death penalty can in no way be shown to serve the criminal's own interests as well, since it destroys the subject of those interests. Thus, from the standpoint of the contract theory, one will have to reject the death penalty, following Beccaria, though not on the ground that the criminal may not be allowed to consent to it, but rather because he is not able reasonably to consent to it for lack of any interest of his own therein. The death penalty is incompatible with a thought basic to any individualistic view of the state, which has been formulated thus by Stammler (*Lehre vom Richtigen Recht*, 208 [c]): "Every legal demand must be maintained in such a manner that the person obligated

[1] METAPHYSIK DER SITTEN (ed. by Vorländer, 1907) 163–164.

[2] Against the arguments following in the text: NELSON, DIE RECHTSWISSENSSCHAFT OHNE RECHT (1917) 135–136.

[c] Translated as THE THEORY OF JUST LAW (Modern Legal Philosophy Series, 1925) 161.]

may be his own neighbor" [i.e., may still think of his own interest as closest to him].[3]

But does not the contract theory prove too much? Does not its argument deny the state any right to ask its members to stake their lives, say, in a war? By no means! Staking, that is, endangering, one's own life may still be shown to be within the interest of the one who, though endangered, may well survive. But sacrificing one's life, certain death, even in wartime is commonly not required by the state as a matter of principle: volunteers are called for in such cases. For the voluntary sacrifice of one's life for an idea is not contradictory even to individualism; it means to realize life's full value in surrendering one's life. Such fulfillment of life by the surrender of life may, indeed, occur also under the death penalty, namely, in a case where the culprit by his own will has accepted the penalty as atonement. Even in that case, however, there remains the conceptual distinction between the death penalty which is imposed and the atonement which is voluntarily accepted.[4]

Death Penalty as Self-Defense. Of greater weight is another objection to the individualistic argument against the death penalty, an objection that was also raised in that speech of Bismarck's: the admissibility of killing in self-defense. The authorities as well as individuals are under some circumstances entitled for preventive purposes to kill an attacker, who need not even be a murderous one — then why should they be prohibited from killing the convicted murderer for repressive purposes? Indeed, Beccaria has considered this objection.[5] He acknowledges the admissibility of the killing of others if it "should really be the sole means of restraining the others from committing crimes"; and in this connection he thinks of "the case of open tumult and uproar which could be quelled instantaneously by killing the rioters who resist." But in such killings he sees "the consequence of a real declaration of war," which could not be founded upon the law and the social contract but only upon power, though upon just and necessary power. Let us think his reasoning through in terms of the contract theory! In the emergency of self-defense, the social contract is inadequate to protect the legal goods for the protection of which it was entered into, because the organs

[3] The same argument as here is used by MESS, NIETZSCHE ALS GESETZGEBER (1930) 70–71.

[4] That the inescapability of the death penalty renders it distinctive in kind from voluntarily staking one's life in any way, no matter how hopeless, is shown in the statement by Dostoevski, quoted by SAPIR, DOSTOJEWSKY UND TOLSTOI 11.

[5] BECCARIA, ÜBER VERBRECHEN UND STRAFEN ([German] ed. by Esselborn, 1905) 108, n. 1, 192.

established by it are not at the moment accessible. Therefore, the state of nature, including the right of self-defense, is restored as of right, yet within the framework of the state of law and with the recognition of the legal order. Thus the right of self-defense is an original right of man that is left to the person attacked, while the right to the death penalty is only conceivable as a right created on the basis of the social contract, or rather is inconceivable as such upon individualistic grounds. But above all, there is still another point to be made against the argument for the death penalty as a right of self-defense: That the right of self-defense is directed toward repelling the attack, or toward destroying the ability to attack, as the case may be, and though it may in fact bring about the attacker's death, it is not specifically directed toward that killing; so even this right is directed not toward destroying but only toward endangering life. On the part of those killed in self-defense or by the death penalty, this conceptual difference is expressed in the very real mental fact that the former believed in the possibility of escape till the last moment while the latter had to suffer the terrible feeling of the inescapability of a death precisely fixed in time.

These discussions have been devoted less to the question of the death penalty itself than to the task of showing the difficulty as well as the fruitfulness of the conceptual form of the social contract in an individualistic doctrine of law. The decisive arguments against the death penalty are to be sought on levels both higher and lower than legal philosophy: on the one hand, in ethical and religious arguments against its admissibility, and on the other hand, in statistical psychological proofs of experience against its necessity.

Section 24

Mercy

The quality of mercy is not strained . . . — Shakespeare

The legal institution of mercy implies a frank recognition of how questionable all law is, with its relations of tension within the idea of law and its possibilities of conflict between the idea of law and other ideas such as the ethical and the religious. For this very reason, during periods of unquestioning confidence in the complete and sole rule of reason, as in the age of natural law and the enlightenment, the power of pardon was opposed: first by Beccaria (*op. cit.*, sec. 20) and, following him, by Kant, who regarded mercy as "the most slippery of all the rights of the sovereign."

Mercy as a Legal Institution. The intrinsic tensions of the idea of law; the contradictory demands of justice, expediency, and legal certainty; the lack of a norm superior to those three aspects of the idea of law, and the resulting indeterminability of their conflicts — all that has been set forth above (sec. 9, pp. 107 *et seq.*). Now the meaning of mercy is to relax the relation of tension between the conflicting elements of the idea of law in a different way and, in the opinion of the holder of the pardoning power, a better way than it was relaxed in the judgment. The task of mercy may be to make justice prevail against positive law, or to make individualizing expediency prevail against the schematic equalization of justice. Its aim may also be to solve the antinomies possible within each of those elements, in a way different from that of the judgment; for instance, to make substantive law prevail against the procedural weight of *res judicata*, equity against justice, or general political expediency, reasons of state, against the specific expediency of criminological policies.

Mercy as thus understood seems to represent a legal institution, a "specific instrument in the service of just law," [1] in the sense of the adages of Germanic law: "Law without mercy is wrong," or "Mercy stands by the law." Against that view, however, objections are to be raised if one includes in the concept of law the generality of its norms, the equality of their addressees with regard to these norms. To be sure, he who wields the pardoning power will endeavor to exercise it not arbitrarily but according to guiding principles. Mercy, too, strives toward general validity of its basic maxims; and repeatedly in legal history new legal rules originated from maxims according to which the pardoning power was exercised, as from the "judging according to mercy" back in the Middle Ages and from the conditional pardon in most recent times. But as soon as guiding principles of mercy have assumed the form of norms ripe for enactment, the competency of mercy, strictly speaking, comes to an end. Such norms of right law ought to prevail by way of legislation, and not by way of mercy at the expense of the law; similarly equity, once it has from the individual cases established general legal rules, ceases to be equity and itself becomes justice. What mercy, although it seeks to attain general validity, is to make prevail is the right of the individual case and not new legal rules.[2] To be sure, it takes an effort hardly to be expected of the holder

[1] Cf. STAMMLER, LEHRE VOM RICHTIGEN RECHTE 131. [Translated as THE THEORY OF JUST LAW (Modern Legal Philosophy Series, 1925) 100.]

[2] In this sense, Wolfgang Heimann in a Heidelberg doctoral dissertation (1931)

of the pardoning power wholly to disregard, say, his general attitude toward the death penalty in deciding about sentences of death or his general view of the punishment of abortion in deciding about sentences for abortion.

Mercy Before Law. But mercy is not exhausted by its function as a legal institution. Those Germanic legal adages which characterize mercy as a better law contrast with others which call mercy "better than law" and say that mercy goes "before the law." Mercy has never been confined to the equalizing of tensions within the law; rather it means a recognition of the fact that this world is not solely a world of law according to the saying *Fiat justitia, pereat mundus,*[a] that there are still other values besides the law, and that it may become necessary to help these values to prevail against the law. When, for instance, happy patriotic events are the occasion for pardons, such a pardon can no longer be founded upon legal values. But the clearest example of such a pardon not founded upon legal values was the right of persons, who were not organs of the legal community, to bring about a pardon. Instances may be found in the story of the pardoning of Barabbas in the Gospels, when the people of Jerusalem at Easter, or in the Middle Ages when religious bodies or cloisters annually, were entitled to ask that a certain number of convicts be set free.[3] Finally, we recall from olden times the role which, in the execution of the death penalty, was played by an accident, or the will of the gods it was presumed to reveal; the delinquent was freed from punishment if the rope burst or the sword failed. We must not regard such institutions of the past (with Stammler) as "mere curiosities of social history," mere "aberrations"; on the contrary it is from them that we may gather essential information about the meaning of mercy.

Mercy in those times was a much richer and softer concept than it is in our time. We carefully weight out even mercy on the scales of the law by ounces and pounds: Mercy has become a legal benefit extended according to principles; justice wants to rule even over mercy, like reason over benevolence. But just as alms once upon time was the free flow of abundance and not a canalized charity, so mercy is not strained —

calls the idea of pardon the idea of "right discretion" (*Willkür* in the sense of Stammler's terminology).

[a] [Let justice be done though the world perish.]

[3] The renewal of the request to set a culprit free is advocated by MESS, NIETZSCHE ALS GESETZGEBER (1930) 28: "Would it not be appropriate in the highest degree if pioneers, who have achieved something extraordinary for mankind by staking their own lives, were to be rewarded by the right to ask for the pardon of a convict?"

not even by the strain of justice. Mercy means not merely a milder form of law; as a lightning flash it strikes into the sphere of law from an utterly non-legal world and makes the frigid gloom of the legal world more clearly visible. Just as the miracle breaks through the laws of the physical world, so mercy is the lawless miracle within the juridical world of law. In mercy, non-legal realms of value penetrate into the midst of the legal world: values of religious compassion, of ethical tolerance. In mercy, the law's claim of comprehensive rationalization is opposed even by the kindly accident, by that lordship of chance which Nietzsche has called the oldest nobility of the world.

So mercy is not exhausted by being "the safety valve of the law," to use Jhering's terms. It stands as a symbol for values in the world that are fed from deeper sources and culminate in higher summits than the law.

Section 25

Procedure

Do you think that a state can survive and is not indeed destroyed when sentences that are pronounced are without force and are invalidated and frustrated by individuals? —Socrates

Purpose, in Jhering's words, is the creator of the entire law. Yet the law has scarcely been created ere it denies its creator; from the beginning it seeks to be valid for the sake of its own existence without regard to the accomplishment of its purpose, to live on as a purpose unto itself according to its own rules. Scrupulously is that autonomy of the law partitioned off from the purposeful activity of the state, adjudication separated from administration. Such is the meaning of the principle of the independence of the judiciary.

Judicial Independence. This principle, then, rests on the assumption that the legal order and the order of the state are not identical, but rather that the law confronts the state as an autonomous world. We have recognized justice, expediency, and legal certainty as the three aspects of the idea of law. While the idea of law is closely connected with the state by the notion of expediency, which after all is mostly the expediency of the state, it transcends the framework of the state with its two other features. For justice demands generality and equality of the norm, as against those affected by the norm, without regard to the expediency of the state; and legal certainty demands the validity of positive law even if it is inexpedient for the state. Whereas the content of the law is predominantly determined by the expediency of the state, the form of the law is outside and above the sphere of influence of the ends of the state.

Now it is true that the law, even as to those of its characteristics which are beyond the influence of the end of the state, is still included in the state; but it is included in the same way that the other cultural values, such as science and art, are raised to tasks of the state, namely, in their whole autonomy, uninfluenced by considerations of expediency. To be sure, for the state the law is only a means to an end, but in the same sense as, for instance, science: the state puts both to its service by serving them. To justice applies what applies to truth; not, indeed, that the expedient is true (as is assumed by pragmatism), but that the true, when it may unfold without regard to any purpose, is eminently expedient. This is why there is both promotion of science by the state and freedom of science from the state. Not without reason do we speak of "cognizance" in speaking of judicial judgments; [a] so judicial independence means nothing else than the freedom of science, transfererd to the field of practical legal science.

The Procedural Legal Relation. The relation here shown between the law and its purpose, viz., the origin of law in purposes and yet the independence of its validity from those purposes, is reproduced in the relation between substantive and adjective law. Procedural law is to serve the purpose of helping to realize substantive law. Yet it is valid unconditionally, hence even to the extent that it does not serve, and indeed may possibly hamper, the purpose of realizing [substantive] law. In all other normative disciplines we contrast categorical imperatives with hypothetical imperatives, that is, with those precepts which are to promote compliance with the former and which for precisely that reason are valid only if and inasmuch as they really achieve that purpose. The law alone knows exclusively categorical imperatives; even the procedural norms which are in the service of substantive law are of categorical and not of hypothetical character. The law's tone of command knows no degrees. The lawmaker never either raises or lowers his commanding voice; whatever he demands he demands throughout with the same absolute obligatory will.

This independence of the validity of procedural law from its expediency as a means of realizing substantive law is expressed dogmatically in the sharp distinction between the procedural legal relation and

[a] [I.e., the court takes "cognizance" of certain facts, or it takes "cognizance" of certain types of cases which fall within its jurisdiction.]

the substantive legal relation which it serves to implement. Manifold practical conclusions are reached on this foundation, most illuminating of which is the decision of the familiar controversy whether counsel for the defense is justified in pleading for the acquittal of an accused whose guilt is known to him personally. Beside the legal rule that the guilty person is to be punished there stands the other rule, of equal value, that only the one proven guilty is to be convicted. So the counsel who advocates the acquittal of one who is guilty but has not been proven guilty still remains an attorney-at-law, not indeed at substantive but at procedural law. But the idea of value which alone can justify such validity of procedural law, even in cases where it contravenes its task in substantive law, is legal certainty.

Res Judicata. Lastly, the relation shown above between law and the purpose of law, and again between substantive and adjective law, appears in the second degree in respect of *res judicata.* Just as the law is valid regardless of whether it satisfies the purpose it has been created for, just as procedural law is valid regardless of whether it serves the substantive law it is intended to serve, so the judgment, which is to settle both the substantive legal situation and the correctness of procedure, results in *res judicata* regardless of the possibility that it may both run counter to substantive law and have originated in incorrect procedure.

Again it is legal certainty that alone can explain why *res judicata* results even from an incorrect judgment. But in respect of *res judicata* there arises a problem that we have already encountered in discussing the legal validity of a statute. We have seen that legal certainty alone may suffice to support the legal validity of wrong law, yet that cases may well be conceived of in which the wrongness of the content of the law, its injustice or inexpediency, are of such a degree as to overbalance the value of legal certainty which is guaranteed by the validity of law once enacted. To that possible invalidity of enacted law because of its wrongness there corresponds the thought of absolute nullity of final judgments because of definite defects of substantive or adjective law. Only in these cases it is not merely the unjust and inexpedient content of the judgment that is opposed to its validity, but rather a conflict that arises within legal certainty: Against the effect of *res judicata*, required by legal certainty, there arises the demand, starting from the very same thought of legal certainty, that substantive and adjective law be effectuated in practice.

So procedural law most impressively illustrates a ground on which all law is questionable, namely, that in the field of law the means tends to become an end unto itself. As the law often conflicts with the idea of law, so procedural law stands in opposition to substantive law, and so finally *res judicata* may conflict with both substantive and adjective law.

Section 26

A Government of Laws [a]

Mistrust yourself, my lord, lest you mistake
Reasons of state for justice. — *Schiller*

How is it possible for the state to be bound by its own law? How are rights of the individual against the state, how are constitutional and administrative law — and constitutional and administrative legal wrong — how is a government of laws, possible? This problem has traditionally been raised by asking whether law "precedes" the state or the state "precedes" law, that is, whether the state owes its power of command, as to its extent and limits, to the law, or whether contrariwise the validity of the law is determined and conditioned by the will of the state.[1]

Priority of the Law or the State. The two possible answers to this question seem to face equally grave objections. The view that the state precedes the law is confronted with the fact that the state is not only a source of the law but is itself a legal institution whose juridical existence results from constitutional law. Again, to the opposite affirmation that the law precedes and transcends the state, it must be objected that to assume a law prior to and above the state means either to revive natural law or to anchor constitutional law in customary law, whereas the very fundamentals of constitutional law are settled not by peaceful legal usage but in the clash of legal views, which can be terminated only by the decision of the will of a recognized state-power.

[a] [This term is used here as an approximate rendering of the German term *Rechtsstaat* (literally, state of law, legal state), which denotes a state in which governmental action must be authorized by laws and its conformity to law must be secured by appropriate safeguards. This is distinguished in German terminology from the *Polizeistaat* (literally, police state), or government by prerogative, in which governmental action may be taken by executive authority of the sovereign. The *Rechtsstaat* is not necessarily *Justizstaat* (literally: judicial state), or government by judiciary, in which the legality of governmental action is reviewed by the ordinary courts; it may provide other safeguards of legality, such as administrative adjudication and review by special administrative courts.]

[1] On this problem, cf. Georg Jellinek, Allgemeine Staatslehre (3d ed.) 364 *et seq.*

Identity of the State and the Law. From this dilemma, salvation is promised by the doctrine of the identity of the state and the law (Hans Kelsen). According to it, the question of the priority of the law or the state is inadmissible because the two are one. As far as the lawyer is concerned, the state exists only to the extent to which and in the way in which it expresses itself by enactments — not as a social power, not as a historical formation, but only as the creator and the content of its enactments. The very word "legislation," like other words with this suffix,[b] signifies both a process and its product, both the action of the will and what is willed. When legislation is observed as the content of a certain action of the will, it presents itself to us as law; when legislation is observed as an action of the will with a certain content, it becomes personified as the state. As organizing order or organization,[c] legislation is the state; as organized order or organization, it is the law. The state and the law are related to each other like the organism and the organizational pattern. The state is the law as enacting activity; the law is the state as enacted pattern; the two are distinguishable but not separable.

According to that view, which identifies the state and the law, the state would always be in the right, the wrongdoing state would no longer be a state. Thus the question whether the state is bound by its law would not indeed be solved but would be made to disappear. For the statement that the state is always in the right must not be mistaken for a pronouncement in favor of government by prerogative.[d] Nor is the statement that the wrongdoing state is no longer a state to be taken for a pronouncement in favor of a government of laws — except in a sense in which the government of *every* state would be a government of laws.[2] The doctrine of identity is of purely analytical significance for purposes of definition but is of no legal philosophical substance for purposes of policy.

Does, then, the doctrine of identity actually succeed in showing that it is a mistake to raise the question of priority as between the law and the state? In a purely juridical view, the law and the state are incontestably identical. In that view, the state is indeed the structure that embodies itself in constitutional law. But besides that legal concept of the state, there is still a concept of the state in its working reality. To be sure, this concept of the state in historical-sociological reality cannot be thought through without resorting to the legal concept of the state; it is

[b] [The corresponding German suffix is *-ung*, in *Gesetzgebung*.]

[c] [The German term is *Ordnung*, showing the suffix "*-ung*."]

[d] [Cf. *supra*, n. a.]

[2] Cf. Kelsen, Allgemeine Staatslehre (1925) 91, 100.

a concept of legal reality, and its structure is that of those concepts of realities related to values. The state as legal reality is nothing else than the substratum on which law, and especially constitutional law, *ought* to be realized, though it by no means has usually been so realized. The state is the substratum as seen from this very viewpoint of realization of law, i.e., the substratum as compared with its legal implementation. The legal concept of the state is related to the concept of the state in reality about as follows: "The holder of the right to rule is transformed from a formal right-bearer under the law into a staff of men who are available for the enforcement of that law; and the right to rule is itself transformed into the chance, i.e., the probability that the commands of the staff will be in fact regarded as legitimate and actually obeyed." [3] Against the objection that the two concepts as thus distinguished ought not equally to claim the name of "the state," it may be pointed out that this is not the only case in which the norm and the substratum of the norm are referred to by the same term. For instance, "art" is both an ideal concept and standard, by which the inartistic is banned from the realm of art, and a concept of reality, which includes all art achievements of a period, artistic as well as spurious ones. So, too, "science" on the one hand means the standard of truth for the activity of gathering knowledge, by which shortcomings in knowledge are measured as unscientific, and on the other hand it means the historical cultural concept which, neutral as to values, embraces scientific truth and scientific error. Again, the very concept of culture may be understood both as an ideal for the historical-social cultural facts and as the inclusive concept of those cultural facts themselves.

However, the distinction between the concepts of the state in law and in reality is further complicated because in addition to the legal concept of the state as above mentioned there is still another legal concept of the state, which more closely touches the concept of the state in reality. In another context (*supra* sec. 15, p. 148) we distinguished two kinds of legal concepts: "genuine legal concepts," by which the contents of legal norms are comprehended, and "legally relevant concepts," which are contained as elements in the legal norms themselves, especially in their definitions of states of facts. This distinction may be illustrated, for instance, by comparing the concept of "ownership," as the concept of a legal institution including all its prerequisites and legal consequences, with the concept of "contract," as characterizing a state of facts which establishes legal rights. In accordance with this terminology, the above mentioned concept of the state is a "genuine" legal concept, namely, the

[3] Cf. Hermann Kantorowicz, *Staatsauffassungen* (1925) 1 JAHRBUCH FÜR SOZIOLOGIE 108, following Max Weber.

content of the legal order, or at any rate of constitutional law, reflected in the state as a being, say, the German Reich as the personified Constitution of Weimar. But the German Reich is found as a bearer of rights or duties in innumerable passages in the legal rules of the Constitution of Weimar itself; the state accordingly is not only a "concept of legal essence" but also a "concept of legal content." [4] The concept of the state as a legal content belongs in the category of "legally relevant" concepts. But legally relevant concepts are concepts of extralegal reality to which the legal order refers, which it possibly points up and transforms in certain respects but the core of which it takes over from life. So, too, the concept of the state as a legal content in the last analysis means the state as a real fact, so that the concept of the state in reality thus reaches into the legal world, as a legally relevant concept.

Now the question of the priority of the law or the state refers on the one hand to the normative concept of the law, and on the other hand to the concept of the state in reality. These two concepts are by no means identical but, on the contrary, involve the highest tension, viz., the tension which usually exists between a norm and a reality but which is here still further increased. For the reality "state," the norm "law" is in a certain sense an inadequate norm, because even the *idea* of law is not identical with the *idea* of the state; the law, besides serving the purpose of the state, may be subservient to an idea that may collide with the more immediate purpose of the state, viz., legal certainty, and to an idea which is originally foreign to the state, viz., justice. To be sure, the state, subsequently as it were, admits even justice and legal certainty among its purposes and is ready in part to sacrifice to them "reasons of state." Thus the essential incompatibility of the law as a standard by which to measure the state, the tension between the law and the state, is again somewhat relaxed.

Self-Obligation of the State by Law. Once more, then, we face the problem of the priority of the law or the state, the attempt having failed to show that there is no sense in putting this question. An effort to reconcile the priority of the state with the obligatory force of law upon the state is the doctrine of the state binding itself to its law (Georg Jellinek). However, as we have seen in our critique of the contract theory, the supposed legal self-obligation is in truth not autonomy but heteronomy; the will does not bind itself but the will of today is bound to the will of yesterday, the will of the empirical subject to the will of a subject conceived as ideal. So, too, in the state supposedly binding itself to its law, the binding self and the bound self are different; the bound self is the

[4] Cf. KELSEN, *op. cit.* 275

state as a legal reality, the binding self is the state as the conceptual content of its law; the former is the state in the sense in which alone it was considered in posing the question, namely, according to its concept in reality, while the latter is the legal order itself. So we face the question, in no way simplified, what norm outside of the state binds the state to its law. The doctrine of the "normative force of the factual," Georg Jellinek's explanation [e] (p. 204), that what ultimately matters is whether or not in the opinion of a particular epoch the state itself is bound by the abstract declarations of its will, does not answer the problem but cuts it off. "Normative force of the factual" is a paradox; an Ought can never spring from an Is; a fact such as the opinion of a particular epoch can become normative only when a norm has attributed to it that normativity.

Solution of the Problem: Obligation by Transpositive Legal Rule. Thus we see ourselves forced beyond both positive law and the state, not indeed into the world of facts but into a world of norms which are no longer positive norms of the state, and which therefore can only be norms of natural law. Indeed, as has been shown above (sec. 10, p. 117), the very positivism of the state and the law, when thought through, presupposes a legal rule of natural law: "If in any community there is a holder of supreme power his orders shall be obeyed." In our consideration of the validity of the law (sec. 10), we have found the justification for the commanding power of whoever at the time holds power in this, that he alone is in the position to decide the conflict between legal views authoritatively, to render his decision valid, i.e., effective — he alone is able to establish legal certainty. But if the legal certainty it establishes is the basis of the current state-power's right to create law, it must also be the limit of that power. Only for the sake of the certain validity of its laws does the state have the right to make laws. But that certainty would be frustrated if the state could free itself from being bound by those laws. The same thought of legal certainty by which the state is called upon to make laws also demands that the state itself be bound by its laws. The state is called upon to make laws only upon the condition that it consider itself bound by its laws. So the natural law rule that whoever at the time holds power has the right to enact law is inseparable from the other natural law rule that that holder of power is bound by his own laws. The holder of power would cease to be entitled to enact law as soon as he himself evaded his laws. With the seizure of the state-power, the obligation of a government of laws is of necessity assumed and cannot be declined. So the state is bound by its positive law by transpositive, nat-

[e] [The reference is apparently to the work cited in n. 1, *supra*.]

ural law, by the same principle of natural law upon which alone the validity of positive law itself can be founded.

Value of a Formal Government of Laws. It has been declared that this self-obligatory minimum, the state's being bound only by the positive law enacted by itself, renders the idea of a government of laws positivistic and empty. It has been pointed out that the idea of a government of laws in its original form implied that the state was bound to the rights of man antecedent to the state and to natural law above the state. It has been demanded that the thought of law ought once again to mean that a definite *idea* of law, not merely the *concept* of law in general, be applied to the relation of the individual to the state.[5] Yet the application of the mere concept of law to the construction of a government of laws must not be underrated. For law is only what means to be justice. But by setting up justice there is set up equality. A command issued by the state, to be valid for particular men and particular cases as such, would not be law but arbitrariness. In political reality, too, this thought is forceful enough to compel arbitrariness and selfish interest at least to dress up as law. That even this means something has been illustrated in another connection (sec. 3, pp. 63 *et seq.*), when it was shown that the freedom demanded by the bourgeoisie in its own class-interest, since it was claimed in the form of law, necessarily benefited the fourth estate as well, even against the interest of the bourgeoisie, as including the freedom to organize unions. Moreover, even arbitrary commands of the state come to be interpreted, by the organs for the administration of justice, as rules of law, that is, in the sense required by the principle of equality. Interpretation, practiced by a class of "lawyer-notables" (Max Weber), whose professional honor includes practicing the craft of law according to rules of art, is the vehicle of that autonomy of the legal form which tears the law from its root in self-interest and eventually makes it prevail even against the interest in which it is rooted. For the sake of that autonomy, even the suppressed class may have an interest in the realization of the law enacted by the ruling class. So in their many struggles for their rights the suppressed class in turn becomes the protector of the very legal order which the ruling class imposed upon it, since that law, while *class* law, is indeed class *law*, since it presents the interest of the ruling class not naked but in the garb of law, and since the form of law, no matter what the legal content, always, indeed, serves the suppressed.

[5] Darmstaedter, Die Grenzen der Wirksamkeit des Rechtsstaats (1930).

SECTION 27

ECCLESIASTICAL LAW

Lawyers are often enemies of Christ, as has been said: "a true lawyer, a bad Christian." — *Luther*

The philosophy of ecclesiastical law is but a sector of the religious philosophy of law; the question of the church and ecclesiastical law is but a part of the problem of religion and law. When Catholicism holds that ecclesiastical law is of God, all law in its view must somehow be of God. When Luther calls law utterly secular, this characterization refers also to ecclesiastical law: it, too, is law without God. Nor can one affirm, with Rudolph Sohm, that ecclesiastical law contradicts the essence of the church without believing, with Leo Tolstoy, that all law contradicts religion and all law is law against God.

Catholicism. In Catholicism, the church in the religious sense and the church in the legal sense are one; the law of the church, just like the teaching of the church, is of religious significance; the legal church, too, rests on divine establishment. Even though the teaching and the law of the church may be related as end and means in the eyes of God, who established them, man is bound by ecclesiastical law, as well as by the teaching of the church, categorically and not merely conditionally. This means that the legal church is not a mere means to the end of religious life but is an end unto itself. Thus it follows from its divine establishment that the church has a value of its own. Its value is not exhausted in serving the religious life of its members; it carries its value within itself quite apart from all its effects upon the salvation of its members. So it is not an individualistic social structure, not even a transindividualistic group personality, but rather a transpersonal community of work — an institution and not a corporation. A symbol of that transpersonal mission of the church is the priest who offers the sacrifice of the mass, not for other believers — whose presence, indeed, is not required — nor even for himself — since the wonder of the eucharist takes place not *ex opere operantis* but *ex opere operato*,[a] but for the sake of the transformation itself. That transpersonal mission again is decisive for the organization of the church, which is built not from below, from the beneficiaries of the blessings of ecclesiastical salvation, but from above, from the participants in the forces of religious salvation, in a

[a] [Not by the working of the minister but by the work administered.]

structure of hierarchy and dominion. But the divine origin of the legal church determines also its attitude toward the state and the law of the state. All law partakes of the divinity of ecclesiastical law. But besides the law revealed by God, on which the legal church is based, there is the natural law instilled into man by God, which the state is called upon to realize. The law of the church and the law of the state, in so far as the latter remains true to its destination, flow from the same divine source and are in so far unable to contradict each other. But should the law of the state become alienated from its divine origin, divine law takes incontestable precedence. Thus in superb coherence a uniform legal world unfolds from the dominating center of revealed divine law.

Sohm, Tolstoy. The dangers of identifying the spiritual and the legal church, the starting point of the Catholic system, have been sharply stated by Günter Holstein:

> If one wishes to secure the word and the spirit by law and office and for that reason always takes law, office, and spirit for interconnected, then in truth one puts law and office above the spirit and the word; then — this is the inescapable consequence — it is ultimately not the word and the spirit that determine the kind and conduct of office, but rather official and legal authority that by its decision determines the kind and content of the world.[1]

Fundamentally, this is the danger which Dostoevsky presents as the essence of the Catholic Church, in his grandiose account of the Grand Inquisitor before the reappearing Savior. This is also the point of departure of Sohm's doctrine of the contradiction between the church and ecclesiastical law. Legal formalism and legal compulsion are incompatible with the essence of the church, which is to be founded upon faith and love, that is, upon inwardness and spontaneity. Legal formalism cannot pass upon one's salvation; legal compulsion cannot enforce a Christian way of life. But in truth that tension between the legal and the religious rests not only on legal compulsion and on legal formalism, but on the fundamental nature of the legal way of thought, its "outwardness," of which compulsion and formalism may be said to be but symptoms. According to the legal way of thought, outward behavior is taken for essential, the mental attitude from which it springs for secondary; behavior that is outwardly lawful is deemed satisfactory without a demand for the corresponding mental attitude; the discharge of a legal duty is viewed only as compliance with the demand and claim of another and with a legal enactment commanding from without. In the religious view, on the other hand, all that matters is the mental attitude,

[1] Holstein, Die Grundlagen des evangelischen Kirchenrechts (1928) 220.

faith and love, neither being enforced by the claim of another person or by the presence of a command but both flowing freely from the abundance of the soul. Moreover, in the law in most cases not only does a duty have a corresponding right but also a right of one person often confronts the right of another, as in bilateral contractual relations. This is the essence of commutative justice, which should be characterized accordingly as a mere equalization between two egoisms. Since it means that one has to serve another's advantage only if he finds his own advantage therein, conforming to *do ut des*,[b] it therefore represents the exact opposite of a relation based on love. But if such contradictions between law on the one hand and love and faith on the other are thought through, they compel us to assume not only an opposition between the church and ecclesiastical law, with Rudolph Sohm, but an opposition between religion and law altogether, with Leo Tolstoy. For the demands of the ethics of Christian love claim validity not only for life within the church but also for life in the world, and here, too, they everywhere collide antithetically with the law. Not only ecclesiastical law, but all law would then be against God.

Luther. Just as in the Catholic view God has prescribed their laws to the church and the world, so according to Rudolph Sohm and Leo Tolstoy the legal structure of the church and the world rests on divine establishment; only this divine establishment, precisely contrary to the Catholic view, is directed toward freedom from all legal regulation, toward an anarchic community of love.

> Catholicism teaches that Christ endowed his church with a legal equipment fixed and unchangeable in its basic outlines. Sohm teaches that Christ at the outset gave his church an unchangeable organization of the kind that excluded, in principle and for all times, any connection with the law. The one is as mistaken as the other.[2]

In the Lutheran view, Jesus neither prescribed nor rejected a legal order of the church; law is neither of God nor against God, but rather is simply without God — and it is against God only when it pretends to be of God and when therefore the legal church invades the field reserved to the spiritual church. Says Luther:

> The secular regimen has laws that extend no farther than to body and goods and what is outward on earth, for over the souls God cannot and will not let anyone reign but Himself alone. So where secular power presumes to lay

[b] ["I give that you give," a formula expressing a type of exchange contract in Roman law.]

[2] Cf. KAHL, LEHRSYSTEM DES KIRCHENRECHTS UND DER KIRCHENPOLITIK (1894) 74.

down laws for the soul it encroaches upon the regimen of God and but seduces and corrupts the soul. Therefore one must carefully separate the two regimens and leave both, one to make people pious, the other to establish peace outwardly and restrain bad works.[3]

To be sure, Sohm and Tolstoy affirm that the law inevitably "presumes to lay down laws for the soul," since the sphere of validity of Christian life is unlimited, yet where the legal way of thought begins, Christian life necessarily ends. But if law should thus be against Christianity, Christianity on the other hand still cannot be without law — a Christianity, at any rate, that does not see its only fulfillment in a heroism of love. Christian ethics itself demands of man not the superhuman but only the human when it asks him to love his neighbor like himself. Therewith it tacitly presupposes a minimum measure of safeguarding self-preservation, and hence the legal institutions required for this purpose. Only when the urge to self-preservation has at least in part been satisfied can the impulse to love one's neighbor enter one's consciousness at all.

So Luther gave progressively more and more room to law beside love, without, however, intending in the least to relax the tension between love and law; rather the tension is put into every individual soul and brought to a head. Christ's teaching of not resisting evil is thought to have contemplated man as a Christian and not as a person in authority. "Christ leaves to authority its right and office pure, but teaches his Christians as individual people without office and regimen how they for their part ought to live so that they desire no vengeance at all, and are so disposed that if someone smites them on one cheek they are ready if need be to turn to him the other also." It is incumbent upon authority to preserve the law, but the injured ought to do nothing about it. "So power ought to help and protect him either on its own or on the suggestion of others, without his complaint, request or suggestion. Where it does not do so, he ought to let himself be oppressed and injured and to resist no evil, as the words of Christ read." Later, however, Luther permitted not only authority but the individual himself to preserve his right:

> A Christian cannot but be some temporal person because he is under Caesar at least with his body and goods . . . , insofar as he has a rank or office, house and home, wife and children, for all that is Caesar's. A Christian you are for your person, but against your servant you are another person and owe him protection. Lo, we now speak of a Christian *in relatione*, not as a Christian but bound in this life to another person whom he has beneath or above or even beside him.[4]

[3] Cf. Köhler, Luther und die Juristen (1873) 8–9.

[4] Cf. Köhler, *op. cit.* 12, 13–14.

The Christian, then, ought to live in two worlds at once: as a Christian in one, as a temporal person in the other; but he ought to live in the world of the law as if he did not live therein.

The law thus remains quite unconsecrated and without essence, unrelated to religion and indifferent to religion. "Secular law is a weak, poor, impure law, which miserably maintains temporal peace and the life of the belly." Nor is there any difference on this score between ecclesiastical law and the law of the state, for in Luther's view ecclesiastical *law* was law of the *state*. His interest was confined altogether to the reformation of the teaching of the church; the law of the church he considered a work of man without any religious significance. The form of the Catholic episcopal church might as well survive as a legal organization without religious significance if only it filled itself with the content of true Evangelical teaching. This it did not do, and so it was necessary for Protestantism to establish a new legal organization outside of the Catholic Church. But Luther, in his apostolic idealism, in his superb and fatal indifference toward all religiously insignificant outwardness, regarded legal organization as not a religious but a secular task, and hence a task not of the church but of the state. The ruler of a territory as an "outstanding member of the church" has the duty to extend the benefits of his ruling power to the church and to organize and govern the church together with and within the state. "The entire law becomes free for the temporal sword and its authority: there are no essentially different ecclesiastical and secular laws." [5]

Constitution of the Evangelical Church. As a consequence of Luther's view of the law (unlike Calvinism), the Protestant spirit at first found no organized expression in its ecclesiastical constitution, which was purely of the state; to the single spiritual church there corresponded a different legal church within each territorial boundary; together with the state, the church came under the dominion of the absolute ruler. To be sure, the state which Luther called upon to organize the church was regarded by him as a Christian state, and its head not only as holder of the state-power but also as a member of the church and thus subject to its obligations. The more the Christian state was secularized, the more the organs of the state must appear as foreign bodies in the constitutional life of the church. So in the juridical and legislative work of centuries the Evangelical church gradually has been separated from the state, it has developed toward independence and unity, arriving at last at the conclusion of the Constitution of Weimar [of 1919], Article 137: "There is no established church of the state." At the same time, the

[5] HOLSTEIN, *op. cit.* 87.

Evangelical church has become more and more conscious of the legal form that corresponds to its essence. Distinct from the Catholic view which takes the church for a value of its own, in the Evangelical view the church is an institution of human expediency in the service of the individual souls who alone are of religious value; accordingly, its constitution is to be built up from below, ·from the individuals. To the organization of the Catholic Church by transpersonal dominion, there corresponds in the Evangelical church a formative will toward individualistic association. If one is permitted to apply political categories to the constitution of the church, one would have to call it both democratic and liberal in its essential features. It is democratic inasmuch as its organization, in accordance with the religious thought of universal priesthood, is in the last analysis supported by the individuals associated in the church; it is liberal inasmuch as it gives room to the sovereignty of faith, that is, the sovereignty of God who works faith, so that it must forgo the exercise of influence where the truly religious life within the church begins.

Here, then, we have arrived at the point where the distinction between the Catholic and Evangelical views of ecclesiastical law consistently unfolds. In Protestantism, the church in the sense of faith cannot assume the form of a legal church, for this faith means not indeed the *fides quae creditur* but the *fides qua creditur*;[c] the faith that is taken for a sum total, not of intellectual truths of the creed, but of individual, voluntaristic-emotional acts of believing, is incapable of legal formulation. In Catholicism, on the contrary, ecclesiastical law as the legal shell of a fixed kernel of truths of the creed is as possible as it is necessary.[6]

Section 28

The Law of Nations

Whereas the community which has come to prevail throughout the peoples of the earth has now reached so far that the violation of law at one place of the earth is felt at all places; the idea of a right of world citizenship is no fantastic and extravagant conception of the law, but a necessary completion of the unwritten code of constitutional as well as international law into a public law of men generally, and thus into eternal peace.—Immanuel Kant

It is essentially inherent in legal order to be universal. The law cannot lay down a partial regulation without, by the very selection of the part of human relations to be regulated, also taking a stand on the unregu-

[c] [Not the creed in which one believes but the creed by which one believes.]

[6] Cf. Barion, Rudolph Sohm und die Grundlegung des Kirchenrechts (Recht und Staat, vol. 8; 1931)

lated part — precisely by precluding legal effects there. Consequently, a "legal vacuum" is always devoid of law only by virtue of the legal order's own will; in the strict sense, it is not at all devoid of law, it is not a field of facts legally unregulated, but one legally regulated in a negative sense, by denying any legal effect. In the alleged legal vacuum the legal order has willed nothing — not, by any means, willed not to will, which would indeed be a contradiction in terms.

The Problem. Thus, what seems to be anarchy beside or above a legal order is in truth anarchical regulation of the field of facts in question by the legal order, its delivery to the free play of the forces working therein. So, too, from the standpoint of a particular legal order, another legal order is valid only because the former has made room for the latter. To be sure, that other legal order in turn claims to be valid of its own strength and in turn to have created the very possibility of other legal orders being valid. Therefore, the claim to validity by any particular legal order embraces the entire globe. Indeed, the fact that "private and penal international law" [a] is an element of the national legal order clearly shows that domestic law claims to deal with all foreign states of facts as well, if in most cases negatively, by denying domestic legal effects. Every legal order raises the claim to be world law; in every legal order there is contained the postulate of the "unity of the normative system" (Kelsen). This, on the one hand, implies a world law to crown the legal order as a matter of conceptual necessity, since each individual national legal order pretends to contain within itself that world law completing the legal system. On the other hand, since each raises that claim in contradiction to all others, the requirement of legal certainty postulates the existence of a law of nations above all national legal orders. Suggested therewith, to be sure, is also what renders the law of nations problematical: Its own universal claim to validity, whereby each legal order can be deemed valid only within a particular sphere, contradicts the universal claim to validity of each national law, which can but resort to its own will to ascribe validity to the law of nations.

Individualism: The World State. In the *individualistic* view of the law, to be sure, this problem is resolved very simply. The individual state is destined to be submerged in the universal state: the individual without individuality and hence also without nationality is born a citizen of the world. The line of thought that starts with the individual without individuality leads irresistibly to the state of mankind without nationality.

[a] [Continental terms embracing conflict of laws in the fields of private and penal laws.]

The segregation of mankind into states and nations is historically accidental and provisional; the individualistic view of the state makes logically possible only the world state which is to embrace all mankind without so much as meeting on its way the nation. "If individualism proceeds consistently it may indeed arrive at the world state by expanding the boundaries of the state — it will not be able to arrive at the law of nations as a legal order above and between the states." [1] It is possible to go back from the world state to the nations as technical administrative subdivisions, as provinces of mankind with a common language; but in the systematic view — not, of course, in the historical view — the nation as thus understood would be because of and after, and not before, the world state, just as the municipality is conceivable only within the state.

> The pure idea of law in and of itself pays no regard to the separation of society into individual states. From the universal validity of the juridical law there directly follows the necessity of a legal community which extends over the whole of society. The existence of a plurality of states, and of bodies politic generally, is legally accidental. It is neither demanded nor rejected by the law. It remains a question of expediency whether and how far separate legal organizations in society are desirable according to such accidental boundaries as are determined by geographical conditions or by language, customs and usages, religion, race, and similar factors.

Thus Leonard Nelson.[2] From such a line of thought there may consistently follow only a decentralized world state but not a league of nations. So, in fact, in Kant's eyes the league of nations, as the looser combination of states, is but a substitute for the impracticable world state.[3] But the world state is marked by the same lack of individuality as the individual without individuality, on whom it is ultimately founded. Just as it springs from abstract humanity in men, so it flows into humanity as abstract universality and not mankind as a concrete whole, into humankind as a "generic name in the natural system" and not as a "generic subject in historical reality" (Scheler). For this reason, Lagarde calls the state of mankind as thus understood the "gray international."

Transindividualism: The Dogma of Sovereignty and the Denial of the Law of Nations. The thought of the world state belongs to an age when the state was conceived solely from the standpoint of the thought of

[1] Binder, Philosophie des Rechts (1925) 562.

[2] System der philosophischen Rechtslehre und Politik (1924) 511 *et seq.*

[3] Herbert Kraus, Das Problem internationaler Ordnung bei Immanuel Kant (1931) 30.

law — as a "union of men under juridical laws" (Kant) — and was not yet connected with the concepts both of the nation and of power. It is the thought of the national power state that found its juridical expression in the dogma of sovereignty. But in the attempts to think of the sovereign state as nevertheless subject to the law of nations there is repeated, move by move, the futile endeavor of the individualistic theory of law to get at the state from the sovereign individual human being with his inalienable rights of man. In both cases, the solution was sought in the thought of self-obligation — by founding the state upon the social contract and the law of nations upon the consensus of states. In both cases, on closer analysis the seeming self-obligation turns out to be obligation from without. "By self-obligation, one may explain everything, except only this, that if there is to be a law of nations there must be obligation from without by virtue of which the free self-absolution from the allegedly free self-obligation would be violative of the law." [4] The very appearance of self-obligation could arise only from substituting for the concrete individuality the abstract individual consistently guided by his true interest alone. From the concrete individuality, the path leads not to the social contract but to anarchy. So, too, from the starting point of the concrete individuality of the state, consistent reasoning leads not to the law of nations but to the anarchy of states. For "anarchical law" (Jellinek) is a contradiction in itself; a "law of coördination" is conceivable only on the basis of a law of subordination, as in private law, and not as a legal order topped by no higher order, like the law of nations. On the basis of anarchical coördination, even the partial self-obligation by a concrete contract is inconceivable. If no higher norm binds my will of today to my will of yesterday it cannot be explained why it should remain bound to it. Just as anarchism in its extreme form — in Max Stirner — denies even the binding force of contracts, so the dogma of sovereignty, by recognizing the *clausula rebus sic stantibus*,[b] leads at least to a considerable loosening of the obligation of international treaties. Thus, from the standpoint of the dogma of sovereignty, consistency requires the denial of the legal nature of the law of nations, indeed, even of the binding force of treaties among states.[5]

But the dogma of sovereignty itself provokes immanent criticism. The

[4] Cf. RICHARD THOMA in JUS NATURAE ET GENTIUM, EINE UMFRAGE ZUM GEDÄCHTNIS DES HUGO GROTIUS (Reprint from (1925) 24 ZEITSCHRIFT FÜR INTERNATIONALES RECHT) 67.

[b] [In treaties, a clause or an implication that the obligation is subject to the condition that the circumstances remain unchanged.]

[5] HELLER, DIE SOUVERÄNITÄT (1927) 161, gives an outright definition of sovereignty as the quality of a state by which, resting on its absolute claim to preserve itself, it "maintains itself absolutely in a given case even against the law."

conception of the law of nations as an anarchical law of coördination starts from the possibility of the simultaneous existence of a plurality of sovereign states. In truth, however, "the state, inasmuch as it is declared sovereign, i.e., taken for absolute and presupposed as supreme legal entity, must be the sole legal enity; that is, . . . the sovereignty of the one state excludes the sovereignty of any other state, and therewith excludes any other state as a sovereign community." [6] "The sovereignty of the one state would immediately exclude that of the other and thus destroy itself as a universal legal principle." [7] Each state is thought of as sovereign for the area of its dominion, but an absolute claim of validity for a limited area of validity is a *contradictio in adjecto*.[c] That sovereignty is incapable of being limited to a definite substantive field has surely become clear on every side in the controversy against the doctrine of the division of sovereignty in federalism. But what applies to the substantive field of validity is no less true for the territorial field of validity. The reason why not every individual sovereign legal order raises the claim to rule over the entire globe is only this, that it stops at the state boundary by virtue of wise self-limitation, and not that at such boundary another legal order bade it stop — for if it had to give way to that it would of course not be sovereign. Every state draws its state boundary for itself, as in the Reich Constitution [of 1919], Article 2; [d] and from the standpoint of the dogma of sovereignty it is nothing but a happy accident that the boundary of a state fixed by itself coincides with the boundaries of adjacent states fixed by themselves. But if accident is what is inexplicable, this implies that the dogma of sovereignty is unable to explain such a simple fact as the mutual compatibility of the constitutions of states fixing boundaries between the states. Moreover, it is unable to explain the mutual recognition of states by each other as subjects of the law of nations and contracting parties to treaties, endowed with equal rights. From the standpoint of the dogma of sovereignty, the same conflicts arise here as, in the relation of the state and the church, between the legality theory and the privilege theory of the concordats: [e] To each state, the recognition of, or the treaty promise to, any other state would appear as a favor granted to the other party by

[6] Thus KELSEN, ALLGEMEINE STAATSLEHRE (1925) 106.

[7] Thus NELSON, *op. cit.* 517.

[c] [Contradictory qualification.]

[d] ["The area of the Reich consists of the areas of the German states. Other areas may be included in the Reich by Reich statute if their populations by virtue of the right of self-determination so desire."]

[e] [According to the former theory, the concordat is valid as a law enacted unilaterally by the state; according to the latter, it is valid as a privilege granted unilaterally by the church.]

way of a unilateral legal act. So the picture of the group of states that the dogma of sovereignty offers is not that of a legal community of subjects of law who are mutually obliged to recognize one another. Rather it is that of an arena full of beasts of prey, each of whom claims to remain sole master of the place, but, unable to destroy or drive out one another, growling and snarling they pass by one another for a while.

The thought of the sovereignty of the state completely resembles that natural law thought of the sovereign individual human being who brings his pre-state right of man with him into the state and claims to form the state in accordance with that right of man. It has since been recognized that man does not as a subject of law enter the state but is elevated to a subject of law by the state only. But sovereignty is nothing else than the quality of being a subject of the law of nations: A state is not a subject of the law of nations because it is sovereign, but it is sovereign because it is a subject of the law of nations. So the concept of sovereignty is to be developed, not out of natural law speculation independent of the law of nations, but precisely out of the law of nations. Worked out by this method, it does not mean that above a state there is no further, legal power on earth (hence, as one would have to conclude, not even a law of nations); rather it means just this, that the state is immediately under the law of nations, that it "of right owes obedience to no other legal norms than those of the law of nations." [8] Therewith a law of nations above sovereign states ceases to be a *contradictio in adjecto*; it becomes, indeed, a tautology.

Transpersonalism: Law of Nations and League of Nations. Sovereign national states, bound together by a law of nations and a league of nations — this is the foreign policy objective set by the transpersonal thought of culture and work. Transpersonalism on the one hand turns against the dissolution of the national states into a world state. It cannot overlook the fact that the individual is culturally creative only in the national community. But it turns just as much against taking the national state for absolute in the form of the anarchy of states; for it is equally unable to overlook the fact that the cultural tasks themselves are international in nature. There is no particular German truth, beauty, or morality to constitute tasks of cultural work. A cultural nation and a national culture cannot be thought of as purposes. The national tinge, like the personal touch, must not even be a secondary thought in cultural work. He who seeks not for the cause but for his own, for the vain

[8] Cf. THOMA, *op. cit.* 69; VIKTOR BRUNS, VÖLKERRECHT ALS RECHTSORDNUNG (Reprint from ZEITSCHRIFT FÜR AUSLÄNDISCHES ÖFFENTLICHES RECHT UND VÖLKERRECHT) 34.

expression of individual or national peculiarity, will fail the cause and yet not arrive at his personality or his nation. Like the personality, the nation belongs to those values which one attains by not striving for them — only by self-forgetful devotion to the cause. It is a symptom, but not a remedy, of immature and weak national consciousness to strive for national character in all one's utterances. Life while it is being lived is subject to the universally valid laws of the good, the true, the beautiful; only the life that has been lived becomes subject to the evaluations of "personality" and "nation." They belong to history; and it is characteristic of a history-minded age to believe that evaluations that belong exclusively to subsequent historical contemplation may be transferred into life to determine goals. National consciousness was always strongest when a nation believed itself to be called upon to be the missionary of a transnational idea. This is the structure of national consciousness: the consciousness of a people to be the first-born carrier of a human value, to be a "people of humanity." Thus national consciousness itself is unaware of the national peculiarity of its postulates and achievements — to determine how far they were nationally conditioned and colored is a later task of history. The only way of a people sure of itself is, not to create a distinct national culture mirroring itself, but to create human values and leave it to subsequent generations to recognize, in what is in substance valuable, the characteristic national handwriting as well. On the one hand, then, culture is directed toward transnational goals; on the other hand, those cultural goals can be realized only in the nation and in national forms. This is the ground on which to call for an international cultural community on the basis of national cultural differentiation, for a uniform but decentralized organization of the world.

The Reality of the Law of Nations. Again, the fundamental tripartite division of legal philosophical standpoints has proved its fruitfulness: Individualism required the world state; the transindividualistic view of the state and the law led to the dogma of sovereignty and the denial of the law of nations; the transpersonalistic view turned out to be the foundation of the law of nations and the League of Nations. To the latter view, then, the trend of the development of reality conforms. For *there is* a positive law of nations, supported by a common will above the states, laid down in express agreements and in tacitly acknowledged customary law. To be sure, only a small part of international legal relations is regulated in one or the other way. But to the filling of gaps there apply the principles of finding the law which are formulated in the classical Article 1 of the Swiss Civil Code.[f] The legal rule to be applied is to

[f] ["The statute applies to all legal questions for which it expressly or construc-

be gathered in the first place from "tried doctrine and tradition," that is, those legal principles, regarded as universally valid, which have taken shape on the basis of natural law and have not ceased to dominate men's minds even after natural law has turned from an absolute necessity of reason into a superb fact of history, and which have thus become part of the positive law of nations.[9] In the second place, he who is charged with a decision under the law of nations is to "decide according to the rule he would lay down as a legislator." This seems to hypostatize right law as positive law and to blur the sharp line between absolute worth and real validity of the law. In truth, that objection does not avail in the application of international law any more than it does in adjudication in national law. For back of the individual legal rule that is creatively found in this way, there stands the common will, of the state and above the states, which supports the whole legal order within as well as above the states: That, as between the individuals, so too between the states, there shall be law; and inherent in this common will for law is the tendency toward universal coherence, tolerating no lacunae or legal vacua, which has been mentioned at the beginning of this section.[10]

But the dogma of sovereignty, vacillating between a reluctant affirmation and an open denial of the law of nations, is characterized by its acknowledgment of the right to war, which accordingly is both a phenomenon and a denial of the law of nations.

SECTION 29

WAR

Pax optima rerum.[a] — *Ancient device of the seal of the University of Kiel*

The value of war must be judged not, as is frequently done, on the basis of its favorable or unfavorable secondary effects, but solely according to how far it satisfies its peculiar function. If really war, and war only, were apt to test and awaken heroic virtues and vital forces, still it could not be judged on this basis any more than legal procedure could

tively provides. If no provision can be gathered from the statute, the judge shall decide according to customary law or, where such is lacking as well, according to the rule he himself would lay down as a legislator. In so doing he follows tried doctrine and tradition."]

[9] Cf. ERNST TROELTSCH, NATURRECHT UND HUMANITÄT IN DER WELTPOLITIK (1923), and my comments thereon in JUS NATURAE ET GENTIUM, EINE UMFRAGE 55 *et seq.*

[10] Cf. BRUNS, *op. cit.* 31.

[a] [The best of things is peace.]

be judged on the basis that it exercises acumen and increases knowledge of the law. Now the specific meaning of war is victory and defeat, hence decision of a dispute; whether this is the decision of a legal dispute or of a dispute of interests, that is, of a collision of values, is to be discussed still further. Criticism of war can result solely from the inquiry whether it represents a meaningful method of deciding disputes.[1]

Ethics of War. Applying to war, then, successively the methodical instruments of all those philosophical disciplines which are concerned with the evaluation of human action, it follows that ethics is unable to solve the problem of war. The ethical value judgment relates not to war and the decision contained therein, but to the part of the individual in the war, his war guiltlessness or his war guilt. But war guilt cannot very well mean anything else but to have wanted the war. Taken in this sense, however, war guilt cannot be determined unequivocally at all. For, as long as war is valid as a legal institution, every diplomatic step involves the *dolus eventualis*[b] of a war, no matter how thinly diluted, and all politics is oriented toward the possibility of war. War, according to the well-known saying, is but the continuation of politics with different means, not so much because politics determines the essence of war as because war determines the essence of politics. The currency of the bank note depends on the bank's gold reserve, without people through whose hands the note passes even remotely thinking of it in most cases. Just so the most trifling diplomatic step, even if accompanied by no thought of the *ultima ratio*,[c] derives its efficacy from the available amount of men and rifles, horses and cannon, airplanes and tanks that may be used if need be to enforce it. Politics is related to war like the threat of violence to violence itself; and it must finally lead to war, even against the will of those carrying on politics, from the same necessity which causes any other threat that remains ineffective to turn into violence. One cannot continually strike against the sword without being compelled in a given case also to strike with the sword.

Legal Philosophy of War. Only the question of war guilt is a question of ethics; but the question of the right to war, of the just war, is a

[1] On the following cf. Radbruch, *Zur Philosophie dieses Krieges*, 44 ARCHIV FÜR SOZIALWISSENSCHAFT 139 *et seq.*; SCHELER, DER GENIUS DES KRIEGES UND DER DEUTSCHE KRIEG (1915), but also SCHELER, DIE IDEE DES FRIEDENS UND DER PAZIFISMUS (1931).

[b] ["Eventual intent." This civil law term refers to criminal intent in cases where the result of the criminal act was contemplated as possible, though not necessary, and was desired or acquiesced in by the criminal.]

[c] [The ultimate argument.]

question of legal philosophy. The legal theories of war seek the criterion of the just war in this, that it is a reaction against an injury suffered or imminent, that is, retaliation, enforcement of a claim, or, especially, self-defense. But if war really were nothing else than the settling of legal questions, then in the eyes of anyone who does not believe in a prestabilized harmony of law and power it would be the most unfit means conceivable to that end, a form of proceeding which national legal procedure has left far behind ever since the abolition of trial by combat. Again, it would certainly not be what it has been glorified for: "the mover of the human race." For, since the law is always on the side of the status quo, to make the right to war depend upon injury suffered or threatened means to award it always to him who aims to preserve, and never to him who aims to change, the traditional system of states; it means to attribute unchangeability for all times, as of right, to the historical accident of what at the time happens to be the division of the surface of the earth. Above all, however, the legal theories of war eliminate the concept of war itself. If the just war were really nothing else but self-defense against injustice, then would the resistance of the opponent, self-defense against self-defense, be absurd and an additional injustice, the war would be a punitive expedition against a morally inferior opponent, the enemy would be a criminal, and the character of war as a duel between opponents of equal rights would be eliminated.[2] Therefore, the task of war cannot be to prove existing law but can only be to create new law. The right to victory is not the presupposition but the effect of the war; only by the war is it gained and proven.

Historical Philosophy of War. Therewith we pass from the legal philosophy to the historical philosophy of war. For evaluating events on the basis of their effects belongs to the philosophy of history. The just war would then be the victorious war. Yet, on the other hand, the question of the just war will call for an answer not by the war only but in advance of the war. The right to war that is then in question cannot be the right to victory, which is established only by the victory, but only the right to enter into the state of war. But at the same time the legal philosophical view of the just war, which always admitted application to one or the other party only, is replaced by the concept of the war that is equally just on both sides. For only if the justice of war is thus referred really to the war in its entirety, and not only to the position of the one or the

[2] The Kellogg Pact, by outlawing wars of aggression, has therefore excluded wars in their previous sense altogether. The defense which even under the Kellogg Pact is admissible against aggression is not a *war* of defense, since it opposes right to wrong, whereas war presupposes opponents of equal rights.

other belligerent, is there a thought on which respect of the enemy and equal rights of the opponents, essential to war, may be based. In the historical philosophical view, on the one hand, the war is justified for the victor by his victory and, on the other hand, entrance into war must have been justified also for the belligerent who is subsequently vanquished. This dilemma is resolved by a reflection upon the difference between "significance" and "meaning." "Significance" we ascribe to an event when "values are at stake," "meaning" we ascribe to it when it originates values.[3] A war that is fought for a "good cause" is significant even if that cause succumbs, though it is not meaningful. According to this terminology, the category of a war just on both sides affirms only the "significance" but not the "meaning" of war. Just on both sides is a war if it involves the decision of a question that on both sides is weighty enough for war, a collision of interests, of values, for the decision of which there is no other means but war.

However, whether this significance, namely deciding a collision of values, may indeed be taken to underlie war, depends upon whether the decision of such collisions of values may as a matter of principle be found in victory. War may be construed as implying a question only if victory is able to furnish the answer to it. Only if victory has a "meaning" may we attribute "significance" to war. So we find ourselves referred back to an examination of the statement which has been suggested before as a hypothesis: that victory realizes a right to victory which is not created but only proved by the actual course of the war. That is to say, we are referred back to the question whether military superiority proves something beyond itself, whether, say, national power may serve as a measure of national culture.

National culture is a purely qualitative determination of the nation, not measurable in quantitative terms. But in the military view the nations become "powers," different and comparable according to the quantity of their power, hence assumed to be qualitatively equal to one another. War, the culminating point of the militaristic view of the state, is at the same time the lowest point of national differentiation. It is symbolical that the manifold colors of the national peacetime uniforms were submerged, during the [First World] War, in the khaki color that was almost the same for all nations. Every fighting nation forces the same means of combat upon the other. To be sure, the power-quantity of the states has been claimed to be the index of the cultural quality of

[3] Thus, differing from our terminology in sec. 1, here the meaning which is related to value but is not necessarily of valuable content, the meaning as *terminus medius* [median term] is called "significance," while the term "meaning" is reserved solely for the significance of valuable content.

the nations; a proportionality of culture and power has been asserted, and war, in which the powers take the measure of one another, has been glorified as the *examen rigorosum* of the cultures also. As a matter of fact, the standing of the natural sciences and technology, of the organization of business and transportation, of education and social ethics may express itself in a corresponding measure of military superiority. Yet by no means the entire, and not even the most essential, store of culture may be transformed into military energies. The cultural values of Goethe, Dante, Shakespeare, Molière cannot be fired off as torpedoes or blown off as poison gases — and if nevertheless torpedoes and poison gases determine what expansion a language and therewith a culture is to enjoy in the world, the decision is not by the divine ordeal of war but by the dice of accident; and if subsequent history-writers praise world history as the world judgment, this is so only because the victor always writes the history, too. The highest cultural values cannot be expressed in figures of military power, or indeed in any quantitative determinations. Culture is not a comparable quantity but an incomparable quality; and he who can see the nations only as competing or even fighting masses of cultures of different size has excluded the cultural nation altogether from his field of vision.

Religious Philosophy of War. So the philosophy of history dismisses us without the possibility of finding in war anything other than a power dispute, possibly indeed with cultural consequences, but without any cultural significance of its own. The apology for war may, therefore, be expected only from that source from which consecration and values ultimately flow to all that exists: from religion. For toward war, as toward all that exists, a threefold attitude is possible: The value-blind attitude of science, the evaluating attitude of philosophy, and the value-conquering attitude of religion. Blind against the value or worthlessness of war, science investigates its occasions, its causes, its inherent laws. Evaluating philosophy seeks to determine the criteria of the just war. But religion finds a value of a higher kind even in the most unjust of wars. In human nature, as one of its most paradoxical features, the metaphysical optimism of the religious attitude surprisingly wells up just when any purely empirical view requires despairing pessimism. Good fortune carries too much apparent value in itself to raise any question as to its true metaphysical value; but bad fortune, just because at first sight it seems to contradict this value, powerfully stimulates the religious disposition innate in all humanity. Yet one must never forget that theodicy, if the presumptuous word be permitted, is a justification of God and not a justification of men; that religious philosophy is not ethics; that religious acquiescence in the accomplished fact is no subsequent justification of those who caused it. The Gospel passage about Judas, calling down woe unto him from whom the evil cometh that needs must come, shows that the result and the deed that called it forth are subject to entirely different laws of evaluation. The religious view of war is similar to that of pain, which it praises as holy because of its purifying power yet the causing of which it condemns.

Religion alone, then, may find a blessing even in war; in any other view, war must remain a calamity that is meaningless and alien to significance. Any approach other than that of religion, to which alone it is given to deliver us from all evil, is bound to see in war only disaster and even in victory only the lesser of two disasters. But acquiescence in war as an inevitable disaster befits the lawyer worst of all. He above all faces the question whether the planet which is entrusted to us men is to be ruled by accident or by reason; whether on the very spot where the fate of the globe is to be decided, law, instead of establishing its sole rule, is weakly to leave the field to anarchy; whether the cathedral of the legal order ought to be topped by a miserable emergency structure, a ruin before its completion, or whether it ought to end and culminate in a proud dome.

III

GENERAL THEORY OF LAW

By JEAN DABIN

1944

Jean Dabin was born at Liège, Belgium, on July 9, 1889. He was awarded the doctorate in law by the University of Liège in 1911 and a special doctorate in civil law by the same university in 1920. He became a professor at that university in 1920, but left it in 1922 to become a professor at the University of Louvain, where he has since remained. He has taught civil law, "encyclopedia" of law, private international law, and political and social science. He has served as an exchange professor at the Universities of Paris, Poitiers, Nancy, Dijon, and Lyon, in France, and at the University of Lausanne. He is a co-editor of the REVUE CRITIQUE DE JURISPRUDENCE BELGE, published at Brussels. Among his many honors are an honorary doctorate from the University of Bordeaux, and membership in the Royal Academy of Belgium, International Institute of Philosophy of Law (Paris), and the Instituto Argentino de Filosofia Juridica y Social. He is an Officer of the Order of Leopold and Commander of the Order of the Crown. The most important of his extensive list of publications are LA THÉORIE DE LA CAUSE (Brussels, 1919), of which a Spanish translation appeared in the BIBLIOTECA DE DERECHO PRIVADO (Serie 12, vol. X, Madrid, 1929); LA PHILOSOPHIE DE L'ORDRE JURIDIQUE POSITIF (Paris, 1929); LA TECHNIQUE DE L'ÉLABORATION DU DROIT POSITIF (Brussels-Paris, 1935); DOCTRINE GÉNÉRALE DE L'ETAT (Brussels-Paris, 1939); THÉORIE GÉNÉRALE DU DROIT (Brussels, 1944), the work here translated; ETUDES DE DROIT CIVIL (Brussels, 1947). He is now (1948) living in Louvain.

FOREWORD [a]

In this book will be found the substance of the ideas developed in my two preceding works: *La philosophie de l'ordre juridique positif* [The Philosophy of the Positive Legal Order], Paris, Sirey, 1929; and *La technique de l'élaboration du droit positif* [The Technique of Elaboration of Positive Law], Bruxelles-Paris, Bruylant and Sirey, 1935. On several important points, however, the doctrine has been rendered more precise or more complete.

In particular, it appeared impossible to trace a sufficient distinction between the law and the other rules of human conduct without underscoring the essential link uniting the two concepts of law and society: The law is a societal rule. This is not to say that there could not be law outside of the state and, *a fortiori*, outside of statutes. The state, in the sense of the civil society, is not the only society. Still, on the temporal plane it is the supreme society and its rule is the supreme rule. Neither is this to say that the concept of an international law would be denied. But it is thought that there will be international law, in the full and true sense of the term "law," only when there will exist an international society, more or less universal and in any case organically constituted.

Again, it was desired to examine more closely the relationships between the concept of law and the concepts of natural law and justice, in order to eliminate incessantly renascent ambiguities. Too often are their levels and viewpoints confounded. Thus it is wrong to put the positive legal order or the civil law (what is here called the law) within the direct and exclusive extension of natural law and of justice.

Finally, as indicated by the footnotes, a systematic epitome was undertaken of the *Summa Theologica* of St. Thomas Aquinas so as to mark convergencies and possibly divergencies that appear between the doctrine of the civil law formulated by the great medieval philosopher and theologian and that which a professional jurist of the modern law may propose.

The theory expounded here is confined to a study of the general system of the law, excluding the problem of the formal sources and of the method of interpretation. It thus makes up the first, and incidentally

[a] [The following is a translation of JEAN DABIN, THÉORIE GÉNÉRALE DU DROIT. (Bruxelles: Établissements Émile Bruylant, 1944.) The text of the book is translated in full; omissions made by the translator in some of the author's footnotes are indicated by three periods.]

the principal, part of a comprehensive course in Jurisprudence. Indeed, the first objective of such a course of introduction to law is to define the meaning and function of the legal discipline, as a whole and in its various branches. Do we have to add that the theory of law is of use not only to law students but to all who in one way or another practice law? For the theory of law is nothing else than the reasoned study of that practice.

LOUVAIN
March 15, 1943

GENERAL THEORY OF LAW

PART ONE

THE CONCEPT OF LAW

INTRODUCTION

1. Justifying the Title. We speak of the "concept of law." That title incontestably lacks clarity. We could have said: Conception of *positive* law, a term used to designate the rule expressed in statutes, customary law, and the case law of courts. Indeed, this is the reality at which we are aiming. Yet from the viewpoint of exactness and, in any case, from the methodical viewpoint, the expression "positive law" is not satisfactory. To begin with, the word "positive" is an adjective which sheds no light on the meaning of the noun it is to qualify. Granted that etymologically and historically "positive" has the well-known connotations of the accidental or of the volitional; the word "law" still remains to be defined. The noun, then, is essential, the more so since there exist "positive" rules other than those of law.[1] On the other hand, to speak of "positive law" is to call forth the question of "natural law," since traditionally the law called "positive" is placed in opposition to law called "natural."[2] Now, before we ask ourselves if there exists a "natural

[1] For example, positive morals, decreed by competent authority: God and the church.

[2] It is appropriate to note, however (and this is a new ground for discarding the expression), that the term "positive law" is often understood today in the sense of the law in force, which is effective and consequently real, as opposed to an ideal law that is merely thought of; thus, e.g., Jèze. Going still farther, certain authors understand it in the sense of efficacious law, that is, law not simply set down and promulgated but effectively applied; thus, e.g., Kelsen. [See his GENERAL THEORY OF LAW AND STATE (trans. A. Wedberg, 1945).] Cf., in the same sense, R. CAPITANT, L'ILLICITE, I: L'IMPÉRATIF JURIDIQUE (Paris, 1928) 114 *et seq.*, at p. 115: "Positive law is the law generally obeyed." Still others take positive law to be that which, in some way or other, results from facts; thus, the intuitive positive law of Gurvitch, a synonym for "normative facts" issuing from the social environment. But with this conception one deliberately draws away from established usage, and the positivity of law serves to disguise a positivistic conception of law, which is reduced to a purely positive science.

law," that is, a non-positive law,[3] it is well to know what is law — or what is understood by "law." There always arises the same initial problem: whether it be natural or positive, what is the meaning of the noun "law"? That is why we maintain the expression "concept of law" despite its neutral character, or because of that very neutrality, while reserving a progressive exploration of the idea which it covers.

2. Choosing a Starting Point. A second difficulty — graver than that of the title — arises at the outset of the analysis: What should our starting point be? For the word "law" is used in several senses which are not unrelated to one another yet which remain distinct, corresponding to distinct realities. Among those different senses we must necessarily choose, if only to determine the sense we have in mind and thus to avoid misunderstanding. Yet that very determination is not without risk: Under the pretext of defining a word, problems related to the thing signified are touched and opened up. For instance, the majority of writers, seeking to define law, start from the idea of justice. But that means one of two things. Either justice is taken as synonymous with law, and then the explanation has not advanced one step, as justice remains to be defined. Or else justice (which will always have to be defined) is taken as synonymous with the *content* of the law, and then one prejudges the solution of a problem which could only be argued after one has defined law in a formal sense.

3. Adopting the Idea of "the Rule"; Philological Considerations. The only method that will stand up under criticism is to set up at the very beginning the idea of the law as order, regulation, norm, or rule of conduct. No matter how the idea of the "rule" may be conceived — as a simple mental representation [4] or as an objective reality, which may or may not be of a phenomenal nature — there is no doubt that the law exists as a certain rule of conduct imposing some sort of action, omission, or attitude.[5]

This is suggestively indicated by the etymology of the word *droit* [the French term signifying both law and right]. The word, derived

[3] On the question of natural law, see below, nos. 200–216. [The cross references indicate the numbered paragraphs.]

[4] See, e.g., H. ROLIN, PROLÉGOMÈNES À LA SCIENCE DU DROIT, ESQUISSE D'UNE SOCIOLOGIE JURIDIQUE (Brussels-Paris, 1911) 2, 73. Cf. A. STOOP, ANALYSE DE LA NOTION DU DROIT (Haarlem, 1927) 80, 184 *et seq.*, who speaks of the content of conscience and even of the subconscious.

[5] See, in the same sense, as to the point of departure, J. LECLERCQ, LEÇONS DE DROIT NATUREL, I LE FONDEMENT DU DROIT ET DE LA SOCIÉTÉ (2d ed. Namur-Louvain, 1933), no. 1, pp. 11–12.

from the Low Latin *directum* and encountered in identical forms in several Indo-European tongues (*diritto*, *derecho*, *Recht*, right), simply suggests the idea of rectitude. Lawful or right is what is correct, that is, conformable, adequate, adjusted to a rule — first in the realm of physics and mathematics (e.g., right angle, upright line), then in that of morals and psychology (e.g., right action, upright character), without the suggested rectitude being limited necessarily to the rectitude of justice alone, in the strict sense of respect for another's right. The same root breaks through in the Latin *regere* (*gouverner*, to govern), *rex* (*roi*, king), *regnum* (*règne*, reign), *regula* (*règle*, rule) — again with no restriction to the justice of the content of the *regula* — the particular shade of meaning being that of a command imposed by a superior power: The rule is not only obligatory because it is a rule, but it proceeds from the outside, from above, from an authority.[6] The word *jus*, which designates law in the classical Roman language, is less revealing because its origin is debatable. But whether we derive it, as some do, from the idea of divine will or power (the root *yos*, *yaus*, *juos*, *jous*, signifying saintly, pure, as in *jurare*, to swear), or as others do, from the idea of a bond (the root *yu*, *yug*, *yung*, as in *jugum*, yoke, or *jungere*, to join),[7] these notions are quite close to the idea of the rule: Do not both the divine will and the bond imply the concept of the obligating norm of conduct?[8] Assuming that the terms *justus* and *justitia*, just and justice, actually derive from *jus*, it may be added that the ideas of "just" and "justice" are also indirectly related to the idea of the rule (through the intermediary ideas of the divine will or the bond); and that relation is obvious in *Gerechtigkeit*, the German term for justice, which is directly derived from the idea of law as rule, or *Recht*.

4. *The Objective or Normative as Against the Subjective, Sense of the Lawful.* In defining law by the idea of the rule, we talk of course of "the law," as objectively lawful (*droit objectif*), and not of any

[6] The Greek Δίκη, which means justice, also derives from the idea of the rule: from the root *Dik* or *Dic*, as in *dictamen* or *indictment*.

[7] See F. Senn, De la justice et du droit (Paris, 1927) 25, n. 1; Van Hove, Commentarium Lovaniense in codicem juris canonici, vol. 1, pt. 1 (Malines-Rome, 1928), no. 1, pp. 3–4.

[8] Beyond these philological considerations, it will be noted that in the classical authors the word *jus* [the law or right] is often taken as equivalent to *lex* [a law or statute]; thus, in the expressions *jus naturale* (= *lex naturalis*), *jus positivum* (= *lex humanitatus posita*), *jus humanum* (= *lex humana*). See, e.g., St. Thomas Aquinas, Summa theologica, *Ia IIae*, qu. 95, arts. 2 and 4. Also *infra* nos. 201–202.

right, as subjectively lawful (*droit subjectif*) — adopting a terminology that is rather unfortunate but has become classic among [Continental] jurists.[a] Subjectively lawful, in this sense, is the faculty (capacity) or the attribute (competence) conferred upon an individual or a collective entity that thus becomes the subject of a right — a subjectively lawful right:[9] E.g., the subjectively lawful right of ownership, which is the sum total of the faculties conferred upon the individual owner; the right of paternal power, which is the sum total of the attributes conferred upon the individual father; the right of the suffrage, with which the citizen is endowed as a member of the state; or the right to draft men into the army, or the right of eminent domain, which belong to the state. Now this conferring of subjectively lawful rights can logically take place only on the basis and by virtue of a norm which is called objectively lawful: It is because the law (objectively lawful) creates them that there are rights (subjectively lawful) of ownership, of paternal power, of the suffrage, of the draft and of eminent domain. The objectively lawful, then, or the law, is primary: In the beginning was the rule.

We do not say, though, that this conferring of rights would be pure creation on the part of the rule. Possibly, the rule may be bound to confer them because they already existed before in some way, in which case the conferring has the character of recognizing or consecrating rather than of creating. Nonetheless, even then, the subjectively lawful right is instituted not by itself, by the very quality of its subjective lawfulness, but because it represents an objective value that is defined as such by a superior principle — superior to the right as much as to the rule that is to consecrate it. Consequently, by any token the objective takes precedence — at least if one stays at the same level.[10] Again, even if the question is merely one of recognition, the subjectively lawful

[a] [The distinction referred to here and in other passages of this work is that between "law" and "legal right." French legal terminology distinguishes law as "objective" from legal rights as "subjective," since both "law" and "right" are expressed by the same French term *droit*. This corresponds to the twofold use of the German term *Recht*; see translator's note b to chap. II of LASK, LEGAL PHILOSOPHY, *supra*, p. 32.]

[9] That there are subjects of objective law, i.e., individuals who are addressed by and subject to the rule, goes without saying, even and especially for those who deny the existence of a subjective right in the sense of a prerogative inherent in the individual, such as Duguit. But we need not here enter into the captious and varied controversies raised by the notion of the subjectively lawful — (are there rights, or only duties and functions?). In still another sense, the expression "objectively lawful" refers to a right (subjective) envisaged from the side of the object, as in the phrase: render to each his lawful due.

[10] On the distinction between subjective rights according to morals and according to law, see M. Réglade, *Les caractères essentiels du droit en comparaison avec les*

right that issues from the superior principle will exist, as a subjective right, with regard to the inferior rule only in so far as the latter has recognized it. It is nonexistent as regards the latter, until the moment of such recognition. From still another side does the objective law (*hoc sensu*)[b] transcend the subjective right. The rôle of the objective law actually is not limited to creating or recognizing subjective rights. It includes the prescribing of obligations or measures of order, either for the profit of another or for that of the obligor himself, without the counterpart of any subjective right in the proper sense of that term, which implies a certain power of enforcement and also a definite holder.[11]

5. As Usually Understood, the Rule Called "Law" Bears Upon Relationships Between Men. But if the law is primarily a rule of conduct, it may at once be more precisely said, since the living usage of words has so decided, that the rule of conduct called "law," taken in its specific sense, is limited to relationships between men; that it does not, or at least not directly, concern either duties of man toward God or duties of man toward himself. As usually understood, law implies that there be another — another human individual — and that is why Robinson Crusoe on his island, while bound by duties toward God and toward himself, is not bound by law. However, the legal rule is not the only rule to govern relationships between men. Other kinds of rules, more or less closely related, or at any rate bearing other names, intervene with some competence in the same field. There is the moral rule, whose field extends to the entire activity of man without excepting relationships *ad alterum*.[c] There is the rule of so-called social manners, which may be common to a whole group (civility, politeness, propriety) or peculiar to certain environments (aristocratic or worldly, professional, sporting).[12]

---

autres règles de la conduite humaine et les lois de la nature, in DROIT, MORALE, MOEURS, IIE ANNUAIRE DE L'INSTITUT INTERNATIONAL DE PHILOSOPHIE DU DROIT ET DE SOCIOLOGIE JURIDIQUE (Paris, 1936) 184–186.

[b] [In this sense.]

[11] Insufficient on this point seems the definition of law proposed by L. LE FUR in his *Essai d'une définition synthétique du droit*, 59 BULLETINS DE LA SOCIÉTÉ DE LÉGISLATION COMPARÉE (1930) 320: "Law is the delimitation of competencies of legal persons effected in conformity with the common good by a qualified authority." We shall return to this point, incidentally; see *infra* nos. 83–85.

[c] [Toward another.]

[12] On these different rules and their proper characteristics, see DROIT, MORALE, MOEURS (Paris, 1936). See also A. DU PASQUIER, INTRODUCTION À LA THÉORIE GÉNÉRALE ET À LA PHILOSOPHIE DU DROIT (Paris-Neuchâtel, 1937) nos. 257 *et seq.*; W. Henrich, *Sur la problématique du droit coutumier*, in 2 RECUEIL D'ÉTUDES SUR LES SOURCES DU DROIT EN HONNEUR DE FRANÇOIS GÉNY (Paris) 277–285.

There are, moreover, certain rules of conduct properly called technical, regarding the pursuit of crafts, professions, or activities [13] susceptible of affecting others for better or for worse.

6. *Defining the Legal Rule.* We are, then, at the crossroads. The point now is to identify, among the systems regulating social life (*sensu lato*) [d] that which constitutes the legal rule, and to detach its distinctive principle. Let us make at once a statement, without adducing the evidence: This distinctive principle will be found only if the idea of law is approached from the idea of the organized group, especially of society. The law is a social rule not merely in that it presupposes a social environment, but in that it exists only in and by society, as the rule of that society. If, then, one chooses among the organized societies the civil society (national and international), the law (*jus politicum*) may be defined as follows: The sum total of the rules of conduct laid down, or at least consecrated, by civil society, under the sanction of public compulsion, with a view to realizing in the relationships between men a certain order — the order postulated by the end of the civil society and by the maintenance of the civil society as an instrument devoted to that end.

7. *Plan of the First Part of the Book.* The commentary explaining and justifying this definition (which is the subject of Part One of this work) will be divided into three chapters, corresponding to the principal elements of the definition. In Chapter I, the legal rule will be analyzed as a social rule set up and guaranteed by civil society. In Chapter II, the concept of a rule of conduct and the characteristics of the legal imperative will be studied. Chapter III will be devoted to determining the "matters" or spheres of human activity that fall within the competence of the legal rule. As to the problem left in abeyance, to wit, the kind of order toward which the law is tending (the final part of the definition), it concerns no longer the formal aspect but the meaning and content of the legal rule. Its study is therefore referred to Part Two of this work, whose subject is the elaboration of the law.

[13] Examples of such activities: driving an automobile or simply moving one's own body in the street, activities which, when badly directed, may lead to collisions and injuries to others.

[d] [In the wide sense.]

CHAPTER I

FORMAL DEFINITION OF THE LEGAL RULE

SECTION 1. THE LAW AS THE RULE OF CIVIL SOCIETY

8. Law Implies Societal Life. For the legal rule to make its appearance it is not sufficient that a man be in a natural or accidental relation with another man, through kindred, neighborhood, or exchange; say, Robinson Crusoe on his island facing a new immigrant. Even a plurality of interindividual relationships is not sufficient. Up to this point, morals alone come in to provide a rule for such relationships, the first precept being that of justice in its inter-individual form.[1] As for the legal rule, it comes into existence only on condition that men form a group, not solely by sharing certain common physical, psychological, or social traits producing mere solidarity (such as men of one nation or one social class), but on the basis of a veritable society, implying a specific social end, organization, and hierarchy. One perceives the gradation: Relation to others, solidarity, society.[2] Better than the term "social," which is vague, the term "societal," despite its awkwardness, would suggest the kind of group here envisaged. The legal rule, then, is the rule that governs the relationships between men thus grouped in organic, organized fashion.

9. Why Societal Life Requires Law. Ubi jus ibi societas.[a] To speak of a legal relation is to speak of a societal relation: There is law, in the specific sense of a rule distinct from morals and manners, only where there is an organized society. The reciprocal statement, by the way, is

[1] In general, legal philosophers have law take its beginning, on the contrary, with the simple relation to others, or the interindividual relationship. They start, then, not from the idea of the rule but from the idea of justice, involving the obligation to respect another's right (*jus suum*). See, e.g., 1 A. BOISTEL, COURS DE PHILOSOPHIE DU DROIT (Paris, 1899), no. 12, pp. 18–19; no. 70, pp. 125–126; no. 74, p. 134; G. del Vecchio, *La justice*, secs. 7–9, *L'éthique, le droit et l'Etat* II, in JUSTICE, DROIT, ETAT (Paris, 1938) 39 *et seq.*, 273 *et seq.*

[2] What characterizes a society and apparently distinguishes it from a community, from any form of community, is the existence of a common goal with a view to which the associated individuals concert their efforts. In the community taken as such (for nothing prevents a society from doubling as a true community of the associates), the common goal is lacking and so, consequently, is legal personality. The members are content to share certain things: common traits or a common life. However, when the community takes the form of a common life, the need for discipline reappears with a view to ordering that common life in the interest of all.

[a] [Where law is, there is society.]

equally true: *Ubi societas ibi jus.*[b] Every organized society calls forth a legal rule. First, in order to constitute itself, to subsist, and to function. For the society exists only due to the human individuals of whom it is composed. They must therefore be kept in allegiance and under obligations inherent in the social state by a rule that determines and sanctions their status as members.[3] Again, the society operates only by the action of individuals, called its "functionaries," officials and subordinates of all grades and employments up to the directing personnel, individuals who in turn are bound by a norm, that of social "service." Finally, as each society must obtain from its members not only some contribution to its existence through obligations properly social, but also some collaboration towards its ends, in larger or smaller measure as the case may be, it is important that there be a rule defining and guaranteeing that collaboration. Hence, a twofold discipline: One constitutive or constitutional, by which the group assumes body and life; the other directing and ordering, by which the group moves its members in the direction of the social ends. Thus the legal rule is not simply the rule for relationships between men taken as such, *ut singuli,*[c] outside of any social qualification or pertinence; in all respects it forms the law of a group, whose conditions and requirements it transfers to the two levels of the *constitution* of the group and the *direction* of its members.[4]

If one prefers another formulation which is rather fashionable today, the legal rule connotes the "institution," in the sense of society or corporation. It is justified by the "institution"; its observance is called for and watched over by the social "institution."[5] Institutional by nature, the legal rule is, however, itself instituted in that it results from a funda-

[b] [Where society is, there is law.]

[3] Of course, the rule is not everything; as noted by Hauriou, *Aux sources du droit*, in CAHIERS DE LA NOUVELLE JOURNÉE no. 23 (Paris, 1933) 49: "The highest forms according to which the directing idea of an institution tends to express itself are not properly legal; they are moral or intellectual." See also G. del Vecchio, *A propos de la conception étatique du droit*, in JUSTICE, DROIT, ETAT 305–306.

[c] [As single individuals.]

[4] In the same sense, see J. Delos, *Notes doctrinales thomistes*, in 1 ST. THOMAS AQUINAS, SOMME THÉOLOGIQUE, *La justice* (French translation by M.-S. Gillet) 234–235. But that author is wrong, it seems, in seeking to integrate justice forcibly with the societal order, since justice may exist outside of this order as commutative justice, assuming mere interindividual relations.

[5] Cf. J. Delos, *La théorie de l'institution*, in ARCHIVES DE PHILOSOPHIE DU DROIT ET DE SOCIOLOGIE JURIDIQUE (1931). For that author, the institutional conception of law is synonymous with a conception of law on social foundations (p. 144). It is interesting to observe that in the language of the natural law writers of the seventeenth and eighteenth centuries the "institutional" was opposed to the "natural": the institution was the positive and arbitrary work of man.

mental operation governed by a certain procedure.[6] Once instituted, it becomes itself an "institution"; the rule then is an institution which in turn emanates from the social institution.

10. The Different Kinds of Societies. However, societies are of many kinds, corresponding to varied principles of division. There are private societies, pursuing private ends (business corporations, nonprofit associations, professional societies, and others),[7] and public societies, pursuing public ends (for instance, the state, the church). There are temporal societies, worldly in purpose (for instance, the state, corporations operating for profit, professional societies), and spiritual societies, otherworldly in purpose (the church, the religious communities, the pious associations). There are national societies, constituted on the domestic national level (for instance, the states, certain so-called national churches), and international or supra-national societies (for instance, the Catholic Church, the various "Internationals," and, to the extent it is organized, the society of nations). Moreover, the diversity of kinds precludes neither jurisdictional conflicts due to the overlapping of ends, nor relationships of subordination or integration. Thus, temporal societies are subordinate in a certain manner (where an encounter occurs) to spiritual societies, private societies are integrated in one respect (that of the "public" interest) with public societies, etc. From still other points of view, one may distinguish necessary societies, to which the individual cannot refuse his adherence without denying his nature as man (such as the state and, in a certain way, the church), and free societies, resulting from the arbitrary will of the founders; again, general societies, uniting all individuals on the sole foundation of their quality as men (such as the state, the church), and special societies, uniting individuals of some determined specialization (such as the professional societies), etc.

11. Each Kind of Society Has Its System of Law. Now each of these societies, to whatever class it may belong, possesses its double set of rules of properly social conduct, those regarding its constitution and

[6] This is so even for the customary rule, although it derives from the people: it is also instituted, founded, as the result of a procedure.

[7] We leave aside the family, which is not really a society for want of a common goal of the two kinds of "conjunctions" which make it up, the relations between spouses and those between parents and children; see, in this sense, ST. THOMAS AQUINAS, SUMMA THEOLOGICA, *IIa IIae*, qu. 58, art. 7 *ad* 3; also J. Dabin, *Sur le concept de famille*, in 2 MÉLANGES VERMEERSCH (Rome, 1935) 229 *et seq*. However, when all the members of the family live together in the *domus* [home], they form a community of life and habitation, implying an interior discipline and authority and, in that sense, a "domestic" law (*supra*, n. 2).

those regarding its discipline (in the sense of group discipline), which are endowed with the formal characteristics of law: The law of private corporations and bodies, the law of the state for the civil society, ecclesiastical law for the religious society (Canon Law for the Catholic Church), international law (to the degree to which the society of nations is organized).[8] This is the natural phenomenon of "social law": The organized groups do not merely exist and tend toward their ends; in order to exist and to attain their ends, they necessarily produce law.[9] Each of these systems of law, moreover, has its domain and its individual subjects, a content and physiognomy, of its own, which are determined by the specific end of the group, by the manner or degree of its organization. Thus, the law of the spiritual societies differs in its spirit and methods from that of the temporal societies;[10] municipal law, corresponding to a more fully developed social state, is fuller and stronger than international law, etc. On the other hand, as the groups are not juxtaposed or parallel but obey a hierarchical order, the law of the dependent groups must harmonize with that of the superior groups. Thus, the public or private bodies integrated in the state could not in their own law contradict or deny imperative dispositions of the law of the state;[11] nor could in an organized international society the municipal law, public or private, of any state be logically admitted to override the principles of the law of nations, etc.

12. Distinct and Eminent Place of the Law of Civil Society. In a study limited to the law of the civil society (*jus politicum*), we do not have to go into that complexity, at least not directly; it was sufficient to indicate that the law of the civil society was not the only existing or possible law. But precisely because the civil society is superior to the other groups, at least on the temporal level and from the domestic angle, it must be emphasized that among the different kinds of law the law of

[8] Cf., in the same sense: DE VAREILLES-SOMMIÈRES, LES PRINCIPES FONDAMENTAUX DU DROIT (Paris, 1899), I, 4, pp. 6–7; G. A. RENARD, LA THÉORIE DE L'INSTITUTION (Paris, 1930) 103 *et seq.*; G. del Vecchio, *A propos de la conception étatique du droit*, secs. VI *et seq.*, *loc. cit.*, pp. 295 *et seq.*

[9] Cf. G. GURVITCH, L'IDÉE DU DROIT SOCIAL (Paris, 1932). In Gurvitch's view, though, the "social law" would comprise, besides the law of organized communities (which we call societal), a law of "unorganized communion" (*op. cit.*, pp. 28 *et seq.*). We shall come back to that point below, no. 14.

[10] On this point, see R.-G. Renard, *La contribution du droit canonique à la science du droit comparé*, in INTRODUCTION À L'ÉTUDE DU DROIT COMPARÉ, 1 RECUEIL D'ÉTUDES EN L'HONNEUR D'EDOUARD LAMBERT, § 9 (Paris, 1938) 108 *et seq.*; the same, LA PHILOSOPHIE DE L'INSTITUTION (Paris, 1939) 37, 279–292.

[11] On this point, and against an anarchical pluralism, see J. DABIN, DOCTRINE GÉNÉRALE DE L'ETAT (Brussels-Paris, 1939), no. 253, pp. 408–411.

the civil society occupies — or ought to occupy — a distinct, eminent place.[12] Whereas the law of the particular societies governs their corporative relations in view of their particular group ends, the law of the civil society (*jus politicum*) is competent to order all activities of the subjects within its territory, including the legal and non-legal activities of the particular groups. In that sense, the civil society is sovereign, it is the commander-in-chief of the individuals and groups, and hence its law, inasmuch as it is supreme, is the sole true law.[13] Moreover, and as a logical consequence, the civil society alone has at its disposal "unconditional compulsion":[14] If the groups have a certain right of compulsion over their members for the defense of their own regulations, that right is exercised only in certain limits and with the reservation of control by the public power.[15] This explains why usually the law of the civil society or, designating the same reality by another term, the civil law should have become synonymous with the law pure and simple: Speaking of the law, one is understood to speak of the law superior to all others, the law of the civil society.

13. The Law of the Civil Society Is Nonetheless a Societal Law. However, like the particular laws of all bodies, the law of the civil society, no matter how eminent, remains a social law, meaning a societal law. This remark is important because it tends to dissipate an ambiguity that would put everything in question again. No doubt, different from the ends of the subordinate societies, which are particular, special, and

[12] Cf. J. Delos, *Les caractères essentiels du droit positif en comparaison avec les autres règles de la vie sociale et les lois de la réalité*, in DROIT, MORALE, MOEURS 209–211, according to whom the legal order is a phenomenon peculiar to the political society. It is true that the political legal order, which is installed by the political society, is the supreme legal order. Of course, there are cases of tension: the state in process of formation may not yet have succeeded in establishing itself, or again the state already formed may lose its authority. (Cf. del Vecchio, *op. cit.*). But we look at it here from the philosophical and not the historical point of view.

[13] In this sense, as regards the law laid down by the father of the family in his house, see ST. THOMAS, *op. cit.*, *Ia IIae*, qu. 90, art. 3 *ad* 3: . . .

[14] The formulation is that of G. Gurvitch, who however regards this "monopoly of unconditioned compulsion" as the sole specific trait of the state. In reality, that trait is but secondary, instrumental: that the state has the monopoly of unconditioned compulsion is due to its having the right to that monopoly; that it has the right is due to its having the mission to establish order in the society. Hence its sovereignty, which constitutes a right and places it above the other groups.

[15] In the same sense, see ST. THOMAS, *op. cit.*, *Ia IIae*, qu. 90, art. 3 *ad* 2; on the right to punish in particular, see qu. 92, art. 2 *ad* 3. On disciplinary law, the "particular penal law of institutions," cf. A. LÉGAL AND J. BRÈTHE DE LA GRESSAYE, LE POUVOIR DISCIPLINAIRE DANS LES INSTITUTIONS PRIVÉES (Paris, 1938), esp. pp. 94–122.

often technical, the end of the civil society or the state is general and human. It is man at whose perfectioning this society aims. By way of a certain public good, embracing within its radiation the universality of human needs, moral and economic, individual and social, the civil society seeks to provide for each and all of its members the good life in all spheres of the temporal order. Now one of the first conditions as well as one of the ends of the public good is that within the total community there should prevail a certain order in the relationships between the individuals and the groups, an order which the law, fixed by the civil society, undertakes to realize.[16] But if that is so, how can it be imagined that law could be defined without any reference to morals, which constitute the fundamental human discipline? How could the place of everyone in the society which is the state be marked without appealing to the principles that govern the rights and duties of man? It is not surprising therefore that the law of the state, which is to order private relations, often takes over as its own, precepts that have already been laid down by morals, especially social morals.

Let there be no mistake, however: The rule thus taken over from morals becomes a societal rule in every respect and not from a formal viewpoint alone. If it becomes a part of the law, if it is laid down and imposed under threat of compulsion, it is not at all by reason of its own value, even if that be absolute, but solely because the end of the state demands it. It matters little that that end is general and human (which justifies the connection of politics and morals); for all that it remains no less a specific end, and consequently the rule inspired by that end preserves its societal character.

14. The Other Rules of Social Life (Morals, Manners) Are Not Societal. It will perhaps be objected that all rules whatever that govern relationships between men are equally derived from society and are equally social. Such is undoubtedly the case as regards the rule of social manners, which is laid down by society (*sensu lato*) on the basis of certain social "conventions" and sanctioned, often quite energetically, by reactions of the social environment.[17] Assuming a sociological morality,

[16] On the state and the end of the state, see J. Dabin, Doctrine générale de l'Etat, nos. 25–36, pp. 34–54. We shall come back more closely to the concept of the common good below, nos. 135 *et seq.*

[17] There would remain for discussion the question of the import of the rule of social manners: does it decree a veritable obligation (*oportet*, if only in the field of decency), like morals and law, or simply a propriety (*decet*)? In our times, at any rate, it is a matter of usages, or habits, whose violation singles out the transgressor and exposes him to a more or less formulated note of reproach on the part of his environment; it is not a matter of strict, categorical duties. Cf. L. Recaséns

such would also be the case as regards the moral rule, which would have no other founder than the society itself dictating for its members the imperatives formulated by the collective conscience.

But even admitting that conception of morality, a radical distinction remains between the legal rule and the other rules of social life. It is very well for the moral rule (under the sociological interpretation) and the rule of social manners (indisputably) to proceed from society or, more exactly, from the social environment by way of repetition of the same attitudes, the same gestures (this is the social fact of custom): Still they have no institutional or societal character, they pursue no institutional or societal end, they do not subserve the institution or society as group laws. In fact, the mode of formation or the origin of the rules matters little. There are rules of customary law, issuing from the social environment in the same way as the rule of social manners, just as there can be (witness history, notwithstanding the sociologists) rules of morals laid down by an authority in the same way as the legal rules of a legislative source.[18] What gives a rule its legal character is that it is consecrated and sanctioned, not in an inorganic fashion by the public in the group, but by the group itself as a body — especially, the state — in the conviction that the rule is required for the good of the group and the attainment of its specific end. The social interest being at stake, social discipline enters the field, and with it the organization of the group in the persons of its responsible authorities: Chiefs, functionaries, and judges, the dispensers and guarantors of discipline. The legal rule is thus bound to the social institution as its cause, a final cause and an efficient cause. That is why it is impossible to speak of a "law of an unorganized communion." [19] "Unorganized communion" may well generate rules of conduct, even supporting them by a reaction against violators; but these rules belong to the category of mores or manners and not the category of law.

15. Customary Law Has Societal Character. Even in making the assumption of a customary legal rule, the societal idea, especially the consideration of the social end, is the determining and distinctive element. The idea acts first upon the public of the group, which sees the social interest involved and calls for law to intervene; then, thanks to the

---

Siches, *Les usages sociaux et leur différenciation d'avec les normes juridiques*, in Droit, Morale, Moeurs, 145 *et seq.*, esp. 160–162.

[18] Thus the law of Moses was a positive law containing many moral precepts; in the same way, the Catholic Church edicts a positive moral legislation for its faithful.

[19] According to G. Gurvitch, *op. cit.* 28 *et seq.*

public, it acts upon the social organization, which institutes the means of execution, the procedures of law and compulsion. What, indeed, is signified by the *opinio juris seu necessitatis*,[d] the constituent psychological factor of custom according to the classical doctrine,[20] if not the conviction that the usage, as practiced, is binding and obligatory with regard to the organized group — especially, the state — because it interests that group? It is that conviction that gives the custom its legal character, differentiating it from simply moral, non-legal customs. Nor is there anything to prevent a custom that originally is a moral one or one of manners from attaining the rank of a legal custom: This phenomenon will be brought about precisely when in the public of the group — including the chiefs, who are parts of the public as well, and who sometimes lead it — there germinates the idea that the effective practice of these morals or these manners touches in some manner upon the life of the group or its social ideal, either as a factor of cohesion among its members or as a distinctive sign of its physiognomy with regard to competing groups. Moral or social conformity thus comes to generate the juridical rule.

There is the possibility or even the certainty that these distinctions are hardly perceptible in the societies whose civilization has not advanced much, where the state has not yet assumed a clear-cut form; it is for the historian or the ethnologist to resolve that question.[21] But as for the society that is ours, they are incontestably known and used not only by the specialists of the law, but also by the mass of the people: They instinctively grasp the difference between what they call "the law,"[e] that is, statutes and official regulations, and the other norms of social life. Possibly too, even in our society, the distinctive criteria might not lend themselves to easy application. Not always is there a neat cut between moral custom and legal custom, since it has happened that the moral custom evolves toward "legality." Yet this is not sufficient to reject a principle of distinction which is solidly based upon the facts of social life as well as upon philosophical reasoning.[22]

[d] [Conviction of rightness or necessity.]

[20] On this doctrine, see 1 F. GÉNY, MÉTHODE D'INTERPRÉTATION ET SOURCES EN DROIT PRIVÉ POSITIF (2d ed.) nos. 109–134, pp. 317 *et seq.*

[21] It has been very justly said regarding the relationships between law and morals that "the confusion began in ancient times when custom was considered at least the principal, if not the exclusive, source of law," H. Dupeyroux, *Les grands problèmes du droit* (dealing with the work of Le Fur), in ARCHIVES DE PHILOSOPHIE DU DROIT ET DE SOCIOLOGIE JURIDIQUE (1938), nos. 1–2, pp. 70–72.

[e] [The French term used here is *le code*.]

[22] On the setting apart of law, cf. F. RUSSO, RÉALITÉ JURIDIQUE ET RÉALITÉ SOCIALE (Paris, 1942) 164–170, and more generally, G. del Vecchio, *L'homo*

SECTION 2. POWER AS THE SOURCE OF THE LEGAL RULE

16. Power Alone Is Qualified To Lay Down the Legal Rule. If law is not simply the rule of social life but the rule of civil society, it could only be laid down by the power, or at least with the approval and consecration of the power, which is qualified to act in the name of the civil society, to wit, public authority. We have here a condition that goes not to the efficacy or the validity of the law but to its very existence.[1]

It is by power that a society exists as a body; it is incumbent on power to order the state and to regulate the conduct of the individuals in conformity with the ends of the state.[2] In saying this, we do not adopt a "dogmatic" or authoritarian conception of the law; we merely recognize the organic and, in this sense, social character of the legal rule. Nothing prevents the authority in the state from being organized in a democratic fashion and exercised directly or indirectly by the nation itself; nothing prevents the authority in the state from being decentralized on a territorial basis or even on the basis of economic and social interests (corporations). All that is a matter of the political constitution.[3] Nor is it to be implied that the authority in the state, whether or not democratic, whether or not decentralized, in working out its rules could not be affected by, or even inspired by, the opinion prevailing among the people.[4] In fact, whatever may be the régime of the government or the way of establishing the legal rule — statute, custom, case law — a great many people without official capacity collaborate in or contribute to the formation of the law: Specialists in the moral and social sciences, professional experts in the fields under regulation, and sometimes the mass of the public. Very seldom are the rules the original and personal work

juridicus et l'insuffisance du droit comme règle de la vie, in JUSTICE, DROIT, ETAT 236–239.

[1] See, in this sense, ST. THOMAS, SUMMA, *Ia IIae*, qu. 90, art. 3 *ad resp.*, art. 4 *ad resp.*, *in fine* (. . .); qu. 95, art. 4 *ad resp.* (*tertio*); qu. 96, art. 5 *ad resp.* Cf. Carré de Malberg, *Réflexions très simples sur l'objet de la science juridique*, in 1 RECUEIL D'ÉTUDES SUR LES SOURCES DU DROIT EN L'HONNEUR DE FRANÇOIS GÉNY 192 *et seq.*

[2] We place ourselves for the moment on the plane of the domestic civil society, i.e., the state. The case of public international law will be considered below, nos. 38–40.

[3] Cf. ST. THOMAS, SUMMA, *Ia IIae*, qu. 90, art. 3: . . .; qu. 95, art. 4 *ad resp.* (*tertio*); qu. 96, art. 5 *ad resp.* It is possible, too, that the form of the political régime influences the determination of the content of public and even private law. Cf. MONTESQUIEU, DE L'ESPRIT DES LOIS, bks. V to VII (ed. Garnier 40 *et seq.*). But see *infra*, no. 138, n. 9.

[4] The relationships between law and opinion will be treated below, in the part devoted to the elaboration of the law, nos. 160 *et seq.*, esp. nos. 164 and 165.

of those in authority; the law develops slowly by largely collective work, in which it is quite difficult to discover rights of authorship. In this genetic sense, the law is social, at least as regards its substantial content: The society underlying the state, or, if one likes, "unorganized communion," exerts pressure upon the state and thus influences its law.[5]

However, law exists only from that moment when the state itself, by its organs, has erected it as a law of the state, explicitly or by implication, directly or by renvoi (to a principle or another discipline). Prior to that moment, the matter might well have been regulated (and it will continue to be regulated) by morals, by social manners, or simply by usages: The legal rule, in the sense of a law of the state, is absent. It does not follow that the subject would then necessarily be free and that his activity in the field which is assumed to be "empty of law" would escape any censure, even on the part of the authorities of the state. It means only that for an appraisal of his conduct from the point of view of social discipline one can find no preëstablished legal rule — whether one of obligation or one of liberty — and that the cognizant judge (or official) will have to work out the applicable norm in the special case, in short, to fill the gap in the law.[6] In such a case, we witness the budding of a new legal rule by way of case law (law *in fieri*).[a]

17. The Courts, Creating Case Law, Constitute Power. Law, precisely, does not always derive from statutes and regulations, which are the direct and *a priori* modes of expression of the law. It may also derive from decisions of cases, especially the case law of courts, and even from custom. It is permissible, then, to inquire in what measure case law and customary law emanate from the public authority which alone is qualified to lay down law.

As regards the case law of courts (judicial or administrative), the difficulty is only apparent. No matter how independent and, in this sense, sovereign they may be, the courts instituted by the state to administer justice in the name of the state are evidently depositaries of a part of public authority.[7] From another aspect, the law they apply is

[5] On the "spontaneous elaboration of the law" and the unfolding by the societies themselves of their natural ends, see F. RUSSO, *op. cit.* 33–37, 45–47, 54 and 55.

[6] The question of how the judge will elaborate the principle of law applicable to the special case is reserved for treatment below, nos. 131 *et seq.*

[a] [Law in the making.]

[7] The observation is obviously valid only for the courts of the state, even where they are corporative courts established or agreed to by the state (system of judicial decentralization). Its validity does not extend to private tribunals, corporative or otherwise. Private decisions belong no more to the category of the law of the state than does private legislation.

very much the law of the state, whether they find it formulated in statutes or, in the absence of statutes, have to work it out themselves. For it is all very well to claim to separate the judicial power from the other powers of the state, the legislative and the executive, under the pretext that the latter two would represent political power while the power of the judge would be of exclusively legal nature. First, it is a mistake to oppose law — the law of the state — to politics: Law, the rule of the political society, is necessarily subordinate to the ends of politics. Further, to the extent that the courts have to work out the law, they have to do so very much as the business of the state and for its ends, which is a political task.[8] Finally, it is illogical to regard as non-political the judicial power when the latter, in the absence of a statutory rule, is allowed to supplement the legislative power, which is eminently political. In effect, the courts are competent, if not to legislate by way of general disposition, at least to evolve case law, actually equivalent to statute law, by the exercise of their jurisdiction. Most of the time, though, such case law is formed but gradually and gropingly; hence it is difficult to spot the instant of the birth of a rule of case law.

18. Custom Needs the Approval of Power. The problem is more delicate for custom as a source of law. He who speaks of customary law doubtless speaks of a societal rule which is conceived as group law,[9] yet withal is established by the society itself rather than by the state. Is it necessary, therefore, to leave the law originating in custom outside of the law of the state?

The question does not arise with regard to customary law proceeding from the authorities of the state themselves — the parliament, the administration, the courts — inasmuch as these authorities, as a result of constant practice that has become imperative, create substantive or procedural rules as to their own activities. Such customary public law remains the work of the state which makes its own rule for itself through its human organs. It will merely be necessary to verify the legitimacy, according to the constitutional régime in force, of such a system of autonomous formation of the law of the bodies and institutions of the state.[10] Contrariwise, the difficulty appears most clearly in assuming a customary rule of private law. Can it still be maintained that

[8] On the political character of the function of the judge in the state, see J. DABIN, DOCTRINE GÉNÉRALE DE L'ETAT, no. 158, pp. 246–248. The opposite opinion proceeds from a certain erroneous conception of politics as the struggle for power.

[9] See *supra*, nos. 8 and 9.

[10] Cf. R. Capitant, *Le droit constitutionnel non écrit*, and C. Girola, *Les coutumes constitutionnelles*, in 3 RECUEIL GÉNY 1 *et seq.*, 9 *et seq.*

that kind of rule emanates from the state? This might be denied on the ground that the rule has issued from the mass of the public, from "unorganized social communion," and not from the community of the state as such. But two observations are susceptible of resolving the contradiction.

In the first place, whatever conception one may have of legal custom, and even if one follows the classical doctrine in admitting that it may exist without the concurrence of any authority [11] — still in the politically organized society custom undeniably is unable to play its rôle if the authorities of the state refuse to attribute to it legal value: The *opinio juris* [b] of those concerned must in effect be adopted by the courts and the law-applying organs of the state.[12] Are these agencies bound to accomplish that adoption, as they are bound to apply statutory legal rules? That is another problem, which belongs both to theoretical jurisprudence and to positive constitutional law. In principle, we see no reason to deny *a priori* obligatory value to customary rules, even in respect to the law-applying organs of the state, as long as these rules do not oppose the end of the political society and the discipline which the state is charged to maintain. He who speaks of law of the state thus does not necessarily imply the elimination of the social environment as a qualified formal source of legal rules. It is necessary yet sufficient that the rule should in fact obtain the consecration of the state. In this sense we speak here of law laid down by the state, without distinction between the law derived from legislative or judicial sources, which issues from the state, and the customary law, which issues from the social environment with the approval of the state.

We may further observe that in modern society, where the state has definitely won its place as ruler of the community, the official sources (statute and case law) are preponderant both in number and in value. That preponderance is not accidental. It has often been shown that the régime of the state tended to cause the ebbing of custom, that it calls forth the system of statutory law, involving not only uniform and impartial legality but also the form of the written statute enacted by public authority. If the statutory law, completed by case law, is not the sole mode of expression of the law of the state, it is the most normal and,

[11] See, *contra*, 1 Ed. Lambert, Etudes de droit commun législatif (Paris, 1903) 111 *et seq.* (*Introduction, La fonction du droit civil comparé.*) A summary of Lambert's ideas will be found in A. Lebrun, La coutume, ses sources, son autorité en droit privé (Paris, 1932), nos. 184–192, pp. 190–198.

[b] [Conviction of rightness.]

[12] Cf. 1 M. Planiol, Traité élémentaire de droit civil (12th ed. by G. Ripert), no. 11: "As for myself, I do not believe at all in the possibility of establishing customary rules with obligatory validity outside of case law."

too, the most perfect mode. Moreover, no one contests that the statute could abolish custom, so that where the latter exists, it is in some way by the grace of the statute.[13] Nor does it take any subtlety to claim that, to the extent that the customary rule satisfies the needs of social discipline, the people instituting it function, in a word, as public authority. Or again, if one likes, the régime of custom is equivalent to a kind of direct democracy: Constitutionally the people, acting by way of custom, would be qualified, as one of the very organs of the state, to produce rules of private law.[14]

19. Diversity and Hierarchy of the Rules According to the Creating Organ. In the vast and necessarily complicated political societies of the type of the modern state, the organs of the public authority, even if we consider only the legislative function, are differentiated and hierarchical. This gives rise to a gradation of equally differentiated and hierarchical rules. In states federal in form, there are federal statutes upheld by federal authority in matters called federal and valid throughout the whole federal area; there are, on the other hand, the statutes of the several federated states, valid within the borders of the area of each of these states. Both in federal and in unitary states, always more or less decentralized, there are, on the one hand, the rules laid down by the organs of the state (the central authority), valid for the entire area; and on the other hand, the rules laid down by the decentralized powers (provinces, municipalities) with the authorization and under the control of the state. The municipalities and provinces of the past have more and more merged with the state; but the latter has left or restored to them legislative jurisdiction in certain matters (provincial and munici-

[13] By virtue of the same fundamental idea (power as the source of the legal rule in the state) it is for enacted law, as the expression of the will of the power, not only to declare itself with regard to such and such a custom but also to regulate the problem of the sources of law, in affirming its own primacy among the sources — without being open to accusation of judging in its own cause and aiming at a problem within the competence of the sociologist and not the legislator (see, in the latter sense, 1 F. GÉNY, MÉTHODE (2d ed.), no. 51, 2 *id.*, nos. 88–90; A. LEBRUN, *op. cit.*, no. 135). It is being forgotten that the mission of politics, of which the enacted law is the organ, is to govern the social, which renders the enactment competent both to give solutions and to settle the problem of the sources of regulation.

[14] It is remarkable that St. Thomas, *supra*, n. 3, puts the power to legislate in the hands of the multitude (grouped in the state) or its representatives. This expression may designate the elaboration of a law by the people meeting in legislative assembly as well as by popular custom. See also, on this point, SUMMA, *Ia IIae*, qu. 97, art. 3 *ad resp.*: . . . ; and on free (i.e., democratic) societies, *ibid.*, *ad* 3: . . . In the same sense, JULIAN in DIG. 1, 3, 32, 1: . . .

pal bylaws and regulations). A hierarchy of the same kind is found in many states, federal or unitary, among the rules originating in the central authorities: In the technical terms of constitutional law, we distinguish between the statute, which is the work of the legislative power, and the (general) order or regulation issued in application of statutes or within the framework of statutes by the governmental [executive or administrative] power (such as a royal order) or even by a minister alone (a ministerial order).

The statutes or enacted laws themselves are divided, in régimes of rigid constitutions, into constitutional laws and ordinary statutes, the former binding all authorities of the state, including the legislator of tomorrow, and subject to abrogation or modification only by a special amending process, more complicated than the ordinary lawmaking process.[15] Another kind of rule can be foreseen, already practiced in certain countries: The rule laid down by the occupational corporation as an organism of public law, authorized to lay down rules in its occupational field as the provinces and municipalities are authorized to lay down rules in the local territorial field.[16] But these varieties, depending on the public law of each nation, leave the essential idea intact: We always deal with rules laid down by the public authority. Still, since the lawmaking public authority is incarnated in different organs, each organ must remain within the framework of its jurisdiction and, moreover, lay down its rule in accordance with the prescribed forms and procedures. Otherwise, the rule will be legally invalid.[17]

20. The Rules Laid Down By Private Individuals Do Not Constitute Law. On the other hand, the rules stemming from the wills of private individuals by way of private legal transactions fall outside of the category of the legal rule (in the sense of the law of the state), not only because their obligating force is limited to the parties of the case,[18] but also because the private will of itself is not competent to lay down rules on the state level. This is true both for individual private acts (unilateral

[15] This hierarchy of rules has given rise to the theory of the formation of the law by less and less general, more and more individual "degrees" (*Stufentheorie*), proposed by Merkl, on which see R. BONNARD in REVUE DU DROIT PUBLIC (1928) 668.

[16] On this form of decentralization — occupational decentralization — see J. DABIN, DOCTRINE GÉNÉRALE DE L'ETAT, nos. 203–209, pp. 331 *et seq.*

[17] Cf., in the same sense, on the significance of the objective validity of legal rules, H. Dupeyroux, *Les grands problèmes du droit*, in ARCHIVES DE PHILOSOPHIE DU DROIT (1938) nos. 1 and 2, pp. 46–48.

[18] This is the question of the *general* character of the legal rule, which will be examined below, nos. 56–58.

acts or contracts, for valuable consideration or by way of gift, among living parties or upon death) and for collective acts incorporating economic or other groups, whatever they may be, which may have a genuine regulatory power over their members. In the latter case of a "private statute," as in the case of an ordinary obligation, it is always the private will that is acting.[19] Supposing, then, that one adopts the theory of the formation of law "by degrees" [of generality or concreteness] starting with the most general and most fundamental law, to wit, the constitution,[20] it will be well not to have the system embrace private legal acts, which represent a principle different from that of the legal rule.[21] This does not mean that the state or the public authority cannot consecrate the obligating force between the parties to private legal transactions, including collective acts. On the contrary, it may do so and, reserving certain conditions, it ought to do so: The law of the state [*étatique*] is not synonymous with a "statist" law that excludes the legitimate autonomies of individuals and groups in the legal field.

However, in decreeing that agreements legally arrived at become the statute of the parties, whether on the inter-individual or the corporative level (as in Article 1134 of the Code Napoleon [c]), the law of the state does not elevate the statute of private parties to the rank of a statute of the state. It maintains it on its subordinate level, but proclaims that the private rule has obligating force as far as the law of the state is concerned, that the latter sanctions the private rule in the same way as the rule of the law of the state. In a word, the law of the state is enriched by a new rule of general import, that of respect for the pledged word: *Pacta sunt servanda.*[d] [22] Furthermore, it is understood that in the case of a private act setting up a society or association endowed with personality, the rule created by the group for its members bears the character of

[19] No doubt St. Thomas groups with "positive law" the cases of private convention as well as of "public convention" (i.e., the law of the state); see SUMMA, *IIa IIae,* qu. 57, art. 2 *ad resp.* But there he defines the concept of positivity, not that of laws. His thoughts about laws are expressed *id. Ia IIae,* qu. 90, art. 3.

[20] See *supra,* n. 15.

[21] As to public legal acts, inasmuch as they lay down general rules, the solution is obviously different: they realize the very concept of the law of the state. Cf. DU PASQUIER, *op. cit.,* no. 125, pp. 95–96; no. 130, p. 101.

[c] [Art. 1134 of the Code Napoleon provides as follows: "Agreements concluded in accordance with the laws shall have the force of law as to those who have made them. They may be revoked only by mutual consent or for causes authorized by law. They shall be executed in good faith."]

[d] [Agreements shall be observed.]

[22] Cf., in the same sense, DU PASQUIER, *op. cit.* no. 101, p. 63; no. 125, pp. 94–95. In a different sense, G. del Vecchio, *A propos de la conception étatique du droit,* in JUSTICE, DROIT, ETAT 292–293.

a legal rule as regards these members, but that this is a rule of corporative law, valid on the sole level of the corporation and otherwise under the control of the state.

21. Transformation of Rules of Private Parties Into Law of the State. However, modern law knows cases of the transformation of private rules into law of the state; such as, in the field of industrial relations, the extension to an entire craft or industry, by means of state approval, of stipulations inserted in collective bargaining agreements.[23] Apparently, the issue is only one as to whom they cover: An agreement brings into effect rights and obligations with regard to persons who have not been parties to it at all. In truth, one has to do with a rule of private origin which is not only incorporated into the law of the state but to a certain extent converted into law of the state. Hence its obligating force for all within the craft or industry regardless of whether or not they participated in the collective bargaining agreements. This is an anomalous and transitional mode of working out the laws of the state, which proceeds by way of extending to everybody a rule first established for some few. Under a régime of free corporations, where the group is formed by those freely adhering to it and keeps the quality of an organism of private law, this process is the only one possible if it is desired at once to create a rule valid for all within the craft or industry and to have those within it participate in the making of the rule. Once the corporation is decreed to be compulsory and recognized as an organ of public law with powers of decision (and not of simple consultation), it may itself directly create obligatory rules as the law of the state, doing so under the control of the state and in application of the idea of decentralization.

SECTION 3. LAW AND PUBLIC COMPULSION

22. As Regards Its Execution, Law Is Guaranteed by the State. The rule of the social discipline of the state, which is laid down and promulgated by the state, is also guaranteed by the state, in the sense that the state institutes certain means designed to realize its rule effectively and to carry out what that rule prescribes as exactly as possible.

This necessarily follows from the idea of a rule or discipline that is social. If the rule were not carried out, the end pursued would not be

[23] See, on this point, J. DABIN, DOCTRINE GÉNÉRALE DE L'ETAT, no. 207 and references. Also H. Capitant, *L'évolution de la conception française en matière de conventions collectives du travail*, in 3 RECUEIL LAMBERT § 171, pp. 515–517.

attained. Now, by hypothesis, it ought to be attained *volens nolens*,[a] since the social order, the very authority of the lawmaking state, is at stake. The life of the law is in its being carried out: Law that is in no way active is dead law. True, the codes contain rules that are not applied or are no longer applied, that are dead branches of legislation. But such cases can only be rare: Normally, obedience should follow the precept and does in fact follow it. Consequently, if the law wants to succeed, if it wants to live, it should be fashioned so as to get itself obeyed, morally by a certain adaptation to common opinion, materially by a complex of measures of execution that may go as far as the use of compulsion.[1]

23. Law That Is Not Obeyed Does Not Lose Its Validity as Law. This is not to say, however, that a rule that is not obeyed would cease to exist and that disobedience would have the power to abrogate law. There are those who define the law, at least as positive law, by speaking of "law generally obeyed." By that they mean that, lacking sufficiently general obedience, law lacks efficacy and, in that sense, reality: This is what they call "positiveness." [2] But the validity of a rule must not be confounded with its efficacy. No matter how necessary the effective realization of the legal rule may be, that rule is nonetheless valid as soon as it has been laid down in the correct manner: Its relative or even total lack of efficacy destroys neither its existence nor its validity. If the contrary were true, the subjects of a law would be promoted to masters of that law, which would mean not only anarchy but the overthrow of the order. Again, how would one recognize and measure the degree of efficacy upon which the obligatory character of a law is to depend? The truth is that a law is valid, of objective validity, independently of the *opinio juris* [b] of the subjects.[3] It is quite another question to know if it is good to lay down or maintain a rule that would only receive disobedi-

[a] [Willy-nilly.]

[1] On the compulsory or coercive character of civil laws, see St. Thomas, Summa, *Ia IIae*, qu. 90, art. 3 *ad* 2; qu. 92, art 2 *ad resp.*, *in fine*; qu. 95, art. 1 *ad resp.* and *ad* 1; qu. 96, art. 5 *ad resp.*, *in fine*, *ad* 1 and *ad* 3. *Contra:* see H. Dupeyroux, *Les grands problèmes du droit*, *in* Archives de philosophie du droit (1938), nos. 1–2, pp. 53–55. But independence of the validity of law from its efficacy does not imply that the valid rule should not also be efficacious, and guaranteed to that end.

[2] Thus, following Kelsen who finds positiveness in the two characteristics of validity and efficacy, R. Capitant, L'illicite, 1: L'impératif juridique 115 *et seq.* . . . Cf. Du Pasquier, *op. cit.* nos. 314 and 318.

[b] [Conviction of rightness.]

[3] See, in the same sense, H. Dupeyroux, *Les grands problèmes du droit*, *loc. cit.* 34–42, dealing with the work of Le Fur. *Contra:* Simonius, *Quelles sont les causes de l'autorité du droit?* in 1 Recueil Gény 204 *et seq.*

ence. But that is a matter of legislative prudence, concerning only those who govern. Inasmuch as the rule is laid down, it is not for the disobedience of the subjects to strike it down with invalidity, indeed with sterility. This is precisely why compulsion is instituted: To insure the observance of the rule against disobedience.

24. Abrogation of Statute Law by Contrary Custom. It is true that according to certain conceptions, which are sometimes accepted in practice, the legal rule, where it has issued from statute law, is susceptible of abrogation by desuetude, which entails a return to liberty; or even of positive replacement by a contrary custom.[4] Now desuetude as well as contrary custom presuppose a failure, deliberate or from negligence, to observe the rule: General and prolonged disobedience thus becomes a source of law. But there would first of all be need to see if the failure to observe the statute did not derive from its inapplicability to those very subjects, so that the disobedience would be but apparent: A statute that from the outset or by change of circumstances is inapplicable could not obligate. No one is bound to the impossible, and the statute that would demand the morally or materially impossible is not, or has ceased to be, a veritable statute.[5] Contrariwise, the true problem appears where the lack of application of the statute would be caused simply by the displeasure or disagreement it brings about. It is precisely here that one may ask himself whether the solution of abrogation of statutes by desuetude or, *a fortiori*, by contrary custom, ought not to be discarded as it puts an official premium on disobedience. No doubt, by hypothesis, the disobedience has ceased to be individual, it has become collective: It is the mass that has become refractory, and therefore the attitude of the individual who acts like the mass no longer has the character of individual disobedience. Nonetheless the point remains that the custom has formed as a result of accumulated individual disobediences and contrary to what legitimate authority had prescribed.

25. Special Case of Desuetude. As regards desuetude, however, we may observe that it never results from the negative attitude of the subjects alone, that in addition it requires concurrence on the part of the

[4] This is the solution proposed, e.g., by ST. THOMAS, SUMMA, *Ia IIae*, qu. 97, art. 3 *ad resp.*, *in fine:* . . . Cf. A. LEBRUN, LA COUTUME, SES SOURCES, SON AUTORITÉ EN DROIT PRIVÉ (Paris, 1932), nos. 433 *et seq.*, pp. 461 *et seq.*, and references *id.* p. 467 n. 1.

[5] Cf., in this sense, ST. THOMAS, *op. cit. Ia IIae*, qu. 97, art. 3 *ad.* 2, arguing from the lack of utility or of adaptation of the law. And see 1 F. GÉNY, MÉTHODE D'INTERPRÉTATION ET SOURCES EN DROIT PRIVÉ POSITIF (2d ed.) 410.

law-administering agencies (officials and judges) who fail to lend themselves to action, prosecution, and sanction. It is the passivity of those agencies that permits, and hence realizes, desuetude, for their intervention would have resulted in interrupting the prescription of the statute.[6] A still graver disobedience then, it will be said. But the aspect of the problem has changed. No longer is it our concern to find out if the disobedience of the subjects can entail the death of statute law: On that point, the answer is in the negative. It is rather our concern to find out if the law-administering agencies enjoy a certain freedom in the application of statute law, a freedom that may go so far as to refuse such application. The question is no longer one of the relationships between the statute and the subjects, but one of the relationships between the different "powers" or agencies in the state, particularly between statute law and the case law of the courts. As for custom prevailing against statute law, the same observation will apply, *mutatis mutandis*;[c] although at the beginning of a custom *contra legem*[d] there is disobedience of the statute, the problem that arises is less one of the validity of the statute in the face of the attitude of the subjects than one of the sources of law. Two sources of law are in conflict: Statute and custom; the question is, which is the predominant source. Again, the question relates to the organization of the power to decree rules in the state, in short, to the constitutional régime.[7]

26. In General, the Law Is Obeyed. Ordinarily, obedience to the law comes about spontaneously, without state intervention, though not always without reluctance. No matter how numerous infractions may appear in the case of laws fettering human passions or imposing pecuniary sacrifices, they represent but a rather small percentage in the total of the unnumbered acts of social life: In general, property and life are respected, debtors pay their debts, taxpayers pay their taxes . . . In short, law on the whole is doubtless obeyed more often than it is disobeyed. And that is fortunate, for otherwise no compulsion would stand the test: The measures of enforcement would be paralyzed under the avalanche of infractions. This is the partial truth involved in the saying: Positive law (in the sense of "real," "realized" law) is the law generally

[6] See, in the same sense, ST. THOMAS, SUMMA, *Ia IIae*, qu. 97, art. 3 *ad* 3, *in fine*, arguing from the toleration of authority in régimes where the people do not have the lawmaking power.

[c] [With changes as the case may be.]

[d] [Contrary to a law.]

[7] It must be recognized, though, that the solution of the problem of the relationships between case law and statute law is delicate and far from clarified.

obeyed. Should disobedience be general, compulsion would be powerless, the law would cease to act and hence to live. It matters little, though, what motive actually dictates obedience. A rule of social discipline is entitled to require only conformity of action, independent of the rectitude or purity of intentions: Speaking socially, and thus juridically, it is the result that counts, and that, by hypothesis, is attained.[8] But clearly the fear of the sanction figures among the most active motivations of obedience to laws, whether as a stimulant for laws containing commands, or as an inhibiting force for laws containing prohibitions. The entire criminal law is founded upon the idea of the intimidating force of punishment: The laws threaten force so as not to have to use it or, at least, to have to use it only as a last resort.[9]

27. Sanction and Compulsion. Where voluntary execution fails, compulsion thus enters the arena. What does this mean? The two notions of sanction and of compulsion must not be confused to the point of never distinguishing them. On the one hand, every rule of conduct ordinarily implies a sanction, without that sanction as such having the character of compulsion that inheres in law: The moral rule has its sanctions — sure sanctions of the life beyond, and more doubtful earthly sanctions, consisting in the reactions of tormented conscience, of outraged nature, of shocked public opinion. As for the rule of social manners, it is sanctioned by the approval or disapproval, manifested or perceptible, of the public environment. Now those diverse reactions have nothing substantially in common with the sanction of legal compulsion. On the other hand, there are in law sanctions that fully deserve that name and yet do not in themselves constitute compulsion. In fact, the state can decree plenty of measures that tend to bring about the execution of its rule, specifically if possible, or else by an equivalent. Among these measures, some are preventive, others compensatory or repressive. Now nothing prevents us from calling these latter measures, which presuppose the violation of the rule, by the name of sanctions. Thus, refusal to discharge the obligation to do a certain act (*facere*) is subject to "sanc-

[8] Cf. St. Thomas, *op. cit. Ia IIae*, qu. 92, art. 2 *ad* 4, who, starting from the idea that the end of every law is to make man (morally) good, remarks that fear of punishment may lead a man finally to obey *delectabiliter et ex propria voluntate* [with pleasure and by his own will]. In any event, the law prescribes but the virtuous thing and not the mode of activity of the virtuous man: . . . , *id.* qu. 96, art. 3 *ad.* 2.

[9] Cf., in this sense, St. Thomas, *op. cit. Ia IIae*, qu. 95, art. 1 *ad resp.* and *ad* 1; qu. 96, art. 5 *ad resp., in fine.* One can say that, modeled upon the law of the Old Testament, a juridical law is and will always be a law of fear and not a law of love, which means that its execution will always have to rest on force.

tion" by contractual damages or by dissolution of the contract; violation of matrimonial obligations is subject to "sanction" by divorce or judicial separation; injury unlawfully inflicted upon another, to "sanction" by damages in tort; theft, to "sanction" by restitution of stolen goods; illegal contracts are subject to "sanction" by nullity, and unlawful associations, by dissolution; the incompetent or malfeasant official is dismissed; the parent betraying his trust is deprived of parental power, etc.

Yet, to speak precisely, it is necessary that these sanctions themselves, like preventive measures if any, and like the precept that is guaranteed by all such measures, be translated into reality. Now they will be so translated, in the absence of voluntary execution, by enforced execution. Contractual and tort damages and restitution will be executed against the goods of the debtor by means of various seizures (executory or conservatory), the dissolved association that tries to reconstitute itself will be dislodged and disintegrated by physical compulsion. Thus the law does not limit itself to providing sanctions; it undertakes their effective realization, and this is equivalent to the enforced execution of the violated precept. In other words, execution is always susceptible of being attained by force, whether directly, in kind, or indirectly, by the equivalent of sanctions. In this, compulsion consists.[10]

28. Punishment and Compulsion. Sometimes, in the gravest or most urgent cases, the law provides a kind of sanction whose character is one purely of satisfaction, tending to avenge the attack upon the law and to prevent its recurrence. This is punishment in its multifarious technical forms: punishment in its proper sense, civil penalty, fiscal penalty, and so on. It is no longer a matter of compelling the effective observance of the violated precept, of going back to the infraction, effacing its result and somehow annulling it, or in short, of enforced execution, in kind or by equivalent. It is rather a matter of prosecuting offenders: The violation remains accomplished, but the outrage inflicted upon the rule by the very violation is compensated for by a reëstablishment of the authority of the law, which is indicated by the punishment. Forced execution will intervene with regard to the punishment, but no longer with respect to the violated obligation. In relation to the execution of the precepts, the rôle of the punishment is only psychological and preventive: Acting by way of threat, it tends to create a motive favorable to spontaneous execution in the future.[11] Then, too, nothing stands in the way of pun-

[10] Cf., as to the distinction between sanctions of compulsion and sanctions of equivalence, J. Bonnecase, Introduction à l'étude du droit (2d ed. Paris, 1931) no. 42, p. 79; Du Pasquier, *op. cit.* nos. 137–138.

[11] There are also uncertain cases: equivalents or substitutes so little adequate

ishment being cumulative with the forced execution of the precept; in other words, the infraction may give rise to both forced execution and punishment, the latter then subjecting to sanction the failure of voluntary execution and itself giving rise to forced execution.

29. Variety of the Forms of Compulsion. Of course, the forms of compulsion and of the procedure of its application vary with the times, the places, and the civilizations. The best compulsion being that endowed with maximum efficacy, and efficacy depending upon contingent circumstances, it will be understood that determination of the procedure of compulsion is subject to the law of variation. It will also be understood, since compulsion comes to grips with the persons of the subjects, that the ideas current about the human personality, its rights and its dignity, influence the régime of compulsion so as eventually to temper solutions deduced from the single viewpoint of efficacy. There was a time when the defaulting debtor was sentenced to imprisonment or handed over to the creditor, whereas in our days execution against the person is replaced with execution against property. The principle *Nemo potest cogi ad factum*,[e] which no doubt is necessary, physically necessary where execution of the obligation is not physically possible without the concurring will of the obligor, has been extended at least in civil matters to the case where violence would have to be done to the person in order to obtain his concurrence in the execution: Specific execution is then replaced by money equivalents. In some countries the death penalty has been abolished, and mutilations of the body — cutting off the hand or the tongue, or castration — are now in use only among barbarous peoples. A more refined sentiment of justice has introduced the idea of a necessary proportion between the gravity of the infraction and the penalty, has banished from the law books the system of collective punishments, and so on

Similarly, the mechanics of invoking the sanction vary with the jurisdictions and subject matters of legislation. Sometimes compulsion is set in motion *motu proprio*,[f] and the police organs see to it that the law is respected without waiting for an order or permssion to that effect; sometimes an action is required, ordinarily judicial action, instituted by the particular injured individual or by any citizen whatever (popular or taxpayer's action) or by a prosecuting organ of the state (the state

in their function of reparation that one may ask if the pretended reparation does not rather have a penal character (such as damages to repair a merely moral injury). See A. Givord, La responsabilité du préjudice moral (Grenoble, 1938).

[e] [Nobody can be compelled to do a thing.]

[f] [Spontaneously.]

attorney). This is not to say that obedience would be optional, but simply that the working of compulsion is subject to special rules, depending upon the nature of the protected interests.

30. Specific Characteristics of Legal Compulsion. But beyond the diversities of foundations or details, legal compulsion is distinguished, on the one hand, by its material character: It is not only psychological, it is physical. The *manus militaris* [g] exerts pressure upon the individual's body or property, he is affected in his liberty, in his estate, or in certain capacities to act (prohibitions against activities in commerce or management). On the other hand, legal compulsion is distinguished by its organized and technical character: At least in states worthy of that name, pressure results from a machinery preconstituted under precise rules, functioning in an impartial, objective, and sure manner.[12] From a formal point of view, that capacity for exaction by force most neatly defines the legal rule, and especially the legal rule of the state.[13] It justifies the designation of "public power" that has been given to the state: The state is power not only because it has the right to sanction its orders by force, but also because it has, and must have, the implements of that power. The order of the state, at the border line and in case of need, is the order of compulsion, of armed force. To satisfy the requirements of compulsion it is not sufficient, therefore, that the ordinance be sanctioned by public opinion reacting in its own diffuse and incoherent manner. A discipline abandoned to the sanction of opinion is a discipline disarmed and consequently deficient from the legal point of view.

This is not to say, though, that force would always succeed in all cases or even with regard to all rules. Despite the power of the state, there are always smart people who contrive to violate the laws without incurring the rigors of compulsion; or, again, certain rules are psychologically or technically awkward to apply, so that the machinery of compulsion lends them but insufficient aid. In any case, actual inefficacy or impotence of compulsion can affect the validity of the rule even less than disobedience: That validity binds, and continues to bind, by virtue of the very disposition made by the rule.

[g] [Armed force.]

[12] But see, to the contrary, 2 L. DUGUIT, TRAITÉ DE DROIT CONSTITUTIONNEL (3d ed.) § 19, pp. 208–209, who wants to retain only the idea of "social sanction," excluding that of public compulsion which to his mind is too precise; also F. RUSSO, *op. cit.* 152 *et seq.*

[13] Cf., in the same sense, DU PASQUIER, *op. cit.* nos. 2 and 3.

31. Special Cases of Legal Rules Without Compulsion. Sometimes, it is true, one finds in the codes *leges imperfectae* [h] which, by design or otherwise, are divested of compulsion and even of sanction.[14] But what do those anomalies matter? Do they not say by designation that they represent "imperfect" law — imperfect by the lack of compelling sanction? In pure logic, compulsion and, generally, measures of execution are but an adventitious element with regard to a rule, adding to it without becoming an integral part of it. The rule is complete and it obliges as soon as it disposes and prescribes; the rest is a matter of execution which does not touch upon the precept. But in law it is otherwise. The execution is tied to the precept because it is the function of law as social discipline to act upon society and hence to realize itself. It is not merely for the individual to realize the law; the law itself must prepare and attain that realization by measures of execution, and especially of compulsion.

As for the obligations called "natural" in civil law, they are essentially foreign to the law: Legally, they do not oblige, since he who is subject to them is free not to carry them out. These obligations are not legal and, in this sense, they concern the law only by reason of the effects which laws attach to their voluntary execution (denial of rescission, denial of the character of a gift) or to their acknowledgment (transformation into an obligatory civil indebtedness), and no less by reason of their origin, since they derive from a degenerated civil obligation (nullity, prescription). Yet, even though consecrated by the law, the natural obligations remain obligations that, in law, do not oblige.[15]

32. Insufficiency of the Formula "Tendency Toward Compulsion." The foregoing considerations enable us to understand why it is impossible to define the legal rule simply by a "tendency toward compulsion." [16] According to that conception, it would suffice that the rule be

[h] [Imperfect laws.]

[14] The *leges imperfectae* of the Roman law are laws prohibiting a legal transaction without sanctioning the prohibition. See F. Senn, Leges perfectae, imperfectae, minus quam perfectae (Thesis, Paris, 1902).

[15] This is so even if one claims a distinction between right and action, or between *Schuld* (*debitum* [indebtedness]) and *Haftung* (*obligatio* [liability]). A right without action, a *Schuld* without *Haftung* do not constitute legal bonds.

[16] In that sense, all adherents of natural law: e.g., 1 F. Gény, Science et technique en droit privé positif, no. 16, p. 51; 4 *id.* p. 252; 1 J. Leclercq, Leçons de droit naturel (2d ed.) no. 11, pp. 45, 50; Du Pasquier, *op. cit.* nos. 282 and 311. Equally so all adherents of the legal rule deduced from common consciousness: e.g., 1 L. Duguit, *op. cit.* (3d ed.) § 8, p. 94 (see the quotation, *infra*, no. 107). — But see the more recent study by F. Gény, *Justice et force*, in Etudes de droit civil à la mémoire de Henri Capitant 241 *et seq.*, whose subtitle indi-

susceptible of sanction by compulsion without such compulsion having to be positively organized. The motive that dictates the solution is evident. One seeks in that fashion to safeguard the idea of a "natural" law distinct from the moral rule and lacking compulsion (if not an obligatory character and, in the special case of justice, the capacity for exaction); to add effective compulsion would be the work, precisely, of positive law. Yet, apart from that attempt to justify natural law, one must confess that "tendency toward compulsion" is a rather strange answer. From the viewpoint of compulsion, that is, in distinguishing rules from that viewpoint, two solutions are possible: Either the rule is sanctioned by compulsion or it is not. *Tertium non datur.*[i] Effective compulsion alone provides the answer. The "tendency toward compulsion" leaves the rule without compulsion; and hence that rule, with regard to a rule sanctioned by compulsion, remains but a rule of another category or, at best, an imperfect legal rule.[17]

33. Legal Compulsion as the Monopoly of the State. Instituted for the ends of protecting the rule of the law of the state, compulsion, and especially the right to punish, belongs only to the state and its competent organs. In this sense, compulsion is, and cannot but be, public. It would be the reign of war and of anarchy if every citizen — or private groups of citizens — had the right to employ force in order to guaranteee the execution of the laws laid down by public power, even under the pretext that those laws would consecrate their own personal interests. Private compulsion is at times excessive and at times insufficient: Insufficient on the part of the feeble against the strong; excessive, or in danger of being so, on the part of the strong against the feeble. In any case, it is disorderly and it provokes disorder. Historically, it was one of the first tasks of the state in its formative stage to substitute its justice and its compulsion for private justice and compulsion and gradually to monopolize the coercive power. That was the logic of its rôle. As for punishment in particular, one conceives the right to punish only as the prerogative of a superior authority and not as a right of an equal against an equal. When one speaks of a private penalty, one deals not at all with a penalty inflicted by a private person but simply with a penalty — or a reparation — called forth to sanction a private wrong, an injury done to a private interest. True punishment can only be

---

cates its tendency: *Pour l'intégration de la force dans le droit* [For integration of force with law].

[i] [There is no third alternative.]

[17] Cf., in the same sense, P. Cuche, *A propos du "positivisme juridique" de Carré de Malberg* in MÉLANGES CARRÉ DE MALBERG (Paris, 1933) 75–76.

public, since only the authority that has laid down the rule is qualified to exact vengeance for its transgression.[18]

34. Special Cases of Private Compulsion. It does happen, however, that private individuals find each other recognizing a certain right to use material pressure — physical or economic force — in order to safeguard the rights they hold by the rule of social discipline (private compulsion). The classical case is that of legitimate self-defense: An individual under attack against his life or his property has the right to defend by force his right to live or his right of ownership. But the question there is less one of compulsion tending to prevent the violation of the rule guaranteeing human life or property than one of instinctive defense of the essential goods that life and property are for everyone. In any case, the right of legitimate self-defense plays a subsidiary part: It is admitted only in the case of necessity, given the inability to have recourse to public force.[19] On the other hand, there are means of economic pressure consecrated by the social rule itself: Such are the right of retention and the *exceptio non adimpleti contractus.*[j] The thing that is due will be delivered only if the opponent in turn has performed his obligation. But, again, there is here not so much a means of compulsion put at the service of the legal rule (notwithstanding its compulsive value, which is by the way rather psychological) as the application of an elementary idea of reciprocity, postulated by justice and good faith. Do we have to point also to the boycott and the blacklist? In cases where they are used legitimately, they represent the exercise of a right of contractual freedom that is no longer put at the service of other rights or of a law, but of mere interests in the field of the competition of life, so that the process no longer offers any analogy to the idea of legal compulsion.

35. Disciplinary Power of Private Bodies. Let us add that the rule of the law of the state alone is susceptible of sanction by compulsion, and above all by punishment. The inferior and subordinate groups may well enjoy what is called "disciplinary" power, authorizing the application of so-called disciplinary penalties on the part of the group against members who have offended against the rule of its internal law. But that disciplinary penal power differs from the power of the state in extent and character. Not only is it limited as to the kind of offenses and the kind of penalties; but even where the authority of the group is competent to

[18] See, in the same sense, ST. THOMAS, SUMMA THEOLOGICA, *Ia IIae*, qu. 90, art. 3 *ad* 2; qu. 92, art. 2 *ad* 3; *IIa IIae*, qu. 60, art. 6 *ad resp.* and *ad* 1.

[19] See, in the same sense, DU PASQUIER, *op. cit.* no. 140. . .

[j] [Plea of non-performance of the contract by the other party.]

step in, there is always reserved an appeal to the state as the judge of last resort.[20] Thus, controversies between husband and wife, parents and children, even in the field subject to the exercise of marital or parental authority, are susceptible to judgment by the state. Little would it avail the father of the family to oppose to it his disciplinary power, which indeed derives from the authority over his family that the state recognizes. That disciplinary power does not withdraw him beyond the control of the public authority, which is superior to it. The same, *mutatis mutandis*, goes for the rights of the authority of a corporate body over its members. Where the state exists, the whole legal system of those groups, including the disciplinary power, is in a certain way subordinate to the legal system of the state, whose mission it is to pare down possible abuses of the authority and disciplinary power of the groups over their members.

The Objections Against This Definition

36. The Rules of Public Law by Which the State and Authority Are Constituted. However, the definition of law which has been proposed and commented upon above is seemingly condemned by the existence of a set of rules everybody calls legal, which are far from corresponding to the traits here presented as essential. Such are several rules of municipal [national] public law and, even more, public international law.

As for municipal public law, one could think first of all of the category of rules by which the public authority itself is constituted (form of government, distribution of powers, etc.). How could the rules organizing authority in the state emanate from that authority which, by hypothesis, does not exist yet? How could they even emanate from the state, which comes into being only with the differentiation of the rulers and the ruled? Logically, the constituted power cannot at the same time be the constituent power. Thus the definition which ties the legal rule to authority and to the state, acceptable as to rules set down by the authority for its subjects, private individuals, and officials, could no longer be accepted as to the rules, logically and chronologically anterior, by which that authority is founded.

Yet upon reflection this is a specious objection. As the principal basis of the constitutive charter of authority and of its statute, one always discovers again an authority, which is a public authority. That authority — a whole people, a fraction of the people, a minority, or a single chief — is doubtless not the *constituted* authority, but it is the *con-*

[20] Cf., in the same sense, A. Légal and J. Brèthe de la Gressaye, *op. cit.* 184 *et seq.*, 321 *et seq.*, 461 *et seq.*

stituent authority. It has no strictly legal title, but it has a moral title, at least to the extent that it can avail itself of certain arguments of legitimacy. On the other hand, that constituent authority is a public authority, even though the state is perhaps not yet constituted, because everything that relates to the state, already constituted or still in the process of constitution, necessarily takes on a public character, at least by intention.[21] In quite the same way one would try in vain to embrace within a single principle, and consequently within the same definition, the law that is made and the competency to make law: At the origin of the law must be a principle which could not be law, a kind of moral and political principle which, if one likes, one may call "natural political law."[22]

37. The Rules of Public Law Governing the Activities of Those Who Hold Authority. More pertinent is the objection that touches upon the category of rules of public law governing the activity of those who hold authority, whatever their functions may be — legislative, administrative, or judicial. For it is understood that in a state under the rule of law there are rules not only for the subjects in their relationships with each other and with the state of which they are members but also for the officials and the rulers, who have to discharge their functions according to jurisdictional, procedural, and substantive norms determined by public law, which is constitutional and administrative law.

Now, whatever the mode of organization of authority may be, whatever precautions may have been taken to prevent abuses of power and to subject each organ of authority to its law, there will always be in the state authorities that are practically irresponsible, which will obey their rule only if they wish, against which at any rate the employment of compulsion is impracticable, indeed inconceivable. This is so for all organs supreme within their branch [of the government].[23] How can public force be mobilized against Parliament, against the Executive, against the Supreme Court or the Supreme Administrative Tribunal?[k] One may well provide sanctions of annulment or restitution against their

[21] Cf. G. GURVITCH, L'IDÉE DU DROIT SOCIAL 119: "There are communities which by one and the same act engender their law and found their existence upon it, which create their existence in engendering the law that serves as their foundation." He adds: "These communities in which constitution through the law and generation of a law coincide are, precisely, normative facts."

[22] As to this concept of political natural law, see *infra*, nos. 205 and 215.

[23] Cf. ST. THOMAS, SUMMA, *Ia IIae*, qu. 96, art. 5 *ad* 3: the prince is beyond the law *quantum ad vim coactivam legis* but not *quantum ad vim directivam legis* [as to the compelling but not as to the directing force of the law].

[k] [The French designations are *Cour de Cassation* and *Conseil d'Etat.*]

acts, measures of recall or punishment against the persons of their incumbents. But the better is often the enemy of the good, and it may happen that sanctions would be more damaging than the illegalities they would strive to remedy. Thus, in countries with rigid constitutions which have no judges to apply sanctions in one way or another to the unconstitutionality of statutes, the ordinary legislature is in fact free to violate the constitution. Again, wherever the judicial power enjoys independence, the supreme organ of that power, the Supreme Court, although subject to the laws and charged with assuring their observance by the courts, is in fact free to violate the law under color of interpreting it.

The question then arises whether such rules, involving neither compulsion nor any organized sanction whatever, still belong to the category of law. The answer has already been given for the *leges imperfectae:* We are dealing with law, not with morals or manners, since we have to do with rules of societal character laid down by public authority; but we are dealing with imperfect law to the extent to which compulsion, the guarantor of effective execution, is lacking.[24]

38. Public International Law: The Lack of Compulsion. More troubling is the case of public international law. Here one views primarily the relationships between states. Now it is a fact that at the present stage of international relations, there exists no organized international society, universal or even regional, capable of laying down for the member states a rule of an inter- or super-state social discipline. Consequently, our definition breaks down in its foundations: No society, no authority to set down the rule, no sanction or compulsion to provide for its realization. And yet everybody talks and keeps on talking of international law.

Let us observe at once that, if law it be, it will be a law imperfect on the side of compulsion. On the one hand, the possible disapproval by international public opinion (represented by the other states and citizens of those states, perhaps also by a fraction of the public of the transgressor state) could not count as a legal sanction.[25] Still less could the protestations of the state that may be victimized do so, nor the reprisals taken by it, war not excepted. War may well have its justification, especially in the case of legitimate self-defense, which is individual by hypothesis;

[24] Thus, authors who exclude organized compulsion from the definition of law are obliged to recognize that from the viewpoint of application (a viewpoint essential in law) "there is law, in the full and complete sense of the term, only when the rule is recognized and protected by the social power": F. RUSSO, *op. cit.* 156. See also F. GÉNY, *op. cit. supra*, n. 16.—To others, compulsion would not be indispensable; . . . see M. Réglade, *Essai sur le fondement du droit*, in ARCHIVES DE PHILOSOPHIE DU DROIT (1933), nos. 3–4, pp. 184–185. . .

[25] See *supra*, no. 30.

but it does not conform to the concept of legal sanction, which supposes compulsion exercised by the authority of an organized group.[26] On the other hand, the efforts made since 1919 to set afoot means of compulsion of a legal character have finally failed: Rightly or wrongly, several states which were bound by the terms of the Covenant of the League of Nations to collaborate in the sanctions decreed by the "societal" authority declined. And no doubt it will take time before a machinery of compulsion is ready to function that is both adapted to the particular features of international life and sufficiently efficacious.

39. Public International Law (Continued): Absence of an International Public Society. But if the lack of compulsion leaves only an imperfect law, does not the absence of an actual and concrete international society cause the very concept of law to disappear, at least as it has been defined, as a law of a group? Despite its logical appearance, the conclusion seems excessive, for the following reasons. No doubt one finds among the states no society as perfected as the various internal political societies in which citizens are grouped together; especially, one meets with no authority here that is properly legislative or executive. Contrariwise, there exist international tribunals (courts of justice and courts of arbitration), creators of rules of judge-made law, and especially a more or less developed international custom, resulting from the constant practice of states in their mutual relationships. Now, just as custom at the domestic level is a source of true law, that is, of an institutional social rule, although it has not been laid down by public authority,[27] just so and *a fortiori* it conserves that character of a generator of law in its proper sense, of an institutional social rule, at the international level.[28] On the part of states, and generally of collectivities, the adoption of a common rule indicates a desire for coördination and organization which one cannot discover to the same extent in the attitudes of private individuals who submit to private custom. At the international level, the phenomenon of custom is more than the foreshadowings of a society of

[26] As to war, the theological tradition is to the contrary: it considers the just war a legal sanction. On the other hand, many sociologists speak of a punishment procedure of primitive law; see, e.g., P. Guggenheim, *Contribution au problème sociologique du droit international*, in 2 RECUEIL LAMBERT § 76, pp. 117–118. But individual, unorganized reactions, even when justified, do not constitute a legal sanction.

[27] See *supra*, no. 18.

[28] See, in the same sense, DU PASQUIER, *op. cit.* nos. 8 and 41. It is wrong, by the way, for certain writers on international law to claim that international custom is to be traced back to a tacit agreement, for custom binds every state regardless of any individual acquiescence.

states: It is at once its bait and its embryo. Among states, the recognition of reciprocal rights and duties, which can only be functional rights and duties,[29] engenders a quasi-society.[30]

40. International Custom Is Subordinate to the Category of Law. Yet, it will be said, are the rules that have issued from international custom really legal rules? Why should one not assign them to the category of morals or that of social manners?

There could be no question here of a rule of the manners of social convenience since, by hypothesis, this is a matter not of convenience but of obligation: The state is bound, in the absolute sense of the word. Neither could there be a question of morals since, in truth, morals govern only individuals and not collectivities, without distinguishing between collectivities that are persons and those not endowed with personality. Often there is confusion here, due to the ambiguity resulting from the expression, "international morals." All human individuals, in whatever field they may act, for themselves or for others, are subject to morals, in their domestic and international public activities as in private business or family life. In this sense, it is true that there exist "international morals" and that there are not two sets of morals, one for individuals and another for states. The "political" lie, the "political" assassination, committed in the name of the state or for political ends (the pretended good of the state or the community) are and remain lies, assassinations — morally and politically. But it does not follow that the states themselves and the public and private collectivities generally, are subjects of morals. The idea of morality, in its exact and complete concept, is inseparable from the idea of personality. Only the real, substantial persons, endowed with their own reason and will and provided with an end of their own, are susceptible to merit and demerit, to an obligation of conscience, a right intent, a moral perfection. Now the collectivities, even where they unite in themselves the conditions of so-called moral personality (which is the case of the states), have only an accidental, functional personality, and this cannot be reduced to the idea of morality.[31]

[29] On this functional character, see J. DABIN, DOCTRINE GÉNÉRALE DE L'ETAT, no. 296, pp. 478–480.

[30] One could add other considerations, drawn from the existence of veritable international laws (act of regulation, lawmaking treaty, act of union), as opposed to an international contractual agreement; see 1 G. SCELLE, PRÉCIS DU DROIT DES GENS 14 *et seq.*

[31] This is the reason, quite exact in itself, why GROTIUS, LE DROIT DE LA GUERRE ET DE LA PAIX [DE JURE BELLI AC PACIS] (translation by Barbeyrac, Basle, 1768) [English translation, by Kelsey, in SCOTT'S CLASSICS OF INTERNATIONAL LAW (1925)] *Discours préliminaire* [Prolegomena] § 41, refused to place international

Contrariwise, nothing prevents us from talking of international law, because states, like individuals, may be subjects of law, actively and passively. Law, viewed from the standpoint of its beneficiary, in effect consists in some prerogative residing in another in a somehow objective manner.[32] That is why a legal title may perfectly well be found in the head of a juristic person, and such a person may perfectly well be bound to respect a legal title.[33] In this sense, there exist an international "justice," which corresponds to law *sensu stricto*,[l] an international fidelity to the pledged word, engendering a law *sensu lato*,[m] and even an international mutual aid, which together form the object of international law in the sense of a norm governing the relationships between states.

CHAPTER II

CHARACTERISTICS OF THE LEGAL RULE

41. Plan of this Chapter. Bound in its concept to the idea of the society-state, which provides its specific environment and framework (see Chapter I), the law is also and primarily, according to our definition, a rule of conduct. This thesis, seemingly clear enough, still requires explanations. It is first of all to be proved that law really is a rule of conduct, thus falling under the category of the so-called normative sciences, and that it can always be reduced to a rule of conduct, at least an underlying one. It is further to be shown what traits distinguish the rule of conduct called "law" from other kinds of rules of conduct even in the social field. It would be surprising, for instance, if the "societal" rôle of the legal rule remained without influence upon the physiognomy of the legal imperative.

---

relations under natural law (which he understood in the sense of the moral law; see *infra*, no. 208): Morals exist only for individuals, while states are subject to the law of nations. Cf. J. Lacroix, *Eléments constitutifs de la notion de civilisation*, in LES CONFLITS DE CIVILISATION (SEMAINE SOCIALE DE VERSAILLES, 1936, *compte rendu des cours*) 105: "Morals cannot apply directly to social forces; they need the mediation of the law."

[32] We shall come back to this characteristic of the law, in dealing with justice, *infra*, nos. 225–226.

[33] Certain writers, to be sure, rejecting the idea of juristic personality, deny that states are subjects of international law; . . . see, e.g., G. SCELLE, PRÉCIS DU DROIT DES GENS, PRINCIPES ET SYSTÉMATIQUE, *passim* . . .

[l] [In the strict sense.]

[m] [In the wide sense.]

Section 1. The Law as a Preceptive, Categorical Rule of Conduct

42. The Two Constitutive Elements of Every Rule: Hypothesis and Solution. Analyzed in its logical structure, the legal rule, any legal rule, consists of two parts, of which one indicates a hypothesis, the other (in a word that prejudges nothing) a [consequent] solution. The hypothesis states the conditions of the application of the rule, which by the way are defined in the abstract: Such and such a situation existing, such and such a solution shall or ought to follow. It matters little whether the hypothesis is set out distinctly in a subordinate clause starting with "if," "in case," "supposing," "on condition," "wherever," or is furtively included in the main clause setting forth the solution. Take the rule: The minor lacks legal capacity. The hypothesis is: If a person is a minor; the solution: He lacks legal capacity. Again, it matters little whether the hypothesis consists in a pure state of facts, a state of law, or a mixed state of facts and law. Take the rule: The spouse (or: The owner, the creditor, the heir, the state, the Belgian citizen) has such and such a right (or obligation). The quality of spouse (or owner, creditor, etc.), which forms the hypothesis of the rule, is a state of law, which again may derive sometimes from facts pure and simple and sometimes from legal transactions. Take the rule of damages for injury caused by fault. The two conditions of the right to damages are one of fact: The injury, and one of law: The fault.[1] Equally little does it matter whether the hypothesis presupposes that another legal rule has come into play. Take the rule obliging the creditor who has been paid by the surety to deliver to the latter the documents to facilitate the exercise of his recourse [of subrogation] against the debtor. That provision presupposes the legal rule that the surety is actually bound to pay for the debtor. Indeed, any rule laying down any sanction whatever — punishment, damages, nullity, or rescission — is based upon another rule, explicit or implied, namely, precisely the one whose violation gives rise to the sanction. But what does that mean? Simply this, that legal rules are not always separated from one another, that on the contrary they are linked together, often forming a set or system; and hence, nothing

[1] Cf. the analysis by Du Pasquier, Introduction à la théorie générale nos. 112–113. The hypothesis may, however, be quite simple and consist only in the existence of a subject, as in the rules which prohibit killing, assaulting, injuring. To bring these rules into play it is enough that one human being be confronted with another human being. See G. del Vecchio, *L'homo juridicus et l'insuffisance du droit comme règle de la vie*, in Justice, Droit, Etat 229, 231.

stands in the way of the hypothesis of one rule being itself deduced from an anterior legal rule.[2]

43. The Legal Solution Is a Norm. But what interests us in the legal rule for the moment is less the hypothesis than the solution. This constitutes the essential element of the rule, the disposition it makes. The question then is, what are the meaning and the nature of the legal solution?

Differing from the scientific solution, which is a statement of fact (*sein*, or the Is), the juridical solution is a norm, an order; that is, it belongs to the category of principles directing conduct. Whatever the origin, objective or subjective, of the legal rule, and even if one derives it from some reality, social or natural, positive or ideal,[3] it *indicates* to everybody what is "to be done," and at the same time it *prescribes* what it indicates. In this respect, the legal laws are in no way comparable to the laws of nature: Nature does not "obey" laws as man "obeys" a law. The material things which together make up nature are just what they are. They have causes and produce effects which in turn are just what they are, their more or less regular, that is, constant sequence assuming the name of natural "laws" or, as far as they are made explicit by the scholar's work of statements, experiments, and interpretations, the name of scientific "laws." But clearly those laws do not impose anything on nature; on the contrary, they are the more or less adequate expression of its being and of the manifestations of its being. Man alone, who is spirit, is subject to laws put before his will and dictating his conduct (*sollen*, or the Ought).

Nor should we confound the so-called sociological laws, which like the laws of nature are laws stating facts (social facts of different orders, economic, psychological, moral, etc.), with the legal or moral laws, which are directing laws, distinct in themselves from the actual behavior of men in society. Even admitting that normal social behavior can create or reveal the directing norm of individual activities, this does not prevent elevation of the fact of common conduct to the level of a norm of conduct for every individual, which signifies a change of plane.[4]

[2] See, in the same sense, Du Pasquier, *op. cit.* no. 115, from whom the illustration from the law of suretyship has been taken.

[3] This is the problem of the origin or the mode of elaboration of the legal rule; see *infra*, Part II.

[4] On all these points, cf. the two recent works of G. Cornil, *Le droit n'est pas une science, mais il y a une science du droit* in 26 Bulletin de la Classe des Lettres et des Sciences morales et politiques de l'Académie royale de Belgique, ser. V (1940) 76 *et seq.*, 83–84; F. Russo, Réalité juridique et réalité sociale (Paris, 1942) 48–60.

44. Criticism of the Contrary View (Zitelmann). This distinction between the laws of nature or, more broadly, of reality, and the rules of human action does not undergo too much discussion, and with rare dissents it is readily admitted by jurists. According to one of those dissenters, however, Zitelmann, "a positive law never contains an order. It is solely a general hypothetical judgment: It affirms that a certain effect will be produced if a certain cause occurs. Consequently, the legal rule should be read thus: If X does such and such a thing, Y will resort to a sanction against him." "Will resort" and not "shall resort": The legal rule is thus reduced to the scheme of the pure scientific law, simply marking the relation between two facts, the fact of the sanction consequent upon the fact of a certain attitude.[5] Reserving our criticism as to the — inexact — fashion in which the relation between the sanction and the rule is presented,[6] we are told: "Y will resort to a sanction." First, that remains to be seen: He will or will not resort to it: Only the future will decide. Normally he doubtless will; but why? Because he ought — or believes he ought — to resort to it, by reason of the rule that charges public officers to take care of the application of the sanction. In a word, there is not only the fact of the sanction, but also and first of all — by definition — the duty of the sanction; at least for the sanction, this restores the idea of the norm which was claimed to have been discarded.[7]

45. The Legal Rule Is Always a Norm of Conduct. The law is a norm of conduct, in the sense that its direct or indirect objective is to govern the conduct of private individuals (private law) and of officers within the state (public law) or of the states themselves in the international realm (public international law).

Opposed to this conception is the thesis of Jèze, who wants to replace the idea of the rule of conduct throughout with the idea of competency:

> Law regulates competencies. It organizes the legal capacity of individuals and the jurisdiction of public officers. That is all it does. Public and administrative law is concerned with the legal régime of the manifestations of wills occasioned by the administration of public services. Legal analysis always leads the observer back to stating the manifestation of the will of an individual and determining the legal effects to which that manifestation of a will may lead. This is true for private law as well as for public and administrative

[5] ZITELMANN, IRRTUM UND RECHTSGESCHÄFT (Leipzig, 1879) 208, 222.

[6] See *infra*, no. 53.

[7] See, in the same sense, the criticism of R. CAPITANT, L'ILLICITE 56–57, and G. del Vecchio, *L'homo juridicus, loc. cit.* 230–231.

law. The law — private law or public law — is always and exclusively concerned with manifestations of the wills of individuals.[8]

Other authors introduce a distinction between the rule of conduct properly so called, "prescribing how everyone ought to conduct himself" (*Verhaltungsrecht*, law of conduct), and the rule determining the structure and functioning of public or private groups or organizations (*Verfassungsrecht*, law of constitutions).[9] In the same sense, but in a more limited fashion, R. Capitant divides the law into "police rules," concerning the substance of law, and "competence rules," qualifying an organ to create law.[10]

46. Criticism of Contrary Views (Jèze, Burckhardt, R. Capitant). But first of all, as already observed,[11] it is inexact to reduce all law to rules of capacity and jurisdiction: Besides powers, proper or functional ones, the law regulates duties, pure duties. Nor is it any more true that the law is concerned only with manifestations of wills: Besides acts of will, a great many other facts, non-voluntary or involuntary, in any case foreign to the will, generate rules. On the other hand, if it is legitimate to distinguish among the legal rules a *Verfassungsrecht* [12] (of which competence rules constitute but a fraction), that *Verfassungsrecht* does not for that reason cease to be a rule of conduct. Groups, although they constitute something distinct from the pure sum of individuals, never are anything but the product of a certain ordering of member individuals who are gathered together and integrated in obedience to the constituent law of the group. To constitute the state, its powers and services, is to decree the rules of conduct to be imposed upon the persons, governing and governed, who constitute the state. That those rules are imposed upon them *qualitate quâ*,[a] by virtue of their relation to the group, detracts nothing from the essential fact that in this field, just as in the field of simply inter-individual relationships, the rule "prescribes how one ought to conduct himself." [13] Furthermore, *Verfassungsrecht*, or the

[8] G. Jèze, Les principes généraux du droit administratif: I. La technique du droit public français (2d ed. Paris, 1925) 7.

[9] W. Burckhardt, Methode und System des Rechts (Zurich, 1936) 132 *et seq.* (according to Du Pasquier, *op. cit.*, no. 116, pp. 86–87).

[10] R. Capitant, *op. cit.* 146–149.

[11] See *supra*, no. 5.

[12] As noted *supra*, no. 9, the societal law is, first, the law by which the society is constituted and functions, and then the law laid down by the society thus constituted.

[a] [In their quality as such.]

[13] See, on this point, J. Dabin, La philosophie de l'ordre juridique positif (Paris, 1929) no. 13.

competence rules, exist only with a view to *Verhaltungsrecht*. Groups are instituted in order to act, jurisdictions, in order to be exercised. Now the principal activity of the state and its organs, outside of material acts, is to direct its subjects by means of legal rules and orders. As R. Capitant says, "the competence rule has meaning only inasmuch as it prepares for a police rule," i.e., a rule of conduct for subjects or for officers. "It is, then, but an indirect rule of conduct. Thus, it is the concept of the police rule that is essential to law, and any definition of the law neglecting that notion is necessarily inexact." [14]

47. *The Legal Rule Imposes a Precept and not Advice.* Not every rule of conduct, however, necessarily involves a precept: The directive may take the form of a wish, an advice, a recommendation, a suggestion. The conduct to be followed is indicated; it is not imposed. It is thus not altogether correct to say that "the word rule is synonymous with imperative." [15] Usually, the rule proceeds by ordering; that it may proceed otherwise is not excluded.[16] But for the legal rule the case is clear: On the one hand, the law is not content to advise or recommend, it commands; on the other, its intervention remains limited to commands without adding advice.[17]

The law commands. Perhaps the authority would get a better response if it used advice rather than precept. That is a matter of national psychology; and there are in fact circumstances where the state, not daring to command, advises or, again, recommends and suggests. Good policy, mindful of efficacy, may require such a mode of intervention. But then the matter is precisely one of policy, in the sense of practical politics, and not of law: It is of the nature of the law to prescribe.[18] So, too, advice would not bring about the necessary social discipline, since the subjects would always be enabled not to follow it. Discipline implies command, with the obligation to submit to it. Nor could there be any question of confining the law to an advisory rôle: It is the right

[14] R. Capitant, *op. cit.* 149.

[15] R. Capitant, *op. cit.* 55.

[16] As St. Thomas says, *op. cit. Ia IIae*, qu. 91, art. 4 *ad* 2, "advice necessarily proceeds from some principles"; like the precept, it gives direction.

[17] Cf., in the same sense, de Vareilles-Sommières, Les principes fondamentaux du droit I, 10(7°) and 12, pp. 13 and 16.

[18] Cf., as regards suggestion, R. Capitant, *op. cit.* 93–97. Conversely it is to be noted that advice sometimes amounts to orders, by reason of the authority of the "adviser" or of certain possibilities of reaction in case of resistance. See, with regard to the *auctoritas* of the Roman Senate over the magistrates, 7 Mommsen and Marquardt, Manuel des antiquités romaines (French translation by P.-Fr. Girard, 1891) 231.

and the duty of authority, its function and its very definition, to direct, no doubt by way of advice but also and in the first place by way of imperative command.[19]

Aside from precepts, morals employ advice, inviting to a higher perfection, which finds a field of application in all spheres of human activity, including the sphere of social relationships. The law does not demand that much: It demands what discipline requires, that is, only the execution of what is commanded. Perfection resides in the exact, prompt observance of the indispensable discipline: Neither more nor less. To go beyond the law would perhaps satisfy morals, moral advice or even commands which are often more exacting than those of law. Or, possibly, it would collaborate with some public policy tending to bring about a certain social result or to encourage a certain "social" attitude. This, added to the legal duty, which undoubtedly is of interest to virtue or to society (ordinarily to both at once), still leaves the law indifferent, since within the margin of its system it is essentially and exclusively preceptive.

48. A Precept Underlies the Disposing and the Permissive Rules. But it is not useless to show that an imperative does indeed underlie all legal rules.[20] This is evident as to many such rules; to wit, those which directly command something (obligation to do) or, what amounts to the same, prohibit something, a prohibition being nothing else than a command to avoid what is prohibited (obligation to abstain). It matters little whether the formulation is in the present or future indicative rather than the imperative (or subjunctive), once the rule really suggests an order.[21] Take, for example, the rules that decree the obligation to register births; to pay one's creditor; to pay damages for wrongful injury; to provide for one's child; to observe prescribed forms; to enter military service; to abstain from any wrong, civil or criminal,[22] from any contract contrary to public policy or morality, or from the admission of inadmissible testimony. Obviously, these are imperative or prohibitive rules in substance as well as in expression.

But there are cases less neat where the imperative remains implied in

[19] Cf., in the same sense, ST. THOMAS, *op. cit. Ia IIae*, qu. 90, art. 3 *ad* 2; qu. 92, art. 2 *ad* 2; also, on the necessity of the laws, especially the penal laws, qu. 95, art. 1 *ad resp.*; qu. 92, art. 2 *ad resp.*, *in fine.*

[20] On the following, cf. ST. THOMAS, *op. cit. Ia IIae*, qu. 92, art. 2.

[21] R. Capitant is wrong in calling laws formulated in the indicative "declaratory laws." Why "declaratory," when they really lay down a precept?

[22] The penal laws are equally imperative laws, commanding abstention from the affirmative or negative act that gives rise to the penalty. They also contain an order, addressed to the organs applying the law, to make the punishment operative.

the legal solution. Take the so-called "disposing" rules. By assumption, they neither command nor prohibit any act; they define interests and rights, capacities and competencies; they determine the conditions on which a certain legal effect begins or the legal effects of a certain situation. Still more generally, they resolve a question concerning the relations among people — in short, they "dispose." For instance, the possessor in good faith of a movable shall be its owner; one's domicile shall be at the place of one's principal establishment; the child born to a Belgian father shall be a Belgian; movable objects which the owner of real property shall have affixed to it for its service and exploitation shall be deemed immovable; the burden of proof falls upon the claimant; the husband is presumed to be the father of his wife's child; the minor shall have no legal capacity; the citizen registered in the electoral lists shall have the right to vote; a certain organ shall have jurisdiction to make a certain legal rule or decision.

Yet every "disposition" involves an injunction to everyone — parties, third parties, officials administering the law — to respect the legal regulation. The thing commanded is here not a particular determined act but obedience to a law according to the terms of its disposition. For instance, when a law declares the possessor in good faith of a movable to be its owner, that "disposition" implies a prohibition addressed to everybody, particularly the dispossessed owner, against contesting or contravening the right of the possessor. When a law fixes the domicile at the place of principal establishment, that "disposition" obliges everybody, interested party or third party, private individual or official, to relate to that place the effects the law attaches to the idea of domicile. As for a rule of jurisdiction, that "disposition" contains at once a prohibition of action by any organ other than that declared competent, a prohibition of the latter exceeding its jurisdiction, and an order to its subordinates to admit the validity of decisions made by the competent organ and to conform their conduct to them.[23]

The case of the so-called "permissive" laws (basically, a variety of the "disposing" laws) is no different. To permit is to recognize capacities to act (or not to act), and therefore to command everyone not to hamper the free use of the recognized capacity.[24]

49. The Supplementing Laws. Stranger appears the case of the laws known in private law as "supplementing laws." These laws intervene in

[23] Cf., in the same sense as regards the laws of competence, R. CAPITANT, *op. cit.* 79–80, 147–148.

[24] See, in this sense, DU PASQUIER, *op. cit.* no. 117, p. 88. Cf. R. CAPITANT, *op. cit.* 78–79, . . .

matters that in principle are left within the realm of the wills of private individuals, who have permission to settle them at their convenience. When the law regulates them it does so only in a supplementing way, in the absence of a contrary will responding to certain previously fixed conditions. But one must not confound "supplementing" and "optional," as if the command degenerated to a sort of advice. The legal rule is competent, and hence exists, only in a subsidiary way. But where its competence is not discarded, it obligates in the same fashion as the rule not susceptible to derogation, viz., by way of an imperative, and with regard to the parties as well as to the judge. In the antithesis: Imperative laws v. supplementing laws, the term "imperative" is to be understood in the special, technical sense of laws not susceptible to derogation, i.e., not supplementing.[25]

50. The "Directives" or "Standards." As for the distinction between the "standard," a new term to designate the supple or "directive" rule,[26] and the legal rule, in the sense of a rigid rule leaving no place for any power of discretion, it is surprising to see it invoked in a discussion with which it has nothing to do. Whether "standard" or rigid rule, the law is always imperative, whatever may be the flexibility or inflexibility of its disposition.[27]

51. The Imperative Character of the Law Does Not Exclude Waivers. Let us note, in conclusion, that the imperative character of the legal rule does not necessarily exclude all capacity to waive facts or even rights. In this connection, it is appropriate to distinguish according to the public or private nature of the interest protected by the rule. Where that interest is public, directly or indirectly, wholly or in part, closely or remotely affecting the good of the state or the public, a waiver is thinkable neither on the part of private individuals, since the public interest is engaged, nor on the part of officials, who are chosen to defend the public interest, not to sacrifice it. Not only is a waiver unthinkable, but the legal imperative will normally be executed through public or

[25] Cf., in the same sense, R. CAPITANT, *op. cit.* 69–74; DU PASQUIER, *op. cit.* no. 118.

[26] See A. A. Al. Sanhoury, *Le standard juridique*, in 2 RECUEIL D'ÉTUDES SUR LES SOURCES DU DROIT EN L'HONNEUR DE FRANÇOIS GÉNY 144 *et seq.* — Inexact: R. CAPITANT, *op. cit.* 86, and DU PASQUIER, *op. cit.* no. 119 *in fine*, . . .

[27] Cf., in the same sense, R. CAPITANT, *op. cit.* 82–85; J. DABIN, LA PHILOSOPHIE DE L'ORDRE JURIDIQUE POSITIF, no. 7; DU PASQUIER, *op. cit.* no. 119. But from another point of view the directive is an intermediate phenomenon between the stability of the juridical and the movement of social life; see F. RUSSO, RÉALITÉ JURIDIQUE ET RÉALITÉ SOCIALE, 140–142, 151.

private organs charged with pursuing such execution. Contrariwise, where the protected interest is solely private, the beneficiary of the rule, as the master of the value it recognizes — property or liberty, right or capacity — is always free not to avail himself of it, free even formally to renounce it. The law remains imperative for everybody, including the beneficiary, who cannot prevent its value from accruing to him or at least being available to him by the sole will of the law; but by virtue of a new, equally imperative rule, by which every person who is of age is master of his rights, he is not obliged to accept the legal benefit or to take it into account.[28]

It is a nice question, though, how to draw the line between the rule of private interest and that of public interest, because of the close interpenetration of the two kinds of interests. Seen from the angle of abstract generality, are not the private values, as human goods desirable for all, matters of public interest?

52. The Legal Imperative Is Categorical and Not Conditioned or Technical. But here is a further distinction: The imperative of the law is categorical.

Apparently this goes without saying, and it may be asked how an imperative could be anything but categorical. But, rightly or wrongly, since Kant one opposes to the straight, so-called categorical, imperative a merely conditional, so-called hypothetical, imperative. Now the legal imperative has nothing conditional about it. No doubt the law is conditioned in the sense that the disposition of the rule is based upon a hypothesis and that the command is unchained only inasmuch as the hypothesis is in fact realized. The realization of the hypothesis thus forms the condition of the application of the disposition; or, more exactly, it is presupposed by the disposition. But while it may happen that the realization of the hypothesis depends upon the will of the subject individual, the same does not hold good for the disposition. Once the hypothesis is realized, the command is binding categorically, independently of any condition whatever that may originate in the subject individual or elsewhere. There exists an "obligation in case . . . ," not an "obligation if . . ."; the disposition is conditioned, it is not conditional.[29] For instance, the rules governing the various kinds of contracts,

[28] Very often private relationships are in fact regulated in a manner different from that provided by the laws. It is for the party "most diligent," hardy, or able, to initiate action; the others, letting things go, approve or tolerate it out of fear of conflicts and misunderstanding. *Vigilantibus jura prosunt* [Rights are useful to those who are vigilant].

[29] See, in the same sense as to this distinction, G. del Vecchio, *L'homo juridicus et l'insuffisance du droit comme règle de la vie*, in JUSTICE, DROIT, ETAT 228–230.

whether under public or private law, whether relating to property or other interests, presuppose the conclusion of the contract, which depended upon the will of the parties; but once the contract has been concluded, the rule of the law or of the agreement (the latter on matters left to the autonomy of the parties) is called into play without condition, at any rate on the part of the obligor.[30] The same goes for rules of competence or jurisdiction, for instance in the field of creating law. The law to be created — that is the hypothesis, which calls into play the competence rule; the latter is conditioned. It does not at all follow that its imperative would be conditional, even with regard to the authorized organ. Although the latter may be free to create the law, that is, to appraise the utility of that creation, it can proceed only according to the rule of jurisdiction imparted to it.[31]

The so-called hypothetical or conditional imperative, on the contrary, is binding only in relation to a certain result of a technical nature; hence its synonymous name, "technical imperative." If one wants to arrive at the result (which for the "technician" is not always optional, for his particular duty, which enters the picture, is morally and often legally categorical), then one must take the means to it. By this token, the means is obligatory and in that sense commanded. Thus whenever the question is one of accomplishing anything, whether a work of manual or of spiritual labor (a scientific, artistic, or even legislative work), the perfect realization of the work commands the employment of certain means determined by the pure and applied science of the work envisaged. Hence the conditional or hypothetical imperative, envisaged as such, is reduced to a technical rule sanction (if one may speak of sanction) by lack of success, by failure.[32]

Never is the legal rule, with regard to its subjects, technical in this manner. Assuredly, any rule whatever, the moral rule and the legal rule as well as the technical, exists only in relation to an end. But there is this capital difference that the technical rule serves the end of a work —

[30] Except for the beneficiary's right not to invoke the rule; see *supra*, no. 51.

[31] Confused by R. CAPITANT, *op. cit.* 147; and by Brunetti, dealing with the Italian Civil Code, art. 401, as cited by G. del Vecchio, *op. cit.* 228. [Art. 401 provides as follows: "The provisions of this Title [On Minors entrusted to Public or Private Assistance, and on Filiation] shall apply to minors who have not completed their eighteenth year and who are children of unknown parents or who are natural children recognized only by their mother who finds it impossible to provide for their upbringing. The same provisions shall apply to minors found in an institution of public assistance, or assisted therein toward their maintenance, education or reëducation, or to those in a state of material or moral abandonment."]

[32] Cf., in the same sense, DE VAREILLES-SOMMIÈRES, *op. cit.* I, 10(3°), pp. 12–13; Del Vecchio, *op. cit.* 231–235; R. Bonnard, *L'origine de l'ordonnancement juridique*, in MÉLANGES MAURICE HAURIOU, 70–72.

a technical, special work, reserved in principle to the technicians, whereas the moral rule and the legal rule serve the end of order — a human order, valid for all men by reason of their quality as men. The human order which is envisaged by morals is the essential human order: That of perfecting man in his moral, spiritual being. Consequently, the rules of end and means translating the conditions of this perfection to which man is called necessarily have categorical character.[33] The same goes for law. The human order envisaged by the law is that of life in common within the framework of the political society. Now, since that life in common forms an integral part of the condition of man, the corresponding rules, even if technical by their material object,[34] have categorical character.[35]

53. The Sanction Does Not Transform the Categorical into the Hypothetical. The sanction, penal or otherwise, which accompanies the legal rule, changes nothing in this analysis. The sanction is decreed not in order to confer upon the subject an option between the disposition made by the rule and the sanction; it is decreed, on the contrary, in order better to guarantee the observance of the dispositon. The rule is the principal; the sanction, the accessory. Far from transforming the categorical imperative of the rule into a hypothetical imperative ("Observe the rule if you want to escape the sanction; nevertheless, if you prefer the sanction, you have the right not to observe the rule"), the rôle of the sanction is to come to the aid of the categorical imperative so as to bring about its realization in conduct as far as possible. Otherwise, the pretended sanction no longer corresponds to the concept of a sanction.[36]

True, certain authors, e.g., Kelsen, claim to distinguish a double imperative in the rule, one categorical, addressed to the public agents charged with applying the law and particularly with making the sanction operative, the other hypothetical, addressed to the subjects on condition that they would avoid the sanction. According to that conception, one would even have to say that the only rule is that addressed to the public agents. But that reversal is as contrary to the requirements of the social order as it is to the principles of logic. If the public agents

[33] Thus prudence — moral prudence — is required by a categorical imperative although it constitutes the virtue charged with adapting means to ends.

[34] Thus, e.g., the rules of social prudence decreed by the legislator in the matter of road traffic have the validity of a categorical imperative although they constitute mere technical means of realization.

[35] Cf. R. Capitant, *op. cit.* 90–91, regarding the norm he calls economic or sociological. . .

[36] Cf., in the same sense, R. Capitant, *op. cit.* 92–93.

have to apply the rule, it is just because the subjects, mere private individuals or officials, did not observe it when they were bound to. There exist in reality two equally categorical duties: For the subjects, to obey the rule; for the public agents, in case of disobedience to apply the sanction. It is not true to say, because the penal law — essentially a law providing sanctions — addressing itself to the repressive judge, decrees that the murderer shall be punished by death, it is therefore permissible for the subjects to commit murder; nor that murder is prohibited only on condition or for technical reasons, such as that one desires merely to avoid the penalty for its repression.[37]

54. The Imperative Remains Categorical Even in "Risk Legislation." Sometimes, however, the legal rule looks as if it contained a merely hypothetical imperative or even left the subjects free to choose between the rule and the sanction. The public registration of conveyances seems to be of that character.[38] The law imposes the obligation of formal registration only on condition that the grantee seeks the result attached to registration, to wit, that the grant in his favor may be relied upon against third parties; the means, registration, is commanded only in so far as the effect, reliability of the conveyance against third parties, is desired. If, for any reason (carelessness or otherwise), the grantee does not seek that effect (sanction), he has the right to be disinterested in it and consequently to do without registration (rule).

But that is an inexact analysis of the system. The imperative is there used in reference to the term registration, whereas in fact it does concern the connection established between the two terms, registration and reliability against third parties. In reality, registration is not commanded, and hence one could not talk of the ineffectiveness against third parties, which is consequent upon failure to register, as a sanction. The law merely decides that in order to have effect with regard to third parties the conveyance must be registered, that a conveyance lacking registration cannot be relied upon against them. There we find the disposition and at the same time the imperative: The effect with regard to third parties is subordinated to registration; the latter is the requisite condition for reliability against third parties. No doubt the grantee has a choice between registration, by which he can rely on the grant against third parties, and failure to register, when he cannot so rely. But this

[37] Cf., in the same sense, R. Capitant, *op. cit.* 97–103. Also, on the secondary character of penal justice, G. del Vecchio, *La justice*, § 10, in Justice, Droit, Etat (Paris, 1938) 49–51.

[38] The reference is to the Belgian system, where such publicity is ordinarily optional.

alternative has nothing in common with that of rule and sanction: The lack of effect against third parties is only the result — by the way, an obligatory, imperative result — and not the sanction of the failure to accomplish the condition, to wit, registration, which remains entirely free. On the other hand, as to the registration, one could not talk of a hypothetical or technical imperative ("Resort to registration if you want to obtain efficacy *erga omnes* [b]"); otherwise, whenever a legal effect is subordinated to conditions depending upon the operation of liberty, the imperative would become hypothetical and technical.[39]

This is not to say that in laying down the rule the legislator would have had no preference as to the effective realization of publicity by registration. He probably even counted upon the disadvantageous effect of the failure to register in inducing the subjects to register; hence the name "sanction" given to the lack of effect against third parties. But the policy of the legislator and the legal rules he can lay down in applying that policy are two distinct things. In this particular case, the legislator did not push his policy to the point of decreeing an obligation to register as a matter of law, or again his peculiarly legal policy lagged behind his economic and social policy. The present subject of our inquiry is the legal rule envisaged in its imperative rôle and not in its intimate relations with the general policy of the state.

55. The Categorical Imperative of the Law Is Binding in the External and the Internal Forums. To affirm the categorical character of the legal imperative is not the same as going into the question, in what manner that imperative is binding: In the internal forum, i.e., before the tribunal of conscience, or in the external forum, i.e., before a human tribunal armed with compulsion. To resolve this new problem we must more closely study the order to which the law belongs. Now, although this order, like that to which morals belongs, is a human order and not at all a technical regulation (whence the categorical trait of the two rules),[40] the human order of the law is a societal order, instituted with a view to a social end, more particularly the end of the society-state, while the human order of morals is the order of individual conduct, in all fields to be sure, including the political and social. Starting from that difference, it will be seen at the outset that, necessarily and in any event, the categorical imperative of the law is binding in the external forum and, necessarily and in any event, the imperative of morals is binding in the

[b] [Against everybody.]

[39] The text rectifies the interpretation proposed in LA PHILOSOPHIE DE L'ORDRE JURIDIQUE POSITIF, no. 12, pp. 48–49.

[40] See *supra*, no. 52.

internal forum. A law which would not be binding in the external forum would no longer be a societal rule, and that is why before the courts and other organs applying the law everyone is responsible for the exact observance of the rule. Morals which would not be binding in the internal forum would no longer be a rule of human life, and that is why morals applies of itself, by its very virtue, to each conscience, which remains free to obey or not, under its responsibility.

But the problem is not thus solved, for interferences have to be taken into account. It may happen, first, that the legal rule borrows one of its precepts from morals. This is a frequent case because order in society presupposes a certain degree of effectively practiced morality. To the prescription of conscience is added the order of the public authority. The converse assumption is more complicated: Can the legal rule which, of itself and immediately, is binding in the external forum also be binding in conscience? An affirmative answer could not be doubtful when the moral rule explicitly or by implication refers back to the legal rule. It does in fact happen that morals leaves it to the public authority and to the legal rule to provide for the determination of the exact content of its precepts depending on circumstances; say, for justice in the different contracts. In that case, the law will be binding in the external forum by virtue of its own nature and in the internal forum by virtue of morals which refers to it.

However, even outside of any thought of reference from morals to law, there is, in principle, ground for acknowledging that the legal rule is valid in the internal forum. The ground is that, as far as the state, a necessary and universal society, is concerned, the societal order is a human order wanted by nature, whence it follows that the rules set forth in the name of this natural human order oblige the subject in his conscience.[41] Man would not be fully man were he not a subject member of society, respecting his obligations as a member, first among which ranks obedience to the rules and orders decreed in the name of the society by competent authority. Morals, then, enjoins upon the citizens to obey the legal rule and makes this a duty of conscience,[42] at least whenever under the circumstances obedience is required for the realization of the ends the legislator has set for himself.[43] Let us add that the duty

[41] See, in this sense, St. Thomas, Summa, *Ia IIae*, qu. 96, art. 4.

[42] Thus the legal rule obliges, not directly by itself and by reason of its own character, but solely through the intermediary of morals which, in a general fashion, provides for obedience to just laws. The moral precepts, on the contrary, oblige by themselves, by reason of the intrinsic value of their particular content.

[43] Indeed, cases must be taken into account where the precept would be of value exclusively as a means and where observation of the precept in the special case would be of no use because the goal would definitely not be involved. Equity then

in conscience to obey a law does not at all imply the duty to find it good, adequate or opportune; else how could the law progress? Equally we reserve the case of unjust laws, which are so by being contrary to the moral rule, for what is immoral could not bind the conscience.

SECTION 2. THE LAW AS A GENERAL RULE

56. The Thesis of the Advocates of the Individual Legal Rule. Is the legal rule always a general one, or can one speak of an individual legal rule?

Until recently, the legal rule was always defined as general and abstract, addressed to the subjects in general, private individuals or officials, or to abstractly determined categories among them; e.g., to males, to minors, to parents, to owners, to creditors, to merchants, to workers, or to the authorities in general or of a certain grade, in short to "whoever shall fulfill a certain condition." [1] But there is a certain trend of recent date among writers who see no inconvenience in admitting a category of purely individual rules, "formulated so as to address one or several specially envisaged subjects." And they thus contrast "objective" legal rules (in the sense of general, impersonal ones) with "subjective" legal rules (in the sense of special, individual ones), or, as it were, in a metaphor, ready-made with custom-made clothing.[2]

Evidently, every general rule is called upon to particularize itself in its application to individuals who are part of the envisaged "generality": The precept laid down for all is valid for everyone in particular, and the application of the general precept is necessarily individual. However, by a general rule we understand a rule established in the abstract, outside

requires that the rule that is a means be binding no longer in conscience; see, in this sense, ST. THOMAS, *op. cit. Ia IIae*, qu. 96, art. 6, and qu. 97, art. 4 *ad resp.* Exception: where the judge, obliged to apply the laws without distinction, has intervened and pronounced sentence.

[1] DE VAREILLES-SOMMIÈRES, *op. cit.* I, 5, p. 9. The generality of the rule is thus by no means synonymous with uniform common law, to the exclusion of all special legislation applying to some social categories; on this point, see J. DABIN, *op. cit.* no. 14, pp. 53–54. Also, on *privilegia* and *leges privatae*, as opposed to *leges communes*, ST. THOMAS, following Aristotle, SUMMA, *Ia IIae*, qu. 96, art. 1 *ad* 1; likewise qu. 95, art. 4 *ad resp.*, *in medio*. Nor is the generality of the rule incompatible with the idea of dispensation; on dispensation, see ST. THOMAS, *op. cit. Ia IIae*, qu. 96, art. 5 *ad* 3, *in fine*, and art. 6, *ad resp.*, *in fine*.

[2] See, in this sense, R. CAPITANT, *op. cit.* 58–68, 153–156; the representatives of the Viennese School (Kelsen, Merkl); R. Bonnard, *L'origine de l'ordonnancement juridique*, in MÉLANGES MAURICE HAURIOU (Paris, 1929) 35–41; H. Dupeyroux, *Sur la généralité de la loi*, in MÉLANGES CARRÉ DE MALBERG (Paris, 1933) 137 *et seq.*

of any consideration of a particular individual and of an individual case. It matters little whether that rule has been set down at one stroke, by the process of statutory enactment, or issued from a series of judicial decisions rendered for particular cases (judicial source). Always the rule, statutory or judicial, is formulated for no one person in particular. On the contrary, the pretended individual legal rule (not to be confounded with the dispensation from a general rule, which is indeed individual but is not a rule) is intended for named individuals, prescribing the conduct to be adopted upon a certain occurrence by one or several persons determined by their singular characteristics.

In fact, the history of political thought knows the system of "government by decree" [3] and the régime of the police [or prerogative] state, both proceeding by way of individual dispositions outside of any pre-established general rule (*jussa de singulis concepta*, edicts or decrees aiming solely at particular cases).[4] But, even outside of those assumptions, and along the lines of the principle of a state under the rule of law, the advocates of the individual legal rule envisage under that term the following situations, by way of example: The administrative decision rendered to the advantage or disadvantage of a person (such as the assessment of a certain taxpayer for a certain amount); the administrative order to a person to take certain sanitary measures on his property; the order given by a superior to a subordinate in the official hierarchy; or the judgment requiring of a certain litigant some performance, some change in status or capacity; or the contract creating rights and obligations specially adapted to the convenience of the parties who have concluded it or adhered to it.[5]

57. *Criticism of the Above Thesis.* But this analysis does not seem exact. That there exist individual legal situations — rights, powers, obligations, and functions — flowing from sources other than the general legal rule, is incontestable and uncontested; the administrative decision, the judgment, the contract, are sources of such situations. It does not

[3] For criticisms directed against this system of government by Aristotle, see M. Defourny, *L'idée de l'Etat d'après Aristote*, in 2 MÉLANGES VERMEERSCH (Rome, 1935) 102–105.

[4] Near this conception one can perhaps place the "decisionism" of a Carl Schmitt (who contrasts it with an allegedly abstract and unreal "normativism"), on which see K. Wilk, *La doctrine politique du national-socialisme: Carl Schmitt*, in ARCHIVES DE PHILOSOPHIE DU DROIT (1934), nos. 3–4, *La crise de l'Etat* 169 *et seq.*

[5] H. Dupeyroux, *op. cit.* no. 9, in MÉLANGES CARRÉ DE MALBERG 161, goes farther. He applies the concept of the individual rule not only to acts rendering the general rule concrete (judgment, administrative decision, contract), but also to legislative acts containing a derogation of the general rule.

follow that the administrative decision, the judgment, the contract, are legal rules. No doubt the administrative decision, the judgment, the contract, imply a command, an individual imperative, valid for the determined individuals, the addressees or contracting parties. But in themselves they constitute orders or sentences, and not rules, norms, or laws,[6] because the legal rule, the norm, the law, called upon to govern many cases, implies generality.[7] Perhaps it does not suffice to note that law, as a social discipline valid for a generality, includes generality.[8] Social and general are not necessarily equivalent: On the one hand, an individual imperative may perfectly well be conceived in a social sense, taking account of the social interest; on the other hand, even in the case of the social disciplines, the ideal would always be the particularized solution, setting out for everyone his rights and duties, "custom-made." But, quite apart from the danger of partiality, of inequality of treatment and of arbitrariness, such a method is altogether impracticable: In the social discipline, above all, it is impossible for the authority to assign to everyone his line of conduct. And this impossibility suffices to justify the principle of the generality of the legal rule.[9]

Again, in the actual state of political organization, the pretended individual legal rules merely put into effect a general rule. If the administrative decision is binding upon the subject, this is so not by its own force but because it is rendered in execution of a rule of public law commanding the administrator to make the decision he has made (without, however, denying him a certain power of appraising discretion). If the losing litigant is bound to comply with the judgment, this is by virtue not of the imperative of the judge but of the imperative of a law on which the mission of the judge and the authority of his judgment are founded. If the contract engenders individual precepts for the parties or adherents to the agreement, it is because the legal rule attaches such effects to the conclusion of contracts: *Pacta sund servanda*, provided they

[6] In themselves, for to the degree that the administration is authorized to issue "regulations" or the courts have the power to render "regulatory" judgments, they become legislators.

[7] See, in this sense, ST. THOMAS, *op. cit. Ia IIae*, qu. 96, art. 1 *ad resp.*, *ad* 1 and 2; DOMAT, TRAITÉ DES LOIS chap. XII, 16, and LES LOIS CIVILES DANS LEUR ORDRE NATUREL title I, sec. I, 21; J.-J. ROUSSEAU, DU CONTRAT SOCIAL, bk. II, chap. II. — According to R. CAPITANT, *op. cit.* 60, n. 1, generality is implied in the concepts of the norm and of laws but not in the concept of the rule. . .

[8] This is the traditional argument; see ST. THOMAS, *op. cit. Ia IIae*, qu. 96, art. 1 *ad resp.*

[9] See J. DABIN, LA PHILOSOPHIE DE L'ORDRE JURIDIQUE POSITIF, no. 14, p. 53. Also, as to the superiority of the system of the general rule over the system of decisions rendered in each particular case, ST. THOMAS, *op. cit. Ia IIae*, qu. 95, art. 1 *ad* 2; qu. 96, art. 1 *ad* 2.

are validly concluded as to form and content.[10] Let us note that the basic law does not merely attribute a competency [to decide or to contract];[11] it is also in some way regulatory. This is clear for the administrative official and the judge, who positively decide the individual case according to a law, applying the general rule to the special situation. It is also clear for the contract, where the autonomy of the parties has the right to act only within the frame of the laws, maintaining respect for mandatory laws and for public policy and morality.

58. The Objection Concerning the Contract with the Force of Law. Concerning the contract, it is true, in the relations between the parties the regulation laid down by private will has the force of a "law" for the parties and the judge, exactly like a law of the state (Code Napoleon, article 1134 [a]), and even to the exclusion of a law of the state when the latter is only a supplementing law.[12] But, precisely, this law is but a private law, contractual or corporative. Now the legal rule which is here in question is the rule laid down by the state. One may say then, if one wishes, that by means of the permission of the state the contract generates individual legal rules, but not that the legal rule laid down by the state could be individual: The state, at least the state under the rule of law, emits general rules only, upon which, however, there will rest the individual imperatives of the administrative and judicial authorities as well as the individual imperative of the contract.[13] In the case of corporative individual rules, emanating from private bodies for their members, the same principle of generality reappears at a subordinate level. The corporative legal rule, too, is addressed to the generality of the members; and the individual orders which the authority of the body decrees are not legal rules on this level either.

Section 3. The Law as a Systematical Rule: The Legal Institutions

59. The Rule as Institution and the State as Institution. The legal rules do not constitute a pile of detached pieces without connection with

[10] Cf., in the same sense, St. Thomas, following Aristotle, *op. cit. Ia IIae*, qu. 96, art. 1 *ad* 1, *in fine*: . . .

[11] As R. Capitant says, *op. cit.* p. 155.

[a] [See *supra*, chap. I, sec. 2, n. b.]

[12] See *supra*, no. 49.

[13] Cf. the considerations developed by Du Pasquier, *op. cit.* nos. 124–125.

one another. On the contrary, they form organic wholes, which we call institutions: Institutions of rules at the service of the institution that is the state. In either case of an institution we are dealing always with some more or less unified body. But the state as an institution is a social body whose elements are human beings, while the legal institution is a body of law whose elements are legal rules. Further, the social body of the state is a real, albeit moral, being, while the body of law has only logical existence.[1] Finally, the state as institution is unique, while the legal institutions are multiple. The legal institution in the singular would be the entire law; but the total law of a people at a given moment of its history is made up of the sum and the synthesis of the particular legal institutions. Inasmuch as they are agents of social discipline and of the end pursued by the state, the legal institutions and rules, the law, must also be counted among the political institutions which are component and integral parts of the institution that is the state.

60. Definition of the Legal Institution. What characterizes the legal institution, as against the legal rule in general, is the systematic note. For instance, the legal institutions of marriage, of guardianship, of ownership, of contract, of documentation, of civil or criminal responsibility, of agency in private or public law, of appeal and appellate remedies, are the hierarchically arranged totalities of legal rules relating to those different matters. As for the legal transactions (e.g., marriage, contract), their conditions of existence, of foundation, of form, of validity against third parties and also multiple effects of a legal order, must be defined; as for the rights, liberties, obligations, and competencies (e.g., ownership or agency), their content and limits and the modes of their acquisition, transmission, and extinction must be determined; as for the machineries (e.g., guardianship or documentation), their structure and functioning must be fixed. Cutting across all this, there is need for organizing the preventive and repressive measures needed to guarantee that the institution become effective in social reality.

Now these diverse problems give rise to a set of rules designed to im-

[1] According to Hauriou's terminology, the constituted bodies are "person institutions" while the legal rule is a "thing institution," i.e., an institution existing in the social environment but not established within its framework, *La théorie de l'institution et de la fondation*, in LA CITÉ MODERNE ET LES TRANSFORMATIONS DU DROIT, 4 CAHIERS DE LA NOUVELLE JOURNÉE (1925) 2 *et seq.* In reality, the two kinds of institutions are radically different by their very subject matter. Only one link unites them: the idea of the organic whole. Cf. the criticism by J. BONNECASE, INTRODUCTION À L'ÉTUDE DU DROIT, no. 46, p. 87, and J. Delos, *Bien commun, sécurité, justice*, in 3 ANNUAIRE DE L'INSTITUT INTERNATIONAL DE PHILOSOPHIE DU DROIT (1938) 36, n. 1.

plement a fundamental idea which constitutes the animating and federative principle of the institution under contemplation. Thus the whole system of the rules of marriage is deduced from the philosophical-juridical idea which the legislator has of marriage with regard to the spouses, the children, and society; the whole system of guardianship is but the implementing of the simple idea of the protection of the minor against his own weaknesses and against the exploitation by third parties by which he could be victimized; and so on.[2] The same concept of the institution is apparent in the distinction formulated by Duguit between the "normative" and the "constructive and technical" legal rules.[3] The former designate not so much a rule properly so called (which cannot be understood without "construction") as the directing and, in this sense, normative principle, which the latter ["constructive and technical"] then set out to put into operation by diverse processes called by Duguit, both too vaguely and too strictly, sanctions or "ways of law." [4] The norm enveloped by constructive rules — that is the equivalent of the legal institution.

61. Hierarchical Arrangement of the Rules Grouped under the Institution. Among the rules thus articulated there prevails a hierarchy whose key is furnished by the end of the institution and by the degree of proximity of the means to the end, the more remote means being subordinate to the closer means and so forth along the line. For instance, the law requires the guardian to act as a good father of a family would (Code Napoleon, article 450 [a]), which is the immediate legal translation of the supreme idea of protection. Consequently, it provides that the guardian shall be obliged to render an accounting (second rule, subordinate; article 469 [b]). In order to avoid the guardian's eluding the accounting, it forbids any agreement between the guardian and the minor who has become of age unless preceded by the submission of a

[2] Cf., in the same sense, J. Bonnecase, *op. cit.* no. 45.

[3] 1 L. Duguit, Traité de droit constitutionnel (3d ed.) § 10, pp. 106–107; § 21, p. 224.

[4] For a criticism of Duguit's formulation, see J. Dabin, La philosophie de l'ordre juridique positif no. 6.

[a] [Art. 450 of the Code Napoleon provides as follows: "The guardian shall take care of the person of the minor and shall represent him in all civil transactions. He shall administer his property as a good father of a family would and shall be responsible for damages which may result from bad administration. He shall not be able to buy any property of the minor, nor to rent it unless the family council shall have authorized a substitute guardian to transfer possession to him as tenant, nor to accept the cession to him of any right or claim against his ward."]

[b] [Art. 469 provides as follows: "Every guardian shall be accountable for his administration upon its termination."]

detailed account (third rule, sub-subordinate), and at the same time it sanctions that prohibition by the relative nullity of an agreement contrary to the law (fourth rule; article 472 [c]). It is by reason of that hierarchy that the "ways of law" always occupy but a secondary place — both in the system and in the obligation — in relation to the rules they in some way guarantee and which are therefore the principal ones; that, particularly, the sanctions could never be envisaged apart from the rule nor put on a footing of equality with a power of choice.[5]

The idea of the legal institution also permits us to correct what could be too radical, and hence deceptive, in the division of the law into compartments. This observation is valid above all for the rules of penal law, which always are but sanctions, of a particular kind indeed, of other rules they presuppose, rules of private or public law, even where the latter are not expressly aimed at by the laws of private or public law. Thus, the penal law punishing homicide is but the sanction of that principle not formulated in the civil law: The right of life. The fact that the infraction is provided for only as a condition of the application of the penalty would tempt one to believe that the penalty is principal and the infraction secondary; the idea of the institution reëstablishes the exact order.[6]

62. Regrouping of the Institutions in Higher Syntheses. Again, the diverse legal institutions themselves are for the most part susceptible to regrouping in a vaster synthesis. Thus, the institution of the sale, as a contract, depends on the institution of the contract, which in turn depends on the institution of the legal transaction; the institution of ownership as a property right depends on the institution of the law of property; the institution of marriage is one of the elements, and a fundamental one, of the whole system of the law of domestic relations; the institution of guardianship is one of the régimes of protection of persons without capacity; and so forth. Seen from another aspect, the same institutions fall under a different synthesis. Thus, the sale can be envisaged, outside of the contractual angle, as an exchange for a valuable consideration, as an act *inter vivos*, etc.; ownership, as an inheritable

[c] [Art. 472 provides as follows: "Any agreement that may have occurred between the guardian and the minor who has come of age shall be void unless it has been preceded by the rendering of a detailed account and the delivery of evidentiary documents, all to be stated at least ten days before the agreement in a receipt of the account rendered."]

[5] See *supra*, no. 53.

[6] For discussion of an application, see J. Carbonnier in REVUE TRIMESTRIELLE DE DROIT CIVIL (1942) 296–298 and decisions cited.

right, a right in personalty or realty, etc. — not to forget the derogations from principles that are justified by the singularity of cases.[7]

Another, more formal, aspect of the systematization of the law is in effect the tendency of jurists to reassemble the rules by starting from more or less general solutions which are said to state "principles" and with regard to which the rules constitute at times a more or less specialized application and at times a more or less radical derogation.[8] In relation to the principle, the derogatory rules are thus displayed as separate branches, but at the same time their place is marked in the logical complex of the law. It is necessary, though, to guard against mistakes of appraisal, and particularly against ranking among the exceptions what would really be but a new principle concurrent with the first one. For example, it is wrong to consider as so many exceptions the cases of responsibility without fault since, in positive law as well as in reason, fault is not the only principle of responsibility.

63. The Legal Institutions and Logic. However, the grouping of rules in institutions does not always satisfy the rules of pure logic. On the one hand, there are institutions with lacunae where the system is incomplete for want of one "constructive" rule or another; such is the incapacity of illegitimate children to inherit more than their statutory share (Code Napoleon, article 908 [d]), a rule which can be circumvented by abstaining from recognizing the illegitimate children whom the testator would want to benefit.[9] In the course of time, the lacuna may be filled thanks to the work of case law; but it may happen that it endures and the institution never arrives at its perfection. On the other hand, there are institutions which suffer from a certain inner discordance: The legislator has not been able to choose between two propositions and has resigned himself to a bastard solution. Take the institution of the incapacity of the married woman as conceived in the Code Napoleon, which is both a consequence of the principle of authority in the family and a measure

[7] The "general principles of law" are not legal institutions in the sense of systematic wholes. They are particular solutions which are, however, general by their application.

[8] On the scientific character of that systematization, see F. RUSSO, *op. cit.* 87 *et seq.*

[d] [Art. 908 of the Code Napoleon provides as follows: "Natural children shall not be able to receive anything by gift *inter vivos* or by will beyond what is accorded them in the Title On Succession."]

[9] See on this point 3 L. JOSSERAND, COURS DE DROIT CIVIL POSITIF FRANÇAIS no. 1423.

of protection of the weakness of the feminine sex.[10] Among the various institutions, at the higher levels of generalization, the same phenomenon of incompleteness or incoherence appears even more often: Certain institutions mark time and coagulate, while others of the same type evolve in a more or less abrupt or rapid manner. How could it be otherwise? The law is the image of life and under its influence. Now life does not proceed in a compact and rectilinear manner; it advances by uncertain, discontinuous steps and not at the rhythm of a mathematical development.

CHAPTER III

THE SUBJECT MATTER OF THE LAW

64. In General. Whereas the moral rule, from the point of view of the good, that is, of the end of man as a spiritual being, governs the entire field of human activity, inward and outward, individual, social, and religious, with no limitation as to level or framework, the field of the law is restricted to the relations of men with men within the perspective of the organized social group, especially the state.[1] On the other hand, all human relations of a temporal order (except, however, spiritual intercourse, particularly that of friendship) fall in different degrees within the competence of the law, whatever their objective — economical, extra-economical, or political — and whatever their form — interindividual or corporative, municipal or international.

SECTION I. EXCLUSION OF INNER ACTS: DUTIES TOWARDS GOD AND DUTIES TOWARDS ONESELF

65. The Inner Acts Are Subject to Morals. The law regulates the relations of men with men; this means that inner acts escape the realm of the law altogether. By inner acts we understand the multitude of psychological processes, of intelligence, will, sensibility, which remain confined to the inner man without being necessarily translated outward by conduct of commission or abstention. These processes are not removed from

[10] On the incapacity of married women and its foundation under the Code Napoleon, see 1 A. COLIN AND H. CAPITANT, COURS ÉLÉMENTAIRE DE DROIT CIVIL FRANÇAIS (9th ed. by Julliot de la Morandière) no. 661.

[1] On the "societal" character of the law, see *supra*, no. 6.

all rules: The rule of reason — in which the principle of morality is epitomized — is competent to govern the inner as well as the outer life, exactly on the same ground and with the same force. Thoughts, sentiments, wishes, can contradict reason as well as can conduct or expressions of attitudes, and conscience has no more trouble in appraising intentions than in judging conduct.[1]

Again, outward acts themselves are susceptible to moral judgment only on account of the inner dispositions which explain them. Right intentions may wholly or in part redeem the objective badness of the acts, as inversely the objective goodness of acts may be diminished or annihilated by malice of intention. How could morality be satisfied if it did not touch that inner world in man where the principle of his being and the root of his action lie? A morals of deeds would be only a surface morals, a hypocritical conformity. The destiny of man, which to a large part is within him, requires the conformity of the heart. The latter goes so far as to demand that the rule be loved not only in what it prescribes but for itself, inasmuch as it is the expression of right reason and, in that sense, of the destiny of the human individual. How could reason suffer man in his innermost heart to detest his own destiny? [2]

66. The Inner Acts Are Not Subject to the Law as a Social Discipline. Quite different is the position of rules such as the legal rule, which represent social disciplines. What can a social discipline require? Merely an order of outward conduct. It is true that in the human world the society is also and essentially a grouping of souls, implying a communion in the same ideal, which is the end of the society. That communion is socially necessary, there being no "living" society without it. Where it is also a matter of necessary societies, such as the state, the communion is morally obligatory: No one has the right in conscience to refuse his soul to life in the state. However, men communicate with one another only through the body, which is the indispensable interpreter of every social relation precisely because man is not pure spirit and the society of men cannot be conceived of as purely spiritual. In the image of man, who is the substantial element of human groupings, the society of men, whatever its end — even if purely spiritual, aiming at the good of the soul — is both spiritual and corporeal. By bodily contact — word, writing, ges-

[1] Even a restitution in spirit, called for to repair a theft in spirit, is known to St. Thomas: "A prelate is able to take property from his church in spirit alone when he begins to have the *animus possidendi*, of possessing the thing as his and no longer in the name of his church. He must then make restitution by abandoning such *animus*," SUMMA, *IIa IIae*, qu. 62, art. 5 *ad* 5.

[2] See, on the superiority of the New Law (the morals of the Gospel) over the Old Law, ST. THOMAS, *op. cit. Ia IIae*, qu. 91, art. 5 *ad resp.*, *secundo*: . .

ture — the human relations, interindividual (e.g., exchanges) or properly social (organized groupings), acquire not only visible form but also real existence in the world of space and time. Manifested attitudes realize the constitutive process of societies: Affiliation of members, nomination of those in titular authority; and also their working operations: Production and distribution of the social good, collaboration of the leaders and members. Consequently, the manifested attitudes which realize the social life are logically subjected to the discipline charged with providing for the requirements of social life.

One must therefore not demand of that discipline that it govern purely inner acts in which the body has no part: It would intervene in vain, and what is more, without competence. How compel man to think justly, to feel and to will rightly, even in the field of social affairs? What competence in the governing of spiritual faculties could a rule claim which exists only in view of external social relations? [3] Assuredly, society has a major interest in its members nourishing "social" feelings, favorable to its work and its discipline, because the adherence of hearts is the best guarantee for the obedience of action. But it is in an indirect manner, by the whole of its policies, particularly in the field of education, that the state may contribute to the formation of the "social" character of its subjects. It will not succeed in that by measures of obligation tending directly to call forth and procure the appropriate sentiments.

67. Application of This Idea; the "Pedagogical Function" of the Laws. Such are the reasons why the penal legislator thinks of punishing an attempt to commit a crime only if it be manifested by beginning its execution: As long as the crime lives only in thoughts the law keeps out and cannot but keep out, however morally illicit the criminal thought may be. Such again are the reasons why the legislator dealing with legal transactions — of private or of public law — prescribes legal effects only for the expressed will (if not, in the technical sense of German law, the "declared" will): A *propositum in mente retentum,*[a] bare of social incidence, could not have any social effect. Whether the inner act be taken immediately as the object of the legal provision (first example) or as the condition of application of that provision (second example), the solution is identical: It does not count in regard to social discipline.

Yet legislators have been known to invade the inner domain and to decree piety or love (of God, of the family) not only in acts but in spirit.

[3] Cf. St. Thomas, *op. cit. Ia IIae*, qu. 91, art. 4 *ad* 3: . . . See also qu. 98, art. 1 *ad resp.*; qu. 100, art. 9 *ad resp.*

[a] [A mental reservation.]

How can that kind of intervention be explained? By the idea of general policy: The state makes use of the prestige of a formal law to inculcate in its people precepts which, despite its intervention, are and remain moral precepts.[4] On the one hand, not every measure nor even every rule laid down by a law is necessarily of a legal character; to be that it must also be juridical in its objective and its content. Now there is no law — no juridical law — where the precept relates to inner acts. On the other hand, the authority has the right to employ any honest means to attain the ends falling within its mission: If there are reasons to believe that the proclamation of a moral precept by the civil law would be such as to favor the practicing of that precept, technical distinctions could not check such a policy, especially since the mass of the people, which cares nothing about jurisdictional divisions, might be shocked by certain cases of silence of the law.[5]

68. In What Sense the Law Is Concerned with Intentions. Still it is true that the law in all its branches is preoccupied with intentions: The intention of subjects and the intention of the legislator himself. Thus, it is intention that qualifies the criminal infraction; that marks the difference between good and bad faith, voluntary and involuntary fault; that governs the interpretation of legal acts or transactions, private and public, including the statutes.[6] So, too, there are notions or criteria of a psychological order whose rôle in law, especially in modern law which has broken with the old formalism, is considerable. But the assumption is different. The question in this case is no more one of pure intentions forming the subject matter for precepts of command or prohibition. It is one of outward acts — nonlegal or legal — which the jurisit tries to connect with the intentions that accompany or explain them, moving from the external to the internal, from the act to the intention. And the procedure is only normal: As the outward acts emanate from man, an intelligent and free being, they could not be envisaged, even by the jurist, in their materiality alone, outside of all considerations of intention. Only in the light of the idea do the acts take on moral and even social significance (since society is composed of men). In fact, society is not indifferent to whether the intentions accompanying or explaining

[4] Aristotle spoke of the "pedagogical function" of a law which instructs and catechizes rather than commands.

[5] For instance, the people might be astonished not to find the precept of mutual love listed among the reciprocal rights and duties of spouses. In fact, however, the laws on the reciprocal rights and duties of spouses prescribe only acts and abstentions.

[6] See, however, to the contrary as regards the interpretation of statutes, 1 J. BONNECASE, PRÉCIS DE DROIT CIVIL (2d ed.) no. 100, p. 96.

acts are innocent or malicious, social or antisocial, and hence the necessity to treat the acts accordingly, to diversify and shade the dispositions of the rules according to the intentions. Neither are society and private individuals indifferent to whether the legal acts or transactions, private or public (contracts, statutes, etc.), are interpreted according to their letter or their spirit, and hence the necessity to seek out the intention in order to set apart the spirit of the disposition from the sometimes obscure, inexact, or incomplete letter.[7]

69. Of the Prudence Required in the Search for Intention. However, prudence is called for. If, unlike pure intention, the intention involved in an act is susceptible of being clarified by the act itself or by the surrounding circumstances, it is no less true that in some particular cases the outward act may betray the real intention: Individual psychologies are often complex and indistinct, which entails the possibility of errors.[8] Let us add that in practice the working conditions of the organs of application of the law — administrative officials and judges — rarely permit a resort to the slow and nice methods of rigorously scientific analysis. That is why prudential reason commands the rejection of psychological investigation in matters where by general statistical laws the variety of individual motives would prevent any sufficiently sure conclusion. Where the intention must normally remain indiscernible, it is preferable altogether to renounce speculative and often deceptive research and to stick instead to the materiality of facts — gestures, words, writings.[9]

From still another viewpoint does a certain "materialization" of the law find its justification. The requirements of social life, particularly of economic life, do not always accommodate themselves to the fatal and damaging insecurity which regard for thoughts and motives entails in relationships. Goods and documents call for rapid and unhampered circulation. Hence the renascence of formalism — a purely utilitarian formalism without symbolic value — which characterizes some parts of the commercial law of today: The legal transaction, embodied in the

[7] Cf., in the same sense, F. Russo, Réalité juridique et réalité sociale 117–118.

[8] Cf., in this sense, L. Josserand, Les mobiles dans les actes juridiques du droit privé (Paris, 1928) 317 *et seq.*

[9] This idea may be applied in the field of moral personality. Scientifically, for moral or legal personality to exist, there must be found that psychological element which forms the soul of the group, to wit, a certain degree of communion among the members. Now the jurist, unable to recognize this element of communion, sticks to compliance with procedures constituent of legal personality in order to establish that there is such personality; he discards the substance to retain but the appearance or color. Cf. F. Russo, *op. cit.* 121–124.

material document, is valid by itself, independently of its antecedents or, to use the technical term, of its *causa*.[b] This formalism has limits, though, for it is characteristic of a materialist civilization systematically to sacrifice the moral to the economic.

70. The Relations of Man with God Are as Such Outside the Competence of the Law. Let us now return to the outward acts which, whether or not they are separated from intentions, constitute the only subject matter of the law. Considered with regard to its objective, human activity is directed either toward God or to the person himself or to other men, which division corresponds to the three kinds of tendencies of human nature: Superior, egoistic, and altruistic ones.[10]

The relations of man with God, his Creator and supreme Good, are governed, as to outward as well as inner acts, by morals, especially under the heading of the virtue of religion.[11] They do not as such belong to law, at least not the law of the civil society. Indeed, when religion itself has been established in society by the ecclesiastical institution (which must give rise to a specifically ecclesiastical law: *Ubi societas ibi jus*), the civil society as such has no competence in religious matters. This follows from the distinction between the spiritual and temporal powers: It does not belong unto Caesar to define the rights of God or to make them his concern. That task belongs strictly to the church and, for those who reject any church, to the individual conscience.

71. Exceptions: Incidence of the Spiritual upon the Temporal. However, account must be taken of the echo of religion, its principles, its worship, its institutions, at the level of temporal civil life. Even in the case of advocates of a religion without a church, religious feeling will not remain locked within the interior of conscience: In a manner both very natural and very legitimate, it will experience the need to externalize itself in individual or collective practices or manifestations. It will then be for the civil authority to proclaim the rule of freedom of worship and to safeguard it against any attack from whatever quarter, on

[b] [*Causa* in the civil law denotes the motivating conditions underlying a contractual agreement; unlike consideration in the Anglo-American common law of contracts, *causa* does not have to be established separately in order to spell out a civil law contract.]

[10] See St. Thomas, Summa, *Ia IIae*, qu. 72, art. 4. Cf. qu. 94, art. 2 *ad resp.*, *in fine*.

[11] On the virtue of religion as an annexed virtue of justice, see *infra*, no. 223. The moral virtue of religion does not however exhaust the whole religious element. According to the teachings of the Gospel, God is reached directly by the theological virtues of faith, hope, and charity.

the part of private individuals or public officials. It is thus that the law comes to know relations of man with God: Through the interpreter of freedom of religion and of worship, which becomes incumbent upon men in their relations among one another.

The safeguard of the law may indeed extend beyond this indispensable minimum. If the state deems it opportune it will lay down rules to prohibit certain acts or attitudes showing ostentatious contempt with regard to religion, e.g., blasphemy, sacrilege, parody of worship. Indeed, acts of that kind have nothing in common with the freedom, guaranteed as such, of sincere antireligious propaganda: Their sole aim is to shock the feelings of the religious part of the population. The injury done to worship recoils to hit the worshipers: The act contrary to religion becomes a blameworthy violation of respect for persons and often an attack upon national unity. Finally, without having to assume the case where the state itself professes a natural or positive religion (case of a state religion), one could quite well understand that the state, acknowledging a practical value of the religious idea by reason of its social benefits, would favor religion, and that this policy would be translated into appropriate rules of public and private law (e.g., compulsory religious instruction in schools, privileges for the clergy, subsidies for institutes and works).

Such, rapidly sketched, are the progressive stages of interferences between the state and religion within the atmosphere of the modern state. Sometimes religion, the rule for the relations of man with God, provides law, the rule for the relations of men among one another in organized social life, with its very subject matter, under the negative aspect of religious freedom to be safeguarded or religious feelings not to be hurt. Beyond that, sometimes it dictates a certain pragmatic way for the law to consider social relations, and consequently their régime, from the angle of the religious idea or simply the religious fact. But the connection is always but indirect: The spiritual intervenes in the law only inasmuch as it touches the social, inasmuch as the religious element affects the relations of men among one another. And this is logical since the state is set up over the temporal while religion as such is a matter of the individuals themselves and of the religious society.[12]

72. The Law Takes No Cognizance of the Duties of Man towards Himself. The same principle of the incidence *ad alterum*, the repercussion upon another, holds good for that category of duties which is called, somewhat dubiously, the duties of man towards himself.

[12] Cf. G. Renard, Le droit, l'ordre et la raison (Paris, 1927) 320 *et seq.* (*Le droit naturel et la religion naturelle*, II).

Strictly speaking, one could not have a moral duty towards one's self any more than a legal indebtedness to one's self, for the two opposed qualities of creditor and debtor are not susceptible of resting on the same head save by an accounting fiction.[13] What is exact is that man has duties whose objects are his own physical and moral person: His body and members, his spiritual faculties, his honor, and by extension his estate, an instrumentality in the service of the person. Morally, man is absolute master neither of his person nor of his property. The person of man with all his powers is subject to a natural and supernatural destiny which imposes upon him his law of perfection and salvation. On the one hand, man is made for God, for Goodness, Truth, and Beauty, the reflections of the divine perfections; on the other hand, man is a social animal, in solidarity with his kind on many grounds in such a way that all that actively or passively concerns his person reflects upon others, those who are in more or less close relations with him.

73. Reservation of the Principle of Incidence "Ad Alterum." By this detour the law once again acquires competence to lay down rules in the field of "duties towards oneself": These duties can double formally as duties towards society. As a member of private groups such as the family and public groups such as the state, the individual is not free to dispose of his person or his goods to the detriment of groups to which he has a service to render, a function to fulfill, and which have a strict right to his collaboration. Once the duty, individual in its immediate objective, takes on a social aspect incidentally, the intervention of the legal imperative is justified on the ground of social discipline. That is why the law may prohibit not only suicide and self-mutilation but also the varied forms of "prostitution" by which the individual would alienate his honor, the abandonment for a consideration or without it of certain essential liberties, particularly those touching upon his vocation: The right to marry, to work, to establish one's self, etc. Any abdication of the human person, his faculties and attributes, even for the benefit of another individual who would claim to derive an advantage for his own person from this sacrifice of the person of another, constitutes a loss of value for the family or national group to which the diminished individual belongs, and for humanity as a whole.

Similarly, this is why it is incumbent upon the law to protect individuals not only against malicious or maladroit undertakings of third persons but also to a certain extent against accidents and even against injury they cause themselves, voluntarily or otherwise, contractually or

[13] Cf., in the same sense, St. Thomas, Summa, *Ia IIae*, qu. 57, art. 4 *ad* 1; qu. 58, art. 2.

extracontractually (cases of defective consent, minority, and other protective incapacities; cases of weak social classes protected by social legislation). Independently of any idea of injustice or abusive exploitation suggestive of a directly antisocial act, the sole element of individual wrong, whatever its form or cause may be (act of a third party, act of the victim, fortuitous event or act of God), engenders the social wrong, and therewith the competence of the legal rule to the ends of safeguarding and eventual restoration.

Section 2. The Social Relations and the Concept of the Legal Relationship

74. The State-Societal Character of the Legal Rule Recalled. So far we have proceeded by elimination: The law governs only relationships between men, directly or indirectly.[1] The time has come to define the field of the material competence of the law in a positive manner.

Let us first recall our point of departure. The legal rule makes its appearance only in a certain environment which provides the reason for its existence and its characteristics, i.e., the organized social environment. The outstanding organized social environment at the domestic level is the political society or state, whatever its legal or historical form (the city-state of antiquity, the free city of the Middle Ages, the modern unitary or federal state). This outstanding rank finds its explanation in the very end of the state-society, whose primary aim is to put order into social relationships, all social relationships of the temporal domain. If the state-society comes into being it is not in order to add a new unity to the various relationships and groupings which prior to its appearance have linked men to each other. Or rather, the state society does make up a new society endowed with its own end and its special organization; but its own end is a purelly formal end in the sense that it aims at introducing a principle of harmony and rational cohesion into society in general, which is multiple, confused, and often divided. Now the first instrumentality of that harmony and cohesion is the legal rule, issued by the superior society charged with disciplining the social activities, i.e., the state. In this respect, there is something synonymous between the state and the law. On the one hand, the supreme law is that laid down by the state, exercising its very function as a state, which is first of all the

[1] It is thus inexact to say with M. Lévy-Ullman, Eléments d'introduction générale à l'étude des sciences juridiques: I, La définition du droit (Paris, 1917) 60–62, that the law would apply to other relationships than those of man with his like . . .

function of order. On the other hand, the law of the state is the only one that is guaranteed by sufficiently efficacious compulsion. That is why, at the domestic level, the environment of the state is the environment in which of logical and factual necessity the legal rule blossoms forth as the typical norm of organized social life.

75. Universal Competency of the Legal Rule in the Field of Human Relations of the Temporal Order. Under this perspective, which is the proper perspective of the law, the competency of the legal system normally embraces all kinds of human relations in the temporal domain, precisely because it embraces all that fall within the competency of the general, governing and directing end of the state. It is by no means claimed, though, that the law would have the obligation to intervene everywhere and always, but rather that it has the faculty to do so: Hence ubiquity of competence and not of intervention. Where human relations function correctly by virtue of customs or of the play of private institutions, such as the family and the corporate bodies, the intervention of the supreme rule will be useless and therefore hurtful. This goes at least for relations other than those which concern the state itself, for as to these latter it is normal that as they find their cause in the existence of the state they should be regulated by the exclusive intervention of the state (statutory law or customary law). As for concrete cases of intervention, the problem arises from another point of view, that of determining the content of the law, and it will be dealt with in that context.[2]

76. Exception: Relations of a Spiritual Nature. The general competency of the law on the subject matter of human relations knows but one exception, to wit, the relations of a purely spiritual character.

By "spiritual" we understand here not the spiritual of religion, the supernatural (by contrast with the temporal), but the natural and temporal spiritual faculties of man: His intelligence and his heart. Man, a social animal even to his spiritual faculties, enters into communication with others naturally, not only on the basis of interests or of the solidarity of the family or nation, but also on the broad and disinterested basis of ideas and affections. Men exchange with other men, learned or unlearned, fellow-countrymen or foreigners, opinions of every kind, religious, philosophical, scientific, political, by means of conversation, correspondence, exhibition and reproduction of works, etc.[3] Man seeks and

[2] See *infra*, Part II, chap. II, especially nos. 156 *et seq.*

[3] Literature and art are not a matter exclusively of the author. The work is intended to reach the public: thus it falls under the principle of spiritual exchange.

often finds the sympathy, comradeship, friendship of his kind. And this spiritual intercourse, which no inner or outer frontier impedes, proceeds through more or less coherent, stable, "instituted" relations, which may even be embodied in organized groups for non-lucrative purposes: Scientific, artistic, fraternal, and "friendly" societies of all kinds. While such relations are not freed from the moral law of charity, honor, prudence, moderation, in short, of reason which condemns all disorder even in the realm of the spirit and of friendship — while they are held to a certain decorum by the environment of policed societies, yet they do not adapt themselves to the discipline of the law inasmuch as they remain in the spiritual state, free from any touch with interests or institutions.

On the one hand, unlike relations of affection founded upon a law of nature (as in the relations of the family and kinship), they are freely tied together and untied, as favored by selective affinities of liking and predilection. Neither are they bound to express themselves in imperatively fixed ritual forms. With the exception of morals and manners, it is spontaneity without rules that constitutes the value of the intercourse of minds and hearts. On the other hand, how could there be compulsion touching the spirit? No doubt it is not a matter of inner acts, since by hypothesis ideas and feelings give rise to external relations and hence outward acts. Nonetheless, these relations have their roots in the spirit, and without constant reference to the spirit they cannot be understood. Now at least any rule imposed from without, if not any discipline whatever, is by nature repugnant to the spirit. It strives especially against every mode of forced execution, not only in kind but also by equivalent, e.g., satisfaction by indemnity. A friendship commanded or "directed" under threat of compulsion would be the negation of friendship. Hence the individual may well fall short of his moral duty or, to a certain point, of usages in the matter of friendship or of spiritual intercourse generally. Legal compulsion, and consequently the legal rule, will abstain from intervening for this basic reason that "the spirit bloweth where it listeth," that it obeys only its own inspiration and not a foreign pressure.[4]

77. *In What Manner the Law Is Concerned with Friendship.* This is not to say, though, that the law would ignore friendship. First of all, it protects it as a value, under the heading of "rights of personality,"

[4] It is thus a mistake to think, as suggested by J. BONNECASE, *op. cit.* no. 41, p. 76, that the relationships between the law and spiritual intercourse, especially friendship, would depend upon the "domain of the law," according to the contingencies of the social environment. Spiritual intercourse as such cannot be reduced to a legal norm. See, in this sense, DOMAT, TRAITÉ DES LOIS chap. V, 11, and chap. VI.

under the name of the interest of affection. The affection which unites relatives or friends is indeed for the beneficiaries a human interest of the spiritual order which third parties do not have the right to aggrieve, whether directly by fomenting discord among the parties or indirectly by causing the death of one of them.[5] From a subjective point of view, friendship is also a generating principle of law in the case of groups with non-lucrative purposes in the service of friendly aims: From friendship proceeds the institution which is to impose upon the members a discipline of rights and duties guaranteed by the state. This, however, requires that the associates had the intention to band together in a legal and not merely a moral and friendly society, it being understood that the social object will be not so much friendship itself, which resists the legal imperative, as the establishment of a favorable environment for cultivating friendship, the ulterior and more or less speculative end of the group.

Still further, friendship, or at any rate "altruistic" intention, provides the psychological basis of liberalities *inter vivos* and by will, and of beneficent contracts (gratuitous bailment for use or deposit, suretyship). If these contracts are binding in law and not merely in morals, this is so by virtue of the moral and social principle which is taken up by the law: *Pacta sunt servanda.*[a] A promise given freely and with the *animus contrahendae obligationis* [b] confers legal character upon anything whatsoever, including the gratuitous gestures of friendship. The law, to be sure, reserves to itself control of the *causa* [c] or motive determining the transaction: Sincere, morally legitimate friendship or unregulated passion.[6] On the other hand, certain contracts with objectives of self-interest are accompanied by a note of friendship which normally calls for a reflection in their legal régime. Such are the contracts of "collaboration" [7] — certain hirings for service and certain associations — where the spirit of collaboration, which is one of the forms of friendship, will sometimes temper the rigor of the ordinary law as shaped by economic considera-

[5] Established law under the cases. If it is exact that "there is no right to affection," that "the idea thereof is not properly conceivable," G. Marty, note in SIREY (1931), 1, p. 151, col. 1, yet affection where it exists figures among the legally protected realities.

[a] [Agreements shall be observed.]

[b] [Intent to contract an obligation.]

[c] [See *supra*, chap. III, sec. 1, n. b.]

[6] See M. BOITARD, LES CONTRATS DE SERVICES GRATUITS (Paris, 1941).

[7] This is a term used by G. Ripert, *Une nouvelle propriété incorporelle: la clientèle des représentants de commerce*, CHRONIQUE, DALLOZ HEBDOMADAIRE (1939) 3: "Besides the contract of employment and the contract of partnership, the contract of collaboration should be studied."

tions, and sometimes on the contrary will surpass its requirements precisely in the name of the friendship which must unite the collaborators.[8]

As an example of the rôle of friendship in the law may finally be cited the principle of "presumptive affections of the deceased," adopted by several jurisdictions as a determining criterion of the order of succession. Whatever place may be accorded in the inheritance system to the idea of a duty derived from the bonds of blood, it seems impossible altogether to exclude from it the principle of affection if one wants to provide a rational justification for testamentary freedom being exercised to the detriment of the heirs.

Hence it is seen that there exist groupings, contracts, statutory rules, in short, legal phenomena, which have their source in relations of the spiritual order such as friendship. Those relations occupy too great a place in life and are too fundamental there not to appear at some turn or other of the law. Yet the fact remains that considered directly by themselves relations of the spiritual order partake of the régime of freedom of inner acts, being in truth but the flowering of such acts in someone else: What is friendship if not the fusion of two minds, two wills, and consequently of two intimacies?

78. The Need for More Precise Explanation of "Social Relations." Outside of the bonds of a spiritual nature, all relations among men are by nature susceptible to regulation by the law. One could adhere strictly to this proposition. However, a more precise statement may appropriately be made, not for the sake of inquiries in sociology or social philosophy with which we are not here concerned, but because such precision is a matter of interest to legal science. First, the notion of "social relations" is based upon essential legal categories such as the concept of "legal relationship" or the division of the law into its diverse compartments or branches. Furthermore, the different kinds of relations are not to the same extent subject to the grip of the law. There are among them some that the law affects only in a superficial or fragmentary way. Thus the following summary sociological observations are justified by way of preliminaries.

[8] For German solutions, see Volkmar, *La revision des contrats par le juge en Allemagne*, in TRAVAUX DE LA SEMAINE INTERNATIONALE DE DROIT (Paris, 1937) 20–22, 29–30. More generally, on the penetration of the "community spirit" in economic-social, and hence legal, relationships, see E.-H. Kaden, *Un exemple de la pratique extra-judiciaire en Allemagne: le contrat de bail uniforme*, in 1 RECUEIL LAMBERT § 41, pp. 511 *et seq.*, esp. at 517–518; K. Geiler, *L'ordre juridique de l'économie allemande*, in 3 RECUEIL LAMBERT § 152, p. 260 (regarding the right to work); L. Dikoff, *L'évolution de la notion de contrat*, in ETUDES DE DROIT CIVIL À LA MÉMOIRE DE HENRI CAPITANT (Paris, 1938) 213–215. And see, on "contract sliding into institution," G. RENARD, LA THÉORIE DE L'INSTITUTION (1930) 435 *et seq.*, esp. at 446 *et seq.*

79. Summary of the Various Kinds of Social Relations. It is a fact of banal experience, corresponding, to be sure, to a requirement of nature, that on the level of action even more than that of the spirit man lives only linked to other men. From the moment of his birth, he is united with his parents, his relatives, his nation, by the indelible bonds of blood and nationality. From his family and his school he receives all the physical, intellectual, and moral care during his formative period that the complex work of education requires. Arrived at the age of maturity, he himself establishes a home, unless he chooses a religious vocation where once again he will find a life in the community. By the fact of proximity of dwellings he is in contact with his neighbors, so much more numerous in our days when the population has increased and become more densely concentrated. Every time he makes use of any freedom whatever — to come and go, to express his thoughts, to work, etc. — he meets on his way with the freedom of somebody else with which he is in danger of colliding. In his economic and occupational activities he deals with suppliers, customers, coworkers and employees, and he is in conflict with competitors who at the same time are his colleagues. As man in isolation is weak, incomplete, ephemeral, he joins forces with his like in more or less durable groups for lucrative and non-lucrative goals. Integrated *volens nolens* in the public societies — the state, the province, the municipality — he owes obedience to authority and takes part in the burdens and the advantages of collective life. The states and the subjects of the various states, in turn, maintain economic, social, and political relations with one another which in their totality make up public and private international life.

80. Attempt at a Classification of These Relations. In view of these examples, social relations are susceptible of several modes of classification, which by the way are cumulative and overlapping.

Regarding their *form,* men are linked together sometimes by simple contact (cases of vicinage, clash of freedoms, competition, or in a less distinct manner repercussion of our attitudes upon somebody else); sometimes by sharing certain specific common traits producing similarity or solidarity (cases of family relationship or of engagement in the same occupation); sometimes by exchanging goods or services, ordinarily for a consideration (all cases of contracts); sometimes by association, private or public, with or without objectives of self-interest — not to omit the family bond, which in certain respects partakes of the above modes (contact, solidarity, exchange) while preserving its essential original significance in the service of life and of the species.

Regarding the persons who are their *subjects,* social relations are immediately concerned sometimes with the individual or physical person, sometimes with the moral being which is the personified public or private body resulting from the union of individuals organized with a view to a certain end. This gives rise to a double set of relations: Internal relations of the moral person with its members, and external relations of the moral person with outside individuals and bodies. Incidentally, it is understood that, as the bodies exist only through the individuals, interindividual relations provide the starting point, logically and chronologically, of corporative relations.

Regarding their *objectives*, social relations refer to extra-economic values or to economic values or to politics. By "extra-economic" values are meant those kinds of values which are not as such measurable in money: First of all the human person and his intangible prerogatives, then the family and its relationships which form an immediate extension of the human person. The economic values indicate the various forms of wealth, the rôle of which is to satisfy the economic needs of individuals, families, and groups. One will however note the interdependence between the two categories of values; for if the economy is subservient to the person and the groups, the economy in turn has the person and the groups contribute to it as producers, distributors, and consumers of wealth. As for politics, it calls forth the state and the system of relations issuing from the state, its constitution, organization, and functioning. In this sense, politics denotes the "public" as against the "private" element: Whereas the personal and family values and the economic values belong above all to the private order, the political values are essentially public since the state by definition is the public society, devoted to the good of the entire community.

Lastly, from another viewpoint, starting with the assumption of the plurality of states, one has to distinguish between the municipal relations, private and public, which move within the framework of the state, and the international relations, equally embracing the private and the public, which transcend the borders of a particular state.

81. Attitude and Rôle of the Law with Regard to Voluntary Social Relations. Now these multifarious contacts, constituting the *social* reality, are not confined to just existing on the factual level and developing their fortunate or unfortunate effects according to the law of arbitrariness, of interest, or of force. They obey rules — undoubtedly the moral rule, possibly the rule of social manners, but also the legal rule, constituting the *legal* reality, which imposes its compulsory norm upon them. From the scientific as well as the practical point of view, it is wrong to try to abolish at least the distinction, if not the differences, between social reality and legal reality. For if the social reality, as human reality, is already incontestably "rich in tendencies and orientations which it seeks by itself to manifest and to satisfy," [9] one still has to appraise that finalism, first in itself, relative to moral verity, to the "natural finalities of social life," and then with regard to the specific conditions, as to substance and form, of the legal system.[10] This suffices to justify the idea of *normative* social sciences.

Faced, then, with the facts of relations submitted to his judgment and his norm, the jurist has to solve a twofold problem. First, a problem of legitimity. Certain relations, factually possible, will be forbidden as fundamentally bad or simply as dangerous for the parties, for third parties, or for the state. In that case, the law sets its prohibition against the positive social reality, it rises and fights against it.[11] Other kinds of relations, though bad or dangerous, are tolerated. For opportunistic reasons or from want of power, the law does not go so far as to forbid, but it refuses to declare permissible; the positive social reality remains at the margin of the law.[12] Still other kinds of relations are recognized as legitimate, eventually encouraged or aided, with or without restrictions, according to the inconveniences they may present. The positive social reality receives legal consecration.[13] Then, there appears a problem of organization or what is called "regularization." As for forbidden combinations, the prohibition is to be sanctioned by repressive, or eventually preventive, measures. As for legitimate combinations, their more or less advantageous regulation is to be fixed by determining their conditions of legal existence (substance, form, proof), on the one hand, and, on the other, their legal effects.

Such is the essentially normative task of the jurist, at least in the case of relations of exchange and association which depend upon the play of human wills. Even under a régime of legal freedom such as ours, where the autonomy of the will constitutes the principle in economic matters, exchanges and groupings do not cease to be subject to the rule, first because this freedom is limited by a mass of substantive and formal prescriptions, and then because it is the solution of the law itself which sets up as a legal norm respect for promises issuing from the free will. Still further, the law continues to govern even where it appears to give

[9] F. Russo, Réalité juridique et réalité sociale 51.

[10] This is recognized by F. Russo, *op. cit.* 53–54.

[11] To cite at random: adulterous relations, contracts contrary to laws, to public policy or public morals; certain contracts between spouses (sale, partnership), or between guardian and ward; associations of criminals; at certain epochs and in certain countries, workers' associations, religious congregations, etc.

[12] E.g., concubinage; certain kinds of unrecognized associations; etc.

[13] E.g., marriage; adoption (at least in certain jurisdictions); exchanges, etc.

way. Its present withdrawal may always be followed by a return with any change in the circumstances which motivated its abstention.[14]

82. Attitude and Rôle of the Law with Regard to Other Categories of Relations. As for communications and groupings of a necessary character, where the will is not autonomous, the function of the law is ultimately none other than to safeguard and maintain them precisely against disordering by particular private wills. Thus, the family, marriage or the union of the sexes, though freely concluded on the ground of freedom of inclinations, is bound to an imperative statute worked out with a view to the task of the family. Thus, the relations between parents and children, which issue from nature alone without the will taking any part, are governed by a statute founded upon the principle of education. Thus, again, there are the relations springing from life in the state, an obligatory society willed by the social and progressive nature of man, whose statute, internal and external, depends on its very objective, to wit, the idea of the public good.

There remain the relations by contact and the relations by similarity, deriving from what is given by fate, somehow mechanically, in social life, economic and otherwise, on the domestic and on the international levels. As for the contacts, which so often degenerate into oppositions, it is for the rule to delimit the respective spheres of action and expansion, to prevent encroachments, and in case of injury to fix responsibilities. Thus, the law establishes obligations between neighbors, decides upon the conflicts of rights and freedoms, and assures damages for injuries and restitution for unjust enrichment at the expense of another. The jurist even endeavors to convert into profitable collaboration contacts which may promote understanding as well as war. As for the similarities, the task of the rule is to define the consequences which on the level of social discipline derive from the solidarity existing in fact. Thus, the law attaches to the solidarity of blood and family relationship a series of legal effects (duty of support, order of descent, etc.). Thus, again, starting from occupational solidarity, the law may go so far as to decree a compulsory corporative body made up of those engaged together in the same occupation, and so on.

83. The Objective and Subjective Interpretations of the "Legal Relationship." In so far as they concern the law or, if one likes, in so far as

[14] One can speak of the quasi-indivisible union, in the same social fact, of compulsion (viz., of the legal rule) and freedom, see F. RUSSO, *op. cit.* 158, 188, only in this sense, that freedom may be commingled with the rule, but not, that the rule is hardly distinguishable from freedom.

the law takes an interest in them, the relations of fact are thus transformed into legal relationships, and one can subscribe to Savigny's analysis: "Every legal relationship is composed of two elements: First, a given subject matter, i.e., the relation itself; second, the legal idea which regulates that relation. The first may be regarded as the material element of the legal relationship, as a simple fact; the second, as the plastic element, which ennobles the fact and gives it the form of law." [15] The actual or potential relations of fact which exist among men become legal relationships from the moment the law subjects them to its dominion. Understood in that way, the concept of the "legal relationship" (just as its corollary, the concept of the "legal situation," signifying the status in law of the parties to the relationship) simply evokes the idea of the rule, the objective rule: The legal relationship is that which is regulated by law. However, another, subjective meaning of the legal relationship, envisaged as a bond from person to person, is found in writers, such as Savigny, whose above quoted text is immediately preceded by the following passage: "Every legal relationship appears to us as a relation from person to person determined by a legal rule, and this determinative rule assigns a field to each individual where his will reigns independently of any foreign will." [16] In other words, every legal rule would presuppose a legal relationship in which one of the parties would be the holder of a subjectively lawful right, a creditor (*sensu lato*), while the other would be charged with a correlative obligation, a debtor (*sensu lato*).

84. Critique of the Subjective Interpretation. But while all relations of fact which constitute the subject matter of the law have, as their termini on the active and the passive sides, persons who may or may not be determined *a priori*, on the contrary one has to deny that the rule of objective law always creates subjective legal rights.[17] The rule orders and consequently decrees an obligation — the obligation to conform to the rule. But to that obligation there does not necessarily correspond the prerogative that is called a subjective legal right. In a word, "the legal relationship" in the subjective sense [of a legal right] "does not cover the whole law." [18] All relationships of fact are legal relationships, governed by objective law; but neither in fact nor in law are these relationships reduced to the single form of the subjective right.

[15] 1 SAVIGNY, TRAITÉ DE DROIT ROMAIN (French transl. by Guenoux, 2d ed. 1855–1856) 324; followed by BONNECASE, *op. cit.* no. 40, p. 75, and no. 45 *bis*, p. 83.

[16] SAVIGNY, *ibid.*

[17] These terms are here taken in the classical sense of jurists (see *supra*, no. 4), without referring to the special conception of Duguit.

[18] DU PASQUIER, INTRODUCTION À LA THÉORIE GÉNÉRALE no. 130, p. 100.

The subjective right (in whatever sense one may understand it: As right, capacity, function, or competency) in effect presupposes a determined — or determinable — person upon whose head it may rest and who is capable of exercising and asserting it. This holds good for the right of the contractual obligee, which authorizes him to demand a service of another, even where the obligation is payable to bearer; for the so-called absolute rights, such as property rights or the rights to one's own self and his faculties (personality rights); for actions in court; for the quasi official rights of private law, such as the marital or paternal authority; or for the jurisdictions of public law. These prerogatives always have a determinate holder, a physical or moral person of private or public law.

But a great many legal rules have no active subject, as in every case where the disposition is laid down in the interest of third parties generally or of the public. For example, take the rule that forbids agreements contrary to public policy or to good morals.[19] To be sure, that rule is established for the public good, and like every measure of the public good it will finally redound to the benefit of the particular individuals who make up the public; yet it has no determined or even determinable beneficiary. To be sure, the right to invoke the nullity of the transaction hit by the prohibition is conferred by the law upon "any interested person." Yet if the action to declare the nullity thus finds one or several active subjects — those persons who will prove to have an interest in the nullity — it does not follow that the rule sanctioned by the action would in turn have any active subject. Again, take the rules relating to domicile. They evidently concern the relationships among men: There would be no need to localize persons at some point in space if they should never enter into relations. Yet one could not say that those rules, which no doubt dispose and consequently command, are creative of subjective legal rights or even of legal relationships. The domicile, which is a place, is not a relationship, even when the domicile provides the subject matter of a rule.[20]

"Everybody" may well be said to be a *passive* subject, where the obligation in question is the general one not to infringe upon the prerogatives of another, as in the case of absolute rights, of jurisdictions, and of offices (valid *erga omnes* rather than binding upon anyone in particular). "Everybody" could not be an *active* subject, the beneficiary of a

[19] Add: all police regulations of traffic, sanitation, etc.

[20] Neither is domicile "the legal relation existing between a person and a place," as defined by Aubry and Rau, following Zachariae. See, for a criticism of that definition, 1 M. PLANIOL, TRAITÉ ÉLÉMENTAIRE DE DROIT CIVIL (12th ed. by G. Ripert) no. 555.

right or holder of a power. For on pain of disorder, activity in any field requires individualization of the subject as the responsible author of the activity.

85. The World of the Law Is Not Limited to a Network of Bonds between Determinate Persons. It is thus a mistake to picture the world of the law as a sort of network of bonds of rights and obligations between actually determined persons, on the strength of the claim that it governs the relationships among men. That picture simplifies the complexity of human relations, which involve not only immediate relationships of active and passive subjects determined at the outset (e.g., between neighbors, between parents and children, between contracting parties, between the state and citizens: This is the legal relationship in the strict and technical sense), but also more indirect, more uncertain relationships of subjects unlimited at the outset, where the public in general — actual or future — or some fraction thereof intervenes as an interested party actively or passively. Moreover, there are legal rules which, while starting with the assumption of human relations and with a view to serving them, establish no legal relationship among determined persons nor among undetermined ones: The rule simply lays down a mandatory solution in matters which are of close or remote concern to human relations. Thus the world of the law is defined less by the idea of the legal relationship than by that of the rule. The world of the law is primarily the world of the rule, no doubt governing the relationships among men, but in a broad sense transcending the concept of the legal relationship in the technical sense.

Section 3. The Different Kinds of Social Relations and the Corresponding Branches of Law

86. The Fundamental Principle of Division is Given by the Existence of the State. However, as has been seen,[1] social relations are of various kinds; hence the different branches and divisions of the law.

While this partition does not destroy the unity of the notion (the idea of law must necessarily be valid without substantial change for all compartments of the juridical discipline), it is understood that the variety of subject matters influences the behavior of the rule with regard to each of them.

Among the principles of division which are suggested by an analysis

[1] See *supra*, nos. 79–80.

of social facts, the most fundamental in our present society appears to be that derived from the existence of the state at the center of human relations. Not only does the state belong to the principle of law — the law under its form of state law [2] — but it also belongs to the principle of any logical division of the law. The existence of the state, indeed, gives rise to the double set of private and public relations, on the one hand, and of municipal and international relations, on the other.

87. Public Relations and Public Law. Once the state appeared as the supreme group devoted to the public good, a new category was added to the category of the theretofore private, interindividual or corporative, relations: That of public or political relations. By them are to be understood relations touching upon the state,[3] which includes, first, the relations through which the state is constituted and organized and through which it acts and functions; then, the relations which the state maintains with the subjects, its members, individuals or groups, private or public (the public groups being such as the provinces, the municipalities, and the corporations of public law, if any). Now then, while private relations call for an appropriate rule, which is the branch of private law, the relations to which the state is a party, at least as public power,[4] belong to the branch of public law. This distinction is incontestable even if, with Duguit and others, one denies the personality of the state. The fact remains that the governing individuals, who are put in the place of the personal state which is deemed fictitious, act not for themselves but *qualitate quâ*, i.e., inasmuch as they are working functionaries of the public good. Whatever the theory by which one represents the state, the two notions of governors and of the public good (and these one finds throughout unless the state itself is denied) are sufficient to bring out the distinction between private relations, which are directed toward the private individual or private bodies, and relations bearing the imprint of the public character.

88. Why the Expression "Political" Is Preferable to "Public." However, the term "public" is equivocal; much better would it be to speak

[2] See *supra*, nos. 8–13.

[3] One would be wary in arguing from the famous passage in ULPIAN, DIG. 1, 1, 1, 2; JUSTINIAN'S INST. 1, 1, 4: *Quod singulorum utilitatem pertinet, — quod ad statum rei Romanae spectat* [What pertains to the use of individuals, as against what regards the status of the affairs of Rome], which is controversial. It is possible that *status rei Romanae* refers not to the Roman state but to Roman public property.

[4] This leaves aside the question whether as to acts done in administering its property the state does not fall under the rule of private law; see J. DABIN, DOCTRINE GÉNÉRALE DE L'ETAT no. 70, pp. 109–110.

of "political" relations and "political" law.[5] For although the political, that is, the state, is subservient to the public, that is, the community of the citizens, the public is not to be confused with the political. On the one hand, private relations are always of more or less interest to the public, directly or incidentally;[6] on the other hand, concern with the public good is not the exclusive monopoly of the state, the incarnation of the political.

That is why one must reject the criterion of certain authors[7] who claim as referable to public law every rule laid down for the safeguarding of a public interest and, by that token, mandatory (in the technical sense: Any disposition of a will to the contrary notwithstanding). That conception results in emptying private law of a great part of its content, and even in a way annihilating it by reducing it to the rôle of a law merely supplementing the will of private persons; at the same time, it fails to understand the existence of a specifically political order, which is the order of the state itself. Moreover, it is a mistake to search for a division of the law in the mandatory, as opposed to the merely supplementary, character of the rules. Sometimes the law consecrates autonomy, sometimes it excludes it, for reasons connected with the elaboration of the substance of the law. Logically, a division of the law could be deduced only from the diversity of the matters dealt with and not from the nature of the solutions applied to the problems.[8]

89. International Relations and International Law. The state also belongs to the principle of another and in certain respects still more fundamental distinction: That between municipal relations, which move within the sphere of each particular state, and international relations. Once the particular states have admitted at least the principle of a rule obligatory on legal grounds in the field of international relations, international law is born — public or political international law where rela-

[5] These are the terms, e.g., of MONTESQUIEU, DE L'ESPRIT DES LOIS, bk. I, chap. 3; bk. XXVI, chaps. 1, 15–18.

[6] In this sense, private law is spoken of as being "publicized" — in the sense of being "socialized" — without involving any confusion or interpenetration of public (in the sense of political) law and private law. Cf. E. Riezler, *Oblitération des frontières entre le droit privé et le droit public*, in 3 RECUEIL LAMBERT § 143, pp. 117 *et seq.*, esp. at 125–126, 130 *et seq.*

[7] Thus the Swiss W. Burckhardt, in the works cited by DU PASQUIER, *op. cit.* no. 171, p. 153, n. 1, and all adherents of the so-called theory of jurisprudence of interests. [See THE JURISPRUDENCE OF INTERESTS (M. M. Schoch, ed., Cambridge, Mass., 1948).]

[8] The more so since it is often difficult indeed to know whether or not the legislator has laid down his rule imperatively. Thus, the line of demarcation between public and private law would be essentially uncertain.

tionships between states as political groups are concerned (law of nations, *inter gentes*);[9] private international law where relationships between private persons are complicated by a foreign element (in persons, property, places). In the latter case a problem of legislative jurisdiction arises which brings into play the respective sovereignties of the states concerned.[10]

90. Penal Law and Adjective Law Are Only Subsidiary Laws. That is all there is to this classification. In particular, there is no ground for introducing the penal law and the various parts of adjective law under the category of public law. Although these branches of the law are related to the authorities of the state — inasmuch as it imposes penalties or administers justice — they seem to be only subsidiary laws, aiming at carrying into execution rules of substantive law, both public and private, municipal and international, without themselves governing any determinate aspect of social life.[11]

91. Private Relations and Private Law. While public relations have no other objective than the state and the relationships at home and abroad which life in the state implies, in short, the body politic,[12] private relations are tied around two great categories of interests: The category of economic, pecuniary interests, so-called property interests, and the multifarious category of extra-economic or non-property interests. Hence the subdivision of private law into the law of property relations and the law of persons and domestic relations. From another point of view, while public relations and the corresponding law are exclusively corporative (at least under the theory of "moral beings"), private relations and private law are sometimes interindividual — when those con-

[9] We keep here to the traditional and simple conception of international law. But see for a more profound study A. Von Verdross, *La loi de la formation des groupes juridiques et la notion de droit international public*, in 2 RECUEIL LAMBERT § 75, pp. 112–115 (concerning branches of the law).

[10] Actually, indeed, the conflict of laws, and generally conflicts rules of any kind, are particular to each state — unlike the law of nations, which is common, at least among civilized peoples.

[11] Cf., on procedure, M. Ricca-Barberis, *Le droit d'agir dans la tradition germanique et dans la tradition latine* (*Klage et Actio*), in 2 RECUEIL LAMBERT § 108, pp. 551 *et seq.* But see, to the contrary, E. Riezler, *op. cit.*, in 3 RECUEIL LAMBERT § 143, pp. 134–136.

[12] Undoubtedly public law, too, involves subdivisions. But they either depend on a formal point of view, such as constitutional law which is the written law of Constitutions (where one finds public law, no doubt, municipal and even international, but also principles of private law, penal law, etc.); or they refer to various aspects of that same life in the state, such as administrative law which governs administrative power, revenue law which governs relationships between the treasury and the taxpayers, election law, or military law.

cerned are physical persons, who may be equal or unequal (the latter by subordination of one to the other, as in the case of a "power," or, better, an authority) — and sometimes they are corporative — when they aim at or start from the existence of a body of private law, whatever may be its end as a group, lucrative or otherwise.[13]

92. Maximum Impact of the Law upon Its Subject Matter in the Field of Economic Relations. If it is true, then, that all human relations — domestic and international, public and private, property and nonproperty, interindividual and corporative ones — fall within the competence of law, it is appropriate to add that, for various reasons, the grip of the rule varies noticeably in degree according to the subject matters.

As regards first of all private relations, which long remained under the grip of customs and private institutions (family, corporate bodies),[14] the penetration of the law is best revealed in the economic field. Not because the selfish interest, the normal motor of economic life, would like to yield to any discipline, on the contrary — nor because all economic liberty ought to be proscribed: The economy requires a large dose of liberty;[15] but rather because law and economics offer structural analogies. On the one side, the economic values are essentially "things," translatable into money, interchangeable, impersonal; on the other, the law is essentially an external discipline, laid down and applied from without. Thus one can understand that such a discipline is pleased with regulating "things" which accommodate themselves more easily to its touch than the personal values whose inner subjectivity escapes it. No doubt the objectivism (or "thing" character) of economics must be well understood. There is no pure economics, and consequently no pure thing. By its origin as by its end, economics is washed through with the human: The wealth of goods is produced or made fruitful by man and is at the service of man, of the collective whole and of everyone individually. Moreover, it happens that things acquire a personal value outside their commercial value; such are the nourishing earth, the ancestral

[13] As to structure, as observed before, the state and private groups are equally corporative bodies and hence fall under a corporative law. Thus, one may speak of "private constitutional law," as the theorists of the institution do, see G. Renard, La théorie de l'institution 163, 271 *et seq.*, 278. But it is understood that the state includes and dominates the private bodies at least as far as the public good requires.

[14] The law of the state has intervened sometimes to remedy abuses of earlier disciplines that have become despotic, sometimes contrariwise to support them with its authority when they have lost some of their force, and sometimes to modify their precepts in a sense more open to the needs of the whole community.

[15] See *infra*, nos. 156 *et seq.*

home, the family jewels. In this sense, the values of property as "patrimony," evoking the idea of the family, are opposed to the economic and commercial values.

As a human discipline, the law will obviously try to take these personal aspects of economics into account, at least as far as its structure as external rule does not hinder it from mastering them. It is this reservation that justifies the jurist against the reproach that he gives property only an insufficient analysis (the famous *jus utendi, fruendi et abutendi*),[a] not exhausting and hardly scratching the surface of the moral and human reality of the relation of the thing to the person.[16] The "moral and human reality of property" is not very accessible to the jurist because he does not have the means to enclose it in a neat rule that gives the owner security: It would be socially intolerable if at every one of his steps the owner could be cross-examined in the name of the moral and human reality of property. Contrariwise, where the economic values are sufficiently detached from any element of personality, as in exchange and commercial transactions,[17] the legal rule works with ease, for it has less trouble in measuring rights and duties where the subject matter as such is measurable, ponderable, calculable.

93. Far Less Impact in the Field of Personal Values. Much less well adapted and less efficacious is the position of the law with regard to extra-economic values, those pertaining to the person and the family.

Neither the human person nor his powers (which are his emanations), neither the soul of man nor his body (which are indivisibly united) are measurable "things," susceptible of seizure from the outside. Hence the powerlessness of the jurist fully to objectivate and fence in the relations which have their direct subject matter in, or touch upon, such values. That powerlessness is to be observed even where the person is made to serve economic ends, as in the contract of employment. Labor is not a commodity precisely because it implies engagement of the person in the work to be accomplished. But how can the extent and value of that engagement be measured exactly so as to render to each what is his due? And outside of the obligation to pay wages, which is a measurable thing (though measurable by the yardstick of the human life), how can the personal relationships, from man to man, between parties to the employment of labor, be regulated in an adequate manner? [18]

[a] [The right to use, enjoy and abuse.]

[16] The statement is by J. Tonneau, *Propriété*, in DICTIONNAIRE DE THÉOLOGIE CATHOLIQUE cols. 738 and 833; the criticism is by F. RUSSO, *op. cit.* 84–86. . . .

[17] With certain reservations even there, for the personal element is never susceptible of complete exclusion, see *supra*, no. 77 with n. 8.

[18] See, e.g., articles 9 and 11 of the Belgian Law on the Contract of Work of

If "rights of personality" are involved under a contract or outside a contract, how are damages to be assured in an adequate manner for violation of such rights? How can such rights even be defined in their inner subjectivity, since the personality is, to a large extent, not communicable? Forget about the "economic personality" of the industrialist or merchant, which if need be may be appraised in economic terms, according to the value of the enterprises (although actually the economic personality is inseparable from the personality as such). But who can be satisfied with the legal treatment of attacks upon the physical side of personality and, above all, upon the moral rights of individuals? No doubt the law sets up rules and reveals its presence: What good would it be if it did not protect persons above all in what is closest to them? But its protection is short, and whatever it may do to improve its means of penetration, it will never go beyond the surface layer of the substance of personality.[19]

94. The Same, in the Field of the Family. Equally remarkable is the insufficiency of the legal approach in the field of the family. The relations between husband and wife, parents and children are infinitely richer and more meaningful than is evidenced by legal definitions. What is marriage for the jurist? Simply cohabitation combined with mutual material aid. Husband and wife live together and have the right to do so as a result of a solemn agreement, which is the act of celebration of the marriage; having contracted the marriage, they are bound to live together in mutual faithfulness and to render mutual aid to each other. Now such a definition, which is limited to the external side of things — the common life, habitation in the same *domus* [b] — is far from expressing the essence or simply the reality of marriage. It barely suggests the carnal union, whereas marriage is the total fusion, body and soul, of two human personalities, man and woman, with a view to the propagation of humankind and to their own perfection. According to scientific and metaphysical verities, marriage suggests a very vast world where love and life, individual and species meet; of this profound and truly mysterious reality the law retains only certain superficial traits which it can capture.[20] The same remark may be made about the "paternal group" linking children to their parents. The obligation to feed, bring up, and maintain children with which parents are charged (Code Napo-

March 10, 1900. The difficulty remains the same if the relationships are conceived on a community level, in the framework of the "community of the enterprise."

[19] See the reproach formulated by G. del Vecchio, *Essai sur les principes généraux du droit*, § VII, in JUSTICE, DROIT, ETAT 145.

[b] [House, home.]

[20] Cf. D. VON HILDEBRAND, LE MARIAGE (transl. by Lavand, ed. Cerf, 1937).

leon, article 203),[c] could in its textual tenor be fulfilled in technically as perfect a manner by an educator as by the parents. Yet the child's progenitors will add to the legal obligation a manner of discharging it, a diligence and tact whose secret lies in that unique sentiment: Fatherly and motherly love. Reciprocally, the docility which children are charged to observe will be fortified by a note of trustful devotion which finds its irreplaceable source in filial love.

In short, domestic relations — and all relations that approximate them, such as the relations between the employer and his collaborators, without falling back for this reason upon "paternalism" [21] — present themselves under a double aspect: A somehow corporal aspect, for which the discipline of law is appropriate, and a psychological and moral aspect, irreducible to a rule proceeding from without, such as the law or the rules of social manners. And it is always the same fundamental doctrine: The internal does not fall under the law, even where the relations under consideration may have a mixed character, both external and internal.[22]

95. Cause of the Relative Powerlessness of the Law in the Field of Political Relations. In the order of political relations, where the powerlessness of the law is equally manifest in certain sectors (the whole field concerning the duties of rulers, the field of international relations), that powerlessness, it is well known, is due less to the subject matter than to the subject individuals. Essentially, it rests upon the impossibility of subjecting the various sovereign authorities to their rule: *Quis custodiet custodes?* [d] [23] By its nature, politics is wholly subject to the law, without distinction between relations of the citizen to the state and relations of the state to the citizen, and without distinction between domestic and international politics. Is not the state in all respects a society devoted to a certain end, and consequently subjected to the laws of that end? Are not its organs and agents functionary, and consequently subjected to the law of their function? The very definition of the state-society assumes the existence of a rule for all who, on whatever ground, are in-

[c] [Art. 203 of the Code Napoleon provides as follows: "The spouses by the sole act of marriage at once contract the obligation of nourishing, sustaining, and raising their children."]

[21] Cf. our observations *supra*, no. 77 (on the note of friendship added to certain contracts for consideration) and no. 90 (on the coefficient of personalism included in the contract of work).

[22] Cf., in the same sense, 1 SAVIGNY, *op. cit.* (transl. by Guenoux, 2d ed.) 324: See equally on the law as the "logical and universal aspect of social life," F. RUSSO, *op cit.* 128–134.

[d] [Who will watch the watchers?]

[23] See *supra*, nos. 36–40.

volved in the relations of the state, for the rulers as well as for the subjects and for the states among each other on the international level. And as the state is a public, hence external, society, no consideration of inwardness can hamper the normal play of the rule here nor localize it in the surface layer of the matter.

96. The Claim that the Nation is Not Reducible to the Legal Rule. True, it is objected that, if that observation holds good for the state, which belongs "to the order of organization, of logic, of the universal," it does not hold good for the nation, which represents "the affective, dynamic, original elements of the life of the political society": Facing the law, there will always be politics, and the sum total of the more personal and intimate relations of national and international life. Thus would be explained the field reserved to the exclusive jurisdiction of states in international law.[24]

But, to begin with, how can that dissociation of the state and the nation be admitted? Is not the state the organized nation itself? [25] And from the moment when the nation is organized in the state, how can it free itself from the state? The state would, by its nature, fall under the law; the nation, in what it involves of the original, the personal, the intimate, would fall under politics. But how can that conception of politics as connected with the nation rather than with the state, and above all that opposition between politics and law, be justified? From the assumption that nations are somehow living beings, moved by forces which one calls political, animated by sentiments — or passions — which one decorates with the name mystical, it does not follow that these living collectives escape all law. The human collectivities, made up of human individuals, are, like the individuals, subject to the law of reason. That their passions are more violent, that in this respect they have not gone beyond the stage of primitivism or infancy, changes nothing in the principle. It will be precisely the rôle of the state to educate its nation, as it does its individuals, to discipline it, to civilize it in such a way that reason outstrips sentiment in the politics of the nation. Nor is there any question of sacrificing national values; on the contrary, the law commands that they be safeguarded and defended against any enemy, internal or external. But the legitimacy of national values is one thing, and quite another is an exacerbated, distrustful, aggressive nationalism which claims to be freed from any norm.[26]

[24] F. Russo, *op. cit.* 129–131.

[25] We are speaking here of the nation in general, without necessarily referring to the principle of nationalities.

[26] Only the principle of the competence of the law in all matters of the political

97. The Illusion of the Sufficiency of the Legal Order. The powerlessness of the law in political matters thus is not due to the political. It is due to the fact that the rule is the work of the state itself, the state being free to decree or not to decree it, and to such effect as the state sees fit, and, having decreed it, always remains free not to observe it. Thus the master of the law and the subject of the law are confounded. The state as legislator is qualified to define and guarantee the obligations of the state as of anyone in the political society; the state as judge is charged with applying to the state the rules imposed upon it by the state as legislator. No doubt, there is nothing to prevent the state as legislator and judge from subjecting to discipline its own organs, the institutions, the powers, the men who exercise the functions of the state. But whatever contrivance may be imagined to escape the circle (division of authority by separation of powers, etc.),[27] a supreme organ will remain, which disposes of the rule and its application in a sovereign manner, yet is itself delivered from any properly legal discipline. The same conclusion applies in the order of relationships between states, in the absence of an organized international society: The states, which by the norm ought to obey a collective discipline, in fact enjoy a freedom legally sovereign, at least in the sense that no compulsion leads it to respect the rule. The difficulty is not at all congenital; in the present state of the international world, it is not surmounted, and its solution seems hardly imminent. Moreover, supposing that international law one day arrives at the fully legal stage, one would be faced on this level with the obstacle encountered in the domestic order: How to obtain submission to the norm of international law by the supreme organ of international legislation.

This is the "hole on top," the fundamental lacuna which shows the illusion of the "plenitude of the legal order": If authentic, specific law is indeed the law that is called positive, one still could not deny that this positive law needs to be complemented by the moral law in order to fill the sphere that is necessarily "empty of law" — empty because of the impossibility of putting under positive law the authority which is the master of positive law. Where, for this reason, politics escapes from law, it remains under the jurisdiction of morals, the sovereign master of all human acts, including the acts of men who "make" politics.

---

order is meant to be raised here without excluding therefrom *a priori* "the more personal and intimate realities of national and international life." The question in what measure and manner the law ought to intervene is not under examination.

[27] Even where the organs of legislative or executive authority are subject to the judiciary they must show themselves discreet so as not to excite reactions hostile to control; cf. note P.L. on the Council of State, decision of May 16, 1941, SIREY (1942), 3, 21, at p. 21, col. 2, and p. 22, col. 1.

PART TWO

THE LEGAL METHOD

CHAPTER I

IS THE LAW "GIVEN" OR "CONSTRUED," THE SUBJECT OF A SCIENCE OR OF A TECHNIQUE?

SECTION 1. STATE OF THE PROBLEM AND PRESENT THEORIES

98. Explanation of the Terms "Given" and "Construed." These are the terms in which Gény has posed the problem,[1] terms no doubt a little simple. But since the formulation has become classic among legal theorists, it seems useful to preserve it while rendering more precise its meaning, which certainly needs explanation.[2]

A thing is given when it exists as an object outside of any productive intervention of man: Such as God, nature, human beings and their relations, the contingent facts of history. A thing is construed when, taken by itself, it has its cause in the efficient activity of man: Such as a house, a poem, a syllogism, the state. It is clear, further, that the "construed," once it has been given reality, becomes something "given" for everybody, including its author: A given relative datum, if one likes the term, whereas the thing that owes nothing to human causality is a given absolute. Now, with regard to the "given," to whatever category it may belong — physical, metaphysical, or historical — the attitude of man is that of knowledge, of science; with regard to the "construed," man, who by definition is the constructor, is operative and, in this sense, makes a work of art or of technology.[3] On the one hand, the attitude of investigation or reception; on the other, creative operation.

This is not to say that the work of knowledge would exclude all con-

[1] See F. GÉNY, in the symposium LES MÉTHODES JURIDIQUES (Paris, 1911) 181–196; also, notably, 1 SCIENCE ET TECHNIQUE EN DROIT PRIVÉ POSITIF (Paris, 1914) nos. 33–34, pp. 96–100; 2 *id.* (1915); 3 *id.* (1921); 4 *id.* (1925). [See also F. GÉNY and others, THE SCIENCE OF LEGAL METHOD (trans. E. Bruncken and L. B. Register, New York, 1917).]

[2] On the ambiguity of the notions of "given," "construed," "technique," in Gény's work, cf. F. RUSSO, RÉALITÉ JURIDIQUE ET RÉALITÉ SOCIALE 30.

[3] Technique, then, is here understood to mean not so much processes (following the definition of technique as a complex of processes) as a result which technique has wrought.

struction: In its raw state, the "given" is difficult to seize for the human mind; at least there is needed for its comprehension an operation of the intelligence which cannot proceed without a certain more or less deforming conceptual elaboration. In relation to the "raw fact," the "scientific fact" is "construed." Yet the whole effort of science tends to as exact as possible a restitution of the real, naturally in accordance with the means at the disposal of science. On the contrary, the work of the man of art or of technology arrives at something new, which may well have retained from the real its materials (by contrast with pure creation) or the reason for its being (by contrast with aimless work), but which nevertheless in its actual form did not before exist in reality.[4] Thus understood, the distinction appears hardly contestable. At bottom, it fits in with the classical distinction between the speculative or theoretical sciences, which confine themselves to considering things from the standpoint of their truth alone, and the practical sciences which, aiming at action, tend to evolve rules of action, which is here called "construing."

99. Extent of the Application of the Idea of the "Construed." Little does it matter, moreover, whether construction refers to *agere*,[a] i.e., to mores (morals and politics) (*agibilia*), or to *facere*,[b] i.e., to the productions, utilitarian or otherwise, of the laborer, the craftsman, the artist, the scholar (*factibilia*).[5] It is true that usage reserves the term "technique" to the minor needs of the various *facere*, and the name "art" to the major needs (especially in the case of aesthetic work),[6] while in the field of mores, the name "prudence" signifies the practical reason concretely discerning things to be done and decisions and alternatives to be taken.[7] But interesting as these distinctions may be, there is no place here for the moment to dwell upon them.[8] In any event, whether "technique," "art," or "prudence" is concerned, it is the practical order that

[4] This is the answer to the objection that any science whatever, even one most positive in its methods, would be construed; see, in that sense, M. Djuvara, *Le but du droit*, in 3 ANNUAIRE DE L'INSTITUT INTERNATIONAL DE PHILOSOPHIE DU DROIT ET DE SOCIOLOGIE JURIDIQUE (1938) 100–101. If science is indeed construed by the human mind, the realities with which it is concerned are not.

[a] [Acting.]

[b] [Making.]

[5] Cf., as to justice, ST. THOMAS, SUMMA THEOLOGICA, *IIa IIae*, qu. 58, art. 3 *ad* 3.

[6] Etymologically, "art" and "technique" (τέχνη) are synonymous.

[7] On the distinction between art and prudence, see especially ST. THOMAS, *op. cit.* *IIa IIae*, qu. 47, art. 2 *ad* 3, art. 5 *ad resp.* Incidentally, art and even technique are not excluded from the domain of *agibilia* but they remain dependent upon prudence.

[8] They will be encountered again at a more advanced stage of the argument, *infra*, nos. 124, 192.

comes into play: Action to be proposed, work to be elaborated, construction and not speculation.[9]

Equally little does it matter who the author of the construction is: Isolated individual or collectivity, professional or nonprofessional. Neither in the field of *agere* nor in that of *facere* do isolated individuals, and that includes the specialists, have a monopoly of construction. As groups of artisans working under the direction of a master have erected cathedrals, so collective reason is able to pose principles of conduct in moral matters. Nor shall we consider what is the psychological process of construction: Spontaneous elaboration (as often in popular work) or reflective elaboration. What counts from our point of view is neither the quality of the actor nor the mode of the activity. It is the aim, the work created. And hence there is no ground for restricting the ideas of the "construed" and of "technique" to the cases of reflective elaboration on the part of so-called technicians alone, excluding spontaneous elaborations of collective origin.[10] What has been construed by life, by the people, remains a human creation by the same token as the individual work of the specialist.

100. Statement of the Question. After these differentiations, with which category is the law to be ranked? Is the law, as regards its content, "given," apart from all human elaboration, or is it rather "construed" by men, by the professional jurist or the people? And, since the terms are interrelated, is the law, as something "given," an object of science, that is, something to be found and registered, or is it, as something "construed," a work of art or of a technique?

Let us first of all remark that the law may be contemplated from two points of view: In its historical existence, and in its essence.

101. In Its Historical Existence, the Law Is "Given." In its historical existence, the law is obviously "given," an object of science, whether we deal with contemporary law or ancient law, with national law, foreign law, or international law. This given law, if it is in force, will no doubt require application to special cases, which belongs to a certain art rather than to science. But with a reservation for application to special cases, the historically given law, in force or not, does present itself as a reality, susceptive of a properly scientific, speculative knowledge.[11] Again, the

[9] Cf. St. Thomas, Comm. Post. An., bk. I, lesson 14: . . .; also Comm. Eth., bk. X, less. 14, *in princ.*; Comm. Polit., bk. I, less. 1: . . .

[10] This seems to be the conception of F. Russo, *op cit.* 32 *et seq.*, . . .

[11] Even the interpretation of the law is a science inasmuch as to interpret the law means to understand it as it is and not to reform or deform it. In all matters, indeed, the real calls for interpretation.

law of a country or of a group of countries or, if that is possible, of the entire world may be studied not as static, at an arrested moment of time, but in its evolution in the course of the ages. This is the viewpoint proper to the historian.[12] Finally the law may be studied from a strictly sociological viewpoint, in its relations with the social life either of a country or an epoch or in general. Anyway, the activity is one of science: The science of the national or foreign law, the science of legal history, the science of the sociology of law. The attempt is made to analyze and to understand certain phenomena as such or by comparison,[13] namely, phenomena of legal rules. This is the science of the established law, which is eventually to complete and crown some general theory: A "philosophy" of such a legal system,[14] a "philosophy" of legal history,[15] "principles" of the sociology of law.[16]

102. But What about Law in Its Essence? But outside of the "existential" law — present, past, future, or merely possible — there is law pure and simple, denuded of any form of concrete existence.[17] It is in relation to the law as thus understood, in the state of essence, that our question is raised. In it one at once discerns the interest in an exact appraisal of the lawyer's mission. If the law is "given," at least for the jurist, it will be enough to gather the "given" thing in the reality that supplies it. According to the more or less "positive" nature of the given, the method of knowledge will vary: Properly scientific or philosophical, even theological (in the eventuality that something given that is juridical has been revealed). But the search always sets itself only one aim: To find out the law where it is, as something given. An appeasing doctrine! The jurist is a man of science: His conclusions have the objectivity and

[12] On the "history of the laws of antiquity" (*antike Rechtsgeschichte*) which in turn is a part of the "universal history of humanity" [*sic*] (*allgemeine Rechtsgeschichte* [properly translated: "universal history of law"]), according to Post and Kohler, see L. WENGER in 1 RECUEIL LAMBERT § 11, pp. 138 *et seq.* Cf. P. KOSCHAKER in 1 RECUEIL LAMBERT § 22, pp. 274 *et seq.*

[13] The allusion here is to the comparative method, in law (comparative law), in legal history (comparative history), and in the sociology of law (comparative sociology of law).

[14] See, e.g., JHERING, ESPRIT DU DROIT ROMAIN (transl. by Meulenaere).

[15] Cf. P. DE TOURTOULON, LES PRINCIPES PHILOSOPHIQUES DE L'HISTOIRE DU DROIT (Paris-Lausanne, 1908–1919) — though that work includes much legal philosophy.

[16] Cf. N.-S. Timacheff, *L'étude sociologique du droit*, in ARCHIVES DE PHILOSOPHIE DU DROIT (1938) nos. 1–2, pp. 209 *et seq.*

[17] On the necessary distinction between comparative method and general theory of law, cf. F. Weyr, *Remarques générales sur la nature juridique de la méthode comparative*, in *Introduction à l'étude du droit comparé*, 1 RECUEIL LAMBERT § 26, p. 311.

certainty of science. The authentic rule, issuing from the given, has the validity of the propositions of science: Imagination is excluded. Contrariwise, if the law is construed, the door is open to the arbitrary subjectivism of the author of the rule. Even if the construction should be subjected to principles, the solutions evolved in applying them could only be vacillating, disputable and disputed.

But whatever may be the security — real or fancied [18] — which one expects from a "scientific" conception of the law, it is impossible to found security upon error. The law will be even more arbitrary, or in any case more tyrannical, if it presents itself in the name of something given that would lack objective reality. It is truth, then, that it matters to seek even when it should appear less agreeable, less comfortable than error.

103. Attitude of Legal Positivism, and Criticism. A whole juristic school adopts an attitude of indifference to the problem, on the stated ground that it would transcend the jurist's sphere of competence. According to them, the science of law would have only the historically given law as its subject, which the jurist as such would only have to outline in scientific form. Such a task alone would be "positive" because it would be attached to the real, and the historically given law alone is real. As for the critique of that law or the search for some principle dominating the positive elaboration, that work, which is not indeed denied to be legitimate, would be "metajuridical," belonging to disciplines other than the law: Political science, sociology, philosophy. Such is the attitude adopted, independently of taking any position in the properly philosophical order, by the adherents of the school of so-called legal positivism, which starts from the positively established law and seeks to know that law only.[19] But even admitting that legal science could be immured in the pure exposition of the law, a non-suit for lack of jurisdiction is not a solution. With legal science defaulting after pleading lack of jurisdiction, another discipline will have to take charge of the problem, which may be, if one likes, the discipline of legal philosophy.[20]

[18] The difficulty of "How to construe?" has its counterpart in the other difficulty, which must necessarily be resolved: "Where to look for the given, and how to interpret it?"

[19] As representatives of this school may be cited notably Jèze in France and Kelsen and his followers in Germany. [See H. KELSEN, GENERAL THEORY OF LAW AND STATE (trans. A. Wedberg, 1945).] On the Kelsen school, see J. Sedlacek, *L'oeuvre de François Gény et la science du droit pur*, in 1 RECUEIL D'ÉTUDES SUR LES SOURCES DU DROIT EN L'HONNEUR DE FRANÇOIS GÉNY 277 *et seq*. Cf. the doctrine of the exegetic school in France in the nineteenth century as summarized in J. BONNECASE, INTRODUCTION À L'ÉTUDE DU DROIT (2d ed. Paris, 1931), nos. 108 *et seq*., pp. 180 *et seq*., especially no. 118, pp. 190–191.

[20] Cf. CICERO, DE LEGIBUS, bk. I, chap. 5: . . . See generally, on the untenable

104. Everybody Recognizes that in Some Part the Law Is "Construed." A first point admits of no discussion: Up to a certain point, more or less considerable according to varying opinions, the law is construed. Thus Savigny, the great master of the historical school, recognized the existence of a scientific elaboration of the law by the jurists, which he called "legal technique" and which he distinguished from the spontaneous creation of the law in the heart of the people.[21] For Duguit, custom, case law, and statute law, being "mere modes of stating the legal rule,"[22] are a matter of "legal art";[23] as for the foundation of the law, it is made up of two kinds of rules, the "normative legal rules, or legal norms properly so called" and the "constructive or technical legal rules," "established as far as possible to assure respect for and application of the normative legal rules."[24] Among the adherents of natural law, none denies that it requires practical realization, which constitutes precisely the original resort of the positive law: The whole system is built upon the logical opposition between an element of law given by nature and a positive element issuing from the will of man.[25] Even the authors most inclined to emphasize the part of the naturally (or scientifically) given within the complex are clearly obliged to admit a limit: "Science," writes Russo — in this case, social science — "has permitted us to remove certain indeterminations, but not all: Some irreducible ones subsist; some social structures are necessary which we have not been able to uncover even by the most penetrating analysis of social life."[26]

105. The Certain Part of the "Construed": Formal Sources; Machineries; Differentiations by Enumeration. In fact, the statutes, the customs, the decisions of cases, inasmuch as they are formal sources of law, are indubitably construed. They are not the law itself but represent

---

character of legal positivism (*hoc sensu*), H. Dupeyroux, *Les grands problèmes du droit* (dealing with the work of Le Fur), in ARCHIVES DE PHILOSOPHIE DU DROIT (1938), nos. 1–2, pp. 14 *et seq.*

[21] On the conceptions of Savigny in this respect, see 3 F. GÉNY, SCIENCE ET TECHNIQUE, no. 180, pp. 5–6, and citations there.

[22] 1 L. DUGUIT, TRAITÉ DE DROIT CONSTITUTIONNEL (3d ed.) § 14, p. 154. [Portions of the work of Duguit were translated in A. Fouillée, J. Charmont, L. Duguit, and R. Demogue, MODERN FRENCH LEGAL PHILOSOPHY (trans. J. P. Chamberlain and E. F. Scott, New York).]

[23] 1 L. DUGUIT, *op. cit.* § 15, pp. 158, 161–162; § 16, p. 173.

[24] 1 L. DUGUIT, *op. cit.* § 10, pp. 106–107; also pp. 154, 225–226.

[25] See, e.g., F. GÉNY, SCIENCE ET TECHNIQUE EN DROIT PRIVÉ POSITIF (4 vols.) *passim*.

[26] F. RUSSO, *op. cit.* 109; see also 40–42.

a certain manner of expressing it and containing it. They are organs, instruments. Now means or instruments are construed. They have their authors — including custom, which is indeed a creation of the people because it derives from their attitudes and conduct. Again to the various organs and instruments of the law there correspond as many particular procedures and techniques: A legislative technique, a technique of case law, and one of custom. Nor is this all. Going beyond the mode of expression, the "construed" enters the content of the law. For instance, the machinery for the protection of minors, at the very least when taken in its concrete determination, outside of the idea of protection, is construed: Any machinery whatever implies construction, including the legal machineries that are translated into rules of conduct (realm of *agere*).[27] Similarly, the precise differentiations by enumeration which one meets in the codes at every step are purely artificial in their concrete determination — viz., the figure chosen. No examination is made as to whether these "constructions" are postulated by any necessity whatever, nor whether they have a law of their own, which is not in doubt. It is merely maintained that they are not at all given, that man establishes them, literally makes them.[28]

106. Divergence of Opinions as to the Nature and Origin of the "Given." Yet following the texts cited above, the law is not construed in its entirety. By general opinion, at the basis of the construed portion, rendered explicit and developed by it, there would repose something "given," an anterior legal reality which the traditional school calls natural law,[29] which others call rational law,[30] the "notion of law" (Bonnecase),[31] the "social reality" seen across its "natural finalities" (F. Russo, taking up an expression by Delos),[32] the "legal rule" or "juridical norm" (Duguit),[33] or the "normative facts" (Gurvitch).[34]

[27] On *agere* and *facere*, see *supra*, no. 99.

[28] That is why the theories of radical objectivism are difficult to understand which claim to exclude any intervention of the will in the domain of the law; see, e.g., R. Bonnard, *L'origine de l'ordonnancement juridique*, in MÉLANGES MAURICE HAURIOU, pp. 48–49.

[29] We shall come back to the "given" of natural law, *infra*, no. 110.

[30] M. Djuvara, *Droit rationnel et droit positif*, in 1 RECUEIL D'ÉTUDES SUR LES SOURCES DU DROIT EN L'HONNEUR DE FRANÇOIS GÉNY 245 *et seq.*

[31] J. BONNECASE, INTRODUCTION À L'ÉTUDE DU DROIT nos. 138 *et seq.*, pp. 217 *et seq.*

[32] F. RUSSO, RÉALITÉ JURIDIQUE ET RÉALITÉ SOCIALE (Paris, 1942) *passim*, esp. 37–40, 48–60, 108–109.

[33] We shall come back at once to the "normative" given of DUGUIT, *infra*, no. 107.

[34] G. GURVITCH, L'IDÉE DU DROIT SOCIAL (Paris, 1932) *passim*. Also the same,

As an essential element of the whole, what is thus given in the law would be primary to and imposed upon the construction, so that according to Duguit the positive law contrary to the "legal rule" would lose all character as law, whereas to the traditional school the contradiction would raise the delicate problem of the "conflict between natural law and positive law." [35]

Unfortunately, agreement among partisans of the "given" in the law ceases when it comes to defining the nature and origin of what is thus given; and the sometimes rather neutral terms they use (such as the "legal rule" of Duguit) really cover divergent conceptions. From the first encounter on, the security that had been counted upon vanishes: The "given" in the law itself becomes the subject of debate! Broadly, two theses are in conflict, determined by the philosophical tendencies of their protagonists: On the one side, positivism, though under varying aspects, psycho-sociological or squarely materialistic; on the other, "metaphysical realism," disguising the basic unity of its doctrine under the diversity of its formulae.

107. The Opinion of Duguit. For Duguit, most eminent representative in France of the psycho-sociological conception of the "given," "a legal rule exists when the mass of the individuals who make up the group comprehends and admits that a reaction against the violators of the rule can be socially organized. That organization may be nonexistent, it may be embryonic and sporadic; that matters little. *At the moment when the mass of minds conceives of it, desires it, provokes its creation, the legal rule appears.*" [36] Thus the legal rule or juridical norm exists from the instant and on condition that the "mass of minds" [37] aspires to a socially organized reaction against the transgressors of that primary, so-called social, norm, which, as analyzed at length by Duguit, consists essentially of the law of social solidarity, in the twofold form of the economic norm (for that which relates to the economy) and the moral norm (for the extra-economic activities). Two factors, according to Duguit, contribute to form the state of conscience from which the law ultimately emerges. They are both facts, and the author, true to his positive method, proposes to utilize them as such only, without searching

---

L'EXPÉRIENCE JURIDIQUE ET LA PHILOSOPHIE PLURALISTE DU DROIT (Paris, 1935) 142 *et seq.*

[35] See F. GÉNY, SCIENCE ET TECHNIQUE, vol. 4.

[36] 1 L. DUGUIT, *op. cit.* § 8, p. 94. Our italics.

[37] Duguit, indeed, rejects as unreal the idea of a "social consciousness" distinct from any individual consciousness; see 1 *op. cit.* § 12, pp. 127 *et seq.*; § 13, pp. 146–151.

for their objective value: They are the feeling of sociality and the feeling of justice.[38] The feeling of sociality is "the feeling existing at a given moment that the bond of solidarity which maintains the social integration would be broken if the respect for a certain economic or moral rule were not sanctioned by means of law." [39] The feeling of justice: Man always and everywhere has the feeling that he is an individual having a certain autonomy, which implies respect for two kinds of particular justice, distributive and commutative, the best definition of which was given by St. Thomas Aquinas.[40]

To sum up, "the consciousness among the mass of the individuals of a given group that some moral or economic rule is essential for maintaining the social solidarity, and the consciousness that it is just to sanction it, these are the two essential elements of the formation and transformation of the legal rule." [41] Hence the work of the jurist is twofold: "A truly scientific work" — one of positive science, where no philosophy, no metaphysics enter — "to uncover under the social facts the legal rule; and a work of technical art, to prepare the customary or written rule, which is the constructive rule tending to determine the scope, and guarantee the realization, of the norm." [42]

108. Theories Searching for the "Given" of the Law in Popular Feeling. In this exposition, one recognizes the guiding theme of the historical school: Basically, the law emanates from the people.[43] Not from the "legal" people, deliberating in its *comitiae* [c] or through the intermediary of its representatives, based on the title of political sovereignty, but from the real people, going about their ordinary occupations, thinking out the law as a function of their experience and from the more or less enlightened ideas they form of the legal ordinance. Another, more empirical formula leaves the definition of the given of the law to public opinion, that is, to the public in general as far as it has opinions in matters of law.[44]

Sometimes the people conceive man and his relationships with an-

[38] 1 L. Duguit, *op. cit.* § 10, pp. 115–116.

[39] 1 L. Duguit, *op. cit.* § 11, pp. 116–117.

[40] 1 L. Duguit, *op. cit.* § 11, pp. 120–122.

[41] 1 L. Duguit, *op. cit.* § 11, p. 125. See, in the same sense, R. Capitant, *op. cit.* 127–132.

[42] 1 L. Duguit, *op. cit.* § 15, p. 162.

[43] See, e.g., Savigny, Système du droit romain § 7: "It is the spirit of the people, living and acting in all individuals in common, that engenders positive law."

[c] [Popular assemblies in classical Rome.]

[44] See, e.g., G. Cornil, Le droit privé. Essai de sociologie juridique simplifiée (Paris, 1924).

other from the angle of the universal — and they will then proclaim abstractly envisioned "rights of man" (individualism) or the principle of social solidarity (solidarism or socialism). Sometimes the people do not look beyond the horizon of national (*völkisch*) [d] man — they will then think out the law nationally, depending upon their peculiarly national temperament and aspirations. Sometimes the people manifest their will themselves by their behavior or by various more or less organized and inherent movements. Sometimes a *Führer* emerges from their mass, an infallible medium rendering explicit in authoritarian form the will latent in the spirit of the people (*Volksgeist*).[45]

But whatever the world-outlook philosophies (*Weltanschauungen*) and the processes, the fundamental conception does not change: Moved by a complex whole of ideas and feelings, interests and wants, the people deem just or desirable some legal solution — in private, public, or international law — which to them seems to merit the sanction of social compulsion. At this precise moment and by virtue of the popular will, the "given" of the law exists, which the jurist or statesman has only to put into form and fit together in the ways of the law. Is the people right in willing what it wills? Is its estimation well founded? That is a matter of personal, rigorously private opinion. At any rate, the jurist, as a scholar devoted to the observable real, or as one of the members of his people, is not qualified to substitute his own judgment for the will of the people. Immanent and transcendental, the "given" of the law resides in this multiple subject, more or less one, the people, public opinion, which forges it as it understands, feels, and wills it.[46]

109. The "Given" of the Law as a Product of Force. Close to those psycho-sociological conceptions inspired by "modern science" may be put the theories, more brutal in form, which at all times in the camp of so-called realistic thinkers reduce the law to the will of the stronger, as the epilogue of a struggle for survival, for riches or for power, between individuals, between classes, between peoples (law of vital competition, historical materialism, political imperialism, in short, all forms of "social

[d] [The term used in German National-Socialist (Nazi) doctrine, denoting folkish or racial.]

[45] See J. Duquesne, *Sur l'esprit du peuple allemand comme source d'origine du droit allemand*, in 3 RECUEIL LAMBERT § 150, pp. 225 *et seq.*

[46] On legal psychologism as a manifestation of "legal romanticism," see J. BONNECASE, INTRODUCTION À L'ÉTUDE DU DROIT nos. 180–182, pp. 278–281; also no. 140, pp. 219–220. But there is no understandable reason for classifying as "legal classicism" the theories which derive the law from "social consciousness" (Durkheim): they equally betray a subjectivist conception, that of the social mass; cf. BONNECASE, *op. cit.* no. 182, pp. 181–182.

Darwinism"). In that struggle which always tends toward conquest or maintenance of a favorable law, victory would naturally fall to the holder of the greatest force, unless the "balance of power" (as they say in international politics) leads to a precarious peace of equilibrium or compromise.[47] The forces at play must not, however, be understood as solely brutal force: To it must be added the force of intelligence or of will — of the will to power: Nietzsche's *Willensmacht* [*sic*] — the force of number or of grouping, economic or political force, etc. Always the law depends upon a weight, a pressure, foreign to the intervention of any reason in the law. Now it is easy to perceive the link that in fact unites the conception of popular law with the conception of law as force. Does not the people represent the greatest force? If its will must prevail, is it not ultimately because it is strongest? Where else than in the force of the people can one find the reason for its right to create the law? Unless one says, which amounts to the same thing: The popular will most often is fused with the preponderant social force, which is predominant in the heart of the mass, thus being able to impose its will upon all.

110. The "Given" of the Law as Issuing from Nature (Natural Law Doctrines). In opposition to those theses which develop the "given" of the law from moving and contingent sources stands the classic, traditional theory of the "given" as something objective, deduced from nature. Its definition may be borrowed from Gény, its most illustrious defender among the jurists of today:

> The given corresponds approximately to the fundamental notion of natural law. It consists of a fund of moral and economic verities which, confronted by the facts, command certain directives for their governance. The objective of these directives, superior to the arbitrariness of wills, is restricted and vague. It centers upon the supreme idea of the "objectively just," representing an equilibrium of interests which sometimes requires auscultation by all our powers of understanding yet which always furnishes but a rather blurred orientation, of a nature more moral than economic, in truth, principally moral. This given . . . furnishes the "rule," the "principle."[48]

[47] For a new edition of these theories, see H. DE PAGE, DROIT NATUREL ET POSITIVISME JURIDIQUE (Bruxelles, 1939). And see the school of *Interessenjurisprudenz*, the jurisiprudence of interests, according to which the law is the product of dominant interests, PH. HECK, GESETZESAUSLEGUNG UND INTERESSENJURISPRUDENZ (1914) 17. [See also the translation by M. Schoch in THE JURISPRUDENCE OF INTERESTS (Cambridge, Mass., 1948).]

[48] F. GÉNY, SCIENCE ET TECHNIQUE EN DROIT PRIVÉ POSITIF, *Conclusions générales*, 147. Also, on what he calls the "rational given," as an essential element of the classical law of nature, 2 *id.* no. 169, pp. 380–384.

Prudent and even a bit hesitant as this formulation may be, one sees proclaimed therein the existence, independent of any free choice by men — private individuals, people, qualified legislator — of a small number of regulative principles of conduct in the moral and economic sphere, principles which the author traces back to the idea of justice. That justice, conceived as an equilibrium of interests, would essentially respond to the concept of natural law. Thus neither morals nor economics nor justice are simply the product of states of consciousness or of opinions. Morals and economics have their laws, different in nature, but similarly endowed with objective value; and if with Duguit one can speak of a "feeling of justice," this is not at all a subjective feeling without correspondence to the real, but on the contrary a more refined sense of the objective idea of justice that has somehow passed to the state of a physical habit. As for the equilibrium of interests that is constitutive of justice, it must, in the spirit of Gény, not be understood as a mechanical balance where the interests are gauged solely by the weights of their constantly variable forces, but a moral balance where the comparison is established in the light and on the basis of a superior, permanent principle, which is precisely the objective idea of justice. Objective, because it has its foundation in nature, especially the nature of man: Inasmuch as it is spiritual, human nature in effect postulates that respect of man for man which lies at the beginning of the equilibrium of "interests," that is, in a word, of human values, wherein justice consists. It is also added that in order to discover that justice, at least in each of its applications, all our powers of understanding may be made to contribute, not only discursive reason, but also intuition, feeling, conscience, not even excluding faith.

Section 2. Examination of the Theories of the "Given" (Duguit, Gény, etc.)

111. Return to the Problem: Is There a Legal "Given"? Such, rapidly sketched, according to some of their typical interpreters,[1] are the

[1] The other interpretations of the "given," explicit or implied, can always be traced back more or less to one of the types summarized in the text. Thus the "notion of law" ("the regulatory principle charged with defining the social harmony in its essence and indicating the means to attain it"), adapted to the "permanent nature of man," according to J. Bonnecase, is related to Gény's natural law, as stated by Bonnecase himself, Introduction (2d ed.), no. 187, p. 209; see also *id.* nos. 112–113, pp. 220–225; no. 184, pp. 283 *et seq.* Russo's "social reality," involving norms according to its "natural finality," *op. cit.* notably p. 53, is equally in line with natural law, which it is to determine and complete by transcending it; for it

present theories concerning the nature of the "given" in the law. But prior to any discussion of the nature of law, the initial question remains: Is it correct to say that the law — the law as here defined, in the sense of a societal rule of the state or between states — is *given*, if only in part? Is the truth not rather that the law is not at all given, that following the logical definition of the "construed" as a work produced by man,[2] the law is wholly "construed," down to its most substantial foundation?

Contrary to prevailing opinion, we would here take the part of the theory of *total* "construction" and try to prove it, first negatively, through a critique of the two kinds of conceptions of the "given," and then in a direct manner, through an analysis of the process of elaboration of the law.

112. Critique of the Doctrines of the Popular "Given." As for the variously shaded theories deriving the "given" from the people, it is easy to reply that the people as such are not qualified in legal matters, any more than in any other matters whatsoever — philosophical, scientific, technical — to decide what is or what ought to be: The true, the good, the just, the useful. Suppose the people have a certain opinion on a point of law, there is nothing to indicate that that opinion would be adequate to juridical truth and that the jurist would therefore be under a duty to accept it as the unobjectionable "given" of the legal regulation. The law is not a matter of the will, of masses or numbers; it is a matter of reason. This, by the way, everyone admits, among the people and even among the legal sociologists: A good many of these recognize that certain popular tendencies, far from imposing obligation, themselves call for redress.[3]

This is not to say that the people will always be wrong, a theory which would result in unduly rejecting all spontaneous elaboration of the law in the heart of societies, notably in the form of custom. On the contrary, it is impossible to deny in a sane people that is endowed with a certain experience, a rather exact sense of the law, its requirements and even its opportunities. As the case may be, the so-called popular

---

embraces not only the ethical values but all social values whatever; see notably *id.* pp. 44–45. As for Gurvitch's "normative facts," defined by him as the rules deriving from the social environment which realizes them, and constituted in an immediate fashion by the intuition of reason ("intuitive positive law"), they belong rather to a sociological conception, yet without breaking with a certain conception of natural law; see *infra*, no. 126, n. 19.

[2] On the notion of the "construed," see *supra*, no. 98.

[3] See, among others, P. Esmein, *Le droit et ses sources populaires*, in BIBLIOTHÈQUE DE PEUPLE (Paris, 1942) 19–20; equally, RUSSO, *op. cit.* 53–54.

law may show itself sometimes inferior and sometimes superior to the law of the jurists.[4] Yet interpreting the law as an organ does not mean creating it as an author. It is inadmissible to assume that the people — the collective consciousness, the great mass of minds, public opinion — are, not merely the more or less well inspired organ of, but the supreme source of, the law, at least as far as the jurist is concerned. Whatever may be the formal origin of the mode of formation of the law, it is valid scientifically only by the amount of legal reason it contains.

In the case of many authors, especially Duguit, the contrary doctrine proceeds from a preconceived method of purely experimental "positive science" which would forbid one to draw the "given" of the legal rule from anything but observable phenomena. And as Duguit refuses to see this "given" in the observable phenomena of statutes, customs, decisions, "simple modes of stating the legal rule," he is reduced to searching for the authentic "given" of the legal rule in the social environment, the state of consciousness of "the great mass of minds." Indeed, on the "positive" level, there is no other choice. Either the legal rule is supremely given in the existing law, which one must take as it is, save for explaining it by its phenomenal causes; or else the legal rule inhabits an equally observable anterior region, which can only be the state of consciousness of the people. But phenomenon for phenomenon, why stop at the state of consciousness of the people rather than at the existing law? Because the latter would always tend to conform to that state of consciousness, which would thus be the first phenomenon determining the other? Yet popular nonconformity may be encountered and is in fact often enough encountered. It even happens that the existing law maintains itself against popular opinion, indeed, that it triumphs over and converts it. Where, then, is the ground for any preference? [5]

Let us add that while sometimes the state of consciousness of the mass may be perceived without too much trouble, it is still more often indiscernible, either because the people are divided in opinion or because they have no opinion on the problem to be solved. Where, then, lies the legal rule if not, in the absence of public opinion, on the side of the law in force, which presents at least the advantage of effective existence? [6]

[4] There is thus no deprecation here of the spontaneous elaboration of the law by the people in favor of the reflective elaboration by sociologists and jurists; cf. RUSSO, *op. cit.* 33 *et seq.* There is reason in the people, and spontaneity does not exclude reason.

[5] Cf., in the same sense, H. Dupeyroux, *Les grands problèmes du droit*, in ARCHIVES DE PHILOSOPHIE DU DROIT (1938) nos. 1–2, pp. 43–45.

[6] There are still other arguments, see RUSSO, *op. cit.* 20–26, who refers especially to the very frequent phenomenon of law borrowed by one people from other peoples, at 24–25, 133–134. On this phenomenon, see also G. del Vecchio, *L'idée*

Indeed, Duguit does not remain true to his own point of view. Further on, and repeatedly, he sets up as the supreme principle of the law, with no reference to the state of consciousness of the mass, the norm of "social solidarity," which, though perhaps debatable, is fully objective.[7]

113. Critique of the Doctrines of Force. The law, say the "realistic" thinkers, is nothing else than the will of the stronger, and assuming competing forces, the solution will be given by the equilibrium of the forces. This time the explanation is neat, almost cynical. As the state of consciousness of the mass, taken by itself, was a cloudy concept, so force is a tangible reality. One clearly sees where the greatest force is — on the side which the pressure indicates. But, once again, force may well impose upon the legislator any legal "given," whatever pleases the interests or passions which it serves. By no means does it follow that force is qualified to "give" to the jurist whatever there is that is valid. Truth to tell, it "gives" nothing, the concept of the "given" implying, after all, the idea of a solution endowed with a virtue of its own. Now force is content to dictate the solution: Force creates it. Hence there is no more room for asking if the law includes a part of the "given"; the distinction no longer makes sense. The law, synonymous with force, is neither "given" nor "construed": It is traced back to an arbitrary pure fact.[8]

114. As for Natural Law, the Question Arises Only with Regard to Juridical Natural Law. If the "given" of the law could not reside in facts — the facts of common consciousness or the facts of power — does one have to discover that "given" in the "fund of moral and economic verities," "commanding certain directions" which "center upon the supreme idea of the objective just," in short, in natural law? [9]

Let us at the outset dissipate an equivocality which risks vitiating the entire discussion. It is certainly legitimate to attribute validity to the notions of natural law and justice in order then to deduce therefrom the rules destined to govern the conduct of man toward others, on the plane of strictly interindividual relationships as well as on the properly social plane (family, state, and other groupings). But the question in that case

d'une science du droit universel comparé, in JUSTICE, DROIT, ETAT 184–185, and the studies brought together in 2 RECUEIL LAMBERT Pt. IV, title 1 (*La réception des droits*), pp. 581 *et seq.*

[7] See, e.g., 1 L. DUGUIT, *op. cit.* § 53, pp. 674–680, . . . See also 2 *id.* § 8, pp. 54–55.

[8] The ideas negating justice have already been sifted by Plato with very penetrating criticism, which is summarized in P. LACHIÈZE-REY, LES IDÉES MORALES, SOCIALES ET POLITIQUES DE PLATON 37–49.

[9] Or in the "notion of law" of Bonnecase. See *supra*, n. 1.

is one of the fundamental human rule, that is, the moral rule, which indeed prescribes respect for the right of another (the subject of commutative justice) [10] and also the constituent principles of the régime of the necessary societies (family and state), the "institutional" part of morals. In this sense there exists an interindividual natural law, a familial natural law, and a political natural law.[11] But the legal rule is something different from the moral rule. The former is the concrete rule laid down by the state-society for its subjects from the viewpoint of its own discipline [12] — which incidentally in no way excludes the realization, not merely of an "ethical minimum," as has been said,[13] but of the maximum possible. It is also, first of all, the rule of constitutional and administrative law concretely organizing the state, the peculiar principle of that discipline.

The question then is, on the specific level of this kind of rule, whether natural law and justice, which indeed constitute the "given" of the moral rule *ad alterum*, will serve equally as the "given" of the legal rule. If the answer is in the affirmative it would have to be admitted that the two rules start from the same "given" and, as the moral rule comes first, that the "given" of the legal rule is nothing else than that of the moral rule. Between the two systems no other differences would subsist than those which result from the diversity of positive determinations. As for the substance of the precepts, the first directions, they would be identical, traceable always to the same idea of natural law and justice.[14]

115. Nature Furnishes the Jurist with No Juridical "Given," No Necessary Rule. Legal experience as it comes from the general practice of legislation, case law, and customs, does not confirm that conclusion. Indeed, it is seen that in certain cases the legal rule does take up the initial "given" of natural law and justice, save for subjecting it to certain adjustments; that in other cases it discards or modifies it, and not only in the details of determination, but also in a much more radical manner by reversing the directive, as for instance when the law lets itself be guided above all by preoccupation with security. Sometimes, indeed, a

[10] On the natural character of the moral duty of commutative justice, cf. ST. THOMAS, SUMMA, *Ia IIae*, qu. 94, art. 2 *ad resp., in fine.*

[11] On these various applications of the idea of natural law, see J. DABIN, LA PHILOSOPHIE DE L'ORDRE JURIDIQUE POSITIF nos. 79–108, pp. 311–395. The concepts of natural law and of justice will be especially studied below, Part III.

[12] See *supra*, nos. 8–13.

[13] G. JELLINEK, DIE SOZIALISTISCHE [sozialethische] BEDEUTUNG VON RECHT, UNRECHT, STRAFE (2d ed. Berlin, 1908) 45–59.

[14] See, e.g., J.-T. Delos, *Les caractères essentiels de la règle du droit positif*, in DROIT, MORALE, MOEURS 212–214: . . . ; see also 218–219.

law consolidates the established or acquired fact, even where such establishment or acquisition may have taken place contrary to natural law and justice (idea of security in society). Sometimes it so disposes and shapes the form of its rule that it may operate surely and with the minimum of arbitrariness even if natural law and justice must suffer thereby (idea of legal security).[15] What is this but to say that the jurist [16] has to consult not solely natural law and justice, that he maintains a certain freedom of choice with regard to them?

Hence the mandatory "given" becomes optional, that is to say, it ceases to be a given, a solution, so as to turn into a datum, viz., one of the elements of the problem. An important and capital element, no doubt, which could even furnish the "rule," the "principle," as Gény says, but which by reason of the possible "exception" leaves no less room for choice, thus destroying the idea of "given." For to choose is to construe, when the jurist "receives" the principle as well as when he "creates" the exception. Even in the first case his rôle is not confined to a passive reception, as with regard to a pure and simple "given," the object to be stated and registered; it takes on a truly active, constructive aspect. In adopting the "given" which he could have discarded, the jurist leaves the indeterminate, creates the decision and therewith the solution.

The same criticism applies to another frequently used formula which calls natural law and justice the inspirational sources of the positive law.[17] To be inspired by a model is not necessarily to copy it. On the contrary, that is to preserve freedom to take it as it is, to modify it, or not to take it at all, according to the circumstances.

Will it be said that even where he appears to be discarding natural law and justice in order to create an exception, the jurist does not cease to conform to natural law and justice, which he translates in his own way, taking account of the needs and requirements proper to the legal order? [18] Notwithstanding its success, this formula badly disguises a false conclusion. To apply an exception to a principle is not to translate it, to be inspired by it, or even to adopt it; it is jolly well to contradict it, at least in the case under contemplation. The principle remains safe; but it is illogical to suggest that in decreeing the exception one continues

[15] On the various applications of the idea of security, cf. G. Radbruch, *La sécurité en droit anglais*, in ARCHIVES DE PHILOSOPHIE DU DROIT (1936) nos. 3–4, pp. 88–89.

[16] It is understood (see *supra*, no. 99) that the term "jurist" includes not only the professional lawyer but all those who, even among the people, collaborate in making law, as in the formation of customary law.

[17] See, e.g., G. RENARD, LE DROIT, L'ORDRE ET LA RAISON (Paris, 1927) 134: . . .

[18] Cf., in this sense, M. Djuvara, *Le but du droit*, in 3 ANNUAIRE DE L'INSTITUT INTERNATIONAL DE PHILOSOPHIE DU DROIT (1938) 97–104, especially concerning "legal technique," at 100 *et seq*. . . .

to apply the principle. Further, if the legal order has its own needs and requirements, capable of influencing the content of its rules to the point of dictating exceptions to the "given" of the principles of natural law and justice, that proves that the legal rule, unlike the moral rule, is not subjected to, nor determined purely by, this "given," that it obeys other laws.

116. Undue and Illogical Extensions of the Idea of the Natural Juridical "Given." True, it is claimed one can escape the difficulty by embracing within natural law and justice not only the law and justice, but also in a general manner all that is required by life in society. Thus, the need of security, in society and in the law itself, is ranged among the requirements of natural law and justice. Is life in society not postulated by nature, and hence do not its requirements belong to natural law? On the other hand, is there not a social justice, to which particular justice is subordinate, and hence do not the social requirements of security take precedence over the particular right? Therefore, when a juridical law consecrates the idea of security, it still realizes the "given" of natural law and justice. In that way it is thought to mask the conflicts, if not the antinomies, of needs and principles which are at the heart of social life; such as the principle of justice on the one hand, which demands respect for and the triumph of the right, and the principle of security on the other hand, which sometimes demands definitive or provisional recognition (or tolerance — it matters little) of a status quo not conforming to justice (an unjust state of facts or even an unjust rule, *hoc sensu*).[19]

But first it will be observed that respect for justice, even particular justice, is as essential to society as is the concern with security. *A priori*, social justice inclines us more to the side of security than to that of particular justice: There remains in each case a choice in the direction of security or of particular justice. Consequently social justice does not "give" any solution, nor even any principle of solution. It simply commands a search for the best solution, taking everything into account, from the viewpoint of the general good. And it is the statesman-jurist, not the theorist of natural law and justice, who will make the choice.[20] Indeed, if the "given" which is invoked does not correspond to any

[19] See, e.g., G. RENARD, LA THÉORIE DE L'INSTITUTION 48 *et seq.*; J.-T. Delos, *Les buts du droit*, 3 ANNUAIRE (*supra*, n. 18) 40–47 . . .

[20] Cf., in the same sense, P. Cuche, *A propos du "positivisme juridique" de Carré de Malberg*, in MÉLANGES CARRÉ DE MALBERG (1933) 76–79; the same, *L'élaboration du droit pénal et l'irréductible droit naturel*, in 3 RECUEIL GÉNY 273–274. M. Cuche has not read me well if he believes I ever maintained anything else; see *Pour une meilleure terminologie*, in ARCHIVES DE PHILOSOPHIE DU DROIT (1931) nos. 1–2, pp. 195 *et seq.*

uniform directive, even an abstract one, if under the sound of a single name — "natural law," "justice" — it assembles multiple directives, of contradictory contents, without furnishing a clue to the choice, it is vain to speak of a "given." This "given," which supplies neither a solution nor the principle of a solution, is no longer really a "given." With regard to the "given," there will perhaps be a general method, complex at best, of elaboration of the law (directive of *method*), but by no means what one expected and was promised, to wit, solutions or principles of solutions indicating the way people are to behave, in short, the precept to be included in the rule (directive of *solution*).[21]

117. Difference Between the Pretended Legal "Given" and the "Revealed Given" of the Theologians. Such is the case, *mutatis mutandis*, as regards the "revealed given" of the theologians, which does seem to have inspired the theme of the legal "given." The "revealed given" consists, indeed, of solutions in the proper sense, verities of dogma and morals which form the entrusted deposit of Revelation committed to the care of the church that is their interpreter. Such is not the case as regards the "given" of natural law and justice in the sense in which it is desired to understand them, natural law covering all that is postulated by nature, and justice covering all that is due, in the widest sense, not only the just but also the useful, the opportune — security as well as right. As is well known, moreover, the "revealed given" presents itself not merely as an inspiring principle susceptible to adaptations or exceptions; without excluding certain determinations or more explicit statements, it is nonetheless given *a priori* in a definitive and intangible fashion. This is what marks the idea of an entrusted deposit.[22]

118. Choice of Concrete Examples. Let us make this somewhat abstract discussion clearer by analyzing concrete examples. These will be taken from Duguit, who invokes them as models of "normative rules" drawn, according to his theory, from the "state of consciousness of the great mass of minds." [23] The adherents of the theory opposing ours will not fail to see in them so many expressions of a legal "given" drawn from natural law and justice.[24] But whatever the alleged source may be,

[21] The same objections militate against the theory of RUSSO, *op. cit.*, according to which the "given" of the law would be constituted by the scientifically analyzed "social reality" . . .

[22] These differences are omitted in the parallel drawn by G. RENARD, LA PHILOSOPHIE DE L'INSTITUTION 299–301.

[23] See 1 DUGUIT, *op. cit.* (3d ed.) § 10, pp. 109–110.

[24] See, as to respect for engagements and reparation of unjustly caused wrong, L.

it will be shown that these solutions are in no way "given" to the jurist, not even by way of general principles susceptible of diverse determinations and exceptions, that they do jolly well belong to the autonomous constructive activity of the jurist. We shall deal with the following three great rules of the Code Napoleon, dominating the law of property interests: Respect for ownership, freedom of contract, and reparation for injuries due to fault.

119. Respect for Ownership. Incontestably the Code Napoleon protects ownership, at least in principle, but not by virtue of a "given."

To begin with, it would be difficult to maintain that the principle of ownership is given in the state of consciousness of the mass. No institution is more strongly debated than ownership, not only in its details but also in itself, since a party exists called communist, whose program contemplates a common ownership of the means of production (socialization, nationalization).[25] Contrariwise, those who hold with natural law and justice have little trouble in proving that private ownership, even extended to the means of production, is indeed required both by the nature of things and by a just consideration of the individual right.[26] Does it follow that the solution is "given" to the jurist, if only in principle and save for exceptions? Not any longer, or at least not *a priori*. There is a divergence between the rule of natural law and justice, which seeks private ownership, and the rule of legal protection of ownership by way of codes, tribunals, and public force. At the outset, passage from the rule of natural law to the legal rule implies a new control and consequently a new judgment. There are no doubt claims that one readily admits, where hesitation is not permitted, so strongly indicated does legal protection appear; thus, the principle of private ownership, and for that matter all elementary applications of the idea of commutative justice, the right to life, to bodily integrity, to honor, etc. The social order would be in peril if the individual right remained without official

---

Le Fur, *La théorie du droit naturel depuis le XVIIe siècle et la doctrine moderne*, in 18 RECUEIL DES COURS DE L'ACADÉMIE DE DROIT INTERNATIONAL DE LA HAYE (1927) 389. Concerning the precepts of natural law among the ancient writers, cf. GROTIUS, LE DROIT DE LA GUERRE ET DE LA PAIX (transl. by Barbeyrac, Basle ed. 1768), *Discours préliminaire* § VIII; J. DOMAT, TRAITÉ DES LOIS CIVILES chap. V.

[25] Will it be said that ownership is consecrated by all legislations and by that token belongs to the *jus gentium*? But the *jus gentium*, the pretended product of collective reason, may have its opponents, today as of old

[26] The "nature of things" and "natural law" are here spoken of in a wide sense, which does not exclude the work of reason. But according to tradition ownership belongs to *jus gentium* rather than to natural law *sensu stricto*, see *infra*, nos 203–204, 212.

defense on the part of public authority. This does not prevent protection from being accorded only in so far as the social order demands it, to the extent and in the form the social order demands, on condition moreover that this protection be realizable and efficacious — in short, conforming to the specific juridical laws.

Once this uniformity is recognized, one may well say that it is the legislator's moral duty — one of natural law and justice — to sanction the principle of private ownership. But it is not because the moral duty commands such an attitude of the legislator in regard to the law that the solution is "given." It is not given by its inherent virtue but solely as the conclusion of a judgment reached by the jurist in the accomplishment of his proper task. Differences of opinion may always entail more or less essential differences in the content of the rules, which is a sufficient foundation for the theory of the autonomy of "positive" law in relation to the "given" of natural law. In other words, and in brief, apart from the philosophical and moral conception of ownership, which is the conception of natural law, there exists a legal conception of ownership, which no doubt borrows from the former but deals with ownership under a certain aspect only, that concerning the particular ends and proper means of the legal discipline.[27]

120. Ownership Is Far from Always Enjoying the Protection of the Law. Furthermore, in some situations very legitimately, for reasons of social order or of legal technique, ownership such as natural law conceives it will not enjoy the protection of the law. Such is the case of prescription in favor of one who is in possession in bad faith, resulting in a denial of protection to the unjustly dispossessed owner,[28] or the case of freedom of contract, implying a denial of protection to the owner unjustly suffering as a result of his contract. Mere "exceptions," it will be said, to a principle that remains intact and continues to impose itself as "given" notwithstanding the exceptions — or again mere "adaptations" of the principle of respect for ownership to the requirements of security. But these are logical artifices, verbal arrangements. The truth is rather that one has to do with a conflict between two principles equally valid on the level of the law — the principle of respect for ownership, and the principle of security — a conflict which the jurist in the particular case resolves by according preference to the

[27] Especially as to the "superficial" character of the legal conception of ownership, see *supra*, no. 92.

[28] See J.-A. Robilliard, *A propos d'un conflit entre le droit civil et la loi de l'Eglise relatif à la prescription acquisitive*, in 1 BULLETIN THOMISTE (1931–1933) *Notes et communications* 193–198: . . .

principle of security.[29] For, it must be repeated, a principle that is given only save for an "exception" to be determined by the jurist (or save for an "adaptation" actually equal to an "exception") may well remain a principle; it is no longer an [inescapable] "given," since it is subject to examination and possible rejection. After the jurist's decision as before, though, the principle of ownership remains "given" as a principle of natural law, binding both the subjects, as to their conduct, and the moralist who construes the moral rule. The proof thereof is that the "given" of ownership continues to bind one's conscience notwithstanding the defect of legal protection, at least until the pronouncement of a judge.[30]

121. Freedom of Contract. This rule [of freedom of contract] means, in law, that contracting parties are free to "do as much and by such contracts as they please," provided that such contracts are lawfully concluded and contravene neither a law (an express provision) nor public policy or public morals. Now it is inexact to claim with Duguit that the principle of contractual freedom would be "given" in the state of consciousness of the mass, since one encounters many a partisan of the "prescribed contract" or at least of one controlled, either by the administration or by a corporative body or by the judge. It would be equally wrong to see in freedom of contract a principle of natural law and justice, if that amounts to interpreting it as a complete immunity excluding, if only in principle, any intervention by an authority to verify the content, motives, or purposes of the contract concluded. A limited contractual autonomy may avail itself of natural law on the ground of the importance of individual liberty, which indeed postulates for the human individual a certain external mastery over his acts and interests. Yet freedom of contract must respect not only laws, public policy, and public morality, but right and justice: Commutative justice which requires equivalence of performances in exchange — just wages, just prices — and social or legal justice which does not tolerate nuisances or dangers to the general good; in short, all that is opposed to a liberal economic régime where pure liberty would be proclaimed as a principle, and particularly as a principle of natural law and justice. Hence no

[29] By the same reasoning must be understood the example of the deposit, taken from CICERO, DE OFFICIIS 3, 25, 95, by ST. THOMAS, SUMMA, *Ia IIae*, qu. 94, art. 4 *ad resp.*, art. 5 *ad resp.*; see also *IIa IIae*, qu. 62, art. 5 *ad* 1; qu. 120, art. 1 *ad resp.* . . . Cf., . . . DOMAT, TRAITÉ DES LOIS chap. XI, 21–22.

[30] See, generally in the same sense, . . . Desqueyrat, *La part d'immuable et de variable dans le régime des libertés*, in LA LIBERTÉ ET LES LIBERTÉS DANS LA VIE SOCIALE, proceedings of SEMAINES SOCIALES DE FRANCE, 30th session, Rouen (1938) 184 *et seq.*

ground of natural law and justice prevents contractual freedom from being subjected in its exercise to a more or less vigorous control or even to various restrictions destined to prevent its abuses. The contrary is true.

However, concretely, natural law and justice prescribe nothing either for or against intervention. Legitimate or even commendable as it may appear in theory, intervention involves multiple inconveniences, notably from the point of view of security in society. Rightly or wrongly, it runs the risk of shaking, in the consciousness of the less enlightened masses, the principle of faith in the pledged word; by attacking the stability of contracts, it runs the risk of introducing an element of disorder in business relations. Thus the principle of freedom of contract, which is in no way "given" to the philosopher or moralist, is no more "given" to the jurist either. On the level of positive realities which is his, it is for him to choose between the solution of freedom and that of intervention. A matter of opportunity, then; and, in fact, he will adopt one or the other policy according to the circumstances of time, place, and case.[31]

122. Reparation for Injuries Due to Fault. The problem here lies less in the principle of reparation for injury done to another than in the conditions of that reparation. The injury, we are told, must be the effect of a fault. Fault as the ground of reparation: Such would be the norm or direction "given" to the jurist in his task of elaborating the legal system of responsibility in part. But again it cannot be at all said that the requirement of fault is admitted by the mass of minds nor yet prescribed by natural law, even in principle. On the one hand, the mass of minds of the twentieth century remains divided between the adherents of responsibility for fault, or subjective responsibility (this is the traditional doctrine), and those of responsibility without fault, or objective responsibility. On the other hand, if all fault by definition implies falling short of a rule of conduct, there is occasion to distinguish between voluntary fault, implying injury caused willfully, and involuntary fault, which implies no will to inflict injury. Now, while philosophers and moralists, speaking in the name of natural law and justice, attach a strict obligation of reparation only to voluntary fault, jurists show themselves more exacting, following an already long tradition: Involuntary fault alone, committed by imprudence or negligence (quasi-delict),[a] gives rise

[31] Thus in our days we observe a tendency to admit breach as the general principle of rescission of contracts, at least of commutative contracts with no aleatory element; see G. RIPERT, LE RÉGIME DÉMOCRATIQUE ET LE DROIT CIVIL MODERNE (Paris, 1936) no. 93, pp. 179–181; E. Demontès, *Observations sur la théorie de la lésion dans les contrats*, in ETUDES DE DROIT CIVIL À LA MÉMOIRE DE HENRI CAPITANT (Paris) 171 *et seq.*

[a] [In the sense of the term in Roman law.]

to civil responsibility in tort, sometimes even to penal responsibility (as in homicide or bodily injuries which are especially grave). A fundamental divergence, the meaning of which can only be the following: If there exists in this case a "given" for the moralist, at least if it is a conclusion deduced from natural law, this "given" does not impose itself necessarily upon the jurist, whose point of view in matters of responsibility for torts could not be copied from that of the moralist.[32]

Furthermore, natural law itself does not impose as the sole principle of reparation the requirement of a fault, whether voluntary or involuntary. There are indeed cases where natural law and justice command reparation in the absence of any fault, by applying an idea of risk creation or again of just distribution of the burdens of common life, as for injuries caused to private individuals by the execution of public works, etc. There is here neither an "exception" from nor an "adaptation" of the principle of fault. The rule is different, by reason of the difference of situations. It is thus wrong to represent the rule of reparation for injuries due to fault as "given" either to the jurist or even to the moralist. Reparation for injuries operates by virtue of diverse principles between which the jurist chooses according to the cases. In this sense, the solution he brings to the various cases is not given in advance: It is "construed," by way of casuistry.

SECTION 3. THE LAW IS "PRUDENCE" AND CONSEQUENTLY CONSTRUED

123. Conclusions Reached Concerning the Legal "Given." To sum up, the theory of a legal "given," consisting of an elementary rule of conduct which would be the subject of purely speculative knowledge, cannot stand the test either of a rational critique or of the realities of the law. As for the "given" of the state of consciousness of the mass, one cannot, apart from a prejudice in favor of positive science or of a sort of religion of the folk (*Volk*), perceive the grounds entitling the mass, not just to translate or express the rule, for instance by custom, but literally to create it by a necessary identification of law and opinion. In fact, the

[32] Thus it does not suffice, as to article 1382 of the Code Napoleon, to speak of a central idea — of security or of justice, according to the interpretations — thought to be at the center of legal terms such as "human act," "fault," or "reparation"; J. Delos, *Les buts du droit*, in 3 ANNUAIRE DE L'INSTITUT INTERNATIONAL DE PHILOSOPHIE DU DROIT (1938) 38; see also 163. Neither could one characterize legal solutions in the matter of civil responsibility as "even morally exceeding the normal requirements of individual or social ethics," F. RUSSO, *op. cit.* 55, *initio*. . . [Art. 1382 of the Code Napoleon provides as follows: "Any human act whatsoever that shall cause damage to another shall oblige him by whose fault it has occurred to repair it."]

law in force does not always coincide with the state of consciousness of the mass: Between the two, a struggle prevails from which [popular] opinion does not always emerge victorious. As for natural law, one cannot well understand this "given" that is obligatory for the jurist but only "in principle," which leaves intact the faculty to judge of the exception and consequently to set aside the principle. Actually, the jurist often makes use of the permission, laying down rules "construed" according to the requirements of his own order, which is the legal order and not the order of natural law or of justice.[1]

To meet this critique, the observation is made that the "given" always implies a certain conceptual elaboration on the part of the understanding intelligence, which is more or less important according to the subject matter, yet the "given" that is thus elaborated does not for that reason merit the name of "construction." [2] A perfectly exact observation: The "given" elaborated by science still remains a "given," as has been said.[3] But contrary to what happens for the theologian, the moralist, the scholar, there is in the case of the jurist not a conceptual elaboration of something "given" — a "revealed given," a "given" of natural law, a raw fact — but a veritable "construction," which is not limited to conceptually elaborating a "given," but which elaborates its object and hence construes it.[4] The legal rule is in no way "given" in or by science, philosophy or morals. In substance as in form and down to its most essential directives, it is the product of a special elaboration which is the law's own work. Thus one can explain why the jurist may affix not only "adaptations" but also "exceptions" to what is claimed to be the legal "given" derived from nature: He is the master of his construction. No matter how "natural" a principle may be morally or socially, the jurist may have valid reasons, not indeed to contradict it, but not to let it pass as a rule in his construction.[5]

124. The Operations of the Jurist Belong to Practical Reason, Especially to Prudence. Is this to say that the operations of the jurist in construing the law (as *pragmaticus legum*) [6] may not be acts of reason?

[1] Contrary to L. Le Fur, *Règles générales du droit de la paix*, in RECUEIL DES COURS DE L'ACADÉMIE DE DROIT INTERNATIONAL DE LA HAYE (Paris, 1936) 185. . . .

[2] R.-G. RENARD, LA PHILOSOPHIE DE L'INSTITUTION (Paris, 1939) 100, n. 2: . . .

[3] See *supra*, no. 98, text and n. 4.

[4] St. Thomas compares the legislator to a weaver, COMM. POLIT., bk. III, lesson 3, and to an architect, SUMMA, *IIa IIae*, qu. 47, art. 12 *ad resp.*, *in fine*.

[5] Cf., in the same sense, Desqueyrat, *op. cit.* in LA LIBERTÉ ET LES LIBERTÉS DANS LA VIE SOCIALE, proceedings of SEMAINES SOCIALES DE FRANCE (Rouen, 1938) 184–191, *passim*.

[6] The expression comes from Vico.

Not at all; but they are acts of practical reason. Tending toward a certain end of practical order, to wit, the good organization of social relationships, the elaboration of the law depends not on speculative understanding, scientific or philosophic, but on judgment. More precisely, as the good organization of social relationships touches upon the good of human life in general, the action ordered to that end belongs essentially to prudence, at least for the substance of the rule if not for its external "make-up." If, according to the ancient definition, the subject matter of prudence is the discernment and effective realization of means most appropriate to ends (*ea quae sunt ad finem*) in the field of moral things (in *operabilibus*),[7] the task of the jurist is that of adapting to the end of the legal system the means which constitutes the legal rule.[8]

Is it not in view of this duty of his status that the lawyer is called "prudent" and that "jurisprudence" is a synonym of law? "Jurisprudence" or "legal prudence" is one of the species of the moral virtue of prudence, that which relates to legal activities, to the establishment of the legal rule and to its application to special cases.[9] For prudential reason is not confined to the disposition of single cases, to professional consultation or the decision of a lawsuit. There is the prudence of legal counsel (the Roman "prudent") and the prudence of the judge, the latter providing the origin for the [French] technical term of *jurisprudence* to designate the work of legal creation and interpretation done by the courts. But there is also a *legislative* prudence, concerning the particular action of elaboration of the general rules designed to govern individual cases.[10] This legislative prudence will guide the operations of all those who, in whatever capacity, collaborate in the building of the law; [11] it will permit them to judge concretely of means and ends, their

[7] See, in this sense, ST. THOMAS, SUMMA, *IIa IIae*, qu. 47, art. 6; also arts. 7 and 8. As opposed to prudence, which works in the domain of human *agere*, including the government of others, art and technique work in the domain of *facere*, see *supra*, nos. 98 and 99, with notes 4, 5, 7.

[8] Cf., in the same sense, ST. THOMAS, *op. cit. Ia IIae*, qu. 95, art. 3 *ad resp.*: . . .

[9] Cf. F. SENN, LES ORIGINES DE LA NOTION DE JURISPRUDENCE (Paris, 1926) 6: . . . , pp. 17–24, 27–30, 45–48.

[10] On political prudence on the part of the rulers, legislative prudence (*legispositiva*), and prudence of government (*regnativa*), see ST. THOMAS, SUMMA, *IIa IIae*, qu. 47, art. 12; qu. 48, art. 1 *ad resp.*; qu. 50, arts. 1 and 2; qu. 57, art. 1 *ad* 2.

[11] If we speak here of legislation and legislative prudence, it is understood (see *supra*, no. 99 and no. 115 n. 16) that the argument is not limited to law derived from legislative sources alone. Whatever its source — legislative, judicial, or customary — whether it derives from professional jurists or from life itself, that is, from the people, the law is prudence. There is a prudence of custom which manifests

value and their opportunity with regard to the ultimate purpose of the legal order.

One may ask if civil legislation is a matter of justice or of prudence.[12] The question is ambiguous, for one must distinguish between the content of the statute and the act of legislating. But even when the statute consecrates justice and embodies it in its content, prudence, not justice or natural law, dictates that decision to it. In the case of the directing legislator, the statute is a work of prudential reason; [13] it is a matter of justice — of legal justice — only in the case of the subjects, inasmuch as they are morally bound to obey the law.[14]

125. To Say "Prudent" Is Not to Say "Arbitrary." From saying that the law is "construed" wholly and down to its foundations [15] it does not follow that construction can take place in an arbitrary fashion or even with the freedom of artistic creation, precisely because it is a work of prudential reason. To say reason is to say submission to truth in all its forms, theoretical and practical. To say prudence is to say, a path to follow and hence a method. No doubt there remains room in the concrete work of elaboration for a certain proportion of arbitrary will. But the margin is enclosed within relatively narrow limits: Those which trace the unbreakable "given" of external realities, on the one hand, and the more supple "given" of the method of elaboration, on the other. We may also note that on reflection the idea of a "given" law no more excludes the arbitrary than that of a "construed" law includes it. All depends on the origin assigned to the "given": If the "given" is in the consciousness of the mass, or *a fortiori* in the will of the strongest, the law thus given will indeed exclude the arbitrariness of the jurist who is bound by that "given," but not that of the consciousness or will of those who created the "given."

But let us look more closely at the limits imposed upon construction.

126. The Factual Presuppositions of the Jurist's Legal Rule. The

---

itself in the spontaneous but nonetheless reflective steps of all men who make the custom; so much so that if custom is not prudent it will represent bad law.

[12] See St. Thomas, *op. cit. IIa IIae*, qu. 50, art. 1 *ad* 1. Cf. qu. 57, art. 1 *ad* 2.

[13] Save for the duty of legal justice incumbent upon the rulers to carry out what legislative prudence dictates to them.

[14] Cf., in the same sense, St. Thomas, *op. cit. IIa IIae*, qu. 50, art. 1 *ad* 1 *in fine:* . . .

[15] It will be seen farther below how it is construed, under what points of view, which will bring out the existence of two stages of construction, one of a political and social nature and one of a specifically regulatory or juridical nature; see *infra*, chap. II, nos. 131 *et seq.*, nos. 191–194.

jurist does not draw his rule *ex nihilo* [a] and he does not build it up in a vacuum. Like any rule whatsoever the law is based upon facts. By "facts," in the widest sense, we understand all realities whatsoever, no matter of what nature they may be or to what discipline they may belong, that are capable of interesting the jurist in elaborating his own system, whether as underlying, substructural facts or as surrounding, environmental facts.

This definition includes, first, the facts properly so called, that is, facts of the Is (*Sein*). These are the facts concerning man, for whom, and also by whom, the rule exists: Physiological, psychological, economic, sociological, political, historical ones; facts concerning things and nature, with which man comes in contact; facts concerning God, the author and sovereign Lord of man and creatures. All the sciences — sciences properly so called, metaphysics, theology — thus become "auxiliary sciences" of law. The truths they propose are for the jurist so many precedent "given" things which in a certain manner always bind him, whether they have the character of necessity or belong to the domain of pure accident.[16]

At the outset, the jurist will accept them as they are, being unable to change anything in them. He will even take them as points of departure of his law, by way of conditions or presuppositions, except for translating the scientific realities into concepts manageable by the use of categories, legal presumptions, and other processes of formal legal technique.[17] In this sense it is exact to say unqualifiedly: *Ex facto oritur jus*; [b] the facts are sources of law, generative elements of legal rules and solutions. For instance, that paternity is not susceptible of being established directly, at least in the present state of science; [18] that material things are divided into movables and immovables; that man is endowed with personality; that he has an instinct of sociability; that in the ranks of society there are individuals of feeble mind, and of various kinds — these are inescapable facts, for the jurist as for everybody, which entail consequences in the field of the legal discipline.

But even where facts depend upon the free will of men, facts of conduct that the jurist with his law could lay his hands on, these facts continue to be present and consequently to bind the jurist by reason of

[a] [Out of nothing.]

[16] Of course there are disputed verities, disciplines the very legitimacy of which is contested by some, such as philosophy or theology. But these problems transcend the competence of the jurist as such.

[17] See *infra*, nos. 166 *et seq.*

[b] [Law grows out of facts.]

[18] The allusion here is to progress that may result from certain new methods of investigation: blood group tests, hereditary bodily traits, etc.

their existence alone. Whether he adapts himself to them or approves them, or again claims to rectify, to correct or repress them, they *are*, and by that token they count. In this sense again the statement is true, this time in a relative manner: *Ex facto oritur jus*. Not because the law would always have to bow before the facts of conduct, since its mission is on the contrary to appraise and govern them; but because these facts can exercise an influence upon the decision to be adopted by the legislator. This is so especially for the facts constituting the social environment, which represent the surrounding air of forces, ideas, interests and wants, always moving, sometimes antagonistic, in the midst of which the law is to evolve. Now, to the extent that the facts constituting the environment are dependent upon human freedom, it is clear that the jurist, before assuming an attitude with regard to them, must endeavor to comprehend them, which presupposes knowledge and experience of that social environment.[19]

127. Moral or Technical Precepts and Existing Law as Presupposed Facts. Nor is this all. The facts composing the "given" that precedes the law embrace not merely the facts pure and simple which are objects of speculative science. They also embrace all the rules of action, without distinction between human activity (*agere, agibilia*) and technical or artistic activity (*facere, factibilia*). There exists a mass of techniques, belonging to the most varied fields: The techniques of business, of banking, of insurance; the techniques of building machines, tools and apparatus; the techniques of ocean navigation and of air navigation; medical and surgical technique; techniques of aesthetic, scientific, literary work, and of legislative work, too, etc. For the jurist, the rules, procedures, and prescriptions of the different arts or techniques are obviously given as facts. In so far as the law is concerned with technical fields the jurist is consequently bound by the "given" of the technique which will provide him with the basic elements of his construction.[20]

The same remark applies to rules of nontechnical human activity: The rule of morals or the rule of already established law (facts of the Ought (*Sollen*)). For the jurist, the moral rule is given not only as to its first principles of natural law and justice but also as to the ultimate conclusions and determinations therefrom, the product of the work of

[19] This is the whole bearing meant to be attributed to the maxim *Ex facto oritur jus*. There is no question of "canonizing" the facts without more and erecting them into law. That is the equivocal implication of Gurvitch's idea of the "normative fact," a purely empirical fact. Cf. F. Russo, *op. cit.* 50 *et seq.*

[20] See, especially as regards the technique of insurance, M. Picard, *L'affaiblissement contractuel du contrat d'assurance*, in 3 Recueil Lambert § 146, pp. 161–162.

specialists in ethics. Although those conclusions and above all the determinations are themselves in part "construed," what is thus "construed" by the moralist becomes "given" for the jurist. The same holds for existing law in relation to the work of elaboration of a new rule: For the construing jurist, the existing law, which is itself in its entirety "construed," becomes a legal "given" inasmuch as it is a historical reality. And it is quite certain that the jurist, in making his rule, could not detach himself from this historical legal "given," whether he wishes to complete or perfect, or even to reform or reverse, the existing law.

But take care to note: These latter "given" factors remain prelegal, subject to auxiliary sciences, the science of natural law and morals, the science of the existing law or of legal history. Though they may very closely touch the elaboration of the law — which precludes their being called "metajuridical" — yet they do not constitute the legal "given" of the rule to be construed. This is obvious for the preëxisting law, since by hypothesis one seeks to modify it; it is also true of the "given" of the moral rule, of natural law, and of justice. The jurist receives morals and moral solutions as "given" at their specific place and level, inasmuch as they are a moral "given." He does not have to receive them as a legal "given," that is, as a completely prepared "given" of his own rule. On this new level, he will make such use of them as is prescribed by the rule of prudence related to his special work, the work of the law to be elaborated. Sometimes, then, prudence will dictate that one sanction the moral "given," sometimes it will command a different attitude: A refusal to intervene or a new arrangement of the moral "given."

128. The Kinds of the "Given" Enumerated by Gény. This is the error, or probably rather the ambiguity or the misunderstanding, in Gény's conception: The various kinds of the "given" which he enumerates, the natural or strictly real "given," the historical "given," the rational "given," the ideal "given," corresponding to the varieties of the "given" envisaged here, are preëxistent not only to "construction" in the sense understood by Gény, but also to the legal rule itself taken in its substance. These kinds of the "given" are in reality but preceding data, each belonging to its species, i.e., scientific, technical, or moral. They figure among the elements of the problem to be resolved by the jurist. They do not furnish the solution or even the principle of the solution, which remains to be chosen and construed in its totality.[21]

[21] This is recognized by Gény without difficulty, at least for the natural or strictly real "given"; see 2 SCIENCE ET TECHNIQUE no. 167, pp. 371–376. Does he not himself speak of the "data" of positive law? See 2 *id.* heading of chap. IX, no. 166, p. 371. See, in a still more explicit manner, G. RENARD, LE DROIT, LA LOGIQUE ET LE

True, one invokes the normative character of these very data: "The moral and economic verities" would give "directions," [22] "the social life is stirred by tendencies, it seeks to attain ends" so that "social science, the study of the positive given, is already to a large part a science of norms." [23] Without failing to understand what there may be of "natural finality" in certain social realities and the consequences following therefrom on the level of the moral and economic conduct of individuals,[24] the question — always the same one — is whether the legal rule is lodged under the same roof. Duguit saw things more clearly when he distinguished the social norm — economic or moral — from the legal norm, requiring in the latter the distinctive sign of a particular "reaction," [25] which in our view is the effect of the prudential judgment of the jurist. To pass over that judgment, claiming that the norm is given in the social reality, is to deprive the legal system of all autonomy, all specific existence.

129. The "Given" of the Method of Elaboration of the Law. But what is given above all, outside of the precedent facts, is a method of elaboration of the law, consisting of certain principles evolved by philosophical reflection or legal philosophy. Different from the *solutions*, which in every case are determined by (legislative juridical) prudence, the *method* is given by science, a science turned toward action since we are concerned with elaborating the law, but a science made up of general, universal principles, which prudence has, precisely, to apply to particular cases. By definition, the principles of that science bind the construing jurist in a necessary, absolute fashion, with no possible derogation of any sort. In the absence of a juridical natural law, there thus exists a *natural legal method*, representing the permanent and invariable principles that preside over the elaboration of the law.[26] This method the legislator must follow; this method, too, the judge must follow to the extent that he has to "act as a legislator" (see Swiss Civil Code, article

---

BON SENS (Paris, 1925) 14; LE DROIT, L'ORDRE ET LA RAISON 139 . . . ; LA THÉORIE DE L'INSTITUTION 48–55, 65–66; LA PHILOSOPHIE DE L'INSTITUTION 30–33, 103–104.

[22] F. Gény as quoted above, no. 110.

[23] Formula of F. RUSSO, *op. cit.* 51.

[24] This conception is basic to the notion of natural law, a rule deriving from the nature of things, that nature being understood moreover in a sense transcending pure empiricism; see *infra*, nos. 203–205.

[25] L. Duguit as quoted above, no. 107.

[26] In this sense — of method and not of solution — must apparently be understood the "rational or scientific law" of LE FUR, LES GRANDS PROBLÈMES DU DROIT (Paris, 1937) 181, n. 1 and citations; equally so the "notion of law" of BONNECASE, INTRODUCTION AU DROIT no. 138, pp. 217–218 . . .

1),[c] whether in the absence of a formally enacted law or in using such discretionary powers as the laws leave with him. The law is prudence and consequently, on the part of him who makes laws, it is action. Yet neither that prudence nor that action is blind. They are preceded by knowledge, particularly knowledge of the field, the end, and the conditions of the action. In this sense, it was possible to write without paradox: "The law is not a science, yet there is a science of the law,"[27] of established law and of the law to be established. The jurist who has to "construe" the rule will begin by respecting the "given" of the rules that govern his own activity: That is the first, preliminary duty of legislative prudence.[28]

What, then, are the laws of legal elaboration? This will be studied systematically in the following chapter.

130. The "Given" of Facts and of Method: The Idea of the "Construed." A last objection confronts us, which will permit us to state more precisely the import of the conclusions of the present chapter. It may be formulated as follows: If the prudence of the jurist must be guided by the "given" of the social facts, on the one hand, and the "given" of the legal method on the other, is not the margin of indeterminacy narrowed down to the point where the pretended "construed" is ultimately reduced to a "given"? The observation will seem to be strengthened if one reflects that among the ways left to the choice of prudence, some are indicated as preferable by reason of better adaptation, which it is precisely for prudence to discern. Now is not to discern that which is more clearly indicated, in effect to know?

We may answer, first, that the twofold determination, of the facts and of the method, does not preclude the indeterminateness of the solutions which, within the framework outlined, are left to the free arbitrament by the prudent; further, that despite the existence of better adapted and therefore preferable means, freedom of choice is far from suppressed, for it is always a matter "of affairs that imply more or less debate and counsel."[29] Let us also recall that the arbitrament of prudence is not arbitrary and that a solution chosen, construed, is not a solution

[c] [Art. 1 of the Swiss Civil Code provides as follows: "The statute applies to all legal questions for which it expressly or constructively provides. If no provision can be gathered from the statute the judge shall decide according to customary law or, where such is lacking as well, according to the rule he himself would lay down as a legislator. In so doing he follows tried doctrine and tradition."]

[27] G. Cornil in the study cited *supra*, Part I chap. II sec. 1, n. 4.

[28] See, in the same sense as concerns moral prudence, ST. THOMAS, SUMMA, *Ia IIae*, qu. 47, art. 3 *ad resp.*: . . . See also art. 6 *ad resp.*, *in fine*.

[29] Cf. ST. THOMAS, *op. cit. Ia IIae*, qu. 47, art. 2 *ad* 3: . . . See also art. 4 *ad* 2.

deprived of a real foundation: The choice is always reasonable, objectively well founded. We maintain only that the content of the solution is in no way given as a truth of speculative science: To discern it is not to see it as true but to adjudge it good, opportune and, in this sense, just. This gives to the conclusions of prudence a character of only relative certainty. One is never absolutely sure that the way chosen by the legislator, the norm adopted by him, is the good or only good one, while a solution given by science would partake of at least approximate, if not absolute, certainty, which is the appurtenance of the scientific truths.[30]

CHAPTER II

THE GUIDING PRINCIPLES OF THE ELABORATION OF THE LAW

Introduction

131. The End of the Law and of Its Processes of Realization. In order to discover the guiding principles of the elaboration of the law, one has to ask one's self, first, toward what end does the legal rule tend? and secondly, by what processes is it called upon to realize itself, in its existence and in its execution? This follows from the idea of construction. If the law is a work of construction, it could be elaborated, in itself and in what it orders, only in view of a certain end,[1] in relation to which it plays the rôle of means,[2] and thanks to an equipment which has itself properties of a technical nature. Legal prudence is essentially subject to these considerations of end and equipment, outside of which the legal rule, like everything construed, would be deprived of meaning. Nor is any distinction to be made according to the sources of the law or the capacity

[30] See, in this sense, on prudence, St. Thomas, *op. cit. Ia IIae*, qu. 47, art. 3 *ad* 2; on human laws, *Ia IIae*, qu. 91, art. 3 *ad* 3, art. 4 *ad resp.* (*secundo*); qu. 96, art. 1 *ad* 3. Cf. G. Renard, Le droit, l'ordre et la raison 139–140.

[1] See, in the same sense, St. Thomas, Summa theologica, *Ia IIae* qu. 95, art. 3 *ad resp.*: . . . ; equally qu. 96, art. 1 *ad resp.*, *initio*. Cf. Jhering, Der Zweck im Recht (3d ed. 1898, transl. by Meulenaere, 1901, under the misleading title L'Évolution du droit), which is epitomized by: "Purpose is the creator of the entire law." [The first volume of Jhering's work was translated by I. Husik as The Law as a Means to an End (New York, 1913).] Others speak of value (understood in an objective sense); thus R. Bonnard, *L'origine de l'ordonnancement juridique*, in Mélanges Maurice Hauriou 58 *et seq.*

[2] St. Thomas, Comm. Polit., bk. IV, lesson 7: . . .

of the persons who participate in legal work. The method of elaboration is the same whether the rule proceeds directly from the statute or indirectly from the courts by way of decisions, whether it emanates from specialists, as statute and case law, or simply from the people, as custom.[3] Always and everywhere one has to respect the laws of the work to be accomplished, failing which the work will be bad or defective.

132. The Instrumental Character of the Legal Rule Differentiates It from the Moral Rule. Let us note this at once: The instrumental character of the law expresses a fundamental difference between law and morals. Notwithstanding the classical definition of the good act (*conveniens medium quo perveniatur ad finem ultimum*),[a] it would be wrong to present the moral rule, even the positive moral rule laid down by an external authority, as a mere means with a view to an end, "a technique of obtaining our full beatitude," as one author puts it. In reality, the moral law, natural or positive, confines itself to translating the requests of the one and only morality, and it translates them as true, without preoccupation with extrinsic finality. "The honesty of an act is one thing, its 'utility' is another, even that spiritual utility by which it yields us the supreme beatitude." [4] No doubt, in conforming to the law, man will arrive at his happiness: The *bene vivere* engenders the *beata vita*.[b] But this eudemonism must be rightly understood. What constitutes the value of morals, and therefore justifies it and makes it binding, is not immediately the beatitude to which it leads as to its goal, and still less as to its rewards; the rational and obligatory value of morals resides in morals itself, inasmuch as it renders explicit what is good and bad with regard to reasonable human nature, the latter being conceived in relation to the natural and supernatural end of man. Morals truly *pursues* no result, no good, not even the moral good: It *fuses* with the moral good, expressing its requirements and conveniences.

The legal rule on the contrary exists in view of a distinct and superior end, which it could quite well fail to attain, which could be attained also in other ways, so that a question may always be raised as to the utility of its provisions or even of its intervention at all in the particular case. It has value as a means and in so far as it realizes the end, the end of the

[3] There are bad customs, with regard to the end of the law, just as there may be bad statutes or bad decisions. There may also be inapplicable customs, due to lack of adaptation to the technical equipment of application.

[a] [The convenient means by which one may arrive at the ultimate end.]

[4] J. TONNEAU in 5 BULLETIN THOMISTE, no. 9 (1939) 604. See equally A. VALENSIN, TRAITÉ DE DROIT NATUREL, vol. 1: LES PRINCIPES (Paris, 1922) 92–98: . . .

[b] [Living in goodness engenders the happy life.]

law. The law is utilitarian, morals is not.[5] The legal rule is subordinate to a system which has itself the value of an instrument: The system of the temporal public good, the state's end and reason of being — while the moral rule, deduced from man, returns to man, the supreme value, to whom it indicates and prescribes the necessary conditions of his vocation as man.

133. The Moral Rule Is Not Concerned with Processes of Realization. Nor is the moral rule dependent upon the technique of any equipment whatsoever of formulation and realization. It is nature, enlightened by reason, that dictates the duty, and it is everybody's conscience, under the inspiration of prudence, that on its own account interprets the dictate of nature.[6] Now the voice of nature and the voice of conscience do not need to reveal themselves through the interpreter of the "formal sources," the concepts, the words, the processes indispensable to the manifestation of an external rule given to man by man. On the other hand, the man who transgresses the laws of morals is responsible for his shortcomings only before his conscience and God (internal forum) and not at all before a human tribunal deciding according to certain indispensable rules of procedure and evidence. From that it follows that in the field of morals the form never checks the substance, and no formal condition could arrest or limit the play of the natural law. This is so even where the precept should have formed the object of a positive (moral) rule. Never is the subject permitted to argue that due to the formal imperfection of the positive enactment he may claim to be freed from any rule. In the absence of the external rule of morality, the internal rule subsists, preserving its power to obligate.

The legal rule on the contrary exists and binds only within the framework of its context, if not the literal, at least the conceptual, one. Outside of this context, which circumscribes the precept more or less widely or by reference to a norm of another kind, moral or technical, the subject preserves his freedom in law.[7] This, precisely, is why the interventions

[5] On the notion of the "purpose of the law," cf. J. Delos, *Le but du droit*, in 3 ANNUAIRE DE L'INSTITUT INTERNATIONAL DU DROIT ET DE SOCIOLOGIE JURIDIQUE (1938) 29–39.

[6] This is not to say that the natural moral law has no legislator. He is God, the author of nature, who promulgates His law *ex hoc ipso quod (Deus) eam mentibus hominum inseruit naturaliter cognoscendam* [by its very insertion (by God) as something that may be known by the minds of men], ST. THOMAS, *op. cit. Ia IIae*, qu. 90, art. 4 *ad* 1.

[7] This is not to say — which is another question — that any conflict of interests not provided for by a law or another formal source would have to remain without a solution. In the relations among private individuals, at the very least, the judge may not refuse to judge, see Code Napeolon, art. 4 [which provides: "The judge

of the law can be useful or efficacious only on the condition that they respect the laws of the structure and the machinery of the legal apparatus by which they are realized.

SUBDIVISION I. THE END OF THE LEGAL ORDINANCE: THE TEMPORAL PUBLIC GOOD

134. "Lex est Ordinatio ad Bonum Commune." If law is consubstantial with the idea of society,[1] the end of the legal rule could only be the end of the society itself, to wit, the common good. And since in the case of the society of the state the common good means the public common good, the rôle of the legal rule is to determine conduct from the viewpoint of the public good: *Lex est ordinatio ad bonum commune.*[a] [2]

This definition, in the traditional philosophical doctrine of laws or rules, is appropriate for all kinds of rules, including the moral rule.[3] But whereas for the moral rule the common good envisioned is that of the moral human nature common to all men,[4] for the rules of groups or of social discipline, such as the law, the common good in question is that which determines the social purpose of the group envisaged, in our particular case, the public good.[5] Politics and law thus join in the same

---

who shall refuse to render judgment on the pretext that the statute is silent, obscure or insufficient may be proceeded against for denial of justice"]. At this point, the question is one of the measure of the legal obligations of the subjects.

[1] See *supra*, nos. 8–12.

[a] [The law is an ordinance for the common good.]

[2] St. Thomas, Summa, *Ia IIae*, qu. 90, art. 4: *Lex "nihil aliud est quam quaedam rationis ordinatio ad bonum commune ab eo qui curam communitatis habet promulgata."* [A law "is nothing else than an ordinance of reason for the common good, promulgated by him who has care of the community."] See also art. 2. This is the guiding motif of the whole Thomist treatment of the law; it recurs many times as basic to the argument.

[3] See, on the *lex aeterna* [eternal law] which governs "the total community which is the universe," qu. 91, art. 1 *ad resp.*; qu. 93, art. 1 *ad* 1; and on the natural law, which is instituted *ad bonum commune naturae* [for the common good of nature], qu. 94, art. 3 *ad* 1.

[4] See, on moderation . . . , St. Thomas, *op. cit. Ia IIae*, qu. 94, art. 3 *ad* 1. Also, man is a political animal, and hence the moral law itself could not disregard that character. See, in this sense, St. Thomas, *Ia IIae*, qu. 90, art. 2 *ad resp.*: . . .

[5] See, on human laws, St. Thomas, Summa, *Ia IIae*, qu. 95, art. 4 *ad resp.*: . . . Elsewhere the reference is to the "common good of the multitude," qu. 96, art. 3 *ad resp.*; the "common good" alone, qu. 95, art. 3 *ad resp.*, *in fine*; qu. 96, art. 1 *ad resp.*, art. 3 *ad resp.*; *IIa IIae*, qu. 58, art. 5 *ad resp.*, *in fine*; "human utility," qu. 97, art. 1 *ad resp.* and *ad* 3, art. 2 *ad resp.*; "common welfare," qu. 95, art. 3 *ad resp.*; qu. 96, art. 6 *ad resp.* But, as the context shows, this is always the common good of the commonwealth, the complex of individuals grouped in the commonwealth (*communitas civitatis*).

end. More exactly, inasmuch as politics is the science and art of the public good,[6] the legal rule is at the service of politics, and the prudence that presides over the elaboration of the law, or legislative prudence,[7] is a part of political prudence.

Section 1. Concept and Characteristics of the Temporal Public Good

135. Definition of the Adjective "Public": That Which Concerns the Public. The notion of "public" good is not less awkward to define for all its indispensability. This is due to the variety of its aspects and also the almost inextricable connection of the individual and the social.

First of all, concerning the "public" element, we deal with the good of the members of the state-society when they are taken together, putting aside the good of the component individuals and groups or even the sum total of such goods. The immediate subject destined to be the beneficiary of the public good is the public in general, i.e., everybody without reference to individuals, social categories, and particular communities, taking account, too, both of the present and of future generations.[1] Just as there exists a "public" opinion, a "public" spirit, a "public" sentiment, which are the opinion, spirit, or sentiment of the public, so there exists a "public" interest or "public" good which is the interest and good of the public. The "whole" of the public does not, however, constitute an entity separate from the component individuals or groups, whether in a substantial or even an accidental fashion; it does not imply, as such, any unity of order, any moral personality. The public simply represents the mixed, motley crowd, the undetermined and undifferentiated mass of individuals and groups, the multitude as opposed to the individuals and groups considered one by one or by adding their mere units.

This public must not, however, be confused with the state itself, which is the association constituted by the individuals with a view precisely to the good of the public. The state, as an association, is a moral person; [2] the public, as such, although its good is the end of the state, is

[6] Often, politics is taken in the sense of the play of political forces, that is, forces fighting for the possession of power. In that case, the law clearly does not serve these forces but on the contrary has the mission to regulate them; see, e.g., F. Russo, *op. cit.* 161. But this is not the philosophical and traditional definition of politics.

[7] See *supra*, no. 124.

[1] On the multiplicity of the community, cf. St. Thomas, *op. cit.*, *Ia IIae*, qu. 96, art. 1 *ad resp.*

[2] On the moral personality of the state, see J. Dabin, Doctrine générale de l'Etat nos. 63 *et seq.*, pp. 97 *et seq.*

not a moral person. Thus the expression "public good" is superior to that of "common good": It not only specifies that the community whose good is in question is the public, i.e., plenary, community (as opposed to particular communities), but it also escapes the equivocation resulting from the use of the term "community," which may signify either the unorganized community, i.e., the public, or the organized community, i.e., the state. The public is not the state since the state-society is at the service of the public; it is the unorganized community or rather, because the idea of community is superfluous, it is everybody, in the sense of the global mass of the individuals outside of any idea of organization and corporation (which finds its realization in the state).

136. The Public Good from a Formal Point of View. From the formal point of view, what the public requires as its own good, what is specifically the good of all without distinction, is a sum total of general conditions under the protection of which the legitimate activities of everyone within the public may be exercised and developed comfortably. Action is the immediate concern of the particular individuals, who are never relieved of the task of themselves providing, within the limits of their abilities — isolated or associated — for the necessities of their lives in all fields (supplementary character of the state in relation to society). At least they may rightfully demand of the state, instituted to this end, that it take care to provide them with the maintenance of an environment — psychological, moral, legal. technical; conceptions. mores, institutions — that is propitious to action and that guarantees the results of action. Thus the public good, like the public itself, is essentially intermediary: The environment it creates is, for the individuals and groups who are the substantial elements of the public, a means by which better to attain their ends. Left to themselves, in a hostile environment or without any framework, they would not arrive at the "perfect sufficiency of life." [3] They would have trouble in acquiring or guarding their own good. The state comes to their aid and serves them through the public good and all the institutions of "public services."

137. The Constitutive Elements of the Public Good: Order, Coördination, Aid. Interpreted in this fashion, the public good presupposes, in the first place, the establishment and maintenance of a certain order in society, generating security and confidence. How would the activities and the very life of the public be possible if the social surroundings

[3] ST. THOMAS, POLITICS, bk. I, lesson 1: . . .

were at the prey of violence, brutal or insidious (in the form of abuse of power), of faithlessness, and of fraud? Here there are general preceding obstacles, the elimination of which in all appropriate ways falls to the competence of the state. It will attain this, particularly, by the organization of a police force charged with preventing and repressing disorder, by the establishment of tribunals charged with adjudging controversies, and by the promulgation of fixed rules in the public and private fields. To make order, law, justice reign within the community is the primordial duty of the state, corresponding to the primordial need of the public. It will be appropriate, too, to inquire how that order, that law, that justice must be conceived in order to be in accord with the very idea of the state and of a rule proceeding from the state.[4] For the moment we confine ourselves to bearing in mind the necessity, felt by the public, of a certain discipline inimical to chaos and arbitrariness, regulative and protective of the rights of each and all.

The liberal school [a] claimed to keep to this stage of negative intervention,[5] refusing to admit that the freedom of the individuals in their so-called private activities could ever be touched in any manner whatever by the state, whether in the form of regulations or in that of subsidies. But one has become aware that in a complex civilization the public good has other enemies than external disorder, to wit, the dispersion of efforts in unregulated competition. On reflection, the life of men, of each man in particular and of humanity in general, can be traced to a perpetual exchange of services, subject to the law of productivity and of equilibrium. Now dispersion prevents productivity and causes a disequilibrium. Hence the necessity of a certain reasoned coördination, a certain adjustment, which is in the interest of the mass of exchanges and therefore within the competence of the state which is set up over the common interest.[6]

Finally, private individuals or subordinate groups are often in need

[4] This problem will be examined further below, nos. 145 *et seq.*

[a] [In the Continental sense of the term, often found in Catholic writers, denoting doctrines of extreme individualism.]

[5] According to a formula alleged to be inspired by the doctrine of Kant in his First Metaphysical Principles of the Theory of Law (1797), the purpose of the law, and therefore of society, is to assure the coexistence of the freedom of everyone with the freedom of all.

[6] Does it have to be added that the realization of this program, which after all implies the collaboration of the subjects, cannot be accomplished without the education of the public? Moral education, which falls especially to the moral authorities; technical education (e.g., with a view to coördination in economic matters, or in matters of road traffic), where the rôle of the state will be more direct, if not exclusive.

of more concrete aid open to all "commoners" once they fulfill its conditions. Certain works that are beyond individual capacities, in the material or the spiritual sphere (communications, sanitation, instruction, culture, etc.), require the collaboration of the state, which is more powerful and better equipped than particular individuals in isolation or grouped in free associations. If a "service" has the characteristic of necessity or urgency with regard to the public good, the state will even be qualified to assume its management so as to replace impotent or insufficient private initiative.

But in any situation, whether presiding over order, coördinating, or providing aid (sometimes to particular individuals), the state has in view the particular good of no one, no individual, no category or class. Even where it protects the rights and interests of individuals and groups within the community, it is the general, impersonal good of the members of the community that motivates, or ought to motivate, its proceedings.

138. The Public Good Covers All Human Values of the Temporal Order. With respect to its content, the public good from its own angle embraces the totality of values of human interest. Whether one considers the good of bodies or the good of minds or souls, economic or extra-economic activities, egoistic or altruistic tendencies, order, coördination, and aid are always useful, in variable measure and more or less efficacious according to the fields. There is but one exception: The religious good, considered under the peculiarly religious aspect, falls within the competence of another society, equally public within its sphere, the religious society. That is why one speaks more precisely of the temporal public good, as opposed to a spiritual or religious public good. To the extent, however, to which religion merges with the temporal, the state regains its competence to maintain a temporal environment favorable to the specifically religious public and private good. In this sense, there exists a religious public good of the temporal sphere.

Hence, according to the kind of interest envisaged, the public good comprises a series of aspects (closely allied, by the way), of which the principal ones are: The economic public good, relating to economic life (production, distribution, consumption of wealth); the moral public good, relating to moral life (virtues and vices); the intellectual public good, relating to education and culture; and the physical or physiological public good, aiming at health, hygiene, sports, etc.[7] From another point of view, one discerns an individual public good devoted to the

[7] The ancient writers distinguished between goods that are honest, useful, and delectable: the public good covers those three kinds of goods. Cf. St. Thomas, Summa, *Ia IIae*, qu. 92, art. 1 *ad resp.*

values that perfect the individual, and beside it a collective, social, communal public good aiming at the development of the population in numbers, in quality, and in the spirit of union and sacrifice: This is the element of the public good which has to do with the collective values, with the greatness and prosperity of nations.

At the service of the different categories of the public good the civil society or state takes its place as the instrumentality to realize them, which gives rise to a new aspect of the public good — the peculiarly political public good, relating to the state itself, its constitution, organization, and functioning. It is indeed evident that the public good will be the better served the better the group established to this end is able to fulfill its mission. In this sense, the political society and its good constitute the first of the elements of the public good, at least in principle, in the sphere of execution (if not of intention).[8] Now the efficiency value of the state implies a series of conditions, of a moral and technical order. These depend both upon the people, whence the state draws its substance, and upon the management of the public authority, above all of the agencies charged with laying down and applying the legal rule.[9]

139. Domestic and International Public Good. Mutatis mutandis, bearing in mind that states are only moral persons and not material beings and also that they are only ephemeral formations whereas the individual is made for eternity, one may transfer to the international order the notions that have just been developed for the domestic order. There exists an international public good, which consists likewise in a

[8] In the sphere of execution and not of intention, since the state, and therefore the political public good, is an instrument related to the public good at large, which is that of the underlying community. And on the other hand it is quite clear that in its specifically political action the state remains subject to the general principles of morality: the end does not justify the means.

[9] If the law must be elaborated as a function of the political régime (in the sense of the form of government: republic or monarchy, democracy or aristocracy), that is so inasmuch as the political régime as established constitutes one of the elements of the political public good and therefore of the public good at large. But it would be wrong to take the political régime for the directing principle of elaboration not only of the political but of the civil laws; cf., in that sense, MONTESQUIEU, DE L'ESPRIT DES LOIS, bks. V–VII. Also: ST. THOMAS, SUMMA, *Ia IIae*, qu. 100, art. 2, referring to Aristotle. Whatever the régime may be, the norm of the law is the public good. The régime may well influence the mode of producing the formal sources of the law (which is all that is meant by the text of ST. THOMAS, *op. cit. Ia IIae*, qu. 95, art. 4 *ad resp., tertio*), but not their content (save inasmuch as the maintenance of the established régime is one of the elements of the public good). The discussion here, by the way, concerns the political and not the social régime, which may legitimately intervene in the determination of distributive justice, based upon proportional equality; see *infra*, no. 234.

certain order, a harmonization of efforts, a common aid in all fields falling within the competence of states, i.e., that public good which they are obligated to provide, each on its own account, for their individual members. Equally, in the service of the international public good there ought to exist an international political organism — preferably a society of states — playing a rôle analogous to (not identical with) that of the state in relation to the domestic public good.

140. Political and Other Values of the Temporal Order. But let us return to the domestic public good, for which it still is less difficult to sketch a synthesis than it is for the international public good. The existence of a specifically political public good, which is the good of the state as an organ, does not preclude politics from having for its objective the public good in general without any exclusion of fields. To preach "separations" or simply distinctions between politics on the one hand and economics, morality, culture, health, etc., on the other, on the pretended ground that these matters are of a private order and therefore do not fall under politics, is to make a great mistake. First, economics, morality, culture, health are not exclusively of a private order. To the extent that individual activities are outwardly manifested, they impinge upon the public by way of incidence or radiation; economics, morality, health, culture, originally and by nature private values, take on a public character, thus opening the way to the competence of politics, the appointed guardian of the public good. Furthermore, the separation or distinction between the political order and other supposed parallel orders destroys the very concept of politics by abolishing its reason for being. Politics in effect has no other reason for being than from the angle of the public good to govern or, if you will, serve the external human activities that are exerted according to their own objectives, economic, moral, sanitary, cultural. Politics and its agent, the state, have no meaning but with a view to order, coördination, and, in short, to propitious environment in all sectors of the temporal domain.

What is exact — it has already been noted — is that the state does not have to take charge, either directly or through the intermediary of organisms dependent upon it in law or in fact, of these different sectors in such a way as to dispossess the individuals and groups thereof, precisely because its rôle in principle is only to guide and motivate and not to manage. The state does not have to make reality of economics or culture any more than of morality or health: These goods are realized only in and by the individuals. Incumbent upon the state is only the making reality of politics, which by the means peculiar to politics will permit the individuals on their account to attain the goods of economics, morality, health, and culture. The state will therefore beware of managing economics or culture, which are the business of the individuals and groups and not of their rulers or officials. But it will have an economic policy, a cultural policy, a policy of morality and of health, by which it will attempt to diagnose and then to translate into facts the requirements of the public good in these different fields.

141. Need for a Philosophy of Values to Discern the Requirements of the Public Good. However, the spheres of human values which the public good covers are not of equal rank, and thus the state will have to take sides. A needless choice, if there were always a means to give satisfaction concurrently and fully to economic and moral, corporal and spiritual, individual and collective, especially political and social, values. Now, whatever has been pretended, in practice these values are often antagonistic. Who will deny that too exclusive preoccupation with material wealth, health, or physical strength conflicts with the true good of the human person? — that excessive care for the collective values runs the risk of compromising the legitimate prerogatives of individuals? — that immoderate devotion to the power of the state as a political organism is prejudicial to the national economy and, above all, to political honesty?

Man is one and his destiny unique, so a synthesis is certainly possible, but only by means of balances and sometimes of breakings which presuppose recognition of a hierarchy of values. Is the spirit superior to matter? Does the individual human being win out over the collectivity, people or nation? Does the state exist for society, or vice versa? Where are the perishable values and those that do not die? For if there are values that do not die, they must take first place even on earth. The world outlook (*Weltanschauung*) is involved, and the choice will necessarily influence politics, its orientations and its concept. The state will then be seen to pursue a materialist or a spiritualist policy, a collectivist or a "personalist" policy, a policy which deifies the state or one which makes it subservient to society.[10] Even where the state, pretending to be neutral between the doctrines, would affirm that it refuses to choose, it would not cease to choose, on pain of condemning itself to inaction and ultimately of negating itself.

[10] Aristotle repeatedly, ETHICS, bk. V, and POLITICS, bks. III and V, speaks of cities founded with a view to wealth, pleasure, liberty, power. In the same way, St. Thomas contrasts régimes (i.e., states) oriented toward the true good, which is the common good regulated according to divine justice (the honest good), with régimes oriented toward the relative good, i.e., the useful or delectable or even the good contrary to divine justice, SUMMA, *Ia IIae*, qu. 92, art. 1 *ad resp.*

To be sure, rulers, untrue to the logic of their principles, do not always follow the policy of their philosophy; and one must congratulate oneself on that if the latter is false or ruinous. To be sure, also, from different ideologies there may sometimes emerge identical solutions (although of different spirit), such as a family policy based sometimes on demographic, "natalistic" considerations and sometimes on arguments of morals and law. Hence, on the immediately practical level, men of realistic sense will meet notwithstanding the divergence of initial conceptions. But the choice cannot be indefinitely eluded. There always comes a moment when the state is led to pronounce itself, in deeds, if not in words. In what sense?

142. Our Philosophy of Values. The answer, inspired by reason and conforming to Christian traditions, may be summarized in three points: Primacy of the spirit over matter (and by "spirit" we understand not only the intellectual values but above all the moral values: Virtue and character); prevalence of the individual human person over every collectivity; subordination of the state-society to society pure and simple. Not that only the spirit should count in man; but the spirit ought never to be sacrificed to matter, which moreover ought to be regulated and sublimated by the spirit.[11] Not that the individual human person could do without the various earthly communities, private and public; but these communities do not constitute ultimate ends, they are themselves, each in its way, established to perfect the individual persons.[12] As for the state, it must be maintained in its rank as the servant of the public good, that is, ultimately of the present and future individuals and groups who form the public: The state exists but by them and for them; it ought to bestow the effectively produced public good upon them by way of distribution.

143. Primarily Moral Character of the Notion of the Public Good. This necessity of a connection with a doctrine of man or, as one says today, a philosophy of (human) values confers an essentially moral character upon the notion of the public good, whatever philosophy may be adopted and however immoral it may be. Despite its intermediary character, the public good is not a merely technical thing because on all levels it is closely related to a certain conception of human ends. This is not to say that it knows no peculiarly technical solutions. For there are many techniques among the matters to which it applies, such

[11] Cf., in this sense, St. Thomas, Summa, *Ia IIae*, qu. 92, art. 1: . . .

[12] Thus the public good prevails over the private good only when it belongs to the same order: . . . St. Thomas, Summa, *IIa IIae*, qu. 152, art. 4 *ad* 3.

as automobile traffic, organization of markets, factories; and even in moral matters the corresponding measures of public good may take on a technical character, as in the fight against prostitution, drunkenness, gambling, and other manifestations of public immorality. In speaking of "good," indeed, one speaks not only of ends but also of means more or less proximate, more or less efficacious in arriving at the ends. Now the means, as such, have a technical character.[13] Still a technique applied to the service of man brings into play principles that touch man, his life and his supreme good.

No more should one pretend to reason from the formal character of the elements of the public good. If the public good tends to introduce order, coördination, and aid in social life, it is clear that these values are not just "for all useful ends," that they imply a direction which is itself determined by a philosophy. On the one hand, the public good is necessary — as a means — because order, coördination, and aid are in all fields the indispensable conditions of the progress of humanity. On the other hand, all politics hangs on something "mystic," i.e., something absolute — an authentic absolute, or something relative built up to an absolute.

144. Relativity of the Applications of the Idea of the Public Good. From that double observation no one should conclude that the public good is not affected with relativity. On the contrary, it is very much so affected, in its concrete applications of ends and means, by reason of psychological, historical, geographical contingencies which furnish the framework and often the subject matter for solutions of the public good. This poses the problem of a science of the public good, the social public good, the peculiarly political public good. To what extent does such a science exist or is it possible?

No doubt there exists a general science of the public good which is devoted to the study of the concept of the public good and is therefore a philosophical science, the most important part of political philosophy. To that science belong the preceding explanations. Penetrating farther, on the side of determinations, one can also recognize the existence of a *special* science of the social and political public good, capable of bringing up solutions of the public good evolved in the light of experience and history. Yet such solutions will always be merely elementary. For instance, it is impossible to say in advance, relying upon scientific conclusions, that the public good requires such and such a form of economic organization or of political régime, valuable in themselves, always and

[13] On the distinction between the two types of legal "constructions" (viz., of legal solutions), ethical as against technical, cf. F. Russo, *op. cit.* 44–45.

everywhere, without regard to contingencies. To political prudence rather than to the science of abstract types must be left the care and responsibility for the concrete solutions of the public good.

The more so as often there is pressure of time, circumstances are abnormal, wisdom tells one to seek the lesser of evils, which will entail certain momentary reversals in the hierarchy of values. The sphere of execution will take precedence over the sphere of intention. And if intention is for the greater part cognizable by science, execution falls solely to prudence (always reserving the rights of morality).

SECTION 2. The TEMPORAL PUBLIC GOOD AS NORM OF THE POSITIVE CONTENT OF THE LAW

145. The Temporal Public Good Differs from Morals; Intersections. By its peculiar objective, which is to dispose and to command, the rôle of the legal rule is thus to order the relationships between men according to the special and shifting requirements of the public good.[1] This is the basic difference between law and morals, which contains and entails all others: While morals prescribes to individual human beings what is the good of human nature and consequently their own good in the domain of mores, on the level of reasonable human activity, including the sector of politics, the law regulates the conduct of individuals, groups, and states as a function of the end of the state-society (or international society), to wit, the public good, in all domains of the temporal order, including the domain of morality.[2] One sees the intersections. On the one hand, morality becomes a matter of public interest inasmuch as politics is charged with providing by adequate measures for the formation of an environment favorable to virtue. On the other hand, the public

[1] The following may be cited as fine syntheses of the argument: . . . ST. THOMAS, IN ETHIC., bk. V, less. 2. Also: SUMMA, *Ia IIae*, qu. 90, art. 2 *ad resp., in medio*. SUMMA THEOLOGICA, *Ia IIae*, qu. 98, art. 1: The end of human laws is the temporal tranquillity of the commonwealth, at which they arrive by repressing external acts which may trouble the peaceful condition of the commonwealth; the end of divine laws on the contrary is to conduct men to eternal felicity.

[2] Cf. Portalis, *Discours préliminaire (au projet de Code civil de la Commission)*, no. 26, in LOCRÉ, LA LÉGISLATION CIVILE, COMMERCIALE ET CRIMINELLE DE LA FRANCE (Bruxelles, 1836) 161, col. 2: . . . See also MONTESQUIEU, DE L'ESPRIT DES LOIS, bk. XXVI, chap. 9, paras. 2–3 (ed. Garnier, p. 440). For a more thorough study, see J. Dabin, *Règle morale et règle juridique. Essai de comparaison systématique*, in ANNALES DE DROIT ET DE SCIENCE POLITIQUE (Louvain, 1936) 135–139. Wrongly, R. Bonnard, *L'origine de l'ordonnancement juridique*, in MÉLANGES HAURIOU 72–74, assigns as ideal to morals "the fulness of the individual being" and to the law "the fulness of the social being" . . .

good becomes a matter of morality inasmuch as the political nature of man enjoins him to fulfill his duties as a member of the state and a collaborator in the public good.[3] But two things remain. First, the determination of the necessities, utilities, and conveniences of the public good, in the sphere of ends as in that of means, falls professionally to the state and not to morals. Second, it is for the state and not for morals to decide upon the legal solutions most capable of bringing about concrete results for the public good; for there is a branch of politics relating to legislation — legal politics — which constitutes one of the most important parts of politics in general.

146. The Norm of the Public Good Governs All Branches of the Law. The norm of the public good dominates all branches of the law, private and public, municipal and international. This is an obvious truth for public and administrative law, whose immediate subject matter is precisely the political, *res publica.* On the one hand, the state, its constitution, its functioning, can be regulated only in accordance with the best efficiency of the state as an instrument of the public good. On the other hand, as to the relationships between the state and its members, the contributions and sacrifices which life in the state imposes upon the citizens can have no other measure than that public good which is their reason for being and the reason for the existence of the state. Even the distribution of the public good among the individual members of the state can take place only under reservation of the principle of the public good, whose realm extends to distributive justice as well as to legal or social justice.[4] Similarly, international law is based upon the international public good, which includes the good of the states themselves taken together and the good of their individual members in so far as they are called upon to enter into international relations.

147. Private Law and the Public Good. What is important to emphasize, however, is that despite appearances the norm of the public good also presides over the elaboration of municipal private law. To be sure, private law is the rule which, governing the relationships between private individuals and groups, defines the rights and duties of everyone with regard to the others. But it does not follow that that definition should be formed exclusively or even primarily from the viewpoint of

[3] This is the moral duty of legal justice, which will be studied *infra,* nos. 235 *et seq.*

[4] On the subordination of distributive justice, which is particular justice, to legal justice, which is general (relating to the public good), see J. DABIN, DOCTRINE GÉNÉRALE DE L'ETAT, no. 272.

the particular good of the individuals or groups. The law that is called private is private as to the sphere of relationships it governs; it is public, or rather — to avoid any confusion with the subject matter of public law or politics — it is social,[5] not only as to its function but also as to its content. This means, no doubt, that in the regulation of private relationships the law that is called private will safeguard "public policy and public morals" (which in a technical sense represent certain elementary requirements of the public good); that, moreover, it will guard the interest of third parties (who, as opposed to the parties concerned, represent the public, frequently interested in particular individual relationships); but still more, that in determining the respective rights and obligations, the legal rule will be conceived with less regard to the rights of the immediate parties than to the good of the entire community. The latter is never a third party in regard to any relationship whatever between individuals, in the sense of an interested outsider; yet it is always a party, in the sense that the parties to the individual relationship are also members of this very community.

Thus the rôle of the public good in law is not merely to provide a barrier, reservation, or counterweight to the play of an individual right created *a priori*, "save for public policy or the interest of third parties." Its rôle is a positively determining one in the sense that for the jurist the consecration of the individual right, the extent and the mode of that consecration as regards all, parties and third parties, depend *a priori* upon the public good. In a word, the rights of the parties are determined not by "mine" and "thine" envisaged separately, but by "ours" — which comprises, beyond the parties, the public, the total community.[6] In his relationships with other individuals as well as with the state, the individual is taken as a member of the public (the state is in charge only of the public), and his rights and obligations are regulated in consequence thereof.[7]

148. The Social Conception of Private Law and the Concern with Individual Rights. Will this doctrine be called "socialist" or statist"? [8]

[5] See *supra*, no. 88 and n. 6.

[6] Cf. G. Renard, La Théorie de l'Institution (Paris, 1930), vol. 1, *partie juridique*, and the formula by Mausbach, *id.* 329, n. 2: . . . Also Natorp, Vorlesungen über praktische Philosophie (1925) 453.

[7] See, in this sense, St. Thomas, Summa theologica, *Ia IIae*, qu. 90, art. 2 *ad resp.*: . . . ; *ad* 1: . . . ; *ad* 2: . . . : see also art. 3 *ad* 3. And see Isidore of Seville, quoted Summa, *Ia IIae*, qu. 90, art. 2, *initio*; qu. 96, art. 1 *ad resp.* Cf. Portalis, *Discours préliminaire*, no. 17, in Locré, *op. cit.* (Bruxelles ed. 1836) 159, col. 2: . . .

[8] Cf., in this sense, J. Bonnecase, *op. cit.* nos. 153, 155, 156, and especially no.

Assuredly it is socialism, at least a juridical socialism, if one maintains that the rule of the jurist is necessarily social, centering on the public good and not the individual good. It is statism, too, if it is for the state to make a sovereign appraisal of the requirements of the public good in matters of the legal rule — and how can that competence of the state be disputed? But neither this juridical socialism nor this statism means a negation of the individual right or a refusal to recognize it. On the contrary, the public good demands that recognition: Have not the individuals been led to band together in the state with a view to safeguarding their persons and property? And how could the public good be derived from what would be evil for the individuals, the component parts of the public: *Totum non est praeter partes.*[a] Historical experience accords with social philosophy in testifying that the public good cannot be realized, cannot be conceived, without having respect for the individual right, or by abolishing the limits between "mine" and "thine."[9] One does not in this way come back to individualism: It remains true that the measure of the individual right or, more exactly, of the protection assured it by the law, is the public good, not the right of the individual. And this thesis is not without practical consequences, as will be seen from the following examples.

149. The Example of Rent Legislation. All Western [European] countries after the World War of 1914–1918 and without interruption since then have known "rent legislation," extending leases and limiting the amount of rent. On account of the critical shortage of living quarters it was necessary to protect tenants of modest means (or business men) from being put out on the street at the expiration of their leases, a situation which would have entailed both iniquities and social disturbances. The solution was obvious: The landlords were compelled to extend their leases beyond the expiration date, with provision for an adjustment of the amount of rent by a percentage which was much less than that of the devaluation of money (50 or 100 per cent increase in rent in relation to 1914, whereas money had depreciated in the proportion of 400 and more). On all the evidence, this legislation sacrificed the right of the

157. And cf. 1 A. Boistel, Cours de philosophie du droit, nos. 40 *et seq.*, pp. 71 *et seq.*; 2 *id.* nos. 383 *et seq.*, pp. 159 *et seq.*

[a] [The whole does not exist outside of the parts.]

[9] Thus it is not only, as has been said, because "injustice would disturb the order of society and entail the danger of revolution" that the common good requires justice, but in a more essential manner because the very idea of the common good is impotent without justice, apart from any idea of disturbance or revolution. Cf. G. Radbruch, *Le but du droit*, in 3 Annuaire de l'Institut international de philosophie du droit (1937–38) 50; but see *id.* 53 *in fine.*

landlord to that of the tenant: From the viewpoint of commutative justice, on the level of "mine" and "thine," the equilibrium was broken. On the one hand, the landlords lost the free disposition of their property; on the other, they did not obtain the just price for providing its enjoyment. It is possible, even certain, that in the minds of some people rent legislation took on the meaning of an attack upon property or, quite bluntly, an election maneuver: Do not the tenants represent the "little men" and therefore the mass of the electorate?

Yet objectively the solution was justified, at least in its principle, as a measure commanded by the public good under the circumstances. The public good, especially concern with public peace and tranquillity, demanded the invasion of the right of the landlord, the break in the equilibrium which actually benefited the tenant. With commutative justice failing, social justice received satisfaction.[10] For social justice may require the citizens to give up certain things not only for the profit of the state under the perspective of public law, but also under the perspective of private law for the profit of other citizens or other social categories, when these particular sacrifices are indispensable for the good of the whole community.[11]

150. The Objection of "Legislation of Circumstance." Will this example be rejected as legislation "of circumstance," exceptional and provisional, and by claiming that normally the determination of private rights would take place on the basis of strictly commutative justice? The objection would not be pertinent. Continually the law has to do with situations that are sometimes conforming and sometimes contrary to normality, and its solutions are made up sometimes of principles and sometimes of exceptions from principles. Now philosophically neither the problem nor the method changes: It is always the public good upon which either the principle or the exception is founded. In normal, i.e., calm, times, the public good will be likely to coincide with the consecration of commutative justice. In abnormal, i.e., troubled, times, and, if you will, on the ground of the policy of the lesser evil, the public good will suggest such more or less grave derogations from the rule of commutative justice.[12]

[10] See another, more tenuous example in the case suggested by J. Carbonnier in REVUE TRIMESTRIELLE DE DROIT CIVIL (1942) 365 (obligation of a higher employee to continue his service while the enterprise is folding up).

[11] Cf., concerning the definition of justice as a moral virtue, CICERO, DE INVENTIONE, 2, 53, 160: . . . , and comment by F. SENN, DE LA JUSTICE ET DU DROIT (Paris, 1927) 44–47. We shall return to this passage *infra*, no. 238.

[12] On the distinction between normal and abnormal times, see M. HAURIOU, PRÉCIS DE DROIT CONSTITUTIONNEL (2d ed. Paris, 1923) 440–441.

151. Examples from the Ordinary Law of Private Institutions: Prescription. Does one nonetheless want to argue from a starting point in normal times? It will not be difficult to discover a number of institutions of private law in the apparently most individualistic codes, where the solution is to be explained by the predominance of the viewpoint of social justice ("ours") over the viewpoint of commutative justice ("mine," "thine"). Such is the rule of prescription, already referred to.[13] It has indeed been attempted to reconcile prescription with individual right through explaining it by a presumption of renunciation: The inaction of the holder of the right during a sufficiently long lapse of time would indicate an intention to abandon the right.[14] Historically and rationally the explanation is factitious. The true reason of prescription lies in certain necessities or conveniences of social life. It matters for the public good that at the end of a certain time accounts should be cleared (liberating prescription or limitation of debts), unused rights in real property detached from ownership should disappear (extinctive prescription of usufructs and servitudes), illegitimate acquisitions of property should become regularized notwithstanding their original defects (case of acquisitive prescription of ownership and real rights). Yet these results contradict the individual right, since they operate so as to transfer value without compensation from one estate to another without the consent of the holder (it is an adage of law and of common sense that "renunciations are not to be presumed"). Commutative justice could not approve prescription precisely because the right is by definition imprescriptible: It is inconceivable according to law and justice, understood in the philosophical sense, that the thief or usurper could ever become the legitimate owner of the thing he stole or usurped. *Res clamat domino.*[b] The assured right of the owner is nevertheless immolated to the public good of security in society.[15]

Will it be said that in fact the normal function of prescription is to clarify normal situations by relieving the beneficiary of an often difficult proof? Incontestably so. But the exactness of the remark does not permit us to neglect the cases, even though they are exceptional, where prescription implements injustice precisely because the law of prescription has stability and not justice in mind

[13] See *supra*, no. 120.

[14] See, e.g., 1 A. Boistel, Cours de philosophie du droit nos. 244 *et seq.*, pp. 401 *et seq.*

[b] [The thing calls for its owner.]

[15] For a detailed defense of this thesis, see J. Dabin, La philosophie de l'ordre juridique positif, nos. 139–141.

152. The Same: Ownership under the Code Napoleon. There are also other examples where one could not argue that the case is exceptional. Take the régime of ownership and rights in real property under the Code Napoleon. The following rules may be taken up at random as inspired in the first place by a concern with the public good (understood in a more or less exact manner): The limitation of the number of rights in real property (article 543),[c] the prohibition of restraints on alienation,[16] the lifelong character of usufructs (article 617, para. 2),[d] and the requirement of an increased value of the dominant estate as a condition for the existence of a servitude (article 686).[e] No motive deduced from respect for everyone's right offers a check to an unlimited variety of modes of utilizing property. But the legislator believed that socially the limitation presented advantages of simplicity and clarity, justifying a restriction upon the freedom of owners to encumber their property with any detached rights they pleased. Similar considerations of a social order explain the prohibition of restraints on alienation. They do not in any way contradict the individual right either on the part of the stipulating party (since he is master of his property) or on that of the obligor (since he has given his acceptance). But it appeared to the legislator that the power of alienation was required by the economic principle of freedom of circulation of goods in the social interest. From the viewpoint of the respective rights, there was nothing to postulate the lifelong character of usufructs or the condition of increased value for servitudes either. But from a general point of view the legislator refused to admit that as important a detached right as a usufruct could in perpetuity paralyze the exercise of the rights of full ownership to the detriment of productive use of the property; or that the service imposed upon an estate, with its real and permanent character, should not be compensated by an augmentation in the value of the benefiting estate.[17]

[c] [Art. 543 of the Code Napoleon provides as follows: "Property rights may be either ownership or a mere right of user or servitudes only."]

[16] A solution evolved by way of interpretation; see PLANIOL AND RIPERT, TRAITÉ PRATIQUE DE DROIT CIVIL FRANÇAIS, vol. 3: *Les biens* by M. Picard, no. 223.

[d] [Art. 617 para. 2 of the Code Napoleon provides as follows: "Usufruct shall be terminated: . . . By expiration of the time for which it has been granted."]

[e] [Art. 686 of the Code Napoleon provides as follows: "Owners are permitted to establish upon their estate or in favor of their estate such servitudes as to them seems fit, provided however that the services established shall be imposed neither upon a person nor in favor of a person, but only upon land and for land, and provided that such services shall not otherwise be contrary to public policy. The use and extent of the services thus established shall be governed by the grant constituting them or, in the absence of such grant, by the following rules."]

[17] There are other examples, such as the rules of accession by incorporation, art. 552. [*Sic.* Art. 552 of the Code Napoleon provides as follows: "Ownership of

Perhaps one will venture to offer this interpretation: Far from deriving from a social idea, the above mentioned rules could be but the affirmation, pushed to a paroxysm, of the individual right of ownership, which the legislator wanted to be absolutely free, notwithstanding the owner's contrary will, just as the prohibition of a contract to work for life is evidence in favor of the absolute conception of the principle of freedom of the person. But, even neglecting the argument of the productive use of property, which has nonetheless been invoked, it will be observed that if the Code Napoleon in fact saw its ideal in free, full, and unhampered ownership, this ideal was in its eyes justified less by the right of the owner considered as such than by the interest of the public in general. It is too often forgotten that liberalism, unlike anarchism, presents itself rightly or wrongly as a social doctrine, by the same token as solidarism or socialism. To the liberal, liberty is fused with, and alone is capable of providing for, the general interest.

153. The Same: Domestic Relations, Succession, Contracts. It is appropriate to generalize: In all fields of private law — the law of domestic relations, of succession, of contracts — one encounters regulations elaborated directly as a function of the public good rather than of the pure individual right. For the law of domestic relations, this is not astonishing. The realization of the human and national ends of the family is radically incompatible with the concept of the right of the individual as such. That is why, for example, marriage is decreed to be indissoluble, at least in principle, and the community of life between the spouses always produces a certain community of property relations, even

---

the soil carries with it ownership of what is above and below. The owner may plant and build above as he shall see fit, save for the exceptions established in the Title On Servitudes or Land Services. He may build and dig below as he shall see fit and draw all products that such diggings may furnish, save for the modifications resulting from the mining laws and regulations and the police laws and regulations."]

The concern with the pure individual right would demand the coexistence (which is not at all impossible) of the two rights, of the owner of the thing to which there is an accession and of the owner of the acceding thing. However, since the coexistence would probably entail conflicts and would hardly be favorable to a fruitful utilization of the property, the Code in the social interest decrees expropriation of the owner of the accessory thing, which will increase the principal thing, though with provision for indemnification. The same system prevails as regards injuries caused to property by industrial establishments: the right of the owners is sacrificed, with indemnification provided. Finally, will it be said that justice drives the law of nations to recognize, in an unjust invader, the rights of an occupant, not only burdensome rights (such as the maintenance of order) but also profitable rights (such as requisitions)?

in case of separation of property,[18] etc. The same social note appears in matters of succession. For if descent may be legitimately related to the descendants' own right (in their quality as members of the family of the deceased, though), the arrangement of the régime reflects preoccupations of a familial, social, and even political order. Is not the mode of dividing estates of interest to the power of the state over its subjects? [19] The law of contracts until recent times, it is true, was construed in substance by means of the classical categories of liberty and property merely tempered by the laws, public policy, and public morals. But how can one with these concepts account for solutions such as the mandatory value of fixed prices? In order to grasp the adequate reason of fixed prices, one must not hesitate to leave the ancient individualist framework and place one's self in the perspective of a socially organized economy, where the retailer is envisaged no longer in his purely legal quality as a contracting party and owner but as invested with an economic function in the mechanism of distribution of products.[20]

154. In the Field of Evidence and Procedure. Even rules as technical as the law of evidence and the law of procedure (at least in civil matters) are rather often turned from their normal ends and transferred to the service of a policy which through them as intermediaries pursues some end of the public good. More or less irrefragable presumptions are instituted which are but distantly related to the probability of the presumed facts. Difficulties of proof are artificially raised where the matter opposes no special resistance to demonstration.

Thus, in the field of filiation, the law multiplies favors to legitimacy, presuming that the ideal it deems desirable is realized; yet it ignores adulterous or incestuous filiation, which cannot be acknowledged in its eyes; and for simple natural filiation it is content with obstacles to proof. Arguments of a social order (safeguards to the peace of families, fear of scandal) win out in the probative system over the concern with an objective and prudent search for the truth.[21] Similarly, in the matter of civil responsibility in tort a tendentious employment of statutory pre-

[18] See on this last point R. Savatier, *L'évolution du régime de la séparation des biens*, in LE DROIT, L'AMOUR ET LA LIBERTÉ (Paris, 1937) 70 *et seq.*

[19] Cf. CH. BEUDANT, COURS DE DROIT CIVIL FRANÇAIS (2d ed. by R. Beudant and P. Lerebours-Pigeonnière), vol. 5: LES SUCCESSIONS AB INTESTAT by R. Le Balle (Paris, 1936), nos. 62–85.

[20] Cf. R. HOORNART, LA POLITIQUE DES PRIX IMPOSÉS (Bruxelles, 1939) . . .

[21] See, on this policy, J. DABIN, LA TECHNIQUE DE L'ÉLABORATION DU DROIT POSITIF (Bruxelles-Paris, 1935) 89 *et seq.* Also A. Rouast, *Les tendances individualistes de la jurisprudence française en matière de filiation légitime*, in REVUE TRIMESTRIELLE DE DROIT CIVIL (1940–41) 223 *et seq.*

sumptions permitted judical decisions to assure an especially favorable régime of reparation to victims of injuries, motivated no doubt by a feeling of pity for the victim but also, from the social point of view, by a policy of preventing injuries: The more severely the authors of accidents — presumed to be at fault or responsible — are treated the more will they redouble vigilance and precaution.[22] Finally, in the field of procedure, do we not see the legislator multiply formalities and delays simply with a view to wearing out actions of which he fundamentally disapproves but which he is obliged to tolerate, as in matters of divorce on specified grounds and above all divorce by mutual consent? The resources of form come to the aid of substance; adjective law concurs in realizing substantive law, in this case, a substantive law of social tendency, preoccupied more with society in general than with particular individuals.

155. In Criminal Law. Is it necessary, finally, to remark that the law of sanctions, especially the penal law, is directly under the dominion of the public good? The same public good that has to decide upon the content of the rules is naturally the judge of the form and degree of the sanctions. If their primary purpose is to assure the effective execution of the precepts of law, through the evil they inflict and the fear that evil may inspire, yet sanctions raise a new problem in relation to the problem of the content of the law. The execution of the law could not be carried out regardless of consequences or even solely with a view to the efficacy of sanctions. Excellent rules might be provided with very efficacious sanctions which, however, would have a deplorable social effect. Certainly, there are sanctions that are obvious, issuing logically from the violation of the rule itself; such is the nullity which "sanctions" contracts made in contravention of a legal prohibition. Such contracts are ordinarily null and void (with reservations, though, as to the scope of these nullities),[23] and one and the same judgment — a judgment of the public good — resolves both the problem of the prohibition of the law and that of its sanction. But there are sanctions which keep less closely to the existence of the precept, such as annulments of transactions, seizures, and above all penalties (which incidentally explains the birth of the penal law as an autonomous branch). Now it is a distinct judgment — always one of the public good — that will raise the question of punishment, a judgment dictated by the social gravity of the infraction

[22] See on this point J. Dabin, La philosophie de l'ordre juridique positif, nos. 155–156.

[23] Ordinarily; for it may happen that the law upholds the forbidden transaction and imposes the sanction of a penalty upon the transgression.

and the social necessity of a more energetic reaction, yet without overlooking the rights of the person of the delinquent, who, despite the punishment, still has the right to be treated humanely.[24]

SECTION 3. THE TEMPORAL PUBLIC GOOD AS NORM OF THE NEGATIVE CONTENT OF THE LAW

156. The Public Good Often Demands Abstention of the Jurist. It would be wrong to believe, however, that the intervention of a legal rule is indicated every time that some attitude conforming to the public good is to be obtained from the subjects, whether private individuals or even official functionaries. The public good, the norm of the positive content of the law, is also and for the same reason the criterion of its negative content; as the master of the mode of intervention, it equally decides in each case upon the principle of intervention.[1] Seen from another angle — that of the realization or the incidences of the rule — it may happen that the requirements of the public good demand of the jurist a more or less complete abstention. And it is understood that we have in mind here not at all the effacement of a statute or custom in favor of the courts, where the judicial source of law is substituted for other sources, but rather the lack of any legal rule, whatever its source, *a priori* or *a posteriori*, in short, a system of more or less complete freedom imposed upon and eventually sanctioned by the judge. Here appears in full relief the mission of the jurist to prefer prudence to justice, even social justice. The "prudent" man does not think exclusively of justice; he seeks what is realizable; failing to obtain the best, he contents himself with less, which is sometimes the lesser evil.

Let us leave aside the assumption of intangible autonomies. There are indeed spheres of activity, even external activity, where the will of individuals is the master of decision and action, save for its responsibility before conscience and God. Universal as the domain of the public good

[24] Cf. P. Cuche, *L'élaboration du droit pénal et l'irréductible droit naturel*, in 3 RECUEIL GÉNY 271–274. Cf. ST. THOMAS, SUMMA, *IIa IIae*, qu. 66, art. 6 *ad* 2: . . . ; and see ST. THOMAS, *op. cit. IIa IIae*, qu. 85, art. 1 *ad* 1.

[1] The definition of law as *ordinatio ad bonum commune*, called upon to serve the "utility of men," as in the passages quoted *supra*, no. 134 and notes 2 and 5, means no doubt that in the first place the law will prescribe what the common good or the utility of men demands, but also that it will abstain from such prescription in cases where the common good and the utility of men would not benefit therefrom. Isidore of Seville, approved by St. Thomas, said that the law *saluti proficiat, expediat saluti* [should "benefit welfare" or "expedite welfare"], SUMMA THEOLOGICA, *Ia IIae*, qu. 95, art. 3.

may be in the temporal order, there are reserved zones prohibited to penetration by the public and the state at least in the form of precepts if not of advice: Those in which the personal destiny of the individuals in this and in the other world is at stake, in a word, the freedom of vocation in the wide sense. This freedom is not only legitimate but also necessary. No reason of the public good could motivate its suppression or limitation because it stems from the nature of the human individual, who is not merely a part of a whole but also a being subsisting in and for himself, and because no attack upon human nature could be useful to a public good which is also basically human.[2]

157. The Dilemma: Freedom or Legal Rule. Let us remain, then, on the level of the competence of the state and the public good. It is not a foregone conclusion that in concrete reality the rule will be a better instrument of a solution than the free will of individuals, in whatever way, incidentally, the latter may proceed, by way of material action or of disposition (legal transaction), unilaterally or by agreement. Seemingly, the rule alone, as emanating from the social authority — rulers or the people themselves acting together — is capable of rising to the level of the good of all while the private will would never go beyond the limited horizon of the particular interest. But if experience condemns the all too optimistic doctrine of a public good flowing by a law of fate from the play of competing freedoms,[3] it would be an exaggeration to claim that, conversely, freedom could never produce anything but damage to the public good — often a positive damage, and in any case a negative one by the very lack of coördination and discipline which results from competition. In these matters, *a priori* doctrines, always extreme and simplifying, weigh less heavily than facts, because we are concerned with registering results and the sole valid method for registering results is statistics or, if you will, more modestly, experience.

The dilemma is thus not one between freedom on the one hand and the public good on the other; it is one between freedom and the rule, both possible instruments in the service of the public good. Freedom has its perils: Disorder or injustice, which are precisely the reason of being of the rule; but the rule in turn is not without inconveniences. Whatever the virtues of external discipline may be from the very viewpoint of the

[2] As to the relation of the individual human being to society and the state, see J. Dabin, Doctrine générale de l'Etat, nos. 212–216, pp. 342–352.

[3] This is the moment to quote the typical formula of Eudore Pirmer in the Belgian Chamber, in 1860, in the debate concerning art. 494 of the Penal Code, repressing usury: "We wrongly oppose the protection of freedom!" Quoted in 2 Nypels, Le code pénal belge interprété (Bruxelles, 1878) 675.

education of freedom,[4] every rule by its inhibiting effect involves a certain attack upon individual energies. Spontaneous enthusiasm is controlled, contained, broken. The excess of discipline kills the spirit of initiative. The fully prepared regulation relieves one of foreseeing and providing; and in the absence of regulation the disoriented subject falls into inertia. From another aspect, discipline laid down in advance always errs through generality, which prevents it from adapting itself to the particularities of cases, while freedom, mobile and supple, knows how to invent exactly adjusted solutions. Lastly, let us not forget that the rule issuing from the will offers this superiority over the imposed rule, that it adds to the abstract force of the obligation the stimulus of personal engagement, which doubles its effective value.

158. Sometimes Freedom Ought to be Preferred, but Not Without Limit or Control. Now these merits of freedom, in action as well as in the regulation of action, are not without repercussions upon the public good. At some point, freedom may be preferred to intervention even if in the special case the solution provided by freedom would be less in conformity with the public good than the solution of the rule. By hypothesis, the advantages of freedom represent on the whole a more appreciable element of the public good than what has been given up for it. More, in the choice to be made between freedom and the rule, the law will begin by laying down the rule of freedom, at any rate as long as it has not been shown that in practice the use of freedom turns generally against the public good. This explains not only the great principle of modern private law that "all that is not prohibited is permitted," but also the principle of the autonomy of the will in the regulation of private interests. The law has greater confidence in freedom than in itself to define the relationships between particular individuals for the best interests of each and all. If it formulates the rule, it does not always impose it, in the sense that it permits liberty to derogate from it by the disposition of a will to the contrary: The rule of the law is then but supplementary.[5]

Of course, freedom from regulation could not be absolute, without limit and without control, which would amount to denying the utility and the very principle of social discipline. At the outset, it is incumbent upon the law to insure the expression of authentic freedom or at the

[4] See, in this sense, ST. THOMAS, SUMMA, *Ia IIae*, qu. 95, art. 1 *ad resp.* and *ad* 2.

[5] On the system of the Code Napoleon, see J. Dabin, *Autonomie de la volonté et lois impératives, ordre public et bonnes moeurs, sanction de la dérogation aux lois, en droit privé interne*, in ANNALES DE DROIT ET DE SCIENCE POLITIQUE (Louvain, 1940) 190 *et seq.*

very least of a sufficient freedom, for a freedom that is psychologically null no longer answers to the concept of freedom. Further, there are matters which are not appropriately treated through freedom, which call for a common measure, objective and uniform, independent of will in general and of any particular dissident will. Lastly, even in the field left to freedom, there will always be room for paring down the abuses and gaps of freedom by adequate measures whenever freedom, positively or negatively — through badly regulated competition — would cause to the public good a damage greater than that which intervention would entail.[6] Even within the framework of a vigorously social conception of the law, this justifies the very large place accorded to the freedom of individuals and groups, a principle often denounced as typically individualistic although its moderate, balanced application is ultimately as beneficial to society as to the individuals.

159. Beneficial Character of Freedom even in the Domain of Public and Administrative Law. Nor is this beneficial character of freedom entrenched in the sector of private law. It shows itself also in public and administrative law, where the public good represents the only valid viewpoint, outside of any consideration of private good. Good management of the state does not systematically require a rule any more than does good management of particular interests. The spirit of initiative and freedom of decision are as indispensable to rulers, functionaries, and officials responsible for the public good as they are to private persons. And hence while in some matter or under some circumstances the public good may demand the subjection of the holders of authority to a more or less rigid rule, there will be other cases where the public good will require that they have a more or less discretionary power, such as, whenever the danger of arbitrariness will appear less prejudicial to the public good than too strict a discipline.

160. The Psychology of the Subjects: Cases Where the Public Good Is Satisfied Without the Intervention of a Law. The shortcomings inherent in the system of regulation are not the only reason for abstention on the part of the rule. Account must also be taken, to a large extent, of the psychology of the subjects.

Suppose, first, that ordinarily they spontaneously execute the order deduced from the public good. The result is here obtained without the

[6] See L. Josserand, *La "publicisation" du contrat*, in 3 RECUEIL LAMBERT § 145, pp. 143 *et seq.*; G. Ripert, *L'ordre économique et la liberté contractuelle*, in 2 RECUEIL GÉNY 347, and LE RÉGIME DÉMOCRATIQUE ET LE DROIT CIVIL MODERNE (Paris, 1936) nos. 137 *et seq.*

rule having to show itself.[7] Now if the legislator makes the claim to intervene, if only to support with a sanction the principle already practiced in fact, the effect of his step could be radically different from what he had thought. Instead of confirming the subjects in their attitude, it may cause a turnabout dictated by a feeling of reaction against meddling that is deemed intolerable. There are individualistic peoples whose caviling temperament goes as far as explicit contradiction; there are defiant peoples who in the course of history have had to suffer many an abuse. A psychology, perhaps regrettable, which yet imposes itself as a fact upon the statesman desirous of avoiding mistakes. The more so since the inopportune proclamation of commonly practiced principles risks awakening the doubt that will end by ruining them. Contrary to the well-known saying, there are things that are better left unsaid.[8] But since under certain circumstances freedom has proved itself, why not trust it as long as it continues to merit the trust? The codes of law are not like catechisms or grammars containing the complete enumeration of what to do and what to avoid. Arranged in them are only the precepts that it is useful to have promulgated because people would tend to transgress them; that is, unless the principles in question are so important that isolated infractions could not be permitted. For instance, there is good reason for the legal rule prohibiting murder and theft, although murderers and thieves are relatively rare. In this case, by the way, such a law lays down the precept only by sanctioning it, by way of the penal law or the law of civil responsibility, since it is useless to announce such a precept: The law does not prohibit murder, it punishes it, this sanction like every sanction naturally implying a prohibition.

161. The Same: Cases Where the Order of the Public Good Would Meet with Resistance. Provision must be made for the converse assumption: The people do not understand the requirements of the public good; they do not practice them and are not disposed to accept them. This occurs especially where the old human passions of unchastity, intemperance, prodigality, cupidity, and pride are at work, against which the state has the duty to fight, by reason of their social harmfulness; or it occurs where the state seeks to introduce ideas of orderly coöperation

[7] Cf., in the same sense, MONTESQUIEU, CAHIERS, 1716–1755, presented by B. Grasset (Paris, 1941) 95: "One should not do by laws what one can do by habits"; "useless laws weaken necessary ones."

[8] This is one of the reasons why the English do not like the system of [Constitutional] "Declarations of Rights": What good is there in proclaiming what goes without saying? For all that, individual rights are not any the less recognized and very energetically sanctioned in England.

in a society of too individualistic leanings. *Quid leges sine moribus?* [a] This still says too little. Disagreement with mores is capable of producing results worse than the futility of laws: Troubles of every sort, economic, social, moral. Now, no matter how just may be the disposition of a law seen only as such and as to its intention, the rôle of that law is not to aggravate a real disorder, which by hypothesis its precept is powerless to extirpate, by adding a new and worse disorder. The legal rule ceases to be of any service when, on the whole and balancing its advantages against its inconveniences, it produces more evil than good.[9] No doubt the people are at fault when in contempt of a formal order they continue obdurately in vicious practices or refuse to make legitimate sacrifices of independence. But the authority in turn commits a political fault when it reacts too late by untimely intervention without first thinking of converting the mass of misled opinion.[10]

The dosage of legal requirements does, however, involve degrees. From the legislator's inability to prescribe the maximum, on account of the state of opinion, it does not follow that he ought to prescribe nothing at all.[11] He will prescribe the minimum, or, more exactly, the maximum of what opinion is able to support. For example, divorce once having entered into the mores, the legislator will not necessarily go so far as to exclude it.[12] Working with the fire, he will only take care to hinder its abuse and even its use by a series of precautions tending to restrain and sterilize the undesirable solution.[13]

[a] [What are laws without morals?]

[9] Cf., in the same sense, St. Thomas, *op. cit. Ia IIae*, qu. 95, art. 3 *ad resp.*: . . . Especially concerning the repression of vices, see qu. 96, art. 2 *ad resp.* and *ad* 2; qu. 77, art. 1 *ad resp.* See also Montesquieu, De l'esprit des lois, bk. XIX; equally Portalis, *Discours préliminaire*, no. 5, in 1 Locré, *op. cit.* (Bruxelles ed. 1836) 154, col. 2: . . .

[10] God Himself has proceeded in this progressive manner, giving the Old Law to a still imperfect humanity, and another more perfect law (the Law of the Gospel) to those who had already been led by the earlier law to a greater understanding of divine matters, St. Thomas, Summa, *Ia IIae*, qu. 91, art. 5 *ad* 1.

[11] St. Augustine, approved by St. Thomas, *op. cit. Ia IIae*, qu. 96, art. 2 *ad* 3: . . .

[12] Divorce may have entered the mores so deeply that the public, in order to reserve the possibility of breaking off relations in case of a suppression of divorce, will forego marriage so as to live in free unions, which is no doubt much worse than divorce. The same difficulty hampers a prohibition of work by married women outside of the home. The desire for independence — and sometimes the necessity to supplement the family income — may turn from marriage to concubinage women who would nonetheless want to work outside.

[13] As examples of this policy, one may also cite the case of numerous rules of the Code Napoleon in the matter of gifts *inter vivos*, showing the hostility of the legislator toward that kind of dispositions, which deprive families of their estates.

162. The Intervention of the Legal Rule Is Not the Only Possible Solution. But let us make no mistake: Silence or tolerance on the part of the legal rule by no means signifies abstention of the authority. There are several ways in which the state may usefully promote the public good. In general, no doubt, it will hardly succeed without laying down a precept. The subjects need to be given commands, and formally the state is the commanding power. But the action of the state by way of command and power is not always the aptest method. Like the father of the family, like any authority whatever, the state may confine itself to encouraging through the grant of advantages or counteracting through "prohibitive" procedures. As long as morality is preserved (for the end does not justify the means), the state has the right and the duty — of political prudence — to choose the means which leads most surely to the goal.[14]

Take, for instance, the fight against alcoholism, an incontestable social scourge, injurious not only to the individuals who yield to alcoholic liquor but also to their offspring and to all of society, since the abuse of alcohol kills the race. Instead of issuing a prohibition pure and simple, sanctioned by a penalty if need be, which is the most direct and most energetic method, the state may intervene by so many limitative regulations (closing down the sale of drinks for certain hours of the day, imposing taxes, etc.) or, in a manner no longer juridical, by favoring the consumption of products competing with alcohol, organizing anti-alcohol propaganda in its own schools, or allotting subsidies to private anti-alcohol groups; in these latter cases, the law gives way to general politics. What about the fight against the high cost of living, another social scourge, or, more precisely, the practice of exorbitant prices? Apart from the direct procedure of fixing ceilings, which often remains a dead letter or results only in producing a shortage of goods,[15] various more or less efficacious procedures are at the disposal of the state to curb the upward movement: e.g., initiating competition by enterprises managed by the public authorities or even suppressing private trade (system of public enterprises (*régies*) and monopolies).[16]

To check the abuses of economic power, the state, instead of itself combating such abuses in a preventive and repressive manner, may

[14] On the efficacy of advice in relation to precepts, cf. St. Thomas, *op. cit. Ia IIae*, qu. 95, art. 1 *ad resp.* and *ad* 1.

[15] Not to forget the special danger noted by Montesquieu, De l'esprit des lois, bk. XXII, ch. 19: "Usury increases in Mohammedan countries in proportion to the severity of its prohibition: the lender indemnifies himself against the risk of violation."

[16] Cf., on the creation of municipal slaughterhouses, French Council of State, Nov. 24, 1933, Sirey (1934), 3, 105, with note by M. Mestre.

stimulate the grouping together of the weak who are the victims or, again, make itself the mediator to bring the parties together. Such has been the policy of the state of the nineteenth and twentieth centuries in the field of protection of labor. While it intervened by protective statutes ("social legislation" properly so called), it lifted the barriers to labor unionism, erected institutions of conciliation and arbitration, and favored collective agreements and mixed commissions. Such a policy, which takes advantage of the play of social forces, offers many benefits. It is economical since it relieves the state of the need for incessant and often delicate policing; it is in accord with the idea of human dignity since it leaves to the interested parties the care of defending their own interests; it aids virtue since it drives toward the recognition of the bond of solidarity which unites the workers among themselves, on the one hand, and capital and labor, on the other. In an analogous order of ideas, we see governments favoring the elaboration and establishment of uniform types of contracts in order to introduce certain reforms that are not yet ripe enough to pass directly into statutes: The state avails itself of extra-judicial practice as a precursor of the requirement of the law.[17] Finally, if one likes an example now on the agenda, it is quite certain that the return of woman to the home, which in every regard represents the social verity, will be attained much less by prohibiting work outside than by a complex of measures destined to influence the external and internal, economic and psychological causes that drive mothers to desert their homes. Do we have to add that most of the time the authority will be led to put all means within its power to work simultaneously, that resort to the method of the compelling imperative does not exclude the use of other, indirect procedures, and vice versa?

163. The Desirable Public Good and the Realizable Public Good. It follows from these explanations that the public good, the norm of the positive legal ordinance, is two-faced, that in a certain sense it even assumes contradictory aspects. Sometimes, the public good commands a rule which erects its requirements into a precept; sometimes, it demands freedom, abstention of the rule with regard to these same requirements. There is the desirable public good, incarnating the ideal, and the realizable public good, depending upon contingencies. Good in its disposition, the rule may nevertheless produce fruits contrary to the public good on account of an unfavorable social environment. Now what matters is the result, the final result, the amount of effectively realized public good. For the legislator, the question is thus not so much to determine what

[17] Cf. E.-H. Kaden, *Un exemple de la pratique extra-judiciare en Allemagne: le contrat de bail uniforme*, in 1 Recueil Lambert § 41, pp. 511 *et seq.*

the subjects owe to the public good as what he is able to obtain from them by means of his rule.[18]

164. Public Good and Public Opinion as Factors of the Elaboration of the Law. In a single glance one grasps the relationship, established in the system of law, between the notion of the public good and the factor of public opinion, the "collective consciousness," the "great mass of minds." Opinion as such is no generator of law because it does not create the requirements of the public good nor the consequences they involve with regard to the law.[19] But if the requirements of the public good are objective, the conception, true or false, which opinion may form of these same requirements in turn constitutes a fact endowed with objective reality. And that fact is of interest to the law in so far as the state of opinion is a factor in the realization of the rule. While a rule in accord with popular feeling is ordinarily assured of success, a rule disavowed by opinion is almost condemned to failure. Now the failure of the rule, signifying disobedience of the subjects, not only damages the law but also affects the public good itself, so that an alternative is raised: Either abstention of the rule, renouncing the benefit it ought theoretically to procure, or inefficacious intervention with its fatal consequences for the prestige of the authority.[20]

In reality, it is true, the dilemma rarely takes so trenchant a form. The failure of a rule is never complete; or even if complete, it does not always entail loss of the prestige of authority. The necessity of a choice remains, the more so as, outside of practical efficiency, the truth of a rule, the ideal it translates, also has its peculiarly social interest. In the eyes of righteous people, and even of others, the silence of the law, passing for indifference or complicity, is capable of engendering a scandal at least as damaging to the prestige of the authority as the lack of success. But no matter what the difficulty of the choice in special cases, it was sufficient to mark the exact place of opinion among the component elements of the legal synthesis. Opinion, in fact, conditions the elaboration of the law; it is the principal factor of success or failure of a legal rule, which requires effective execution in terms of its own nature and accord-

[18] Following Isidore of Seville, St. Thomas teaches that a law must be necessary, useful, and beneficial to the public good, SUMMA THEOLOGICA, *Ia IIae*, qu. 95, art. 3 *ad resp.* and *ad* 1.

[19] See *supra*, no. 112.

[20] Cf. MONTESQUIEU, CAHIERS 96: "One must know the prejudices of his century well so as neither to shock them too much nor to follow them." "One must do nothing but the reasonable; but one must be very careful not to do everything that is reasonable."

ing to the essential vow of the public good.[21] Before a legal requirement of a nature to shock opinion can be established in an efficacious manner, it will be appropriate to await the conversion or neutralization of such opinion. Normally, the social action of education, exerted together by the state and by private initiative, will precede properly legal action.

By the name of public opinion we understand of course a consistent and compact social force. Often the alleged opinion is only that of a minority of writers whose theses find no echo in the public, or still again, the pretended opinion is divided into hostile currents and counter-currents. Nothing then prohibits the authority from taking advantage thereof and, by a bold decision, dictating the solutions it deems well founded. Its very intervention will often have the effect of rallying the indifferent, the undecided, and even some from the opponents.

165. The "Problem of Interventionism" Does Not Arise in Morals, at Least Not in Natural Morals. By all these traits, again, the legal rule is distinguished from the moral rule. There is no "problem of interventionism" in morals. Whereas for the public good the question of the realization and consequently of the utility of the rule is absolutely capital, the moral good exists and is binding independently of any consideration of success or opportunity. It is true that the moral legislator will guard against prescribing for the people a degree of perfection that would be above their strength. In the purely positive portion of the rules, and even in the conclusions deduced, through the rational work of the moralists, by starting from the requirements of nature, care will be taken to adapt his precepts to the contingencies, foremost among which is the level of conscience or of moral formation of the mass.[22] Such is the margin of "legislative prudence" in the domain of morals. But as to the first precepts resulting from the natural law itself in its immediately given terms,[23] they are what they are and they oblige everyone coming into this world, notwithstanding the opinion of the people, notwithstanding the legislator of morals himself, whose rôle is but to translate the "given" of nature without altering it by any modification or curtailment whatsoever.[24]

[21] This very reservation of human laws as regards things they are not capable of governing in an efficacious manner is the work of an eternal law, says St. Thomas, *op. cit. Ia IIae*, qu. 93, art. 3 *ad* 3. In other words, this impotence is part of the divine plan.

[22] See St. Thomas as cited *supra*, n. 9, applying to human laws in general, moral and juridical.

[23] On the distinction between virtue in general, prescribed by nature, and the specifications of virtue, which are not always prescribed by nature, cf. St. Thomas, Summa theologica, *Ia IIae*, qu. 94, art. 3 *ad resp.*, *in fine.*

[24] On the prescriptions added to the rule of natural law *ad humanam vitam*

SUBDIVISION II. THE MEANS: THE TECHNICAL EQUIPMENT OF THE LAW[1]

INTRODUCTION

166. The "Formal Realizability" or "Practicability" of the Law. Like any rule of social discipline, the law calls for effective realization, in the sense that its precepts are intended to pass into the conduct of the subjects or at least the general mass of them. This necessity, as above indicated, suggested consultation of the state of public opinion, whose eventual hostility could entail the failure even of a rule excellent in itself: That is the assumption, which has just been examined, of a lack of "material realizability" of the law.[2] But outside of that assumption, which concerns the substance of the precepts (of end and of means), the powerlessness of a rule may be due to other reasons, which concern the very form of the precepts (case of the "formal realizability" of the law).[3] The legal rule is indeed subject to application. This is to say not merely that it ought to be obeyed, but also that it needs to be carried into execution through the intermediary of external organs, which are, besides the subjects themselves, the officials and the judges. This is the consequence of the societal character of the rule. Different from morals, the law does not confine itself to prescriptions while leaving to each person the mastery and responsibility of application of the precept to his case. On the contrary, this application may open the way to action and prosecution; it is guaranteed by material sanctions, of which the mechanism is not automatic; it calls forth or may call forth proceedings which must find their decision before a human tribunal.

167. The Theoretical Value of the Rules Is Distinct from Their "Practicability." Thus the truth of the law, resulting from its adequacy to the end of the public good, does not suffice to fulfill the ideal of the good rule. In addition, the law must be applicable, practicable, manageable, by corresponding to the peculiarly technical conditions of carrying it into execution.[4] The two orders of ideas, complementary in fact, are

utilia [useful to human life], see ST. THOMAS, *op. cit. Ia IIae*, qu. 94, art. 5 *ad resp.* and *ad* 3.

[1] Term used by G. RENARD, LE DROIT, LA JUSTICE ET LA VOLONTÉ (Paris, 1924) 87, 123, 124.

[2] See *supra*, no. 164.

[3] The formula of the distinction between two sorts of "realizability" is by 1 JHERING, ESPRIT DU DROIT ROMAIN (transl. by Meulenaere), sec. 4, pp. 51–52.

[4] We may recall the passage from St. Thomas, *supra*, no. 164, n. 21.

nonetheless logically and really distinct, though this has sometimes been disputed.[5] The theoretical value of a rule may well be conceived outside of its "practicability": An impracticable rule is not at all an intrinsically bad rule, and an intrinsically good rule is not necessarily practicable. Essential as the formal legal technique is in that it assures the penetration of the law into life, it does not by that token constitute a part of justice, either the justice of the philosopher or the justice of the jurist (which is ours). For the technical side of the law is governed not by the idea of "substance of the law" but by the idea of rule, of discipline. Independently of any content, it is because the law is the rule of social discipline that it ought to be practicable and therefore managed with a view to that practicability.

Now the two elements often enter into competition, the practicability of the rule postulating certain sacrifices or, as they say in sugared terms, certain "adaptations" of the solution in substance deduced from the sole consideration of the public good. No doubt, the law as the jurist envisages it does not dwell in the state of the disembodied ideal. By definition and by function it is applied to living matter, at least to normal life, *ut in pluribus accidunt*,[a 6] if not to altogether singular cases. But the formal realizability of the law answers to a different concept, which is that of application in *lived life*, i.e., of effective execution, of the *living* applications of the idea of justice. Even related to life, a rule does not become applicable, realizable, from our point of view, except on the condition that it respect certain specific principles of a technical nature governing the applicability of rules.

What are these principles?

Section 1. The Definition, or Legal Conceptualism

168. Inconveniences of an Insufficiently Defined Law. The first factor of the practicability of the law consists in sufficient definition. An undefined or insufficiently defined law is not at all practicable in that its application will occasion hesitations and controversies which generate insecurity. Subjects and judges will ask themselves what exactly is the rule, and even if there is a rule. Now insecurity in relations, from what-

[5] Thus M. Djuvara, *Le but du droit*, in 3 Annuaire de l'Institut international de philosophie du droit (1938) 102–104, especially the conclusion at p. 104: . . . The same tendency to "minimize" the distinction is found in F. Russo, *op. cit. passim*, especially p. 31: . . . ; pp. 61 *et seq.*, and conclusion at p. 108.

[a] [As it happens in the majority of cases.]

[6] St. Thomas, *op. cit. Ia IIae*, qu. 47, art. 3 *ad* 2.

ever cause it may stem — above all, where that cause is the uncertainty of the law — is a grave evil which paralyzes activities and leads to stagnation. Speaking socially, the total absence of any rule where one is necessary, or a rule imperfect in the substance of its disposition, is often preferable to an uncertain rule. Those solutions have at least the merit of clarity, and at worst certain arrangements will permit paring them down, while uncertainty adds to the disorder of conduct a more monstrous disorder, to wit, the disorder in the very ordinance that pretends to make order rule.[1]

169. Lack of Definition on the Part of the Formal Sources of the Law. A lack of definition of the law may be found, first, in the formal sources, the assumption being that the existence of the rule is in doubt, either because in the régime in force the problem of sources may not be resolved or because the authorized sources may themselves suffer from the vice of indeterminacy.[2] It is the great advantage of the system of statutory sources to do away with these perplexities. On the one hand, the statute by the sole fact that it is the rule enacted by the authority in the state is necessarily preëminent over the other sources, at least in principle; on the other hand, the statute is born at a precise moment in time, it is published and easy to prove.[3] True, there remain the difficulties of interpretation. But the doubt in this case bears upon the content of the rule and no longer upon its existence, an assuredly lesser evil which by the way is inevitable and common to all sources. Yet the system of the statutory rule is not the universal and only one. Certain countries or certain branches of the law know hardly anything but customary law, as among little developed peoples or in international law. Or again a cumulation of sources is established, including statutory, customary, and case law, where primacy does not always belong to the statute. In any event the statute, the work of an essentially limited human reason and foresight, is by itself incapable of assuming the whole task of legal regulation. Case law and possibly custom have a rôle to play supplementing the statute. Now case law, which proceeds by successive stages and by the haphazard bringing of suits, remains uncertain

[1] Cf., in the same sense, the qualities of the positive law according to Isidore of Seville, approved by St. Thomas, Summa theologica, *Ia IIae*, qu. 95, art. 3, *initio: . . .* , and *ad resp.*, *in fine: . . .* Also G. Radbruch, *La sécurité en droit anglais*, in Archives de philosophie du droit (1936) nos. 3–4, pp. 86 *et seq.*

[2] On the social necessity of setting the law apart among the rules of social life, cf. F. Russo, Réalité juridique et réalité sociale 164–170.

[3] It is of course assumed that the laws are "well made," which is not always the case.

for a rather long time while its often laborious formation is continuing.[4] As for custom, issuing from habitual usage recognized as law, the difficulty is to discover it in both of its elements, the *usus* and the *opinio juris.*

No doubt it would be vain to hope to banish such wavering lines altogether, the more so since against its advantage of security the statute presents the inconvenience of a frozen edge which embarrasses the adaptation of the law to the transformations of life and the singularity of special cases. But, short of complete security, nothing prohibits tending to the maximum of security compatible with suppleness, by submitting to the statutory system such matters as call primarily for treatment by a precise rule. Neither is a division excluded between prerogatives of the statute, on the one hand, and of custom and case law, on the other, the latter being enabled to create precise solutions within a certain framework previously outlined by the statute. It is the task of the legal sociologist to search for the fields of application of the various sources of the law and the modalities of their coöperation.[5]

170. Indeterminacy of the Applicability of the Law in Time or Space. Another cause of perplexity in the realm of the formal sources comes from the very frequent indeterminacy of the extent of the applicability of the rule in time and space.

Where there are two laws successive in time of which the second is to abrogate or modify the first, what are the respective spheres of application of the two rules? Notwithstanding the probably superior quality of the new, juster, better adapted or more practicable statute, the security of social relations demands respect for rights acquired under the rule of the old statute. But the notion of "vested right," seemingly clear, becomes obscured in the presence of facts, acts, or situations that are permanent, at least in their effects. Hence the utility of special "transitional provisions" other than the essentially vague norm of the "transitional" or "intertemporal" law that is called the non-retroactivity of statutes.

As for space, the question, by reason of the multiplicity of states and the competition of national statutory systems, is what is the competent

[4] On the disadvantages of elaboration of the law by the courts, see R. Savatier, *Le gouvernement des juges en matière de responsabilité civile* (history of art. 1384, § 1, *in fine* [of the Code Napoleon]) II, in 1 RECUEIL LAMBERT § 37, pp. 461–466. [Art. 1384, § 1 provides as follows: "One is responsible not only for injury which one causes by one's own act, but also for that which is caused by the actions of persons for whom one is responsible or of things which one has in one's custody."]

[5] On this point, cf. 3 F. GÉNY, SCIENCE ET TECHNIQUE, no. 199, pp. 83–84.

rule in the case of a legal relationship made up of elements belonging to different nationalities: The place where the relationship was formed, the place where the property is located, the nationality or the domicile of the parties. This is the problem of the so-called conflict of customs, statutes, or laws. Now the answer is not identical in all countries, and even in each country it is far from unanimous concerning either particular solutions or the general method of solution. Almost entirely left to writings and decisions (and to the struggles of national interests), this branch, conflict of laws, is debated in greatest uncertainty. Despite that anarchy, conflicts should not necessarily be resolved to the advantage of the law which in reason presents a superior title to competence; for it may happen that the rationally competent law represents a very uncertain source compared with its competitors. Thus, from motives of pure practicability, one could in the field of contracts [relating to property] adopt the law of the place of the location of the property, which is easier to determine than that intended [by the parties] under the principle of autonomy, at least where the parties did not express their choice.[6] Without entering into an examination of that view, one could not in any case reject it on the ground that it is without pertinence to an exact legal philosophy.

171. The Lack of Precision of the Law in Its Formal Content. The insufficiency of definition may be found, further, in the very context of the law as transmitted by the sources. The rule exists, undeniable in its existence and applicability, whatever its origin, statutory, judicial, or customary; but its terms are indecisive, to the point where it escapes easy and sure management. Let us note that this is not a lack in the determination of the "ways and means," of the multifarious measures — processes, procedures, sanctions of every kind — called upon to put the central idea of a system into operation, such as an incomplete organization of guardianship, of the policing of warehousing, or of the system of proof. These insufficiencies, which affect the substance of the law, involve a lacuna in the law rather than a defect in definition. What leaves something to be desired in such a case are the "constructive rules," the "ways of the law," as Duguit says; the institution in its organic, systematic import remains incomplete. In the case of indeterminacy we are discussing here, on the contrary, the institution may be complete; but the concepts figuring in the rule — whatever they are, of purpose or means — without being incomprehensible to the mind through obscurity of thought or language, are not drawn in lines firm and recognizable

[6] See H. Battifol, note, in Sirey (1935) 1, 257, esp. at p. 259, col. 2, and p. 260, col. 1.

enough for the practical end of putting the rules into application. In a word, the vice is in the conceptual mold, the external configuration of the law.

Sometimes it affects the portion of the rule indicating the hypothesis, or the conditions of application of the disposition. Such would be the rule that would place under the clearly determined régime of guardianship individuals "incapable of managing their affairs by themselves" (how is that incapacity to be defined or discerned in practice without too much risk of error for each individual?), or again the rule that would condemn to a clearly determined penalty of imprisonment individuals guilty of "acts contrary to public peace" (how is the "contrariety to public peace" to be defined or discerned in practice without too much risk of error for each act?).[7] Sometimes and more rarely the lack affects the portion of the rule enouncing the disposition, the precept or sanction. Such would be the rule that would lay down a penalty against the author of a determined act without any precise statement of the nature or duration of the penalty. The conditions of application of the rule are well determined; but the solution is in every case left to the judge, charged with arbitrating *ex aequo et bono*, according to equity, reason, or expediency. So the rule offends neither against the public good nor against justice, on the contrary; neither does it incur the blame of containing a lacuna, save precisely for the lacuna of indeterminacy of its concepts, attributable to the inexperience of the legislator who has neglected to construe them in manageable form, or to the resistance of a matter naturally rebellious against being put into such form.

172. Examples: The Injustice of Usury or Illicit Speculation. Take the fight against the injustice of usury, at least in certain kinds of commerce and at certain periods.[8] Quite apart from the reactions of opinion among those concerned — often on the part of both the sellers desirous of enriching themselves and the buyers desirous of acquiring goods at any price — the difficulty lies in having a Protean injustice, which varies essentially with economic and social circumstances, with localities, and with weeks and sometimes days, circumscribed in a concrete manner, otherwise than by a philosophical formula. There is no doubt

[7] One can imagine (and "revolutionary" periods have effectively instituted) other examples: laws forbidding criticism of acts of the government, prohibiting luxury, or prohibiting women from taking up any work proper to men. What is "criticism," "luxury," or "work proper to men"? Cf. MONTESQUIEU, DE L'ESPRIT DES LOIS, bk. XXIX, chap. 16.

[8] We have in mind commerce in things indispensable to life (food, shelter), and abnormal periods where no natural regulatory mechanism is functioning. Also, "usury" is taken in a wide sense, not limited to loans at interest.

from the viewpoint of the public good: The civil and even penal repression of usury, which is a social scourge, would be legitimate and probably, taking everything into account, opportune. But to characterize the injustice of usury by the tests of the "illegitimacy," the "excessiveness," or even the "abnormality" of the gain, as several recent statutes and cases have decided, is actually to renounce the furnishing of a criterion. In order to be able to grasp that injustice it would be important to state its measure, to indicate the limit, beyond a certain figure, which realizes the illegitimacy, the excessiveness, the abnormality, *hic et nunc*.[a] Now one is content with a verbal definition, by which the notion to be defined is reproduced in different terms: It is clear *a priori* that the injustice of usury is something illegitimate, excessive, and, let us hope, abnormal. Still the educational argument must be kept in mind, which may make it advisable for the legislator to inscribe upon his books the duty of contractual justice, thus conferring thereon the sanction of his moral authority. But as long as the precept has not been rendered practicable through clear formulation it will very closely resemble, if not a "scarecrow," [9] at least a mere invitation to moderation.

173. Examples (Continued): Grave Insult as a Cause for Divorce. Another actual case of this difficulty is that of the "grave insult" which has been made a "determined" cause of divorce by the Code Napoleon. Even if one takes account of the text which refers to a *direct* insult "by one of the spouses against the other" (article 231),[b] it seems the legislator could not have used an expression at once more exact and more loose to indicate the idea that is truly basic to the institution of divorce as he conceives it. For what renders the breaking of the conjugal bond legitimate under the doctrine of the Code and hence deserves to be a cause for divorce is in effect any shortcoming of a certain gravity in any duties whatever, moral or legal, that issue from marriage. Such a shortcoming does constitute an insult leaving the injured spouse with a grievance and a complaint. But was not such a formula bound to lead to an excess of abuses in practice? And if the legislator intended to authorize divorce, which he considered a necessary evil, only as an ultimate remedy — this is the case for the Code Napoleon — one may measure the distance

[a] [Here and now.]

[9] The word is used by M. RIPERT, LE RÉGIME DÉMOCRATIQUE ET LE DROIT CIVIL (Paris, 1936) no. 147, p. 291. In the United States there exist governmental commissions charged with regulating the rates of power companies. But they have been faced with the difficulty of determining the "fair return" on the "fair value" of the enterprises. They have not succeeded, and still less have the courts, in setting up exact principles, so that the attempt at regulation is nearly frustrated.

[b] [Art. 231 of the Code Napoleon provides as follows: "Spouses may ask for

which in practice may separate the *ratio legis* from the effective result. Whereas divorce was not to occur but for a "determined cause," the pretendedly determined cause of the "grave insult" with no other precise term functions in fact as an indeterminate cause for divorce.[10] For want of a clear determination, the mechanism of security does not work. The system of divorce, in whatever *restrictive* features it has, ends in failure. One will hold the interpreter responsible for this: Why should a rule calling for strict interpretation be indefinitely extended? But the interpreter is what he is, inclined to loose and tendentious interpretations. It is for the legislator by added precision to prevent the abuse which may be made of his formulations.[11]

174. Examples (Continued): The Aggressor in Public International Law. As a final example of delicate if not impossible definition may be cited that of the war of so-called "aggression." It will be recalled that there was discussed in Geneva the "outlawing" of the state guilty of aggression with regard to another state, member or nonmember of the League of Nations. An excellent idea, fully conforming to the requirements of public international order, although in the state of national psychologies the realization of the idea could have seemed chimerical. But a definition of the aggressor had to be "construed." To what acts, attitudes, or steps was the characteristic, aggression, to be attached? On the one hand, there are disguised ways of attacking or preparing an attack, and these disguised ways, which fall under a professional technique, are legion. On the other hand, there are acts of apparent aggression whose real signification is far from always corresponding to the appearance, subjectively or even objectively. Consequently, this is an equivocal matter, full of clouds and detours; the experience of these last few years has shown it only too well. Now, to be valid, the definition of things by the jurist as constructor must satisfy the double condition of truth and practicability. First, the chosen characteristic must effectively reveal the

---

divorce from each other on the grounds of physical violence or grave insults by one against the other."]

[10] See 1 M. Planiol, Traité élémentaire de droit civil (12th ed.) no. 1158. On grave insults under art. 955, no. 2 [of the Code Napoleon; see *infra*, n. 22], cf. Savatier in Revue trimestrielle de droit civil (1940–41) 307–308.

[11] The general formula of the German Civil Code ("profoundly shattering the marital relation") is hardly more satisfactory, with the difference that the legislator has not claimed to "determine" the grounds for divorce. [Sec. 1568, par. 1 of the German Civil Code provides as follows: "A spouse may sue for divorce when the other spouse by grave violation of matrimonial duties or by dishonorable or immoral conduct has been guilty of so profoundly shattering the marital relation that the [complaining] spouse cannot be expected to continue the marriage."]

idea it claims to translate, at least in the majority of cases. Second, it must be easy to identify, without in every case necessitating inquiries and discussions which would enervate the force of the rule by retarding its application.[12]

175. Special Difficulty of Definition of Qualitative Values. A great many things are better understood by not being defined; such are the values of the spiritual and moral order, which are of a qualitative kind. In the more or less concrete evaluation, feeling decides there with more penetration and refinement than the logical reason armed with its always crude categories. That is why these sorts of things, as has been noted,[13] are less docile and pliable than quantitative values in conforming to the legal rule, because they are almost indefinable and in part incommunicable. This matters little for the moral rule, whose working requires no application in the mechanical and external sense: Conscience and God will make their appraisal freely and without any intermediary. But as to the law, a social discipline, socially applied and sanctioned, the rules which rely upon the sole appraisal of the interpreter, whether subject or judge, are not without danger. Intelligence, guided and in a certain manner bound by the categories, takes less risk of going astray than judgment, which is always more or less subjective, especially in certain periods in the life of peoples when the justness of feeling is even more "off its axis" than the logic of minds.[14]

Take the repression of obscene shows, an incontestable cause of public immorality. How make the distinction between the show which is obscene and that which is not? A question of fact, no doubt, rather than of definition. But what will the feeling of the judge be? One tribunal will show itself indulgent, another one, rigorous; without a criterion that can be grasped, precision is impossible. The problem — of political prudence — then is to find out where the lesser evil lies: In the indeterminacy of a rule which in practice is exposed to erring by

[12] Under the Geneva Protocol of 1924, the state which would refuse to submit the controversy to a pacific procedure was to be deemed the aggressor. Other projects made their appearance in which an effort was made to enumerate direct or indirect acts of aggression. A problem of the same order arose before the Disarmament Conference which assembled under the auspices of Geneva: that of distinguishing between offensive armaments subject to prohibition and defensive ones which would be authorized.

[13] See *supra*, nos. 93–94.

[14] On the danger of arbitrariness of the judge, see St. Thomas, *op. cit. Ia IIae*, qu. 95, art. 1 *ad* 2: . . . On the dangers of the system of directives (standards) in particular see J. Maury, *Observations sur les modes d'expression du droit: règles et directives* nos. 10 *et seq.*, in Introduction à l'étude du droit comparé, 1 Recueil Lambert § 35, pp. 425 *et seq.*

excess or by deficiency, thus casting confusion into a branch of socially useful activity, or in the license accorded to the producers of indecent shows to corrupt their public with impunity. An exact comprehension of the hierarchy of values will doubtless lead to preferring the second alternative: So much the worse for the socially useful activity of the theater if its functioning is in a certain manner linked to the demoralization of the people. One will nonetheless regret the absence of a categorical definition allowing a reconciliation of all legitimate interests and affecting only the really obscene shows.[15] This is by no means to say, though, that the obstacle is insurmountable. The jurist has the duty unceasingly to perfect his instruments and in the light of science and experience to search for the formula adhering as closely as possible to truth while providing the maximum of practicability.

176. The System of Broad Definitions: Advantages and Inconveniences. Typical and necessary as it may be, the definite character of legal rules is on the whole a matter of the golden mean and, for each rule to be elaborated, a matter of the special instance. Definition thus is required only to a certain degree — that below which the rule, being decidedly too loose, is unmanageable. Moreover, definition is not without inconvenience. A law too exactly defined, above all by features of pure form, is an incomplete law, for it leaves outside of its grasp factual situations which are not formally provided for although they are in substance identical.[16] Besides, it is often ill adapted, in the absence of a margin for singular cases in derogation from the norm. It provides an adjustment only for the situation envisaged, and provided that the individual case in no way deviates from that assumed situation. But social life, infinitely multifarious, complex, changing, could not be reduced to a collection of assumptions *a priori* for which the law would have to provide as many uniform solutions. Instituted to discipline the living subject matter, the law is bound to espouse the plasticity of life — as far as the requirements of security permit. Hence in every age, and especially in our epoch which is smitten with realism in the social as in the natural sciences, the favor accorded to the method of broad definitions, whose suppleness permits all cases, foreseeable or not,

[15] In vain would one claim to ask for an answer from natural law; cf. P. CUCHE, CONFÉRENCES DE PHILOSOPHIE DU DROIT: LE MIRAGE DU DROIT NATUREL (Paris, 1928) 30–32. Natural law offers only the very first principles of morality; see *infra*, no. 204.

[16] A significant example is that of the repression of usury in loans of sums of money . . . On the realistic character of the penal law as compared with the conceptual formalism of private law, cf. L. Hugueney, note in SIREY (1942) 1, 149 (§ 2), on *Crim.*, Oct. 9, 1940.

to be embraced and yet allows each one to be granted its appropriate treatment.

177. Examples: Public Policy; Article 1382 of the Code Napoleon. The most striking illustration of this method in private law is that of "public policy." There we have a notion which, except in certain of its applications, is nowhere defined either by statute or by case law or by custom. One understands at one stroke that public policy synthesizes the essential normative principles of social and political life; but nothing is revealed as to the determination of these essential principles. Now the rôle of "public policy" in the law is of capital importance, not only as one of the criteria of the so-called mandatory laws, derogation from which is prohibited, but also in itself as an insurmountable barrier to the autonomy of wills: Everything is permissible for the will of the subjects short of encroaching upon "public policy." [17] Of this "public order," which is more or less variable with time and place, the judge ultimately is the arbiter, under the sole control of the highest court, the interperter of "public policy" in the absence of a statute. How, indeed, could it be permitted that, outside of the very incomplete cases where the statute has come to state precisely such and such a requirement of "public policy," the subjects would be free to contravene any principle whatever of "public policy," even if it be an unwritten, unforeseen one? The principle of a certain law, though it is itself required by the public good, is obliged to give way to a superior principle of public policy, to wit, the maintenance of the social and political life based on respect for all the values composing "public policy." [18]

Another example of a broad definition is furnished by article 1382 of the Code Napoleon: "Any human act whatsoever that shall cause damage to another shall oblige him by whose fault it has occurred to repair it." "Any human act whatsoever," provided it is injurious and also faulty, by infraction of no matter what rule of morals, law, social manners, or (mechanical or social) technique: Unlike other bodies of legislation, the Code neither enumerates nor specifies in any manner the faulty activities or abstentions. "To repair": The statute indicates neither the mode nor the extent of the reparation, an amount of money or other value of replacement. Thus the rule confines itself to setting up the general and abstract principle of reparation of injuries due to fault;

[17] On "public policy," see J. Dabin, *Autonomie de la volonté et lois impératives, ordre public et bonnes moeurs*, in ANNALES DE DROIT ET DE SCIENCE POLITIQUE (Louvain, 1940) 190 *et seq.*

[18] The same remarks apply to the notion of *bonnes moeurs* or public morality; see observations by Savatier in REVUE TRIMESTRIELLE (1940–41) 303–305.

it is the judge who will work out the determination of the principle according to the cases. Thereby is guaranteed the fullness of application of a rule judged to be true and useful in its very generality and whose functioning would be hampered by a system of more or less strict definition.

178. Examples in the Field of Public and Administrative Law. The same method prevails, even much more widely, in public law, constitutional and administrative, for the norms guiding legislative, executive, and administrative activities. If the public authority incontestably has no right or jurisdiction save along the line of the public good,[19] it is impossible to have the line of conduct to be followed in every case fixed in advance in a rigid fashion as one would for private relations. Public life, especially the life of administration, is filled with unforeseen situations which must be pared down and provided for by exactly adapted solutions.[20] Hence the resort to broad rules within the frame of which the authority can move at ease with the reservation of an eventual control of the legality of its decisions.[21]

179. But Not All Matters Lend Themselves Equally to Broad Definitions: The Penal Law. However, to proceed by "directives" does not fit all matters without distinction. There are those matters where the need for security prevails over the considerations of truth and expediency, as in every case where the law provides for penalties, forfeitures, or other measures punitive in character.[22] In a society respectful of the rights of man, it would be intolerable to have the most precious human goods — life, honor, liberty — depend upon the free appraisal of one

[19] On the degree of the impact of the law upon politics, see *supra*, nos. 95–96.

[20] One may generalize and extend the conclusion to rules whose subject is any authority whatever, public or private (such as the head of the family) . . .

[21] An eventual control; the control is not always actually established, e.g., the control of the constitutionality of statutes and even in some countries of the legality of administrative rules.

[22] E.g., the ingratitude of the recipient of a donation giving rise to revocation of the gift (Code Napoleon, art. 955) or the unworthiness of the heir giving rise to exclusion from succession (art. 727). [Art. 955 provides as follows: "A gift *inter vivos* may be revoked on the ground of ingratitude only in the following cases: (1) If the donee has encompassed an attack upon the life of the donor; (2) If he has become guilty of violence, delicts, or grave insults against him; (3) If he refuses to give him alimony." Art. 727 provides as follows: "The following are unworthy to inherit and are thus excluded from succession: (1) He who shall be convicted of having killed or attempted to kill the deceased; (2) He who has brought an accusation of a capital offense against the deceased which shall be adjudged to have been slanderous; (3) The heir who, being of age, and advised of the murder of the deceased, shall not have reported it to the agencies of justice."]

or several men, even if these be qualified public functionaries such as the judge or administrator. *Nulla poena sine lege. Odiosa sunt restringenda.*[c] The rule must determine both the fact which occasions the penalty and the nature of the penalty.[23] This follows from the principle of a government of laws.[24] So, again, in the field of contract, where the principle of scrupulous observation of engagements has its necessary counterpart in a scrupulous definition of the respective rights and obligations — by the contract, by usages, or by statute — where the security of the creditor calls correlatively for the security of the debtor.[25] So, equally, in the field of procedure or in matters of form not only are the stages indicated that are to be gone through and the formalities that are to be complied with, but also the details of the procedure and forms are clearly designated from a conceptual point of view.

180. The Jurist Does Not Cease to Search for the Strict Definition. Precision in the law answers to so natural a tendency that even in matters subject to the régime of directives, judges and lawyers exert themselves to banish the vagueness of concepts by introducing notes of specification. So a division of labor is established at the end between the statute which from above formulates the "directive" and the other sources, closer to the concrete, which with lesser, and also variable, authority set forth its applications in detail. In the case of article 1382 [of the Code Napoleon],[d] we then see the catalogues of factual acts and the listings of damages: It is "established doctrine" and "established by cases" that some kind of attitude is reprehensible either from the moral or social point of view or from that of technical skill; or that some sort of injury to persons or property, material or moral, opens the way either to a certain amount of money damages or to a certain mode of

[c] [No punishment without a law. Burdens must be restricted.]

[23] This is not to say that the penal law knows only rigorously defined concepts. Thus, in offenses based on habitual practices (usury, etc.), the law does not define the number of acts constituting a habit; cf. A. Lebrun, note in DALLOZ CRITIQUE (1941) *Jurisprudence* 78 *et seq.*, especially at 80–81. Sometimes, however, the law fixes a number; see the Belgian Law of Social Defense of 1930, art. 25, para. 2, where three infractions are required "as constituting a persistent tendency to delinquency." On the other hand, there are many psychological concepts in penal law which are not susceptible of determination *a priori*, such as malice.

[24] However, a government of laws has not always existed; see some references in G. del Vecchio, *Essai sur les principes généraux du droit* § VI, in JUSTICE, DROIT, ETAT 140, n. 2. Today, the principle is again contested not only in practice but also in theory.

[25] Cf., in this sense, J. Maury, *Observations sur les modes d'expression du droit: règles et directives* no. 12, in 1 RECUEIL LAMBERT § 35, p. 426.

[d] [See *supra*, no. 177.]

reparation such as the publication of the judgment of reparation in the newspapers.[26] Another famous example, drawn from administrative law, is that of the French Council of State,[e] rendering decisions, making determinations, regulating its own discretionary power within the framework of the good of the service, by means of more or less strict directives or categories.[27] The human mind, as much as social life, thirsts for precision. If the rule does not provide it, the mind creates it; the directive evolves into a rule.[28]

181. Cases Where the Law is Obliged to Renounce All Definition. There are, however, matters where the law is constrained to renounce any definition whatever and, for that reason, any intervention: That is, when the very science of these matters speaks reservedly. The realities which are basic to the rules always have a scientific character in the sense that, "given" by life, they are in the first place subjects of scientific knowledge. Through the intermediary of science, grasped and defined by science, they reach the jurist.[29] Now it may happen that scientifically the matter is not clarified, that the science furnishes the jurist neither with a directive nor with anything certain as given. A typical case is that of medical fault: Despite the general competence to judge any fault whatsoever in no matter what field, which the statute grants the courts, they ordinarily refuse to pronounce upon the fault committed by physicians and surgeons, at least where it is properly medical or surgical, relating to the very technique of the medical or surgical art.[30] Medical science is not always in agreement as to the value and expediency of a treatment or a surgical operation: *Grammatici*

[26] As concerns the calculation of injuries, see the tables in 1 PIRSON and DE VILLÉ, TRAITÉ DE LA RESPONSABILITÉ CIVILE EXTRA-CONTRACTUELLE (Bruxelles, 1935) nos. 186–219, *passim*, pp. 416–529.

[e] [The supreme tribunal of administrative law in France.]

[27] See on this point M. Hauriou, *Aux sources du droit*, in CAHIERS DE LA NOUVELLE JOURNÉE no. 13 (1933) pp. 147 *et seq.*

[28] See, in the same sense, J. Maury, *op. cit.* nos. 16–17, in 1 RECUEIL LAMBERT § 35, pp. 428–430.

[29] It is understood that "science" is taken here in a wide sense, meaning not only the sciences properly so called but also philosophy and the technologies; see *supra*, nos. 126–127. But one must leave aside history, whose subject is the existence of singular, purely contingent facts, which poses a question of proof that the jurist will eventually resolve by a legal presumption; one must also leave aside morals, for the perplexities of the moralist cannot prevent the jurist from giving to problems a specifically legal solution deduced from the sole requirements of the public good.

[30] See the exposition in 2 R. SAVATIER, TRAITÉ DE LA RESPONSABILITÉ EN DROIT FRANÇAIS (Paris, 1939) nos. 777 and 790.

certant.[f] How then should the legislator or the judge take sides on the questions disputed among scholars in the field? Simple prudence prohibits the jurisprudent from venturing into regions where the science — which by hypothesis is alone competent — hesitates to make its pronouncement. The impossibility of a scientific definition upon which to base a sure solution thus condemns the jurist to an attitude of abstention.[31]

In other such cases, it is true, the jurist intervenes instead of abstaining, but he does so without taking sides, as in the matter of artistic and literary protection. Incontestably, from the social viewpoint as well as in reason, only work of an artistic character confers rights upon its author. A work lacking artistic character is without interest for the jurist as well as for the public; it is not worth the trouble of an effort at protection. But the difficulty consists in judging the artistic character of a work. The "canons" differ and the principles of aesthetics are even more vacillating than those of the medical art: *De coloribus non disputandum*.[g] Yet the jurist intervenes in the particular case because a refusal of intervention would have the inadmissible result of depriving the author of the true work of art of protection; he would suffer unjustly from an indifference based on principle. That is why the law keeps to a purely empirical criterion for the determination of the work of art: The work that presents itself with the pretension, whether or not justified, of constituting a work of art, legally belongs to art. On the basis of this criterion, the law extends its protection to any creation whatever, artistic or pseudo-artistic, leaving to the aestheticists and the public the task of separating the grain from the chaff.

182. Summary of the Technical Processes of Definition: Simplification. The processes of definition used by the law for purposes of "practicability" are more or less radical. On principle and in a general fashion the jurist uses simplification, neglecting the exceptional cases, little embarrassed by shades of meaning, preferring to cling to the superficial and obvious aspect of things. In this respect, one may compare the definitions, given respectively by the jurist and the scholar in the field, of the notions of "worker" or "salaried employee," which are basic to social legislation or laws on associations, or of the notion of "defects in consent" [*vices du consentement*], as grounds for the avoidance of legal acts. Whereas the sociologist endeavors by minute and complicated

[f] [The grammarians differ.]

[31] This abstention is not, however, a refusal to judge or denial of justice as proscribed by Code Napoleon, art. 4 [see *supra*, no. 133, n. 7] . . .

[g] [One should not argue about colors.]

analysis to depict the characteristic traits of the diverse social types of the "worker" or the "salaried employee," the jurist simply decrees [32] that for him the "worker" is a man whose occupation is manual labor, at least principally, while the work of the "salaried employee," on the contrary, is principally of an intellectual nature.[33] Whereas the psychologist and the moralist endeavor to depict the numerous factors of mental deficiency capable of influencing the validity of acts, the corresponding chapter of legal psychology distinguishes itself by a rigid and poor "schematism" where only certain elementary, narrowly designated defects find acceptance.

No doubt modern law becomes more and more preoccupied with psychology and sociology, and the inherited categories of the [Roman] Institutes have become happily more supple through the contact with a more exacting and refined science.[34] But, whatever one may do or want to do, the legal definition will always remain more or less approximate, expeditious, and summary. To grasp the phenomena in their logical or historical entirety and continuity, and *a fortiori* to penetrate into the

[32] In the absence of the legislator, who has not pronounced upon the point; see the [Belgian] Law on the Contract of Work of March 10, 1900, art. 1, and Law on the Contract of Employment of August 7, 1922, art. 1.

[33] Right here is one of the rocks of all "pluralistic" legislation which diversifies statutes according to social categories or classes, viz., the difficulty of a definition of types both exact and commodious enough. See on this point J. DABIN, DOCTRINE GÉNÉRALE DE L'ETAT, no. 271, p. 438.

[34] Thus it is appropriate to take account of the introduction in many special statutory provisions of new and more supple categories in matters of legal psychology, such as the notion of the abuse of the weaknesses, passions, wants, or ignorance of the contracting party. See, e.g., sec. 138, para. 2 of the German Civil Code [which provides as follows: "In particular, any legal act shall be void by which a person through exploiting the plight, the light-mindedness, or the inexperience of another shall cause pecuniary gains to be promised or afforded to himself or to a third party for a consideration which they exceed so far in value as to be conspicuously disproportionate in the circumstances"] and art. 1907 *ter* of the Belgian Civil Code (Royal Ordinance no. 148 of March 18, 1935) [which provides as follows: "Without prejudice to the application of the provisions protecting incompetents or relating to the validity of contracts, where the lender, abusing the wants, weaknesses, passions, or ignorance of the borrower, stipulates for such interest or other advantages as manifestly exceed the normal interest and the coverage of the risks of the loan, for the benefit of the lender himself or of another, the judge upon the request of the borrower shall reduce his obligations to the repayment of the borrowed capital and payment of statutory interest. The reduction shall apply to past payments of the borrower, provided that his request is made within three years from the day of any such payment."] See generally on the tendency of contemporary law to become "socialized," and in this sense "individualized," G. Radbruch, *Du droit individualiste au droit social*, in ARCHIVES DE PHILOSOPHIE DU DROIT (1931) nos. 3–4, pp. 387–398.

essence of things is not, and never will be, the forte of the jurist, because his task is not to establish scientifically correct definitions but to elaborate applicable rules, and the practicability of the law seeks relatively simple, manageable definitions.[35]

183. Some Artifices of Simplification. The tendency to simplification is shown in particular in the employment of certain means which manifestly have no other rôle than to cut short any wavering in the application of the law. Such are the means of prescribing figures, for concepts representing quantitative values, and the means of enumeration of species, for concepts representing qualitative values. For instance, when the jurist decrees that the period of prescription is thirty years, that figure is fixed by reason not of its truth, for it is arbitrary, but of the certainty which it confers on the rule of prescription by lapse of time. When the law draws up the list of transactions subjected to forms of some sort or other, or that of dangerous, obnoxious, or unsanitary establishments subjected to administrative authorization, it sacrifices the fullness of the idea, expressed generically, to the convenience of particular cases.[36]

Still further, where there is the problem of a precise determination that is deemed both indispensable as a guarantee against interpretative aberrations and unrealizable by the normal device of "reduction to the quantitative," the jurist does not hesitate to replace the inconvenient concept with a substitute less exact in substance but more easily grasped, ordinarily with its indicia or its sign. Thus, the age, or duration of the physical existence, of the individual (a quantitative value susceptible of statement in figures from the date of birth) is taken for the irrefragable sign of mental maturity, justifying full freedom and legal capacity; the real estate character of a transaction (according to the nature of its object) is taken for the irrefragable sign of the degree of seriousness of the acts, justifying a reinforcement of the system of protection afforded those lacking legal capacity; the standard of living of the taxpayer, disclosed by certain indicia (kind of dwelling, servants, etc.), is taken for the irrefragable sign of the importance, always hard to evaluate, of his income from the viewpoint of revenue.[37]

Under the law of large numbers — or of probability — it is doubtless

[35] Cf. in a rather different sense F. Russo, *op. cit.* 65 *et seq.*, 99 *et seq.*, 109–110, 192 *et seq.*

[36] On the process of "reduction to the quantitative" by statement of figures or enumeration, see J. Dabin, La technique de l'élaboration du droit positif 121 *et seq.*

[37] In systems of taxation based upon external indicia. However, even in systems based on controlled tax declarations or returns, the process remains; save for the

permissible to suppose that in the particular case the sign faithfully translates the underlying reality. But the moment the contrary is possible and, on the basis of an irrefragable presumption, the proof of that contrary is inadmissible, the substitution amounts to a conscious and deliberate sacrifice of the truth at least for those assumed cases which deviate from *quod plerumque fit*.[h] For the others, contrariwise, which form the majority, the rule will work with a sure aim, in a quasi-automatic fashion and without negating truth. Such is the advantage of a judiciously calculated misstep: In the majority of cases it combines the advantages of the truth of the law and of its practicability.[38]

SECTION 2. THE APTNESS FOR PROOF OF THE FACTS THAT ARE SUBJECT TO A RULE

184. The Social Necessity of Proof. A second factor of the practicability of the law consists in the aptness for proof of the facts established as conditions of application of rules.[1] Let it be noted that this is a distinct factor of the definition: The conditions of application of rules can be perfectly defined in their concept without thereby solving the problem of proof. In order that the rules find their application it does not indeed suffice that their conditions of application are actually realized: That effective realization must also be proved, that is to say, objectively shown by elements engendering conviction either in the party bound to perform or, in case of contest, in the organs of application of the law. The bound party who knows that the conditions are realized no doubt can — and most of the time he is under a duty to — perform spontaneously; but in the absence of spontaneous performance the necessity of proof enters the arena, and it must be maintained by any social organization on pain of installing an "impressionistic," partial, arbitrary justice. The private or public party who demands the application of a legal rule or, in other words, the operation of the sanction after violation of a rule, thus has the burden of establishing the existence in the particular case of the conditions of application of the disposition made by the rule. Normally, this burden of proof is upon him and he will dis-

---

risk of a control which is, moreover, often not very effective, taxation is based on the declaration alone which takes the place of the indicia.

[h] [What occurs in most cases.]

[38] On the process of substitutions of concepts, see J. DABIN, LA TECHNIQUE DE L'ÉLABORATION DU DROIT POSITIF 144 *et seq.*

[1] On the technique of proof, see J. DABIN, LA TECHNIQUE DE L'ÉLABORATION DU DROIT POSITIF 77 *et seq.*

charge it by his own strength alone or with the more or less active aid of the judge; [2] if he fails, his claim must normally be rejected.

185. The Difficulties Inherent in Proof. However, not all facts are equally apt for proof. There are among them some which escape demonstration due to the lack of sufficiently sure means of investigation.[3] How in that case is one to avoid embarrassment? No doubt the law may supply the deficiency, not only by requiring a certain formality or by preconstituting proof (where the matter lends itself thereto), but also by setting up simplifying presumptions. Thus, the statute relieves the child of a married woman, conceived during marriage, of the proof of paternity, which is the condition of application of the obligations and effects of paternity. In its eyes, and consequently in the eyes of all, the woman's husband is the father of the child, at least until proof to the contrary by the party who contests the paternity.[4] Still, in order rationally to justify the presumption, it must be supported by probabilities. The law can presume, even rebuttably, only what is normal. Otherwise the presumption degenerates into a fiction: The legislator presumes what he desires or likes rather than what is; he prejudges and, to that extent, he rebels against reality, he resorts to fiction.

But usually the matter defies legal presumptions; varied and singular reality obeys no constant factor, which explains the exceptional character of the presumptions of the law. The duty of proof reappears. Now let us assume it is impossible to produce proof, if not always in an absolute manner, at least in the forms of its production in court, before the organs of application of the law. For example, the facts to be proved, though external or externalized, are of such a nature as to occur without witnesses, leave no traces, lend themselves to disguise; or they are

[2] This depends upon the legal system. Some procedural laws allot an active part to the judge in the conduct of even civil proceedings; others establish in principle the system of judicial passivity (inaptly so-called "neutrality").

[3] We confine ourselves to this assumption, which is the most frequent one. But there are also cases where the proof of the fact (or the method of investigation) would be too scandalous. This explains the elimination in French civil law of impotence as a ground for the nullity of marriage or even for an action disavowing paternity, Code Napoleon, art. 313, *initio* [which provides as follows, as amended by the Belgian Act of March 20, 1927: "The husband may not disavow the child by alleging his natural impotence; he may not even disavow him on the ground of adultery unless the birth has been concealed from him, in which case he is allowed to submit all facts tending to show that he is not the father."] Between the scandal of proof and the scandal of silence of the law, the law chooses silence.

[4] We are talking here only of simple presumptions admitting proof to the contrary (*juris tantum*), for irrebuttable presumptions (*juris et de jure*) regulate no question of proof . . . See J. DABIN, *op. cit.* 241 *et seq.*

covered by professional secrecy, a value deemed superior to the manifestation of the truth; or again, where the matter involves an appraisal of the significance, the bearing or the influence *in casu* [a] of certain subtle facts (which is still to be proved), the estimation of facts cannot be made. The jurist then has no other resource than to eliminate these facts as conditions of application of the rule and, in the case where they would have to form its sole condition, — as for penal repression or for taxation — to sacrifice the very rule called upon to govern them. It is logically and socially impossible to base any regulation, command, or proceeding upon facts which by their nature or by reason of an unfavorable environment escape all control.

186. Sometimes These Difficulties May Lead to Total Abstention by the Law. Such is the attitude adopted universally by legislatures, even in countries with brutal "birth" policies, with regard to Neo-Malthusianism.[5] Independently of the demoralization of which it is both a result and an agent, Neo-Malthusianism constitutes an essential social evil, synonymous with the extinction of the race, of society, and of the state. On the other hand, the concept does not offer any difficulty in its definition: It is known what Neo-Malthusianism is and in what practices it consists. The sole obstacle resides in proof. To mark the facts of propaganda, circulation of equipment or abortion does not go beyond the possibility of inquiry: [6] It is enough if the prosecutors and courts dare to act. But how can contraceptive activities, too, be tracked down? That is why the law at the outset renounces the struggle, at least under the direct form of prohibitive intervention. The same obstacle of proof, added to that of definition, will hamper the repression of usury. The usurer uses simulation and dissimulation ("palliated usury"); his victims, both ashamed and grateful, refrain from complaining, which renders proceedings delicate. In civil law, the legislator refuses to take account of misrepresentation as a cause of nullity of marriage, in part because in such a matter the constitutive elements of misrepresentation are hard to grasp, to estimate and to prove.[7]

[a] [In the case.]

[5] However, PLATO, LAWS, bk. VI, 783 d *et seq.*, provided for inspectresses of marriages. . . See P. LACHIÈZE-REY, LES IDÉES MORALES, SOCIALES ET POLITIQUES DE PLATON (Paris) 216–218.

[6] On propaganda, see French Law of July 31, 1920, DALLOZ PÉRIODIQUE (1921) 4, 167.

[7] Fear of fraud has led to limiting to descendants the persons entitled to family allotments; see Rodière, *Pour quelles personnes les allocations familiales sont-elles dues?* DALLOZ HEBDOMADAIRE, *Chronique* (1939) 25.

187. The Law Eliminates the Element Resisting Proof. Elsewhere, the jurist discards the element resisting proof in the complex of facts basic to the disposition of the law, retaining only the circumstances capable of discovery. Thus, the legislator of revenue law is seen first proclaiming his intent to strike at certain operations "speculative in character" (in the sense of productive of benefits), then he is abandoning this condition as too delicate of proof, so as finally to tax the operations taken in their materiality, leaving out the element of speculation. The latter subsists only on the logical plane, by virtue of a legal construction, as the irrefragable presumption of speculation; from the rank of a condition of application, speculation is pushed back to the level of a reason or motive, incapable by that token of influencing the working of the precept: *Finis legis non cadit sub praecepto.*[b] [8] Again, in imposing liability for injury resulting from multiple causes among which there is a fault, the more or less decisive character of the fault in relation to the other causes of the injury is neglected. The individual at fault is made responsible, and in full, since his fault has contributed to producing the injury, if only partially or even mediately. This solution, which is called "equivalence of conditions," may seem unjust since it does not respect distributive justice in distributing the burden of the injury. But it is justified by saying that it is "the only one that appears susceptible of resolving the problem of the causal relation in practice." [9] In other words, the theoretically true law yields to the practical consideration of proof.

The same surrender is noticeable in numerous rules of civil law, and sometimes of penal law, where there is a disregard of the psychological state of the acting person, of the intention with which he acted, his good or bad faith, and so forth. For as long as the psychological inquiry is practicable (and with the reservation that no harm be done those parties or third parties who could have legitimately relied on the appearances created), it is no doubt desirable. But from the moment it meets obstacles of proof, renouncing psychology is not at all turning to a materialist objectivism; it is merely showing a sane realism, conscious of the practical ends of the law.

[b] [The end of a law does not fall within its precept.]

[8] The case chosen as an example is that of a Belgian Law of June 14, 1937, as construed by the [Belgian] Court of Cassation in decisions of March 6, 1940, with conclusions of the [Belgian] Advocate General Hayoit de Termicourt, PASICRISIE (1940) I, 140; of November 12, 1940, PASICRISIE (1940) I, 290; etc.

[9] 2 H. DE PAGE, TRAITÉ ÉLÉMENTAIRE DE DROIT CIVIL BELGE (2d ed.) no. 958, p. 904. But see G. Marty, *La relation de cause à effet comme condition de la responsabilité civile*, in REVUE TRIMESTRIELLE DE DROIT CIVIL (1939) 685 *et seq.*

SECTION 3. THE CONCENTRATION OF LEGAL MATTER

188. Reduction of the Mass of Rules through Classification. A third factor of the practicability of the law consists in a certain dose of reduction and concentration of legal matter. Although this factor has less (and more remote) importance than the two preceding ones, it is nonetheless interesting inasmuch as concentration facilitates the management of the law.

In pure logic and according to pure justice, even social justice, each particular case should have its particular solution modeled upon the case. Whether it be taken from the viewpoint of the individual or of society, justice is always individual, measured by the individual case. But this "individualization" which is possible for the internal forum is not practicable for the external forum. Rules, that is to say, *general* dispositions, are necessary, formulating the hypothesis in a general manner, on the basis of a presumption of conformity of the single cases to the norm, and also the solution in a general manner, notwithstanding the more or less noticeable differences between the cases.[1]

That first, and also most essential, simplification is still insufficient: The sum total of the rules must itself not exceed a certain limit. Hence, in particular, the classifications of hypotheses and [legal] solutions under certain common predications, erected into so many principles of division. The rôle of classifications in the law is to diminish the number of the rules so that the interpreter does not feel overwhelmed with an excess of scarcely differentiated prescriptions. Indeed, the more abundant the rules, foreseeing and disposing in a special manner of indefinite quantities of hypotheses, the heavier the instrument to be moved and the harder to find the rule applicable to the particular case.[2] Thus are to be explained the cut and dried classifications that are intended as exhaustive: Things are movable or immovable, acts are for valuable consideration or gratuitous, rights are property rights or non-property rights, interests are public or private; intermediate or mixed cases are

[1] Cf. in this sense, ST. THOMAS, SUMMA, *Ia IIae*, qu. 96, art. 1 *ad resp.:* . . . Equally, art. 6 *ad resp.* (*in medio*) and *ad* 3. But see, as to the ground derived from the common good, our observations above, no. 57.

[2] Is it sufficiently well known that in America the Laws of New York cover 2751 pages for 1911, 1377 pages for 1912, and 2220 pages for 1913? That the decisions of the courts in the United States cover probably 12,000 to 13,000 volumes as of 1928? That a million decisions are summarized in the AMERICAN DIGEST? (According to R. VALEUR, DEUX CONCEPTIONS DE L'ENSEIGNEMENT JURIDIQUES: LES FACULTÉS FRANÇAISES DES SCIENCES SOCIALES, LES ÉCOLES PROFESSIONNELLES DE DROIT AUX ETATS-UNIS (Thesis, Lyon, 1928) 137–138.

perforce placed in one of the two classes.[3] Similarly, the [legal] solutions are divided into limited classes: The systems of protection for those lacking legal capacity are divided into representation and assistance or authorization; the nullities sanctioning irregular acts are absolute or relative. Each one of these categores entails a more or less inseparable set of [legal] consequences.

No doubt, once again, perfection lies in the golden mean. Too simple classifications will produce an inadequate and therefore unjust law. Here again the realistic, scientific spirit of contemporary jurists is inclined to render the heads of classification more supple so as to bring law closer to life, which is wholly in gradations. But the requirements of the manageability of the law oppose their veto to an excessive multiplication of headings, which if carried to an extreme would have the effect of ruining the utility and even the principle of classifications. So, too, even where the jurist sees fit to introduce shadings into his divisions, he ordinarily does so by the detour of exceptions, which is a way of maintaining the rigid classification at least as a principle. Sometimes the jurist goes farther: In the same manner in which he bends definitions by substitution or amputation, he forces classifications either by extension to categories foreign thereto or by inversion of the natural order of attachment. Thus, the classification of movables and immovables is extended to contractual rights and copyrights, or certain movables, the so-called "immovables by destination," are attached to the class of immovables. Whatever the value in the particular case or even the expediency in general of such alterations, they always tend to the same result, to wit, an economy, at least an apparent one, in the tremendous profusion of legal rules.[4]

189. The Process of "Legal Constructions." To the same concern with concentration relates the so-called process of "legal constructions." By this is understood a systematization of the law by way of dialectics, starting from a simple idea whose corollaries then radiate over the entire matter so as to unify and often to fecundate it.[5] For systematization on

[3] On half onerous, half gratuitous mixed contracts, cf. M. BOITARD, LES CONTRATS DE SERVICES GRATUITS 159–160, 171–175.

[4] On the process of classification, see J. DABIN, LA TECHNIQUE DE L'ÉLABORATION DU DROIT POSITIF 163 *et seq.* Also, regarding classified types of conflicts of laws, P. LEREBOURS-PIGEONNIÈRE, PRÉCIS DE DROIT INTERNATIONAL PRIVÉ (3d ed.) no. 219, p. 253.

[5] "Legal construction" thus has nothing in common with the "construction" of the law in the sense determined before, nos. 98 *et seq.* Legal construction proceeds from given rules with a view to systematization, while the construction of the law works out the rules themselves.

the basis of the *real* explanation is not always satisfactory to the mind, by reason of the often fugitive or complex character of the *ratio legis*; the latter mingles considerations of law and fact, of reason and expediency, not to forget history, which by its accidents or survivals so powerfully influences the content of the law. Hence the recourse to an ideal principle — a popular notion or a juridical category — more or less close, more or less artificial in relation to the real explanation, but whose synthesis-value brings simplicity and clarity into the diffuse mass of rules. Such is the idea that the heir continues the person of the deceased, or the idea of a mandate, tacitly conferred by the husband upon the wife, to manage the affairs of the household. Let us add that the idea, playing the rôle of the hypothesis in science, constitutes a means of developing the law in that it may suggest solutions on new points not foreseen by the existing rule. If, then, materially construction does not result in diminishing the sum total of the rules, if it even happens that by its fecundating power the idea augments their number, reduction nevertheless operates intellectually, by virtue of the unifying principle of which the rules are henceforth but logical determinations or corollaries.

But it must be said at once that the process of constructions is dangerous, precisely to the extent that the idea, withdrawing from the social, moral, and legal realities which condition the law, risks sacrificing the law's substance to a factitious unity. The logical coherence of the rules is a facility for the interpreter and also for the subjects — and therefore in certain respects a secondary quality which could not prevail over the essential, to wit, the truth, expediency, and immediate practicability of the law.[6]

190. Preserving a Just Measure in Evaluating "Practicability." So, too, if, following Jhering, Gény, and the theorists of technique in the law, the idea of practicability has been insisted upon, particularly under the aspect of the definition of the concepts and their aptness for proof, this is not intended to create the impression that concern with such practicability should block all efforts toward the theoretical ideal, which is the rule conforming to the public good in accordance with the possibilities of the environment. First, it has been intended only to establish a principle, to wit, the necessity of considering in the law the practicability of the rules. The examples have been chosen only to document this, by way of underscoring the obstacles without claiming them to be altogether insurmountable even in the cases cited. It has been remarked,

[6] On "legal constructions," see J. DABIN, *op. cit.* 186 *et seq.*

moreover, that the principle of practicability was subject to compromise. A lesser practicability might suffice where the intrinsic virtue of the precept, supported by the moral authority of the legislator, would be of a nature to convince the subjects. Still more: Every consideration of practicability must be effaced where the silence of the law would take on the appearance of a scandal, a social evil more serious than the lack of practicability. Further, it must not be forgotten that the impracticability of today can disappear tomorrow or find its remedy, thanks to the progress of science in the definition of its concepts, to the perfecting of the technique of proofs, to a more logical distribution of the subject matter of the law. Thus, for instance, the uncertainty in the field of medical fault may give way to surer appraisals; resort to statistical procedures may lead to a more exact measurement of social facts; the discovery of the so-called "blood-group test" has permitted us to circumscribe, if not to eliminate, the mystery of paternity; the system of organic laws and codifications diminishes the inconveniences of the multiplicity of rules, etc.

CONCLUSIONS ON THE LEGAL METHOD AND COROLLARIES

Section 1. Dual Aspect of Technique in the Law

191. As to Substance, a Social and Political Technique; as to Form, a Logical Technique. At the end of this detailed exposition of legal method, we have in hand the somewhat experimental proof for the thesis which has previously been developed *a priori*, that everything in the legal rule, whatever its source, including custom, is construction and, in this sense, a work of technique. As will have been noted, this technique is of a twofold kind. First, as to substance, that is, as to the content of the rules, the appropriate technique is of a social and political nature. Of a social nature, because the subject matter and the aim of the law are to order the social relationships between individuals and groups and between states. Of a political nature, because that ordering must take place under the inspiration and within the framework of domestic and international politics. Then, as to form, the appropriate technique is of a logical nature, indeed of a special logic, to a peculiarly utilitarian end, to wit, the practicability of the rules.

192. It Is a Mistake to Reduce Technique in the Law to the Sole Idea of Practicability. Gény may be criticized for having neglected the distinction between these two compartments and to relate the whole technical side of the law to the idea of practicability.[1] Is it not for social science,[2] or rather for politics, which governs the social, to decide upon all that concerns the public good, upon the value and the expediency of the measures, legal or otherwise, which it may require, recommend, or support? Interpolated between the natural law as conceived by Gény, reduced to a minimum of economic or moral principles which provide the basic ideas, and the working out of a practicable form, there is the phase of organic and adapted development of the first principles, no doubt the most important and the most typical phase of elaboration. This is where the law is essentially subordinate to social science and politics, where all those who contribute to building it up work as sociologists and political scientists. It is agreed, also, that the expression "technique" is not well chosen to designate this task. It is valid — and has here been accepted [3] — only in a quite relative sense, as opposed to science. In reality, as has been explained,[4] the determination of the content of the law, being a matter of governing others and therefore of moral action, belongs not to a technique, nor to an art, but above all to one of the kinds of prudence, political prudence, and still more especially, juridical prudence. It is this juridical prudence that makes the choice between legal solutions — in the spheres of ends, of means, of sanctions, of proofs [5] — without excluding the concurrence, in a subordinate rank, of a certain social and political art.

The practicability of the law, on the contrary, raises no other problem than that of a certain "fashioning" of the rule under its conceptual aspect, which renders it apt for application first by the subjects and then by officials and judges. Now this problem as such is foreign to social science and politics, which no doubt dominate the practicability of the law as a principle but leave the task of realizing it to the technician of regulatory form. Hence the term "formal legal technique" or "legal technique properly so called," to designate this latter phase of construction of the law: Formal technique, since it concerns only the

[1] As to this criticism, see J. DABIN, LA TECHNIQUE DE L'ÉLABORATION DU DROIT POSITIF 348; in the same sense, F. RUSSO, RÉALITÉ JURIDIQUE ET RÉALITÉ SOCIALE 31–32, 61 *et seq.*

[2] "Social science": sometimes we shall speak of "sociology," using the two terms synonymously.

[3] See *supra*, nos. 98, 99.

[4] See *supra*, no. 124.

[5] Upon suggestions which appear well founded, J.-P. Haesaert, *La technique juridique*, in ARCHIVES DE PHILOSOPHIE DU DROIT ET DE SOCIOLOGIE JURIDIQUE (1939) nos. 1–2; F. RUSSO, *op. cit.* 69–70, the matter of sanctions and of proofs is here detached from formal legal technique so as to attach it to political and social technique; see J. DABIN, *op. cit.* 58 *et seq.*

working out of a practicable form — plain legal technique since it owes nothing immediately to sociology and politics. And this time the expression is adequate, for it is no longer a matter of acting (in the moral sense) but one of making (in the technical sense).

Incontestably, too, sociology and politics outrank the working out of the form, at least in the sphere of intention: Before thinking of rendering his rule practicable the jurist must endeavor to construe it as socially good and expedient. Substance prevails over form, and the value of the rule over its execution. That is why no one will complain of a frankly bad rule (if not an imperfect one) being in addition impracticable: Granted that the legislator's prestige must suffer thereby, the latter corrects the former. But it is understood that the discovery in the law of a social and political viewpoint underlying the formal viewpoint of practicability leaves the law as something construed, even at the social and political level, and that at this level it is still a matter of technique (in the sense of prudence) and not of science.

193. The Law Is Not Solely Social Science. Recently, however, in a remarkable work already often cited,[6] one has claimed discovery of the basis for a contrary position. Whereas Gény, noting the part of technique in the law, perceives it only from the narrow angle of practicability and not of sociology and politics, our author, F. Russo,[7] contrariwise underlines wonderfully the rôle of sociology in the law (he omits any mention of politics) but tries to view it only from the aspect of science and not of technique. Without denying that the law adds something to social reality, especially an element of structure, he in effect maintains that the law is essentially a science, not only by the content of its dispositions, but also down to its practicability, which itself belongs to social science rather than to a properly legal or regulatory technique. Thus almost the entire law would be given, a "given" of social science, and technique would have lost almost all its standing. But that thesis contradicts the process of the elaboration of the law as it has just been retraced. The law is, and can only be, construed, and in this sense is a work of technique, because it is the product of the combination in variable proportions of the diverse points of view which must all come into balance in the composition of the rules. No one of these points of view, taken in isolation, imposes in advance a solution as given by science, nor *a fortiori* the satisfactory equilibrium of these points of view. It is easy to show that.

[6] See *supra*, no. 81 and notes 9 and 10; no. 104 and note 26; no. 106 and note 32; no. 111, note 1; no. 116, note 21; no. 128 and note 21.

[7] F. Russo, Réalité juridique et réalité sociale (Paris, 1942).

In the first place, to determine what the public good may require, advise, or tolerate regarding legal rules in such and such circumstances of environment and cases is not a matter of a statement, even upon reflection, about an anterior social reality, the subject of scientific or philosophical knowledge. It is a matter of practical, prudential reason, starting from facts and principles and evolving therefrom the conclusions which the public good effectively requires under the circumstances. No doubt, as Russo observes, social reality is not limited to purely empirical facts (although these constitute no negligible part of it and, too, are susceptible of being traced back to laws). Studied more deeply, sometimes in the light of a science superior to empirical science, to wit, social philosophy, social reality manifests tendencies and orientations, it unfolds values and norms.[8] But, first, supposing they are authentic,[9] these values are of diverse kinds, moral, economic, psychological, properly technical, and often they compete; then, most of the time, they are true only in a general and abstract sense; finally, even admitting that they furnish certain solutions to the sociologist and moralist, there still remains the proper task of the jurist, which is to appraise to what extent the transmutation of these socially good solutions into legal rules is of such a nature as to augment the real sum total of the public good.

194. The Jurist Knowingly Deforms the Real Through His Technique. Nor is this all. To determine after that first choice if the solution positively advantageous to the public good is practicable, and eventually to amend this solution so as to make it practicable, from the standpoint of definition or of proof, is less than ever a matter of science; it is exclusively a matter of technique. True, Russo objects that the technical procedures used by the jurist to render the law practicable "did not radically modify the social reality which served as the basis for legal elaboration, but impressed upon it only certain deformations which left its essential content unaltered." [10] But the moment the deformation is recognized there is the avowal of a difference between the legal method, which deforms, and the scientific method, which endeavors not to deform. The jurist simplifies, structuralizes, presumes. In a sense, he does

[8] See F. Russo, *op. cit.* notably p. 55: "The effort of knowledge of social realities can be accomplished only through affirming finalities and values." In other words, social science must find its completion in a social philosophy.

[9] See Russo himself, *op. cit.* 54, according to whom there is a distinction between the constitution of the value and the judgment upon the value. In many cases "the judgment of value will only too late detach the values from their primordial connection with the facts," Gurvitch, L'Expérience juridique 125.

[10] F. Russo, *op. cit.* 103, as to conceptualism, and immediately following (second paragraph of his text) as to presumptions.

not at all go against the real: Simplification, structure, presumption, keep within the area surrounding reality. Yet to the extent that the real undergoes a deformation, even a nonessential one, the definition of the jurist is more or less removed from that of the scholar.

Russo further objects that the scholar, too, uses concepts and presumptions: "It is not rare that even in the exact sciences one is content with probable data obtained by indirect means when faced with the impossibility of making a direct observation." [11] But the question is not one of knowing if one uses certain procedures; it is one of knowing under what conditions and to what end one uses them. Now there is this capital difference, stressed at the outset of our observations about the problem of the "given" and the "construed" in the law,[12] that the scholar does not cease to keep his eye on science, that is, the exact and complete knowledge of reality; that, if he uses approximative — and deformative — procedures, he does so for want of better instruments and owing to the actual state of technique in his science. The deformation performed by the jurist, on the contrary, has no necessity from the scientific point of view. So it happens that the reality fully grasped by, or at least within the grasp of, science is deformed by the legal rule, which comes to simplify or alter the very conclusions of scientific observation. Thus, it is the motive of the deformation that is decisive. The *scientific* deformation proclaims the powerlessness, at least for the moment, of the scholar; it calls forth correctives which he hastens to apply to the matter. The *legal* deformation as such is a technical device, a procedure sought in order to attain the practicability of the law. Now then, to sacrifice scientific truth, no matter how little, to purely practical ends is not scientific, it is technical.

SECTION 2. RELATIVE CERTAINTY AND VARIABILITY OF THE LAW

195. As Products of Prudence Legal Solutions Have Only Relative Certainty. Such being the nature of the legal discipline — prudence, art, and technique from beginning to end — how could one be surprised by the character of merely moral or even relative certainty that adheres to the so-called positive legal solutions? Exactly to appraise the situations of fact that give rise to regulation, to discern the concrete requirements of the public good in its relationships with the legal rule, to recognize the state of public opinion, to measure the degree of practica-

[11] F. Russo, *op. cit.* 104.
[12] See *supra*, no. 98.

bility of the solutions and give them their exact measure — these are so many questions that cannot be solved summarily with certainties of a mathematical or scientific order. Aristotle has written, with the approval of St. Thomas Aquinas, that "in such matters attention must be paid to undemonstrable propositions and opinions of experts, elders, and prudent men, no less than to demonstrated verities."[1] If, then, there exist solutions of law which offer themselves with a sufficient character of certainty in the eyes of people of judgment, there are many others which are open to argument, founded upon more or less probable opinions.

196. The Different Causes of Variation of the Law. The analysis of legal method allows us on the other hand to understand better why the law is indeed necessarily variable with times and places, and also why the competent authority must change the law, not only when it is bad or imperfect from the outset but also when its dispositions have ceased to be in accord with those of the directing elements of elaboration, whose nature is to change.

The law is called upon to undergo change, first, by reason of the variations in the subject matter of regulation. *Ex facto oritur jus.*[a] Every rule no doubt imposes its form upon a preëxistent matter; but the latter reacts upon the form inasmuch as the rule is bound to impress upon the matter the form appropriate thereto.[2] More precisely, relations and ways of conduct are subjected to a law only in dependence upon the constitution of the matter, which thus imposes its "given" — the "given" of inescapable fact — upon the law. Therefore, if the "given" of the matter is diversified or modified, the resulting legal solutions will feel its repercussions.[3]

The second cause of variation lies in the public good, the fundamental norm of the legal system, the requirements of which are changeable in space and in time.[4] While one may discover common principles of the common good, of a philosophical, scientific, or technical order, valid for any society, whatever may be its historical physiognomy (climate, soil, the physical, intellectual, and moral aptitudes of its members),[5] with

[1] St. Thomas, Summa, *Ia IIae*, qu. 95, art. 2 *ad* 4; also citations *supra*, no. 130, note 30.

[a] [Law arises out of facts.]

[2] See *supra*, nos. 126, 127.

[3] See, in the same sense, St. Thomas, *op. cit. Ia IIae*, qu. 97, art. 1 *ad* 2: . . . See also qu. 95, art 2 *ad* 3.

[4] See, in the same sense, St. Thomas, *op. cit. Ia IIae*, qu. 97, art. 1 *ad* 3: . . .

[5] This is the problem of a "science" of the public good, suggested *supra*, no. 144. On the universal and the national in the law, cf. F. Russo, *op. cit.* 129–132; G. del

respect to applications of these principles, Pascal's whimsical remark may justly be employed: "Truth on this side of the Pyrenees, error on the other." The different political groups have their particular traits, which necessarily influence the applications. Thus, the requirements of the public good are not the same in rudimentary societies as in those of refined civilization. Again, in a society of the agricultural type, the public good of agriculture represents a more considerable value within the total public good than does the industrial public good, and vice versa. Reflecting this diversity, the law will take on a primitive or peasant stamp here and an urban, commercial, industrial stamp there according to the character of the population embraced within the state. That state itself, charged with the task of the public good, is more or less "strong," more or less well organized and equipped, politically speaking, so that its interventions in the field of the law cannot surpass the level of its powers of command and execution.

Essentially variable, too, are the reactions of public opinion with regard to the rules: Favorable in a certain environment and in a certain epoch, hostile elsewhere or in other times. Now this variation in reactions must entail different and sometimes contradictory legal régimes — on the one hand liberal or tolerant, on the other more or less regulated, and regulated in more or less divergent ways. The state of opinion, moreover, weighs upon the "practicability" of the law (in the formal sense) in so far as the difficulties of definition or of proof may be aggravated by the refusal of the public to collaborate in the practical application of the rules.

197. The So-Called "Conservative Function" of the Law. Such are the reasons why the law, the so-called positive law, is not always and everywhere the same: The subject matter changes, the public good and the relationship between the law and the public good change, public opinion is modified.[6] No part or branch of the law escapes this rule, not even the most fundamental provisions of public or private law, though admittedly the foundations are ordinarily of greater stability than the superstructures. So when social changes or, *a fortiori*, social upheavals

Vecchio, *La communicabilité du droit et les doctrines de G.-B. Vico*, in 2 RECUEIL LAMBERT § 111, pp. 591 *et seq.*

[6] This is the basic theme of Montesquieu's work, DE L'ESPRIT DES LOIS, the design of which is laid out in bk. I, chap. 3 (ed. Garnier, pp. 8–9). Cf. by contrast the criticism of bk. XXIX of the ESPRIT DES LOIS in 1 CONDORCET, OEUVRES (ed. Arago) 378: . . . Also the extracts from the preparatory work for the Code Napoleon, reported in 1 TAULIER, THÉORIE RAISONNÉE DU CODE CIVIL 251–253. But Condorcet confuses speculative truth and practical truth; on this distinction, see ST. THOMAS, *op. cit. Ia IIae*, qu. 94, art. 4.

occur, the law is logically and normally obliged, if not to be taken in tow by the movement, at least to revise its attitude in the light of the new fact.[7] That is why it is inexact or at the very least equivocal to speak of a "conservative function of the law." [8] The law has neither to conserve itself, in the sense of maintaining the legal status quo, nor to fight against life, once the change (supposing that it depends on the will of men) offers nothing socially reprehensible. It would be better on the contrary to speak of a duty of adaptation and thus of renewal of the law.[9]

It is true, the organs authorized to interpret and apply the laws do not always have the competence to modify it, to the ends of readaptation. In this sense, their mission is to conserve the rules of enacted law and to maintain them against deformations as well as against violations pure and simple. But, to begin with, the maintenance of enacted statutory rules does not necessarily involve the stagnation of the whole law. The readaptation may be the work of other modes of expressing the law than statutory enactment. Above all, it is for the legislator himself to reform his statute, to improve it where it is imperfect, to bring it up to date where it lags behind life. It is also true that any mutation of the law, to the ends of perfecting or of readapting it, must be governed by the norm of prudence.

198. Necessity of Prudence in Change. At the outset, prudence commands one to conserve what one has gotten as long as one is not sure of the value of what one will get. Any change, concerning the future, involves an unknown: What will be the real effect of the new law? Better or worse than the old? The most probable calculations may be destroyed by the intrusion of the famous "imponderables." It is true that risk is inherent in action and the fear of risk would prevent any change. But the risk to be run does not dispense with prudence, at least in calculating the chances of success.[10]

Prudence further commands one to remember that any change in the laws, even when justified in itself, provokes a crisis and consequently an evil: Juridical habits are disturbed; business arrangements are frustrated; more or less respectable, and in any event vested, interests are affronted. And the crisis will be the graver the more the rules in

[7] See, in this sense, St. Thomas, *op. cit. Ia IIae*, qu. 97, art. 1 *ad resp.*: . . .

[8] See G. Renard, Le droit, la justice et la volonté (Paris, 1924) 211 *et seq.*

[9] On stability and movement in the law, cf. F. Russo, *op. cit.* 147–150, 183.

[10] Cf. Montesquieu, Cahiers 120: "Such is the nature of things that abuse is very often preferable to coercion, or at least that the good once established is always preferable to the better that is not established."

question are fundamental, endowed legally or factually with "constitutional" value.[11] Hence, as always, the question is one of balancing assets and liabilities, discounted advantages and expected disadvantages of the change. If the disadvantages outweigh the advantages, one will have to stick to the status quo, notwithstanding its insufficiency or shortcomings. Although perfection is the ideal to be attained, it is not always expedient to try to realize it *hic et nunc*,[b] in spite of all obstacles: Often in practice the better is the enemy of the good. That is why the laws will be changed only in case of "very grave and absolutely obvious utility" or of "extreme necessity" in order to abolish a manifest injustice or any injurious rule.[12] Even on this assumption, prudence may advise certain arrangements, certain temporizations or "transitional measures," so as to attenuate the brusqueness of the shock and to get our minds used to the novelty.

[11] This is the explanation of the system of "rigid constitutions," where amendment of so-called constitutional provisions is subject to a special procedure more complicated than the ordinary [legislative] one. On this process, see J. DABIN, DOCTRINE GÉNÉRALE DE L'ETAT nos. 99 *et seq.*, pp. 151 *et seq.*

[b] [Here and now.]

[12] This is the formula of ST. THOMAS, *op. cit. Ia IIae*, qu. 97, art. 2. See, in the same sense, Portalis, *Discours préliminaire*, no. 5, in 1 LOCRÉ, *op. cit.* (Bruxelles ed. 1836) 154, col. 2; 155, col. 1. It must be added, too, that life today changes and renews itself much more rapidly than it used to and hence readjustment of the law will be more frequent.

PART THREE

NATURAL LAW, JUSTICE, AND THE LEGAL RULE

INTRODUCTION

199. Statement of the Problem. Truth to tell, the question of the relationships between natural law and justice, on the one hand, and the law, on the other, has already repeatedly been touched upon. At the outset of our exposition, we have encountered the thesis that the study of the concept of law should begin with the idea of justice rather than with the idea of the rule, a method that anticipates the solution in affirming the fundamental identity in content of law and of justice.[1] Later on, in dealing with the problem of the "given" and the "construed" in the law, we have been led to contradict the conception of a natural legal "given," or natural law, defined as the objectively just, which would represent the substantial element of the legal regulation.[2] Finally, treating of the method of elaboration of the law, we have evoked and analyzed the concept of the public good [3] which, while altogether distinct from natural law and justice, cannot fail to have close ties to these latter concepts: Can one conceive of the public good turning its back on natural law and justice? But these ties, evident *a priori*, are now to be examined more closely. The problem arises as follows: What place do the concepts of natural law and justice occupy within the "complex" of the law? If they are located neither at the starting point nor at the center of the system, how and on what ground do they figure therein? What is their rôle as factors in the elaboration of the law in the previously defined sense of a rule laid down by the civil society? [4]

200. Objective Value of the Ideas of Natural Law and Justice. It is useless to discuss these problems unless one begins by recognizing a meaning in the concepts of natural law and justice as norms of reason, endowed with objective value. True, some claim that men — individuals and collectivities — in their behavior would not let themselves be guided by any ideal principle detached from their passions and their self-interest.[5] Especially in their relationships with others they would obey

[1] See *supra*, no. 2.

[2] See *supra*, nos. 114 *et seq.*

[3] See *supra*, nos. 134 *et seq.*

[4] See *supra*, nos. 8–13.

[5] This is an allusion to the systems of Hobbes, Nietzsche, and others. Compare

only the "law of the jungle": *Homo homini lupus.*[a] The statutes and customs making up the positive law would indeed be but the product of the physical or economical superiority of the actual holders of power or, at least, the expression of the balancing of antagonistic forces in a determinate moment of history.[6] To others, natural law and justice do indeed exist as either idea-forces driving humanity, or as an ultimate aid against the established law; but that ideal would be only a "myth" or at least a gratuitous hypothesis.[7] Now, if that is so, everything comes tumbling down at once: Natural law and justice, undoubtedly, and also the norm of a public good prevailing over the individual interest, and the very principle of a subjection of the law that is called positive to a rational method of elaboration. The established law is what it is, nothing more; it is valid by itself, by the power of those who have laid it down. The despotism of the legislator rules and replaces the despotism of the individual.

The vast majority of men, however, ignorant or thoughtful, are communicants of the cult of natural law and justice, and they believe therein as a reality of the philosophical and moral, if not of the peculiarly scientific, order. Unfortunately, save for a unanimity in principle as to the ethical character of the two concepts, disagreement prevails among specialists as to the exact definition of each. That is why a comparative study as broached here must logically begin with an attempt to point up the paralleled concepts. These concepts are also so important in the sphere of the moral sciences that the jurist should not regret the time devoted to their analysis, even independently of their rôle on the properly legal plane.

CHAPTER I

THE CONCEPT OF NATURAL LAW

SECTION 1. THE TRADITIONAL CONCEPTION

201. Natural Law as a Norm of Human Conduct. According to the most generally accepted use of the term in our time, the noun "law" in

---

the theories already refuted by Plato, as set forth in P. LACHIÈZE-REY, LES IDÉES MORALES, SOCIALES ET POLITIQUES DE PLATON (Paris) 39–49.

[a] [Man is a wolf to his fellow man.]

[6] See *supra*, no. 109.

[7] In this sense, see among others the two pamphlets by H. DE PAGE, L'IDÉE DE DROIT NATUREL (Bruxelles, 1936) and DROIT NATUREL ET POSITIVISME JURIDIQUE (Bruxelles, 1939).

the expression "natural law" is taken in the sense of a certain rule of conduct with man as its subject and imposed in a categorical fashion upon his activities, and not of a scientific law or a technical rule. That is why we exclude at once the idea of a natural law constituted by economic laws,[1] which are scientific laws and are also capable of technical utilization; and we exclude also the idea of a natural law common to men and animals (inasmuch as man is an animal) [2] or common to all creatures, both animate and inanimate.[3]

202. "Jus Naturale" and "Lex Naturalis" Are Synonymous Terms. However, the subject matter of the rule of human conduct which constitutes natural law is not specified *a priori: Jus naturae* and *jus naturale*, on the one hand, and *lex naturae* and *lex naturalis*, on the other, are interchangeable terms.

It is true that sometimes the terms "natural law" and "natural right," on the model of the plain words "law" and "right," are taken to mean the naturally just. Thus, St. Thomas Aquinas, in dealing with the virtue of justice, defines justice as the virtue which has as its object the lawful right of another (*jus suum*),[4] which lawful right may be natural (*jus naturale*) or positive (*jus positivum*).[5] "Lawful" there signifies what the [Continental] jurists call the subjectively lawful or legal right, as opposed to the objectively lawful, objective law or norm of law.[6] However, at the end of the same article, St. Thomas evokes a *jus divinum* which, similar to the *jus humanum*, decrees precepts concerned with morally good things (*bona*) and prohibitions concerned with morally bad things (*mala*), wherefrom it follows that the *jus divinum* in question is nothing else than the *lex divina* (this term is also found there).[7] In the following article, trying to classify the *jus gentium*, St. Thomas considers hy-

[1] See, in this sense, E. LAMBERT, UN PARÈRE DE JURISPRUDENCE COMPARATIVE (Paris, 1938) — or even Gény's definition paraphrased above, no. 110, which is concerned with a "fund of moral and economic verities," though "principally" moral ones.

[2] See, e.g., ULPIAN, DIG. 1, 1, 1, 3. Cf. ST. THOMAS, SUMMA, *Ia IIae*, qu. 94, art. 2 *ad resp.*, art. 3 *ad* 2. On the *jus naturale* common to men and animals, see F. SENN, DE LA JUSTICE ET DU DROIT 59–73.

[3] See ST. THOMAS, SUMMA, *Ia IIae*, qu. 91, art. 2 *ad* 3: The law being a matter of reason, only what participates in eternal law in the reasonable creature properly merits the name of law.

[4] ST. THOMAS, *op. cit.*, *Ia IIae*, qu. 57, art. 1.

[5] ST. THOMAS, *op. cit. Ia IIae*, qu. 57, art. 2. In the same sense, see also CICERO, DE INVENTIONE 2, 53, 161: . . . ; also 2, 22, 65.

[6] See 1 A. COLIN AND CAPITANT, COURS ÉLÉMENTAIRE DE DROIT CIVIL FRANÇAIS (9th ed. by Juliot de la Morandière) no. 1, p. 1.

[7] ST. THOMAS, *op. cit. Ia IIae*, qu. 57, art. 2 *ad* 3.

potheses of adjustment altogether foreign to any lawful right of another, such as the adjustment (*commensurationem*) of the male to the female to the ends of procreation, and still further the idea of a *jus naturale* common to men and animals (there is no duty of justice between animals),[8] so that *jus naturale* and *jus positivum* end up by merging into altogether general concepts of *lex naturalis, lex divina, lex humana.* The same, by the way, goes for the term *jus civile,* which embraces all dispositions whatever of the civil law and not only those concerning justice. Finally, in dealing with laws as rules, St. Thomas prefers to use the term *lex naturalis* but, in the same context, also happens to make use of the term *jus,* not only as one of the possible objectives of the legal rule (the law of the just) but also as synonymous with the rule apart from its content.[9] All this justifies the assertion of one of the most authoritative commentators upon Thomistic thought: "Conforming to the usage of the time, St. Thomas employs these two terms indifferently." [10] The usage of that time, incidentally, has been maintained through the ages — in the modern period by the theorists of the "law of nature and of nations" school [11] as well as by Domat; [12] in the contemporary period, in the majority of treatises on moral philosophy and natural law.

203. Characteristics of Natural Law: A Norm That Issues from Nature, Universal and Immutable. On the other hand, as the adjective "natural" indicates without too great ambiguity, the rule of human conduct that is called natural law is deduced from the nature of man as it reveals itself in the basic inclinations of that nature under the control of reason,[13] independently of any formal intervention by any legislator whatsoever, divine or human. Natural law is thus distinguished from another law, which is called "positive" (or "voluntary," or "arbitrary") and is supposed to have been established by the will of God or of men. Natural law, furthermore, dominates positive law in the sense that, while positive law may add to natural law or even restrict it, it is prohibited

[8] On the discussions about this subject in antiquity, see F. SENN, *op. cit.* 70–73.

[9] See ST. THOMAS, SUMMA, *Ia IIae,* qu. 95, art. 4: . . .

[10] O. LOTIN, LE DROIT NATUREL CHEZ ST. THOMAS ET SES PRÉDÉCESSEURS (Bruges, 1926) 52 and notes 34 and 35.

[11] As follows from the statements paraphrased below, no. 208 and notes 2 and 3.

[12] DOMAT, TRAITÉ DES LOIS, chap. XI, 9 *initio,* 33 *in fine*; LES LOIS CIVILES DANS LEUR ORDRE NATUREL, Prelim. bk., title I, sec. I, 2 and 3.

[13] This is not the place to set forth the process of knowing the rule of natural law, notably the mechanism of the anguish of conscience. Let us note only that, like reason, it is also "natural" in man; see ST. THOMAS, SUMMA, *Ia IIae,* qu. 94, art. 4 *ad resp.* and *ad* 3.

from contradicting it.[14] How could the legislator, or at least the human legislator,[15] have the power to rebel against the "given" of human nature?

From the characteristics of human nature flow the characteristics of natural law. As human nature is identical in all men and does not vary, its precepts have universal and immutable validity, notwithstanding the diversity of individual conditions, historical and geographical environments, civilizations and cultures. As, on the other hand, nature cannot deceive itself nor deceive us, its precepts, inasmuch as they are authentic, have a validity that is certain, suffering neither doubt nor discussion.[16]

204. First Principles and Secondary Precepts. As to the extent of the "given" of nature and of what must therefore be referred to natural law, views are divided. The traditional school reserves the name natural, with the characteristics of universality, immutability, and certainty inherent in that quality, to altogether general and necessary "first principles," distinguishing them even from "secondary precepts" or "particular conclusions quite close to the first principles." [17] Other interpretations, of later date, include within natural law not only the first principles, but the more or less close conclusions evolved from the first principles by way of rational argumentation.[18] So there exists, historically at least, a "minimalist" conception of natural law, limited to the strict and direct "given" of the inclinations of nature, and another, "maximalist" one, extending to the solutions that are the proper work of reason in starting from the natural "given," [19] without, however, any

[14] See St. Thomas, *op. cit. Ia IIae*, qu. 94, art. 5 *ad resp.* and *ad* 3.

[15] For the divine legislator, the question is disputed whether God Himself could change or abrogate a law of nature whose author He is. In Catholic theology the answer is negative.

[16] This is the idea indicated by Cicero in his famous definition, De inventione 2, 53, 161, and 2, 22, 65: *Natura jus est quod non opinio genuit sed quaedam innata vis inseruit* [Law by nature is what has not been produced by opinion but inserted by some innate force].

[17] See St. Thomas, *op. cit. Ia IIae*, qu. 94, art. 5 *ad resp.*, with reference to art. 4, art. 6 *ad resp.*; qu. 95, art. 2 *ad resp.*, art. 4 *ad resp.*

[18] *Per rationis inquisitionem* [By inquiry of reason], said St. Thomas, Summa, *Ia IIae*, qu. 94, art. 3 *ad resp.*, *in fine*. This extensive interpretation is found not only in the authors of the seventeenth and eighteenth centuries (Grotius, Domat, or Puffendorf) but also in some modern treatises on natural law, as, e.g., J. Leclercq, Lecons de droit naturel, I: Les fondements du droit et de la société (2d ed.), no. 11, pp. 58–60.

[19] Cf. J. Leclercq, *op. cit.* no. 11, p. 56, according to whom natural law is all that the social nature of man involves, neither more nor less . . .

clearly traced boundary lines between the successive zones of first principles, secondary precepts, and their more or less close conclusions.

The disadvantage of the strict conception evidently is to reduce the concrete content of natural law to rather vague generalities, which gives rise to the objection (an unjust one, incidentally) of useless verbalism; the dangers of the broad conception lie in lending the validity of natural law, that is, absolute authority, to solutions endowed with truth merely relative to the cases. The present tendency is toward the minimum conception.[20] On the one hand, one fears being unable to account for the "legitimate variation" of positive rules. On the other hand, one mistrusts logical apriorism in the domain of the moral and social sciences.

205. Subject Matter of Natural Law: The Totality of the Duties of Man. As regards the subject matter of natural law, or equally of the natural legal rule with which it is synonymous, it embraces all orders of duties imposed by nature, and consequently not only the duty of justice (*suum cuique tribuere*) [a] or, more broadly, the duties *ad alterum*,[b] but also the duties toward God, the duties toward oneself, the duties deduced from the idea of the family (giving rise to the concept of natural family law), the duties of the political order, incumbent upon subjects as well as upon rulers, at home and abroad (natural political law). Adopting another principle of division, St. Thomas Aquinas classifies "the natural inclinations from which the order of the precepts of natural law flows" as follows: An inclination, common to all substances, toward the conservation of their being according to its proper nature; an inclination, common to men and animals, toward the union of the male and female, the education of the youth, and similar things; an inclination, proper to man, toward the goods conforming to his nature as a rational being, such as the desire to know God and to live in society, which impels him to avoid ignorance, not to do wrong to his neighbor with whom he must maintain relations, and other things of that kind.[21] It is not hard to recognize in that classification the principles corresponding to the totality of the duties of man: Toward himself, toward his family, toward God, toward his neighbor, toward society.

206. Tendency to Emphasize the Duties "Ad Alterum." Contrary to what is sometimes said, even the theorists of the "state of nature"

[20] See, in this sense, notably 2 F. GÉNY, SCIENCE ET TECHNIQUE EN DROIT PRIVÉ POSITIF nos. 159 and 176; also H. CAPITANT, INTRODUCTION À L'ÉTUDE DU DROIT CIVIL (4th ed.) no. 9, pp. 35-36.

[a] [To render to each his own.]

[b] [Toward another.]

[21] ST. THOMAS, SUMMA, *Ia IIae*, qu. 94, art. 2 *ad resp.*, *in fine*.

guarded against excluding the social duties from their natural law. It did not escape them that human nature is not only individual, that it is also social and political. Under the name of the "state of nature" they merely proposed (on the dialectical level, incidentally) to disregard all positively established economic, social, and legal institutions proceeding from the actual and concrete functioning of the diverse particular societies.[22] More than that, one observes a tendency, precisely in the "law of nature and of nations" school, to put into clear relief, side by side with the "rational nature," the "sociable nature" of man, with the duties *ad alterum*, both interindividual and properly social, which follow from it.[23] No doubt the natural law, or its rule, continues to extend over all orders of duties, including the duties toward God and toward oneself; but the emphasis is upon the duties which life in society imposes. Are we to see in this insistence (rather uncertain, to be sure) the bait for a deviation from the first idea of natural law, which would slide imperceptibly from the plane of moral and social science, where it had first been installed, to the adjoining plane of specifically legal science?

Section 2. Is There a Juridical Natural Law?

207. The Ambiguity of the Concept of Natural Law. For here at last is the ambiguity which has not ceased to befog the concept of natural law from the day the state began to legislate: To what sort of regulation is the natural law related? To the regulation which, aiming at the moral perfection of men, obligates them before their conscience and before God to practice the good and avoid the bad, in short, the moral rule? Or to the regulation of societal origin, laid down by (domestic or international) public authority with a view to the temporal public good (of individuals or states), in short, the legal rule? Or again to both sorts of rules cumulatively, whether they are considered as distinct at

[22] See, in this sense, PUFFENDORF, LE DROIT DE LA NATURE ET DES GENS [*De jure naturae et gentium*] (transl. by Barbeyrac, Basle ed., 1771) [English transl. by C. H. and W. A. Oldfather, in SCOTT'S CLASSICS OF INTERNATIONAL LAW (1934)], bk. II, chaps. II and III, § XXII and n. 1 by Barbeyrac § XXIV. In general, concerning the conception of the "state of nature," see PH. MEYLAN, JEAN BARBEYRAC (Lausanne, 1937) 189 *et seq.*, 202 *et seq.*

[23] See, in this sense, GROTIUS, LE DROIT DE LA GUERRE ET DE LA PAIX [*De jure belli ac pacis*] (transl. by Barbeyrac, Basle ed., 1768), *Discours préliminaire* [*Prolegomena*], §§ VIII–IX; PUFFENDORF, *op. cit.*, bk. II, chap. III, § XV, art. 3, and bk. I, chap. VI, § XVIII. Generally on the law of nature school, see PH. MEYLAN, *op. cit.* 189–190. The same exclusively social conception of natural law in J. LECLERCQ, *op. cit.* no. 15 (general plan of the work).

least in form or taken for inseparable at least up to a certain point? In a word, is natural law the directing principle of morals or of law?

The question no doubt was less important practically in periods of not very complex civilization when the civil law was most often content with the rôle of servant and executor of morals. But in our times, with the threefold phenomenon of the increase of wants, above all material wants, the development of technology, and the emergence of the masses, the civil law is led to formulate many requirements which bear no more than an indirect relationship to morality. Hence the present interest of the problem as to the order of regulation to which the rule of conduct called natural law belongs.

208. Historically, Natural Law Provides Principles of Moral Conduct. With terminology, as has been seen,[1] offering no ground for argument either way, since the words "law," "right," and "rule" may refer indifferently to the moral rule and the juridical or legal rule, the answer is supplied by history: What one has always sought of "natural law" is principles of moral conduct, it being understood that man is a social and political being and that morally he has social and political duties. Natural law, the Schoolmen tell us, dictates to man what he must do to arrive at the ultimate end of human life, that is, happiness; it is the rule and measure of peculiarly human actions; its first principle and first precept is that one ought to practice the good and avoid the bad.[2] The traditional teaching is echoed by the "law of nature and of nations" school. According to Grotius, for instance, the law "obliges to what is good and praiseworthy and not merely to what is just, since law, according to the idea we attach to it here, is not confined to the duties of justice but also embraces what makes up the subject matter of the other virtues."[3] Hence this definition: Natural law "consists in certain principles of right reason, which causes us to know that an action is morally honest or dishonest according to its necessary agreement or disagreement with a rational and sociable nature."[4] The connection is clear: Natural law figures among the first notions of moral philosophy or general ethics in the chapter on laws, side by side with the theory of human acts; and the treatises of natural law, where the applications of the rule of natural law to the different matters are set forth and discussed, are nothing else than treatises on special ethics.

[1] See *supra*, no. 202.

[2] See ST. THOMAS, SUMMA, *Ia IIae*, qu. 90, art. 1 *ad resp.* and *ad* 1, art. 2 *ad resp.*; qu. 94, art. 2 *ad resp.*

[3] GROTIUS, *op. cit.* bk. I, chap. I, § IX, 1.

[4] GROTIUS, *op. cit.* bk. I, chap. I, § X. See generally on the law of nature school, PH. MEYLAN. *op. cit.* 52: . .

209. Natural Law and Special Morals. It matters little, moreover, that the morality of acts requires an element of right intention, without which there can be neither good nor virtue in the actor. Only the objective materiality of the precepts, outside of the dispositions of the soul, is here considered. Materially, then, natural law and special morals dictate the same rules, found the same institutions, or, according to the restrictive conception of the Schoolmen, natural law furnishes special morals with its first principles. Indeed, no difference has ever been established between interindividual natural law and interindividual morals, between the natural law of sexual union, generation, and education, and family morals, between political natural law and political morals, save that, in speaking in strict terms, natural law, expressing the requirements of nature, represents the source from which the solutions of morals in those various matters are derived.

Nor is there any distinction between two parts in morals: A morals of rules of action, which would be morals properly so called, and a morals of institutions, or "institutional morals," which would govern the relations dominated by a peculiarly social idea and which would be called "law." Not only would such an interpretation be novel, involving a rejection of the expressions "family morals," "political morals," and even "social morals"; not only would even the formal dissociation of law from morals run the risk of leading to their separation; but the distinction is also really factitious and, despite appearances, superficial. Morals indeed governs everything human, including the human that is social, directly and without any interpreter. And if, with regard to the social and in view of the human, morals is called upon to establish institutional structures of an objective and to a certain degree formal nature [5] — such as the one and indissoluble marriage, marital authority, and state power — these structures, which by the way can be traced back to rules of conduct,[6] have the same moral and natural character as the dispositions that directly command, forbid, or advise. One can thus conclude in the clearest manner that natural law is nothing else than the moral rule taken in its homogeneous totality, without exclusion of any matters, but is limited to indicating their basic nature, in anticipation of developments provided by the positive moral rule and by the scientific work of the moralists.

210. Relationships between the Natural Moral Rule and the Legal Rule. To be sure, natural law in the sense just defined, i.e., as the natu-

[5] In this sense, and in this sense only, we have spoken above, no. 114, of an "institutional part of morals."

[6] See *supra*, no. 46.

ral moral rule (at least as to first principles), is not unrelated to law, in the sense of the rule established by the state. Under the name of "human law" St. Thomas shows us the civil law coming to the aid of natural law "in order by force and fear to compel perverted and ill-disposed men to abstain from evil, at least so that in ceasing to do evil they leave others in peace." [7] On the other hand, the civil laws are called upon to complete natural law, either by way of conclusions derived from the first principles (as in the case of the *jus gentium*) or by way of concrete determination of the first principles (as in the case of the *jus civile* properly so called). For instance, the law of nature prescribes that he who shall commit an offense shall be punished and the civil law defines the kind of penalty.[8] The same analysis is found in the authors of the law of nature school: The rôle of the civil law is to sanction natural law, in particular in so far as it prescribes what is just. Is it not the first end of the state, and therefore of the law set down by the state, to guarantee "the peaceful enjoyment of one's rights"? [9] It is natural law, moreover, which either on the ground of the necessity of political society (man is a "political animal") or on the ground of the "social contract" (the faith of promises) gives the civil laws their foundation and justifies the subjects' duty of obedience.[10] Finally, everybody admits that civil laws contrary to natural law are bad laws and even that they do not answer to the concept of a law.[11]

211. But These Relationships Entail No Confusion of the Disciplines. But what conclusions are to be drawn from these necessary ties of dependence and derivation of the civil law with natural law?

Let us note first of all that the phenomenon is not peculiar to the civil law. All positive rules, institutions, and prescriptions whatsoever, human and even divine, in some manner depend upon and derive from natural law. No doubt the civil law does so, both private and public, municipal and international law; but so too, in the religious and ecclesiastic domain, do the canon law (as regards, say, the worship to be rendered unto

[7] St. Thomas, Summa, *Ia IIae*, qu. 95, art. 1 *ad resp.*

[8] St. Thomas, *op. cit. Ia IIae*, qu. 95, art. 2 *ad resp.*

[9] Grotius, *op. cit.* bk. I, chap. I, § XIV, 2. See also Puffendorf, *op. cit.* bk. VII, chap. IX, § VIII, and especially bk. VIII, chap. I, §§ I–V, *passim*; Vattel, Dissertation on the question: *La loi naturelle peut-elle porter la société à la perfection sans le secours des lois politiques?* in 1 Le droit des gens par Vattel (ed. by Pradier-Fodéré, Paris, 1863) 35 *et seq.*

[10] See, e.g., Grotius, *op. cit. Discours préliminaire* § XVII: . . . ; see also § XVI.

[11] See, e.g., St. Thomas, *op. cit. Ia IIae*, qu. 92, art. 1 *ad* 4; qu. 93, art. 3*ad* 2; qu. 95, art. 2 *ad resp.*, *initio*; qu. 96, art. 4 *ad resp.*; *IIa IIae*, qu. 60, art. 5 *ad* 1.

God in application of the natural virtue of religion) and above all the positive moral laws laid down by the competent authority — God and the Church — the rôle of which is to render precise and complete the "given" of the moral rule of nature.

Thus, the civil law cannot claim a monopoly in natural law as the principle of its special discipline. On the contrary, natural law is necessarily found at the base of every regulatory norm of human conduct, such a norm being conceivable only along the line of nature. But whereas the influence of natural law is direct in the case of morals, it is only indirect in the case of the civil law. And this is logical. Morals alone is placed immediately and exclusively upon the plane of human nature; its solutions alone, as to its first principles, possess the universality, immutability, and certainty which characterize the requirements of nature; the moral rule alone can be called natural in this sense. As for the other disciplines regulative of conduct, they partake of nature only through the intermediary of morals and only in their principles, not in their positive solutions.

What does it matter, after all, that the civil law borrows a number of its precepts from natural law? From this it follows neither that natural law would cease to belong to the category of morals so as to become the primary "given" or the nucleus of the civil law, — nor that the civil law would have lost its proper nature so as to become the lining or the "supplement" of natural law. Notwithstanding interpenetrations or mutual aid, their essences will remain distinct as long as the differences of their ends and functions subsist. Now, if the end and the function of natural law, rendered explicit, developed, and fecundated by moral science, are to define the good and the just in conformity with the "given" of nature, the end and the function of the civil law are to contribute to the public good, which no doubt in large part comprises the defense and safeguard of the good and the just (reserving however possibilities of environment and technique) but also many other measures besides, aiming at "things useful to human life," invested by human reason and not given by nature.[12]

212. Extension of the Concept of Natural Law: "Natural Jurisprudence." It is true that often the concept of natural law is stretched to include precisely these "useful" things, foreign as such to the category of good and just, which permits assigning a "given" of natural law to

[12] Cf. St. Thomas, *op. cit.*, *Ia IIae*, qu. 94, art. 5 *ad resp.* and *ad* 3, who attaches to positive law the solutions, added to natural law, *ad humanam vitam utilia* [useful to human life] . . . , *ad bene vivendum*, to the morally good life, qu. 94, art. 3 *ad resp.*, *in fine* . . .

the entire civil law, even in those of its dispositions which more or less closely relate to "usefulness to human life." For instance, Grotius suggests a "natural jurisprudence," common to all times and places, detached from anything dependent upon an arbitrary will, a science capable of forming a complete body where one could find treated laws, tributes, judicial duty, conjectures (or presumptions of will), proofs, presumptions, etc.[13]

That link does indeed bridge the hiatus. Natural law no longer represents — or no longer solely or principally represents — the first principles of morality, of the good, the just; it represents — or equally represents — the first principles of civil legislation in the concern for all values whatsoever with which the latter is charged, that is, not only the moral values but also the properly economic or social values, even if they be of a technical nature and in themselves morally indifferent. According to that conception, it is natural law, in the sense of the natural civil law, that will tell the jurist to what extent and in what manner he ought to intervene with his rule, or at least will offer him the first principles of his ordinance, in the same manner as natural law in the moral sense offers to the moralist the first principles of his special morals.[14] In that way one arrives at placing under natural law not only the institution of private ownership, although "differences in wealth are not imposed by nature," [15] but even much more contingent solutions, such as the institution of prescription, the rules of evidence, and the like,

[13] GROTIUS, *op. cit. Discours préliminaire* § XXXII. As for the conception of "immutable or natural laws," cf. DOMAT, TRAITÉ DES LOIS, chap. XI, and the comment by R.-F. VOETZEL, JEAN DOMAT, 1625–1692 (Thesis, Nancy, 1936) 180 *et seq.* According to Domat, the natural laws have been gathered in the Roman law, which represents "written reason," at least in general, TRAITÉ DES LOIS, chap. XI, 19. Other authors will speak of "natural legal reason," the "natural juridical"; see, e.g., G. del Vecchio, *Essai sur les principes généraux du droit* §§ 9 and 11, in JUSTICE, DROIT, ETAT 157 and 170.

[14] The great work of Puffendorf is entitled: LE DROIT DE LA NATURE ET DES GENS OU SYSTÈME GÉNÉRAL DES PRINCIPES LES PLUS IMPORTANTS DE LA MORALE, DE LA JURISPRUDENCE ET DE LA POLITIQUE [THE LAW OF NATURE AND OF NATIONS, OR GENERAL SYSTEM OF THE MOST IMPORTANT PRINCIPLES OF MORALS, JURISPRUDENCE, AND POLITICS]. According to DOMAT, TRAITÉ DES LOIS chap. XI, 34, the natural laws are found both among the "laws of police" (i.e., the law of the state) and among the "laws of religion" (comprising, according to him, rules relating to faith and morals, worship and church discipline, in short, the moral laws and the canon laws). The same vacillation appears in Portalis, *Discours préliminaire au projet de Code civil*, in 1 LOCRÉ, *op. cit.* (Bruxelles ed., 1836) 156, col. 1; 159, col. 1; 160, col. 1.

[15] As to private ownership, see ST. THOMAS, SUMMA, *Ia IIae*, qu. 94, art. 5 *ad* 3; GROTIUS, *op. cit.* bk. I, chap. I, § X, 4; PUFFENDORF, *op. cit.* bk. II, chap. III, §§ XXII and XXIV.

designed to bring about, sometimes with certain sacrifices of justice,[16] the security of social relations, which is incontestably "useful to human life." [17]

213. But This Extension Contradicts the Original Concept of Natural Law. But this broader interpretation rests upon a double contradiction.

What did natural law mean originally? A rule inscribed in human nature, aiming at the absolute good and just, at honesty. What does the "new style" natural law mean? A quite different concept: A rule invented by man, aiming at things useful to human life in a given social state. No doubt the nature of man is rational and therefore inventive of useful things; it is sociable and therefore concerned about things useful not only to the individual man but also to the society of men. Yet originally it was intended precisely to place in opposition to each other inventive reason and nature, and an express distinction was made between the good and the just, on the one hand, and the useful, on the other. The social was not excluded; on the contrary — but in the social the search continued to be for the absolute good and just and not the contingent useful. That the useful itself, once established, opens up the rule of the good and the just, binding as to the consequences of such establishment,[18] changes nothing in the situation. Thus, prescription and the other rules of security in society remain what they are, to wit, useful and invented solutions, although natural law enjoins us to submit to them — as to every decision made by authority and for the public good. That the useful involves nothing contrary to natural law [19] is obvious but does not justify any confusion. To natural law belongs what is provided by it by precept or by faculty or permission, and not what at the outset escapes its concept, such as the category of the useful.

Will it be said that in the social domain at the very least the useful rejoins the just and the good, and hence natural law? Social and political morals indeed command the rulers to make provision for everything, and the subjects to act always according to the public good, even prior to any intervention of positive law.[20] Now the public good, which itself

[16] See *supra*, nos. 115, 149–155.

[17] As to prescription, see GROTIUS, *op. cit.* bk. II, chap. IV, § IX; PUFFENDORF, *op. cit.* bk. II, chap. III, § XXII, and bk. IV, chap. XII, §§ I, VII–IX; also DOMAT, TRAITÉ DES LOIS, chap. XI, 8. It is a question, incidentally, whether all peoples have applied acquisitive prescription.

[18] Cf. GROTIUS, *op. cit.* bk. I, chap. I, § X, 4: . . . Cf. ST. THOMAS, SUMMA, *Ia IIae*, qu. 94, art. 5 *ad* 3.

[19] Cf. GROTIUS, *op. cit.* bk. I, chap. I, § X, 3: . . . In the same sense, ST. THOMAS, *op. cit. Ia IIae*, qu. 94, art. 5 *ad* 3. For a criticism of this viewpoint, cf. PUFFENDORF, *op. cit.* bk. II, chap. III, § XXII.

[20] We shall come back to this point in speaking of legal justice; see *infra*, no. 239.

is a means or intermediary good finally ordered for the good of the individuals, covers all that is useful to the community. From this it follows that a morally indifferent attitude may acquire obligatory value, in the name of social justice, upon the basis of utility alone: The socially useful good merges with the just, moral, honest good. But this argument neglects a capital point: That the useful in the special case is prescribed not simply as useful but first as just, moral, honest. It is just, moral, honest, and therefore a matter of natural law, that the rulers fulfill the duty of their station, which is to dispose of everything with a view to the public good, that is to say, of general utility. It is just, moral, honest, and therefore a matter of natural law, that the subjects, members of the social whole, collaborate in that general utility. The useful becomes the just only because previously the natural, human just did command devotion by everybody, rulers and subjects, to the community.[21] Also, natural law uses restraint here: It leaves to the inventive reason of the rulers and subjects the task of discovering the socially useful solutions and attitudes. Thus, the distinction between natural law and useful invention does not yield in any way.

Those premises, then, are overthrown when, under color of "derivation" from natural law or simply of "conformity" to natural law, the rules of positive law consecrating solutions of social utility are annexed to natural law as issuing definitively from the rational and social nature of man.

214. The Extension Contradicts the Concept of the Legal Rule. Not only the concept of natural law, in the sense of a rule proceeding from nature, is found altered and overthrown in the system under criticism. It has been shown previously in what way the conception of a natural law of a juridical kind, dictating to the civil legislator the content of his precepts at least in a general way, violated the very concept of the civil law.[22] It is contradictory to speak of "natural jurisprudence" because "jurisprudence," down to its most general rules and their aims — not only the useful but also the good and the just — is a matter of prudence, and prudence is a matter of rational appraisal according to the cases and not a matter of inclination of nature. Even if it is assumed, for example, that natural law prescribes to the civil law the punishment of every offense,[23] at least of every offense against the social life which is

[21] In the same way, incidentally, as beneficence continues to belong to the category of morals although the benefactor endeavors to be useful to another (the useful good) or to give him pleasure (the delectable good).

[22] See *supra*, nos. 114 *et seq.*

[23] Cf. St. Thomas, Summa, *Ia IIae*, qu. 95, art. 2 *ad resp.*, *in fine*, . . . ; Grotius, *op. cit. Discours préliminaire*, § VII, . . .

the first concern of the civil law, it remains for the prudential judgment to decide not only upon the mode of repression but also upon its social utility in the particular case. If it is said in reply that in deciding to refrain from repression in the particular case the civil law confines itself to restricting natural law without making a change in it,[24] it is to be observed that precisely there lies the proper rôle of the jurist establishing the civil law: To discern what of natural law it is appropriate to retain and what to omit, according to the requirements of the public good.[25] Thus, natural law does not dictate any decision to the jurist except negatively, to bring out no precept contrary to moral natural law, and affirmatively, to regulate everything as a function of the possible and realizable public good, the first principle of political natural law.[26]

215. Moral and Political But No Juridical Natural Law. To sum up. First, there exists a moral natural law which is fundamental to the moral conduct of individuals as well as to the positive moral rule, and in every domain including the social domain (social morals) and without distinction between outward and inner acts. This rule of itself obliges only in the internal forum and not before the state, its police and its courts. Second, there also exists a political natural law which, based upon the political instinct of man, establishes political society and all that is essential to it, especially the public authority and the civil law, the latter being considered not in its concrete dispositions but in its principle and its method of elaboration. This political natural law is undoubtedly dependent upon moral natural law because morals governs everything human. But it is in turn the starting point of a new system of properly social (indeed, societal) institutions and rules, inspired by the idea of the public good (at once moral, utilitarian and technical) and governing only the outward acts of man as a member of the group. Third, there exists no juridical natural law in the sense of solutions or even mere directives given in advance to the authority charged with the establishment of the civil law according to the public good. No doubt there are principles commonly accepted in the laws of the countries of the same level of civilization: *Jus gentium* or "general principles of law." But one could not without ambiguity and danger credit natural law with principles which, on the one hand, are very heterogeneous, since one finds there commingled rules of morals, of common sense, and of social utility — and which, on the other hand, lack the characteristics of necessity

[24] Cf. ST. THOMAS, *op. cit. Ia IIae*, qu. 94, art. 5 *ad resp.*

[25] See *supra*, nos. 131 *et seq.* and citations.

[26] Cf. VICO, DE UNO UNIVERSI JURIS PRINCIPIO ET FINE UNO, c. LXXXIII: . . .

and universality inherent in the idea of nature. The practice of civilized countries, even supported by wisdom and experience, is not synonymous with natural inclination.[27]

216. The Dualism of "Natural Law — Positive Law" Replaced by "Morals — Law." If these views are correct, they yield an important result concerning the statement of the problem here under discussion. One must no longer speak of relationships between natural law and positive law (at least when by positive law one understands, as is customary, the law of the jurists, the civil law, and not the positive moral law or rule). One must speak of relationships between morals, not only natural but also positive, and the civil law, that is to say, the law. This statement does correspond to reality. On the one hand, what makes its appearance throughout natural law is indeed morals.[28] On the other hand, the law has relationships with kinds of values other than the ethical values.[29] By comparison, the traditional statement errs both by lack of precision and by confusion. It does not bring out with precision that natural law above all signifies morals. At the same time, that statement leads us to believe that natural law covers all values whatever of interest to the jurist.

CHAPTER II

THE CONCEPT OF JUSTICE

Section 1. The Existing Conceptions; Especially, on the Conception of Aristotle and St. Thomas Aquinas

217. The Modern Conception of Justice as a Specifically Social and Juridical Value. For one trying to analyze the relationships between natural law and justice, on the one hand, and the law in the sense of the civil law, on the other, the concept of justice, too, calls for clarification.

[27] See, *contra*, on the "general principles of law," which he understands in the sense of "data of natural law or of *naturalis ratio*" (at p. 156), G. del Vecchio, *Essai sur les principes généraux du droit*, in JUSTICE, DROIT, ETAT 114 *et seq.*, esp. 155 *et seq.*

[28] See, *contra*, F. Gény, *La laïcité du droit naturel*, in ARCHIVES DE PHILOSOPHIE DU DROIT (1933) nos. 3–4, p. 8, n. 1. . .

[29] Cf., in this sense, F. RUSSO, *op. cit.* 44–45.

Perhaps, despite certain appearances, the difficulty of a clear view is even more considerable for the concept of justice than for that of natural law. The latter has at least a sufficiently determined technical character and is enclosed within certain traditional limits. If it occasions misunderstandings, it is not impossible to find again the currents of doctrine from which the divergent interpretations proceed. As regards justice, on the contrary, whose name is invoked by all — by the man of the world, ignorant or cultured, private or public, as well as by the specialists of the various moral sciences, philosophers, moralists, jurists, historians — how is one to discover the guiding thread which will show the path of the acceptable interpretation?

Reading some legal philosophers, it would seem as if the concept of justice was indissolubly tied to the notions of society and of laws. Consulting only their particular discipline, those authors look at justice only across society and across the laws. Justice to them is the substance, the aim, the ideal of the law, law being understood as positive legal organization. Such is, for instance, the point of view of Gény:

> The legal rules aim necessarily, and I believe exclusively, at realizing justice, which we conceive at the very least under the form of an idea, the idea of the just . . . At bottom, the law finds its proper and specific content only in the notion of the just. This primary, irreducible and indefinable notion seems essentially to imply not only the elementary precepts of doing wrong to no one (*neminem laedere*) and rendering to everyone his own (*suum cuique tribuere*), but also the deeper thought of an equilibrium to be established between conflicting interests with a view to assuring the order essential to the maintenance and progress of human society. Now this notion is easily distinguished from the notions of the beautiful and the true, which answer to quite different concepts, and even from that of duty and the good, which suggest the rules either of religion or of morals.[1]

To De Tourtoulon, justice forms the substance of the law; but this heterogeneous substance is composed of three elements: An individual element, the *suum cuique tribuere* (individual justice); a social element, the changing foundation of prejudgments upon which civilization reposes at any given moment (social justice); and a political element, which is based upon the reason of the strongest, represented in the particular case by the state (justice of state).[2]

In turn, Gurvitch in a certain fashion opposes justice to the moral ideal.

> Unlike the moral ideal, which always goes beyond the value of realization,

[1] F. Gény, Science et technique, no. 16, pp. 49–50.

[2] P. de Tourtoulon, Les trois justices (Paris, 1934).

justice is called upon to realize itself by the institution of an effective equilibrium between the claims of some and the duties of others. Justice, as a transition between the pure qualities and a certain degree of quantity, as a substitution of general rules and common types for the absolute individuality of the moral ideal, as a schematic stabilization of its creative movement, in short, as a logicalization of the moral ideal, precisely establishes security and "the social order" as indispensable means of guaranteeing the realization of that ideal. Thus, peace, security, established order, are immanent in justice, which requires the positiveness of all law.[3]

218. According to Tradition, Justice Is Primarily a Moral Virtue. But that lesson of a justice conceived as a specifically social and juridical value, which, without excluding morals (or even the moral ideal), tempers it by an admixture of factors foreign to morals (social prejudgments, positiveness and efficiency, reason of state), is not the primary lesson of justice. We are here witnessing the same slipping from the moral to the legal plane as in the matter of natural law (moral natural law degenerating into juridical natural law),[4] with the aggravating circumstance that juridical justice becomes synonymous no longer even with the essential legal *solution* of an equilibrium between the interests (Gény), but simply with the formal elements which preside over the elaboration of the rules, in short, with the legal *method* (De Tourtoulon, Gurvitch). We do not say that that method is badly developed and, in particular, that juridical justice does not require peace, security, established order, positiveness, efficiency; witness our preceding exposition.[5] We only observe that before there were organized societies and laws to govern them there was some justice, and today there still exists some justice which is not necessarily that of the laws. In the practice of peoples as in the history of doctrines, justice is first a moral virtue, bringing into play the moral perfectioning of the subject without necessarily implying life in political society. The latter may well add specifications or even new orientations, of a properly social character, to the duty of moral justice; [6] it does not bring justice into being, either as its efficient cause or as a condition of its existence. In short, justice is contemporary not with the idea of political society and the civil law but with the idea of the good, of which it constitutes one of the essential categories, one

[3] G. Gurvitch, *Droit naturel ou droit positif intuitif?* in ARCHIVES DE PHILOSOPHIE DU DROIT ET DE SOCIOLOGIE JURIDIQUE (1933) nos. 3–4, p. 70. Also G. GURVITCH, L'IDÉE DU DROIT SOCIAL (Paris, 1932) 93 *et seq.*; L'EXPÉRIENCE JURIDIQUE ET LA PHILOSOPHIE PLURALISTE DU DROIT p. 226.

[4] See *supra*, nos. 207 *et seq.*

[5] See *supra*, nos. 131 *et seq.*

[6] This point will be made more precise in dealing with legal or social justice; see *infra*, nos. 235 *et seq.*

among the highest: No man can claim to be good and honest unless he respects justice "with firm and enduring will." [7]

219. Justice in the Broad Sense of the Good and the Just. What, then, is the place of justice within the frame of morals, and what is its proper object?

Here one finds several accepted meanings. In the widest sense, justice merges with morality itself: It corresponds to the fulfillment of all duties prescribed by honesty, without distinction of domain or virtue, in the private life of the individual or family and in social life, public or political. In this sense, the honest man, the good man, the saint, are "just." This meaning appears not only in the Scriptures, where the just man is the one obedient and faithful to the law, the whole law (natural and positive, moral and legal),[8] but also in some philosophers, pagan or Christian, ancient or modern,[9] and even in the Digest [of Justinian] under the introductory title, *De justitia et jure*. Having noted that the name *jus* derives from *justitia*, Ulpian indeed defines *jus*, after Celsus, as *ars boni et aequi* [a] (*Dig.* 1, 1, 1, *princ.*). Similarly, Paulus: *Jus pluribus modis dicitur: Uno modo cum id quod semper aequum et bonum est jus dicitur, ut in jus naturale, altero modo quod omnibus aut pluribus in quaque civitate utile est, ut est jus civile* [b] (*Dig.* 1, 1, 1, 1). Thus, *jus* embraces not only the *aequum* but also the *bonum*, that is, the moral good;[10] at any rate, the *aequum* is inseparable from the *bonum*. Further on, the same Ulpian, after having defined justice by the *jus suum cuique tribuere*,[c] enumerates the following *praecepta juris*: *honeste vivere, alterum non laedere, suum cuique tribuere* [d] (*Dig.* 1, 1, 10, 1). Thus the first precept of the law is honesty, that is, observance of the moral law. And even if it is noted that "frequently a definition is characterized first by the statement of the wider field to which the object to be defined

[7] Cf. St. Thomas, Summa, *IIa IIae*, qu. 58, art. 3 *ad resp.*, art. 10 *ad* 1.

[8] The "just men" of the Old Testament, St. Joseph the "Just," "justification" of the sinner, etc.

[9] On this subject, see G. del Vecchio, Justice, Droit, Etat, Part I: *La justice* (Paris, 1938) §§ 2–4, pp. 5–19, with citations.

[a] [The art of the good and equitable.]

[b] [We speak of law in several ways: in one way when we call law that which is always equitable and good, as in natural law; in another way, that which is useful to all or to most people in any commonwealth, as in civil law.]

[10] F. Senn, De la justice et du droit 29, translates *bonum* into *common* good, which is taken for the end of justice. But this interpretation rests on no argument. *Bonum*, without further specification, signifies above all the *moral* good.

[c] [To render to each his own right.]

[d] [Precepts of law: to live honestly, not to injure another, to render to each his own.]

belongs so as to arrive at the statement of the field proper to that object," [11] it still remains that justice is an integral and specially noble part of the *honestum*.[12]

Not that the Roman lawyers ignored the distinction between law and morals; as Paulus remarks, grappling with a practical case for which he seeks a solution: *Non omne quod licet honestum est* [e] (*Dig.* 50, 17, 144, *princ.*): There are things the law permits or tolerates which do not conform to honesty.[13] But the problems of law, justice, and legal enactment were discussed in the first place by the philosophers, who envisaged them from the viewpoint of the good of the soul (morality) and also from that of the good of the city or state (politics), for in classical antiquity particularly one did not conceive of an honest man who would not at the same time and first of all be a good citizen.[14] The lawyers in their legal philosophical definitions were content to reproduce the teachings of the masters of philosophy without seeking to correct or amend them from the point of view of their own discipline.

220. *Justice in the Strict Sense of the Virtue Attributing to Everyone His Right.* There is, however, a narrower meaning of justice, yet still a moral one, which limits that virtue to the domain of relations with another. According to a classification inherited from the Stoics, the *honestum* is composed of four principal parts: Justice, prudence, moderation, and fortitude. Unlike the latter three, which are defined by being related to the very person whose passions they tend to regulate and measure, justice has its proper function in ordering the conduct of man in matters relative to another. Justice essentially supposes that there be another (*alietas*); only metaphorically can one speak of injustice toward oneself.[15] Hence the two classical definitions — that reported by Ulpian: *Justitia est constans et perpetua voluntas jus suum cuique tribuendi* [f] (*Dig.* 1, 1, 10, *princ.*), and that given by Cicero: *Justitia est habitus animi, communi ultilitate conservata, suam cuique tribuens dignitatem* [g]

[11] F. SENN, *op. cit.* 40–41 and n. 1. But in the particular case it is a matter not so much of a definition by proximate generic kind and specific difference as of an enumeration of the precepts included in justice.

[12] F. SENN, *op. cit.* 41–42.

[e] [Not all that is permitted is honest.]

[13] Also PAULUS, DIG. 50, 17, 197: . . .

[14] Cf. P. LACHIÈZE-REY, *op. cit.* 30 *et seq.*

[15] See F. SENN, *op. cit.* 39–43, and n. 1 at p. 43. Also ST. THOMAS, *op. cit. IIa IIae*, qu. 57, art. 1; qu. 58, arts. 1, 2, and 11; qu. 106, art. 3 *ad* 1.

[f] [Justice is the constant and perpetual will to render to each his own right.]

[g] [Justice is the habit of the mind which, reserving common utility, allots to each his own worth.]

(*De inventione* 2, 53, 160). Justice attributes to everyone his right, his dignity.[16] But at once two questions arise. Who is to be understood by that other one or everyone (*cuique*)? What is that right (or that dignity) (*jus, dignitatem*) which is his (*suum*) and on that ground is due to everyone? Later, the meaning of the reservation *communi utilitate conservata* will be studied.[17]

221. The Wide Interpretation of the Debt of Justice (the Stoics, Cicero). Following a first interpretation, which represents, as Senn puts it, "the great traditional lesson of justice,"[18] from the Stoics to the Fathers of the Church, passing through Cicero and the lawyers, justice would embrace all that is due to another, without distinction between equal situations and unequal situations, and even where it would be impossible for the debtor to render the equivalent of what he owes — and without any distinction between the so-called "legal" debt, that is, the debt capable of being exacted, and the merely "moral" debt, which is not susceptible of exaction. In this sense, one will put under justice not only the duty of not injuring and that of respecting the *cuique suum* between equal and independent persons, but also a series of other virtues implying a debt toward other beings, even if placed upon different planes: Religion, by which man renders unto God the homage and worship he owes Him; piety, by which we venerate and serve all those united to us by blood as well as our country; gratitude, by which benefits are recognized and repaid; vindication, by which any violence or injustice coming from another is rebuffed; respect (*observantia*), which is incumbent with regard to men superior in merit or dignity; and lastly truthfulness, which says what is and which keeps promises.[19] All these virtues, above the diversity of the respective conditions and circumstances where they intervene, in effect realize the *aequum*, that equality or proportional adjustment to the claim of another which is the essential characteristic feature of justice. If the parties are unequal in dignity,

[16] Synonymous terms, according to F. SENN, *op. cit.* 19–20. See, however, 1 G. RENARD, LA THÉORIE DE L'INSTITUTION 25–29, especially n. 1 at p. 28, according to whom Ulpian referred to individual justice and Cicero to institutional justice. Other substantially similar definitions by Cicero may be found in G. DEL VECCHIO, JUSTICE, DROIT, ETAT 37, n. 3.

[17] See *infra*, no. 238.

[18] F. SENN, *op. cit.* 5–7, 47. Also, by the same author, *Des origines et du contenu de la notion de bonnes moeurs* (in Rome), in 1 RECUEIL D'ÉTUDES SUR LES SOURCES DU DROIT EN L'HONNEUR DE FRANÇOIS GÉNY 53 *et seq.*, esp. 57, 60–63.

[19] This is Cicero's list in DE INVENTIONE, 2, 53, 161 and 2, 22, 65, certain elements of which are taken up in DIG. 1, 1, 2 (Pomponius: religion and *pietas*) and 1, 1, 3 (Florentin: *vindicatio*). Texts and comments may be found in F. SENN, *op. cit.* 21–32.

as in religion, piety, respect, the debt will be adequate to that inequality of the persons; if the debt cannot by its nature be exacted, if need be by compulsion, as in gratitude, vindication, truthfulness, it remains nonetheless a veritable debt, required by the formal principle of equality of proportion.

222. Distinction between the Principal Virtue (Justice in the Narrow Sense) and the Annexed Virtues (Aristotle, St. Thomas Aquinas). Following another interpretation, developed by Aristotle and resumed by St. Thomas Aquinas, it would be appropriate to introduce certain classifications in the category of justice in the general sense of a virtue rendering to everyone his due,[20] which would bring out essential particulars omitted in the somewhat amorphous systematization of the preceding interpretation.

In justice, as in the other virtues, St. Thomas distinguishes "integral parts," which are the "true and principal" justice,[21] and "potential parts" or annexed virtues, which in essentials answer to the concept of justice but get away from it on one point or another.[22] The "potential parts" or annexed virtues of justice are divided into two groups: On the one hand, religion toward God, piety toward parents and country, respect for superiors; on the other, truthfulness, gratitude, vindication, liberality, and affability or friendship.[23]

Upon what points do the annexed virtues of justice fall short of the principal virtue? They approximate and even realize it inasmuch as they aim at rendering to another his due following the principle of a certain equality. But that realization is imperfect, sometimes on the score of equality, as for the annexed virtues of the first group, and sometimes on the score of the debt, as for the annexed virtues of the second group.[24]

223. Annexed Virtues Which Fall Short of Justice on the Score of Equality. On the score of equality: How are we to render to God, to our

[20] St. Thomas gives several definitions of justice; but among them he admits and declares good that of the DIGEST, see SUMMA, *IIa IIae*, qu. 58, art. 1.

[21] ST. THOMAS, *op. cit. IIa IIae*, qu. 80, single art. *ad resp.* and *ad* 4.

[22] We do not speak of equity in the sense of ἐπιείκεια, defined by Aristotle as "the correction of a law by reason of its generality," because this equity intervenes in moderating all positive laws whatsoever, not only laws understood with a view to the common good and creating a duty of legal justice, but also all others, including the laws of positive morals. Cf. St. Thomas, *op. cit.* qu. 120.

[23] See ST. THOMAS, *op. cit. IIa IIae*, qu. 80, single art.; qu. 81, *prol.* It will be noted that St. Thomas reproduces the enumeration and definitions of Cicero textually, save for the last two virtues which, by the way, he adds to the list with a certain hesitation; see the citations below, no. 225 and n. 39.

[24] See ST. THOMAS, SUMMA, *IIa IIae*, qu. 80, single art.

parents, to our country, the equivalent of what is their due? No doubt it is a duty of justice for the creature to render to his Creator the homage of his entire submission and his worship. God has rights over man since He is his author and, being God, could have created him only for His glory. The gratuitous love He bears for His creature, the plan He has conceived to associate him with His innermost life, change nothing in that fundamental position of dependence. In this sense, the duty of religion is a duty of justice toward God.[25] But, precisely on account of that dependence, how could man return to God what would be equal to what comes to him from God? The more so since what he would thus return to Him would not have ceased to belong to God, beginning with the very principle of his activity which God continues generously to dispense to him every day by sustaining him in being. It is true that man has been created free, free even not to render homage to God. But, on the one hand, that freedom rests, in an indirect and indeed mysterious manner, within the free grant of the Sovereign Lord of all things; on the other hand, the total homage of that freedom to which man is in justice obliged does not constitute an equivalence. "And that is why the divine law is not properly *jus* but *fas*;[h] for God it suffices that we should fulfill with regard to Him what we are able to."[26]

The same argument in a lesser degree applies to piety toward one's parents and one's country. From our parents, from our nation we have our being and our whole physical, intellectual, moral formation.[27] How can we make our acts of reverence and assistance equal to the greatness of the benefits received? To this imperfection in equality is added, in the case of parents, an imperfection in the matter of being "another": Between parents and children, because of the fact of generation and education, the distinctness of persons is not absolute. The son has "something of his father," he is "somehow a part" of him physically, intellectually, morally. Now in so far as this solidarity exists and in the matters in which it ought to be taken into account,[28] there is a short-

[25] On the virtue of religion, see St. Thomas, *op. cit. IIa IIae*, qu. 82 *et seq*. . . .

[h] [The Roman term *fas* designates a divinely pronounced law as distinguished from *jus*, the ordinary term for law and right.]

[26] St. Thomas, *op. cit. IIa IIae*, qu. 57, art. 1 *ad* 3; qu. 80, single art. Cf. F. Senn, *op. cit.* p. 26, n. 2.

[27] See generally on parents and country as the principles of the individual's existence, St. Thomas, *op. cit. IIa IIae*, qu. 101, arts. 1, 2, 3, *passim*. Especially on one's country, see *IIa IIae*, qu. 101, art. 3 *ad* 3: . . . In the same sense, also, G. del Vecchio, Justice, Droit, Etat 63–64.

[28] As human individuals, father and son obviously remain distinct and, on this plane, their relations belong to justice properly so called; see St. Thomas, *op. cit. IIa IIae*, qu. 57, art. 4 *ad* 2.

coming in the perfection of justice, for there is perfect justice only between men independent of each other by nature (if not by function).[29]

Lastly, the respect due to persons of dignity (and, by extension, to every greatness: Of virtue, of spirit, of age) is likewise not capable of being lifted to the level of their quality, by reason of the quasi-paternal rôle of all authority.[30]

224. Annexed Virtues Which Fall Short on the Score of the Debt (Moral, Not Legal, Debt). The shortcoming in respect of perfect justice may in the second place be found in the character of the debt. Something is due and the equivalence can indeed be realized; but the claim of the creditor is consecrated merely by morals (*debitum morale*) and not by the rule of positive law (statute or custom) (*debitum legale*), so that the creditor is left without the right to obtain execution. Again, this lack of the possibility of exaction seems to follow less from the lack of consecration by the law than from the very nature of things which intends debts of this kind to remain merely moral debts. They are nonetheless due in the most rigorous manner: The man who does not recognize them is no longer an honest man. But how can he who has received a benefit be *forced* to the duty of gratitude? Not only does that duty lack a precise content, but also the intervention of compulsion would deprive it of all moral value and of its very meaning as a gracious act. By definition, the debt of gratitude is among those which can only be discharged freely.[31] The same goes for the act of (private) vindication which, riposting to an unjust evil, must proceed from an act of free determination if it is to remain a virtue.[32] The reasoning is identical as to truthfulness, as a debt to another, and faithfulness to promises, a special form of truthfulness: As such, neither the manifestation of truth to one who has the right to know it, nor the fulfillment of what has been promised engenders any debt that may be exacted by another. Disloyalty is not injustice, and the disloyal person, the liar or breaker of promises, is merely called dishonest.[33]

Finally, in the last rank of debts connected with honesty is placed a group of virtues belonging to civility rather than decency, contributing

[29] See St. Thomas, *op. cit. IIa IIae*, qu. 57, art. 4 in its entirety; qu. 58, art. 7 *ad* 3: between parents and children, husband and wife, master and slave, there is only an "economic" (i.e., familial) justice.

[30] See St. Thomas, *op. cit. IIa IIae*, qu. 102, art. 1.

[31] See St. Thomas, *op. cit. IIa IIae*, qu. 106, art. 1 *ad* 2; art. 4 *ad* 1; art. 5 *ad resp.*; art. 6 *ad resp.* and *ad* 3.

[32] See St. Thomas, *op. cit. IIa IIae*, qu. 108, art. 2 *ad resp.* and *ad* 1.

[33] See St. Thomas, *op. cit. IIa IIae*, qu. 109, art. 3 *ad resp.* Also, touching upon the properly social viewpoint, *infra*, no. 257 and n. 11.

to a certain rounding out of honesty without, however, being indispensable to it. Such are liberality, affability or friendship, and virtues of the same nature, which Cicero passes over in silence on the ground that "they have little of the reason of debt." [34] At this extreme, though, the analogy turns almost into an antithesis. Thus, affability, a debt of pure honesty, has its principle far more on the side of the person bound to treat another suitably than on that of the opposite party who might have some right thereto.[35] Thus, again, liberality, far from giving another what belongs to him, as justice does, gives him of one's own [36] and does so in consideration of the good of one's own virtue rather than of the good of another.[37] The difference is so much stronger than the resemblance that St. Thomas hesitates at the end: *Et ideo liberalitas* a quibusdam *ponitur pars justitiae, sicut virtus ei annexa ut principali.* [i] [38]

225. Justice in the Strict Sense Must Be Defined by "Aequalitas" Rather than by the "Aequum." Whatever may be the objections in detail which these analyses may raise, the Aristotelian-Thomistic effort to pull the concept of justice together within narrower bounds deserves approval because it is inspired by a distinction that is not at all factitious but is founded upon reality.[39] Without overlooking the bond that unites the annexed virtues with justice, without depreciating their moral value, superior to that of justice as far as scruple or "inwardness" are involved, or their peculiarly social value, by reason of the sociability they promote,[40] the virtue that renders to everyone his right or his dignity deserves to be defined, in the strict sense, not merely by the loose idea of equity (*aequum et bonum*) but by the mathematical idea of equality (*aequalitas*). In this sense, justice equalizes the attitude of the subject to what is the rigorous right of another individual or collectivity, a right covering and protecting an innate or acquired good, which for its holder is in a certain manner his own, whence it follows that he may exact respect for it if need be by force. If this "his own" is lacking, there is no right that can be exacted, no equality to be realized, and therefore

[34] St. Thomas, *op. cit. IIa IIae*, qu. 80, single art.; qu. 117, art. 5 *ad* 1, *in fine*.

[35] See St. Thomas, *op. cit. IIa IIae*, qu. 114, art. 2 *ad resp*.

[36] St. Thomas, *op. cit. IIa IIae*, qu. 117, art. 5 *ad resp*.

[37] St. Thomas, *op. cit. IIa IIae*, qu. 58, art. 12 *ad* 1.

[i] [And therefore liberality is *by some* taken for a part of justice, as it were, a virtue annexed to it as to the principal one.]

[38] St. Thomas, *op. cit. IIa IIae*, qu. 117, art. 5 *ad resp.*, *in fine*.

[39] This is why 1 L. Duguit, Traité de droit constitutionnel (3d ed. Paris, 1927) § 11, pp. 120–122, expressly takes up the Thomistic definitions of commutative justice and distributive justice; see *supra*, no. 107. Also J. Bonnecase, La notion du droit en France au XIXe siècle (Paris, 1919) 104–105.

[40] See on this point R. Bernard, Appendix II, in St. Thomas d'Aquin, Somme théologique. Les vertus sociales (transl. by J.-D. Folghera) 434.

no justice. If there exists "his own," but without any possibility of equalization on account of the basic inability of the debtor, the debt will no longer be one of justice, since it remains outside of the equality postulated by justice. This is not to say that it could not give rise to legal effects, e.g., in the form of the "natural obligation," or even directly to a civil obligation. That is another question, which concerns the determination of the content of the civil law and not the definition of justice.[41]

226. In the Case of Justice, the "Just Mean" Constitutive of All Virtue Is Real or Objective. From this it will be seen what is mistaken in the conception of some modern authors,[42] according to whom justice would be an equilibrium tending to harmonize antagonistic interests. Justice is not just any equilibrium. That equilibrium has its principle and its rule, which is equality: It matters that each of the interests present be given exactly what is coming to it, neither more nor less. In this consists the famous "just mean" peculiar to the virtue of justice. This just or golden mean is objective (*medium rei secudum se*),[j] taken from the side of the other person and his objective right, while the just or golden mean of the other virtues lies in each subject himself and is determined in purely rational fashion (*medium secundum rationem quoad nos*).[k] [43] Moderation and fortitude rectify, measure, and proportion the passions of man, which are internal, according to the indications of (moral) prudence in the particular case, which may yield solutions varying with the ways of life, vocations, and dispositions of people. Justice, on the contrary, rectifies, measures, and proportions the "outward operation," that is, the acting of the subject person, by a right which is found in another, whatever its object may otherwise be (*res, personae, opera*),[l] which therefore demands satisfaction by the sole fact that it exists, outside of any consideration of circumstances or dispositions relating to the debtor: *Et ideo medium justitiae consistit in quadam proportionis aequalitate rei exterioris ad personam exteriorem* [m] (that is, to another).[44]

[41] It seems that this confusion lies at the origin of the mistrust shown by F. Senn with regard to the Thomistic doctrine of justice . . . see *op. cit.* 47, n. 1 *in fine*, p. 54 . . . See also *infra*, nos. 259 *et seq.*

[42] See, among others, the definition by Gény, reported *supra*, no. 217.

[j] [The mean of the matter according to itself.]

[k] [The mean according to reason with regard to us.]

[43] ST. THOMAS, SUMMA, *IIa IIae*, qu. 58, art. 10. Also art. [qu.] 57, art. 1 *ad resp.*; qu. 58, arts. 8 and 9; qu. 60, art. 1 *ad* 3, *initio*; qu. 61, art. 2 *ad* 1.

[l] [Things, persons, works.]

[m] [And therefore the mean of justice consists in a certain equality of proportion of an external thing to an external person.]

[44] ST. THOMAS, *op. cit. IIa IIae*, qu. 58, art. 10 *ad resp.* See also art. 11, *ad resp.*; qu. 61, art. 3 *ad resp.*

227. Confusion to Be Avoided in Interpreting the Concept of the "Real Mean." Yet the objectivity of justice must be rightly understood, and it must by no means be exaggerated by always tracing it back to an equality "of thing to thing," calculated by a "purely arithmetical proportion." [45] One would thereby disregard not only the person subject to the virtue, which is required by the *medium rei*, but also the "other" one, as if what is due him could never be proportioned to the individual personality of the other and therefore never vary according to persons. In reality, what is due will be established from thing to thing where this is indeed involved in the matter. Thus, he who has received a thing on the ground of deposit or of loan ought to restore that thing or its value; similarly, in exchanges the rights of the parties are measured by the value of the things exchanged, which is objective. But in other matters what is due will be proportioned to the subjective condition of the creditor. The grounds and qualities vary and so, consequently, do the rights and the duties correlative to the rights. What is due to one according to equality is not necessarily due to another according to the same equality. Thus the *objective* just mean is far from always coinciding with arithmetical proportionality. The proportionality of justice will sometimes be arithmetical and sometimes geometrical, the mean not ceasing for that reason to be objective.[46] This is brought out by St. Thomas in a concrete example. To the objection that the just mean is called rational because it varies relative to persons and that the same phenomenon is to be observed in justice, where he who strikes a king is not punished with the same penalty as he who strikes a private person, St. Thomas replies: That the proportion not being the same in the injury, the penalty could not be the same under the two assumptions, which proves indeed, he adds, that the difference lies in the things and is not merely rational.[47] Moreover, is not so-called distributive justice, which as a special form of justice is bound to reproduce the general definition of justice, subject to a principle of merely geometrical proportionality? [48]

Let us not forget either that, even in the case where the equality is one of thing to thing, justice brings into relation human persons. What is due someone is "his own," that is, a good that depends more or less closely upon the person of the creditor. What the debtor owes in turn is

[45] The formulations of St. Thomas, *IIa IIae*, qu. 58, art. 10 *ad resp.* . . . and Aristotle, cited there, . . . to the contrary are valid only (subject also to explanations) for one of the kinds of justice, the most typical to be sure, commutative justice; see qu. 61, art. 2 *ad resp.*

[46] Erroneously: Senn, *op. cit.* 47, n. 1, and p. 52. . . .

[47] St. Thomas, *op. cit. IIa IIae*, qu. 58, art. 10 *ad* 3.

[48] See St. Thomas, *op. cit. IIa IIae*, qu. 61, art. 2 *ad* 2: . . .

an act, the rendering of a thing or service, or an abstention, which engages the person of the debtor. On the other hand, the value of goods, including that of merchandise, could not be appraised fundamentally except by reference to their human value, as means for a man to provide for his wants of every sort, so that the equality of justice, even where it is arithmetical, remains of a moral nature.

Section 2. The Three Kinds of Justice

228. Enumeration and Classification. Aristotle and St. Thomas did not confine themselves to distinguishing justice from the annexed virtues. Pursuing their analysis, they divided justice into three kinds, according to the kind of quality of the other persons concerned.

When these are private persons (or acting in such quality), the justice which links them is called "commutative." When the persons in question are a collectivity and its members, especially the state and its citizens, justice is called "distributive" as to what is due from the collectivity to its members, and "legal" as to what is due from the members to the collectivity. As opposed to legal justice, where the immediate object is the collectivity, commutative justice and distributive justice, with their immediate objects being particular private persons, are called particular. But distributive justice, though particular, is nonetheless like legal justice of the collective and societal type — and where the state (or the society of states) is concerned, of the political type — since it is based upon the organized collectivity, while commutative justice, as such, belongs to the individual or interindividual type.[1]

229. Commutative Justice; Its Possible Subjects: Physical or Moral Persons. The simplest, most elementary form of justice, and apparently the only one aimed at in the definitions of Cicero and Ulpian,[2] is commutative justice. Indeed, for this to make its appearance it suffices that there be two human beings, considered individually, whether or not belonging to the same state (two fellow citizens or two persons of different nationalities) or even (a theoretical assumption) participating in no state, no community, such as Robinson Crusoe on his island confronting a second immigrant. Still, as has been seen,[3] it is necessary that between

[1] See generally, as to these distinctions, St. Thomas, *op. cit. IIa IIae*, qu. 58, art. 5 *ad resp.* and art. 7; qu. 61, art. 1.

[2] See *supra*, no. 220 and n. 16 . . . [On] the definition of Cicero . . . see *infra*, no. 238.

[3] See *supra*, no. 223.

these two human beings there be no physical solidarity, as in father and son, nor even family solidarity, as in husband and wife, for such solidarity partly frustrates the quality of being another person.[4] It matters little, though, whether the parties to the relationships are physical or moral persons. From the viewpoint of the debt, if not from that of morality,[5] commutative justice on the active and passive sides binds collectivities as well as individuals, with no distinction between private and public collectivities nor between the domestic and the international levels. Thus, the relationships between individuals and public collectivities, even those of which they are members as long as in the relationship they do not figure in their quality as members,[6] fall under commutative justice; so do the relationships between independent collectivities, such as two private societies or two states.

Still it is necessary that the collectivities under contemplation belong to the category of organized societies, and on that account enjoy moral personality, without which justice would lack an active or passive subject of a right. Outside of moral personality, indeed, either the collectivity is nothing or it is but a collection of individuals, physical persons who themselves are the subjects of rights. It follows that the family, which is not a moral person, could not as such be a party in the relationship of justice, whether with regard to those called its members or with regard to outsiders: Only the physical persons who are members of the family — spouses, parents, children, other relatives — can hold rights and obligations, obviously taking account of that family state which determines a special personal status for them, in their reciprocal relationships (idea of familial justice) as well as in their relationships with third parties and with the state.[7]

230. The Object of Commutative Justice: The "Suum" in Its Diverse Forms. The object of the right of another in commutative justice is what belongs to each one from the outset and is coming back to him in consequence of some commutation.[8] What belongs to each one from the outset: His physical and moral being, the properties of his being, his relations and qualities of every sort, familial, economic, commercial, the material or spiritual works of which he is the author, the external

[4] This is not to say that offenses among members of the same family would be of lesser gravity than injustice against a stranger, for attacks against solidarity are graver than attacks against the relation to others.

[5] See *supra*, no. 40.

[6] As to this distinction, see St. Thomas, *op. cit. IIa IIae*, qu. 61, art. 4 *ad* 2.

[7] See *supra*, no. 10, n. 7.

[8] As to different kinds of exchanges regulated by commutative justice, cf. St. Thomas, *op. cit. IIa IIae*, qu. 61, art. 3 *ad resp.*; also qu. 62, art. 1 *ad* 2.

goods to which he has acquired a right of ownership or of use. This immediate *suum* has an absolute character: It imposes itself upon the respect of all and gives rise only to an obligation of abstention, sanctioned in case of violation by a right to restitution or reparation (this is the *neminem laedere*). However, in the case of delivery of a thing to another under a limited title (loan for use, deposit, etc.), the respect for the *suum* implies the personal obligation of restitution of the thing to its owner.

The *suum* also comprises what, without belonging to another from the outset, is coming to him ultimately through the workings of commutations (communications and contacts), voluntary and involuntary ones. Such is the thing or service due on the ground of exchange, or on the ground of reparation of injury inflicted, or on the ground of compensation for enrichment without cause at the expense of another, in short, choses in action (*jura in persona*) representing the equivalent of the original *suum*.[9] Unlike the latter, the choses in action engender a right only with regard to a determinate person, the beneficiary or author of the commutation, bound by the positive obligation to reëstablish the broken equality (this is the *tribuere cuique*).[10] Curiously enough, commutative justice derives its name from this second assumption, probably because it is based on action while the first resolves itself into an abstention. But it is clear that the second assumption is the logical consequence of the first: There would be no room for rendering to another what is coming to him if before any commutation he were not the master of certain rights in which he could not be touched, without his consent, by anyone. It is understood, too, that the concepts of right (*jus*) and even of belonging or mastering (*suum*) have a meaning only relative to another, representing the eventual opponent.

231. In Commutative Justice, Equality Is Determined as of Thing to Thing. If that is the object of commutative justice, it must be concluded that in this kind of justice equality is taken to be one of thing to thing, or in Aristotle's terms, that its real mean is determined according to an arithmetical proportion of a purely quantitative nature. The creditor of justice has a right to what belongs to him or is coming to him simply because the thing is his, and it is his regardless of any consideration of his personal quality.[11] Consideration of the person will intervene only

[9] On restitution in case of violation of commutative justice, see ST. THOMAS, *op. cit. IIa IIae*, qu. 62, art. 1 *ad resp.* and *ad* 2.

[10] On the integral parts of the virtue of justice, cf. ST. THOMAS, *op. cit. IIa IIae*, qu. 79, art. 1.

[11] ST. THOMAS, *op. cit. IIa IIae*, qu. 61, art. 2 *ad resp.* and *ad* 2; art. 3 *ad resp.*, *in fine*; art. 4 *ad resp.*, *in fine*.

where the condition of the person produces a difference in the things, and St. Thomas again takes up the example of the injury: The injury to persons is more or less grave according to the condition of the injured person. However, even in this case the proportion remains arithmetical because the condition of the person is an element that is to qualify the injury (*conditio personae facit ad quantitatem rei*).[a] [12] Contrariwise, the condition of persons becomes altogether irrelevant where the question, for instance, is to determine what the user of the thing of another ought to restore or what the buyer [of a thing] ought to pay.

232. With Distributive Justice the Societal Plane Is Reached. With distributive justice, which is particular like commutative justice, one reaches the societal plane, and especially, with the state-society, the political plane. Not that there could be no question of distribution between particular independent individuals or groups. Such a distribution is encountered every time there is an undivided whole and one proceeds to divide the capital or the profit, as in the case of the division of the product or benefits of work done in common, on the basis of a contract of partnership or collaboration. But these cases of distribution are generally attached to commutative justice, and rightly so, for we are concerned here ultimately with nothing else than rendering to each his own according to a rigorously arithmetical proportion: The divided equivalent of his undivided quota, the equivalent in money or in kind of his share in the collaboration.[13] For distributive justice to emerge in its specific form, it must be envisioned in the relationships between a society forming a body, on the one hand, and its members, on the other, the latter being taken at the outset not as particular individuals but as members of the body.[14] Although the concept of distributive justice may be set into the frame of any society whatever, private or public, domestic or international (provided it forms a body),[15] it is ordinarily viewed in the framework of the domestic political society, the state. There, it is the pendant to legal justice, which with its typical characteristics [16] is encountered only in the supreme, eminently legal society that is constituted by the state.

[a] [The condition of the person matters for the quantity of the thing.]

[12] St. Thomas, *op. cit. IIa IIae*, qu. 61, art. 2 *ad* 2.

[13] Cf. the old adage: "Equality is the soul of sharing," meaning a mathematical equality which tolerates no violation.

[14] See St. Thomas, *op. cit. IIa IIae*, qu. 61, art. 1 *ad resp.*

[15] Cf. St. Thomas, *op. cit. IIa IIae*, qu. 61, art. 1 *ad* 3, *in fine*, where the principle is applied (wrongly) to the familial society.

[16] On these characteristics, see *infra*, nos. 235–239.

233. The Subject Matter of Distributive Justice: The Various Kinds of Distributions. The subject matter of distributive justice consists of the various kinds of distributions which every social body is called upon to effect among its members. First, where the society is one with purposes of self-interest, established with a view to the good of its members, this means distribution of the social benefits. That in turn means, in the case of the state, participation in the advantages of the public good resulting from the action of the state and its services, protection of rights, aid to interests, etc.[17] Then, distribution of the functions and employments that are at the disposal of the body, which indeed acts only through individuals. Lastly, allocation of the contributions of every nature that are indispensable to social life, for the body lives only by what its members bring in to it. Now these distributions, active and passive, could not take place except according to a principle of equalization as to the rights and faculties of everyone, which is a rule of justice.

In confronting the society with his claim for his just part in the social benefits, the member claims what is due him as his own in his quality as a member. No doubt before distribution those benefits are the property of the social body which has produced them, while in commutative justice the good due is from the outset the personal property of the creditor, directly or by equivalent.[18] But since by hypothesis the body exists only for its members, the benefits it produces are rightfully due its members under its statute. It cannot without injustice retain them or divert them from their destination or distribute them in a partial manner; and thus, "when something of the common goods is distributed among the members, every one of them receives in a way what belongs to him." [19] The solution is identical as regards the burdens: When the society claims a heavier contribution from one of its members than is in justice incumbent upon him, it violates, if not the member's own right (which would transfer us to the terrain of commutative justice), at least his right to the just distribution of the burdens.

234. Difference between Distributive Justice and Commutative Justice. However, the position of the member with regard to the social body is not the same as that of one independent individual with regard to another. First, his right is by definition that of a member, that is, of a part in relation to a whole, and therefore his right in distributive justice remains entirely subordinate to the requirements of the good of the body in its entirety. Thus, if the good of the body demands it, the benefits of

[17] On the public good and its constituent elements, see *supra*, nos. 135 *et seq.*

[18] See St. Thomas, *op. cit. IIa IIae*, qu. 61, art. 1 *ad* 5: . . .

[19] St. Thomas, *op. cit. IIa IIae*, qu. 61, art. 1 *ad* 2 . . . Cf. qu. 62, art. 1 *ad* 3.

private corporations are withheld from distribution and applied to the reserve fund or in other ways;[20] among candidates for public offices, the ablest will not always be preferred; in revenue assessments, fiscal justice may be moderated. In a word, distributive justice is directly subject to legal justice, which expresses the supreme right of the body.[21]

Furthermore, the right of the member with regard to the body could logically be measured only according to an equality proportional to the "dignity," the rank of the member in the body. Now the ranks in the body are not equal. "That is why in distributive justice the mean is not taken according to an equality of thing to thing but according to a proportion of things to persons, so that if one person is superior to another what is given to him ought to exceed what is given to the other. And that is why Aristotle says such a mean is one according to a geometrical proportion, where equality is a matter not of quantity but of proportion." [22] What then is the determining principle of the hierarchy? It is multifarious and also depends upon the diversity of social and political régimes. In modern states, among the criteria of distributive justice there must be counted, besides merit and services rendered, weakness, meaning not only physical weakness, which has always been entitled to a privilege,[23] but also economic weakness. Is it not legitimate that in the political community the weakest benefit from special protection and aid from the state? [24] As to justice in imposing burdens, equally governed by the rule of proportionality, the determining principle is that of ability to contribute to what is required, so that the more fortunate will contribute a larger amount than the less fortunate. Thus, actively and passively, the shares of everyone are calculated by a measure individual to each. But since the calculation always takes place under the same principle, the equality constitutive of justice is maintained.

235. Legal Justice: Its General Concept. The third and most complex form of justice is legal justice.

Conversely to distributive justice, which moves from the society to the members, legal (or social) justice goes from the members to the

[20] On the moderation which is to be imposed in distribution, cf. St. Thomas, op. cit. *IIa IIae*, qu. 61, art. 1 *ad* 1.

[21] See St. Thomas, *op. cit. Ia IIae*, qu. 96, art. 4 *ad resp.*: . . .

[22] St. Thomas, *op. cit. IIa IIae*, qu. 61, art. 2 *ad resp.* See also art. 4 *ad resp.*, *in fine*.

[23] Thus, as for minors, lunatics, and feeble-minded persons.

[24] See in this sense Leo XIII, Encyclical *Rerum Novarum*: "*Quocirca mercenarios, cum in multitudine egena numerentur, debet cura providentiaque singulari complecti respublica*" [As the wage-earners are numbered in an indigent multitude, the state ought to surround them with singular care and providence].

society, especially, as the word "legal" indicates,[25] the political society. Legal justice, though, is a *moral* virtue in what concerns man if not groups, because "it is impossible that a man be good if he is not proportioned to the common good." [26] Is it not the vocation of man to live and perfect himself in and through political society? The holder of the right here is not indeed the community or the public in general, but the state, which is both the organization that encloses the national community (civic or political viewpoint, corresponding to the aspect of the political public good) and that same community in its corporate form (social viewpoint, corresponding to the aspect of the social public good).[27] The debtors of legal justice are the private individuals and groups, who are bound in their quality as members, whatever their rank in the state — rulers or ruled — to render to the social whole what is coming to it on the part of its members. The "ordination for the common good," which is the object of legal justice, is thus traced back to respect by the members for the strict right of the community against them. This ordination of the parts to the whole is the community's due as a right that may be exacted.

236. What the Citizen Owes the State as Organization. To the state as organization the citizen owes in the first place what is necessary to its existence, its independence, the constitution and good functioning of its organs: Revenue, military service, a certain participation in public functions, in short, the "aid and subsidy" which the state, a moral person, can draw only from its members who are physical persons. To the state the individual citizen further owes the exact and faithful discharge of his functions if he is ruling, and obedience to the laws and legitimate orders of the authority if he is ruled. These are so many properly social requirements, valid for any private or public society whatsoever.

237. What the Individual Owes the Community Organized in the State: "Generality" of Legal Justice. But this is not all. It is even in some respects secondary if one takes into account that the state organ-

[25] The thought of Aristotle and St. Thomas is indeed concerned here not with laws in general but with the positive laws of the state.

[26] St. Thomas, *op. cit. Ia IIae*, qu. 92, art. 1 *ad* 3.

[27] St. Thomas assigns the *bonum commune* as the end of legal justice; see notably *IIa IIae*, qu. 58, art. 5 *ad resp.* But, first, this common good is the good of an organized community, since the question is one of the whole and the part, *loc. cit.* and art. 7 *ad* 2, or of the prince and the subjects, qu. 58, art. 6 *ad resp.* Furthermore, this organized community is that embracing the *multitudo*, art. 6, obj. 3, or in short, the state; see also art. 7 *ad* 2: *bonum commune civitatis.* The *bonum commune* thus is the good of the community integrated in the state, including both the extra-political good of that community and its political good,

ization is but a means in the service of the community. To the community of the individuals associated in the state the individual member owes, besides, the adjustment of his private conduct, the submission of his particular good to the common good of the public as defined above in its elements of order, coördination, and aid, radiating over the universality of values of the temporal order.[28] This is what differentiates the state from private societies. The latter pursue but special, particular, limited ends. Their members are parts of the whole, and have duties toward the whole, only for these special ends; otherwise, they retain their independence. In the case of the state, on the contrary, whose end is absolutely general, merging with the good of all in the various sectors of the temporal, the individual member is wholly ordained, as regards the temporal, to the community of the members of the state. It is not enough that he fulfill his civic, political, societal duty toward the state organization. He must also fulfill his social duty, in subordinating all that pertains to him, in his personal activity and his property, to the good of the society grouped in the state.[29]

In a sense one may say that the individual in the state is never done with doing his duty morally, since after having "contributed" to the maintenance of the state and submitted to the laws he remains in justice bound to take the supreme rule of the public good for the norm of his outward life and even his thoughts and wishes [30] on the plane of the temporal. This is expressed in the remark that legal justice is a general virtue (hence its other name, general justice). Through its subject matter it comprises the exercise of all the virtues — undoubtedly the virtues *ad alterum* (particular justice, both commutative and distributive, and annexed virtues, including liberality),[31] but also the other virtues, religion and virtues concerning the person himself who is their subject (moderation, fortitude, prudence). Indeed, due to the phenomenon of interdependence of the "private" and the "public," clearly the exercise of any virtue whatsoever is more or less useful to the public good (*referibile ad bonum commune ad quod ordinat justitia*),[b] as every vice, every moral fault whatsoever has more or less injurious repercussions upon the public good.[32] Yet legal justice remains distinct from

---

which is the good of the state as an instrument for the realization of the extra-political common good.

[28] On the notion and elements of the public good, see *supra*, nos. 135 *et seq.*

[29] See St. Thomas, *op. cit. Ia IIae*, qu. 96, art. 4 *ad resp.*, cited *supra*, n. 21.

[30] On inner passions, cf. St. Thomas, *op. cit. IIa IIae*, qu. 58, art. 9 *ad* 3.

[31] On the annexed virtues of justice, see *supra*, nos. 222–224.

[b] [Referable to the common good, as to which justice ordains.]

[32] See St. Thomas, *op. cit. IIa IIae*, qu. 58, art. 5 *ad resp.* Cf. *Ia IIae*, qu. 92, art. 1 *ad* 3.

the particular virtues inasmuch as it commands them and ordains them for what is its proper object, to wit, the public good.[33]

238. In What Legal or General Justice Remains Special. And this "ordination" is not confined to a mere acceptance. Not only does legal justice prescribe the acts of all the virtues, even where they have the private good as their immediate objective; not only does it require one to put those virtues to the direct service of the public good;[34] but also it happens that it influences the determining elements of the virtuous just mean. This is so at least for the virtues where the just mean is "real," external to the person who is their subject,[35] that is, the two particular justices, the commutative and distributive. Indeed, it is according to the public good and in taking account of the parties remaining members of a whole [36] that the extent of the right of the particular private person toward the particular private person will be fixed in commutative justice, and of the citizen with regard to the state in distributive justice.[37] As expressly stated in the definition of Cicero (perhaps under the influence of Aristotle), the attribution to everyone of his dignity takes places only *communi utilitate conservata*, which may eventually entail certain sacrifices of one's own right on the altar of the public good.[38] It happens likewise very frequently that legal justice commands or prohibits acts which do not directly touch any particular right or interest, which as such do not fall under any virtue or any vice, and which have moral value exclusively by their reference to the good of the total community. These are, in short, technical values — values of social technique — which their end alone endows with morality. In this case, as in the case of the properly societal duties,[39] legal justice

[33] See St. Thomas, *op. cit. IIa IIae*, qu. 58, art. 6 *ad resp.* and *ad* 4.

[34] See St. Thomas, *op. cit. Ia IIae*, qu. 96, art. 3 *ad resp.* and *ad* 3. . . .

[35] On the "real mean," see *supra*, no. 226.

[36] See St. Thomas, *op. cit. IIa IIae*, qu. 61, art. 1 *ad resp.*

[37] On the necessary subordination of distributive to legal justice, see *supra*, no. 234. As for commutative justice, it may be added that the state, which is in part the author of rights inasmuch as it guarantees their acquisition and conservation, is on that ground qualified to limit them as a function of the public good.

[38] For comment on this formula, see F. Senn, *op. cit.* 44–47 and notes.

[39] It is impossible to claim, as has sometimes been done by an exaggerated application of the idea of "generality" of legal justice, that the payment of a tax constitutes as such a liberality toward the state, though belonging to legal justice by its relationship to the common good, inasmuch as the state is the necessary instrument of the common good . . . On the contrary, restitution or reparation can hardly be thought of where the violation of legal justice consists of a refusal to adjust one's private conduct to the public good. In such a case only the sanctions of punishment or nullity are involved.

ceases to be general so as to find again a special subject matter, proper to itself, directly ordained for the good of the whole.

239. Meaning of the Adjective "Legal" in the Expression "Legal Justice." True, it is for the state to determine the obligations of its subjects not only toward itself as an organization but also toward the associated community of which it is the responsible manager. And that is why this justice is called "legal." [40] But it would be wrong to conclude that legal justice coincides with obedience to the rules of public law, revenue law, private law, penal law, and so forth, which determine those two sets of obligations. The laws [41] are indeed far from covering the totality of the requirements of the public good. For multifarious reasons of expediency or regulatory technique, the legislator is often obliged to abstain or keep out, even in the domain of properly societal obligations. For instance, the state, not daring to demand its full impost, will appeal for voluntary contributions in the form of government bonds. Now then, where the requirements of public justice show themselves without ambiguity, the subject is bound by legal justice, notwithstanding the silence or discretion of the law. Where the latter expresses but a part of legal justice, the moral virtue of legal justice takes charge of the rest.

Contrariwise, where the law satisfies the public good, nothing prevents the subjects from going beyond their duty of legal justice and showing themselves generous toward the community in their services and goods. On the part of its members, the state may in justice demand only what the public good requires. As to what goes beyond that measure, the right common to the particular virtues *ad alterum*, especially liberality, resumes its dominion in favor of collectivities as well as of private individuals.

Section 3. The Natural Just and the Positive Just

240. The Right of Another Is Sometimes Natural and Sometimes Positive. A last question arises which, to be sure, concerns justice in general but for which the solution will appear easier after the study of the diverse kinds of justice.

The object of justice is the right of another individual or collectivity. What, then, brings about the determination of that right, qualitatively and quantitatively? The Schoolmen answer that the right — the ques-

[40] See St. Thomas, *op. cit. IIa IIae*, qu. 58, art. 5 *ad resp.*, *in fine*; also the remark *supra*, n. 25.

[41] By "laws" are here understood all positive rules, whatever may be their formal sources.

tion turns on the right of another and not the law, as in the expression "natural law" [1] — that the right of another is sometimes natural and sometimes positive. It is natural when, not only in its principle but also in its measure and form, it is fixed by the very nature of things as resulting from the relationship under contemplation, outside of any intervention of the will of man as private person or public authority. It is positive when, in its determination if not in itself, it results from the will of man proceeding according to the diverse modes of agreement, of judgment or arbitral award, of custom or statute.[2] Where it issues from agreement, judgment, or arbitral award, the positive determination is particular, valid solely for the individual case; where it issues from custom or statute, it has general validity for all cases.

241. The Distinction Recurs in All the Kinds of Justice. Contrary to certain appearances, the two sorts of the just, the natural and the positive, are encountered in all the kinds of justice. In matters of commutative justice, it is nature that at once determines the right of everyone with respect to his life, his works, his legitimate property, the restitution of the thing deposited or the amount of money loaned. There is no need at all in these cases for any arrangement of will whatever to state the exact measure of the right of the one and, correlatively, the obligation of the other. Contrariwise, it is an agreement of the parties or a judgment, more rarely a custom or a statute (system of taxation), that determines the price of things or services or the amount of reparation due.

In matters of distributive justice and legal justice, although normally the determination of the rights of private persons against the state and of the state against private persons is the work of the state itself, especially of rules of law, it may nevertheless occur that nature brings about the determination. Thus, nature, even in the absence of a law, accords to every citizen the right of protection by the police and the right of access to the courts (a matter of distributive justice); nature, even in the absence of a law, obliges the citizen to defend his country even at the sacrifice of his life (a matter of legal justice). One will therefore avoid confusing the hypothesis of the legal just with the category of legal justice. There is a legal just whenever rules of law determine the just, even in matters of commutative justice, while legal justice is that kind of justice which lays down the rights of the state against the citizen, whether or not they be determined by a rule of law.

[1] On this initial distinction, which is not always observed, see *supra*, no. 202.

[2] See in this sense ST. THOMAS, *IIa IIae*, qu. 57, art. 2 *ad resp.*; qu. 60, art. 5 *ad resp.*

242. Positive Determination Is Not, However, Arbitrary. Nevertheless, where positive determination intervenes it is not purely arbitrary. In matters of commutative justice the standard of values, whether from the point of view of exchange or of reparation, is established according to complex considerations of morals, economics, sociology, among which common estimation ranks high. Similarly, in matters of distributive justice, the appraisal of claims in the division of benefits, advantages, and burdens of collective life takes place according to objective and impartial criteria. Finally, in legal justice, again, the requirements of the public good under the circumstances furnish the principle of the solution. This means that if the contractual just, the judicial just, the customary or statutory just deviate from the bases of the natural just as outlined here, they are far from collaborating toward justice, they institute injustice. One must not therefore proclaim, with Fouillée: To say contractual is to say just — nor indeed with the Legists: [a] To say statutory is to say just. The contract or the statute states the just only inasmuch as it determines the just; neither could create it against the natural just or even at the margin thereof.[3]

It is true that there exist, in addition to things that are commanded because they are just (*praecepta quia bona*), things that are just because they are commanded (*bona quia praecepta*).[4] But this does not at all mean that the precept in itself would have the power to engender the just. If it creates justice it is always because in some manner it determines a preëxisting just. As such, the object of the precept was by hypothesis indifferent to justice; hence the necessity of the legal command to make it obligatory. But the command in turn could not be brought forth except because that object was, by hypothesis, "referable to justice." This is properly the case of legal justice under the aspect where it is called "general": The act foreign to particular justice or even to any virtue is invested with the character of justice inasmuch as it is required by the public good and on that ground prescribed by a rule of law.[5] It is also true that it is for legal justice eventually to modify the natural equality of the two particular justices, the commutative and distributive, so as to bend them to the supreme norm of the public

[a] [The term Legists denotes those who base rights and obligations upon the existence of a *lex* in the sense of an enacted law or a positively established legal rule.]

[3] Cf. generally St. Thomas, Summa, *IIa IIae*, qu. 57, art. 2 *ad* 2; especially on justice in exchanges, qu. 77, art. 1 *ad* 1. . . . [Cf.] an observation by J. Tonneau in 5 Bulletin thomiste (1938) 447.

[4] St. Thomas, *op. cit. IIa IIae*, qu. 57, art. 2 *ad* 3. . . .

[5] On the "generality" of legal justice, see *supra*, nos. 237–238.

good.[6] But there again the rule of law which breaks the equality by no means acts as having power over natural justice. It only translates a superior justice, equally natural in its superiority, implying the subordination of the particular good to the general good and, therefore, of the justice due to private individuals to the justice due to the collectivity.

243. The Margin of Indeterminacy in Justice. To sum up, the legal just never is anything but the determination, by a rule of law, of the natural just, that is, of the right of another in the three forms of commutative justice, distributive justice, and legal justice. No more in matters of legal justice than of commutative or distributive justice is a rule of law the creator of justice: The law confines itself to rendering the content of justice more precise according to contingencies. Yet it must be recognized that legal justice leaves a much more considerable margin of indeterminacy than does commutative or even distributive justice, so much so that it takes its name from the determination which the law brings to it. But what makes up the subject matter of legal justice is the society instituted with a view to realizing the public good, whose rôle is the discovery and promotion of the concrete requirements of that public good. The concept of the public good is "given," but its applications are not.[7] More, it still remains to make an appraisal how far these applications ought to pass into the law. And this is the whole problem of the law, which confronts us with a justice properly juridical, the content of which does not necessarily coincide with legal justice. If the public good has its requirements so does the civil law, and these are not the requirements of every law whatsoever.

CHAPTER III

THE "GIVEN" OF NATURAL LAW AND OF JUSTICE IN THE ELABORATION OF THE LAW

244. Restatement of the Problem. We are now in a position, after this long preamble, to define the exact rôle of the two factors of natural law and justice in the elaboration of the law.

To sum up. Natural law represents the category of the moral rule; and although the concept is technically limited to the first principles of

[6] See *supra*, no. 238.
[7] See *supra*, no. 144.

morality, that limitation is without interest to the jurist, who is bound to accept all of morals as given, not only in its first principles but in the subordinate conclusions and determinations evolved by moral science and eventually by the positive rule of the moral law. That is why hereafter natural law will be spoken of in the sense of the moral norm, and vice versa. As to justice, it represents one of the principal rules of morals, that which regards the right of another to be respected and satisfied, either that of particular private persons (particular justice: Commutative and distributive) or that of the public community (legal justice), the latter form of justice outranking the particular justices which are subordinate to it as the parts are to the whole.

Now the elaboration of the law proceeds by considering, first, the public good of the community under contemplation,[1] and secondly, the resources and "possibilities" of the implementation of the law.[2] The question proposed, then, reduces itself to the study of the relationships between natural law (i.e., morals) and justice, on the one hand, and the social-political element of the public good and the technical element of regulation, on the other. Furthermore, nothing new is to be expected of this comparison, for the principles have been set forth in the chapter on the method of elaboration of the law, and we are concerned with nothing more than putting certain aspects thereof into fuller relief.[3]

Section 1. Morality and the Temporal Public Good

245. There Could Be No Public Good Against Morals. A first point could arouse no controversy: A legal rule positively contrary to morals must be condemned as contrary to the public good. For notwithstanding the difference of the concepts, there is no conceivable divorce of the demands of morals from the requirements of the public good. There is no public good against morals because morals governs man and the public is composed of men. By what route or détour could that which would be bad for man be transformed into a good for the public? It is irrelevant in this regard that the public good is but an intermediary good, consisting simply in an environment favorable to the action of individuals and groups. How could that environment be useful to man, not only from the moral but also from the material point of view, if it

[1] See *supra*, nos. 134 *et seq.*

[2] See *supra*, nos. 166 *et seq.*

[3] For a more detailed study of the utilization of moral data (natural law and justice) in the elaboration of the law, see J. Dabin, La philosophie de l'ordre juridique positif nos. 121 *et seq.*, pp. 431 *et seq.*, nos. 129–187, pp. 456–632.

is the result of measures reproved by morals? The advantage will be but illusory or fugitive, and ultimately it is man who will pay the price of immoral policies. It also matters little that the public good has purely temporal or even material and technical aspects. Morals does not reign solely over virtue, or rather, everything is a matter of virtue, including the activities of the purely temporal, material, and technical order. More, the first condition of the public good in all domains is respect for the moral rule, both of precept and of counsel, in the choice of means as of ends. And there is no room for distinctions according to the orders of relations. Whether the relationships involved are of the private or of the political order, on the domestic or on the international plane, any legal rule that violates morals at the same time violates the public good. No solution is politically good that would be morally bad: An immoral or amoral conception of politics is a politically false conception, always for the reason that politics is human and all that is human is, if not moral, at least subject to morals.

As concerns justice especially, a conflict with the public good is even less conceivable inasmuch as justice, in the form of legal justice at any rate, is defined by the public good: Justice is what is demanded by or conforms to the public good, always reserving the rights of morality in general. Therefore, all that is laid down by the law in conformity with the public good is at once in conformity with justice. This conformity, moreover, is presumed to exist, for it is the prerogative of authority to benefit from "previous obedience": [1] Until proof to the contrary the authority is deemed to be right.

246. Examples and Cases of Application. In applying these principles it can be said, in the first place, that the law cannot command what morals forbids, nor can it forbid what morals commands. The classical example, although it concerns a precept for a particular case and not a statutory rule, is that of Antigone. Creon's edict forbidding the burial of the corpse of Antigone's brother was immoral and unjust as contrary to *pietas* (εὐσέβεια) toward the dead of the family and the infernal gods (Sophocles, *Antigone*, verses 745, 749, 924). But there are other historical or imaginable examples: Laws enforcing sacrifices to false gods or prohibiting worship of the true God; laws requiring apostasy, dueling, abortion, euthanasia; laws prohibiting acts of liberality *inter vivos* or by will. The contradiction does not have to be immediate. It suffices that the law by its disposition tends to discourage the virtuous act in setting up *impedimenta* (formalities, delays, taxes) or to encourage the vicious

[1] See M. Hauriou, Principes de droit public (2d ed. Paris, 1916), Appendix 804, 806.

act in setting up advantages (prizes, remissions). It also suffices that the law turns away from action which morals merely counsels, or that it impels toward the commission of what morals calls imperfection: In each of these ways the moral ideal is being checked. Other laws are immoral by contradicting the principles of "institutional morals," being that part of morals which governs the natural social structures; [2] such are the laws admitting a free union instead of or besides marriage, or those ignoring the authority of parents over their children. Finally, there are the laws that are immoral by attacking the principles of political morals: Oppressive laws which under the pretext of the good of the community or the state deprive individuals, nationals or aliens, of their essential liberties, such as the right to marry or not to marry; or partial laws which violate distributive justice to the detriment or in favor of a fraction of the public (party, class, race, or any social category whatever).

Most of the time, no doubt, the legislator enacting an immoral rule believes it to be moral. But it also happens that he thinks he will be able to attain a certain goal of the public good, for instance, an addition of power for the state, without having to concern himself with the moral value of the means, or by persuading himself that every useful means is necessarily moral. This, precisely, is the amoral or immoral conception of politics in its repercussion upon the law.

247. Confusions to Be Avoided in Appraising the Immoral Character of Laws. But one must understand the assumption correctly, and not qualify as "contrary to morals" a policy or a law that would not merit that reproach. Everything permitted by morals, whether as being indifferent by its object or on the ground of a capacity for choice left to the individual, need not necessarily receive the consecration of the law. It is the right and the duty of the legislator to declare illicit the morally indifferent act which under the circumstances would be prejudicial to the public good. By virtue of that very prohibition, the morally indifferent act becomes morally bad, for the act contrary to the public good, denounced as such by a law charged with watching over the public good, is from the outset an immoral act.[3] In the same way, a capacity to act which morals sanctions but which under the circumstances would be prejudicial to the public good could be legitimately suppressed by a law, and that suppression would be binding even in conscience.

On stronger grounds, one must not call legislation immoral that would regulate the rights of everyone toward other private persons, or

[2] On "institutional morals," see *supra*, nos. 114 and 209.

[3] See *supra*, no. 242.

toward the state as functioning for the good of the total community rather than of the right of everyone taken in isolation. There will perhaps result from such regulation some diminution of the right of the one correlative to an augmentation of the right of the other. But there is nothing immoral in that modification, because morals itself prescribes the subjection of the particular good to the general good (moral virtue of legal justice); [4] provided, however, that the law leave the particular person favored by its disposition free to renounce the advantage or in other ways to reëstablish the equilibrium. For the solutions of the public good are not incompatible with practicing the virtues of moderation and equity; the contrary is true.[5]

248. The Law Is Not Bound to Consecrate Every Rule of Morals. Is this to say that, everywhere and always, where morals commands or forbids, the law is under an obligation to follow and sanction the prescription of morals? Not at all. The prohibition of contradicting does not involve the obligation of sanctioning; and the public good, which is not compatible with any kind of immoral law, does not necessarily require the intervention of a law in order to compel respect for morals. No doubt every virtuous act is useful, every vicious act is harmful, not only to its author but to the entire community, inasmuch as it contributes to the formation of a public environment either virtuous or vicious. Such an environment could indeed result only from the acts of particular individuals, who always originate what is public. But the question is not whether the practicing of every virtue and every vice influences the public. The question is whether it is good for the public that every virtue give rise to a legal imperative, every vice to a censure or repression. Now, in the first place, morals imposed under threat of compulsion no longer is morals. Objectively, materially, the precept will perhaps be obeyed and morals, in this sense, satisfied. But by reason of the compulsion and inasmuch as the obedience is due only to the compulsion, the observance of the rule has lost all moral value. Hence one may ask if a law serves the public good when its intervention has the effect of sacrificing the subjective to the objective element in morals, in short, of suppressing morality under color of saving morals.

249. The "Discipline of the Laws" and Virtue. To be sure, one may invoke the necessity of a "discipline" for the perfection of virtue, and

[4] See *supra*, no. 238.

[5] This preoccupation may even be translated into law by the laying down of a "natural obligation"; on this point, see J. Dabin, La philosophie de l'ordre juridique positif nos. 186 and 187, pp. 628 and 632.

the educational action of laws which would engender a habit favorable to the spontaneous fulfillment of duty.[6] But that is a matter of experience, depending upon the mentality of peoples. In fact it often happens, especially in our modern times, that the result of the intervention is rather negative. When virtue claims to impose itself by force, if only by the force of a law, it runs the risk of arousing a state of mind hostile to the law and to virtue, which is a pity both for morality and for legality: In such a case, a moralizing law becomes in all respects demoralizing.[7] No doubt, again, the effect of every law, including every civil law, is to render men good not only inasmuch as they obey that law (for it is virtuous to obey a just law) but also inasmuch as it imposes upon them what the public good prescribes.[8] But it does not follow that a law, or at least a civil law, is qualified to repress all vices and to command actions fulfilling all virtues. It is incumbent upon moral laws to render man good as regards all virtues because their competence, in matters of virtue, is direct and general. As to civil laws, "bearing upon the governance of commonwealths," [9] their moralizing effect is limited to the virtue which concerns the public good, to wit, legal justice. Civil laws render men good as regards the virtue of legal justice, the requirements of which they show them and make more precise, at least to the extent of what they are in a position to obtain from the subjects and therefore to impose upon them. Thus civil laws do not even render men good as regards the totality of legal justice; they render them good as regards that justice only according to the possible, taking account of the moral level of the people,[10] the state of public opinion, and the principle of efficiency proper to the civil law. Again, what matters from our point of view is less the effect of a law than its end; or, if one prefers, the effect can be legitimately pursued only within the framework of the end. Now the end of civil laws is not immediately to moralize man; it is to procure the public good, that is to say, an environment, an intermediary good, and moreover an effective public good, therefore, one calculated by the standard of realities.[11]

[6] See in this sense St. Thomas, Summa, *Ia IIae*, qu. 95, art. 1 *ad resp.* . . . Cf. qu. 92, art. 1 *ad* 1, referring to Aristotle: . . .

[7] This is well noted by St. Augustine in a passage reported in Summa, *Ia IIae*, qu. 91, art. 4 *ad resp.* (*quarto*). See also the citation *infra*, n. 9.

[8] See St. Thomas, *op. cit. Ia IIae*, qu. 92, art. 1 *ad resp.*

[9] St. Augustine, quoted and approved by St. Thomas, *op. cit. Ia IIae*, qu. 96, art. 2 *ad* 3: . . .

[10] On this last point, see St. Thomas, *op. cit. Ia IIae*, qu. 96, art. 2 *ad resp.*; *IIa IIae*, qu. 77, art. 1 *ad resp.*

[11] See in this sense, on the whole, St. Thomas, *op. cit. Ia IIae*, qu. 96, art. 3 *ad resp.*; qu. 98, art. 1 *ad resp.* Equally, Barbeyrac, *Discours sur la permission des*

250. The Law and the Ideal Type of the Family. The same maxim must guide the laws in the elaboration of the legal régime of the natural groups, particularly the family. For instance, institutional morals is not content with just any marriage implying a certain stability, as a rule for the union of sexes; its ideal is that of the one and indissoluble marriage, which alone perfectly realizes the individual and familial ends of marriage. But how can one expect the laws to escape from realities where the mores are not, or not yet, at the height of this ideal — to proscribe polygamy among polygamous peoples, to restore the indissolubility of marriage among peoples accustomed to divorce? Has the Church not taken centuries to make the barbarian peoples accept its matrimonial legislation,[12] to abolish slavery (encouragement of emancipations), to extirpate the scourge of private wars (institution of the Truce of God)? Before commanding in an imperative manner by its legislation, the Church recommended, preached, educated, often compromised with the "hardness of hearts."

251. The Capacity of Morals for "Ordination to the Public Good." The problem of the relations between law and morals finds its definitive answer in the following formulation: The jurist will retain only those of the rules of morals whose consecration or confirmation by the law will in fact under the circumstances be found useful to the public good and practicable with regard to the technical equipment of the jurist. On the one hand, none of the divisions or parts of morals, none of its rules or its virtues, is excluded from the possibility of consecration; on the other, the latter will take place only as far as the public good in the particular case will derive an advantage from it and the technique will oppose no obstacle to it. The capacity for "ordination" to the public good in its different forms — political public good where the state is concerned, social public good where the community embraced within the framework of the state is concerned — this is the first essential condition of the "subsumption" of morals into law.[13] This first condition, indeed, implies the second, relating to technique, for a rule technically inapplicable and hence useless will very rarely be advantageous to the public good. It will have been noted that the criterion is not only conformity to the public good of the *attitudes* to be required of the

---

lois, in 2 PUFFENDORF, LES DEVOIRS DE L'HOMME ET DU CITOYEN (transl. by Barbeyrac, new ed., Amsterdam, 1756) 291 *et seq.* Also PH. MEYLAN, JEAN BARBEYRAC 203–204.

[12] On this patience of the Church, see A. ESMEIN, LE MARIAGE EN DROIT CANONIQUE (2d ed. by Génestal), 2 vols. *passim.*

[13] See ST. THOMAS, SUMMA, *Ia IIae*, qu. 96, art. 3 *ad resp.*, *in fine*: . . . On this distinction between the political and the social, see *supra*, nos. 138 and 237.

subjects, but also and above all conformity to the public good of the *intervention* of a law prescribing for the subjects such attitudes, even if these conform to the public good. Besides the content of a law, the very principle of its intervention must therefore be considered.

Section 2. Justice as the Normal Matter of the Legal Rule

252. The Moral Precepts Susceptible of Consecration by the Law. What, then, are the moral precepts that may be ordained for the public good by the intermediary of the laws? Here political prudence comes in, and especially legislative prudence, whose rôle is precisely that of discerning solutions most adequate to the circumstances of times, places, and cases. Although these solutions are variable in concrete cases, it is not impossible to assign to the work of prudence, if not an inflexible method, at least a marching order of general though provisional value.

Among the rules of morals, the jurist constructing civil laws will at the outset introduce a distinction between the rules governing relationships with others and the rules regarding duties toward God and toward one's self. On the one hand, the duties toward God and the duties toward oneself exist independently of any form of social life; on the other hand, the legal rule is a social rule, and therefore one presupposing other persons. It is clear that the public good, the end of the legal rule, is more directly concerned with the relationships between men than with the relationships of man with God or his conduct toward himself. These latter spheres of duties can affect the public only indirectly, incidentally.[1] Now logic commands one to apply one's self in the first place to what makes up the direct and immediate subject matter of the law, unhampered by any ulterior view of the "incidental" matter.

In the second place, the jurist will distinguish among the moral rules governing the relationships among men those implying something due which is capable of exaction: The debt of justice in its three forms, commutative, distributive, and legal, and also the debts that may be called familial, between spouses, between parents and children, and between relatives, in which the necessary institution of the family consists. As for moral prescriptions other than those of justice, the measure of interest the jurist accords them will depend on the degree of their proximity to justice: A closer interest for the annexed virtues of justice, by reason of their analogy to the principal virtue; a more remote inter-

[1] See *supra*, nos. 70–73.

est where the ground of the debt decreases or disappears, as in the case of beneficence and liberality.

253. Justice as the Precept Most Obviously Fit for Consecration. On several grounds, justice is somehow the natural subject matter of the legal system. First, because fulfillment of the moral duty of justice is most indispensable to the public good. As for injustice among private persons, it is in reaction to this "common evil" that the concept of a public good was born in which the first element is order and peace guaranteed by the force of the community organized in the state. At all times justice has been placed in the first rank of that *ratio qua societas hominum inter ipsos et vitae quasi communitas continetur*.[a] [2] The state would fail in its mission, the public good would not be realized, if justice between individuals was not respected.[3] What about legal justice and distributive justice? Here the question does not even arise. Legal justice is the virtue most necessary to the public good precisely because its object is the public good (of the state or of the public). It is in legal justice that law and morals meet so closely as almost to merge. Is not the object of the moral precept of legal justice that which is fixed by a law? The same goes for distributive justice. The state may well produce the most abundant public good and yet its effort will turn into civil war, that is, public evil, if it distributes it contrary to equity. Neither is it conceivable that a civil law could depart from distributive justice, because the latter is the moral norm to which the rulers, the authors of the civil law, are subject in their professional capacity.

It is true that the two justices, commutative and distributive, which refer to the particular good, are like every particular virtue subordinate to legal justice, which is qualified to regulate the content thereof, that is to say, the particular right of everyone, according to the requirements of the public good. But that subordination is not the work of civil laws. It results, as has been said,[4] from morals itself, which demands the subordination in the temporal order of the particular [private] good to the public good so that on this point the harmony between the two rules is complete.

[a] [Reason by which society among men and, as it were, the community of life is held together.]

[2] CICERO, DE OFFICIIS I, 7, 20; still other passages are reported by F. SENN, *op. cit.* 46, n. 1.

[3] See ST. THOMAS, *op. cit. Ia IIae*, qu. 96, art. 2 *ad resp.*, *in fine*: . . . ; also *ad* 1. See also *Ia IIae*, qu. 95, art. 1 *ad resp.*, . . . ; *Ia IIae*, qu. 98, art. 1 *ad resp.*, . . . ; *IIa IIae*, qu. 77, art. 1 *ad resp.*: . . .

[4] See *supra*, no. 242.

254. Exceptional Rectification of the Two Particular Justices on the Ground of Legal Justice. Yet it would be a mistake to believe that the solutions given by commutative and distributive justice on the basis of the individual right alone would always or even frequently call for rectification on the ground of legal justice. Not only is there no necessary opposition between the public good and the particular justices, but such opposition is also relatively rare. The public good in application will on the contrary demand respect for the particular justices.[5] It must not be forgotten that individuals are the beginning and the end of the state and the public good — that one must therefore start from them as one must finally revert to them. That is why on the methodical level the jurist constructing the law will at once proceed to the solutions of particular justice: Commutative for the relationships among private persons, distributive for what is due to the citizens from the state, thus consecrating the particular right *a priori* according to the title of each one considered individually. Nor will any rectification whatever be operative on the ground of the public good except where proof has been made beyond any doubt that the consecration of the right of the individual according to the standard of particular justice either involves positive damage to the public good in the special case or does not permit the attainment of an advantage remotely compensating the evil inherent in any rectification of justice.

Therefore, when it is recommended that the jurist take justice in its three forms for the basic matter of his rules, it is appropriate to make this more precise by the following complementary distinction. In the relationships between private persons, the justice primarily to be considered is commutative justice; in what concerns the rights of citizens against the state, it will be distributive justice — the domain of legal justice being provisionally limited to the obligations of the citizen toward the state (societal justice). Legal justice as general justice which governs the other virtues, including the two particular justices, will be called upon only secondarily, after demonstration of the insufficiency of the solutions of the particular justices with respect to the public good. Ordinarily, the public good is best served when every one of the members of the public sees what constitutes his own right consecrated in the most exact manner.

255. Special Structural Adaptability of Justice for the Legal Rule. Justice is the preferred matter of the legal order for a second reason, which has to do with its particular structure. Indeed, justice is distinguished by the characteristics of objectivity, externality, and clarity,

[5] See *supra*, no. 148.

which render it eminently adaptable for the legal imperative. On the one hand, unlike the virtues which relate to the passions, justice governs the action of the subject relative to the right of another.[6] Now to decree respect for the right of another, and at the same time to assure the execution of that precept, is undoubtedly less difficult than to foresee and prescribe the environment conducive to virtue in the matter of passions. No civil law could reach them except in acts that translate them outwardly,[7] whereas operative action — of commission or omission — alone suffices to satisfy justice, at least materially. Moreover, the object of justice, to wit, the right of another, is a thing given in external reality, while the virtues regulating the passions have their seat in the subject himself. By reason of this objectivity, the solution of justice has general validity, like the legal rule, obligating everybody uniformly, without distinction according to the subject who is under obligation, while the just measure in respect to passions is a matter of the special case, depending upon individual situations and circumstances.

On the other hand, unlike the other virtues *ad alterum,* justice shows the peculiarity of clear determination as to persons and things. Its beneficiary is the determinate person, individual or collectivity, in whom the right exists; the debtor is either everybody or such and such an individual or collectivity. Similarly, the object of the right is determined or determinable: Such and such a thing, service, or attitude; that alone is someone's due because it alone is "his own." Now again this clarity lends itself to the logical and precise mechanism of the legal rule. True, the determination is far from being as perfect in the two justices of the political order, legal and distributive justice, as in commutative justice. There is some leeway in the appraisal of what is due to the state and the public (legal justice) or what is coming to each one in the distribution of the public good (distributive justice).[8] Nevertheless, the principles according to which prudence must make the concrete determination are outlined in an objective manner. It is indeed the reason of being of the state and of the laws to lay down terms for the original indeterminacy of all that falls within the political.

256. Like the Legal Duty, the Duty of Justice Is Capable of Exaction. Justice is the obvious matter of the legal order for a third reason, to

[6] On the "real mean" proper to justice, see *supra,* no. 226.

[7] On the incompetence of the law in the matter of inner acts, see *supra,* nos. 65–69.

[8] Even in commutative justice, the determination of the right of another is more delicate when the value at stake is of a moral, non-pecuniary kind; see *supra,* no. 93.

wit, that the debt of justice is capable of being exacted. Because its object is the right of another and that right of another is its holder's own, he has the right to exact respect for it if need be by force. Morally, by its nature, justice implies the right to repel unjust aggression: This is the case of vindication which may be permissible and sometimes is a virtue, according to the circumstances.[9] Now, similarly, by its nature the legal rule is capable of exaction and proceeds by way of compulsion: What is required by the public good or decided upon in conformity with it calls for being carried out, voluntarily or by force. Thus when the law takes over on its account the moral precept of justice, the compulsion with which it accompanies it does not constitute an innovation. Especially as regards commutative justice, the consecration of a law does nothing but replace the very insufficient (and for the public good deadly) mode of private compulsion with the regulated mode of public compulsion. The change touches only the form of compulsion and not its principle. Contrariwise, the moral duties incapable of exaction are as such repugnant to compulsion, which is foreign to them and even denatures them. Beneficence and liberality imposed by compulsion remain benefits materially; they have lost their character of virtuous acts. It requires precisely a basis in legal justice to render legitimate a command which makes them — on this new ground — capable of exaction.

257. The Law and the Annexed Virtues of Justice, Especially Faith in Promises. By the very reason of their participation in justice, the annexed virtues of justice,[10] at least those among them which embody more fully the objective structure of justice, participate in the aptness of their principal virtue for legal consecration. What we have here especially in mind is faith in promises. Not only does the party who violates his promise offend the other contracting party to whom he owes his pledged faith, but also all social life is impossible if promises made are not kept at all. Confidence and credit have their sole basis in faith; and faithlessness in promises is undoubtedly as damaging to the public good as are attacks against the right of another.[11] From that side, the situation is clear: The intervention of the laws to sanction faith in promises is not only justified but required. From the side of formal realization of the intervention, the situation is no less clear. The object of faith in promises can be "grasped" quite as much as the object of

[9] See ST. THOMAS, *op. cit. IIa IIae*, qu. 108, art. 1 *ad* 4: the purely personal insult must be borne patiently *si expediat* — according to the circumstances.

[10] On the virtues annexed to justice, see generally *supra*, nos. 222–224.

[11] See ST. THOMAS, *op. cit. IIa IIae*, qu. 109, art. 3 *ad* 1: . . . See also qu. 114, art. 2 *ad* 1.

the debt of commutative justice — even more so, for the promise has formally determined it. The only difference is in respect to exaction. Contrary to what is due in justice, what is promised to another is not coming to him as something that belongs to him, directly or by equivalent; hence the strict exaction of justice cannot enter the arena.[12] Yet faith in promises is so much required by the public good that one should not be astonished to see the laws confer upon it the capability of exaction which it does not of itself possess. In that manner, the moral debt of honesty, which engenders faith in promises, is transformed into a legal debt, which may henceforth be exacted on the ground of legal justice.

258. The Law and the Constituent Principles of the Family. Lastly, among the moral principles whose place is marked in the law, there are to be counted the constituent rules of the family, the rules which define the family as an institution. Family relationships — between spouses, between parents and children, even between relatives — bear a double aspect according to whether they are viewed from within or from without. Seen from their inner or intimate side, family relationships belong above all to that part of morals which governs sentiments and acts resulting from sentiments. In the first rank of these sentiments we find love, a special love of familial character, which is further differentiated according to the diverse psychological and moral categories of conjugal love, paternal and maternal love, filial love, fraternal love, etc. But the law is powerless with respect to the duty of love and even, to a degree, the duty of familial piety inasmuch as it involves love.[13] Contrariwise, with regard to the traits by which the family is set apart as an institution and which belong to the institutional part of morals, the powerlessness of the law disappears.[14] It is not impossible for a law to decree that only the legitimate union, that is, marriage, shall be endowed with legal effects; that this union shall be one and indissoluble, at least in principle; that it shall entail reciprocal duties of cohabitation, faithfulness, aid, and support; that parents ought to give their children during their formative period nourishment and education; that children in turn are under the obligation of docility; that the family group shall have a head, the husband and father, charged with authority — and responsibility — toward his wife and children, — all this according to the moral conceptions prevalent in the people under contemplation.

To what extent do the constituent principles of the law of domestic

[12] See *supra*, no. 224 and note 33.
[13] Concerning familial piety, annexed to justice, see *supra*, no. 223.
[14] On this distinction, see *supra*, no. 94.

relations approach the type of justice? In the absence of justice toward the family as a body (because the family, while forming a group and a community, is not a moral person),[15] it is not forbidden to speak of a sort of justice between spouses, which gives them rights that may be exacted from one another, or a sort of justice between parents and children, which makes them creditors (or debtors) of education, nourishment, docility, etc.[16] But this matters little from our point of view. It is enough that the constituent principles of the family evidently concern the "public." Now it may be affirmed beyond doubt: The family concerns the public good at least as much as it concerns justice, as clearly and as closely. Is the family not one of the bases of the social and political order of a country? Is it not the root of life, and thus of peoples and states? Does one not find it omnipresent, actively and passively, with regard to the particular individuals who are subjects of justice? That is why the law will at once come to the aid of the familial institution, as it comes to the aid of individuals in commutative and distributive justice, and of the state and the public in legal justice.

259. Yet the Normal Order of Consecration Is Subject to Derogation. It is granted, again, that these interventions of the law take place not directly in favor of justice, or in favor of the family, but inasmuch as these values — and their legal protection itself — effectively realize the public good in the circumstances, and on the condition also that the intervention should not be technically incapable of realization. Such being the point of view of the jurist, it is possible that the marching order outlined above in a theoretical manner, starting *de eo quod plerumque fit*,[b] must undergo certain derogations in practice. Thus some moral rules that would normally require the consecration of the law might have to go without it, while others which normally would not require it would have to obtain it.

There could be no question here of drawing up a systematic list of these exceptional cases, their general theory having been presented. Let us confine ourselves to some suggestions, limited to the law of private relations, since in the relationships of the political order the rule of the law itself undertakes, by order of morals, to determine the requirements of legal and distributive justice.

260. Cases Where the Law Abstains from Consecrating Justice. It has already been observed, with supporting examples, how commutative

[15] See *supra*, no. 229.

[16] See in this sense G. del Vecchio, *La justice* § 12, in JUSTICE, DROIT, ETAT, pp. 62–63.

[b] [From what happens in most cases.]

justice (and equally so its annex, faith in promises) often enough had to withdraw before more or less urgent considerations of the social order: Economic, political, psychological (such as the concern for security).[17] Even in morals, general justice normally prevails over particular justice. But there is another set where the law foregoes sanctioning commutative justice. Either it refers for the determination of their respective rights to the regulation agreed upon between the interested parties although this may not always conform to natural justice.[18] Or again it leaves the field free to individual activities, where these usually work spontaneously in the direction of justice,[19] or where political prudence or the insufficiency of legal equipment makes it advisable to tolerate them wholly or in part even though they are unjust.[20]

261. Cases Where the Law Goes Beyond the Framework of Justice. Also, contrariwise, the law pushes beyond commutative justice, sanctioning moral rules other than the rule of justice. It draws first of all upon those virtues *ad alterum*, annexed to justice, where the debt is but moral: Not only fidelity to the pledged word, which is as indispensable to social life as is strict justice, but also, for instance, gratitude and sometimes beneficence and liberality.[21] So-called "social legislation" is full of precepts imposing obligations upon employers to which on the part of the workers no strict right corresponds and which often fall within gratuitous assistance.[22] But these virtues are eminently "social," more social in certain respects than justice. For if justice is the necessary condition of life in society in rendering to each his own, the social virtues, by their disinteresed altruistic character, positively tighten the social bond. Hence it will be seen that the law, concerned with concord and fraternity among the members of the group, is led to promulgate statutes "of social solidarity," where the required attitudes become a matter of legal justice by reason of their "ordination" for the public good.[23] Furthermore, social relations do not exist solely between

[17] See *supra*, nos. 147 *et seq.*; also nos. 114–122. This is why certain natural law writers such as MEYER, INSTITUTIONES JURIS NATURALIS 92 *et seq.*, 104 *et seq.*, speak of combining natural law with the conveniences of the general good.

[18] See *supra*, nos. 156–159.

[19] See *supra*, no. 160.

[20] See *supra*, nos. 161 *et seq.*

[21] See *supra*, no. 224.

[22] This is so even if one accepts the idea of the [industrial] enterprise as a community or institution. Even within the frame of that conception there are acts of assistance beyond the requirements of communal or institutional justice, because the enterprise integrates men into its system only as workers, employees, collaborators, and not men as men.

[23] See in the same sense F. RUSSO, *op. cit.* 54, *in fine*, and 55, *initio*. For an ap-

equals: At their basis is authority. That is why the law prescribes obedience to authorities not only in the state but also in the private groups, in the first place the family. Although obedience is but an annexed virtue of justice,[24] it will be seen that laws come to the aid of the hierarchies which make up the organic unity of social life.

But the law does not entrench itself in the field of the virtues *ad alterum*. Stepping beyond the circle of justice and the social virtues, it represses some shortcomings in duties toward one's self (e.g., the attempt at suicide, drunkenness, certain alienations of essential rights or liberties), some shortcomings in duties toward God (e.g., blasphemy, sacrilege, perjury), or again acts of cruelty to animals. Why? Not because commutative justice would be involved, but because these offenses affect the public, causing trouble or damage in the social environment.[25]

Lastly, beyond justice and even morals, one will have to indicate the innumerable measures of prudence laid down by the law to the end of preventing the violation of the moral precepts it has taken up and sanctioned. Such are the regulations designed to police traffic, industry and labor, and commerce, whose aim it is no doubt to facilitate the activities of traffic, industry, commerce, but also to protect the rights of the persons engaged in those activities against encroachments. Now these preventive measures, though in part ordained for justice, are in themselves means indifferent to justice.

262. "Just Laws" and Laws Consecrating Justice Are Not Synonymous. Finally, one will have to guard against confounding just laws and laws which consecrate justice. A law is just when it prescribes what is within its rôle to prescribe. In this sense, a just law is a law adjusted to its end, the public good, and to its proper means of realization, in short, a law conforming to the legal method. This, the rule of natural law being unaffected, is the *regula rationis* [c] in matters of positive law.[26] Now while ordinarily a just law is a law which consecrates justice, this is not always so. That is all the difference between the lawyer's justice, which is a matter of prudence, and the moralist's justice, which is a matter of truth or science.

plication, cf. A. Rouast, *Le risque professionnel et la jurisprudence française*, in 3 Recueil Gény 228 *et seq.*

[24] On obedience, see St. Thomas, Summa, *IIa IIae*, qu. 104, arts. 1 and 2.

[25] See in this sense, on suicide, St. Thomas, *op. cit. IIa IIae*, qu. 59, art. 3 *ad 2*; on moderation, *Ia IIae*, qu. 94, art. 3 *ad 1*.

[c] [The rule of reason.]

[26] Cf. St. Thomas, Summa theologica, *Ia IIae*, qu. 95, art. 2 *ad resp.*: . . . See also qu. 95, art. 3 *ad resp.*, *in fine*: . . .

TABLE OF STATUTES AND INDEX

TABLE OF STATUTES

INDEX

(The references are to pages)

Bei Fragen zur Produktsicherheit wenden Sie sich bitte an:
If you have any questions regarding product safety,
please contact:

Walter de Gruyter GmbH
Genthiner Straße 13
10785 Berlin
productsafety@degruyterbrill.com